OXFORD

GCSE Maths

For Edexcel

SPECIFICATION A

FOUNDATION PLUS

Linear

Dave Capewell
Geoff Fowler
Peter Mullarkey
Katherine Pate

OXFORD
UNIVERSITY PRESS

OXFORD
UNIVERSITY PRESS

Great Clarendon Street, Oxford OX2 6DP
Oxford University Press is a department of the University of Oxford.
It furthers the University's objective of excellence in research, scholarship, and education by publishing worldwide in
Oxford New York
Auckland Cape Town Dar es Salaam Hong Kong Karachi
Kuala Lumpur Madrid Melbourne Mexico City Nairobi
New Delhi Shanghai Taipei Toronto
With offices in
Argentina Austria Brazil Chile Czech Republic France Greece
Guatemala Hungary Italy Japan South Korea Poland Portugal
Singapore Switzerland Thailand Turkey Ukraine Vietnam
Oxford is a registered trade mark of Oxford University Press in the UK and in certain other countries

First published 2010

British Library Cataloguing in Publication Data
Data available
ISBN 9780199139491
10 9 8 7 6 5 4 3 2 1
Printed in Spain by Cayfosa (Impresia Iberica)

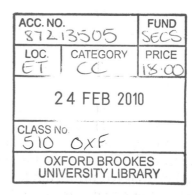

Paper used in the production of this book is a natural, recyclable product made from wood grown in sustainable forests. The manufacturing process conforms to the environmental regulations of the country of origin.

Acknowledgements
The Publisher would like to thank Edexcel for their kind permission to reproduce past exam questions.
Edexcel Ltd, accepts no responsibility whatsoever for the accuracy or method of working in the answers given

The Publisher would like to thank the following for permission to reproduce photographs:
p2-3: J A Giordano/CORBIS SABA; **p16-17**: OUP; **p25**: OUP/Corel; **p28-29**: Joggie Botma/Dreamstime; **p33**: Humanities & Social Sciences Library/New York Public Library/Science Photo Library; **p46-47**: Kuzma/Shutterstock; **p50**: Tom Brakefield/Stock Connection Blue/Alamy; **p62-63**: OUP; **p69**: OUP; **p80-81**: Bhe017/Dreamstime; **p83**: Andrew Palmer/Alamy; **p98-99**: Slobodan Djajic/Dreamstime; **p120-121**: Jeremy Broad/Dreamstime; **p129**: Science Source/Science Photo Library; **p134-135**: Harish Tyagi/epa/Corbis; **p139**: Elmtree Images/Alamy; **p145**: Robert Estall/Corbis; **p146**: Raja Rc/Dreamstime.com; **p152-153**: Soleg1974/Dreamstime; **p155**: Ashley Cooper/Alamy; **p162-163**: Ivan Cholakov/Dreamstime; **p168**: David Martyn Hughes/Alamy; **p173**: Honda; **p182-183**: Jakub Krechowicz/Dreamstime; **p185**: Jag_cz/Shutterstock; **p196-197**: Doug Steley A/Alamy; **p214-215**: Gregory Sams/Science Photo Library; **p228-229**: Ivan Kmit/Dreamstime; **p244-245**: 4774344sean/Dreamstime; **p258-259**: Dgareri/Dreamstime; **p272-273**: Jordan Rusev/Dreamstime; **p275**: Melinda Fawver/Dreamstime; **p290-291**: The London Art Archive/Alamy; **p292**: OUP; **p300**: Raja Rc/Dreamstime.com; **p304-305**: Andres Rodriguez/Dreamstime; **p313**: Williammpark/Shutterstock; **p319**: Sint/Shutterstock; **p322-323**: David Touchtone/Dreamstime; **p334**: Andrew Brown/Corbis; **p340-341**: SHOUT/Alamy; **p358-359**: Juan Fuertes/Shutterstock;**p371**: Alexander Rochau/Dreamstime; **p380-381**: Ivonne Wierink/Shutterstock; **p394-395**: Dbpetersen/Dreamstime; **p401**: Araldo de Luca/Corbis; **Background**: Clint Cearley/Dreamstime.

The Publisher would also like to thank Anna Cox for her work in creating the case studies. The charts on pages 44-45 are reproduced courtesy of the Meteorological Office; the bar chart on page 150 is reproduced courtesy of Defra; the data on page 392 is reproduced courtesy of the IAAF.

Figurative artwork is by Peter Donnelly

About this book

This book has been specifically written to help you get your best possible grade in your Edexcel GCSE Mathematics examinations. It is designed for students who have achieved a secure level 5 at Key Stage 3 and are looking to progress to a grade C at GCSE, Foundation tier.

The authors are experienced teachers and examiners who have an excellent understanding of the Edexcel specification and so are well qualified to help you successfully meet your objectives.

The book is made up of chapters that are based on Edexcel specification A (linear) and is organised clearly into a suggested teaching order.

Functional maths and **problem-solving** are flagged in the exercises throughout.

- In particular there are **case studies,** which allow you apply your GCSE knowledge in a variety of engaging contexts.
- There are also **rich tasks,** which provide an investigative lead-in to the chapter – you may need to study some of the techniques in the chapter in order to be able to complete them properly.

Also built into this book are the new **assessment objectives:**

AO1 recall knowledge of prescribed content
AO2 select and apply mathematical methods in a range of contexts
AO3 interpret and analyse problems and select strategies to solve them

AO2 and AO3 are flagged throughout, particularly in the regular **summary assessments,** as these make up around 50% of your assessment.

Finally, you will notice an icon that looks like this: 

This shows opportunities for **Quality of Written Communication,** which you will also be assessed on in your exams.

Best wishes with your GCSE Maths – we hope you enjoy your course and achieve success!

Contents

N1	**Integers and decimals**	2-15
N1.1	Place value	4
N1.2	Reading scales	6
N1.3	Adding and subtracting negative numbers	8
N1.4	Multiplying and dividing negative numbers	10
N1.5	Rounding	12
	Summary and assessment	14
G1	**Length and area**	16-27
G1.1	Metric and imperial measures	18
G1.2	Perimeter and area of a rectangle and a triangle	20
G1.3	Area of a parallelogram and a trapezium	22
G1.4	Surface area	24
	Summary and assessment	26
A1	**Linear graphs**	28-43
A1.1	Functions	30
A1.2	Drawing linear graphs 1	32
A1.3	More linear graphs	34
A1.4	Horizontal and vertical graphs	36
A1.5	Equation of a straight line	38
A1.6	Midpoint of a line segment	40
	Summary and assessment	42
Functional Maths case study 1: Weather		**44**
N2	**Decimal calculations**	46-61
N2.1	Mental addition and subtraction	48
N2.2	Written addition and subtraction	50
N2.3	Mental multiplication and division	52
N2.4	Written multiplication and division	54
N2.5	Order of operations	56
N2.6	Estimation	58
	Summary and assessment	60
G2	**2-D shapes**	62-79
G2.1	Angle properties	64
G2.2	Properties of triangles	66
G2.3	Angles in quadrilaterals	68
G2.4	Properties of quadrilaterals	70
G2.5	Angles in parallel lines	72
G2.6	Using parallel lines	74
G2.7	Symmetry	76
	Summary and assessment	78

N3 Fractions, decimals and percentages 80-95

N3.1 Equivalent fractions 82
N3.2 Fractions, decimals and percentages 84
N3.3 Ordering fractions, decimals and percentages 86
N3.4 Fraction of a quantity 88
N3.5 Percentage of a quantity 90
N3.6 Percentage increase and decrease 92
Summary and assessment 94
Functional Maths case study 2: Sandwich shop 96

D1 Probability 98-119

D1.1 Probability 100
D1.2 Probability scale 102
D1.3 Mutually exclusive outcomes 104
D1.4 Two-way tables 1 106
D1.5 Expected frequency 108
D1.6 Relative frequency 110
D1.7 Two events 112
D1.8 Two events again 114
D1.9 Probability revision 116
Summary and assessment 118

A2 Expressions 120-133

A2.1 Algebraic expressions 122
A2.2 Indices 124
A2.3 Brackets in algebra 126
A2.4 Simplifying expressions 128
A2.5 Factorising 130
Summary and assessment 132

D2 Collecting data 134-149

D2.1 Frequency tables 136
D2.2 Observation, controlled experiment and sampling 138
D2.3 Surveys and questionnaires 140
D2.4 Grouped data 142
D2.5 Two-way tables 2 144
D2.6 Databases and random sampling 146
Summary and assessment 148
Functional Maths case study 3: Recycling 150

G3 3-D shapes 152-161

G3.1 3-D shapes 154
G3.2 Volume of a cuboid 156
G3.3 Volume of a prism 1 158
Summary and assessment 160

A3	**Real-life graphs**	162-181
A3.1	Drawing linear graphs 2	164
A3.2	Real-life graphs 1	166
A3.3	Conversion graphs	168
A3.4	Drawing conversion graphs	170
A3.5	Compound measures	172
A3.6	Distance-time graphs	174
A3.7	Average speed	176
A3.8	Real-life graphs 2	178
	Summary and assessment	180
N4	**Ratio and calculator methods**	182-193
N4.1	Introducing ratio	184
N4.2	Calculating with ratio	186
N4.3	More ratio problems	188
N4.4	Calculator methods 1	190
	Summary and assessment	192
Functional Maths case study 4: Holiday		**194**
G4	**Transformations**	196-213
G4.1	Reflections	198
G4.2	Rotations	200
G4.3	Translations	202
G4.4	Congruence	204
G4.5	Enlargements	206
G4.6	More enlargements	208
G4.7	Similar shapes	210
	Summary and assessment	212
A4	**Sequences**	214-227
A4.1	Term-to-term rules	216
A4.2	The general term	218
A4.3	Finding the nth term	220
A4.4	Pattern sequences	222
A4.5	More pattern sequences	224
	Summary and assessment	226
N5	**Integers, powers and roots**	228-241
N5.1	Factors and multiples	230
N5.2	Squares and square roots	232
N5.3	Cubes and cube roots	234
N5.4	Powers	236
N5.5	Prime factor decomposition	238
	Summary and assessment	240
Functional Maths case study 5: Business		**242**
D3	**Displaying and interpreting data**	244-257
D3.1	Diagrams and charts 1	246
D3.2	Grouped frequency diagrams	248
D3.3	Stem-and-leaf diagrams 1	250
D3.4	Time series graphs	252
D3.5	Scatter graphs 1	254
	Summary and assessment	256

A5 Equations 1 258-271

A5.1 Solving equations using function machines 260
A5.2 Solving two-step equations 262
A5.3 Solving equations using the balance method 264
A5.4 Solving equations with brackets 266
A5.5 Equations with the unknown on both sides 268
Summary and assessment 270

G5 2-D and 3-D shapes 272-287

G5.1 Interior angles of a polygon 274
G5.2 Exterior angles of a polygon 276
G5.3 Tessellations 278
G5.4 Plans and elevations 280
G5.5 2-D and 3-D measures 282
G5.6 Scale factors 284
Summary and assessment 286
Functional Maths case study 6: Radio Maths 288

N6 More fractions and decimals 290-303

N6.1 Adding and subtracting fractions 292
N6.2 Multiplying and dividing fractions 294
N6.3 Mental methods with decimals 296
N6.4 Written methods with decimals 298
N6.5 Calculator methods 2 300
Summary and assessment 302

A6 Formulae and inequalities 304-321

A6.1 Formulae, equations and identities 306
A6.2 Substituting into formulae 308
A6.3 Writing formulae 310
A6.4 Changing the subject of a formula 312
A6.5 Inequalities 314
A6.6 Two-sided inequalities 316
A6.7 Graphs of quadratic functions 318
Summary and assessment 320

G6 Constructions and loci 322-337

G6.1 Bearings 324
G6.2 Constructing triangles 326
G6.3 Perpendicular lines 328
G6.4 Angle bisectors 330
G6.5 Loci 332
G6.6 Maps and scale drawings 334
Summary and assessment 336
Functional Maths case study 7: Art 338

N7 Proportionality 340-357

N7.1 Proportion 342
N7.2 Unitary method 344
N7.3 Ratio and proportion 346
N7.4 Exchange rates 348
N7.5 Percentage problems 350
N7.6 Interest 352
N7.7 Proportional problems 354
Summary and assessment 356

D4 Averages and charts 358-379

D4.1 Types of data and the range 360
D4.2 Averages 362
D4.3 Charts and tables 364
D4.4 Comparing data 366
D4.5 Grouped data 368
D4.6 Diagrams and charts 2 370
D4.7 Diagrams and charts 3 372
D4.8 Stem-and-leaf diagrams 2 374
D4.9 Scatter graphs 2 376
Summary and assessment 378

A7 Equations 2 380-391

A7.1 More equations with brackets 382
A7.2 Equations with fractions 384
A7.3 Finding solutions from graphs 386
A7.4 Trial and improvement 388
Summary and assessment 390
Functional Maths case study 8: Sport 392

G7 Measures and Pythagoras 394-405

G7.1 Circumference and area of a circle 396
G7.2 Volume of a prism 2 398
G7.3 Pythagoras' theorem 400
G7.4 More Pythagoras' theorem 402
Summary and assessment 404

Formulae 406

Answers 407

Index 438

Finding your way around this book

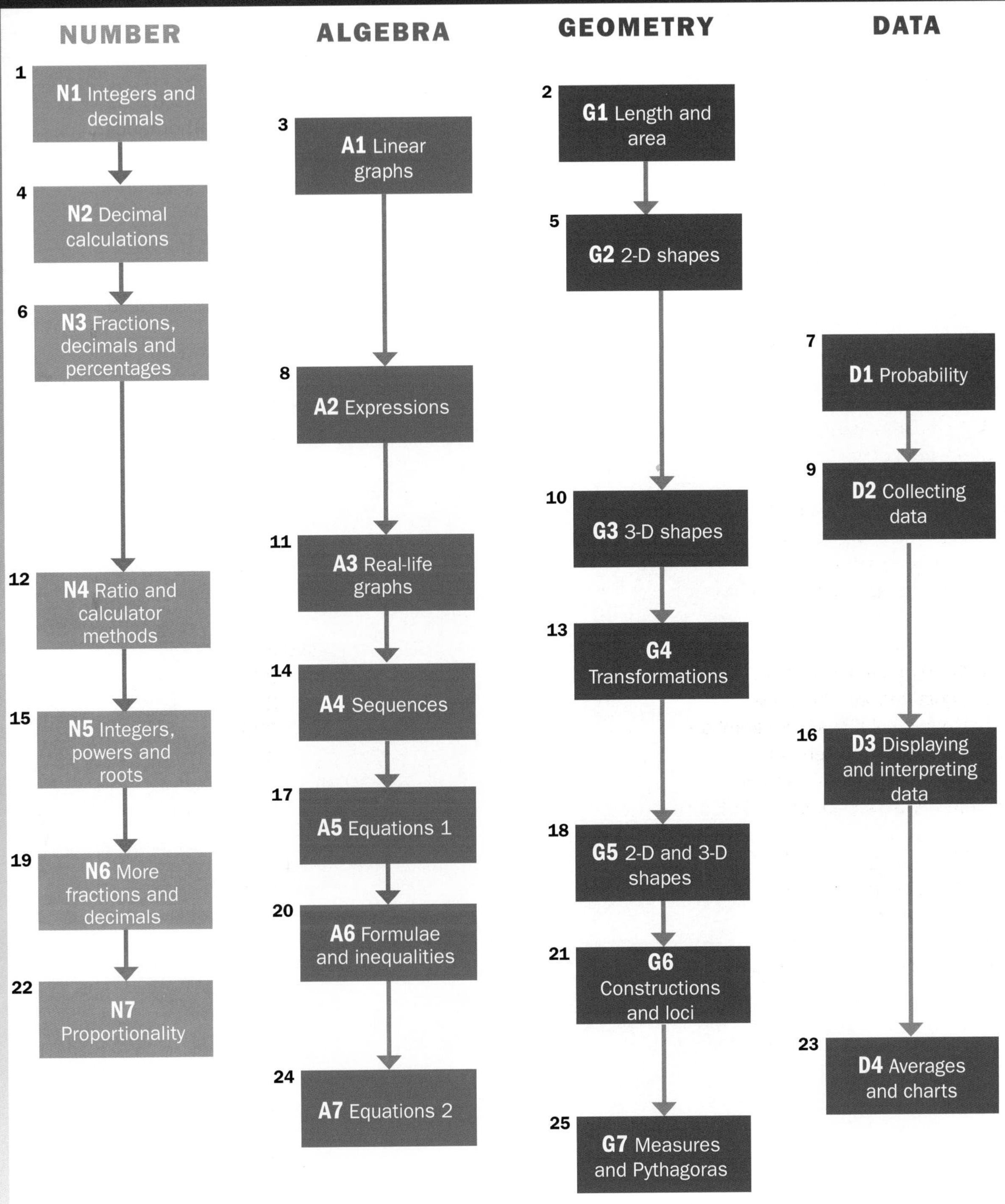

N1 Integers and decimals

Introduction

Negative numbers have been a source of controversy in the history of mathematics. Because negative numbers did not seem to represent real quantities, people were reluctant to accept them. The Greeks called any equation with a negative solution absurd!

What's the point?

In the present day, negative numbers have lots of 'real' meanings such as sub-zero temperatures, stock market losses, and indicating reverse flow.

Check in

1 Put these numbers in order starting with the smallest.
$-8, -1, 2, -5, -3, 4$

2 Calculate
a $10 - 3$ **b** $-6 - 4$
c $3 \times (-4)$ **d** $-6 \div 2$

3 Write all the factors of 48.

Orientation

What I should know		What I will learn		What this leads to
Key stage 3	→	■ Understand place value ■ Read scales, dials and timetables ■ Calculate with negative numbers ■ Round numbers to significant figures	→	N2

Rich task

You can predict the answer to $51^2 - 49^2$ without using a calculator. Investigate.

N1.1 Place value

This spread will show you how to:

- Understand place value and order numbers, representing them as positions on a number line
- Multiply and divide numbers by powers of 10

Keywords
Decimal
Digit
Order
Place value

- In the **decimal system**, the value of each **digit** in a number depends upon its **place value**.

In the number 37.65:

Thousands 1000	Hundreds 100	Tens 10	Units 1		tenths $\frac{1}{10}$	hundredths $\frac{1}{100}$
		3	7		6	5

You write this number in words as thirty-seven point six five.

The digits stand for: 3 tens 7 units + 6 tenths 5 hundredths

$$37.65 = 30 + 7 + \frac{6}{10} + \frac{5}{100}$$
$$= 30 + 7 + 0.6 + 0.05$$

You can use a place value table to compare or order two or more numbers.

Example

Put these numbers in order from lowest to highest.
0.47 0.5 0.512 0.55 0.52

Look at each number to see the place value of the first non-zero digit.
0.47 0.5 0.512 0.55 0.52
You can see that 0.47 is the smallest number. The other four numbers all have a 5 in the first decimal place, so now look at the second digit.
0.50 0.512 0.55 0.52
You can now order the numbers: 0.47 0.5 0.512 0.52 0.55

The digit 4 stands for 4 tenths and the digit 5 stands for 5 tenths.

You can use a place value table to multiply and divide.

- To multiply a number by 100, move all the digits two places to the left.

6.7 × 100

Hundreds	Tens	Units	•	tenths	
		6	•	7	× 100
6	7	0	•		

6.7 × 100 = 670

The 0 holds the digits in place.

- To divide a number by 10, move all the digits one place to the right.

73.2 ÷ 10

Tens	Units		tenths	hundredths	
7	3		2		÷ 10
	7		3	2	

73.2 ÷ 10 = 7.32

Exercise N1.1 Grade F

1 Write each of these numbers in words.

a 456 **b** 13 200 **c** 115 020
d 460 340 **e** 4 325 400 **f** 55 670 345
g 45.8 **h** 367.03 **i** 4503.34
j 2700.02

2 Write each of these numbers in figures.

a five hundred and thirty-eight
b two thousand and thirty-one
c fifteen thousand, six hundred and three
d two hundred and eighty thousand, four hundred and fifty-three
e four hundred and seventeen point three
f one million, seven hundred and seventeen thousand, three hundred and thirty-eight
g five hundred and thirty-seven point four zero three
h three and three hundredths

DID YOU KNOW?

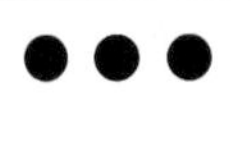

The decimal system is not the only number system. The ancient Mayans had a system based on the number 20.

3 What number lies exactly halfway between

a 25 and 26 **b** 1.8 and 1.9 **c** 30 and 70
d 4.9 and 5 **e** 1.25 and 1.5 **f** 0.7 and 0.71?

4 Put these lists of numbers in order, starting with the smallest.

a 5.103	5.099	5.2	5.12	5.007
b 0.545	0.55	0.525	0.5	0.509
c 7.302	7.403	7.35	7.387	7.058
d 0.4	4.2	0.42	42	2.4
e 27.6	26.9	27.06	26.97	27.1
f 13.3	14.15	13.43	13.19	14.03

5 Calculate each of these without using a calculator.

a 3.2×100 **b** 0.4×10 **c** $152 \div 100$
d $14.6 \div 100$ **e** 2.37×10 **f** 24.3×100
g $1.23 \div 100$ **h** $45.9 \div 10$ **i** 3.4×1000
j 13.56×10 **k** $0.236 \div 10$ **l** 1.745×10
m 0.0392×10 **n** $72.8 \div 100$ **o** $12.4 \div 1000$
p 0.0814×100

6 Use the information given to work out each of these calculations without using a calculator.

a $23 \times 42 = 966$ What is 2.3×42?
b $91 \times 103 = 9373$ What is 9.1×103?
c $39 \times 57 = 2223$ What is 0.39×57?
d $34 \times 71 = 2414$ What is 340×71?

N1.2 Reading scales

This spread will show you how to:

- Represent decimal numbers as positions on a number line
- Read scales, dials and timetables

Keywords
Estimate
Number line
Scale
Timetable

- You can represent decimal numbers as a position on a **number line**.

The arrow is pointing between 4 and 5.

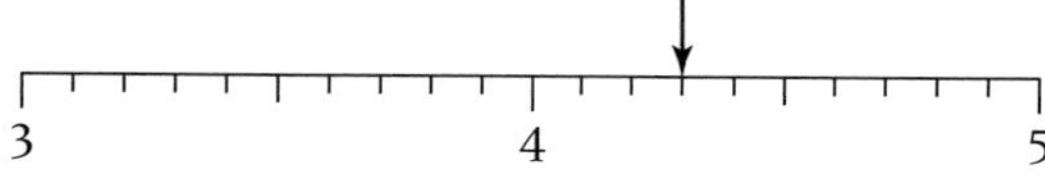

There are 10 spaces between 4 and 5.
10 spaces represent 1 unit.
1 space represents $1 \div 10 = \frac{1}{10} = 0.1$ unit.
The arrow is pointing to 4.3.

The arrow is pointing between 2.2 and 2.3.

There are 10 spaces between 2.2 and 2.3.
10 spaces represent 0.1 unit.
1 space represents $0.1 \div 10 = 0.01$ unit.
The arrow is pointing to 2.27.

You can write 2.2 as 2.20, and so on.

You can **estimate** a measurement from a **scale**.

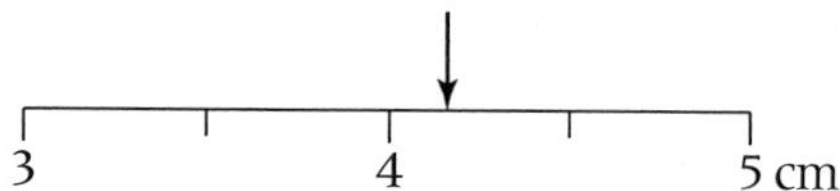

The reading is between 4 and 5 cm.
There are only two spaces between 4 and 5 cm.
The pointer is a little under a quarter of the way between 4 and 5.
A good estimated reading is 4.2 cm.

Most of the scales you read are number lines.

You need to be able to read **timetables** for buses and trains.

Example

How long does it take for the 07:40 train from Clitheroe to get to Colne?

Station	Time of leaving	Team of leaving	Time of leaving
Clitheroe	07:10	07:40	08:10
Blackburn	07:28	07:58	08:28
Nelson	08:23	08:53	09:23
Colne	08:41	09:11	09:41
Bradford	09:52	10:22	10:52

The train leaves Clitheroe at 07:40.
It arrives at Colne at 09:11.

From 07:40 to 08:00 = 20 minutes
From 08:00 to 09:00 = 60 minutes
From 09:00 to 09:11 = 11 minutes
Total journey time = 91 minutes = 1 hour 31 minutes

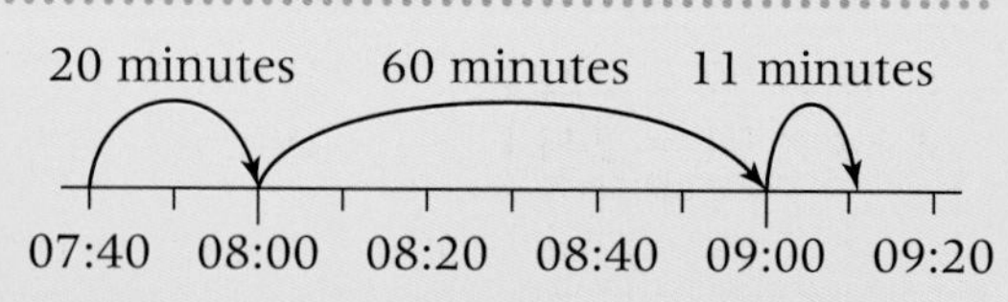

Exercise N1.2

Grade F

1 Write the number each of the arrows is pointing to.

a

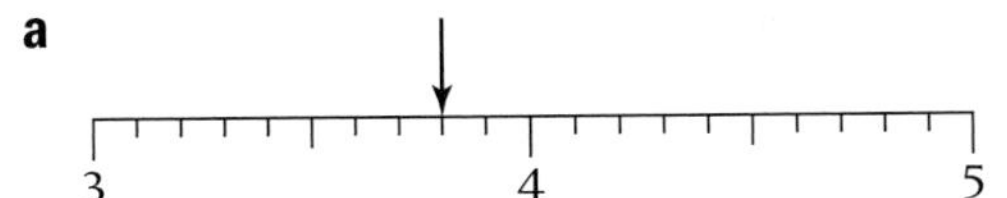

b

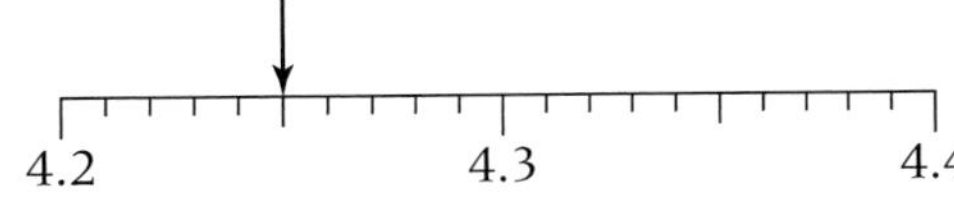

c

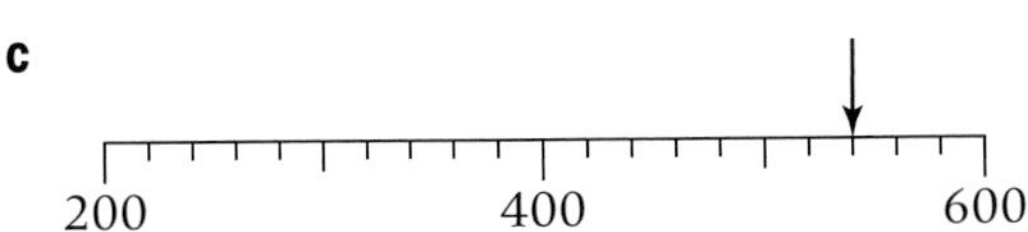

d

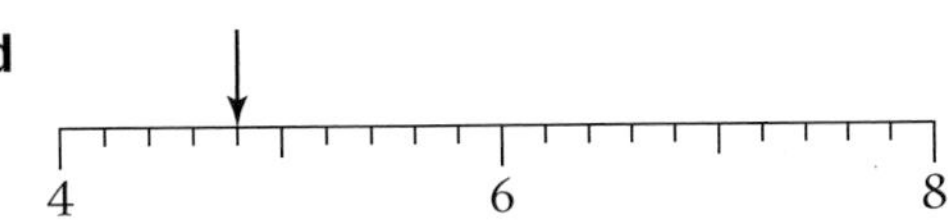

2 Write the reading shown on each scale.

a

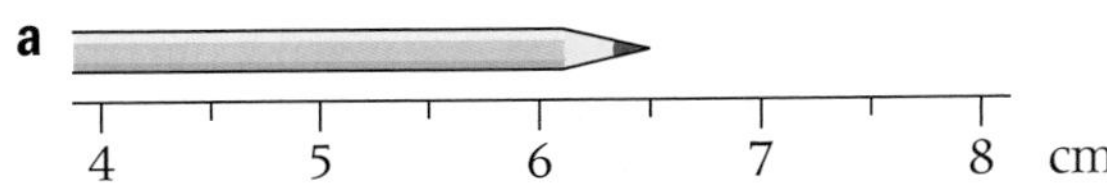

b

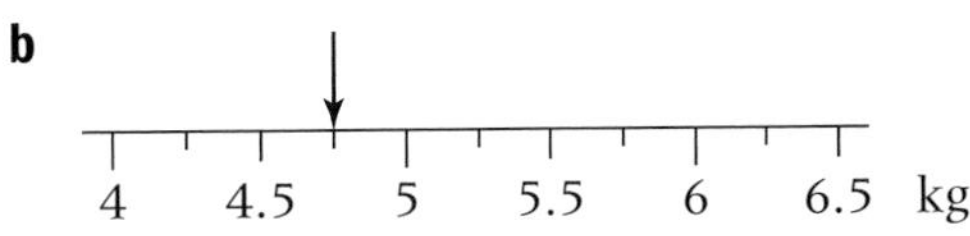

c

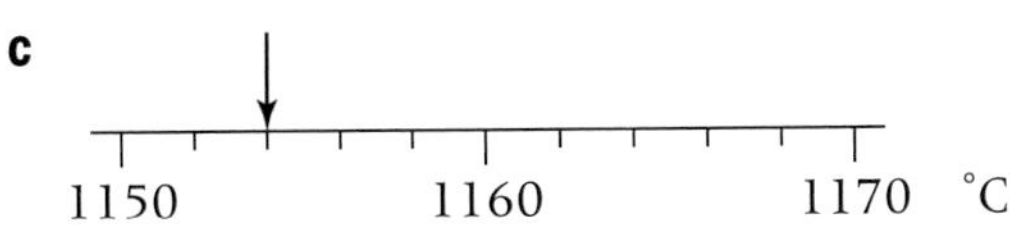

d

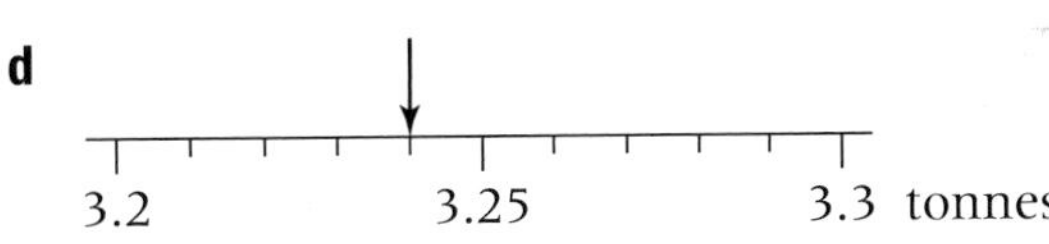

3 Use the scales to write a good estimated reading for each question.

a

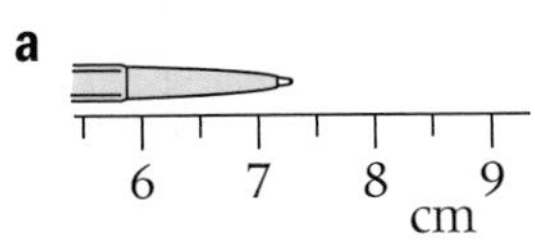

b

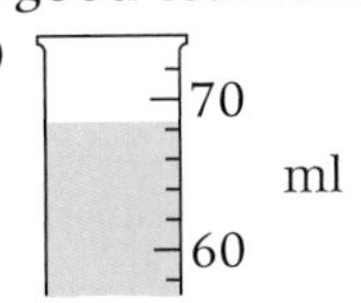

c

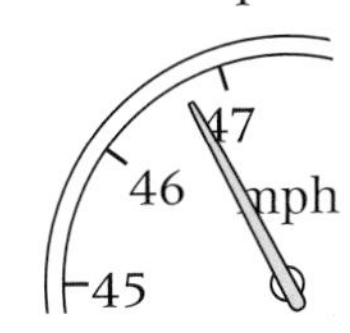

d

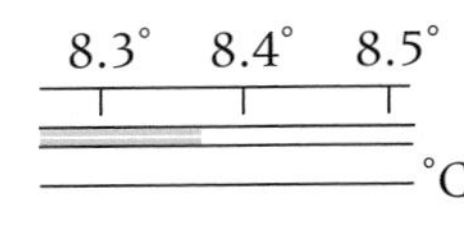

e

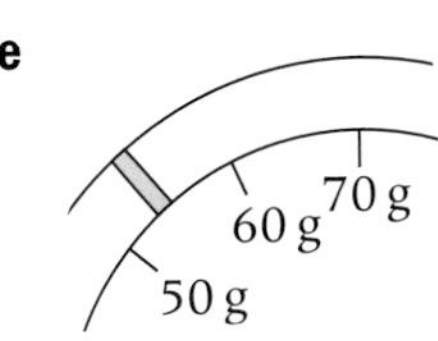

f

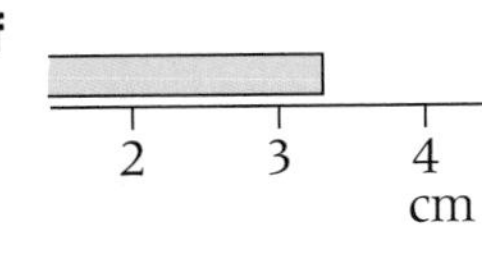

g

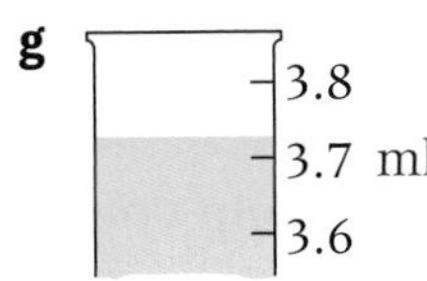

h

000°C

2000°C 4000°C

AO2 Functional Maths

4

Carlisle–Hexham bus timetable			
Carlisle	09:25	11:50	15:00
Crosby on Eden	09:41	12:11	15:21
Lanercost Priory	09:58	12:28	15:38
Birdoswald Fort	10:10	12:40	15:50
Chesters Fort	11:18	13:48	16:58
Hexham	11:32	13:59	17:09

a What time does the 11:50 bus from Carlisle arrive at Hexham?

b What time does the 15:50 bus from Birdoswald Fort leave Crosby on Eden?

c How long does it take the 09:25 bus from Carlisle to travel to Hexham?

d Harry catches the 12:28 bus at Lanercost Priory. He gets off at Chesters Fort. How long is his journey?

N1.3 Adding and subtracting negative numbers

This spread will show you how to:

- Order negative numbers using a number line
- Add, subtract, multiply and divide with negative numbers

Keywords
Add
Negative numbers
Order
Subtract

- **Negative numbers** are numbers below zero.

The temperature in the fridge is −5°C or 5 degrees below freezing.

You can order negative numbers using a number line.

Example

Place these numbers in **order**, starting with the smallest.
−13, −14, 2, −5, −3, 4

−14 −13 −5 −3 2 4

−15 −10 −5 0 5

The correct order is −14, −13, −5, −3, 2, 4.

−14 is further away from zero than −13, so it is smaller.

You can use a number line to help you **add** or **subtract** from a negative number.

To add, move right.
To subtract, move left.

Example

Calculate **a** 5 − 12 **b** −3 + 8 **c** −5 − 4

a Start at 5 and subtract 12 (move to the left).

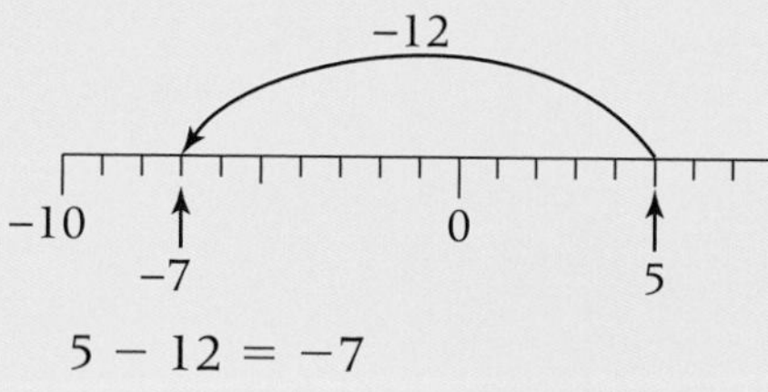

5 − 12 = −7

b Start at −3 and add 8 (move to the right).

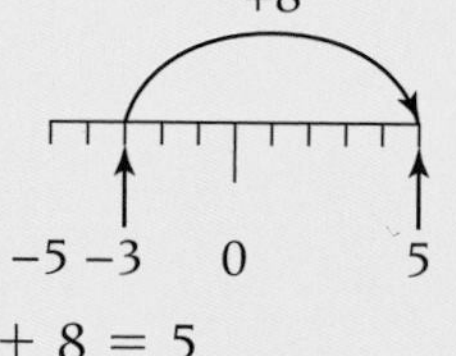

−3 + 8 = 5

c Start at −5 and subtract 4.

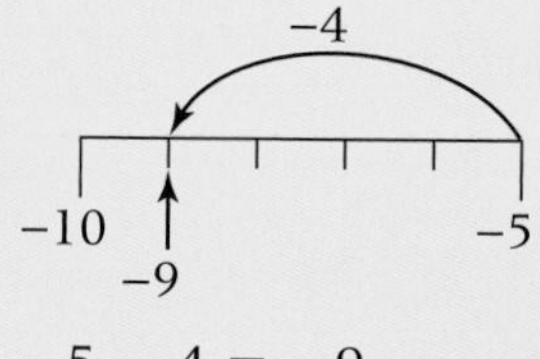

−5 − 4 = −9

There are two rules for adding and subtracting negative numbers.

- Adding a negative number is the same as subtracting a positive number.

18 + −3 = 18 − 3 = 15

- Subtracting a negative number is the same as adding a positive number.

18 − −3 = 18 + 3 = 21

Exercise N1.3 Grade G

1 Put these lists of numbers in order from lowest to highest.

a −13	−6	0	17	−12	15
b 0	−5	−6	−8	−3	−7
c 2	1	−2	4	3	−5
d −1.5	3	9	−3	2	−8
e −3	2	−5	−4.5	3	−2
f 3	8	6	−9	−1	2
g −1	−3	0	−4.5	5.5	−2.5
h −5	−5.1	−6	−5.8	−5.7	−5.4

2 Calculate

a $4 + 12$ **b** $5 - 12$ **c** $7 - 3$
d $14 + 23$ **e** $34 - 17$ **f** $8 - 15$
g $-3 + 12$ **h** $-23 + 12$ **i** $-15 + 7$
j $-13 + 34$ **k** $-5 - 3$ **l** $-5 + 3$
m $-12 - 6$ **n** $21 - 17$ **o** $-8 + 3$
p $-4 + 8 - 2$ **q** $-12 - 3 - 5$ **r** $13 - 8 + 5$
s $-5 + 4 - 7$ **t** $-12 - 4 - 12$

3 Find the number that lies exactly halfway between each of these pairs of numbers.

a 28 and 34 **b** −5 and −17 **c** −6 and 14 **d** −18 and 4
e 3 and 8 **f** −4 and 9 **g** −20 and 35 **h** −3.5 and 2.5

4 Copy and complete each of these number patterns.

a	**b**	**c**	**d**
7 + 3 = 10	7 − 3 = 4	12 + 3 = 15	12 − 3 = 9
7 + 2 = 9	7 − 2 = 5	12 + 2 = 14	12 − 2 = 10
7 + 1 = 8	7 − 1 = 6	12 + 1 = ___	12 − 1 = ___
7 + 0 = 7	7 − 0 = 7	12 + 0 = ___	12 − 0 = ___
7 + −1 = ___	7 − −1 = ___	12 + −1 = ___	12 − −1 = ___
7 + −2 = ___	7 − −2 = ___	12 + −2 = ___	12 − −2 = ___
7 + −3 = ___	7 − −3 = ___	12 + −3 = ___	12 − −3 = ___
7 + −4 = ___	7 − −4 = ___	12 + −4 = ___	12 − −4 = ___

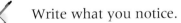

Write what you notice.

5 Calculate

a $13 + -5$ **b** $6 + -8$ **c** $12 + -3$
d $4 + -4$ **e** $-5 + -8$ **f** $-3 + -11$
g $-11 + -3$ **h** $15 - -5$ **i** $4 - -8$
j $-2 - -5$ **k** $-12 - -7$ **l** $-14 - -8$
m $-16 - -20$ **n** $-13 + -12$ **o** $-13 - -12$
p $13 + -12$ **q** $-12 + 7 - 4$ **r** $-12 + -7 - 4$
s $-12 + -7 - 4$ **t** $-12 - 7 + -4$

N1.4 Multiplying and dividing negative numbers

This spread will show you how to:

- Add, subtract, multiply and divide with negative numbers

Keywords
Divide
Multiply
Negative number

You can use a number line to help you multiply or divide **negative numbers**.

- -2×4 can be represented on a number line as four lots of -2.

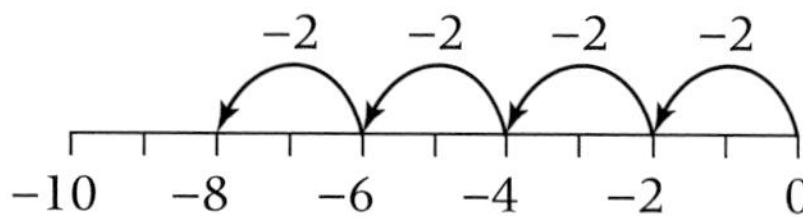

$-2 \times 4 = -2 + -2 + -2 + -2 = -8$

- **Negative number** × positive number = negative number.

- $-16 \div -4$ can be represented on a number line as 'how many lots of -4 are needed to make -16?'

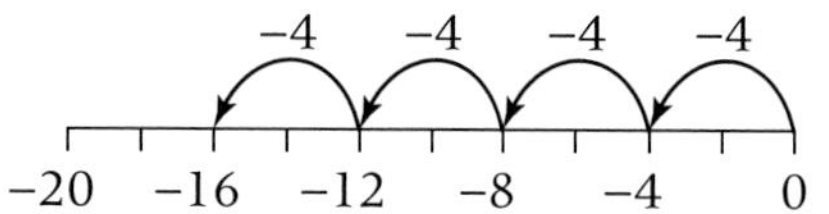

$-16 \div -4 = 4$

- Negative number ÷ negative number = positive number.

To **multiply** a negative number by a negative number, look for patterns in multiplication tables.

$-5 \times 2 = -10$
$-5 \times 1 = -5$
$-5 \times 0 = 0$
$-5 \times -1 = 5$

As you multiply -5 by smaller and smaller numbers, the answer gets bigger. The pattern indicates that -5×-1 is 5.

- Negative number × negative number = positive number.

Remember these rules:

- Negative × positive = negative
  $-2 \times 4 = -8$
- Negative × negative = positive
  $-2 \times -4 = 8$
- Positive ÷ negative = negative
  $-8 \div -2 = -4$
- Negative ÷ positive = negative
  $-8 \div 2 = -4$
- Negative ÷ negative = positive
  $-8 \div -2 = 4$

If the signs are different the answer will be negative. If the signs are the same the answer will be positive.

Exercise N1.4 — Grade G

1 Copy and complete these multiplication tables.

a
$4 \times 3 = 12$
$4 \times 2 = 8$
$4 \times 1 = 4$
$4 \times 0 = 0$
$4 \times -1 = -4$
$4 \times -2 =$ ___
$4 \times -3 =$ ___
$4 \times -4 =$ ___

b
$-7 \times 3 = -21$
$-7 \times 2 = -14$
$-7 \times 1 =$ ___
$-7 \times 0 =$ ___
$-7 \times -1 =$ ___
$-7 \times -2 =$ ___
$-7 \times -3 =$ ___
$-7 \times -4 =$ ___

A03 Problem

2 Choose a number card to make each of these calculations correct.

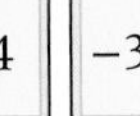
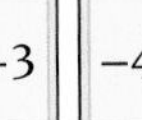
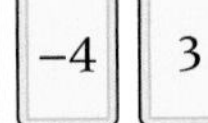

−2 | 2 | 4 | −3 | −4 | 3

a $7 \times \square = -14$
b $-30 \div \square = -15$
c $-5 \times \square = 15$
d $-27 \div \square = -9$
e $\square \times -5 = 20$
f $-6 \times \square = -24$

3 Calculate

a 3×-2 **b** 6×5 **c** 3×-7
d -4×-2 **e** -5×4 **f** -6×-4
g 8×-3 **h** -6×-7 **i** -8×-2
j -5×-10 **k** $-10 \div -2$ **l** $-40 \div 5$
m $-30 \div -6$ **n** $-45 \div -9$ **o** $54 \div -6$
p -9×7 **q** -7×7 **r** -8×-9
s $72 \div -8$ **t** $-42 \div 7$ **u** $-12 \div 3$
v $100 \div -10$ **w** $-81 \div -9$ **x** -7×8
y $-130 \div 10$

4 Here is a set of multiplication and division questions that have been marked by the teacher.
Explain why each of the answers that has been marked wrong is incorrect and write the correct answer.

a $4 \times -5 = 20$ ✗
b $3 \times -2 = -6$ ✓
c $-5 \times -6 = -30$ ✗
d $-14 \times -2 = -28$ ✗
e $7 \times -3 = -21$ ✓
f $8 \times 5 = 20$ ✗
g $7 \times -5 = 35$ ✗
h $-40 \div -5 = -8$ ✗
i $30 \div -5 = -6$ ✓
j $-14 \times -5 = -70$ ✗

5 Calculate these, using either a mental or a written method.
Remember to check the sign of your answer.

a -8×15 **b** -12×-11 **c** 25×-9
d 21×-7 **e** -9×13 **f** -19×7
g -23×18 **h** $-240 \div 6$ **i** $221 \div -17$
j -21×3.2

N1.5

Rounding

This spread will show you how to:

- Round numbers to any number of significant figures
- Use rounding to estimate answers to calculations
- Recognise the inaccuracy of rounded measurements

Keywords
Approximate
Decimal places
Estimate
Rounding
Significant figures

You can round a decimal number to a given accuracy.
To round 718.394 to 2 **decimal places**, look at the **thousandths** digit.

The **thousandths** digit is **4**, so round down to 718.39.
718.394 ≈ 718.39 (to 2 decimal places).

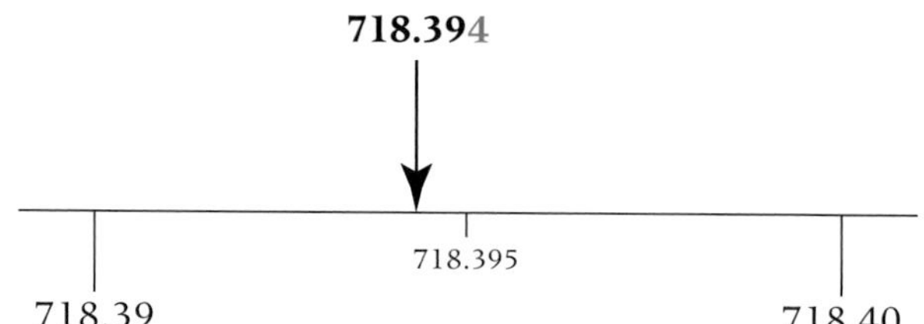

When **rounding** numbers to a given degree of accuracy, look at the next digit. If it is 5 or more then round up, otherwise round down.

To round 54.76 to 2 **significant figures**, look at the 3rd significant figure.

Tens	Units	•	tenths	hundredths
5	4	•	7	6

The first **non-zero** digit in the number is called the **1st significant figure** – it has the highest value in the number.

The **3rd significant** figure is **7**, so the number is rounded up to 55.
54.76 ≈ 55 (to 2 significant figures).

- You can **estimate** the answer to a calculation by rounding the numbers.

Example

Estimate the answer to $\frac{6.23 \times 9.89}{18.7}$.

You can round each of the numbers to 1 significant figure.

$$\frac{6.23 \times 9.89}{18.7} \approx \frac{6 \times 10}{20} = \frac{60}{20} = 3$$

p.58

Exercise N1.5 Grade E

1 Round each of these numbers to the

i nearest 10 **ii** nearest 100 **iii** nearest 1000.

a 3487 **b** 3389 **c** 14 853 m **d** £57 792

e 92 638 kg **f** £86 193 **g** 3438.9 **h** 74 899.36

2 Round each of these numbers to the nearest whole number.

a 3.738 **b** 28.77 **c** 468.63 **d** 369.29

e 19.93 **f** 26.9992 **g** 100.501 **h** 0.001

3 Round each of these numbers to the nearest

i 3 dp **ii** 2 dp **iii** 1 dp.

a 3.4472 **b** 8.9482 **c** 0.1284 **d** 28.3872

e 17.9989 **f** 9.9999 **g** 0.003 987 **h** 2785.5555

4 Round each of these numbers to the nearest

i 3 sf **ii** 2 sf **iii** 1 sf.

a 8.3728 **b** 18.82 **c** 35.84 **d** 278.72

e 1.3949 **f** 3894.79 **g** 0.008 372 **h** 2399.9

i 8.9858 **j** 14.0306 **k** 1403.06 **l** 140 306

5 Write a suitable estimate for each of these calculations.
In each case, clearly show how you estimated your answer.

a 4.98×6.12 **b** $17.89 + 21.91$ **c** $\frac{5.799 \times 3.1}{8.86}$

d $34.8183 - 9.8$ **e** $\frac{32.91 \times 4.8}{3.1}$ **f** $\{9.8^2 + (9.2 - 0.438)\}^2$

AO2 Functional Maths

6 **a** Estimate the cost of 206 bottles of water which cost 30 p each.

b A box of 12 ice lollies costs £1.89.
Estimate the cost of a single ice lolly.

N1

Summary

Check out

You should now be able to:

- Understand place value and order decimals
- Multiply or divide by powers of 10
- Order, add, subtract, multiply and divide negative numbers
- Round numbers to a given number of significant figures
- Read and interpret scales, dials and timetables

Worked exam question

The table shows part of a bus timetable from Shotton to Alton.

Shotton	07 30	08 00	09 00	10 00	11 00
Crook	07 45	08 15	09 15	10 15	11 15
Prudhoe	07 58	08 28	09 28	10 28	11 28
Hexham	08 15	08 45	09 45	10 45	11 45
Alton	08 30	09 00	10 00	11 00	12 00

A bus leaves Shotton at 07 30

a What time should it arrive at Alton? (1)

Another bus leaves Prudhoe at 08 28

b How many minutes should it take to get to Hexham? (1)

Serena lives in Crook.
She has to be in Hexham by quarter past 11

c What is the time of the latest bus she can catch from Crook to arrive in Hexham by quarter past 11? (1)

(Edexcel Limited 2009)

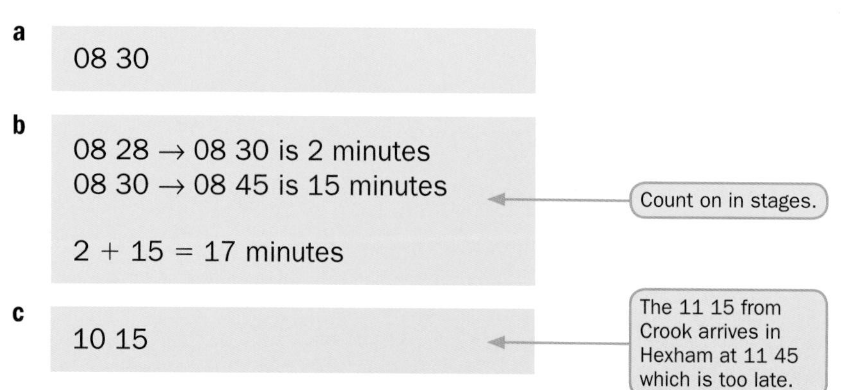

a

08 30

b

08 28 → 08 30 is 2 minutes
08 30 → 08 45 is 15 minutes

2 + 15 = 17 minutes

Count on in stages.

c

10 15

The 11 15 from Crook arrives in Hexham at 11 45 which is too late.

Exam questions

1

City	Temperature
Cardiff	−2 °C
Edinburgh	−4 °C
Leeds	2 °C
London	−1 °C
Plymouth	5 °C

The table gives information about the temperatures at midnight in five cities.

a Write down the lowest temperature. (1)

b Work out the difference in temperature between Cardiff and Plymouth. (1)

c Work out the temperature which is halfway between −1 °C and 5 °C. (1)

(Edexcel Limited 2009)

2 **a**

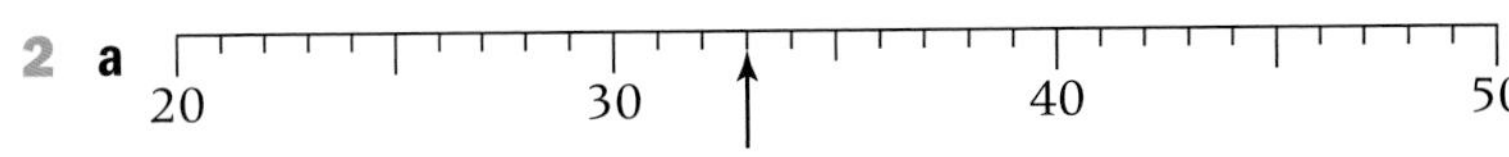

Write down the number marked by the arrow. (1)

b

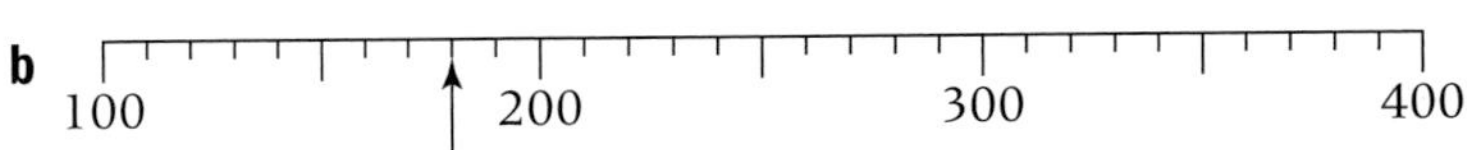

Write down the number marked by the arrow. (1)

c

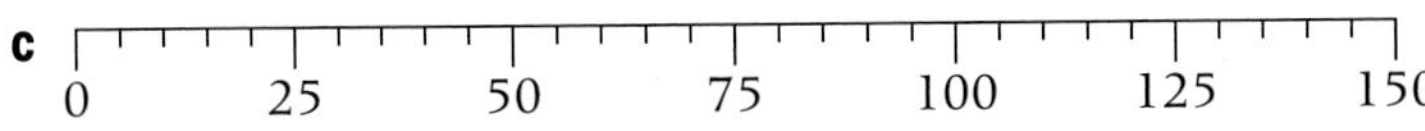

Find the number 110 on the number line.
Mark it with an arrow (↑). (1)

d

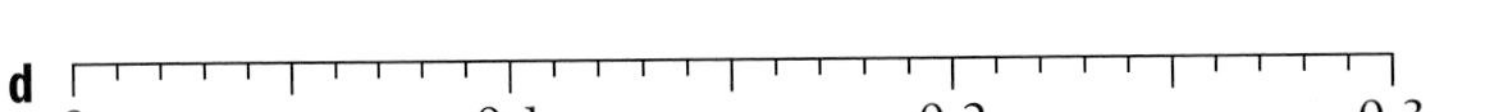

Find the number 0.27 on the number line.
Mark it with an arrow (↑). (1)

(Edexcel Limited 2009)

A02

3 Music videos cost £1.79 to download.
Rehan downloads 21 videos.
Estimate how much money Rehan pays.
Show your working clearly. (3)

Introduction

The United Kingdom is not a very regular shape. However, cartographers have managed to work out its area as 244 820 km^2.

What's the point?

Cartographers use lines of latitude and longitude to divide countries into much smaller regular shapes, such as trapeziums. They can then calculate the area of each of these smaller pieces, and add them together to calculate the area of the country.

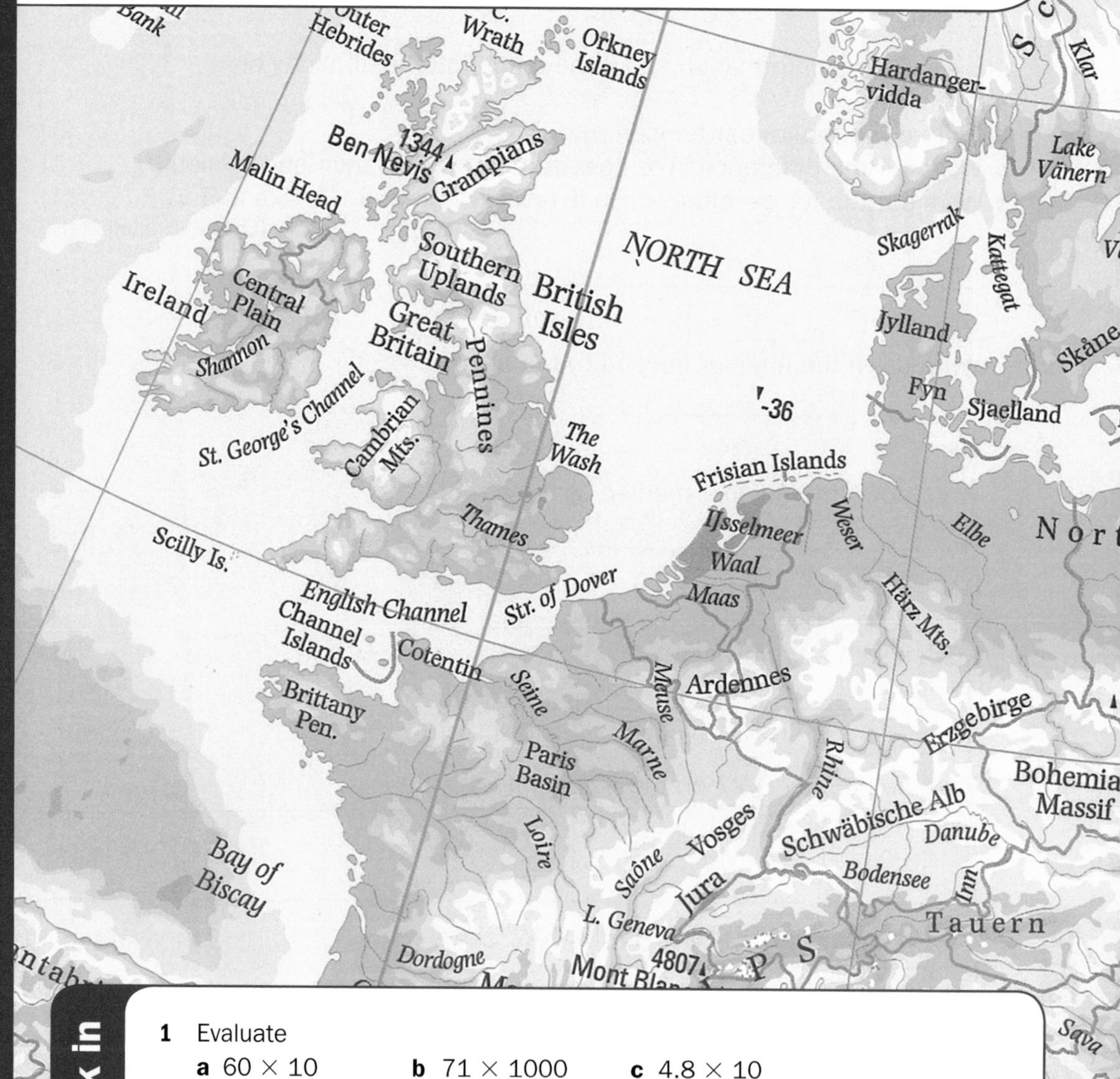

Check in

1 Evaluate

a 60 × 10	**b** 71 × 1000	**c** 4.8 × 10
d 26.3 × 100	**e** 4.5 × 1000	**f** 600 ÷ 100
g 750 ÷ 10	**h** 6500 ÷ 1000	**i** 32 ÷ 10

2 Evaluate

a 5.8 + 2	**b** 14.8 + 0.7	**c** 6.4 + 2.6

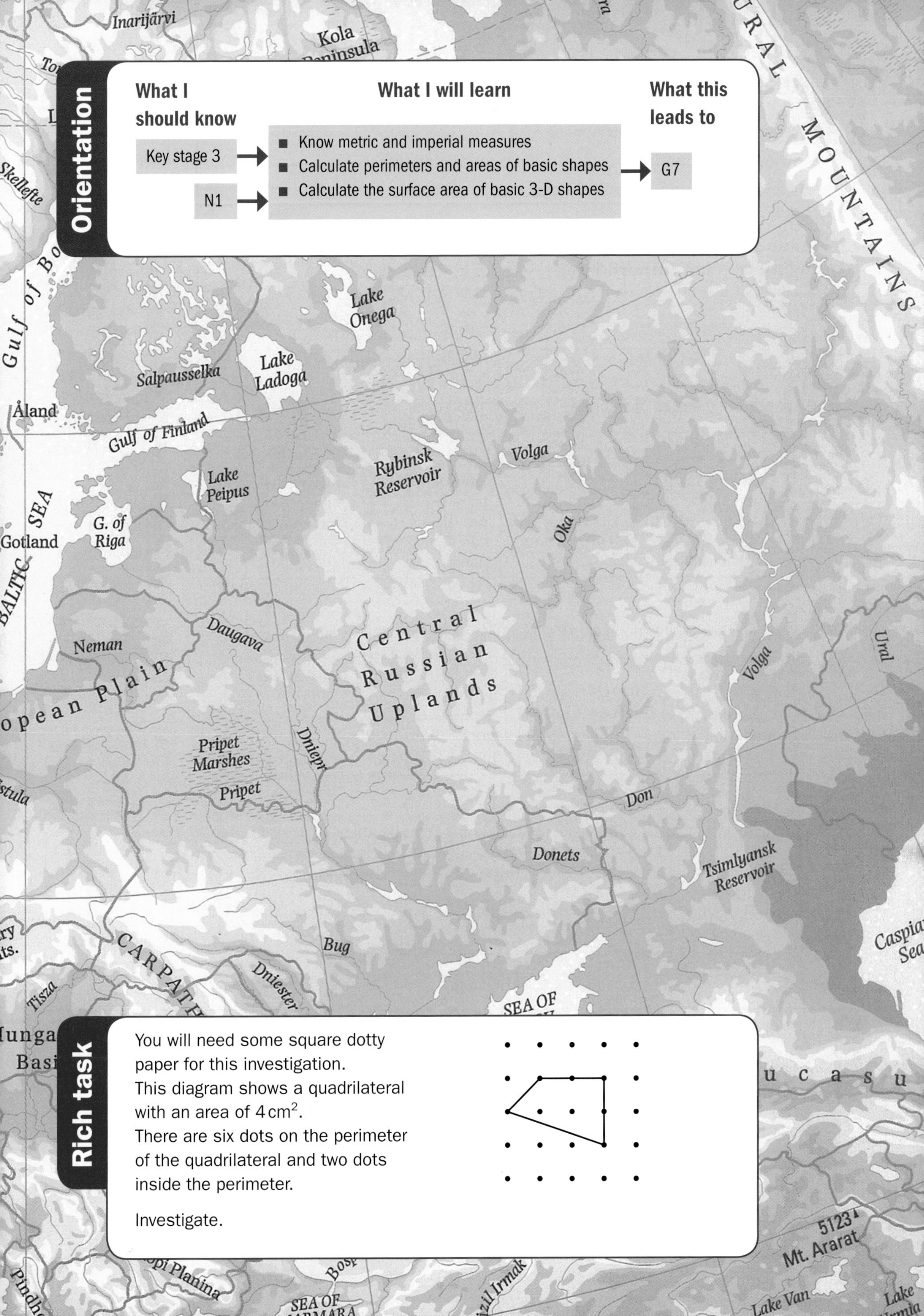

Orientation

What I should know		What I will learn		What this leads to
Key stage 3	→	■ Know metric and imperial measures ■ Calculate perimeters and areas of basic shapes ■ Calculate the surface area of basic 3-D shapes	→	G7
N1	→			

Rich task

You will need some square dotty paper for this investigation.

This diagram shows a quadrilateral with an area of 4 cm^2.

There are six dots on the perimeter of the quadrilateral and two dots inside the perimeter.

Investigate.

G1.1 Metric and imperial measures

This spread will show you how to:

- Know rough metric equivalents to imperial measures
- Convert measurements from one unit to another

Keywords
Capacity
Convert
Equivalents
Imperial
Length
Mass
Metric

You can measure **length**, **mass** and **capacity** using **metric** and **imperial** units.

1 lb of bananas

Paris 40 km

- **Length** is a measure of distance.

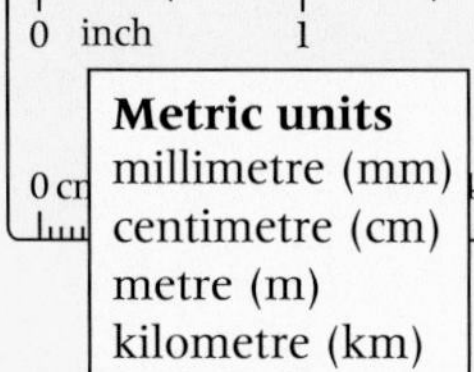

Metric units		Imperial units	Equivalents
millimetre (mm)	10 mm = 1 cm	inch (")	5 miles ≈ 8 km
centimetre (cm)	100 cm = 1 m	foot (')	1 inch ≈ 2.5 cm
metre (m)	1000 m = 1 km	yard (3 ft = 1 yd)	1 yard ≈ 1 m
kilometre (km)		mile	1 foot ≈ 30 cm

≈ means approximately equal to.

1 metre is a bit longer than 1 yard.

- **Mass** is a measure of the amount of matter in an object. Mass is linked to weight.

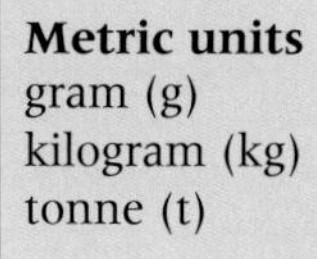

Metric units		Imperial units	Equivalents
gram (g)	1000 g = 1 kg	ounce (oz)	1 ounce ≈ 30 g
kilogram (kg)	1000 kg = 1 tonne	pound (lb)	1 kg ≈ 2.2 lb
tonne (t)		stone	
		ton	

1 lb of jam

1 kg of sugar

- **Capacity** is a measure of the amount of liquid a 3-D shape will hold.

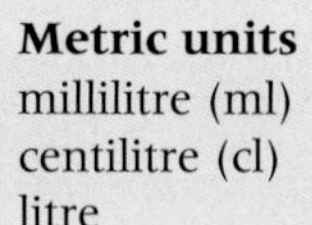

Metric units		Imperial units	Equivalents
millilitre (ml)	1000 ml = 1 litre	pint	1 pint ≈ 600 ml
centilitre (cl)	100 cl = 1 litre	gallon	1.75 pints ≈ 1 litre
litre			1 gallon ≈ 4.5 litres

1 pint of milk

1 litre of lemonade

Example

Calculate the approximate length of a 12 inch ruler in

a centimetres **b** millimetres.

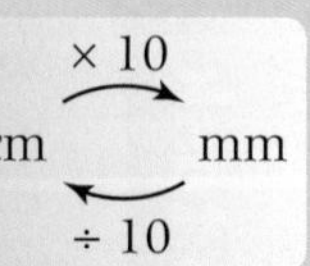

a $1'' \approx 2\frac{1}{2}$ cm

$12'' \approx 2\frac{1}{2} \times 12 = 30$ cm

b 1 cm = 10 mm

30 cm = 30 × 10 = 300 mm

Exercise G1.1 — Grade F

1 Choose one of these metric units to measure each of these items.

millimetre	gram	millilitre	centimetre
kilogram	centilitre	metre	tonne
litre	kilometre		

a your height
b amount of tea in a mug
c your weight
d length of a suitcase
e weight of a suitcase
f distance from Paris to Madrid
g quantity of drink in a can
h amount of petrol in a car
i weight of an elephant
j weight of an apple.

Write the appropriate abbreviation next to your answers.

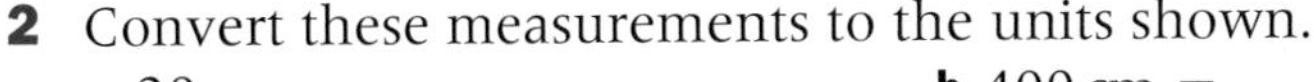

2 Convert these measurements to the units shown.

a 20 mm = ___ cm
b 400 cm = ___ m
c 450 cm = ___ m
d 4000 m = ___ km
e 0.5 cm = ___ mm
f 4.5 kg = ___ g
g 6000 g = ___ kg
h 6500 g = ___ kg
i 2500 kg = ___ t
j 3 litres = ___ ml

3 Convert these distances to miles.

a Berlin 16 km
b Dusseldorf 40 km
c Bonn 88 km
d Dresden 84 km

4 Convert these measurements to centimetres.

a 1 inch
b 5 inches
c 6 inches
d 12 inches
e 36 inches

5 Use 1 kg $\approx$ 2.2 lb to convert these weights to pounds.

a 2 kg
b 40 kg
c 50 kg
d 0.5 kg
e 2.5 kg

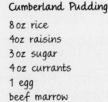

A02 Functional Maths

6 Use 1 oz $\approx$ 30 g to convert ounces to grams in these recipes.

a Lemon Curd
6 oz butter
12 oz caster sugar
6 lemons
6 eggs

b Cumberland Pudding
8 oz rice
4 oz raisins
3 oz sugar
4 oz currants
1 egg
beef marrow

c Chocolate Crunchies
6 oz self-raising flour
2 oz cornflour
2 oz cornflakes
1 oz drinking chocolate
6 oz margarine
3 oz sugar

7 The speed limit on a motorway in the UK is 70 miles per hour. Calculate the speed limit in kilometres per hour.

G1.2 Perimeter and area of a rectangle and a triangle

This spread will show you how to:

- Calculate the area and perimeter of rectangles and triangles

Keywords
Area
Base
Perimeter
Perpendicular height
Square units

- The **perimeter** of a shape is the distance around it.

Perimeter is a length, so it is measured in mm, cm, m or km.

- The **area** of a shape is the amount of space it covers.

Area is measured in **square units**: mm^2, cm^2, m^2 or km^2.

You can find the area of a rectangle using:

- Area of a **rectangle** = length × width

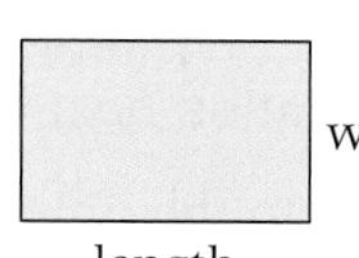

This formula also works for a square.

You can find a formula for the area of any triangle.

For this triangle ...

base

complete the rectangle ...

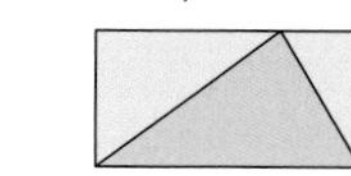

the area has doubled.

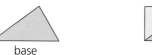

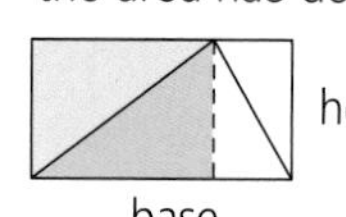

The area of a triangle is half the area of the surrounding rectangle.

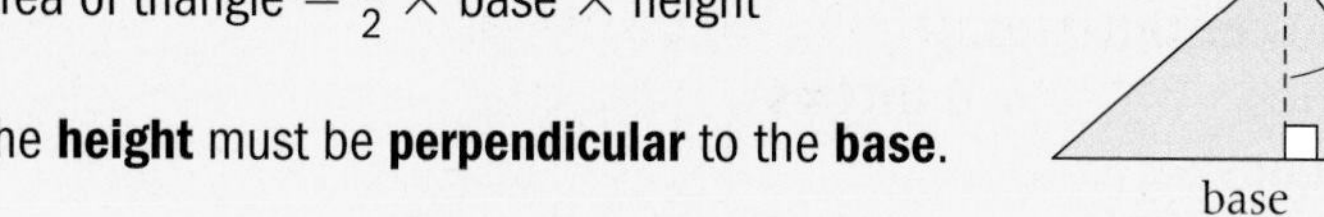

- Area of triangle = $\frac{1}{2}$ × base × height

  The **height** must be **perpendicular** to the **base**.

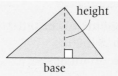

height

base

Perpendicular means at right angles.

You can find the area of a compound shape by splitting it into rectangles and triangles.

Example

Calculate the perimeter and area of each shape.

a

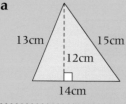

13cm, 15cm, 12cm, 14cm

b

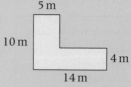

5 m, 10 m, 4 m, 14 m

The two missing lengths are:
10 − 4 = 6 m
and
14 − 5 = 9 m

a Perimeter = 15 + 13 + 14
= 42 cm

Area = $\frac{1}{2}$ × base × height
= $\frac{1}{2}$ × 14 × 12
= 84 cm^2

b Perimeter = 5 + 6 + 9 + 4 + 14 + 10
= 48 m

Area = area of green rectangle
+ area of orange rectangle
= 10 × 5 + 9 × 4
= 50 + 36 = 86 m^2

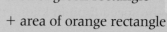

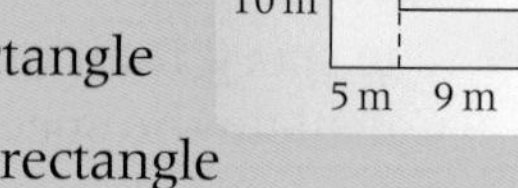

Exercise G1.2 Grade D

1 Calculate the perimeter and area of each rectangle. Give the units of your answers.

a 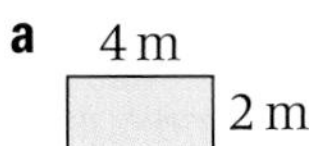

b 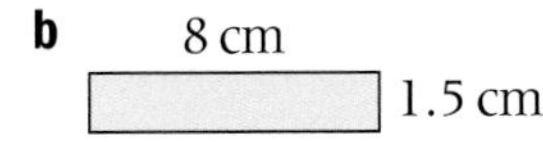

c 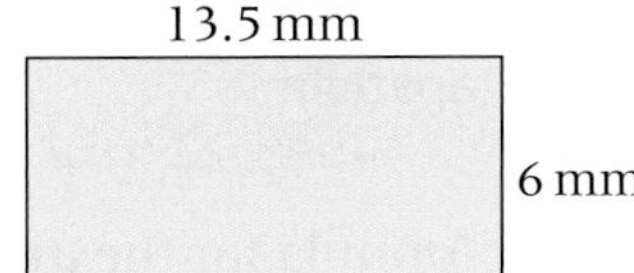

d 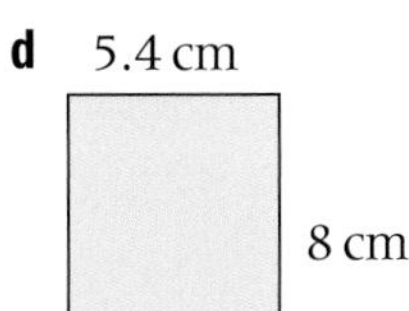

e 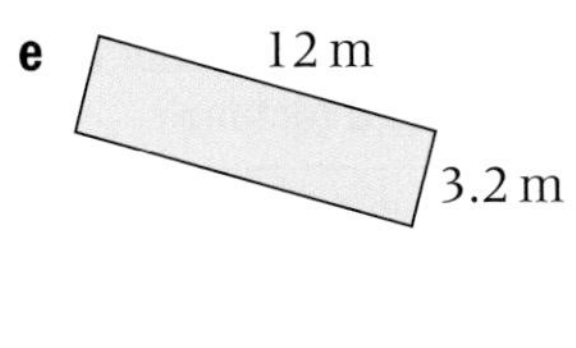

2 Calculate the area of each triangle.

a 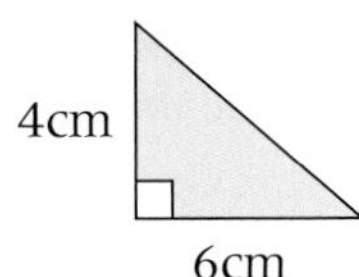

b 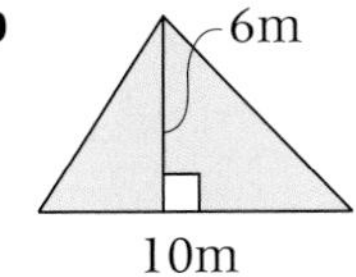

c 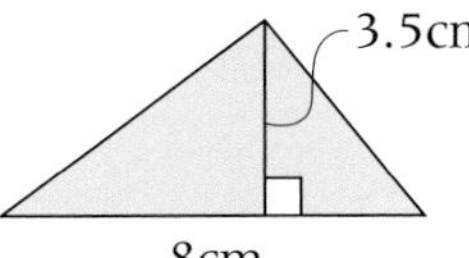

d 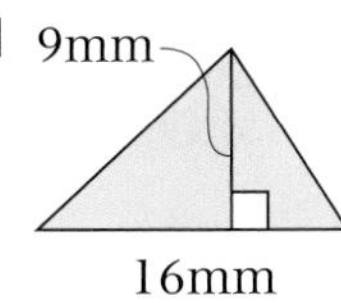

e 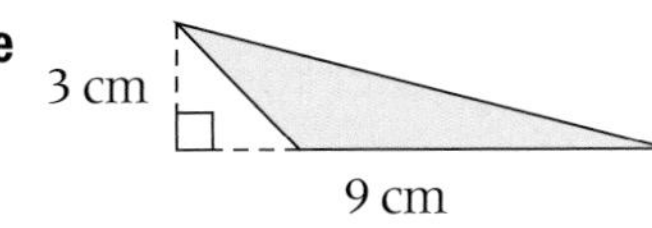

Problem AO3

3 Calculate the missing lengths. Give the units of your answers.

a 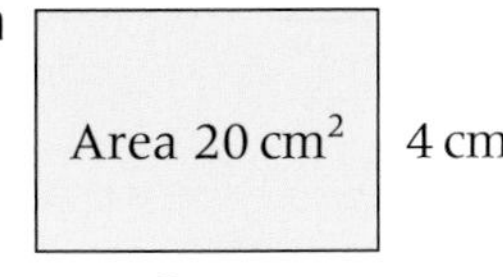

b 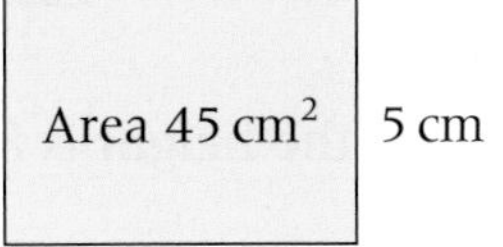

c 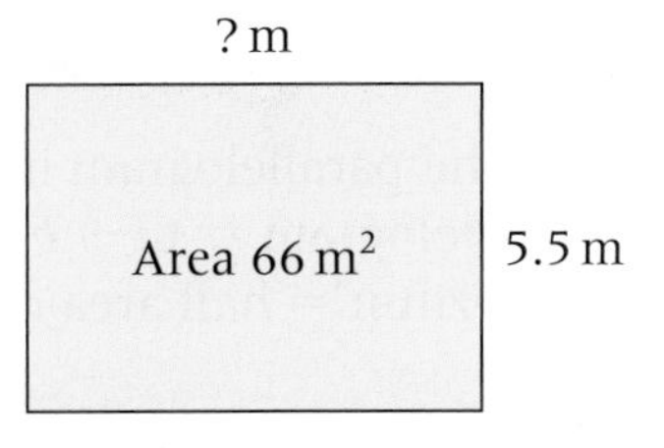

4 Calculate the perimeter and area of each shape. State the units of your answers.

a 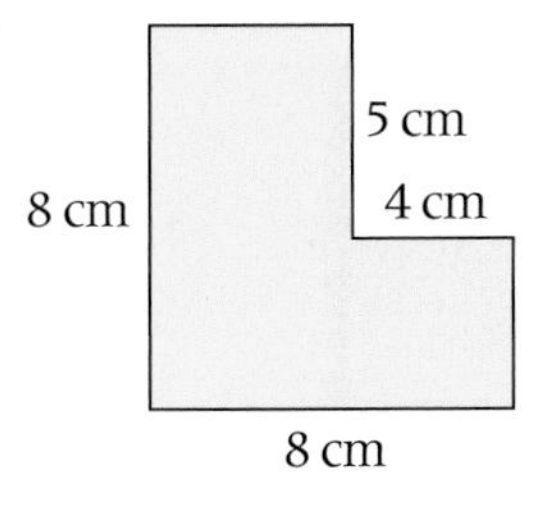

b 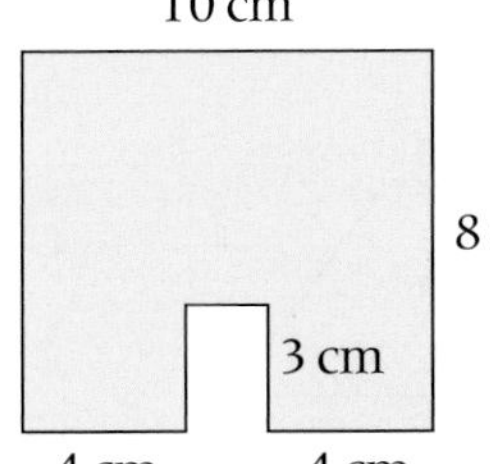

c 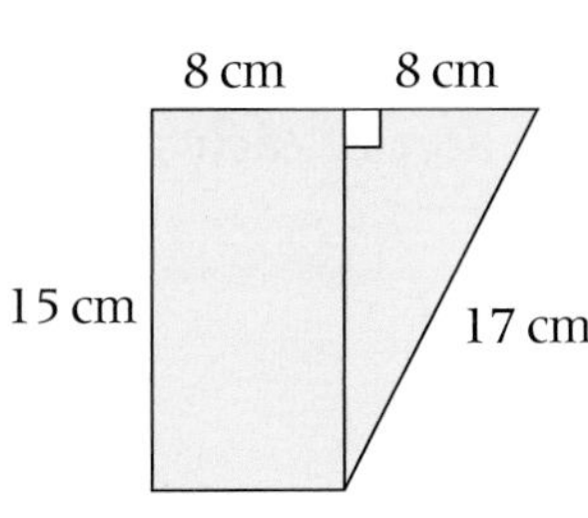

G1.3 Area of a parallelogram and a trapezium

This spread will show you how to:

- Use the formula to find the area of any parallelogram
- Use formulae of rectangles, triangles and parallelograms to find the area of any trapezium

Keywords
Area
Base
Parallelogram
Perpendicular height
Trapezium

You can find the formula for the **area** of any **parallelogram**.

For this parallelogram ...

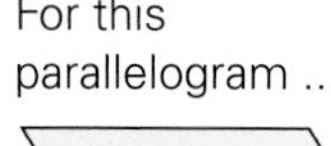

cut off one triangle ...

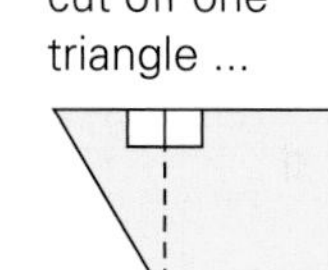

and fit it on the other end ... to make a rectangle.

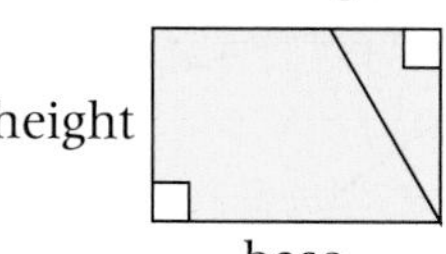

- Area of parallelogram = **base** × **perpendicular height.**

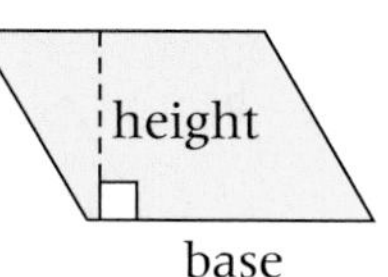

The height must be perpendicular to the base.

You can find the formula for the area of any **trapezium**.

You can fit two **congruent** trapeziums together to make a parallelogram.

Congruent means identical.

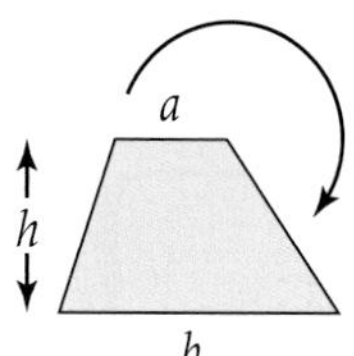

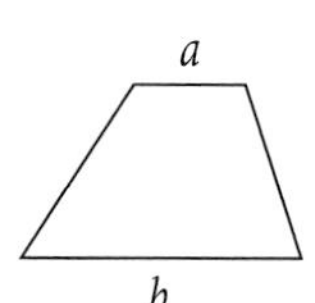

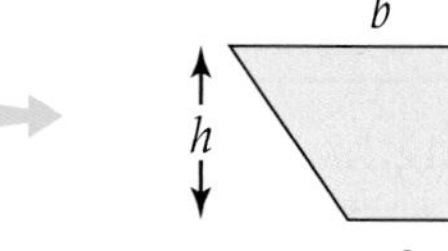

The base of the parallelogram is $a + b$ and the height is h.
Area of parallelogram = $(a + b) \times h$
Area of trapezium = half area of parallelogram.

- Area of trapezium $= \frac{1}{2} \times (a + b) \times h$

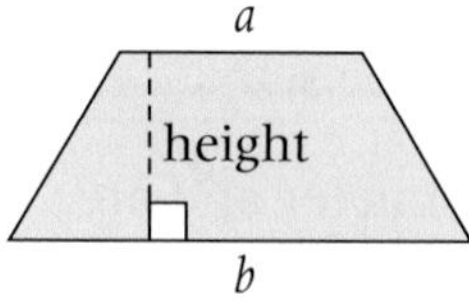

The height is the perpendicular distance between the parallel sides.

Example

Calculate the area of each shape.

a

3 cm
5 cm

b

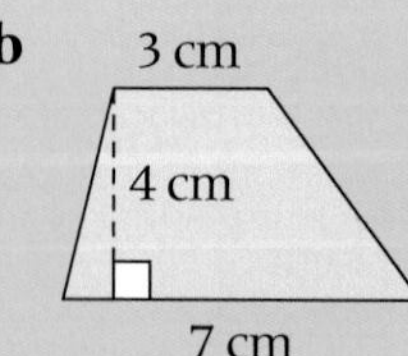

a Area of parallelogram $= 5 \times 3$
$= 15\,\text{cm}^2$

b Area of trapezium $= \frac{1}{2}(3 + 7) \times 4$
$= 5 \times 4$
$= 20\,\text{cm}^2$

Always include the units in your answer.

Exercise G1.3 Grade D

1 Calculate the area of each parallelogram.

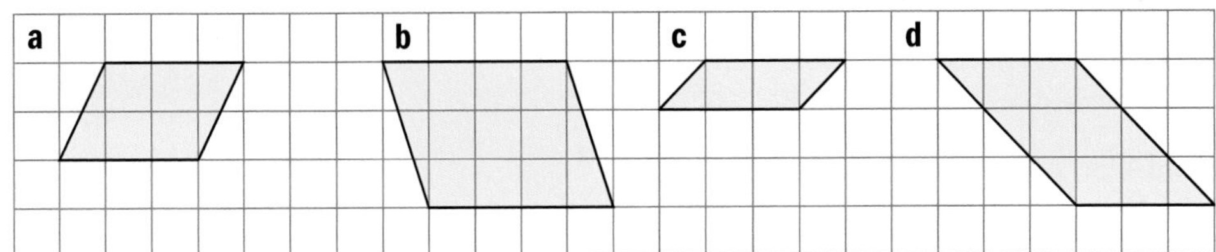

2 Calculate the area of each trapezium.

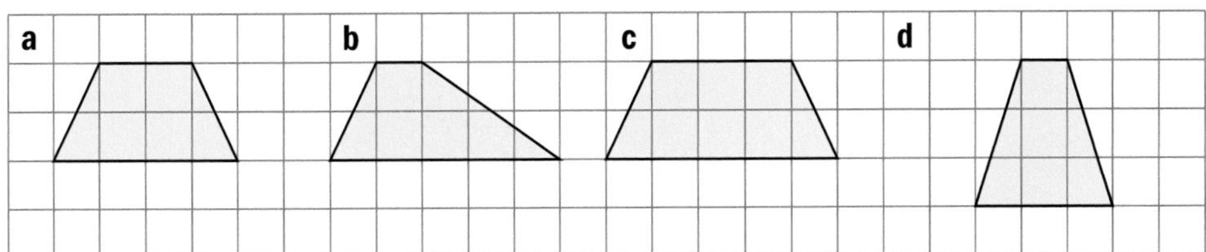

3 Calculate the area of each parallelogram. State the units of your answers.

a 8cm, 10cm

b

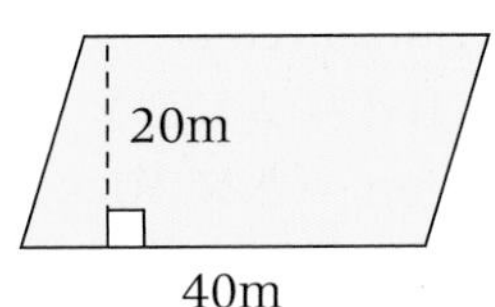

c

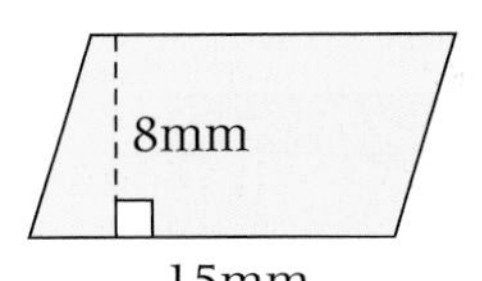

d

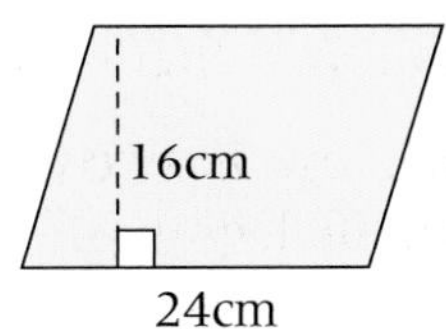

4 Calculate the area of each trapezium. State the units of your answers.

a

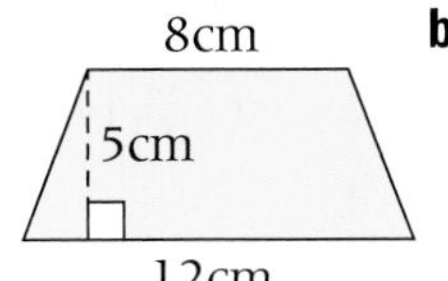

b

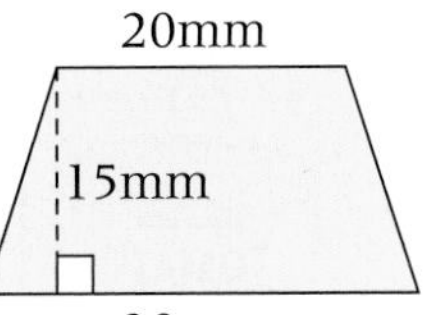

c

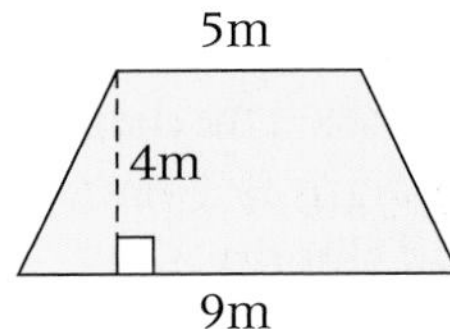

d

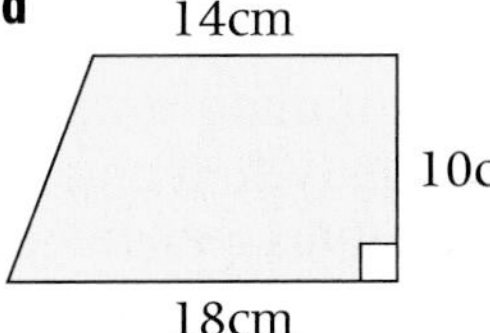

Problem A03

5 The areas of these shapes are given. Calculate the unknown lengths.

a

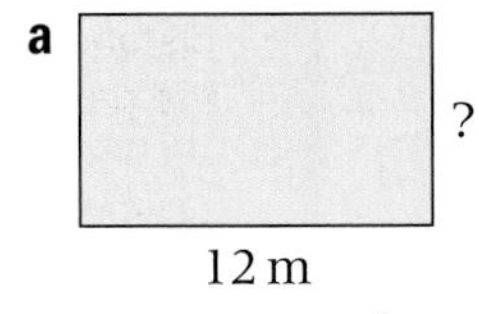

b

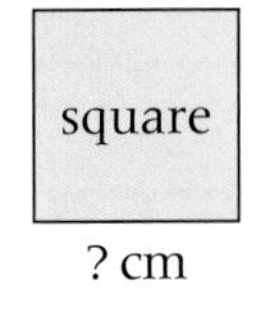

c

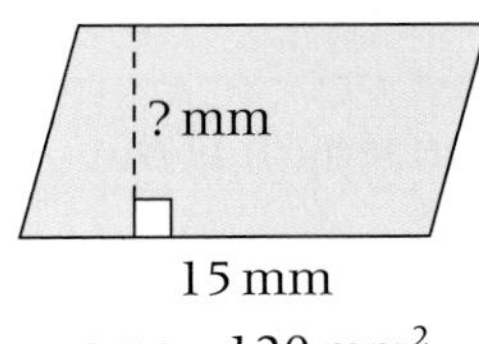

d

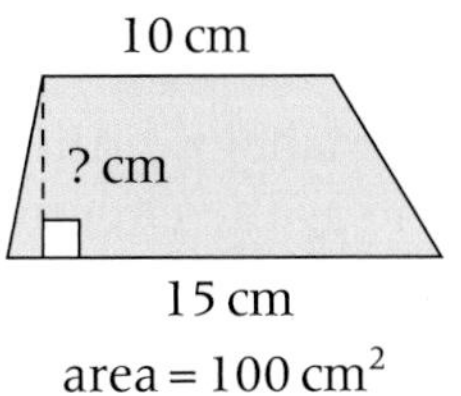

6 **a** Calculate the area of this shape using the formula for the area of a trapezium.

b Calculate the area by adding the areas of the triangles and the square.

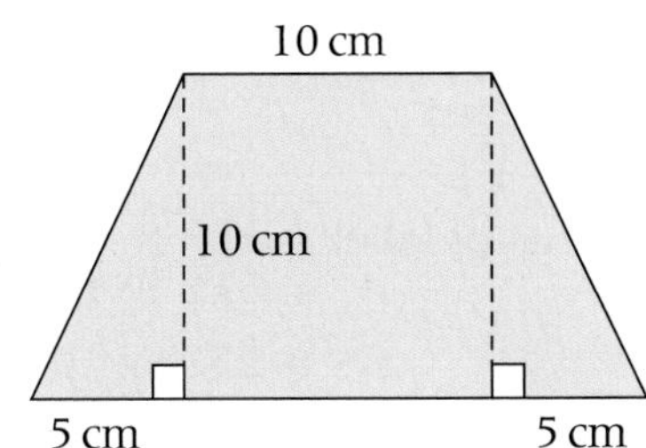

G1.4 Surface area

This spread will show you how to:

- Find the surface area of simple shapes using the area formulae for triangles and rectangles

Keywords
Face
Net
Surface area

When you unfold a shape its **net** is formed.

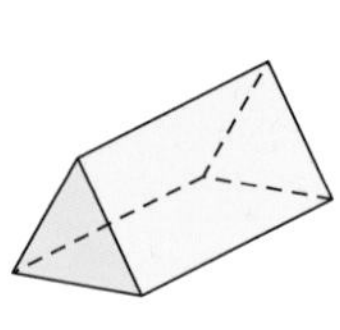

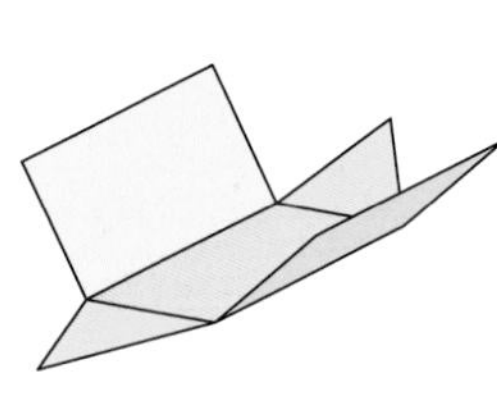

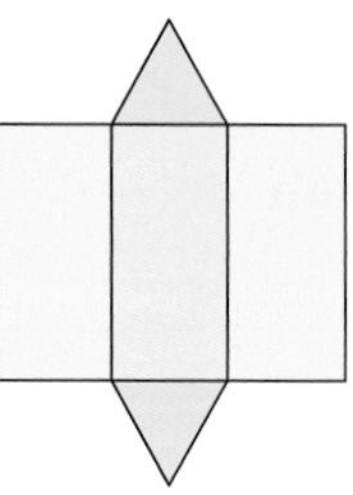

The area of the net is called the surface area.

- The **surface area** of a 3-D shape is the total area of its **faces**.

Units of area are cm^2.

A cuboid has 6 faces. They are in pairs.

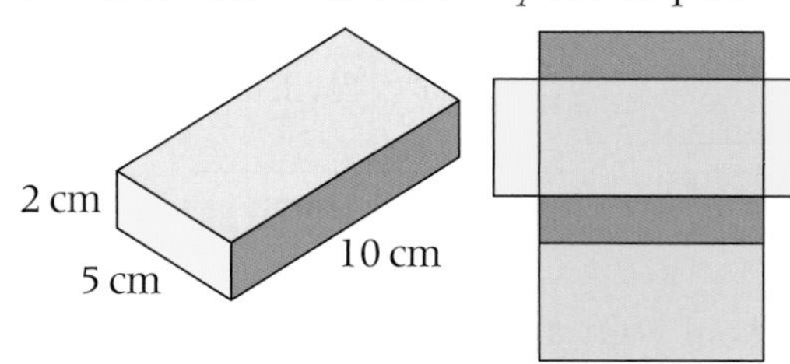

The surface area is

$$
\begin{aligned}
2 \times \text{red} &= 2 \times 2 \times 10 = 40\text{cm}^2 \\
2 \times \text{green} &= 2 \times 10 \times 5 = 100\text{cm}^2 \\
2 \times \text{yellow} &= 2 \times 5 \times 2 = 20\text{cm}^2 \\
\text{surface area} &= 160\text{cm}^2
\end{aligned}
$$

Example

A tin of tomato soup is shown. The diameter of the circle is 8cm and the height is 10cm. The label fits exactly round the tin.

Calculate the area of the label.
Give your answer to a suitable degree of accuracy.

$\pi = 3.14...$

If the label is unfurled, the length is the same as the circumference.

The label is a rectangle.

Circumference of a circle $= \pi \times d$

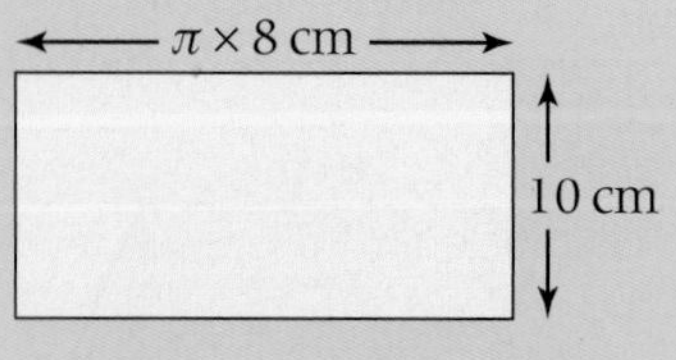

Area of label $= \pi \times 8 \times 10$
$= 251.327\ 41$
$= 251\text{cm}^2$ (to nearest whole number)

Exercise G1.4 — Grade D

1 A 4 cm by 6 cm by 8 cm cuboid is shown.
Calculate
a the area of the red rectangle
b the area of the orange rectangle
c the area of the green rectangle
d the surface area of the cuboid.

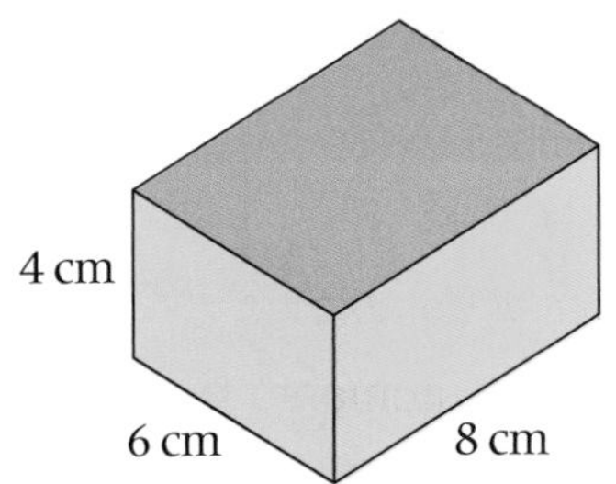

2 Calculate the surface area of these cuboids.

State the units of your answer.

a

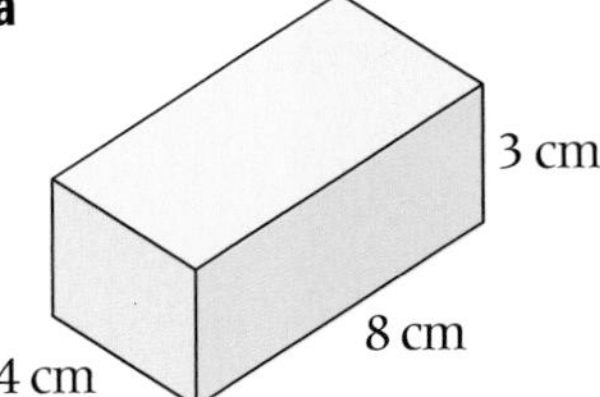

b

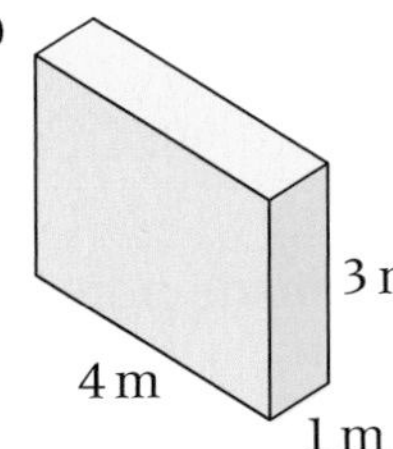

c

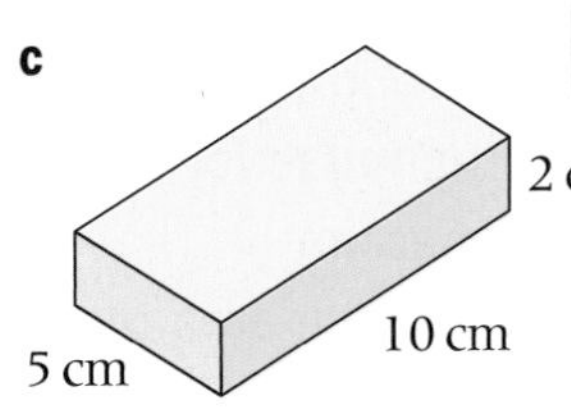

d

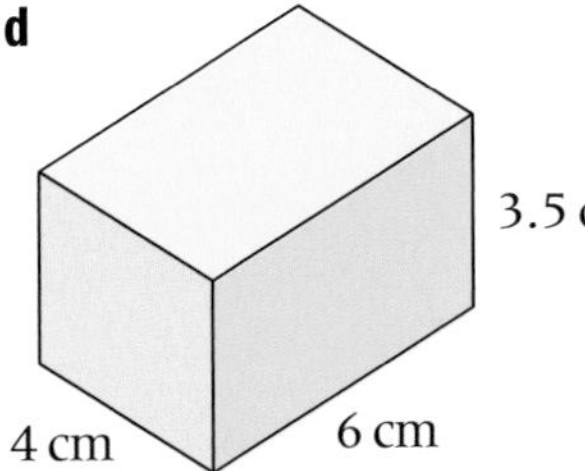

e

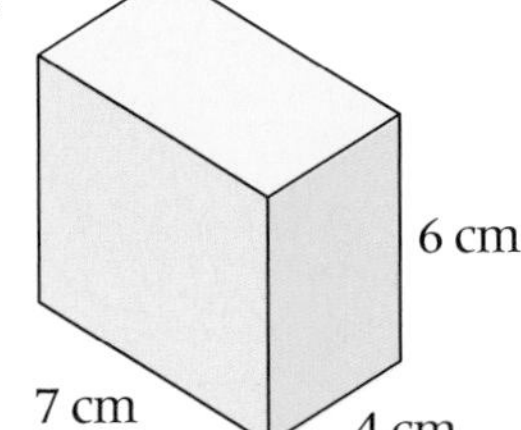

3 Two views of the same triangular prism are shown.

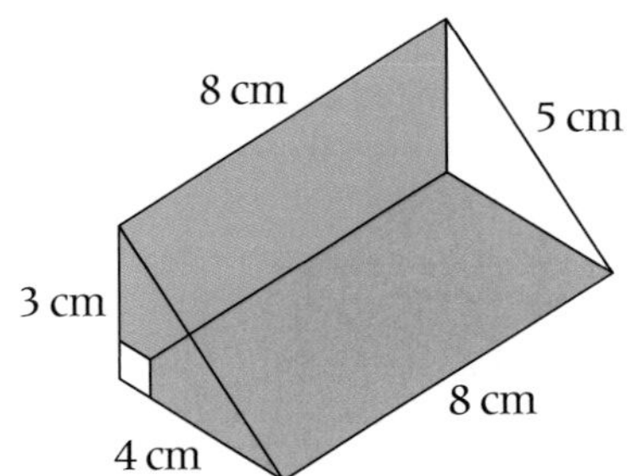

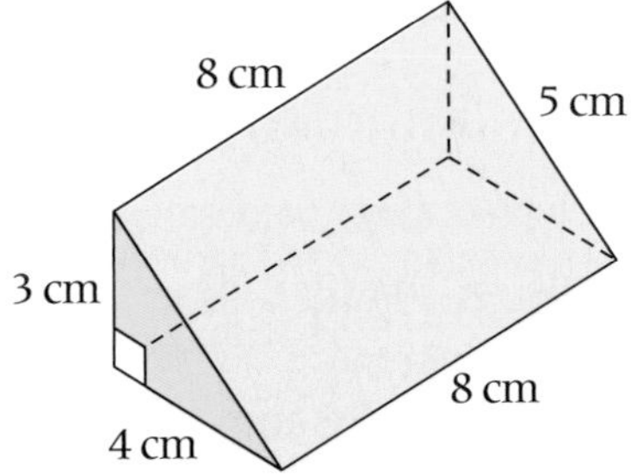

Calculate the area of the
a red rectangle **b** grey rectangle **c** green rectangle
d orange triangle **e** the surface area of the triangular prism.

4 Calculate the surface area of these shapes.

a

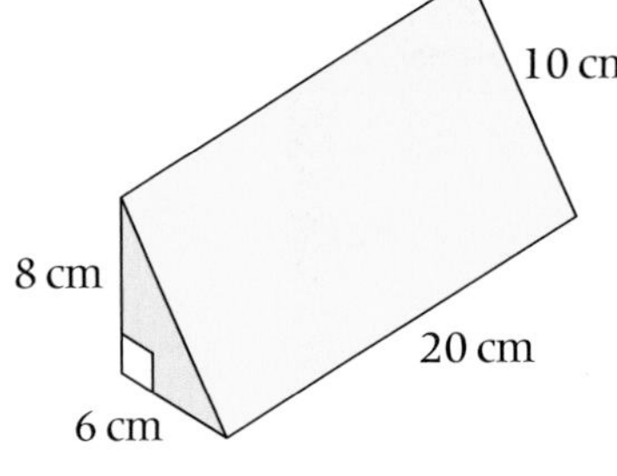

triangular prism

b

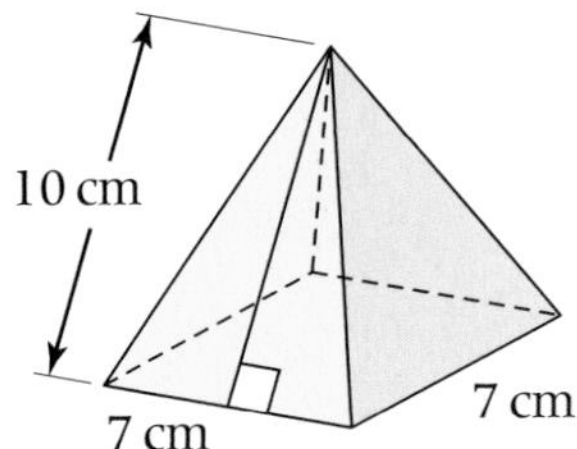

square-based pyramid

DID YOU KNOW?

The Great Pyramid of Giza was 145.75 m tall with four 229 m long bases when it was built. That's a surface area of 66 753.5 m^2!

G1 Summary

Check out

You should now be able to:

- Convert measurements from one unit to another
- Know rough metric equivalents of imperial units
- Calculate the perimeter and area of shapes made from rectangles and triangles
- Use the formulae for the area of a triangle, a parallelogram and a trapezium
- Find the surface area of shapes made from rectangles and triangles

Worked exam question

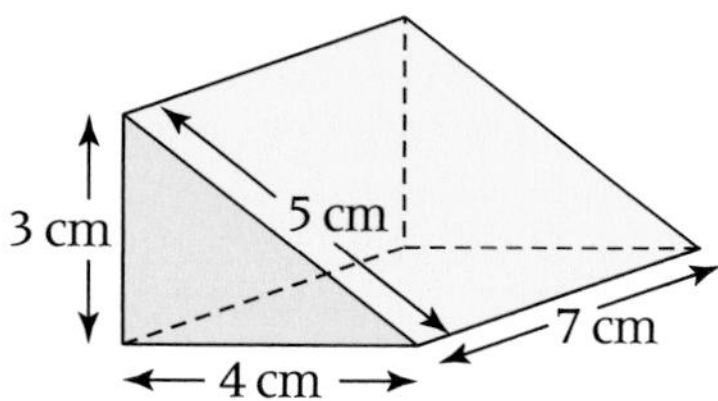

Diagram NOT accurately drawn

Work out the total surface area of the triangular prism. (3)

(Edexcel Limited 2008)

Area of one triangle $= \frac{1}{2} \times (3 \times 4)$
$= 6\,\text{cm}^2$
Area of the other triangle $= 6\,\text{cm}^2$
Area of the 4 cm by 7 cm rectangle $= 4 \times 7$
$= 28\,\text{cm}^2$
Area of the 3 cm by 7 cm rectangle $= 3 \times 7$
$= 21\,\text{cm}^2$
Area of the 5 cm by 7 cm rectangle $= 5 \times 7$
$= 35\,\text{cm}^2$
$6 + 6 + 28 + 21 + 35 = 96\,\text{cm}^2$

Show the calculation for each area.

Show the addition of the 5 areas.

Exam questions

1

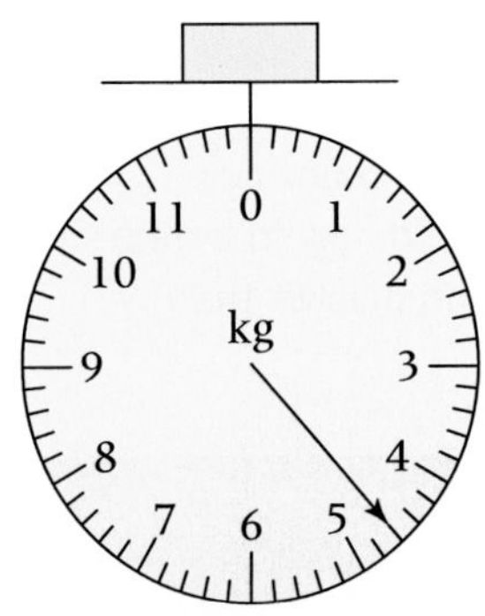

a Write down the weight in kg shown on the scale. (1)

b i How many pounds are there in 1 kg?

The weight of a baby is 5 kg.

ii Change 5 kg to pounds. (2)

(Edexcel Limited 2008)

A03

2

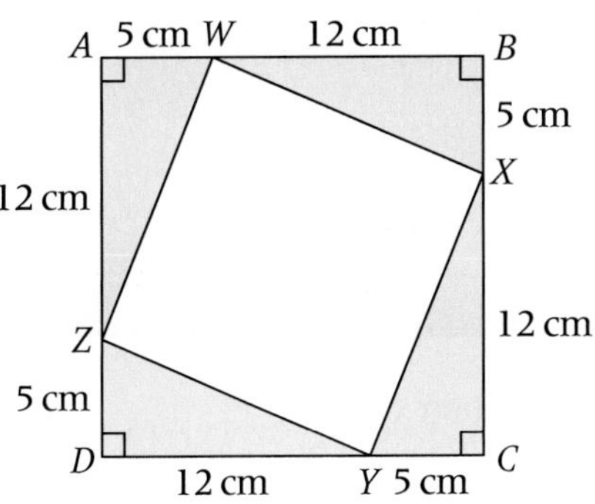

Diagram NOT accurately drawn

Work out the area of the quadrilateral *WXYZ*. (5)

A02

3 James and Sam went on holiday by plane.

The pilot said the speed of the plane was 285 kilometres per hour.

James told Sam that 285 kilometres per hour was about the same as 80 metres per second.

Was James correct?

Show working to justify your answer. (3)

(Edexcel Limited 2005)

A1 Linear graphs

Introduction

When you hire a car, the price often increases in equal amounts for each extra day of hiring. This is an example of a linear function, and the graph will be a straight line.

What's the point?

Linear functions occur commonly in man-made situations, such as in currency conversion and in working out tariffs and charges. If you understand how to create and use linear graphs, you can often solve real-life problems much quicker than calculating from scratch.

Check in

1 Work out the value of each expression when $x = 4$.

a $x + 5$ **b** $x - 6$ **c** $3x$ **d** $\frac{x}{2}$

2 Plot these coordinates on a copy of this grid.

a (3, 4)
b (1, 3)
c (−1, 2)
d 4, −5)
e (−3, −4)
f (−3, 2)

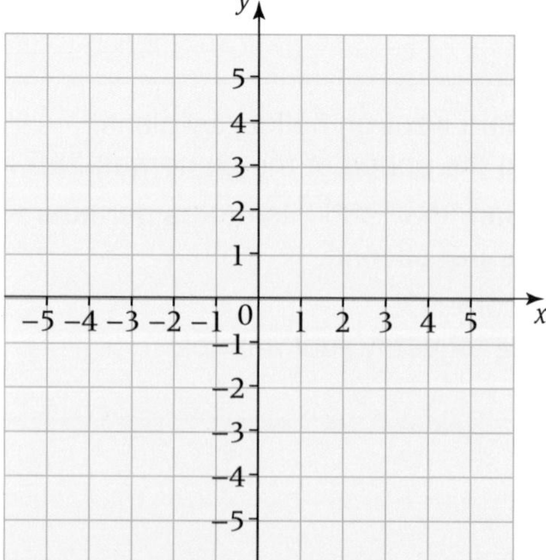

Orientation

What I should know		What I will learn		What this leads to
Key stage 3	→	■ Write an equation to represent a function ■ Plot straight line graphs of functions ■ Recognise the equation of a straight line ■ Calculate the coordinates of the midpoint of a line segment	→	A3

Rich task

To win a game of '4-in-a-line', a player needs to have placed four of their pieces in a line. In this game the winning line of four is clearly marked.

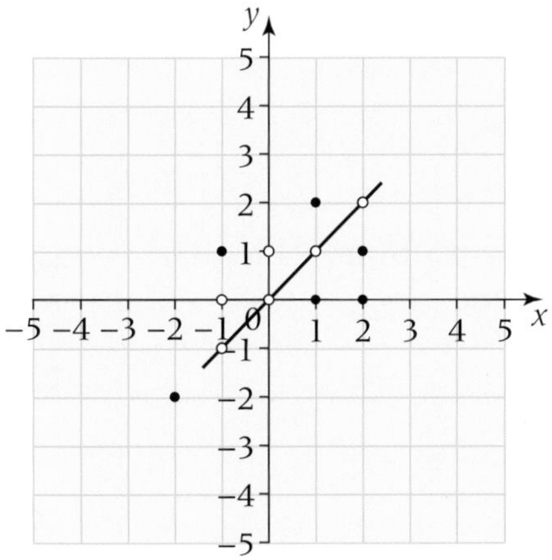

What is the connection between the x and y coordinates of the points on the winning line?

Investigate other winning lines of four that are possible on the grid.

A1.1 Functions

This spread will show you how to:

- Write an equation to represent a function
- Write the input and output values of a function as coordinate-pairs

Keywords
Equation
Function
Map
Substitute

- A **function** is a rule that **maps** one number to another number.

You can draw a function machine and work out the outputs for different inputs.

Example

Draw a function machine for the function $x \to 4x + 7$.
Work out the outputs for the inputs −2, −1, 0, 1, 2.

Input, x		Output, y
−2		−1
−1		3
0	→ $4x+7$ →	7
1		11
2		15

$4x + 7$
$x = -2$
$4 \times -2 + 7 = -8 + 7$
$= -1$

Substitute the input value for x in the function machine.

- You can write an **equation** to represent a function.

For the function $x \to$ $4x+7$ $\to$ the equation is $y = 4x + 7$.

The function links the two variables x and y.

Each input value x gives an output value y.

- You can write the input and output values as **coordinate pairs** (x, y).

Example

This function machine is for the function $x \to 2x - 9$.

Input $x \to$ $2x-9$ $\to$ Output

a Write an equation to represent the function.
b Work out the output values, y, for input values of x from −3 to +3.
c Write the inputs and outputs as coordinate pairs.

x-values from −3 to +3 are: −3, −2, −1, 0, 1, 2, 3.

a $y = 2x - 9$

b

Input		Output	**c**
−3		−15	(−3, −15)
−2		−13	(−2, −13)
−1		−11	(−1, −11)
0	→ $2x-9$ →	−9	(0, −9)
1		−7	(1, −7)
2		−5	(2, −5)
3		−3	(3, −3)

Exercise A1.1

Grade E

1 Find the outputs for the inputs given in these function machines:

a

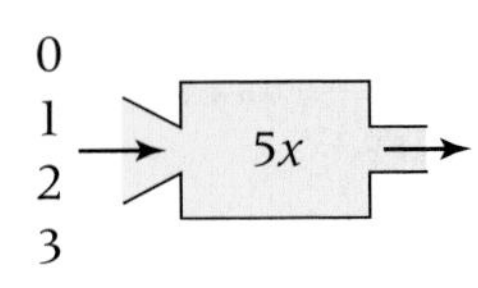

b

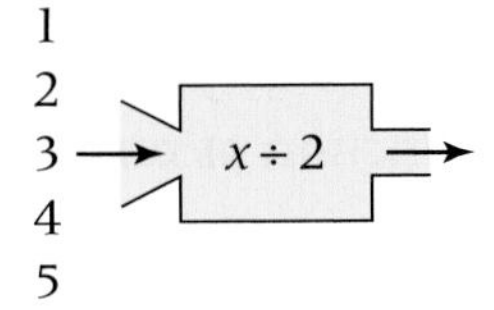

c

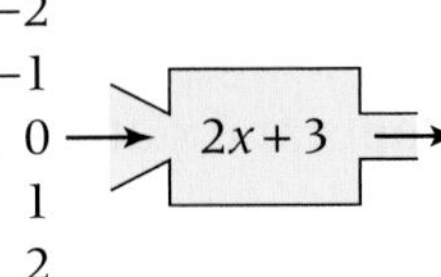

d

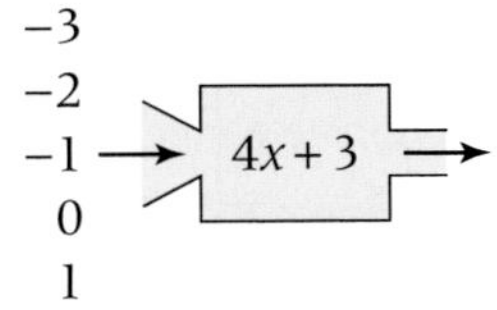

e

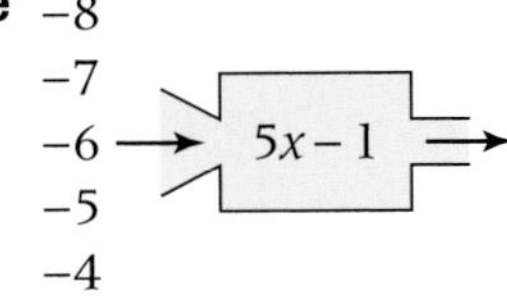

f

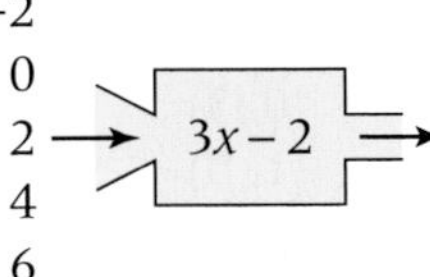

2 For each function

i draw a function machine

ii work out the outputs for the inputs −2, −1, 0, 1, 2.

The first one is started for you.

a $x \rightarrow 3x + 2$

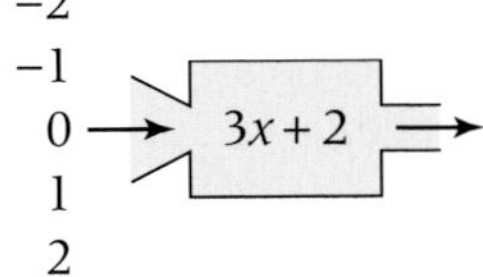

b $x \rightarrow 5x + 2$

c $x \rightarrow 2x - 3$

d $x \rightarrow 4x + 7$

e $x \rightarrow \frac{1}{2}x + 3$

f $x \rightarrow 3x - 11$

g $x \rightarrow \frac{1}{2}x - 2$

3 **a** Draw the function machine for $x \rightarrow 2x + 6$.

b Write an equation to represent the function.

c Work out the output values, y, for values of x from −3 to +3.

d Write the inputs and outputs as coordinate pairs.

4 Repeat question **3** for the function $x \rightarrow \frac{1}{2}x - 1$.

AO3 Problem

5 Match each equation to a function machine and a set of coordinate pairs.

Equation	Function machine	Coordinate pairs
a $y = x + 3$	(i) $2x+1$	(1) (−2, −2), (−1, 1), (0, 4), (1, 7), (2, 10)
b $y = 2x + 1$	(ii) $x+3$	(2) (−2, −9), (−1, −7), (0, −5), (1, −3), (2, −1)
c $y = 3x + 4$	(iii) $4x-1$	(3) (−2, 1), (−1, 2), (0, 3), (1, 4), (2, 5)
d $y = 4x - 1$	(iv) $2x-5$	(4) (−2, −9), (−1, −5), (0, −1), (1, 3), (2, 7)
e $y = 2x - 5$	(v) $3x+4$	(5) (−2, −3), (−1, −1), (0, 1), (1, 3), (2, 5)

A1.2 Drawing linear graphs 1

This spread will show you how to:

- Plot straight line graphs of functions

Keywords
Graph
Linear

You can write the inputs and outputs of a function as **coordinate pairs**.
For example, $y = 2x + 3$

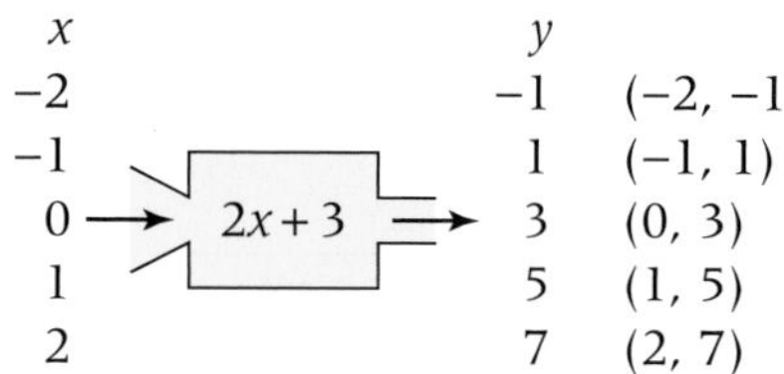

You can write the coordinate pairs for a function using a table.

x	−2	−1	0	1	2
y	2 × −2 + 3 = −1	1	3	5	7
	(−2, −1)	(−1, 1)	(0, 3)	(1, 5)	(2, 7)

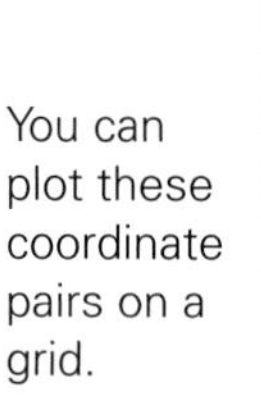

You can
plot these
coordinate
pairs on a
grid.

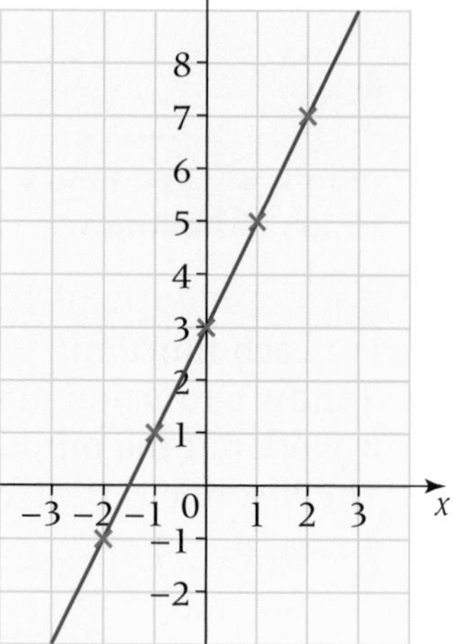

- A function is **linear** if its **graph** is a straight line.

Example

a Copy and complete the table of values for $y = 3x - 2$.

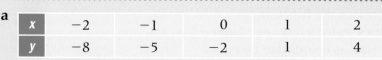

x	−2	−1	0	1	2
y					

b Write the coordinate pairs. **c** Draw the graph of $y = 3x - 2$.

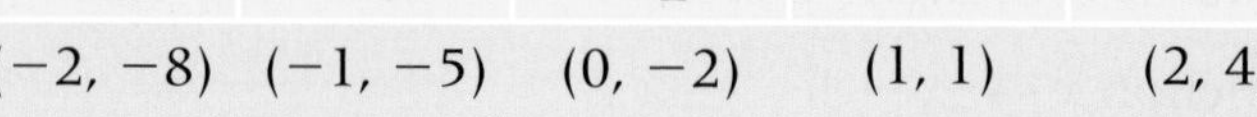

a

x	−2	−1	0	1	2
y	−8	−5	−2	1	4

b (−2, −8) (−1, −5) (0, −2) (1, 1) (2, 4)

c

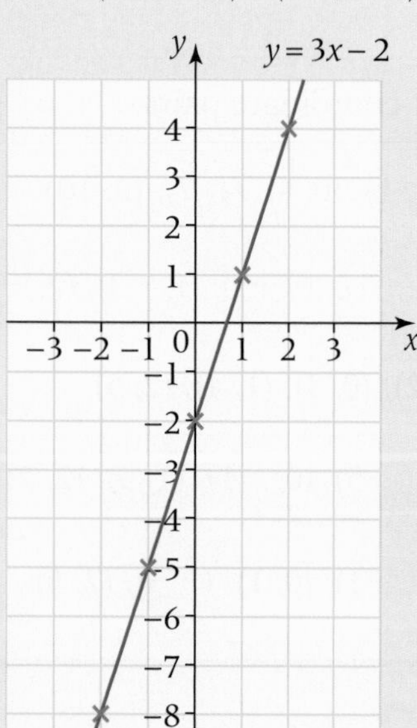

p.164

Exercise A1.2 Grade D

1 **a** Copy and complete the table of values for $y = 3x + 3$.

x	-2	-1	0	1	2
y		0			9

b Write the coordinate pairs.
c Copy the coordinate grid on the right on to square grid paper.
d Plot the coordinate pairs from part **b** on your grid.
e Join these points with a straight line.
f Label the line with its equation.

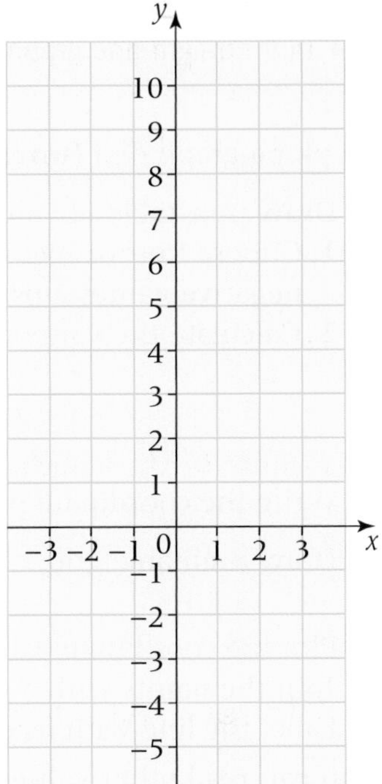

2 **a** Copy and complete the table of values for $y = -x + 3$.

x	-2	-1	0	1	2
y	$-1 \times -2 + 3$ $= 2 + 3 = 5$			2	

b Write the coordinate pairs.
c Copy the coordinate grid from question **1** on to squared grid paper.
d Plot the coordinate pairs from part **b** on your grid.
e Join these points with a straight line.
f Label the line with its equation.

3 **a** Copy and complete the table of values for $x + y = 6$.

x	-2	-1	0	1	2
y	8		6		

b Write the coordinate pairs.
c Copy the coordinate grid from question **1** on to square grid paper.
d Plot the coordinate pairs from part **b** on your grid.
e Join these points with a straight line.
f Label the line with its equation.

Did you know?

The coordinate system that you use is called the Cartesian coordinate system, invented by the mathematician and philosopher René Descartes in the 17th century.

4 **a** Copy and complete the table of values for $y = 2x - 5$.

x	-2	-1	0	1	2
y	-9			-3	

b Write the coordinate pairs.
c Draw an appropriate coordinate grid on to square grid paper.
d Plot the coordinate pairs from part **b** on your grid.
e Join these points with a straight line.
f Label the line with its equation.

A1.3 More linear graphs

This spread will show you how to:
- Plot straight line graphs of functions

Keywords
Explicitly
Implicit form
Implicitly
Subject

To plot a graph of a **function** — For example, $y = x - 2$

- Draw up a table of values.
  1 Choose four or five values of x, including negative values, positive values and zero. — $x = -2, -1, 0, 1, 2$
  2 Calculate the value of y for each value of x. — $y = x - 2$

x	−2	−1	0	1	2
y	−4	−3	−2	−1	0

- Write the coordinate pairs. — (−2, −4) (−1, −3) (0, −2) (1, −1) (2, 0)
- Draw a suitable grid. — The x-axis needs to go from −2 to 2. The y-axis needs to go from −4 to 0
- Plot the coordinate pairs on the grid.
- Join the points with a straight line.
- Label the line with its equation.

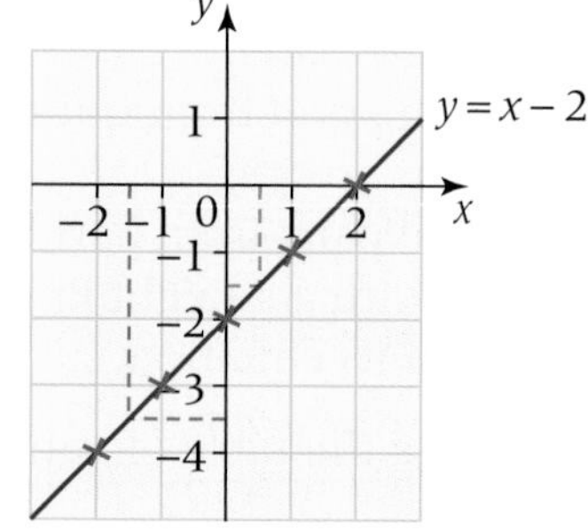

You can read other values from a graph.

When $x = 0.5$, $y = -1.5$
When $y = -3.5$, $x = -1.5$

You can also work these out from the function

When $x = -0.5$, $y = 0.5 - 2 = -1.5$
When $y = -3.5$, $-3.5 = x - 2$
$2 - 3.5 = x - 2 + 2$
$-1.5 = x$
$x = -1.5$

- An equation gives y explicitly in terms of x when y is the **subject** of the equation.
  $y = x - 2$ gives y explicitly in terms of x.

The subject of an equation is the letter on its own, on one side of the =.

- An equation gives y implicitly in terms of x when y is **not** the subject of the equation.
  $x + y = 4$ gives y **implicitly** in terms of x.

For an equation in **implicit form** — $x + y = 4$

- Draw up a table of values.
- Calculate **a** the value of y when $x = 0$ and **b** the value of x when $y = 0$.

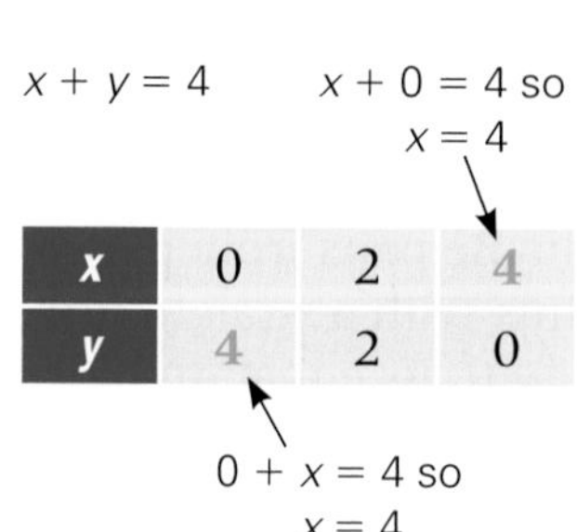

x	0	2	4
y	4	2	0

Exercise A1.3 Grade C

In each of these questions choose values of x from -2 to 2. Work out the values of y, then draw appropriate axes.

1 Draw a graph of each of these functions.

a $y = 3x + 1$ **b** $y = 2x - 2$

c $y = \frac{1}{2}x + 6$ **d** $y = -3x + 2$

2 Draw a graph of each of these functions given in implicit form.

a $x + y = 5$ **b** $y - x = 3$

c $2x + y = 6$ **d** $5x + y = 10$

3 Draw a graph of $y = -2x + 3$.
Use your graph to find
- the value of y when $x = 0.5$
- the value of x when $y = 0$.

4 Draw a graph of $y = 4x + 1$.
Use your graph to find
- the value of y when $x = -0.5$
- the value of x when $y = 7$.

5 Draw a graph of $y = \frac{1}{2}x + 3$.
Use your graph to find
- the value of y when $x = \frac{1}{2}$
- the value of x when $y = 3\frac{1}{4}$.

6 Draw a graph of $x + y = -2$.
Rearrange the equation to find
- the value of y when $x = -2$
- the value of x when $y = -5$.

Use your graph to check your answers.

AO3 Problem

7 Draw graphs of these three functions on the same grid.

a $y = 2x + 1$ **b** $y = 2x - 2$ **c** $y = 2x + 3$

What do you notice?

8 Draw graphs of these three functions on the same grid.
What do you notice?

a $y = -2x + 1$ **b** $y = -2x - 2$ **c** $y = -2x + 3$

Compare your graphs from questions 7 and 8. What do you notice?

9 A straight line has the equation $y = 3x + 5$.

a The point P lies on the line. P has x-coordinate 3.
Find the y-coordinate of point P.

b The point Q also lies on the line. Q has y-coordinate -4.
Find the x-coordinate of point Q.

A1.4 Horizontal and vertical graphs

This spread will show you how to:

- Understand the equation forms of horizontal and vertical graphs

Keywords
Horizontal
Vertical
y-intercept

The points on this **horizontal** graph are
$(-3, 2)$ $(-2, 2)$ $(-1, 2)$ $(0, 2)$ $(1, 2)$ $(2, 2)$ $(3, 2)$

The y-coordinate is always 2.
The equation of this graph is $y = 2$.

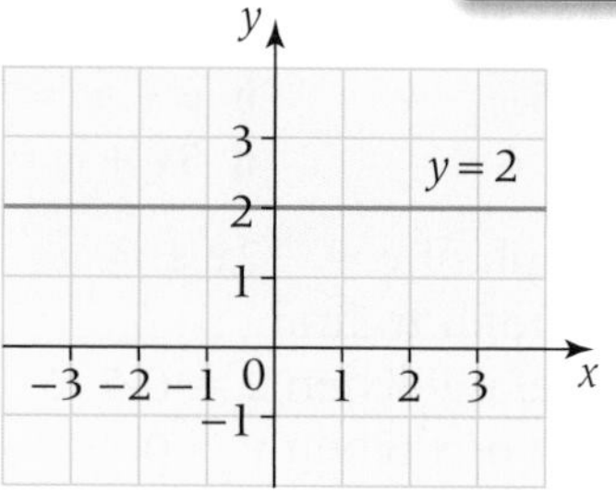

Where a graph cuts the y-axis is called the **y-intercept**.

- The equation of a horizontal graph is always y = a number.

To find the number, look at where the graph cuts the y-axis.

The points on this **vertical** graph are
$(-1, -3)$ $(-1, -2)$ $(-1, -1)$ $(-1, 0)$ $(-1, 1)$
$(-1, 2)$ $(-1, 3)$

The x-coordinate is always -1.
The equation of this graph is $x = -1$.

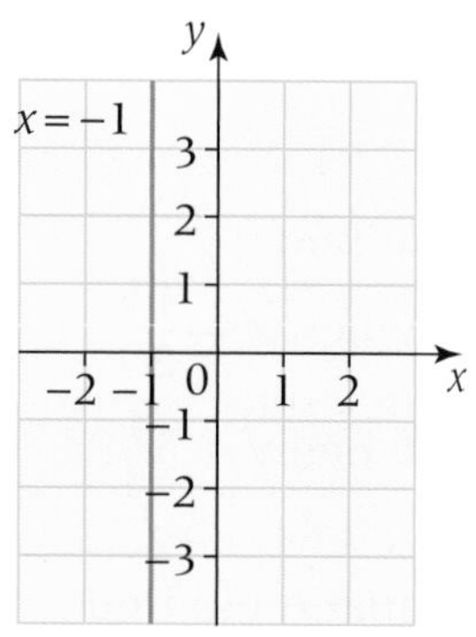

- The equation of a vertical graph is always x = a number.

To find the number, look at where the graph cuts the x-axis.

Example

a Draw the graphs of $y = 3$ and $x = 2$ on the same pair of axes.

b Find the coordinates of the point P where the two graphs cross.

a

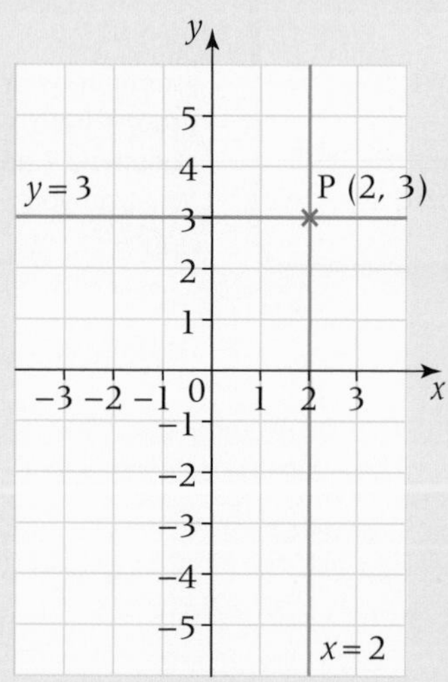

$y = 3$ is a horizontal graph.
It cuts the y-axis at 3.
$x = 2$ is a vertical graph.
It cuts the x-axis at 2.

b The coordinates of P are $(2, 3)$.

Exercise A1.4 — Grade D

1 Write down the equations of these horizontal and vertical graphs.

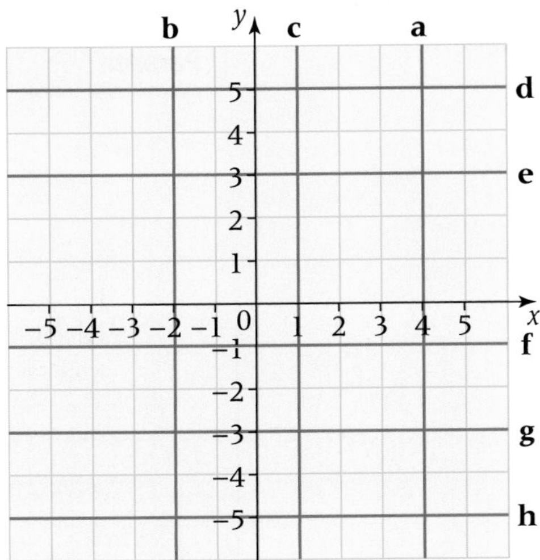

2 Copy the grid from question **1** without the graphs.
Draw these graphs on the same grid.
a $y = 4$ **b** $x = 5$ **c** $y = -2$ **d** $x = -2$ **e** $x = -4$

AO3 Problem

3 Draw a table like this:

Horizontal lines	Vertical lines

Write these equations into the correct columns of your table:

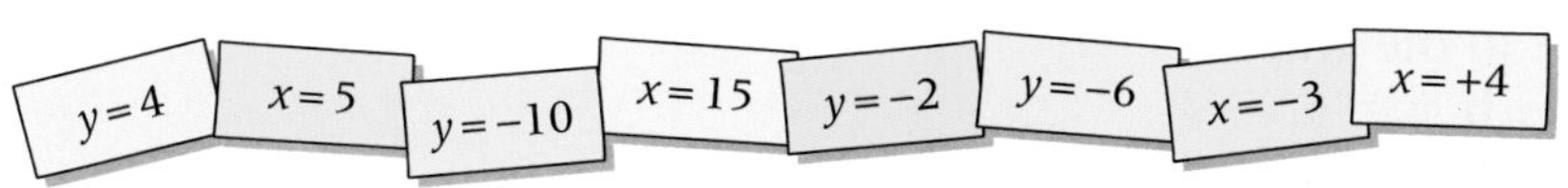

4 Use your graphs from question **2** to find the coordinates of the points where these pairs of graphs cross.
a $x = -2$ and $y = 4$ **b** $x = 5$ and $y = -2$ **c** $x = -4$ and $y = 4$

5 Write the coordinates of the points where these pairs of lines cross.
a $x = 2$ and $y = -3$ **b** $x = 1$ and $y = 6$ **c** $x = 3$ and $y = -1$

6 **a** Copy the grid from question **1** without the graphs.
b Draw a square on your grid using two vertical and two horizontal lines.
c Write the equations of the four lines.

7 **a** Draw a grid with the x-axis and the y-axis going from -5 to $+5$.
b Draw the line $y = 0$ on your grid. What is another name for this line?
c Draw the line $x = 0$ on your grid. What is another name for this line?

8 **a** Draw the graph of $y = 3x + 1$.
b On the same grid, draw the graph of $y = 7$.
c Write the coordinates of the point P where the graphs cross.

A1.5 Equation of a straight line

This spread will show you how to:

- Understand the equation form of a general straight line graph
- Understand that parallel lines have the same gradient

Keywords
Gradient
Intercept
Parallel

- Straight line graphs can be vertical, horizontal or diagonal.
  Examples of vertical lines: $x = 1$, $x = 5$, $x = -2$, ...
  Examples of horizontal lines: $y = 2$, $y = 7$, $y = -1$, ...

The line $y = 2x + 1$ is a diagonal line.

You can describe a diagonal line by

- how steep it is and
- where it crosses the y-axis (the y-**intercept**).

Gradient measures steepness.

The graph $y = 2x + 1$ has gradient 2.
For every 1 unit across, the graph goes up 2 units.

The graph $y = 2x + 1$ has y-intercept 1.
It crosses the y-axis at (0, 1).

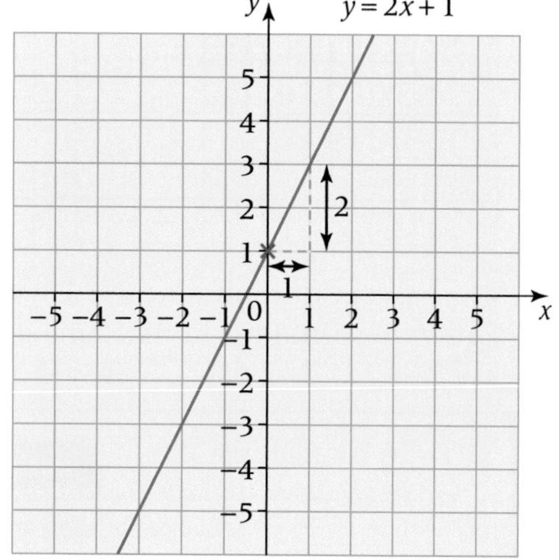

- Diagonal lines have an equation of the form

  $\boldsymbol{y = mx + c}$ where m is the gradient and c is the y-intercept.

Example

Match the equations to the graphs.

a $x = 2$ **b** $y = 3$
c $y = 3x + 2$ **d** $y = 3x - 1$

a → **iv** ($x = 2$ is a vertical graph)

b → **i** ($y = 3$ is a horizontal graph)

c → **ii** ($y = 3x + 2$ has y-intercept 2)

d → **iii** ($y = 3x - 1$ has y-intercept -1)

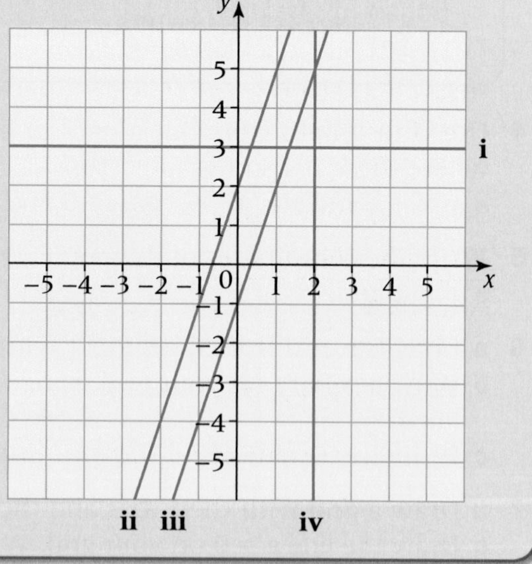

In the example above, the graphs of $y = 3x + 2$ and $y = 3x - 1$ are **parallel**.

- Parallel lines have the same gradient.

Exercise A1.5

Grade C

1 Write the gradient and y-intercept for each of these equations.

a $y = 3x - 1$ **b** $y = 2x + 5$ **c** $y = 4x - 3$

d $y = \frac{1}{2}x + 2$ **e** $y = 5x + 1$ **f** $y = -3x + 7$

2 Match the equations to the graphs.

a $y = 3x + 1$ **b** $y = 3$ **c** $y = 2x + 4$

d $x = -2$ **e** $y = x + 3$

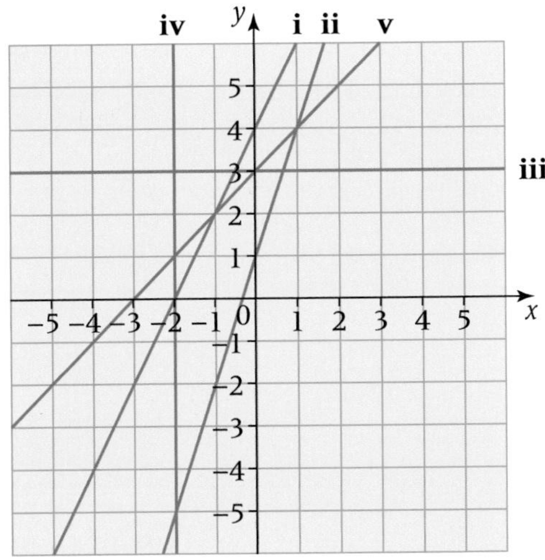

3 Rearrange these equations in the form $y = mx + c$.

a $x + y = 5$ **b** $y - x = 3$ **c** $x + y = -2$ **d** $x - y = 3$

e $2x + y = 6$ **f** $5x + y = 9$ **g** $3x + y = -2$ **h** $y - 2x = 5$

i $2y + x = 4$ **j** $2y - x = 8$ **k** $2x + 4y = 16$ **l** $6x + 2y = 8$

4 List the equations from question 3 whose graphs are parallel to

a $y = x$ **b** $y = -x$ **c** $y = -3x$ **d** $y = -\frac{1}{2}x$

5 Here are the equations of four straight lines.
Which two are parallel?

a $y = 2x + 4$ **b** $2x - y = 3$ **c** $y + 2x = 7$ **d** $4y + 2x = 8$

6 Write these equations for straight lines in order of steepness, starting with the least steep.

$y=4x+3$	$y=2x-2$	$y=3x+1$	$y=\frac{1}{2}x-9$	$y=x+11$

7 Write the equation of a straight line that is parallel to $y = 3x - 1$.

8 Write the equation of a straight line that is parallel to $y + 4x = 2$.

9 Write the equation of the straight line that is parallel to $y = \frac{1}{2}x - 3$ and passes through the point (0, 4).

AO3 Problem

10 Draw the graph of $y = -x$.
What can you say about the slope of the graph?
Is this true for all graphs with negative gradient?
Draw more graphs to test your idea.

Midpoint of a line segment

This spread will show you how to:
- Calculate the length and midpoint of the line AB

Keywords
Coordinates
Line segment
Midpoint

- The **midpoint M** of a line AB is halfway along it.

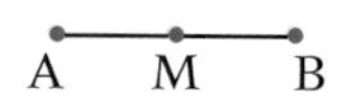

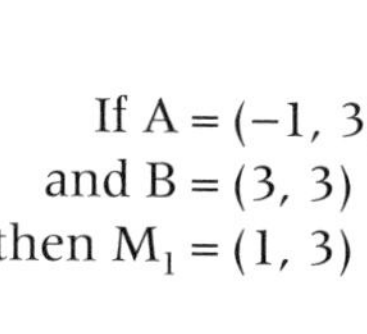

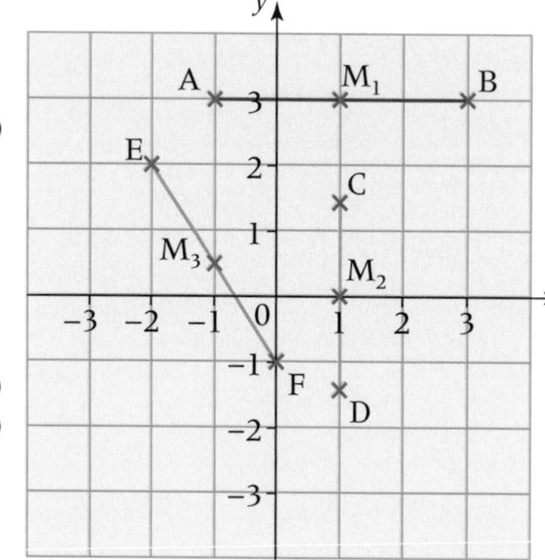

If A = (−1, 3) and B = (3, 3) then M_1 = (1, 3)

If C = $(1, 1\frac{1}{2})$ and D = $(1, -1\frac{1}{2})$ then M_2 = (1, 0)

If E = (−2, 2) and F = (0, −1) then $M_3 = (-1, \frac{1}{2})$

M is the midpoint.

- If $A = (x_1, y_1)$ and $B = (x_2, y_2)$

  then $M = \left(\frac{x_1 + x_2}{2}, \frac{y_1 + y_2}{2}\right)$

The midpoint of AB is the mean of the **coordinates** of points A and B.

Example

Calculate the coordinates of the midpoint between the points

a (7, 1) and (−3, 5) **b** (4, −1) and (2, −2)

a $(7, 1) = (x_1, y_1)$ and $(-3, 5) = (x_2, y_2)$

Midpoint $= \left(\frac{7-3}{2}, \frac{1+5}{2}\right)$

$= \left(\frac{4}{2}, \frac{6}{2}\right) = (2, 3)$

b $(4, -1) = (x_1, y_1)$ and $(2, -2) = (x_2, y_2)$

Midpoint $= \left(\frac{4+2}{2}, \frac{-1-2}{2}\right)$

$= \left(\frac{6}{2}, \frac{-3}{2}\right) = (3, -1\frac{1}{2})$

Sometimes you can find the coordinates of points given by geometrical information.

Example

A rectangle ABCD has coordinates A(−4, −1), B(−2, −1) and C(−2, −2).

a Find the coordinates of the point D.

b Find the midpoint of the line segment BD.

a A sketch shows that D has coordinates (−4, −2)

b Midpoint M $= \left(\frac{-2 + -4}{2}, \frac{-1 + -2}{2}\right) = \left(-3, -1\frac{1}{2}\right)$

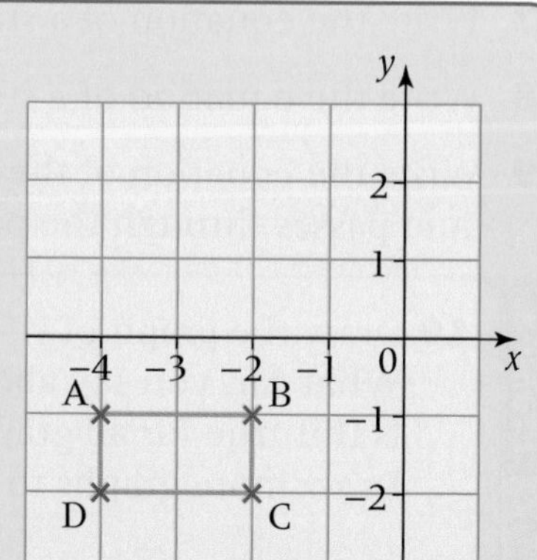

Exercise A1.6

Grade C

1 **a** Draw the points A(1, 3) and B(5, 1) on a copy of the grid.

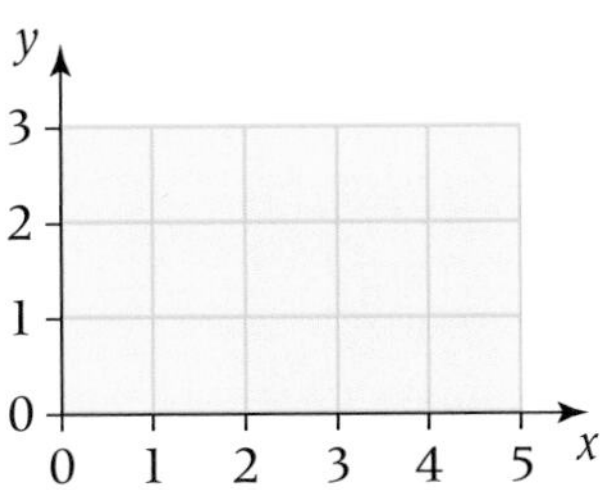

b M is the midpoint of the line AB.
Find the coordinates of the point M.

2 Calculate the coordinates of the midpoint between the points

a (3, 1) and (3, 5)
b (0, 4) and (4, 4)
c (2, −2) and (2, 4)
d (3, 1) and (7, 7)
e (−2, −1) and (6, 7)

3 The point (3, 4) is the midpoint between (x, 6) and (1, y).
Find the values of x and y.

4 A square ABCD has coordinates A(2, −3), B(3, −4), C(2, −5).

a Find the coordinates of the point D.
b Find the coordinates of the midpoint of the line segment BD.

5 A kite WXYZ has coordinates W(2, 5), X(3, 4) and Y(2, 1).

a Find the coordinates of the point Z.
b Find the coordinates of the midpoint of the line segment XZ.

Summary

Check out

You should now be able to:

- Write the input and output values for a function as coordinate pairs
- Plot straight line graphs of functions in which y is the subject
- Recognise the equation form of a straight line graph
- Read values from a graph
- Find the gradient of a straight line from a graph
- Find the coordinates of the midpoint of a line segment

Worked exam question

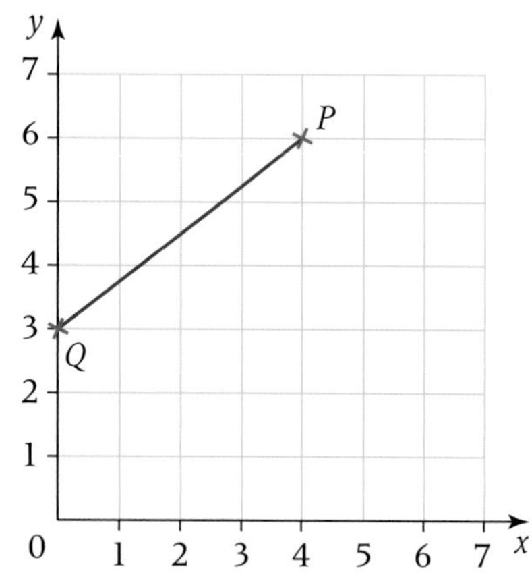

a Write down the coordinates of the point P. (1)

b Write down the coordinates of the point Q. (1)

M is the midpoint of the line from Q to P.

c Find the coordinates of M. (2)

(Edexcel Limited 2009)

---

a The point P is (4, 6)

b The point Q is (0, 3)

c $\frac{4+0}{2} = \frac{4}{2} = 2$ and $\frac{6+3}{2} = \frac{9}{2} = 4\frac{1}{2}$ ← You should show these calculations.

The point M is $(2, 4\frac{1}{2})$

Exam questions

1 **a** Complete the table of values for $y = 2x + 1$

x	-2	-1	0	1	2	3
y		-1	1			

(2)

b On the grid, draw the graph of $y = 2x + 1$

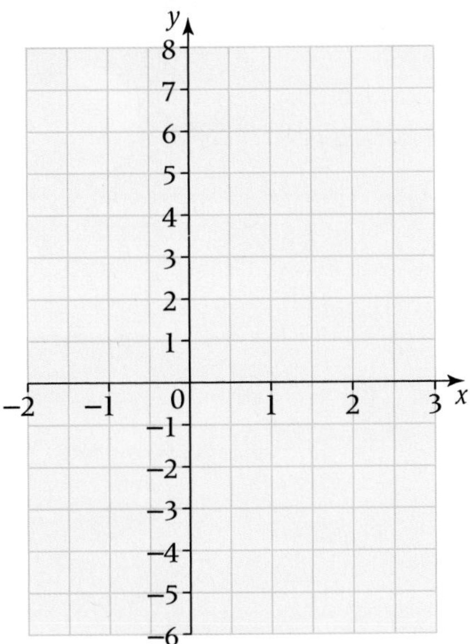

(2)

c Use your graph to find

i the value of y when $x = -1.5$

ii the value of x when $y = 6$ (2)

(Edexcel Limited 2007)

A03

2 A is the point (1, 1)
B is the point (3, 7)
A straight line passes through the points A and B.
What is the equation of the straight line? (3)

Functional Maths 1: Weather

Before creating a weather forecast, data is collected from all over the world to give information about the current conditions. A supercomputer and knowledge about the atmosphere, the Earth's surface and the oceans are then used to create the forecast.

Write down the temperature shown on each of these thermometers:

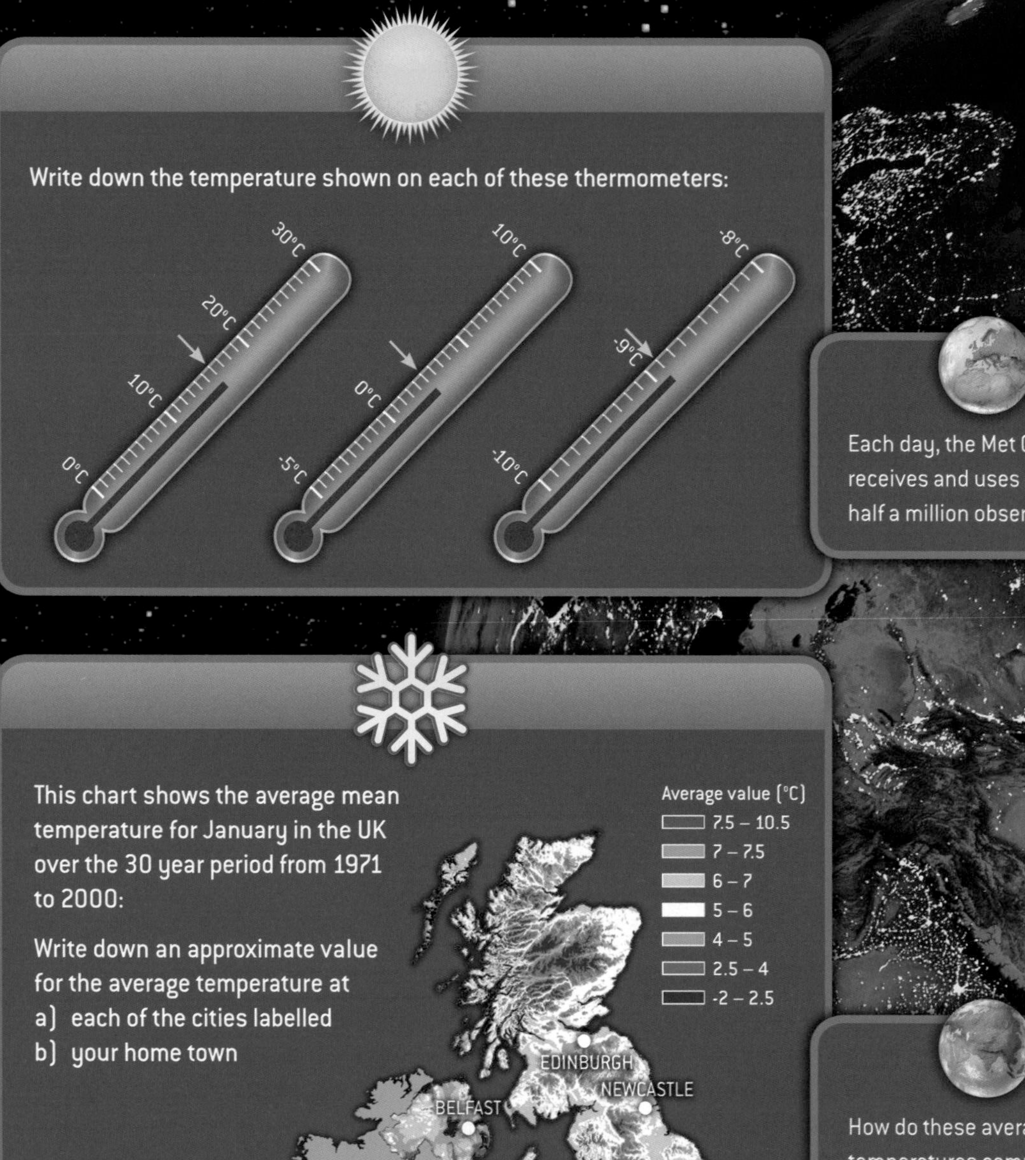

Each day, the Met Office receives and uses around half a million observations.

This chart shows the average mean temperature for January in the UK over the 30 year period from 1971 to 2000:

Write down an approximate value for the average temperature at

a) each of the cities labelled

b) your home town

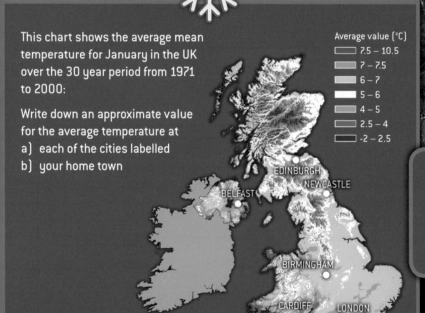

Which area(s) had the

c) highest

d) lowest average temperature?

What is the difference (approximate, in °C) between these temperatures?

How do these average temperatures compare to the temperatures in the UK this January?

Wind direction is measured in tens of degrees relative to true North and is always given from where the wind is blowing. In the UK, wind speed is measured in knots, where 1knot = 1.15mph, or in terms of the Beaufort Scale.

Research the Beaufort Scale using the internet.

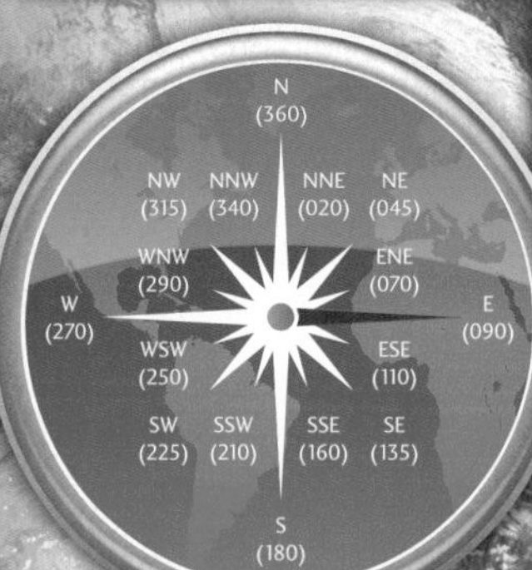

Easterly wind, 090°

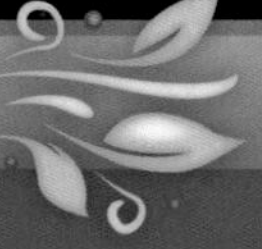

Describe the wind speed (in knots) and direction (in tens of degrees and in words) shown by each of these arrows:

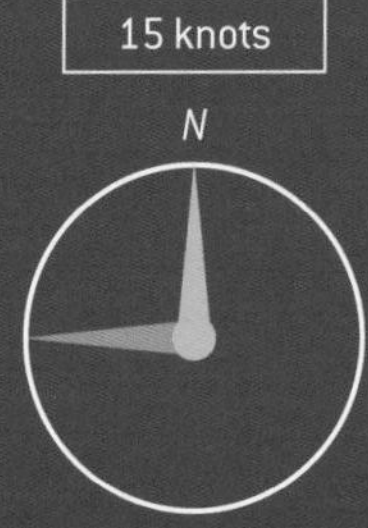

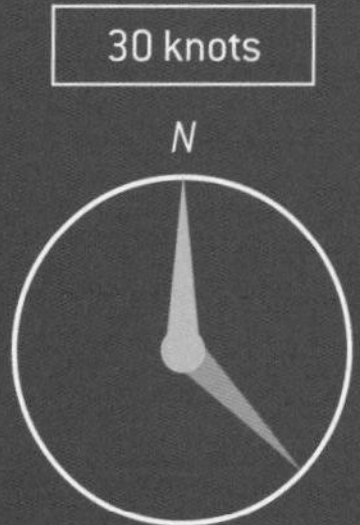

Observed data can be used to make predictions, but there is always some level of uncertainty. This graph shows the range of uncertainty in temperature in Exeter with some indication of the most probable values:

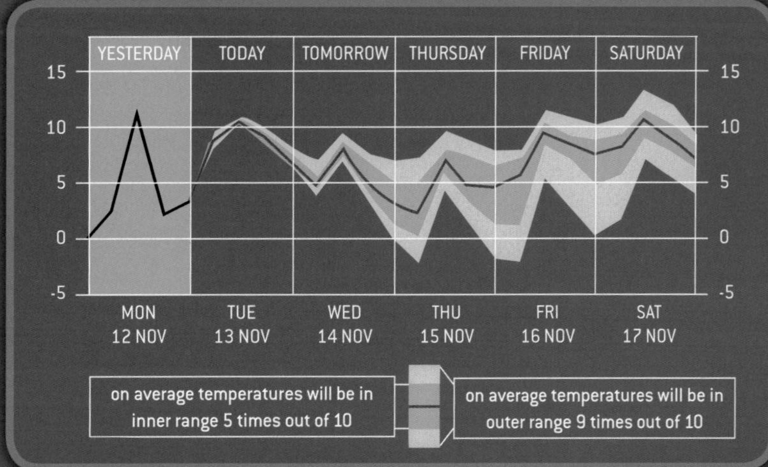

What predictions do you think a weather forecaster would have made about the temperature in Exeter during the week shown?

Justify your response by referring to the graph.

Introduction

In many professions it is vital to perform mental checks on answers that have been calculated. These include doctors working out the dose of medicine to give a patient, pilots checking the fuel required for a flight, or civil engineers calculating the amount of material required to construct a building.

What's the point?

If doctors, pilots and engineers don't check that their answers are sensible, things could go badly wrong and it will affect other people.

Check in

1 Calculate

a $257 + 178$ **b** $375 - 189$

2 Calculate

a 9×8 **b** 42×10

c $72 \div 6$ **d** $143 \div 30$

e 29×48 **f** $204 \div 12$

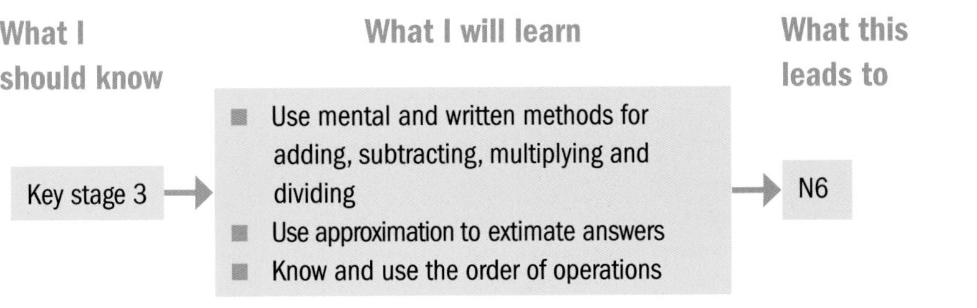

Orientation
What I should know
What I will learn
What this leads to
Key stage 3
Use mental and written methods for adding, subtracting, multiplying and dividing
Use approximation to extimate answers
Know and use the order of operations
N6

Rich task

The number 16 can be split into pairs of numbers such as (16, 0), (15, 1), (14.5, 1.5)

Multiply the two numbers together:

$16 \times 0 = 0$ $15 \times 1 = 15$ $14.5 \times 1.5 = 21.75$

The products are different.

a Find the **maximum product** of a pair of numbers that add together to make 16.

b Choose a starting number of your own and investigate the maximum product.

N2.1 Mental addition and subtraction

This spread will show you how to:

- Use a range of mental and written methods for addition, subtraction, multiplication and division

Keywords
Compensation
Complement
Mental methods
Partitioning

There are lots of **mental methods** to help work out additions and subtractions of whole numbers. You could:

- Use **partitioning** to split the numbers you are adding or subtracting into parts.
- Use **compensation** when the number you are adding or subtracting is nearly a whole number, a multiple of 10 or a multiple of 100.

p.296

Example

Calculate **a** 19.5 − 7.2 **b** 5.8 + 4.8

a 19.5 − 7.2 = 19.5 − 7 − 0.2
= 12.5 − 0.2
= 12.3

Split smaller number into parts.
Subtract the units from the highest number.
Subtract the tenths.

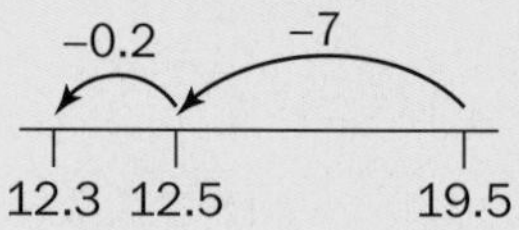

b 5.8 + 4.8 = 5.8 + 5 − 0.2
= 10.8 − 0.2
= 10.6

Round 4.8 to the nearest whole number, 5.
Rewrite **add 4.8** as **add 5 − 0.2.**
Add the 5 to the highest number.
Subtract 0.2.

For most calculations, there is more than one way to work it out. Use the method that you are most comfortable with.

You could count up from the smallest number to the largest number.

Example

Hetti runs in a 3500 m race. She has already covered 1792 m. How far does she have left to run?

3500 m − 1792 m

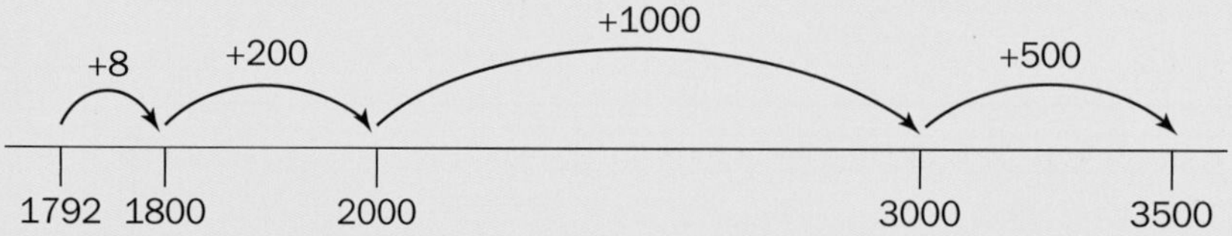

3500 m − 1792 m = 8 + 200 + 1000 + 500
= 1708 m

Exercise N2.1 — Grade G

1 Write the answer to each of these calculations.

a 150 + 120 **b** 170 − 90 **c** 160 + 170
d 130 − 90 **e** 1900 + 1900 **f** 210 − 140
g 320 + 110 **h** 510 − 120

2 Find the missing number in each of these calculations.

a 37 + ? = 100 **b** ? + 0.4 = 1
c 0.31 + ? = 1 **d** 7.3 + ? = 10

3 Use a mental method for each of these calculations.
Write the method you have used.

a 257 + 98 **b** 448 + 112 **c** 427 + 523
d 256 + 552 **e** 354 + 213 **f** 561 + 328
g 16.2 − 1.9 **h** 5.8 + 14.9

4 Copy and complete this number addition square.

+	2.9	4.8	3.9	2.5	5.9	?
3.1						
?		11.3				12.2
8.2						
?		9.7				
7.1						
9.6						

Functional Maths AO2

5 Use a mental method of calculation to solve each of these problems.

a Charlie has to travel 435 km. After 2 hours he has travelled 187 km. How much further does he have to travel?

b Emma has to write an assignment of at least 500 words. After 15 minutes she has written 237 words. How many more words does she need to write to complete her assignment?

c In a test, Alex scores 93 marks, Sophie scores 75 marks and Louise scores 97 marks. How many marks did the girls score altogether?

d Luke downloads 355 minutes of music from the internet. By accident he deletes 186 minutes. How many minutes of music does he have left?

Problem AO3

6 Copy and complete each of these addition pyramids.

a

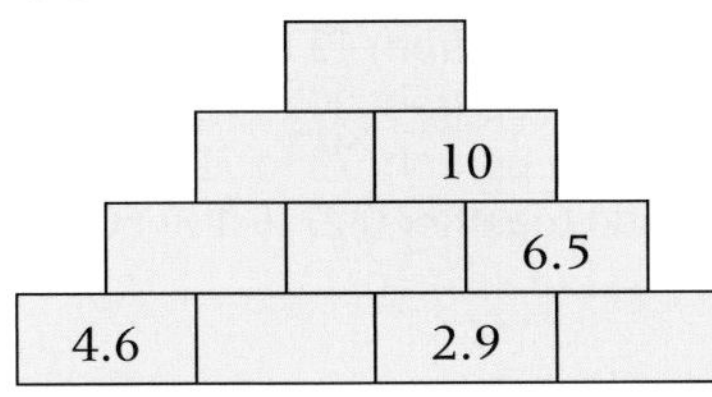

b

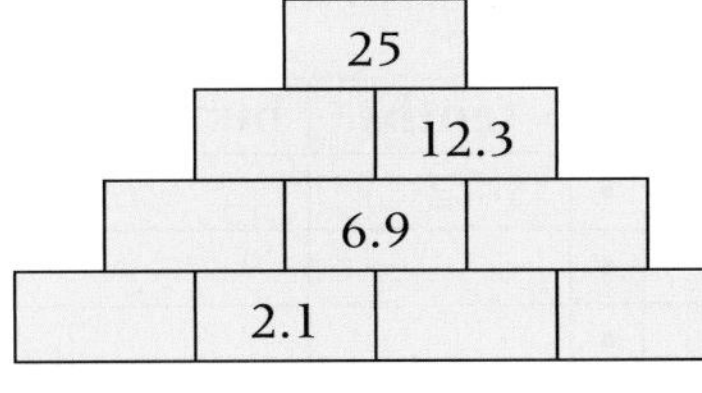

Each number is the sum of the two numbers beneath it.

N2.2 Written addition and subtraction

This spread will show you how to:
- Use a range of mental and written methods for addition, subtraction, multiplication and division

Keywords
Addition
Decimals
Subtraction
Written method

When numbers are too difficult to add or subtract in your head, use a **written method**.
The standard written method for **addition** is based on partitioning.

Example

Hera the baby gorilla weighs 21.62 kg, and Horace her brother weighs 46.34 kg. Henna, the mother, weighs 186.7 kg.
What is the combined weight of the gorillas?

$21.62 + 46.34 + 186.7 \approx 20 + 50 + 190$ (rounding to the nearest 10)
≈ 260 kg

You should always estimate the answer first.

Set out the calculation in columns, making sure you line up the decimal points.

	Hundreds	Tens	Units	•	tenths	hundredths
		2	1	•	6	2
		4	6	•	3	4
+	1	8	6	•	7	
	2	5	4	•	6	6

The combined weight = 254.66 kg.

There is an informal written method for **subtraction**.

Example

A crate is packed full of tins. The total mass of the tins and the crate is 72.6 kg.
When the tins are removed the crate weighs 18.73 kg.
What is the mass of the tins?

Estimate: $72.6 - 18.73 \approx 73 - 19$ (rounding each number to the nearest 1)
≈ 54 kg

This is a standard method for subtraction:

$$\begin{array}{r} {}^{6}\not{7}\,{}^{1}\not{2}\,.\,{}^{15}\not{6}\;{}^{1}\not{0} \\ -\;1\;8\;.\;7\;3 \\ \hline 5\;3\;.\;8\;7 \end{array}$$

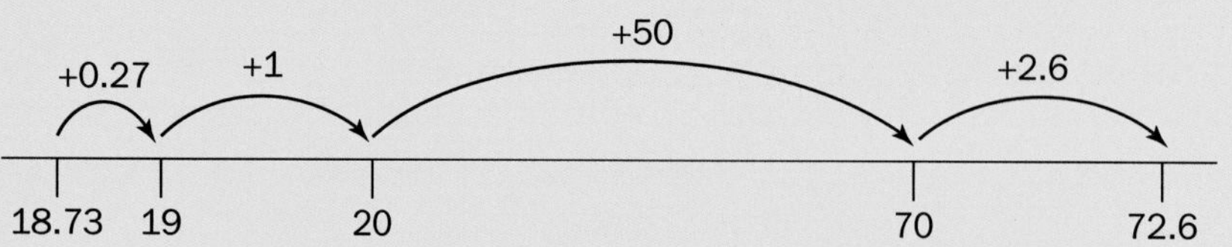

$72.6\text{ kg} - 18.73\text{ kg} = 0.27 + 1 + 50 + 2.6$
$= 53.87$ kg

Count up from 18.73 to 19.
Count up from 19 to 20.
Count up from 20 to 70.
Count up from 70 to 72.6.
Add together 0.27 + 1 + 50 + 2.6.

	Tens	Units	•	tenths	hundredths
		0	•	2	7
		1	•		
	5	0	•		
+		2	•	6	
	5	3	•	8	7

Exercise N2.2 Grade G

1 Use a mental or written method to work out these calculations.

a 23.4 + 13.4 **b** 24.6 + 53.7
c 19.7 + 7.4 **d** 27.8 + 14.3

2 Use a mental or written method to work out these calculations.

a 9.6 − 3.4 **b** 16.7 − 9.6
c 16.3 − 7.8 **d** 61.7 − 33.8

3 Use a written method to work out these additions.

a 4.32 + 6.4 **b** 16.32 + 3.4
c 4.5 + 13.61 **d** 73.2 + 68.79

4 Use a written method to work out these subtractions.

a 16.3 − 8.25 **b** 12.6 − 7.87
c 67.3 − 28.56 **d** 47.38 − 28.7

5 Use a written method for each of these calculations.

a 25.3 + 8.76 **b** 38.1 + 6.61
c 8.31 − 4.8 **d** 15.8 + 8.79
e 25.46 − 7.48 **f** 47.39 − 18.5

6 Calculate these using a mental or written method.

a 12.3 + 2.7 + 7.08 **b** 38.76 + 16.9 − 8.32
c 61.3 + 14.85 + 7.02

AO2 Functional Maths

7 Use a mental or written method to solve each of these problems.

a Lindsey sells cheese. On Monday she sells 28.6 kg; on Tuesday she sells 33.38 kg. How much cheese has she sold?

b Keir earns £298.17 a week. He pays £76.37 each week in tax. How much money does he have left after paying his tax?

c Jess needs three pieces of wood to build a wooden frame. The lengths are 2.32 m, 1.8 m and 1.75 m. What is the total length of wood she will need to buy?

d A box full of bottles weighs 34.6 kg. It is taken to the recycling centre. The bottles are thrown into the bottle bank. The box now weighs 3.87 kg. How much did the bottles weigh?

e Lucce is making a Tuscan bean casserole for 8 people. Here is his recipe:

Kidney beans	1.6 kg
Red onions	0.375 kg
Celery	0.15 kg
French beans	0.2 kg
Tomatoes	1.2 kg

What is the total weight of the ingredients?

N2.3 Mental multiplication and division

This spread will show you how to:

- Use a range of mental and written methods for addition, subtraction, multiplication and division

Keywords
Factor
Multiple
Mental method
Partitioning

To work out multiplications and divisions in your head, you can use **partitioning** to split the numbers into parts.

Example

Calculate **a** 8.2×11 **b** $368 \div 16$

a $11 = 10 + 1$

$8.2 \times 11 = (8.2 \times 10) + (8.2 \times 1)$
$= 82 + 8.2$
$= 90.2$

b $368 = 320 + 48$

$368 \div 16 = (320 \div 16) + (48 \div 16)$
$= 20 + 3$
$= 23$

You split one of the two numbers up to make the calculation easier.

You can re-write a number as a product of two of its **factors**.

Example

Calculate **a** 5.6×20 **b** $156 \div 6$

a $5.6 \times \mathbf{20} = 5.6 \times \mathbf{2} \times \mathbf{10}$

$5.6 \times 2 = 11.2$
$11.2 \times 10 = 112$

$5.6 \times 20 = 112$

b $156 \div \mathbf{6} = 156 \div \mathbf{2} \div \mathbf{3}$

$156 \div 3 = 52$
$52 \div 2 = 26$

$156 \div 6 = 26$

Here are some other methods you can use:

- Use compensation when the number you are multiplying by is nearly a multiple of 10.

  $14.2 \times 19 = (14.2 \times 20) - (14.2 \times 1)$
  $= 284 - 14.2$
  $= 269.8$

- Double one of the numbers and halve the other.

  $12 \times 6.5 = 6 \times 13$
  $= 78$

- Double both of the numbers before you divide.

  $18 \div 1.5 = 36 \div 3$
  $= 12$

Example

Alan needs to stack 168 tins of peas. Each tray holds 12 tins of peas.
The 12 tins on each tray weighs 11 kg.
What is the weight of the tins Alan has to stack?

This problem can be broken down into two parts.

i Find the number of trays needed for 168 tins.

$168 \div 12$
$168 \div 4 = 42$
$42 \div 3 = 14$

Alan needs to stack 14 trays.

ii Find the total weight of the trays.

$14 \times 11\text{ kg} = (14 \times 10) + (14 \times 1)$
$= 140 + 14$
$= 154\text{ kg}$

The 168 tins weigh 154 kg.

Exercise N2.3 Grade F

1 Calculate

a 8×7 **b** $72 \div 10$ **c** 2×4.7 **d** $480 \div 2$
e 9×8 **f** $6.75 \div 10$ **g** $930 \div 2$ **h** 7×9

2 Calculate each of these without using a calculator.

a 4.6×100 **b** $170 \div 100$ **c** 12.7×10 **d** $0.82 \div 100$

3 Use an appropriate **mental method** to calculate these.

a 14×6 **b** 14×9 **c** $105 \div 5$ **d** $78 \div 3$
e 17×11 **f** 31×9 **g** $192 \div 6$ **h** 29×6
i 13×14 **j** 29×21 **k** 31×29 **l** 15×99

4 Use the mental method of partitioning to calculate these. Show the method you have used.

a 1.6×11 **b** 21×8 **c** 7.2×11 **d** 31×2.8
e 18×7 **f** 12×6.4 **g** $618 \div 3$ **h** $316 \div 4$

5 Use the mental method of compensation to calculate each of these. Show the method you have used.

a 17×9 **b** 23×9 **c** 2.3×11 **d** 11×8.9
e 4.2×11 **f** 21×5.3 **g** 12.7×9 **h** 23.1×31

6 Use the mental method of factors to calculate each of these. Show the method you have used.

a 4.3×20 **b** $132 \div 6$ **c** 142×4 **d** 27×8
e $192 \div 6$ **f** 237×4 **g** 3.2×30 **h** $420 \div 15$

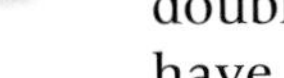

7 Use the mental method of halving and doubling (multiplication) or doubling (division) to calculate each of these. Show the method you have used.

a 4×61 **b** 16×2.25 **c** 16×8 **d** $36 \div 1.5$
e $63 \div 4.5$ **f** 3.4×4.5 **g** 4.2×2.5 **h** 2.44×5

8 Use an appropriate mental method to calculate each of these.

a 22×2.1 **b** 2.3×20 **c** 13×1.4 **d** 8×7.5
e $7.5 \div 1.25$ **f** 75×29 **g** $4.5 \div 1.5$ **h** $4.5 \div 0.15$

A02 Functional Maths

9 Use an appropriate mental method to solve each of these problems.

a The average weight of a piglet is 7.5 kg. A pig has a litter of 12 piglets. What is the total weight of the 12 piglets?

b Four friends win £124 on the lottery. They share their winnings equally. How much money does each friend receive?

Written multiplication and division

This spread will show you how to:

- Multiply and divide integers and decimals
- Use approximation to estimate answers to problems

Keywords
Dividend
Divisor
Estimate
Grid method
Standard method
Whole number

You can use different written methods to multiply numbers together.

Example

Simone buys 16 packets of biscuits.
Each packet costs £1.28. How much does this cost in total?

Estimate:

$16 \times 1.28 \approx 20 \times 1$ (rounding 16 to the nearest 10 and 1.28 to the nearest whole number)
$\approx £20$

You rewrite the calculation 16×1.28 as $16 \times 128 \div 100$.

Grid method

x	100	20	8
10	10 x 100 = 1000	10 x 20 = 200	10 x 8 = 80
6	6 x 100 = 600	6 x 20 = 120	6 x 8 = 48

16 x 128 = 1000 + 200 + 80 + 600 + 120 + 48
= 2048

Answers: Simone spends 16 x £1.28 = 16 x 128 ÷ 100
= 2048 ÷ 100
= £20.48

Standard method

Write the calculation in columns:

	128
	x 16
10 x 128	1280
6 x 128	+ 768
	2048

Standard 'chunking' method
This method involves subtracting multiples of the **divisor** from the **dividend** until you cannot subtract any more.

Example

A box will hold 16 glasses. Howard needs to pack 752 glasses into boxes. Calculate the number of boxes he will need.

Estimate:

752 ÷ 16 ≈ 800 ÷ 20
= 40 boxes

(rounding 752 up to the next multiple of 100 and 16 to the next multiple of 10)

p.298

16)752	
−640	16 × **40**
112	
−112	16 × **7**
0	

752 ÷ 16 = **47**

Howard will need 47 boxes.

Exercise N2.4 Grade F

1 Use an appropriate method of calculation to work out each of these.

a 27×8 **b** 7×84 **c** 9×327
d 13×28 **e** 26×28 **f** 25×35
g 14×115 **h** 24×162 **i** 38×272
j 22×211 **k** 40×133 **l** 29×318

2 Use an appropriate method of calculation to work out each of these. Where appropriate leave your answer in remainder form.

a $156 \div 6$ **b** $184 \div 8$ **c** $165 \div 5$
d $266 \div 7$ **e** $333 \div 9$ **f** $544 \div 8$
g $125 \div 8$ **h** $325 \div 7$

3 Use an appropriate method of calculation to work out each of these.

a 16×2.4 **b** 4.7×23 **c** 6.4×23
d 13×9.3 **e** 48×3.2 **f** 7.3×89

4 Use an appropriate method of calculation to work out each of these.

a 13×1.54 **b** 16×1.73 **c** 17×1.93
d 25×1.38 **e** 87×1.63 **f** 38×1.62
g 34×2.45 **h** 54×9.48

5 Use an appropriate method of calculation to work out each of these.

a 13.9×23 **b** 45×15.3 **c** 82×14.7
d 23.7×34 **e** 46.1×73 **f** 38.7×43

DID YOU KNOW?

Modern arithmetic, using the decimal system, began in India with mathematicians such as Brahmagupta in the 7th century AD.

AO2 Functional Maths

6 a Skye buys 18 packets of rice. Each packet costs £1.17. How much does this cost in total?

b 1 litre of petrol costs 81.9 pence. On a journey Kai uses 45 litres of petrol. What is the total cost of the petrol for the journey?

c Laura buys 27 CDs. Each CD costs £7.49. How much is this in total?

d Kieron runs 32 laps of a track. Each lap takes him 73.2 seconds. What is his total time to run 32 laps?

e Kimberley buys 48 troll dolls. Each doll costs £1.67. What is the total cost of the troll dolls?

7 Use an appropriate method of calculation to work out each of these.

a $192 \div 16$ **b** $234 \div 13$ **c** $342 \div 18$
d $483 \div 21$ **e** $899 \div 31$ **f** $987 \div 47$

8 Use an appropriate method of calculation to work out each of these.

a $26.6 \div 7$ **b** $35.4 \div 6$ **c** $67.2 \div 8$
d $74.4 \div 6$ **e** $118.8 \div 9$ **f** $123.2 \div 8$
g $109.6 \div 8$ **h** $248.4 \div 9$

Order of operations

This spread will show you how to:

- Know and use the order of operations, including brackets

Keywords
Brackets
Index
Order of operations
Power

When you do long calculations you must work them out according to the **order of operations.**

Order of operations
(BIDMAS)

Brackets
Work out the contents of any **brackets** first.

Powers or **I**ndices
Work out any **powers** or roots.

Division and **M**ultiplication
Work out any multiplications and divisions.

Addition and **S**ubtraction
Finally, work out any additions and subtractions.

To calculate $\frac{(6+4)^2}{5} + 8 \times 2$

$\frac{(6+4)^2}{5} + 8 \times 2 = \frac{(6+4)^2}{5} + 8 \times 2$ (work out the contents of the bracket)

$= \frac{10^2}{5} + 8 \times 2$ (work out any powers)

$= \frac{100}{5} + 8 \times 2$ (work out any divisions and multiplications)

$= 20 + 16$ (work out any additions and subtractions)

$= 36$

Brackets are used when you need to do an operation in a different order to normal. Calculations with brackets need to be thought about carefully.

Example

Calculate **a** $\frac{34 \times 8}{5 + 11}$ **b** $11 + 13(8^2 - 47)$ **c** $30 \div (15 - (12 - 7))$

a $\frac{34 \times 8}{5 + 11} = \frac{(34 \times 8)}{(5 + 11)}$

$= (34 \times 8) \div (5 + 11)$ (work out the brackets)

$= 272 \div 16$ (work out the division)

$= 17$

Always write the calculation a line at a time, so you can see each operation clearly.

b $11 + 13(8^2 - 47) = 11 + 13(8^2 - 47)$ (work out the brackets)

$= 11 + 13(64 - 47)$ (work out the index)

$= 11 + 13 \times 17$ (work out the multiplication)

$= 11 + 221$ (work out the addition)

$= 232$

c $30 \div (15 - (12 - 7)) = 30 \div (15 - (12 - 7))$ (work out the innermost brackets)

$= 30 \div (15 - 5)$ (work out the next set of brackets)

$= 30 \div 10$ (work out the division)

$= 3$

Exercise N2.5

Grade D

1 Calculate these using the order of operations.

a $2 + 8 \times 3$

b $4 \times 11 - 7$

c $4 \times 3 + 5 \times 8$

d $5 + 12 \div 6 + 3$

e $(2 + 9) \times 3$

f $(1.5 + 18.5) \div 4$

g $(12 + 3) \times (14 - 2)$

h $5 + (3 \times 8) \div 6$

2 Calculate these using the order of operations.

a $(4 + 3) \times 2^2$

b $3^2 \times (15 - 7)$

c $(6^2 - 16) \div 4$

d $2^4 \times (3^2 - 2 \times 4)$

e $128 \div (2 + 2 \times 3)^2$

f $(8^2 - 7^2) \times 5$

3 Copy each of these calculations.
Insert brackets where necessary to make each of the calculations correct.

a $5 \times 2 + 1 = 15$

b $5 \times 3 - 1 \times 4 = 40$

c $20 + 8 \div 2 - 7 = 17$

d $2 + 3^2 \times 4 + 3 = 65$

e $2 \times 6^2 \div 3 + 9 = 33$

f $4 \times 5 + 5 \times 6 = 150$

4 a Karen and Pete answered the same question. Who is correct?

b Duncan said $(5 \times 4)^2$ means the same as 5×4^2.
Is this correct? Explain your answer.

c Use your calculator to work out $(2.4 + 1.65)^2 \times 3.4$.

i Write all the figures on your calculator display.

ii Round your answer to 1 decimal place.

5 Calculate

a $\dfrac{7^2 - 9}{5 \times 8}$

b $\dfrac{4 \times 8}{4^2}$

c $\dfrac{15 \times 4}{6 \times 5}$

d $\dfrac{2 \times (3 + 4)^2}{7}$

e $\dfrac{(6 + 4)^2}{20} + 7 \times 5$

f $\dfrac{6 + (2 \times 4)^2 + 7}{11}$

6 Calculate

a $12 + 6 - 4$

b $5 \times 4 \div 2$

c $40 \div 10 \div 2$

d $28 - 12 - 4$

e $13(2 + 5)$

f $14(2 + 6)$

g $5^2 + 9(8 - 3)$

h $4^2 + 3(16 - 9)$

i $4 + (12 - (3 + 2))$

j $120 \div (8 \times (7 - 2))$

7 Solve each of these calculations.

a $(15.7 + 1.3) \times (8.7 + 1.3)$

b $\dfrac{7^2}{(2.3 \times 4)^2}$

c $\dfrac{(7 + 5)^2}{(25 + 7 \times 8)}$

Decide whether to use a mental, written or calculator method. Where appropriate give your answer to 2 decimal places.

N2.6 Estimation

This spread will show you how to:

- Multiply and divide by powers of 10 and by decimals between 0 and 1
- Use checking procedures, including approximation to estimate the answer to multiplication and division problems

Keywords
Approximate
Estimate

- You can multiply or divide a number by a power of 10.
  Move the digits of the number to the left or to the right.

$$1.8 \xrightarrow[]{\times 10 \text{ or } \div 0.1} 18 \qquad 18 \xrightarrow[]{\div 10 \text{ or } \times 0.1} 1.8$$

$$12.4 \xrightarrow[]{\times 100 \text{ or } \div 0.01} 1240 \qquad 1240 \xrightarrow[]{\div 100 \text{ or } \times 0.01} 12.4$$

× 0.1 is the same as ÷ 10.
× 0.01 is the same as ÷ 100.

÷ 0.1 is the same as × 10.
÷ 0.01 is the same as × 100.

- You can multiply and divide by any decimal between 0 and 1 using mental methods.

Example

Calculate **a** 12×0.3 **b** $36 \div 0.04$ **c** $2 \div 0.05$

a $12 \times 0.3 = 12 \times 3 \times 0.1$
$= 36 \times 0.1$
$= 36 \div 10$
$= 3.6$

b $36 \div 0.04 = 36 \div (4 \times 0.01)$
$= 36 \div 4 \div 0.01$
$= 9 \div 0.01$
$= 9 \times 100$
$= 900$

c $2 \div 0.05 = \frac{2}{0.05}$
$= \frac{200}{5}$
$= 40$

You can **estimate** the answer to a calculation by first rounding the numbers in the calculation.

Example

Estimate the answers to these calculations.

a $\dfrac{8.93 \times 28.69}{0.48 \times 6.12}$ **b** $\dfrac{17.4 \times 4.89^2}{0.385}$

p.12

a $\dfrac{8.93 \times 28.69}{0.48 \times 6.12} \approx \dfrac{9 \times 30}{0.5 \times 6} = \dfrac{270}{3} = 90$

b $\dfrac{17.4 \times 4.89^2}{0.385} = \dfrac{20 \times 5^2}{0.4} = \dfrac{20 \times 25}{0.4} = \dfrac{500}{0.4} = \dfrac{5000}{4} = 1250$

A good strategy is to round each number in the calculation to 1 significant figure.

Exercise N2.6

Grade C

1 Round each of these numbers to the nearest **i** 1000 **ii** 100 **iii** 10.

a 1548.9 **b** 5789.47 **c** 17 793.8 kg

d €35 127.35 **e** 236 872

2 Round each of these numbers to

i 3 dp **ii** 2 dp **iii** 1 dp **iv** the nearest whole number.

a 4.3563 **b** 9.8573 **c** 0.9373 **d** 19.4963

e 26.8083 **f** 19.9999 **g** 0.004896 **h** 3896.6567

3 Calculate

a 3×0.1 **b** $15 \div 0.1$ **c** 8×0.01 **d** 2.8×100

e $3.8 \div 0.1$ **f** 0.4×0.1 **g** $9.23 \div 0.1$ **h** $44.6 \div 0.01$

Problem AO3

4 Here are five number cards.

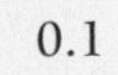

0.01 | 1000 | 10^2

Fill in the missing numbers in each of these statements using one of these cards.

a $3.24 \times ? = 324$ **b** $14.7 \times ? = 0.147$

c $6.3 \div ? = 630$ **d** $2870 \div ? = 2.87$

e $0.43 \div ? = 4.3$ **f** $2.04 \div ? = 204$

5 Round each of these numbers to **i** 3 sf **ii** 2 sf **iii** 1 sf.

a 9.4837 **b** 27.73 **c** 46.73 **d** 387.63

e 2.4058 **f** 4905.81 **g** 0.009 483 **h** 3489.7

i 9.8765 **j** 25.1407 **k** 2314.17 **l** 237 415

6 Work out these calculations using a mental method.

a 12×0.2 **b** 8×0.07 **c** $15 \div 0.3$

d $3 \div 0.15$ **e** 1.2×0.4 **f** $28 \div 0.07$

7 Write a suitable estimate for each of these calculations.
In each case clearly show how you estimated your answer.

a 3.76×4.22 **b** 17.39×22.98

c $\dfrac{4.59 \times 7.9}{19.86}$ **d** $54.31 \div 8.8$

8 Write a suitable estimate for each of these calculations.
In each case clearly show how you estimated your answer.

a $\dfrac{29.91 \times 38.3}{3.1 \times 3.9}$ **b** $\dfrac{16.2 \times 0.48}{0.23 \times 31.88}$

c $\{4.8^2 + (4.2 - 0.238)\}^2$ **d** $\dfrac{63.8 \times 1.7^2}{1.78^2}$

e $\sqrt{(2.03 \div 0.041)}$ **f** $\sqrt{(27.6 \div 0.57)}$

Summary

Check out

You should now be able to:

- Use a range of mental and written methods for addition, subtraction, multiplication and division of decimals
- Multiply or divide by powers of 10 and by decimals between 0 and 1
- Know and use the order of operations, including brackets
- Use rounding to estimate answers to calculations

Worked exam question

Kaysha has a part-time job.
She is paid £5.40 for each hour she works.
Last week Kaysha worked for 24 hours.

Work out Kaysha's total pay for last week. (3)

(Edexcel Limited 2008)

5.40×24

$5.40 \times 10 = 54$
$5.40 \times 10 = 54$
$5.40 \times 4 = 21.60$
£129.60

$10 + 10 + 4 = 24$

OR

```
                540
                 24 ×
540 × 20      10800
540 × 4        2160
              12960      £129.60
```

The decimal point is put in after the calculation.
An estimate is £5 × 20 = £100

OR

×	500	4	0
20	10000	800	0
4	2000	160	0

£129.60

```
 10000
   800
  2000
   160 +
 12960
```

You need to show your working whichever method you use.

Exam questions

AO2

1

Waxworks

Adult ticket: £8.50

Child ticket: £4.50

Mr and Mrs Jones take their three children to the Waxworks.
Mrs Jones pays for 2 adult tickets and 3 child tickets.
She pays with a £50 note.

How much change should she receive from £50? (3)

(Edexcel Limited 2007)

AO2

2 Complete this bill.

Michael's Cycle Repairs			

Description	**Number**	**Cost of each item**	**Total**
Brake blocks	4	£4.12	£16.48
Brake cables	2	£5.68	£ ....
Pedals	2	£	£45.98
Labour charge $1\frac{1}{2}$ hours at £12.00 hour			£ ....
		Total	£ ....

(4)

(Edexcel Limited 2008)

3 Beth says $20 - 5 \times 3$ is 45.
Pat says $20 - 5 \times 3$ is 5.

a Who is right?
Give a reason for your answer. (1)

b Work out $(12 + 9) \div 3$ (1)

(Edexcel Limited 2007)

4 **a** Work out £3.75 × 24 (3)

b Divide £135 by 20 (3)

(Edexcel Limited 2007)

5 Work out an estimate for $\frac{10.02 \times 398}{2.04}$ (3)

Introduction

A fractal is a geometrical shape that can be split into parts so that each part is a smaller copy of the whole shape. The von Koch Snowflake fractal is constructed from an equilateral triangle. On the middle third of each side is built another equilateral triangle and the process is repeated over and over again.

What's the point?

Fractal geometry is a fairly new branch of mathematics that is finding new applications all the time. The von Koch snowflake can be used to model the reception of an antenna.

Check in

1 Use a protractor to measure these angles.

a

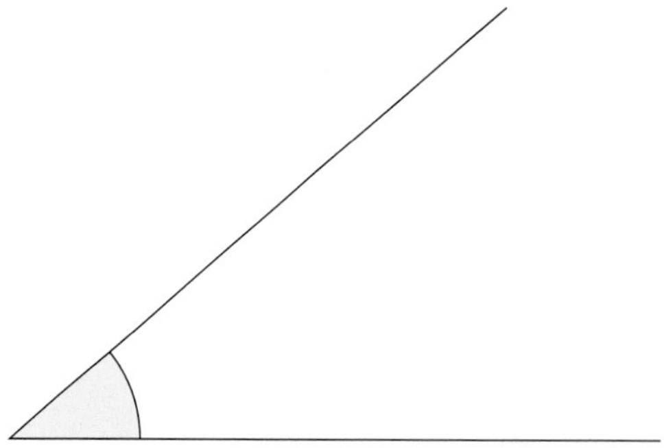

b

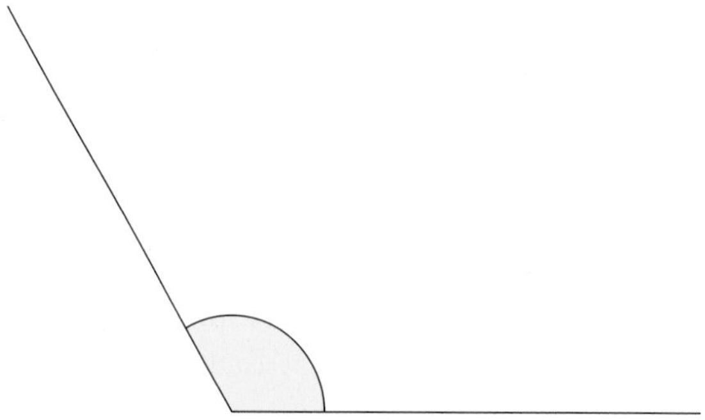

Orientation

What I should know		What I will learn		What this leads to
Key stage 3	→	■ Understand the geometrical properties of triangles and quadrilaterals ■ Calculate with angles in parallel lines	→	G5

Rich task

In this 6-sided polygon every vertex has been joined to every other vertex by a line. There are nine diagonals.

If the polygon had 12 sides how many diagonals will you need to draw?
What if it had 100 sides?

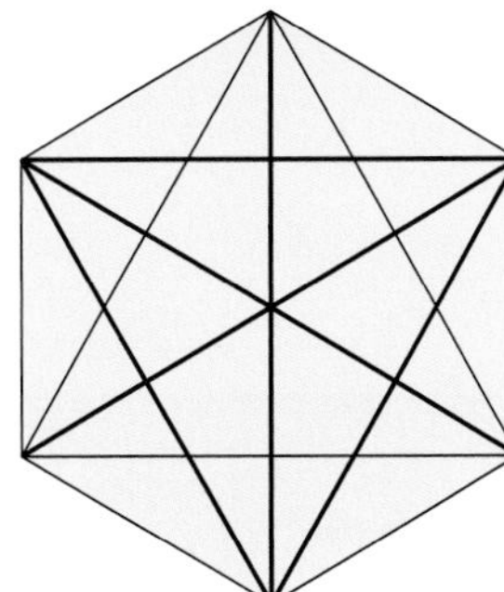

G2.1 Angle properties

This spread will show you how to:

- Recall and use properties of lines and angles
- Recall the geometric properties of triangles

Keywords
Angle
Degree (°)
Straight line
Triangle
Vertically opposite

You should know these facts:

There are 360° at a point.

180°

There are 180° on a straight line.

Vertically opposite angles are equal.

Example

Calculate the values of x, y and z. Give a reason for each of your answers.

a

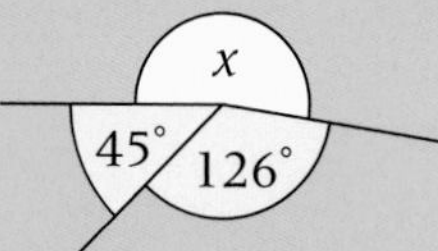

b

c

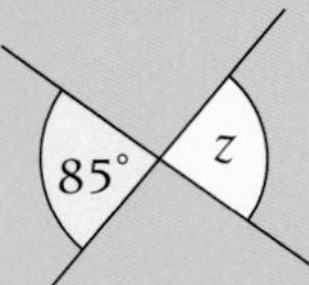

a $126° + 45° = 171°$
$360° - 171° = 189°$
$x = 189°$
(angles at a point add to 360°)

b $54° + 90° = 144°$
$180° - 144° = 36°$
$y = 36°$
(angles on a straight line add to 180°)

c $z = 85°$
(vertically opposite angles are equal)

You should know the names of these triangles:

Right-angled

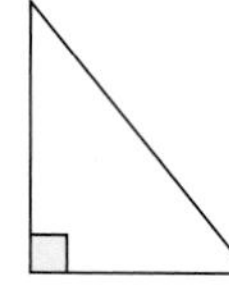

One 90° angle, marked ∟

Equilateral

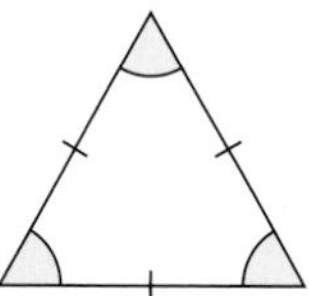

3 equal angles
3 equal sides

Isosceles

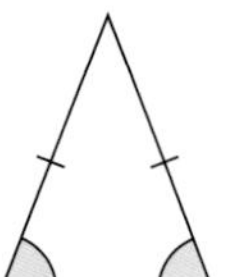

2 equal angles
2 equal sides

Scalene

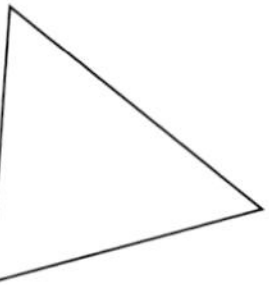

No equal angles
No equal sides

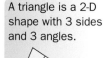

A triangle is a 2-D shape with 3 sides and 3 angles.

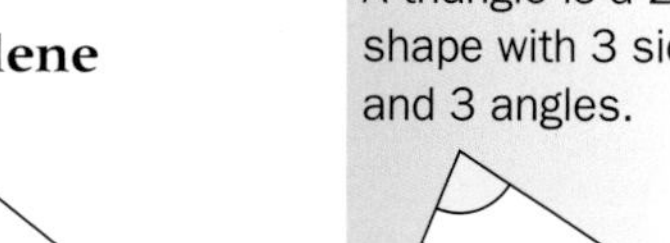

- The angles in a triangle add to 180°.

Draw any triangle, tear off the corners,

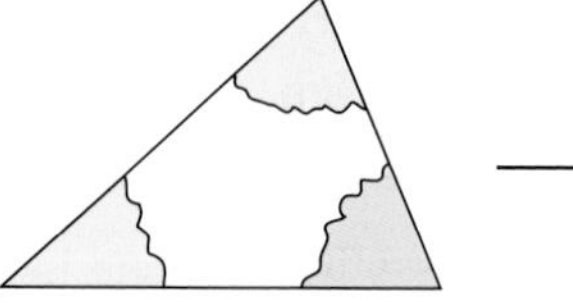

and put them together to make a straight line.

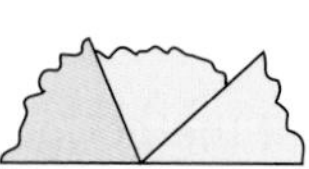

Example

Calculate the value of p.
Give a reason for your answer.

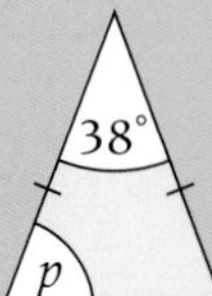

$180° - 38° = 142°$ (angles in a Δ add to 180°)
$142° \div 2 = 71°$ (two equal angles in an isosceles Δ)
$p = 71°$

Exercise G2.1 **Grade E–F**

1 Calculate the size of the unknown angles in each diagram.
Give a reason for each answer.

The diagrams are not drawn to scale.

a

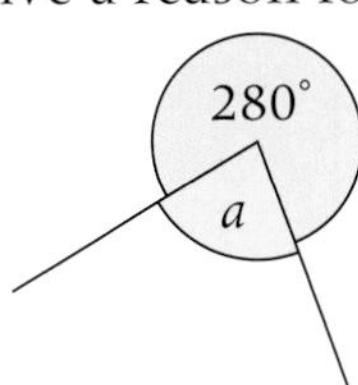

b

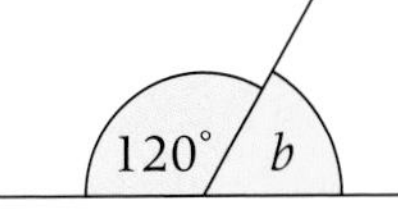

c

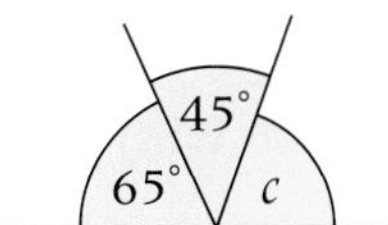

d

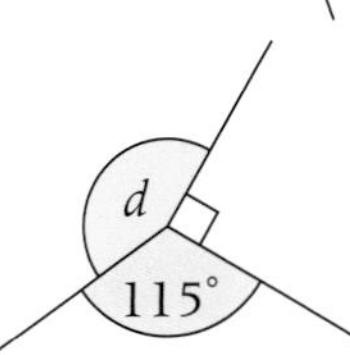

e

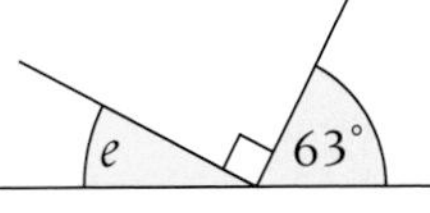

f

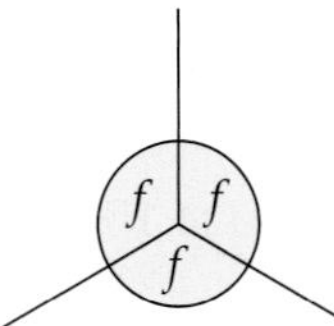

2 Calculate the size of the angles marked by letters in each diagram.

a

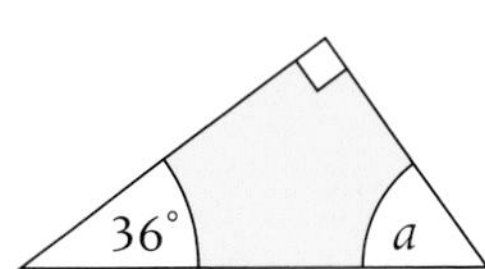

b

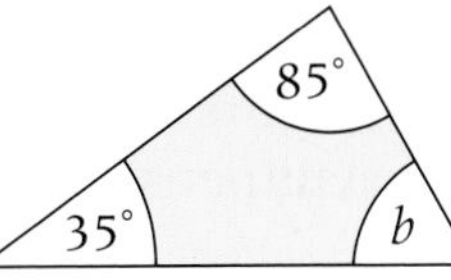

c

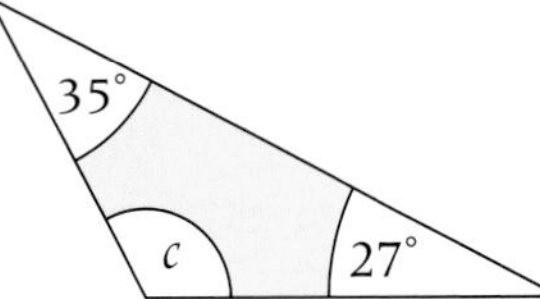

d

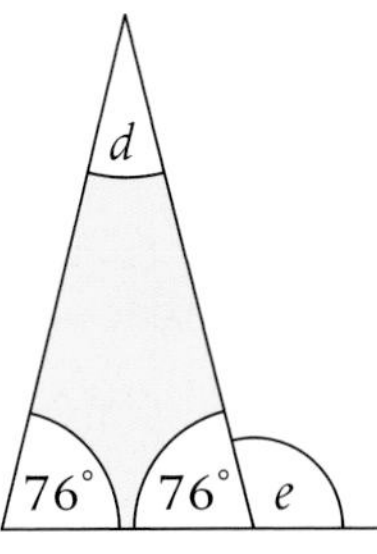

e

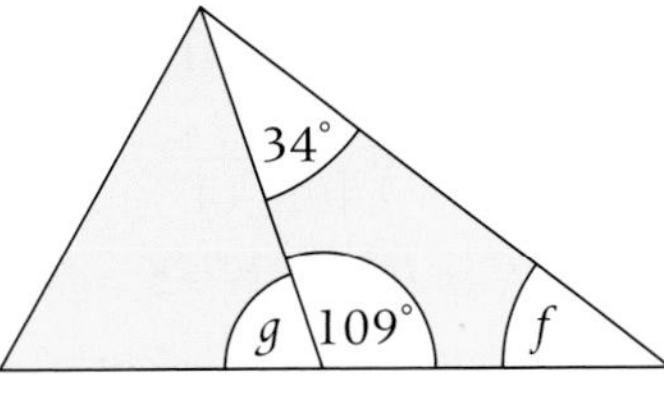

3 Find the unknown angle and state the type of triangle.

a

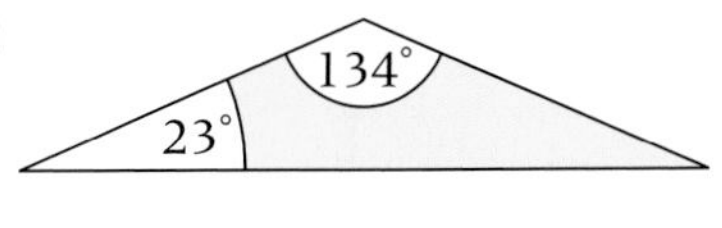

b

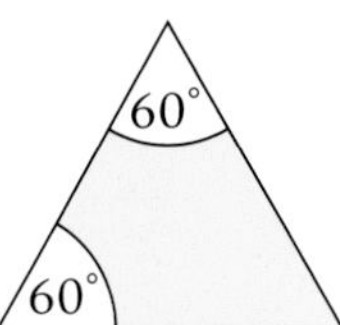

c

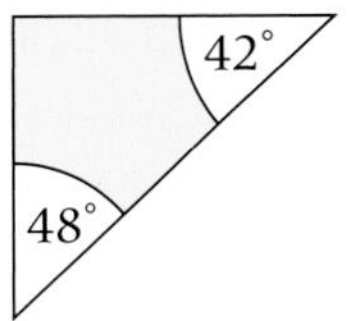

4 Calculate the size of the angles marked with letters in each diagram.

a

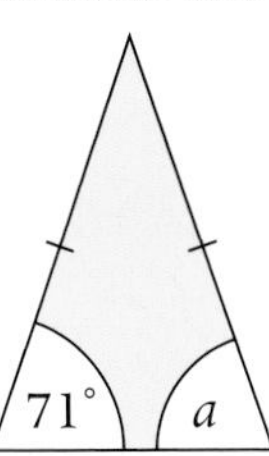

b

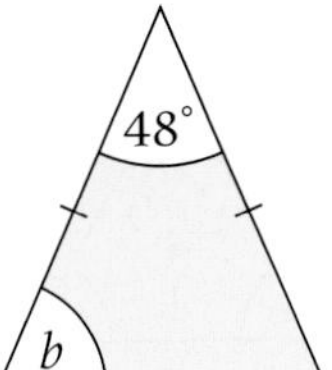

c

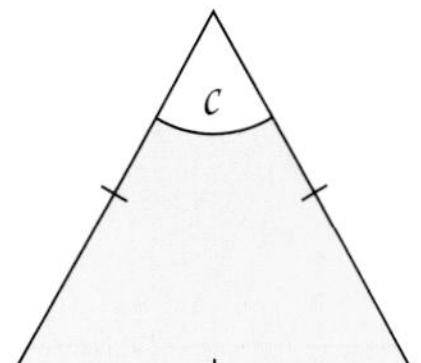

G2.2 Properties of triangles

This spread will show you how to:

- Use angle properties of equilateral, isosceles and right-angled triangles

Keywords
Equilateral
Isosceles
Regular
Right-angled triangle
Scalene
Triangle

A **triangle** is a 2-D shape with 3 sides and 3 angles.

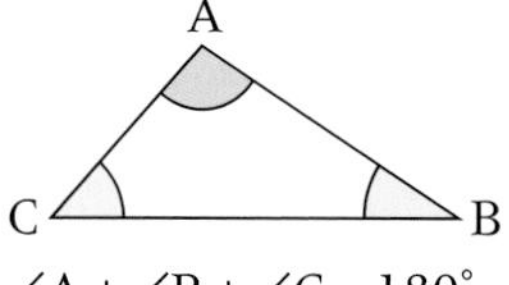

$\angle A + \angle B + \angle C = 180^\circ$

- The angles in a triangle add to 180°.

You need to know the properties of these triangles.

Triangle	Properties	Reflection symmetry	Rotational symmetry
Right-angled	One 90° angle marked ∟	No lines of symmetry	Order 1
Equilateral	3 equal angles 3 equal sides	3 lines of symmetry	Order 3
Isosceles	2 equal angles 2 equal sides	1 line of symmetry	Order 1
Scalene	No equal angles No equal sides	No lines of symmetry	Order 1

The equilateral triangle is a **regular** shape as it has equal sides and equal angles. All its interior angles are 60°.

Example

The side lengths of this spinner are equal.

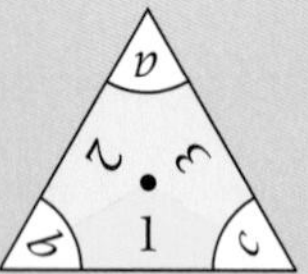

The spinner is rotated about the dot.
What does this rotation show about the angles in the triangle?

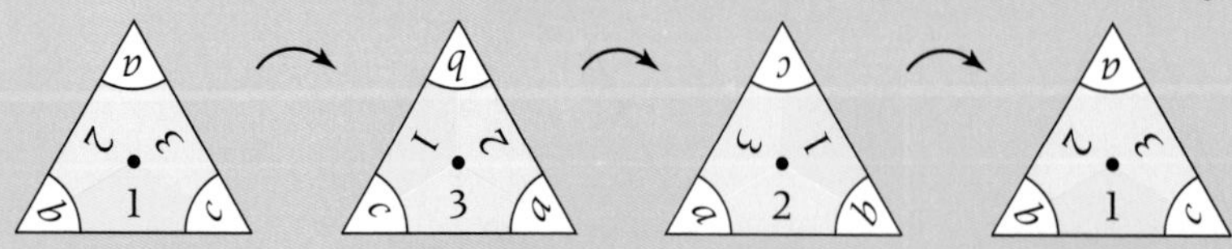

Each position looks identical to the previous one.
The angles are exactly the same.

Exercise G2.2 **Grade E**

1 Calculate the third angle of each of these triangles and state the type of triangle.

a 60°, 60° **b** 37°, 53° **c** 114°, 33°
d 53°, 48° **e** 45°, 90°

2 The points A(−1, −2) and B(3, −2) are shown. Give the coordinates of a point C, so that triangle ABC

a is isosceles
b is right-angled but scalene
c is right-angled and isosceles
d is scalene
e is equilateral (only an approximate value of *y* is possible)
f has an area of 4 cm^2.

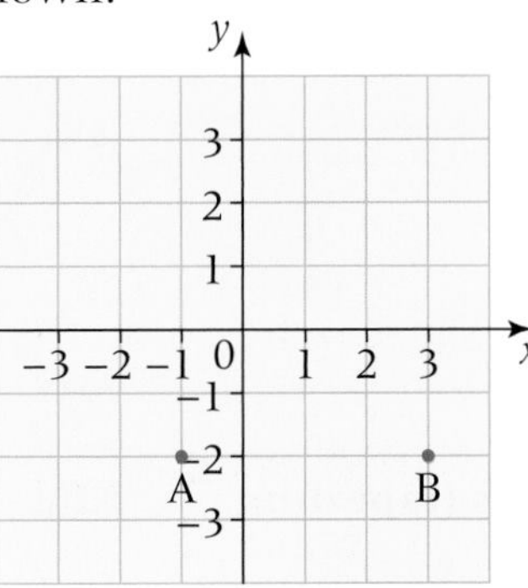

DID YOU KNOW?

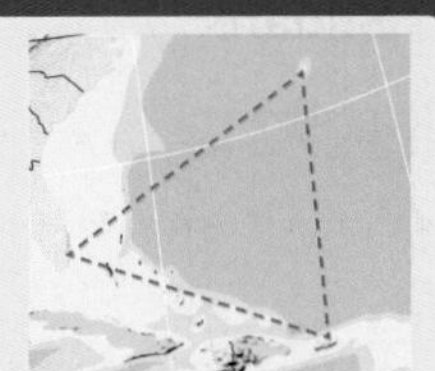

The Bermuda Triangle is a region of the Caribbean sea that forms a roughly isosceles triangle between Bermuda, Puerto Rico and Florida. A large number of ships and planes have disappeared in mysterious circumstances in this area and many theories abound.

3 Here is a regular hexagon. The yellow triangles are equilateral. The green triangles are isosceles. Calculate the three angles in the

a yellow triangle
b green triangle.

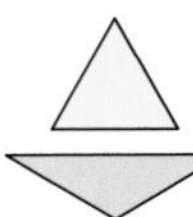

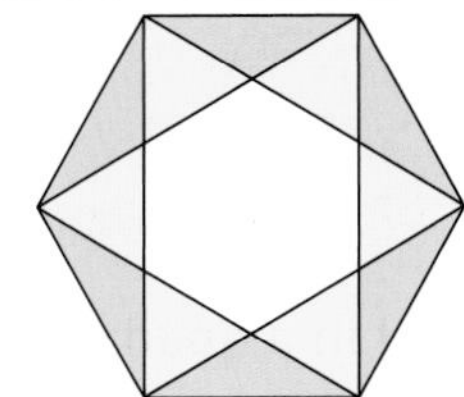

4 A regular pentagon is shown. Find the number of isosceles triangles with each of these designs.

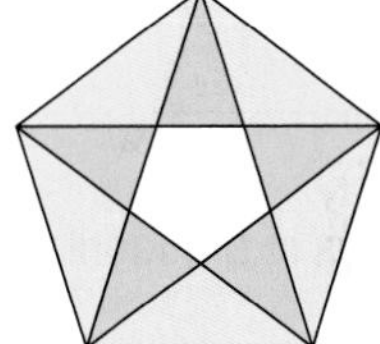

a **b** **c**

d

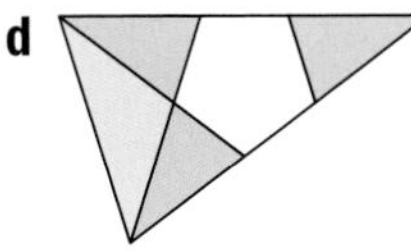

e

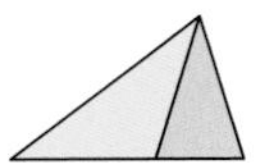

f

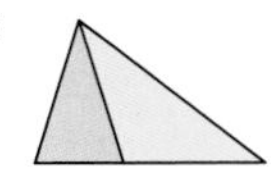

5 Calculate the area of triangle

a ABC
b ABD
c ABE
d ABF
e ABG.

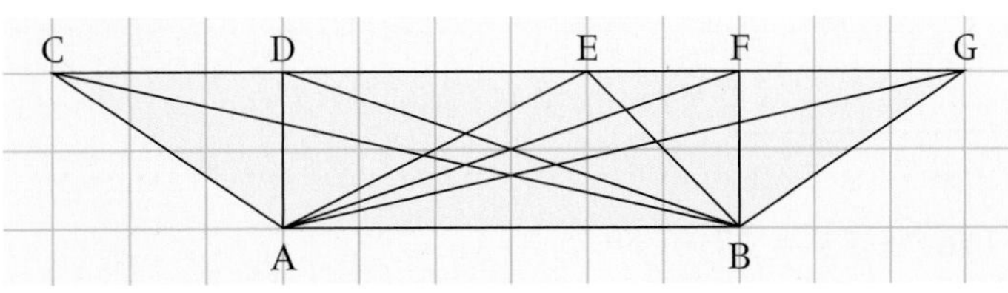

AO3 Problem

6 Can a triangle have a reflex angle? Justify your answer.

G2.3 Angles in quadrilaterals

This spread will show you how to:

- Explain why the angle sum of any quadrilateral is 360°

Keywords
Angle
Degree (°)
Diagonal
Point
Quadrilateral
Triangle

- A **quadrilateral** is a 2-D shape with 4 sides and 4 angles.

Square **Rectangle** **Rhombus** **Parallelogram**

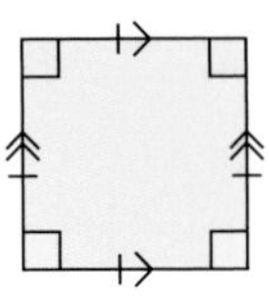

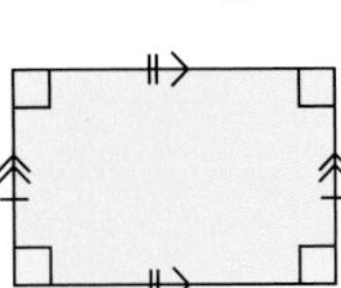

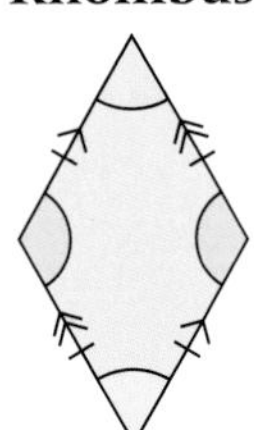

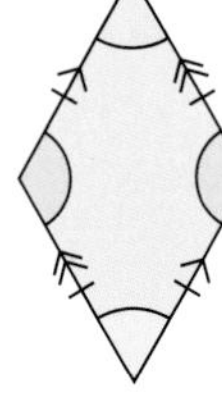

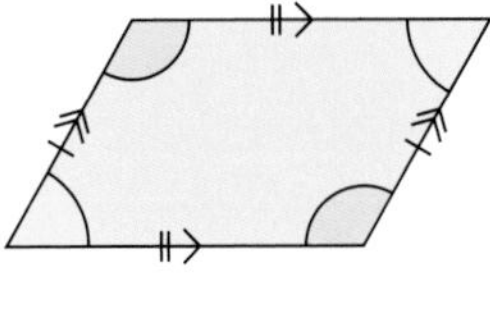

The equal angles are coloured the same.

Trapezium **Isosceles trapezium** **Kite** **Arrowhead**

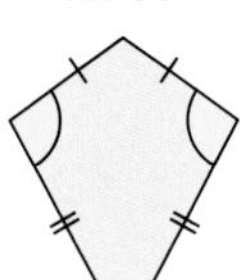

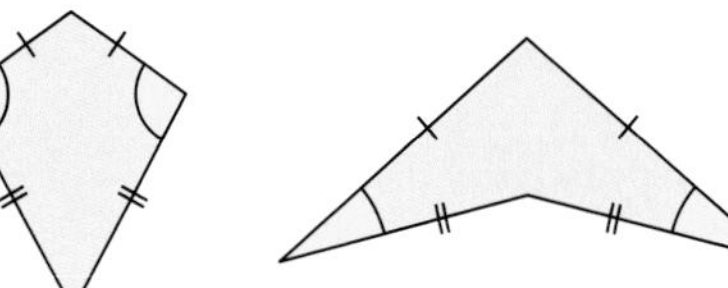

You can draw a diagonal in a quadrilateral to form two triangles.

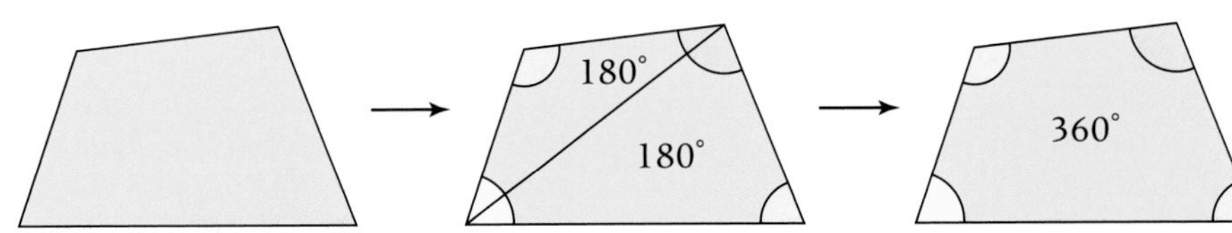

The angles in each triangle add to 180°.
$2 \times 180° = 360°$

- The angles in a quadrilateral add to 360°.

Example

Calculate the values of x, y and z. Give a reason for each of your answers.

a

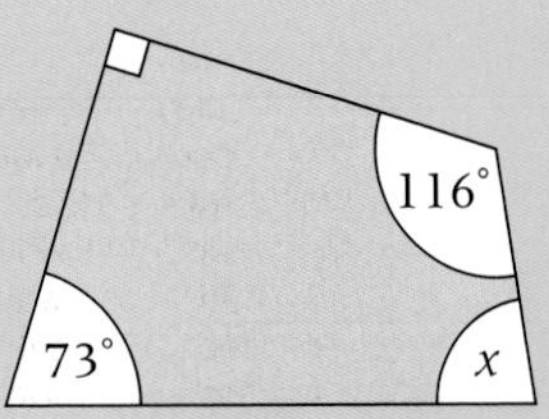

b

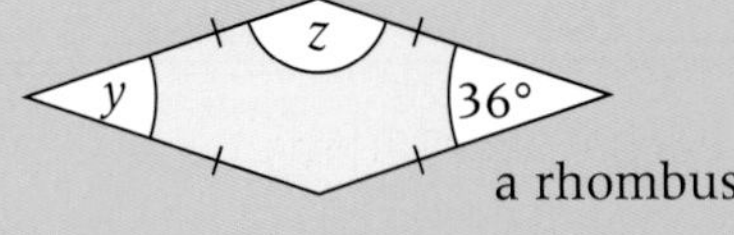

a $90° + 116° + 73° = 279°$

$360° - 279° = 81°$

$x = 81°$ (angles in a quadrilateral add to 360°)

b $y = 36°$ (opposite angles of a rhombus are equal)

$36° + 36° = 72°$

$360° - 72° = 288°$ (opposite angles of a rhombus are equal and angles in a quadrilateral add to 360°)

$288° \div 2 = 144°$

$z = 144°$

Exercise G2.3

Grade E

The diagrams are not drawn to scale.

1 Calculate the size of the unknown angles in each diagram.

a

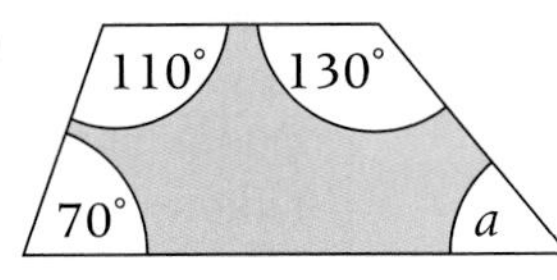

b

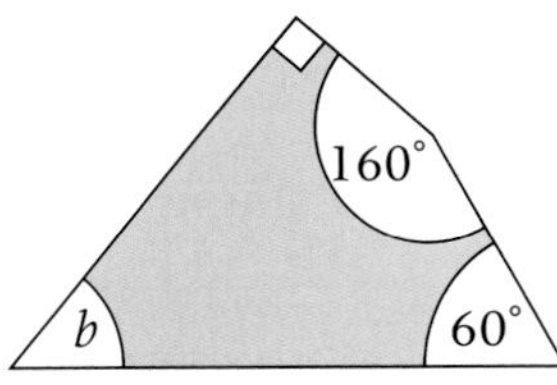

c

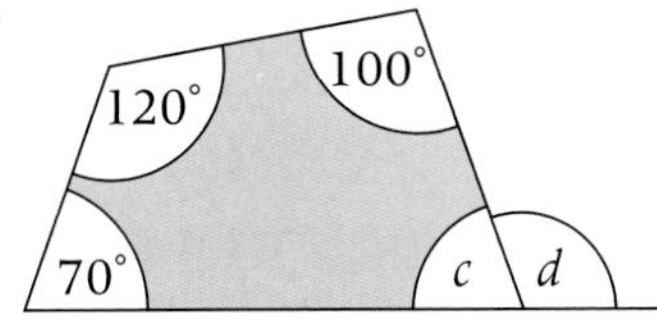

d

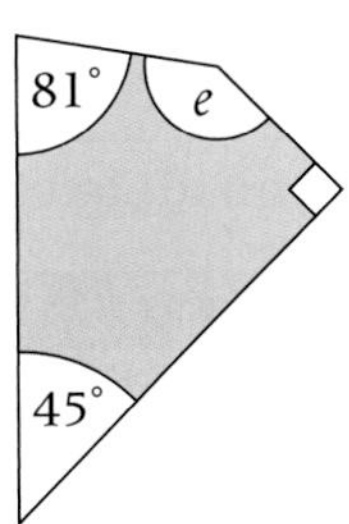

e

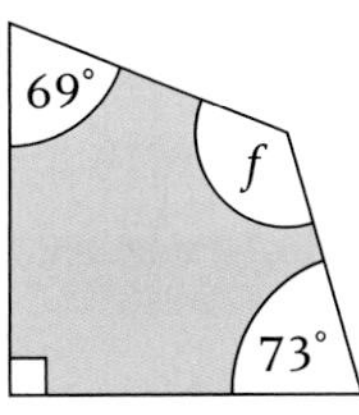

2 Find the unknown angles in each quadrilateral and state the type of quadrilateral.

a

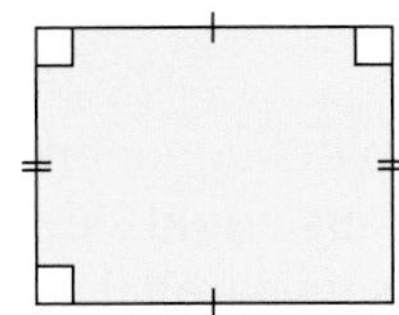

b

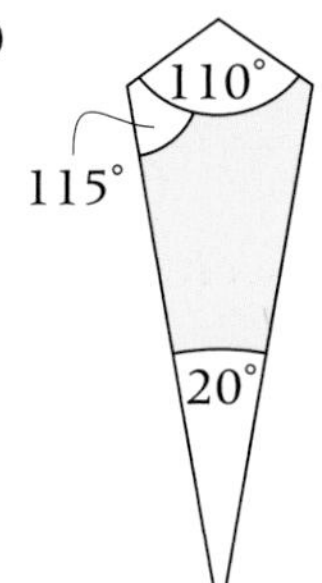

c

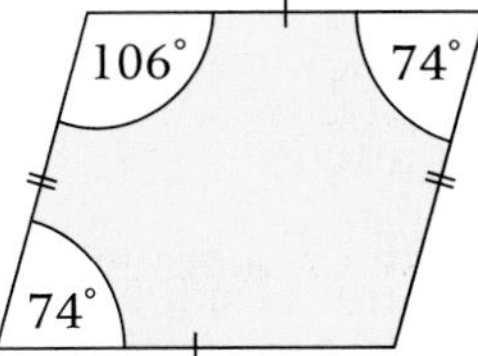

d

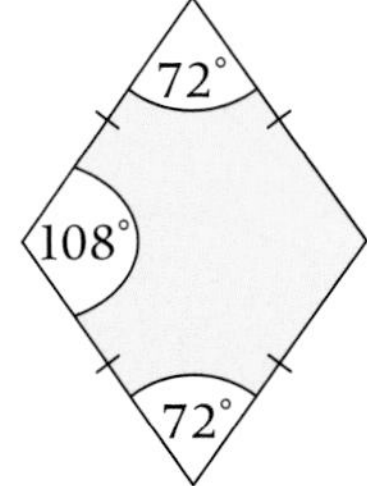

e

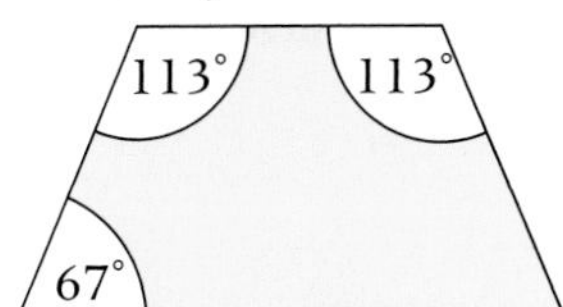

Did you know?

A quadrangle is a rectangular courtyard often associated with university colleges. Oxford University Press, where this book was produced, has its own quadrangle as shown above.

3 Calculate the value of x for each quadrilateral.

a

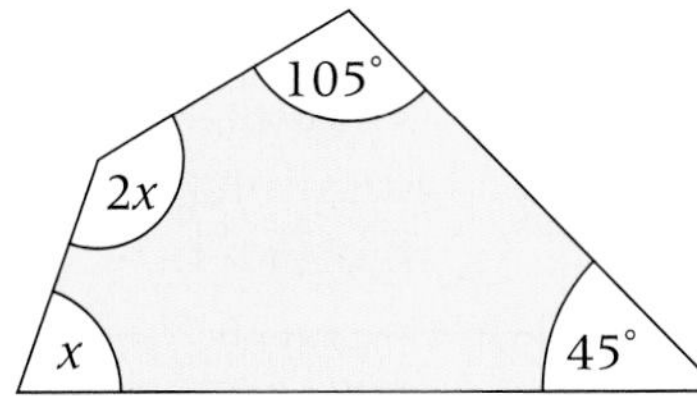

b

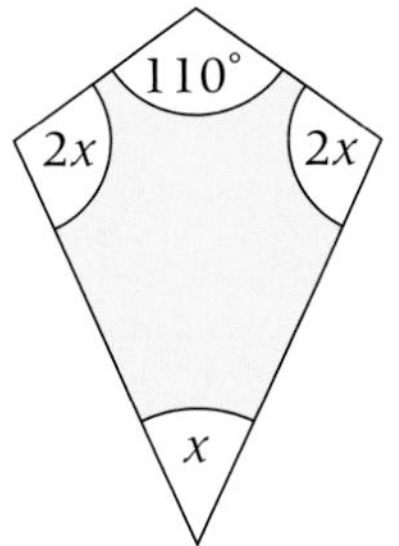

c

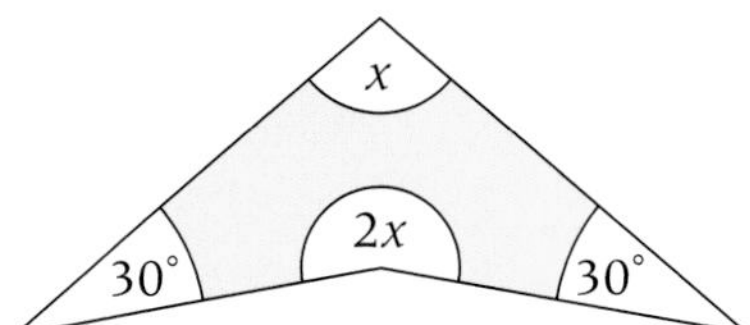

G2.4 Properties of quadrilaterals

This spread will show you how to:

- Recall the geometric properties of quadrilaterals

Keywords
Diagonal
Parallel
Quadrilateral
Line symmetry
Rotational symmetry

You know that a **quadrilateral** is a 2-D shape with 4 sides and 4 angles.

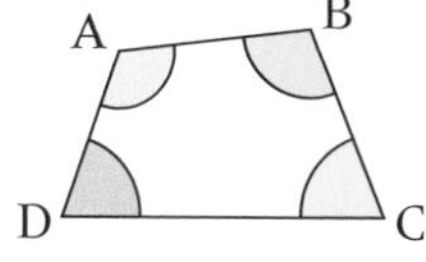

- The angles in a quadrilateral add to 360°.

$\angle A + \angle B + \angle C + \angle D = 360°$

You need to know the properties of these quadrilaterals.

Square	Rectangle	Rhombus	Parallelogram
4 right angles 4 equal sides 2 sets parallel sides 4 lines of symmetry Rotational symmetry of order 4	4 right angles 2 sets equal sides 2 sets parallel sides 2 lines of symmetry Rotational symmetry of order 2	2 pairs equal angles 4 equal sides 2 sets parallel sides 2 lines of symmetry Rotational symmetry of order 2	2 pairs equal angles 2 sets equal sides 2 sets parallel sides No lines of symmetry Rotational symmetry of order 2

Trapezium	Isosceles trapezium	Kite	Arrowhead
1 set of parallel sides No lines of symmetry Rotational symmetry of order 1	2 sets equal angles 1 set equal sides 1 set parallel sides 1 line of symmetry Rotational symmetry of order 1	1 pair equal angles 2 sets equal sides No parallel sides 1 line of symmetry Rotational symmetry of order 1	1 pair equal angles 2 sets equal sides No parallel sides 1 reflex angle 1 line of symmetry Rotational symmetry of order 1

Example

a Plot the points A(−2, −1), B (1, −3) and C(3, −1) on the grid.
b Give the coordinates of the point D, so that ABCD is a kite.
c Draw any lines of symmetry for the kite.

a,c

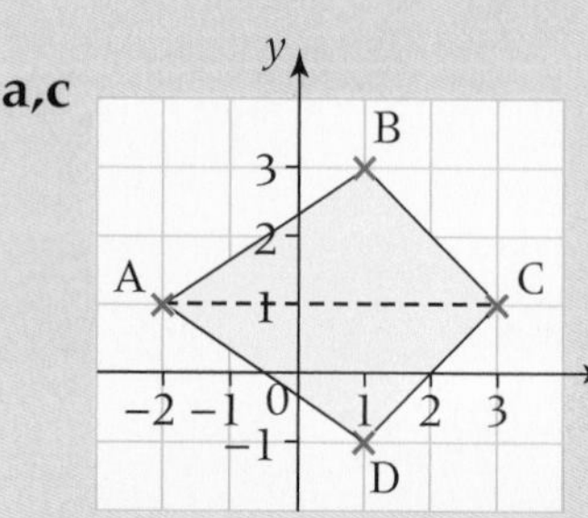

b D(1, −1)

Exercise G2.4 Grade D

1 State the value of each unknown angle.

a

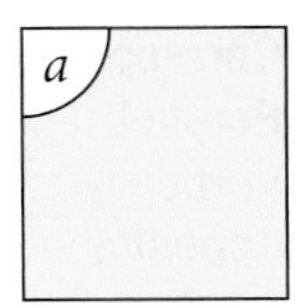

square

b

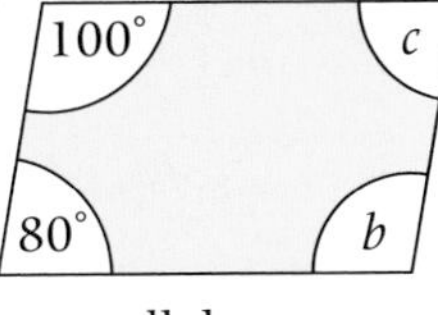

parallelogram

c

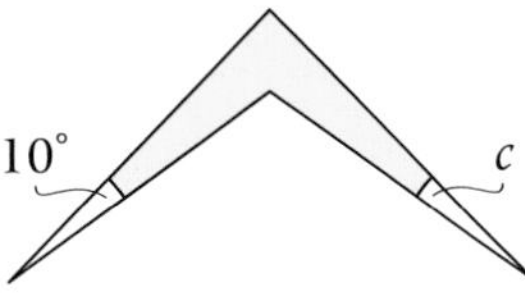

arrowhead

d

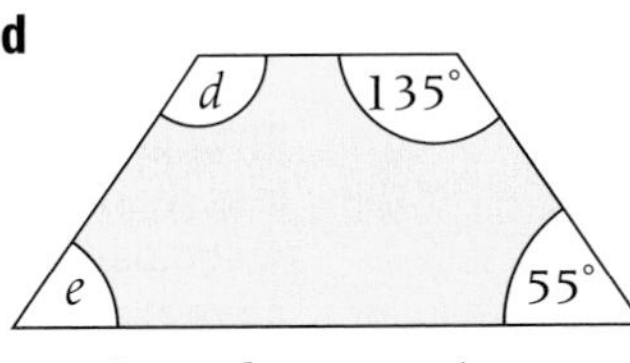

isosceles trapezium

e

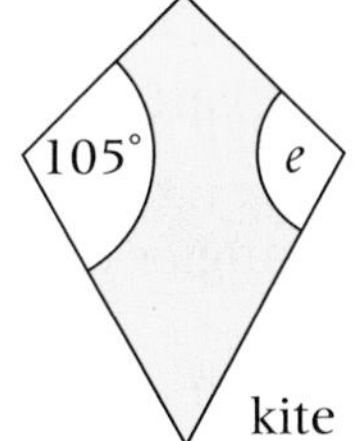

kite

f

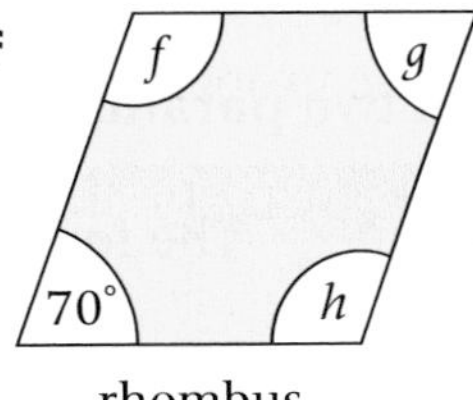

rhombus

2 The **diagonals** of a rectangle

- are equal in length
- bisect each other
- are not perpendicular.

Copy and complete the table of results for the diagonals of these shapes.

Shape	Equal in length	Bisect each other	Perpendicular
Rectangle	✓	✓	✗
Kite			
Isosceles trapezium			
Square			
Parallelogram			
Rhombus			
Ordinary trapezium			

AO3 Problem

3 Plot the points $(-2, -1)$, $(0, -1)$ and $(1, 2)$ on a copy of this grid.
These points are three vertices (corners) of a parallelogram.

a Write the coordinates of the fourth point.

b Draw the parallelogram.

c Calculate the area of the parallelogram.

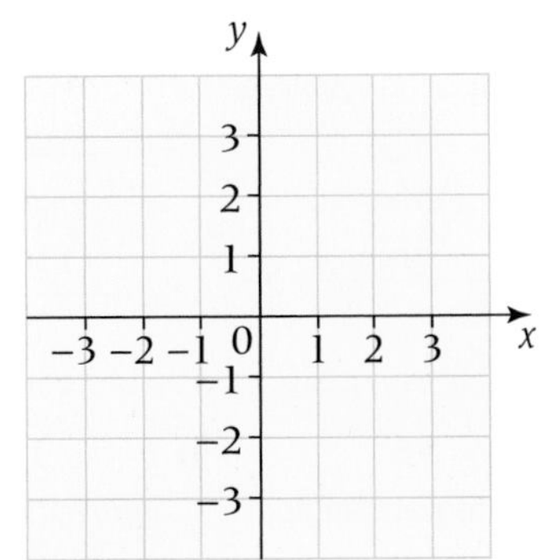

G2.5 Angles in parallel lines

This spread will show you how to:

- Use parallel lines, alternate angles and corresponding angles

Keywords
Alternate
Corresponding
Parallel
Vertically opposite

When two lines cross, four angles are formed.

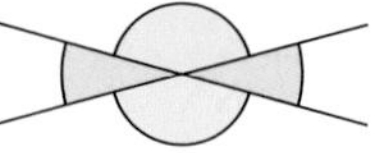

- **Vertically opposite** angles are equal.

Parallel lines are always the same distance apart.

When a line crosses two **parallel** lines, eight angles are formed.

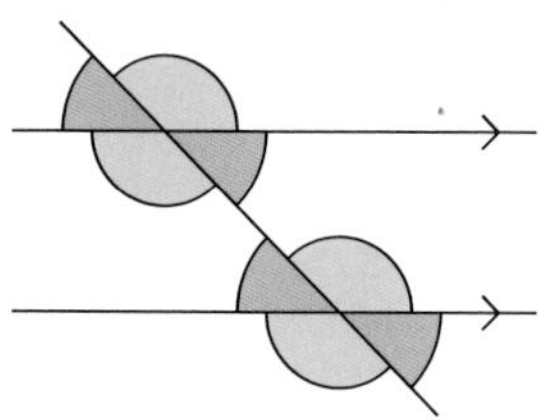

The four red **acute** angles are equal.

The four purple **obtuse** angles are equal.

Acute + obtuse = 180°

An acute angle is less than 90°.
An obtuse angle is more than 90° but less than 180°.

- **Alternate** angles are equal.

They are called Z angles.

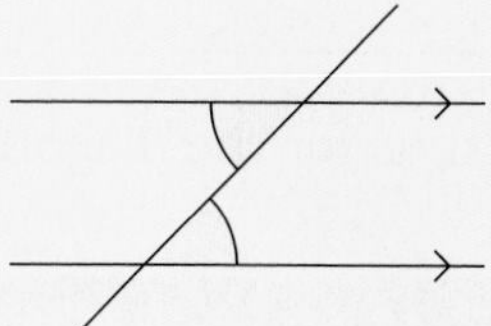

The Z shape can take several forms.

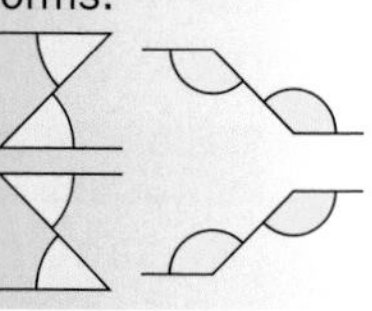

- **Corresponding** angles are equal.

They are called F angles.

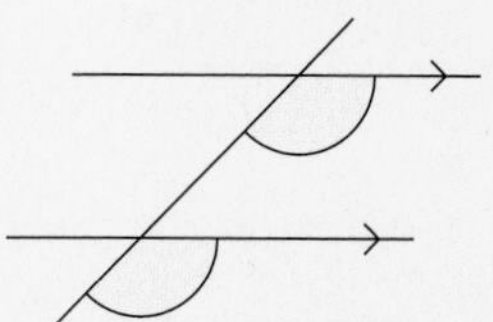

The F shape can take several forms.

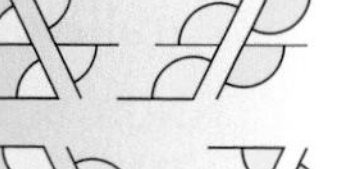

Example

Find the unknown angles in these diagrams.
Give reasons for your answers.

a

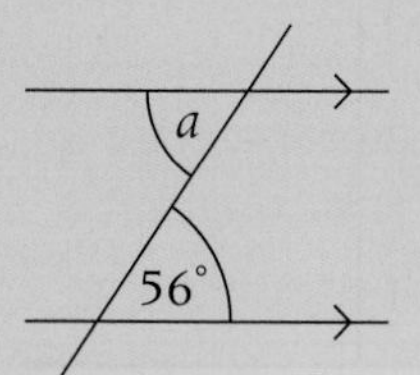

b

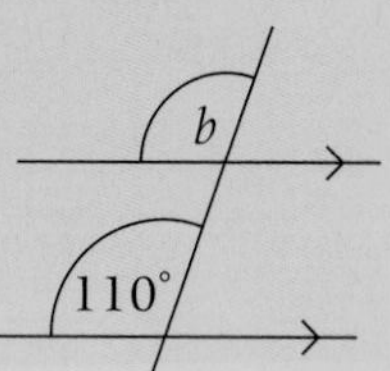

c

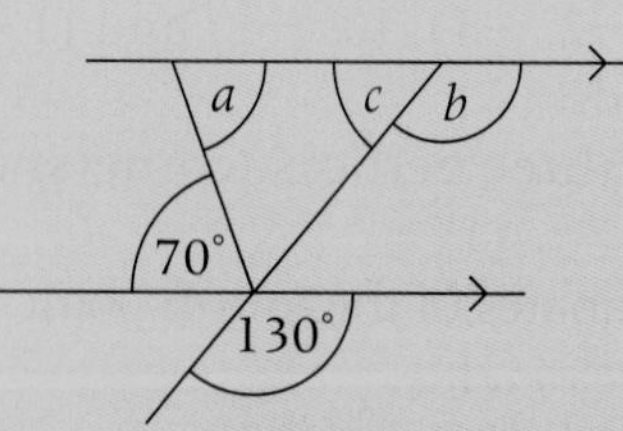

a $a = 56°$
(alternate angles)

b $b = 110°$
(corresponding angles)

c $a = 70°$ (alternate angles)
$b = 130°$ (corresponding angles)
$c = 180° - 130°$
(angles on straight line add to 180°)

Exercise G2.5 Grade D

1 Calculate the size of the angles marked by a letter in each diagram.
Give a reason for each answer.

a

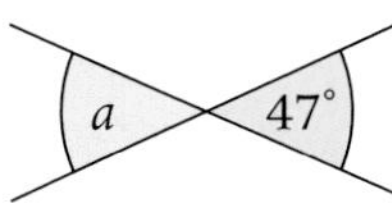

b

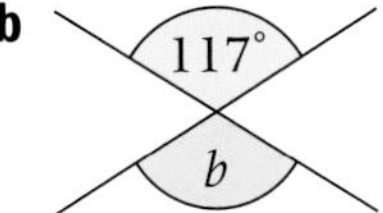

c

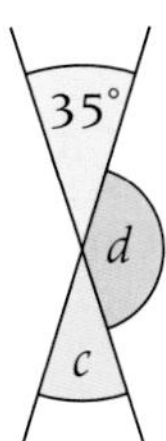

d

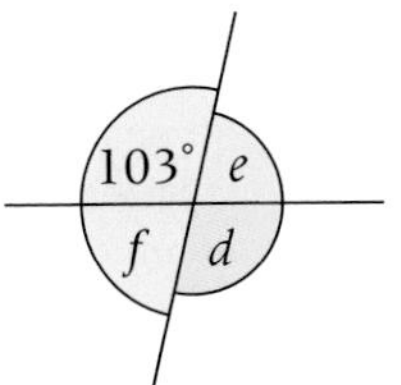

e

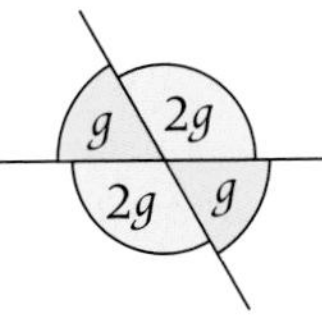

2 Find the value of each angle marked with a letter.
Give a reason for each answer.

a

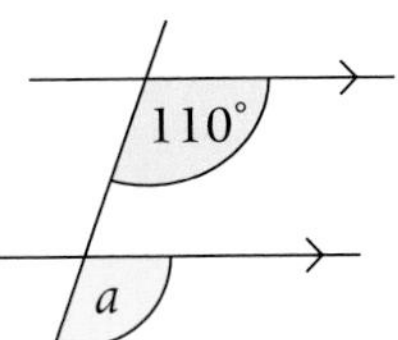

b

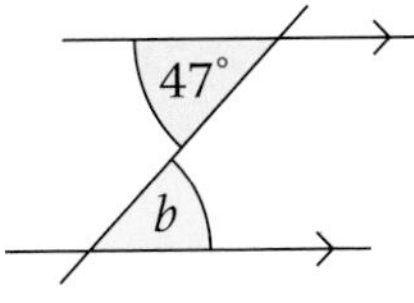

c

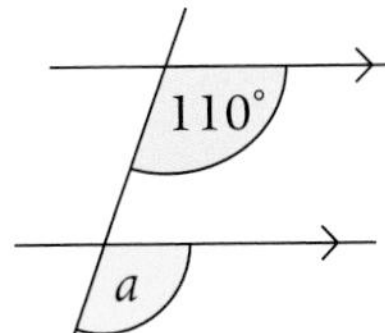

d

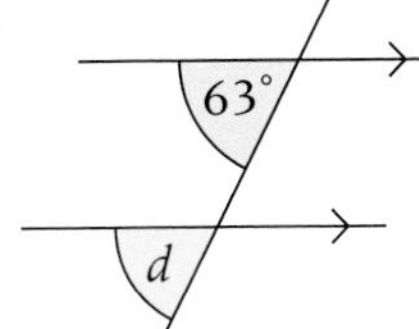

e

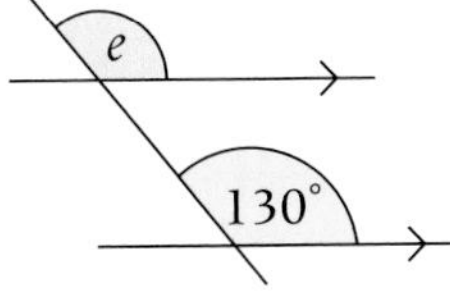

f

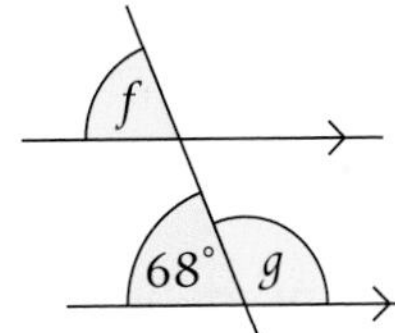

g

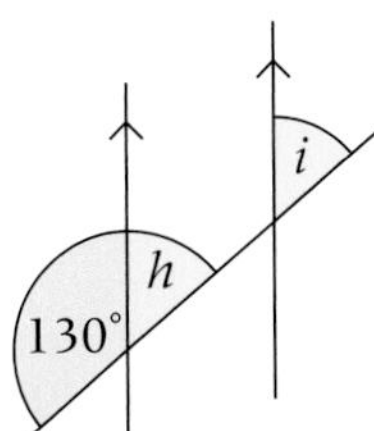

h

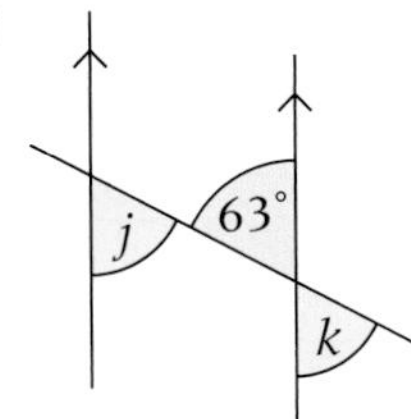

i

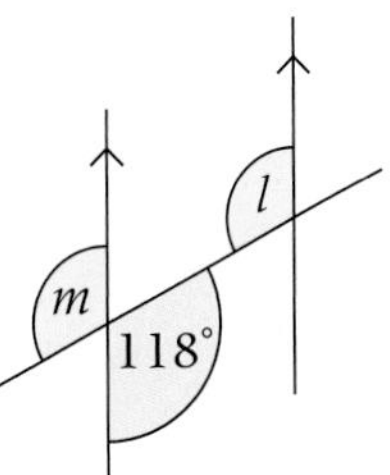

3 Find the value of each angle marked with a letter. Give a reason.

a

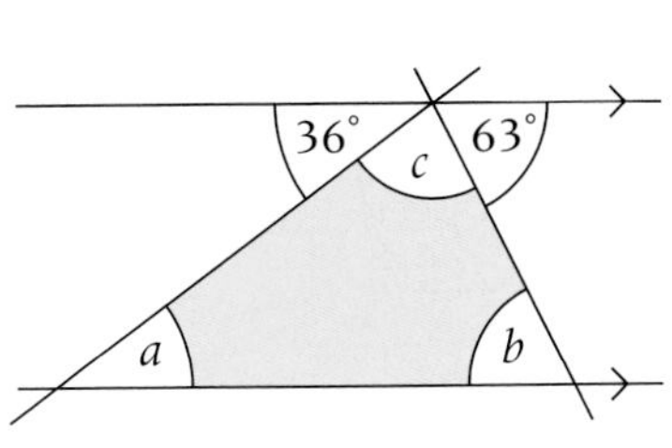

b

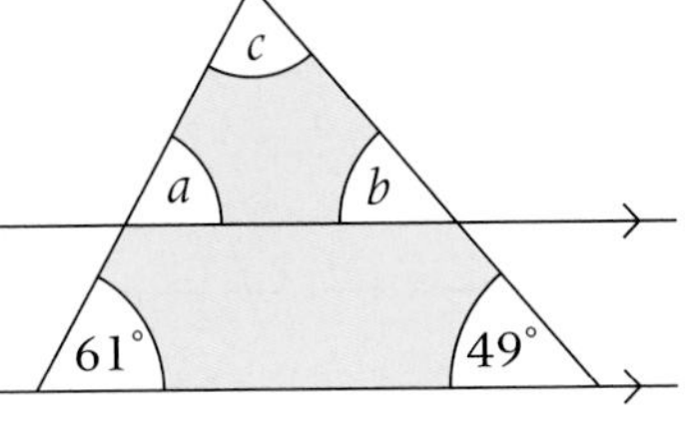

c

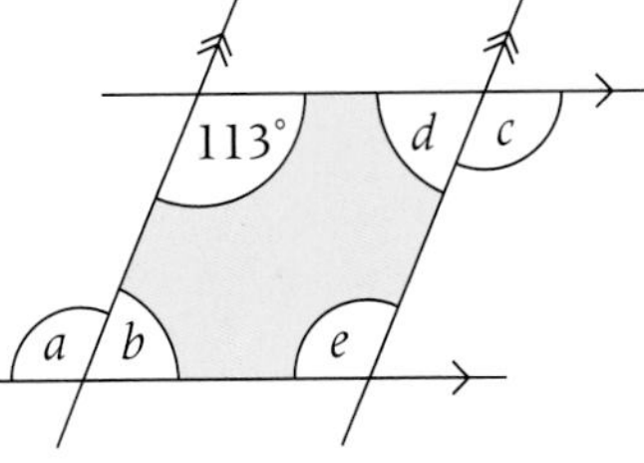

G2.6 Using parallel lines

This spread will show you how to:

- Understand and use angle properties

Keywords
Alternate angles
Corresponding angles
Exterior angle
Interior angle
Parallel
Parallelogram
Proof

When a line crosses **parallel** lines, eight angles are formed.

- **Alternate angles** are equal
- **Corresponding angles** are equal

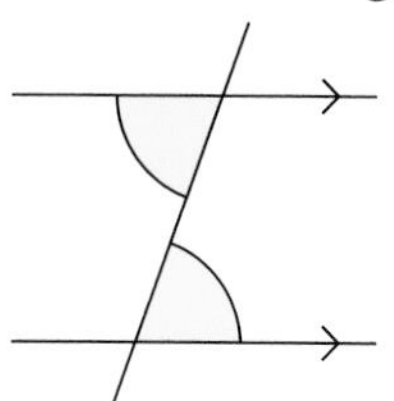

These are Z angles

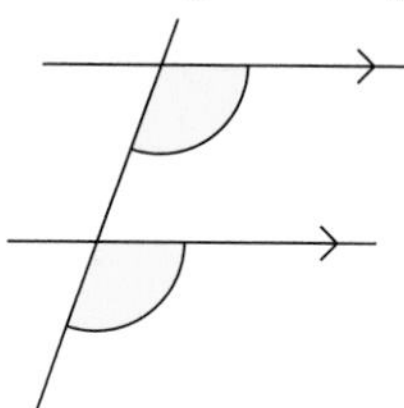

These are F angles

You can use these parallel line angle properties for three **proofs**.

Proof 1

The **exterior angle** of a triangle is equal to the sum of the **interior angles** at the other two vertices.

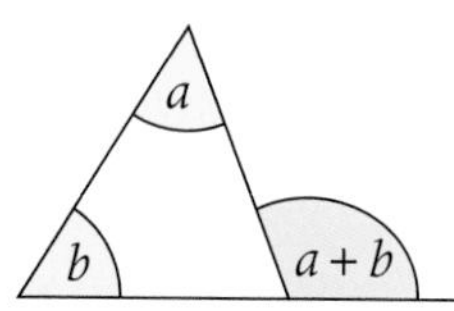

An exterior angle is formed by extending a side.

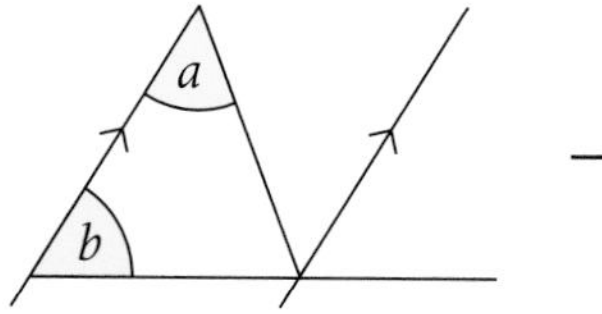

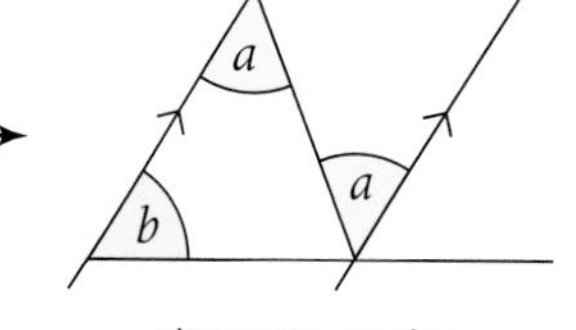

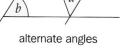

alternate angles

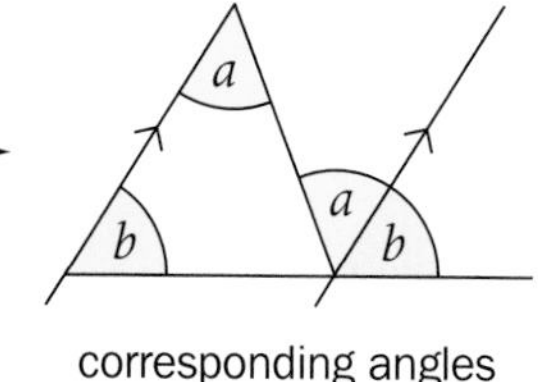

corresponding angles

Proof 2

The sum of the interior angles of a triangle is 180°.

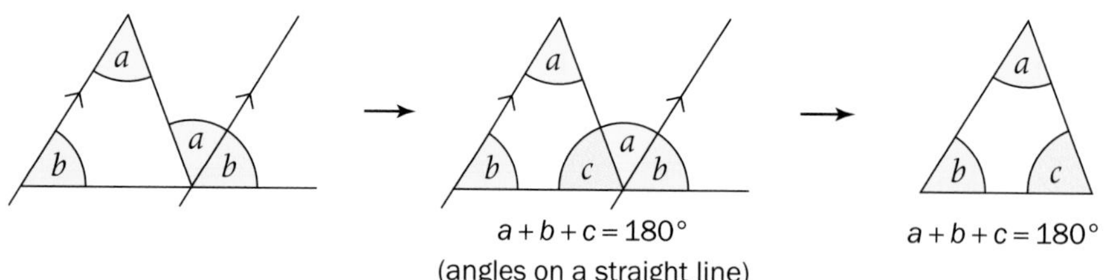

$a + b + c = 180°$
(angles on a straight line)

$a + b + c = 180°$

Proof 3

The opposite angles of a **parallelogram** are equal.

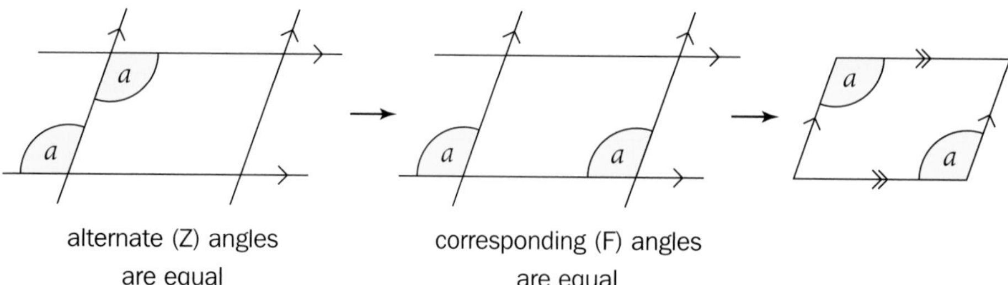

alternate (Z) angles are equal

corresponding (F) angles are equal

Exercise G2.6

Grade D

1 Find the value of the angles marked by a letter. Give a reason for each answer.

a

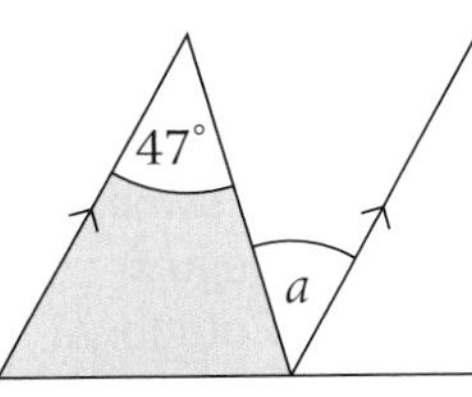

b

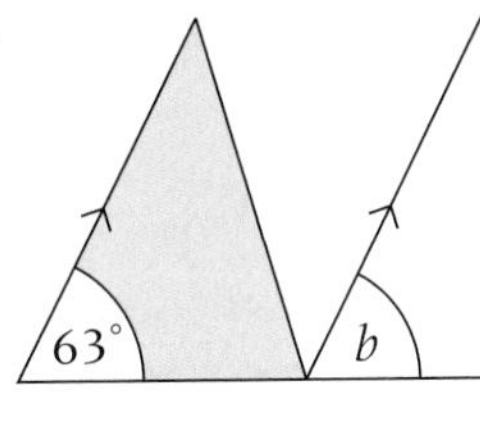

c

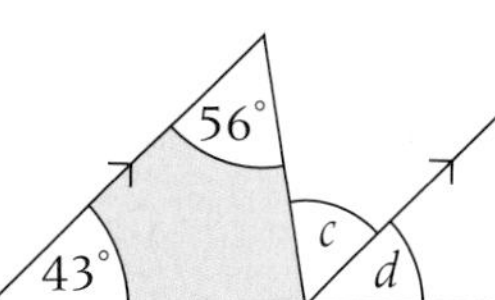

d

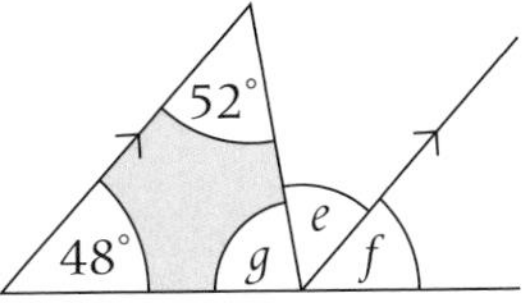

e

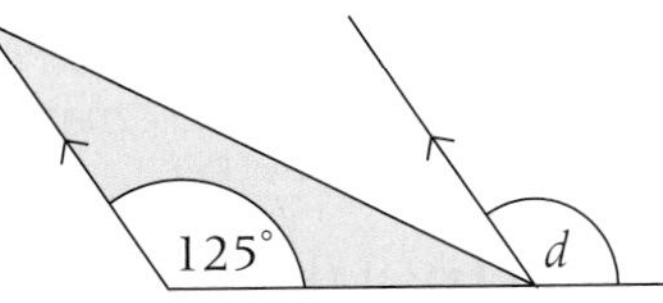

2 Find the value of the angles marked by a letter.

a

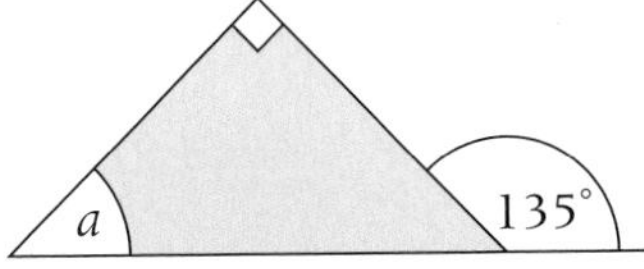

b

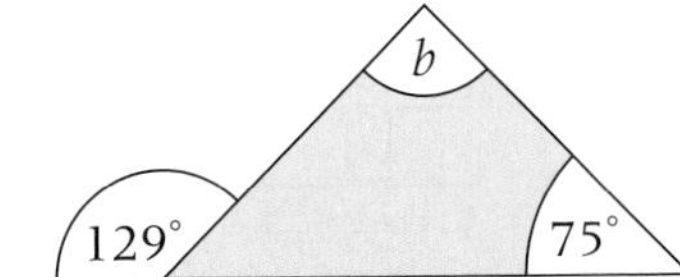

c

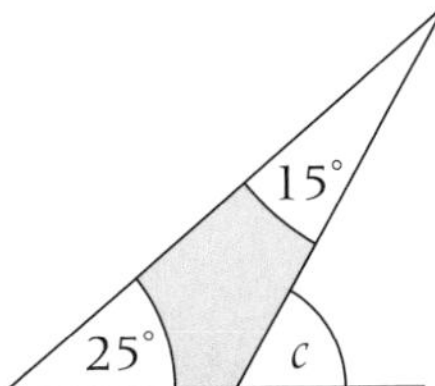

d

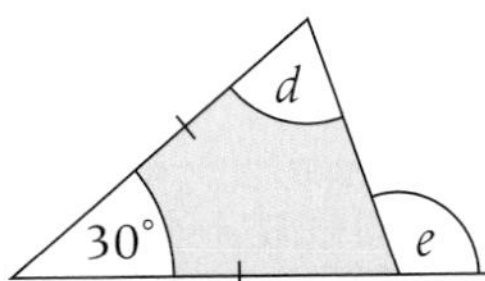

e

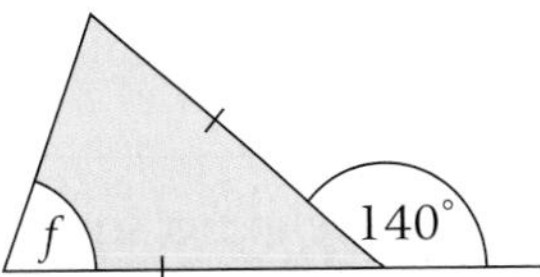

3 Find the value of the angles marked by a letter.

a

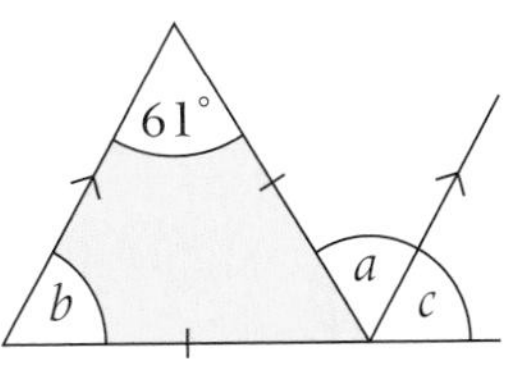

b

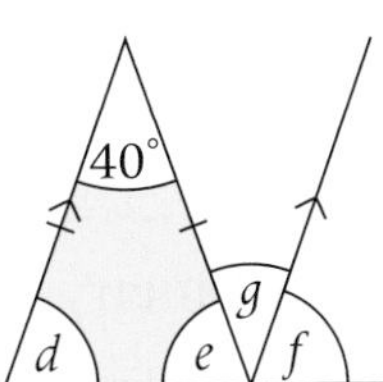

c

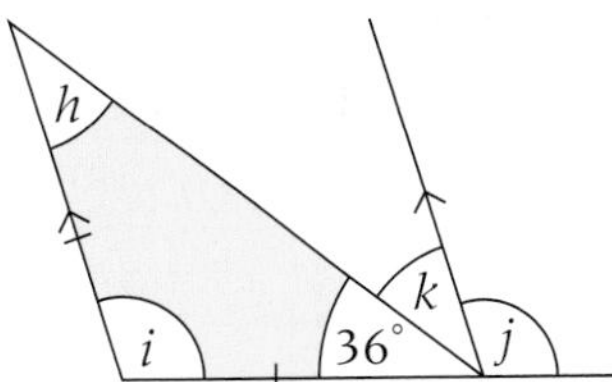

d

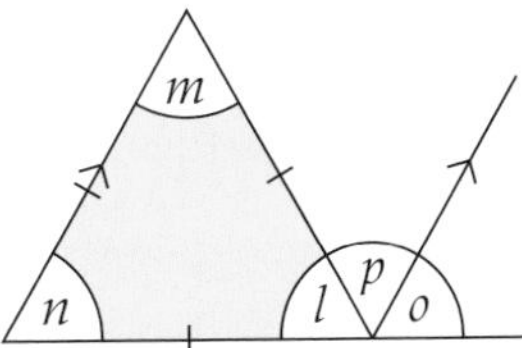

e

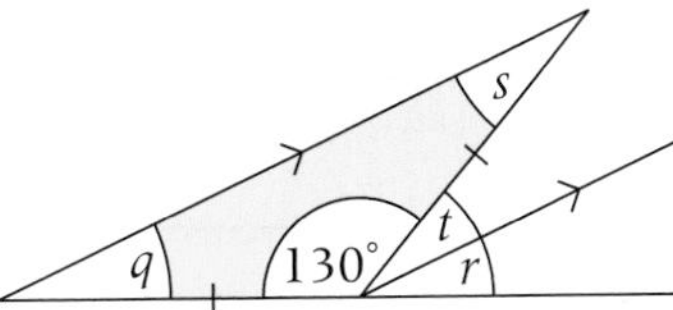

4 Find the value of the angles marked by a letter.

a

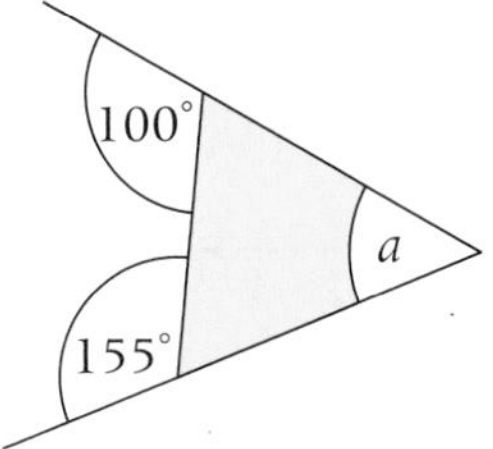

b

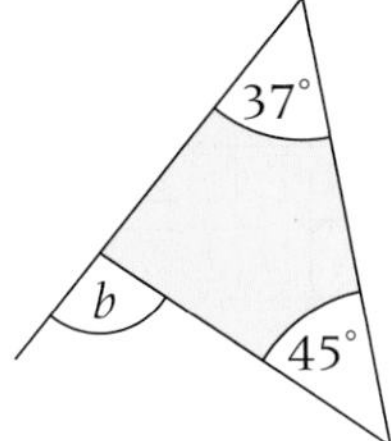

c

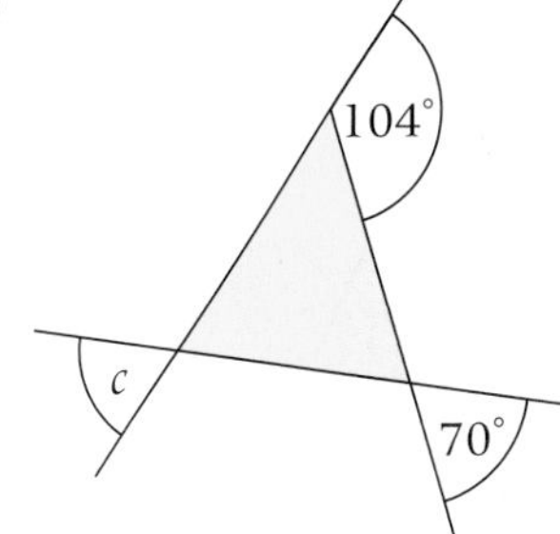

G2.7 Symmetry

This spread will show you how to:

- Recognise reflection symmetry and rotational symmetry of 2-D shapes

Keywords
Line of symmetry
Polygon
Reflection symmetry
Regular
Rotational symmetry

You can describe shapes by their **symmetry**.

A shape has **reflection symmetry** if the shape divides into two identical halves.

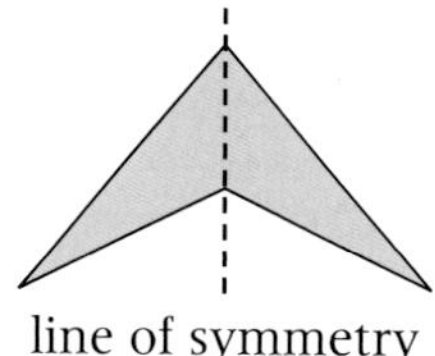

line of symmetry

The **line of symmetry** divides the shape into identical halves, each of which is the mirror image of the other.

A shape has **rotational symmetry** if the shape looks like itself more than once in a full turn.

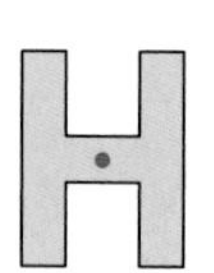
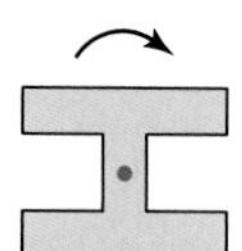
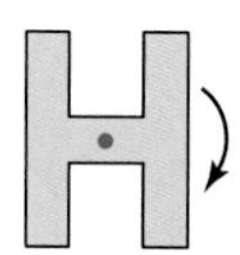
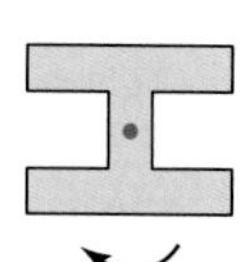
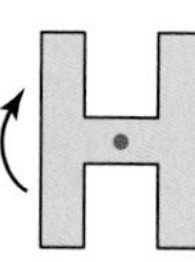

The order of rotational symmetry is 2.

- The **order of rotational symmetry** is the number of times a shape looks exactly like itself in a complete turn.

Example

a Add one extra square so that the shaded shape has 2 lines of symmetry.
b Draw the two lines of symmetry.
c State the order of rotational symmetry of the final shape.

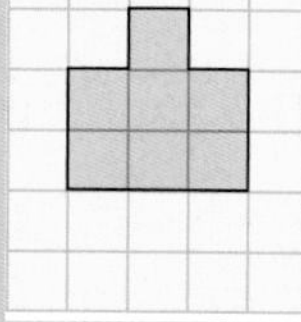

a, b

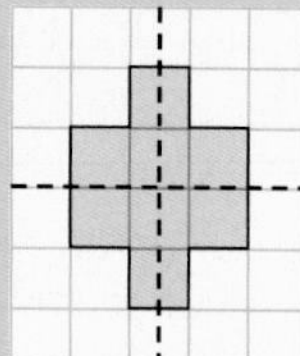

c Rotational symmetry of order 2

A line of symmetry can be given as an equation.

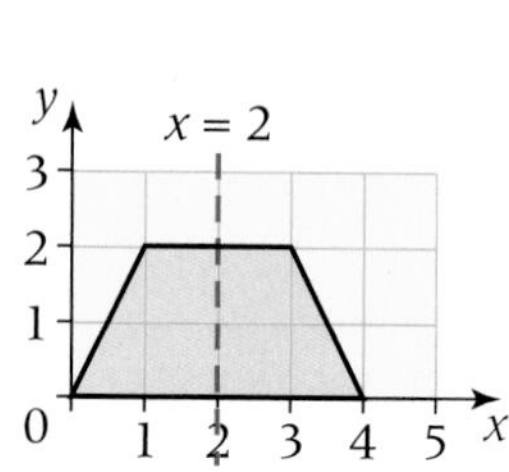

The line of symmetry is $x = 2$.

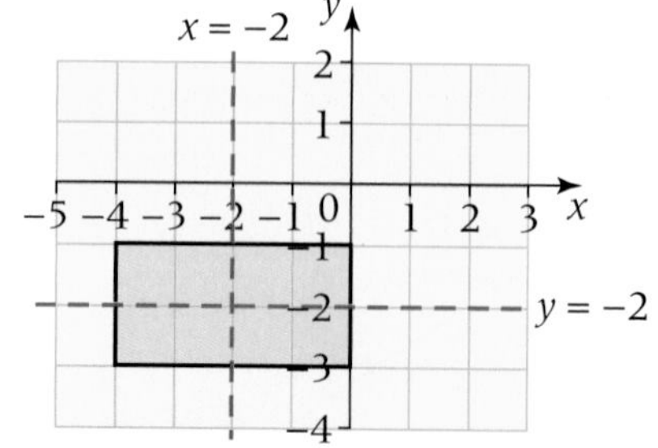

The lines of symmetry are $x = -2$ and $y = -2$.

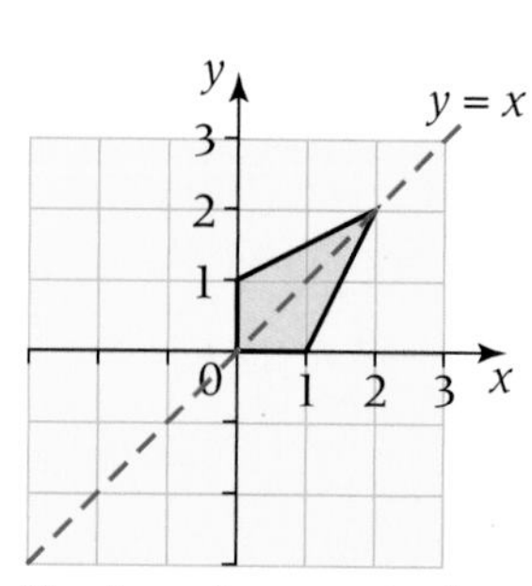

The line of symmetry is $y = x$.

Exercise G2.7

Grade D

1 **a** Write the 26 letters of the alphabet, in upper case.
b Draw any lines of symmetry on each letter.

2 State the order of rotational symmetry of these 2-D shapes.

a
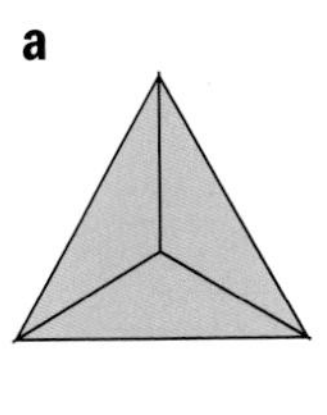
b

c

d

e

f

g
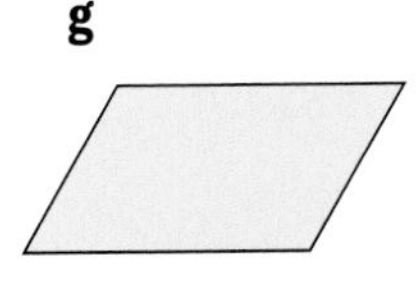
h
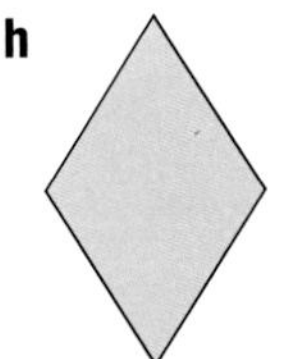
i
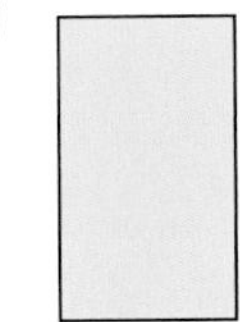
j
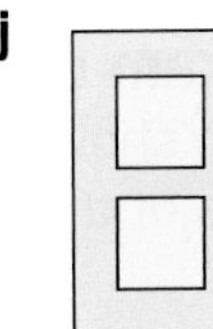

3 Copy these regular polygons.
a Draw the lines of symmetry for each shape.
b State the order of rotational symmetry for each shape.

A regular polygon has equal sides and equal angles.

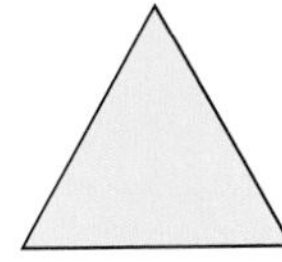
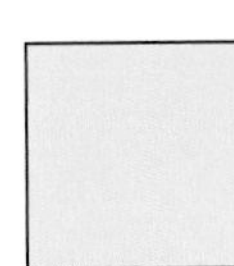
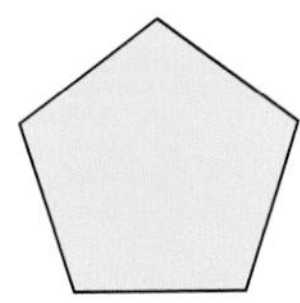
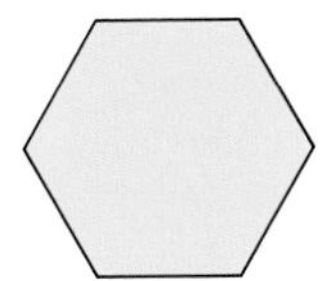
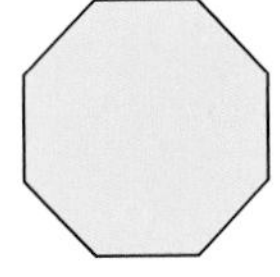

AO3 Problem

4 Make two copies of this grid.
a On one copy, shade in squares so that there are two lines of symmetry.
b On the other copy, shade in squares so that there is rotational symmetry of order 4.

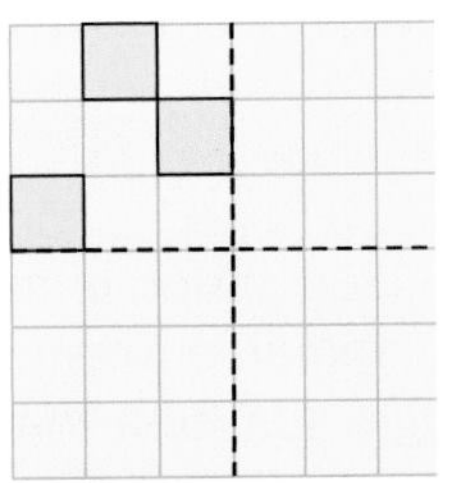

5 Find the equation of the line of symmetry for each of these shapes.

For part b, you will need to find the line of symmetry for yourself.

a
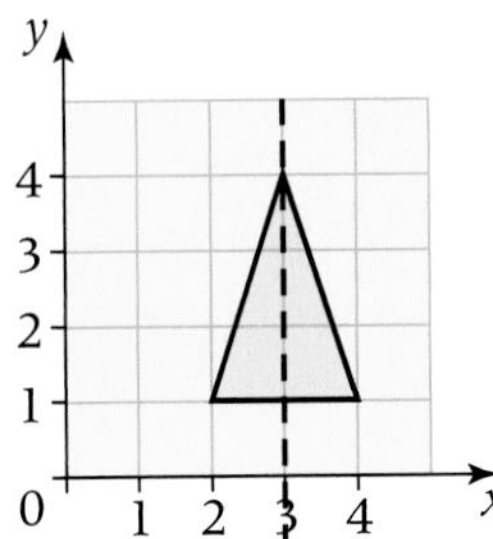

b
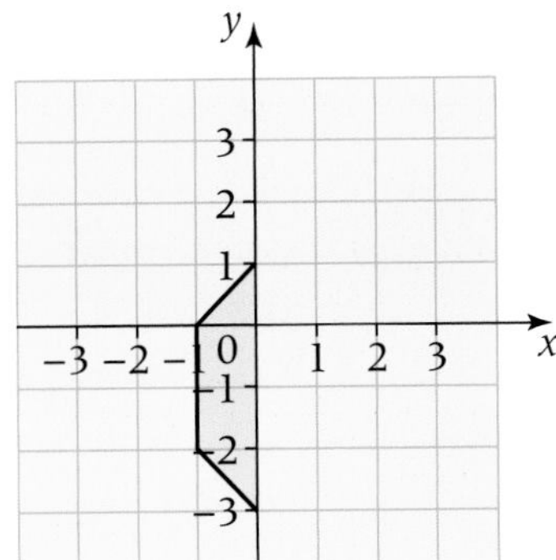

Summary

Check out

You should now be able to:

- Know the properties of special types of triangles and quadrilaterals
- Understand and use the angle properties of parallel lines
- Recognise symmetry of 2-D shapes

Worked exam question

The diagram shows a 5-sided shape.
All the sides of the shape are equal in length.

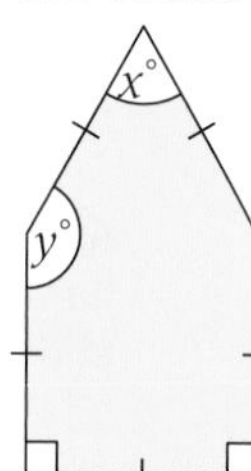

Diagram NOT accurately drawn

a **i** Find the value of x.
ii Give a reason for your answer. (2)

b Work out the value of y. (2)

(Edexcel Limited 2005)

a

i $x = 60°$

ii The 5-sided shape is made from a square and an equilateral triangle.
The angle sum of a triangle is 180°
$180° \div 3 = 60°$

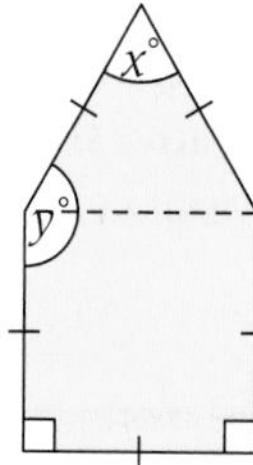

b

$$\begin{array}{r} 90 \\ 60\,+ \\ \hline 150 \\ \hline \end{array}$$

$y = 150°$

Draw the extra line on the diagram, state the triangle is equilateral and show the division $180° \div 3$

Exam questions

1

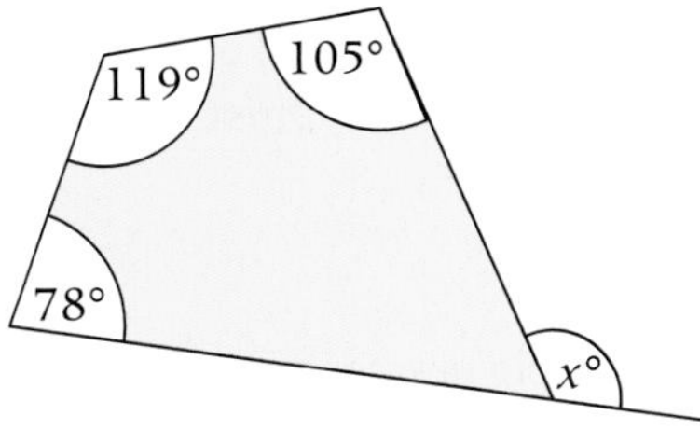

Diagram NOT accurately drawn

Work out the value of x. (3)

(Edexcel Limited 2007)

2

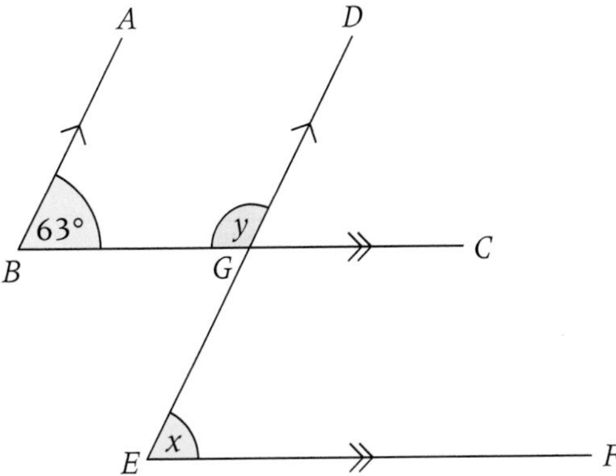

Diagram NOT accurately drawn

BA is parallel to *EGD*.
BGC is parallel to *EF*.
Angle *ABC* = 63°.

a **i** Find the size of angle x.
ii Give a reason for your answer. (2)

b Work out the size of angle y. (1)

(Edexcel Limited 2007)

A03

3 Copy the shape on the grid.

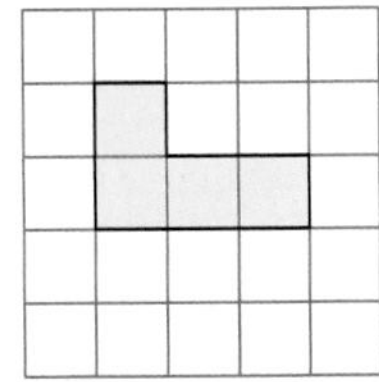

Draw exactly two extra squares on the shape so that it has rotational symmetry order 2. (2)

N3 Fractions, decimals and percentages

Introduction

In modern society, people often want to buy their own house, own a new car or go to university. To do these things they often need to borrow money from a bank or building society. These organisations lend the money but charge a fee (called 'interest') that is calculated as a percentage or fraction of the amount borrowed.

What's the point?

Being able to solve problems involving percentages gives people greater control of their finances. It allows them to budget properly and be aware of the risks involved in borrowing too much money, which can lead to debt and bankruptcy.

Check in

1 Copy and complete.

$10\% = \frac{1}{10} = ?$ $25\% = ? = 0.25$

$50\% = ? = ?$ $? = ? = 0.23$

2 Calculate, using a mental, written or calculator method:

a $3 \div 8$ **b** $150 \div 180$

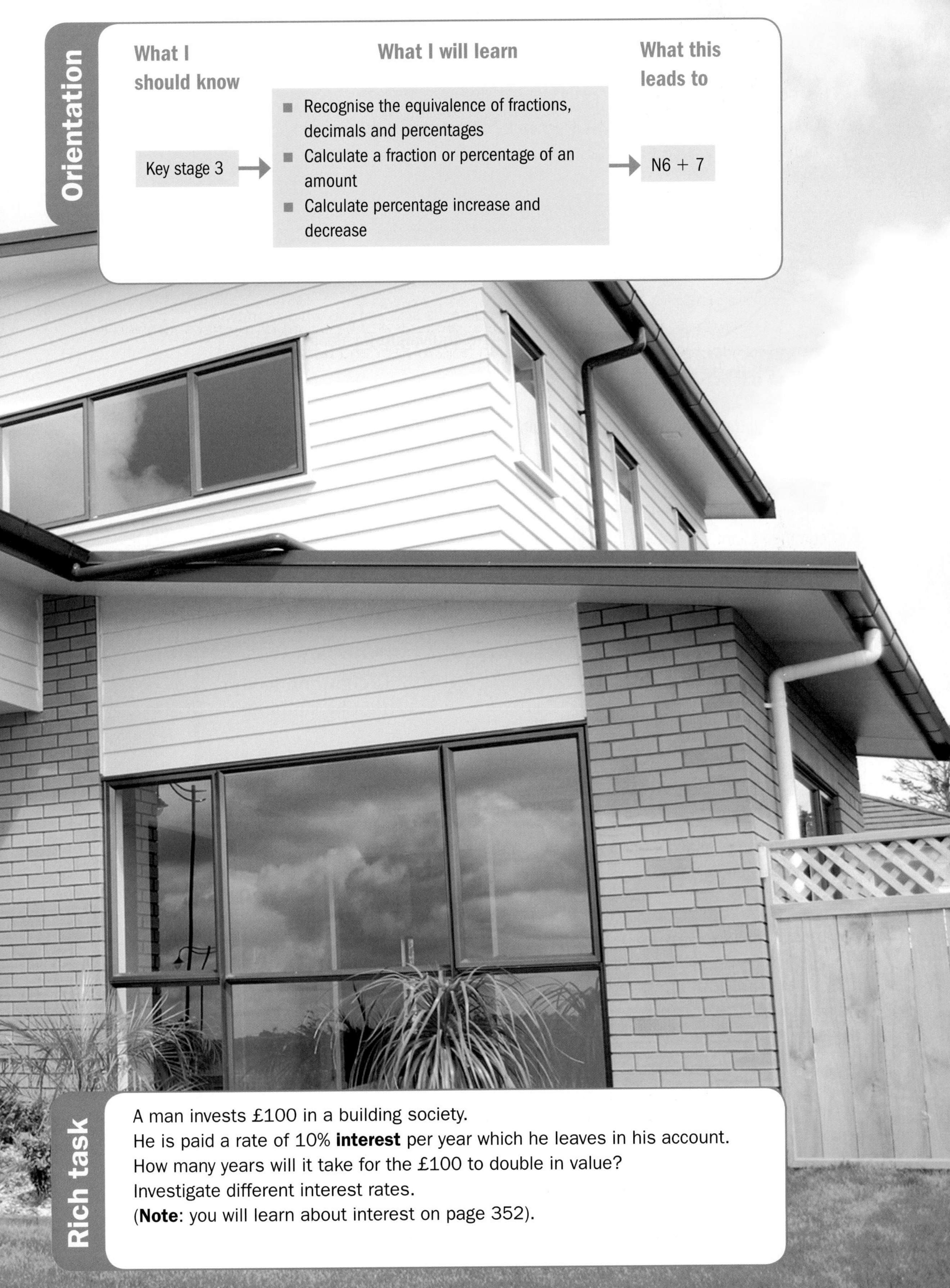

Orientation

What I should know		What I will learn		What this leads to
Key stage 3	→	■ Recognise the equivalence of fractions, decimals and percentages ■ Calculate a fraction or percentage of an amount ■ Calculate percentage increase and decrease	→	N6 + 7

Rich task

A man invests £100 in a building society.
He is paid a rate of 10% **interest** per year which he leaves in his account.
How many years will it take for the £100 to double in value?
Investigate different interest rates.
(**Note**: you will learn about interest on page 352).

N3.1 Equivalent fractions

This spread will show you how to:

- Compare, order and simplify fractions, converting between mixed numbers and improper fractions

Keywords
Denominator
Equal
Equivalent
Fraction
Improper fraction
Mixed number
Numerator

This sandwich is divided into 12 parts.
Adam takes $\frac{3}{12}$ of the whole sandwich.

Adam's portion is also $\frac{1}{4}$ of the whole sandwich.
$\frac{3}{12}$ and $\frac{1}{4}$ are **equivalent** fractions.

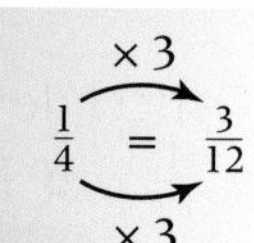

- **You can find equivalent fractions by multiplying or dividing the numerator and denominator by the same number.**

- **You can simplify a fraction by dividing the numerator and denominator by a common factor.**

This process is called cancelling down.

Example

Write each of these fractions in its simplest form.

a $\frac{18}{30}$ **b** $\frac{64}{80}$ **c** $\frac{13}{27}$

a

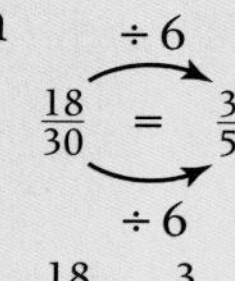

$\frac{18}{30} = \frac{3}{5}$

b ÷4 ÷4

$\frac{64}{80} = \frac{16}{20} = \frac{4}{5}$

÷4 ÷4

$\frac{64}{80} = \frac{4}{5}$

c Has no common factors. It cannot be simplified.

- **You can compare and order fractions by writing them as equivalent fractions with the same denominator.**

p.292

Example

Which is bigger: $\frac{3}{7}$ or $\frac{4}{9}$?

You need an equivalent fraction for both $\frac{3}{7}$ and $\frac{4}{9}$.

×9: $\frac{3}{7} = \frac{27}{63}$ ×9

×7: $\frac{4}{9} = \frac{28}{63}$ ×7

$\frac{27}{63} < \frac{28}{63}$ so $\frac{3}{7} < \frac{4}{9}$

The common denominator of these equivalent fractions will be $7 \times 9 = 63$.

Fractions can be used to describe numbers which are bigger than 1 as **mixed numbers** like $1\frac{2}{3}$ and **improper fractions** like $\frac{5}{3}$.

Example

a Change $\frac{13}{8}$ into a mixed number. **b** Change $1\frac{3}{5}$ into an improper fraction.

a $\frac{13}{8} = \frac{8}{8} + \frac{5}{8}$
$= 1 + \frac{5}{8} = 1\frac{5}{8}$

b $1\frac{3}{5} = 1 + \frac{3}{5}$
$= \frac{5}{5} + \frac{3}{5} = \frac{8}{5}$

Exercise N3.1 Grade E

1 **i** Write the fraction of each of these shapes that is shaded.
ii Write your fraction in its simplest form.

a 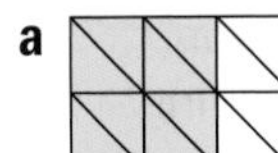

b 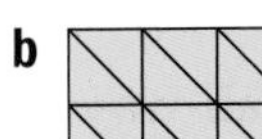

c 

d 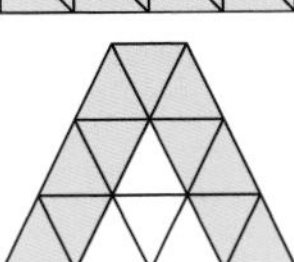

2 Cancel down each of these fractions into its simplest form.

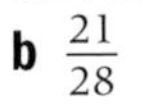

a $\frac{4}{12}$ **b** $\frac{21}{28}$ **c** $\frac{24}{40}$ **d** $\frac{28}{63}$ **e** $\frac{45}{72}$ **f** $\frac{42}{126}$ **g** $\frac{64}{144}$ **h** $\frac{23}{93}$

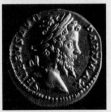

3 Change each of these fractions to an improper fraction.

a $1\frac{1}{2}$ **b** $3\frac{2}{3}$ **c** $4\frac{3}{8}$ **d** $2\frac{2}{9}$ **e** $5\frac{6}{7}$ **f** $7\frac{4}{5}$ **g** $8\frac{8}{11}$ **h** $12\frac{4}{7}$

4 Change each of these fractions to a mixed number.

a $\frac{5}{4}$ **b** $\frac{8}{5}$ **c** $\frac{11}{7}$ **d** $\frac{9}{4}$ **e** $\frac{11}{5}$ **f** $\frac{20}{7}$ **g** $\frac{23}{5}$ **h** $\frac{28}{9}$

5 Find the missing number in each of these pairs of equivalent fractions.

a $\frac{2}{3} = \frac{?}{12}$ **b** $\frac{3}{4} = \frac{?}{36}$ **c** $\frac{5}{7} = \frac{40}{?}$ **d** $\frac{7}{8} = \frac{?}{64}$

e $\frac{12}{30} = \frac{?}{5}$ **f** $\frac{6}{7} = \frac{?}{105}$ **g** $\frac{5}{4} = \frac{?}{68}$ **h** $\frac{?}{10} = \frac{154}{220}$

Did you know?

The ancient Romans used a system of fractions based on the number 12. $\frac{1}{12}$ was called an *uncia*, and this is where the words 'inch' and 'ounce' come from.

6 **a** Here are two fractions, $\frac{1}{3}$ and $\frac{2}{5}$.

Explain which is the larger fraction.

Use the grids to help with your explanation.

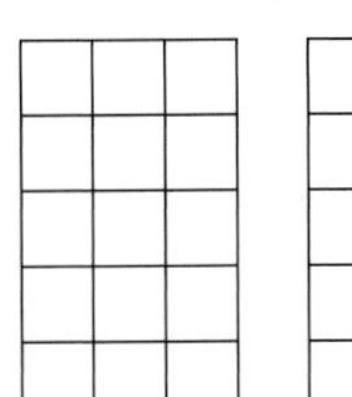

b Write these fractions in order of size.

Start with the smallest fraction.

$\frac{7}{18}$ $\frac{4}{9}$ $\frac{1}{3}$

7 For each pair of fractions, write which is the larger fraction.
Show your working.

a $\frac{3}{8}$ and $\frac{2}{5}$ **b** $\frac{3}{5}$ and $\frac{2}{3}$ **c** $\frac{4}{7}$ and $\frac{2}{5}$

d $\frac{5}{6}$ and $\frac{7}{9}$ **e** $\frac{5}{9}$ and $\frac{4}{7}$ **f** $\frac{7}{5}$ and $\frac{10}{7}$

Convert each of the fractions to an equivalent fraction with the same denominator.

8 Put these fractions in order from smallest to largest.
Show your working.

a $\frac{2}{5}$, $\frac{3}{15}$ and $\frac{1}{3}$ **b** $\frac{4}{7}$, $\frac{15}{28}$, $\frac{1}{2}$ **c** $\frac{4}{7}$, $\frac{5}{8}$ and $\frac{9}{14}$

N3.2 Fractions, decimals and percentages

This spread will show you how to:

- Recognise the equivalence of fractions, decimals and percentages

Keywords
Decimal
Equivalent
Fraction
Recurring
Percentage

Percentages, fractions and decimals are all ways of writing the same thing.

$$40\% = \frac{4}{10} = \frac{2}{5} = 0.4$$

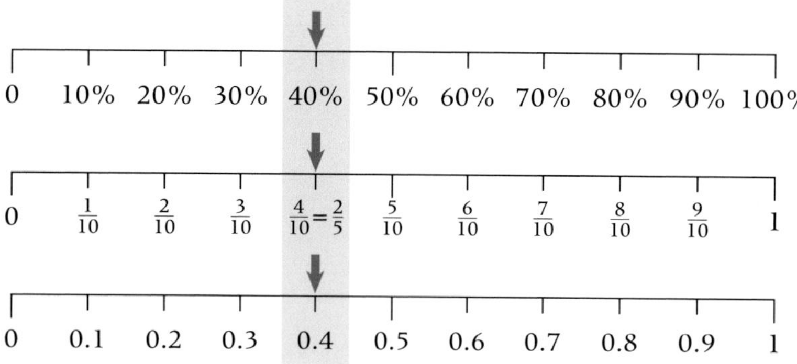

Some useful equivalents to remember:

$10\% = \frac{10}{100} = \frac{1}{10} = 0.1$

$20\% = \frac{20}{100} = \frac{1}{5} = 0.2$

$25\% = \frac{25}{100} = \frac{1}{4} = 0.25$

$50\% = \frac{50}{100} = \frac{1}{2} = 0.5$

$75\% = \frac{75}{100} = \frac{3}{4} = 0.75$

You can write a **terminating decimal** as a fraction.

$$3.42 = 3 \text{ units} + \frac{4}{10} + \frac{2}{100} = 3\frac{42}{100} = 3\frac{21}{50}$$

A terminating decimal ends after a definite number of digits.

$\frac{4}{10} + \frac{2}{100}$ is the same as $\frac{40}{100} + \frac{2}{100} = \frac{42}{100}$

- You can convert a fraction into a decimal ...

... using equivalent fractions

$$\frac{3}{5} \overset{\times 2}{=} \frac{6}{10} = 0.6 \qquad \frac{7}{40} \overset{\times 5}{=} \frac{35}{200} \overset{\div 2}{=} \frac{17.5}{100} = 0.175$$

... using division

$$\frac{7}{40} = 7 \div 40$$
$$= 0.175$$

You can convert between percentages and fractions.

$$145\% = \frac{145}{100} = \frac{29}{20} = 1\frac{9}{20}$$

percentages and decimals.

$$5.4\% = \frac{5.4}{100} = 0.054 \quad (5.4 \div 100)$$

To cancel down a fraction, divide the numerator and denominator by a common factor.

- A **recurring decimal** has digits that keep repeating.

$\frac{1}{3} = 1 \div 3 = 0.333333 \ldots$

You can write this as $0.\dot{3}$

$\frac{4}{33} = 4 \div 33 = 0.121212 \ldots$

Write this as $0.\dot{1}\dot{2}$

Sometimes a whole string of digits recur: $\frac{1}{7} = 0.142857142857 \ldots$

Write this as $0.\dot{1}4285\dot{7}$

The dots show which digits repeat.

- All recurring decimals are exact fractions. $0.\dot{1} = \frac{1}{9}$

However, **not** all exact fractions are recurring decimals. $\frac{1}{5} = 0.2$

Exercise N3.2 Grade C

1 Write each of these decimals as a fraction in its simplest form.

a 0.3 b 0.6 c 0.64 d 0.45
e 0.375 f 1.08 g 3.2375 h 3.0625

2 Change these fractions to decimals without using a calculator.

a $\frac{3}{10}$ b $\frac{11}{25}$ c $\frac{26}{25}$ d $\frac{124}{200}$
e $\frac{27}{60}$ f $\frac{39}{75}$ g $\frac{42}{150}$ h $3\frac{21}{60}$

3 Change these fractions into decimals using an appropriate method. Give your answers to 2 decimal places where necessary.

a $\frac{22}{50}$ b $\frac{2}{3}$ c $\frac{27}{20}$ d $\frac{11}{15}$
e $\frac{8}{7}$ f $1\frac{2}{5}$ g $2\frac{11}{66}$ h $\frac{11}{13}$

4 Write each of these percentages as a fraction in its simplest form.

a 40% b 90% c 35% d 65%
e 1% f 362% g 15.25% h 2.125%

5 Write each of these fractions as a percentage without using a calculator.

a $\frac{27}{50}$ b $\frac{2}{5}$ c $\frac{17}{20}$ d $\frac{13}{25}$
e $\frac{2}{3}$ f $\frac{48}{200}$ g $1\frac{3}{15}$ h $\frac{33}{75}$

6 Write these percentages as decimals.

a 37% b 7% c 189% d 45%

7 Write these decimals as percentages.

a 0.72 b 0.2 c 1.25 d 0.03

8 Write these fractions as percentages. Give your answers to 1 decimal place as appropriate.

a $\frac{48}{70}$ b $\frac{16}{25}$ c $\frac{17}{19}$ d $1\frac{11}{12}$ e $\frac{5}{19}$

Try converting the fraction into a decimal first!

9 Write these fractions as recurring decimals, using the correct notation:

a $\frac{2}{3}$ b $\frac{3}{11}$ c $\frac{2}{9}$ d $\frac{3}{7}$

A03 Problem

10 Investigation

All fractions can be turned into a decimal by dividing the numerator by the denominator. Some produce recurring decimals.

For example $\frac{1}{3} = 1 \div 3 = 0.333\ 333\ 333\ ...$

a Convert each of the fractions less than 1 with a denominator of seven into a decimal using your calculator. Write down all the decimal places in your answer.

For example $\frac{1}{7} = 1 \div 7 = 0.142\ 857\ 142\ ...$

$\frac{2}{7} = 2 \div 7 = ...$

b Write what you notice about each of your answers.

c Repeat for all the fractions less than 1 with a denominator of 13.

N3.3 Ordering fractions, decimals and percentages

This spread will show you how to:

- Recognise the equivalence of fractions, decimals and percentages, ordering them and converting between forms using a range of methods
- Express a number as a percentage of a whole

Keywords
Decimal
Equivalent
Fraction
Order
Percentage

You can convert between **fractions**, **decimals** and **percentages** using a range of mental and written methods.

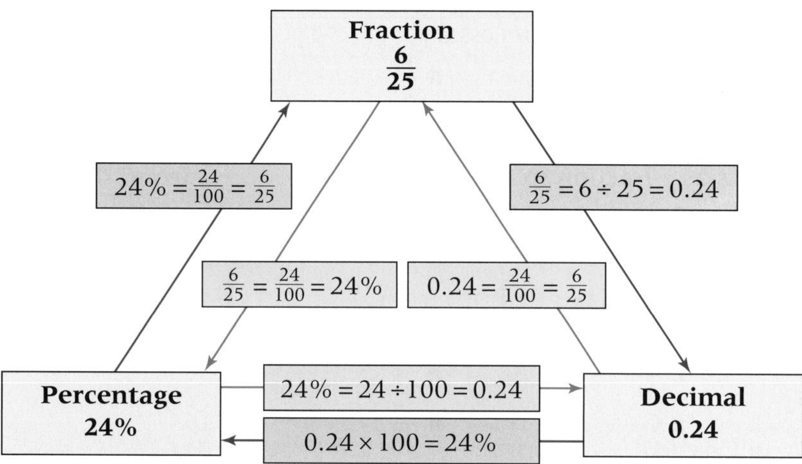

You can write something as a percentage by first finding the fraction.

Example

a What percentage of this shape is shaded?

b In a class there are 40 students. 24 of them are boys. What percentage of the class are boys?

a There are 16 equal parts.
7 of the parts are shaded.
The fraction shaded is $\frac{7}{16}$.
% shaded $= \frac{7}{16} = 0.4375 = 43.75\%$

b There are 40 students in the class.
24 of the students are boys.
The fraction of boys is $\frac{24}{40}$.
% of boys $= \frac{24}{40} = \frac{12}{20} = \frac{60}{100} = 60\%$

- You can **order** fractions, decimals and percentages by converting them into decimals.

Example

Write these numbers in order of size. Start with the smallest number.

0.8   70% $\frac{7}{8}$ $\frac{3}{4}$

$70\% = \frac{70}{100} = 0.7$ $\frac{7}{8} = \frac{35}{40} = \frac{175}{200} = \frac{875}{1000} = 0.875$ $\frac{3}{4} = 0.75$

Place the decimals in order: 0.7   0.75   0.8   0.875

70% $\frac{3}{4}$ 0.8 $\frac{7}{8}$

Rewrite $\frac{7}{6}$ as an equivalent fraction with a denominator of 1000.

Exercise N3.3 Grade C

1 Copy and complete this table.

Fraction	Decimal	Percentage
$\frac{3}{8}$		
	0.28	
		15%
	0.375	
$\frac{4}{5}$		
		17.5%

2 For each pair of fractions, write which is the larger fraction. Show your working.

Convert each of the fractions into a decimal.

a $\frac{5}{8}$ and $\frac{3}{5}$ **b** $\frac{4}{5}$ and $\frac{2}{3}$ **c** $\frac{5}{7}$ and $\frac{3}{5}$ **d** $\frac{3}{8}$ and $\frac{4}{11}$

e $\frac{10}{7}$ and $\frac{16}{11}$ **f** $\frac{14}{9}$ and $\frac{17}{11}$ **g** $1\frac{2}{7}$ and $1\frac{7}{23}$ **h** $2\frac{7}{12}$ and $2\frac{8}{11}$

3 Copy each pair of fractions, decimals and percentages and insert '>' or '<' in between them. Show your working out clearly for each question.

a $\frac{3}{5}$ 0.7 **b** $\frac{7}{15}$ $\frac{30}{65}$ **c** $\frac{5}{9}$ $\frac{7}{13}$ **d** $2\frac{2}{3}$ 265%

4 Put these fractions, decimals and percentages in order from smallest to largest. Show your working.

a 47%, $\frac{12}{25}$ and 0.49 **b** $\frac{4}{5}$, 78% and 0.81

c $\frac{5}{8}$, 66% and $\frac{7}{12}$ **d** $\frac{5}{16}$, 0.3, 29% and $\frac{7}{22}$

AO2 Functional Maths

5 In each of these questions express the answer first as a fraction, then convert the fraction to a percentage using an appropriate method.

a In a class there are 28 students. 19 of the students are right-handed. What percentage of the class are right-handed?

b In a survey of 80 people, 55 said they would prefer school to be compulsory until the age of 18. What percentage of the 80 people preferred school to be compulsory until the age of 18?

c In a football squad of 24 players, 5 of the players are goalkeepers. What percentage of the football squad are not goalkeepers?

d In a mixed packet of 54 biscuits, 36 of the biscuits are covered in chocolate. What percentage of the biscuits in the packet are not covered in chocolate?

6 a Jo scores 68% in his French exam and gets $\frac{37}{54}$ in his German exam. In which subject did he do the best? Explain your answer.

b In a school survey 23% of the students said they did not like eating meat. In Sarah's class $\frac{7}{31}$ students said they did not like eating meat. How do the results of Sarah's class compare with the rest of the school?

N3.4 Fraction of a quantity

This spread will show you how to:

- Express one number as a fraction (or proportion) of another number
- Use fractions and percentages as operators

Keywords
Denominator
Fraction
Numerator

You can express one number as a **fraction** of another number.

Example

In a class there are 32 students. 20 of the students are girls. What fraction of the class are boys? Give your answer in its simplest form.

There are 32 students in the class altogether.
Number of boys = 32 − 20 = 12
Fraction who are boys = $\frac{12}{32} = \frac{3}{8}$

p.342

You can calculate a fraction of a quantity using a variety of methods.

Mental method

To calculate $\frac{3}{8}$ of 32 children:

$\frac{1}{8}$ of 32 children $= 32 \div 8$
$= 4$ children
$\frac{3}{8}$ of 32 children $= 3 \times 4$
$= 12$ children

Written method

To calculate $\frac{3}{7}$ of 63 kg:

$\frac{3}{7}$ of 63 kg $= \frac{3}{7} \times 63$
$= 3 \times \frac{1}{7} \times 63$
$= \frac{3 \times 63}{7}$
$= \frac{189}{7}$
$= 27$ kg

Calculator method

To calculate $\frac{7}{11}$ of £90:

Decimal equivalent of $\frac{7}{11}$
$= 7 \div 11 = 0.636\,363\ldots$
$\frac{7}{11}$ of £90 $= \frac{7}{11} \times$ £90
$= 0.636\,363\ldots \times 90$
$=$ £57.2727
$=$ £57.27

Example

Meagan is 150 cm tall. Piper is $\frac{6}{5}$ of the height of Meagan.

a Calculate the height of Piper.
b What fraction of Piper's height is Meagan?

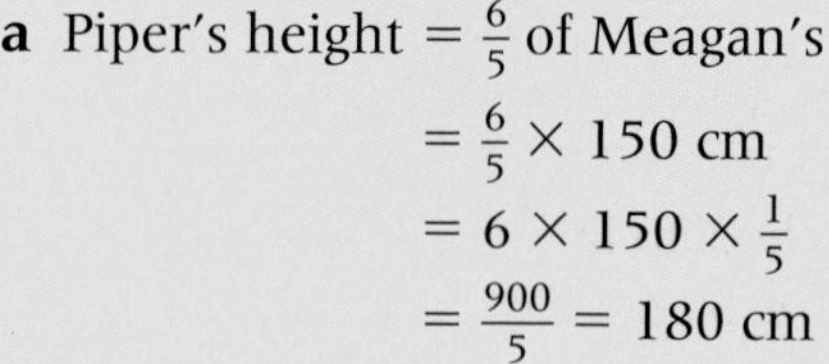

a Piper's height $= \frac{6}{5}$ of Meagan's height
$= \frac{6}{5} \times 150$ cm
$= 6 \times 150 \times \frac{1}{5}$
$= \frac{900}{5} = 180$ cm

b Meagan's height as a fraction of Piper's height $= \frac{150}{180}$ cm
$= \frac{150}{180}$ cm
$= \frac{5}{6}$

Meagan is $\frac{5}{6}$ of the height of Piper.

In the last example, $\frac{5}{6}$ and $\frac{6}{5}$ are **reciprocals** of each other.

- The reciprocal of a number is 1 ÷ that number

The reciprocal of 4 is $\frac{1}{4}$
The reciprocal of 0.2 is $1 \div 0.2 = 5$
The reciprocal of $\frac{2}{5}$ is $\frac{5}{2}$.

This key point is equivalent to the one above.

- A number multiplied by its reciprocal = 1

Exercise N3.4

Grade D

1 Calculate each of these, leaving your answer in its simplest form.

a $5 \times \frac{1}{2}$ **b** $8 \times \frac{1}{4}$ **c** $8 \times \frac{1}{3}$
d $13 \times \frac{1}{7}$ **e** $\frac{1}{12} \times 24$ **f** $\frac{1}{3} \times 4$

2 Calculate each of these, leaving your answer in its simplest form.

a $6 \times \frac{2}{3}$ **b** $5 \times \frac{3}{4}$ **c** $6 \times \frac{2}{3}$ **d** $4 \times \frac{7}{6}$
e $5 \times \frac{9}{20}$ **f** $\frac{4}{5} \times 28$ **g** $\frac{4}{9} \times 30$ **h** $\frac{11}{18} \times 14$

A02 Functional Maths

3 Calculate each of these, leaving your answer in its simplest form.

a What is the total mass of four packets that each weigh $\frac{1}{5}$ kg?
b A cake weighs $\frac{7}{20}$ of a kg. What is the mass of 10 cakes?
c What is the total capacity of 12 jugs that each have a capacity of $\frac{3}{5}$ of a litre?
d What is the total mass of 16 bags of flour that each weigh $\frac{9}{10}$ kg?

4 Use a mental or written method to work out these. Leave your answers as fractions in their simplest form where appropriate.

a $\frac{3}{10}$ of €40 **b** $\frac{2}{5}$ of £70 **c** $\frac{3}{4}$ of 50 m **d** $\frac{4}{7}$ of 64 km
e $\frac{3}{8}$ of £1000 **f** $\frac{5}{6}$ of 70 mm **g** $\frac{11}{12}$ of 1500 m **h** $\frac{4}{13}$ of 60 g

5 Use a suitable method to calculate each of these. Where appropriate round your answer to 2 decimal places.

a $\frac{8}{15}$ of 495 kg **b** $\frac{9}{10}$ of \$5000 **c** $\frac{5}{9}$ of 8 kg
d $\frac{7}{9}$ of 1224 cups **e** $\frac{13}{18}$ of 30 tonnes **f** $\frac{4}{15}$ of 360°
g $\frac{12}{31}$ of 360° **h** $\frac{13}{15}$ of 1 hour **i** $\frac{17}{15}$ of £230

6 Express each of these as a fraction in its simplest form.

a 40 kg as a fraction of 60 kg **b** 15 m as a fraction of 25 m
c 40 cm as a proportion of 2 m **d** 55p as a fraction of £3

A02 Functional Maths

7 a A shirt normally costs £40. In a sale the price is reduced by $\frac{2}{5}$. What is the new price of the shirt?
b Benito receives £20 a week pocket money. He saves $\frac{3}{8}$ of it. How much money does he save each week?
c Karen rents out her holiday cottage to tourists for $\frac{4}{5}$ of the 365 day year. For how many days is her cottage empty?

8 Find the reciprocal of each of these numbers.

a 10 **b** 8 **c** $\frac{1}{3}$ **d** $\frac{3}{4}$ **e** 0.8

Percentage of a quantity

This spread will show you how to:

- Use equivalent fractions and mental methods to calculate simple percentages
- Calculate a fraction and percentage of an amount using a variety of methods

Keywords
Percentage
Fraction

You can calculate simple **percentages** of amounts in your head using equivalent fractions.

Example

Calculate **a** 10% of £83 **b** 5% of 164 m.

a 10% of £83 is the same as working out $\frac{1}{10}$ of £83 $= \frac{1}{10} \times 83$
$= 83 \div 10$
$= £8.30$

b 10% of 164 m $= \frac{1}{10}$ of 164 m
$= \frac{1}{10} \times 164$
$= 164 \div 10$
$= 16.4$ m

5% of 164 m $= \frac{1}{2}$ of (10% of 164 m)
$= 16.4 \div 2$
$= 8.2$ m

$10\% = \frac{10}{100} = \frac{1}{10}$

$\times \frac{1}{10}$ is the same as $\div 10$

To find 5% of something:
- Find 10% of it
- $\div 2$

Harder percentages of amounts can be worked out using a written or calculator method.

Written method

Change the percentage to its equivalent fraction and multiply by the amount.

9% of 24 m $= \frac{9}{100} \times 24$
$= \frac{9 \times 1 \times 24}{100}$
$= \frac{9 \times 24}{100}$
$= \frac{216}{100}$ 2.16 m

9% of an amount
$= \frac{9}{100}$ of it
$= 9 \times \frac{1}{100}$ of it.
This is the same as $\times 9$ and $\div 100$, so you work out $9 \times 24 \div 100$.

Calculator method

Change the percentage to its equivalent decimal and multiply by the amount.

To calculate 37% of £58:

37% of £58 $= \frac{37}{100} \times 58$
$= 0.37 \times 58 = £21.46$

0.37 × 58
21.46

Exercise N3.5 Grade E

1 Calculate these percentages without using a calculator.

a 50% of £300 **b** 50% of 4 kg **c** 50% of £80
d 50% of 37 kg **e** 1% of £30 **f** 10% of 342.8 m

2 Calculate these percentages without using a calculator.

a 5% of £180 **b** 20% of 410 kg **c** 20% of $25
d 25% of £3 **e** 75% of £42 **f** 5% of 3.8 m

3 Calculate these percentages using a mental or written method.

a 15% of £340 **b** 60% of 120 Mb **c** 60% of £75
d 80% of £50 **e** 30% of 455 m **f** 2.5% of £880
g 70% of 1570 mm **h** 15% of 42 kg **i** 45% of 70 mm

4 Write the method you would use to calculate each of these without using a calculator.

a 15% of anything **b** 5% of anything **c** 35% of anything
d 17.5% of anything **e** 95% of anything

AO2 Functional Maths

5 **a** Paul downloads a file from the internet. The file is 16 Mb. After 2 minutes he has downloaded 70% of the file. How much of the file has Paul downloaded?

b Winston has to move 24 tonnes of hardcore. In the morning he moves 55% of the hardcore. How many tonnes of hardcore has he moved?

c A train journey is 395 km long. Lola is travelling on a train that has completed 23% of the journey. How many kilometres has Lola's train travelled?

d At Herbie's school there is a charity race night. The evening raises £234. 58% of the money raised goes to charities and the rest is given to the school. How much money is given to the school?

6 Calculate these using a mental or written method. Show all the steps of your working out. Give your answers to 2 decimal places as appropriate.

a 12% of £17 **b** 16% of 87 km **c** 8% of £38
d 32% of €340 **e** 17% of 65 m **f** 73% of 46 cm
g 85% of 148 m **h** 2% of £76.40 **i** 25% of £85

Revise the work you have done previously on mental and written methods of multiplication:
partitioning
compensation
doubling and halving
grid method
standard method.

Percentage increase and decrease

This spread will show you how to:

- Calculate percentage increase and decrease using a range of methods

Keywords
Decrease
Increase
Percentage

Percentages are used in real life to show how much an amount has increased or decreased.

- To calculate a **percentage increase**, work out the increase and add it to the original amount.
- To calculate a **percentage decrease**, work out the decrease and subtract it from the amount.

Example

a Alan is paid £940 a month. His employer increases his wage by 3%. Calculate the new wage Alan is paid each month.

b A new car costs £19 490. After one year the car depreciates in value by 8.7%. What is the new value of the car?

p.350

a Calculate 3% of the amount.
Add to the original amount.

Increase in wage = 3% of £940 = $\frac{3}{100} \times £940$

$= \frac{3 \times 940}{100} = \frac{2820}{100}$

Increase in wage = £28.20 per month

Alan's new wage = £940 + £28.20 = £968.20

The percentage calculation has been worked out using a written method.

b Calculate 8.7% of the amount.
Subtract from the original amount.

Depreciation = 8.7% of £19 490

$= \frac{8.7}{100} \times £19\,490$

$= 0.087 \times £19\,490$

Price reduction = £1695.63

New value of car = £19 490 − £1695.63 = £17 794.37

The percentage calculation has been worked out using a calculator.

You can calculate a percentage increase or decrease in a single calculation.

Example

a In a sale all prices are reduced by 16%. A pair of trousers normally costs £82. What is the sale price of the pair of trousers?

b Last year, Leanne's Council Tax bill was £968. This year the local council have raised the bill by 16%. How much is Leanne's new bill?

a Sale price = (100 − 16)% of the original price

= 84% of £82

$= \frac{84}{100} \times 82$

$= 0.84 \times 82$

= 68.88

= £68.88

b New bill = (100 × 16)% of the original bill

= 116% of £968

$= \frac{116}{100} \times £968$

$= 1.16 \times £968$

= £1122.88

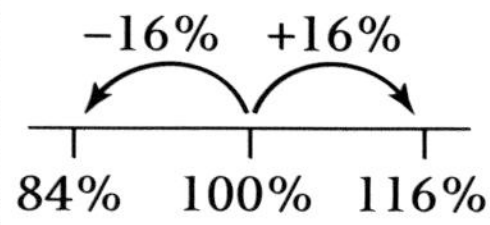

Exercise N3.6

Grade D

1 Calculate these amounts using an appropriate method.

a 25% of 18 kg **b** 20% of 51 m **c** 15% of 360°

d 2% of 37 cm **e** 65% of 510 ml **f** 17.5% of 360°

g 28% of 65 kg **h** 31% of 277 kg **i** 3.6% of 154 kg

j 0.3% of 1320 m^2

2 Calculate each of these using a mental or written method.

a Increase £350 by 10% **b** Decrease 74 kg by 5%

c Increase £524 by 5% **d** Decrease 756 km by 35%

e Increase 960 kg by 17.5%

3 Calculate these percentage changes. Give your answers to 2 decimal places as appropriate.

a Increase £340 by 17% **b** Decrease 905 kg by 42%

c Increase £1680 by 4.7% **d** Decrease 605 km by 0.9%

e Increase $2990 by 14.5%

A02 Functional Maths

4 These are the weekly wages of five employees at Suits-U clothing store. The manager has decided to increase all the employees' wages by 4%.
Calculate the new wage of each employee. Give your answers to 2 decimal places as appropriate.

Employee	Original wage	Increase	New wage
Hanif	£350	350 × 1.04 = ?	
Bonny	£285.50		
Wilf	£412.25		
Gary	£209.27		
Marielle	£198.64		

5 Use an appropriate method to work out each of these.
Give your answers to 2 decimal places as appropriate.

a A drink can contains 440 ml. The size is increased by 12%.
How much drink does it now contain?

b The price of a coat was £185.
The price is reduced by 10% in a sale.
What is the sale price of the coat?

c A house is bought for £195 000. During the next year, the house increases in price by 28.3%. What is the new value of the house?

d The number of students in a school is 940. Next year the school expects the number of students to increase by 15%.
How many students does the school expect next year?

N3

Summary

Check out

You should now be able to:

- Recognise the equivalence of fractions, decimals and percentages
- Convert between fractions, decimals and percentages
- Order fractions, decimals and percentages
- Express a number as a fraction of another number
- Calculate a fraction and a percentage of an amount
- Calculate percentage increase and decrease

Worked exam question

A hotel has 56 guests.

35 of the guests are male.

a Work out 35 out of 56 as a percentage. (2)

40% of the 35 male guests wear glasses.

b Write the number of male guests who wear glasses as a fraction of the 56 guests.
Give your answer in its simplest form. (4)

(Edexcel Limited 2007)

a

$$\frac{35}{56} = \frac{5}{8}$$
$$= 0.625$$
$$= 62.5\%$$

OR

$$\frac{35}{56} = \frac{35}{56} \times 100\%$$
$$= 62.5\%$$

Show this calculation.

b

40% of 35 male guests $= \frac{40}{100} \times 35$
$= 0.4 \times 35$
$= 14$ male guests

Show this calculation.

OR

40% of 35 male guests $= \frac{2}{5} \times 35$
$= 14$ male guests

$$\frac{14}{56} = \frac{1}{4}$$

Write $\frac{14}{56}$ as well as the simplified answer.

Exam questions

A02

1 36 students each went to one revision class.

$\frac{1}{6}$ of the students went to the physics revision class.

$\frac{2}{9}$ of the students went to the biology revision class.

All of the other students went to the chemistry revision class.
How many students went to the chemistry revision class? (3)

(Edexcel Limited 2009

A02

2 A tin of cat food costs 40p.
A shop has a special offer on the cat food.

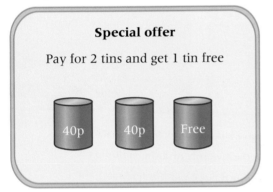

Special offer

Pay for 2 tins and get 1 tin free

40p 40p Free

Julie wants 12 tins of cat food.

a Work out how much she pays. (3)

9 of the 12 tins are tuna.

b Write 9 out of 12 as a percentage. (2)

The normal price of a cat basket is £20
In a sale, the price of the cat basket is reduced by 15%

c Work out the sale price of the cat basket. (3)

(Edexcel Limited 2008)

A02

3 Plain tiles cost 28p each.
Patterned tiles cost £9.51 each.

Julie buys 450 plain tiles and 15 patterned tiles.

a Work out the total cost of the tiles. (3)

b Express 15 as a fraction of 450
Give your answer in its simplest form. (2)

(Edexcel Limited 2007)

Functional Maths 2: Sandwich shop

The manager of a catering company can use data about customer numbers in order to spot trends in customer behaviour and to plan for the future.

mply Sandwiches

Simply andwiches

iches, paninis, baguettes and salads

Simply Sandwiches

Customer numbers at 'Simply sandwiches' takeaway over a given two-week period were:

Day	Number of Customers	
	Week 1	Week 2
Monday	50	54
Tuesday	68	60
Wednesday	47	53
Thursday	58	57
Friday	52	56
Saturday	76	70
Total		

Simply Sandwiches

Use the data in the table to construct a bar chart to show how many customers visit the sandwich shop on each day during this two-week period.

Copy and complete the table.

During this two-week period,

a) which is the busiest day at the sandwich shop

b) what is the range of daily customer numbers?

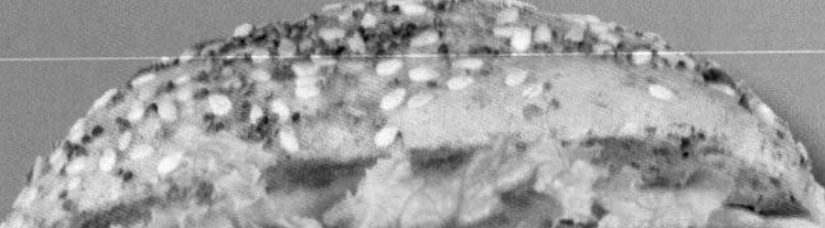

This bar chart shows customer behaviour over a different two-week period. Compare the two sets of data, including reference to the quietest/busiest days and the spread of the data. Give possible explanations and justify your response with reference to the data.

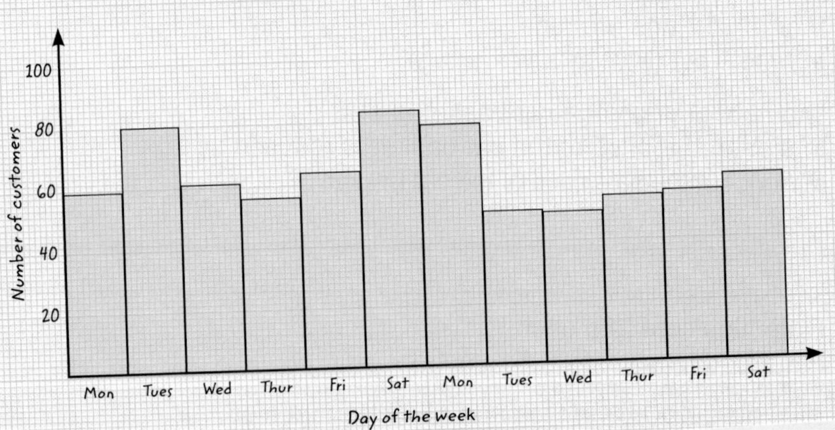

Is data collected over a two-week period enough to be able to estimate customer numbers for any given week? Justify your answer referring to the information.

A manager can use data about customer numbers to help estimate how much stock to order each week. In reality, limitations due to space and the shelf life of products also apply.

In the second week of the two-week period at 'Simply sandwiches', sales of the different varieties of sandwiches were:

Variety	Mon	Tues	Weds	Thurs	Fri	Sat	Total	Average
Ham	14	16	13	14	17	18		
Cheese	9	11	12	10	8	12		
Hummous	6	5	7	4	6	8		
Tuna	7	6	6	8	6	9		
Chicken	18	22	15	21	19	23		
Total								

Copy the table and fill in the missing values.

The manager does a weekly stocktake every Sunday before placing the order for the following week.

The stocktake figures for this week were:

Product	Stock (packs)	Portions per pack	Portions left	Stock needed	Amount to order
Bread	6	20			
Ham	2.5	10			
Cheese	3	10			
Hummous	2	14			
Tuna	1.5	8			
Chicken	1	10			

Copy and complete the table to show an estimate of how much of each product the manager should order to last for the following week.

The stock will be delivered on Wednesday morning.

Estimate how much (if any) of each product the manager will have in stock when the order arrives.

Comment on how well the manager estimated the order for the previous week.

Justify your answers by referring to the data.

Simply Sandwiches

sandwiches, paninis, baguettes and salads

Introduction

There are many things in life which are uncertain. Will it be sunny tomorrow? Will my football team win the Premier League? Will I be able to afford a house in the future? The mathematics used to deal with uncertainty is called probability.

What's the point?

When the Met Office gives a weather forecast, they use a complex mathematical model to predict the probability of sunshine in a particular region.

Check in

1 Cancel these fractions to their simplest form.

a $\frac{6}{9}$ **b** $\frac{5}{10}$ **c** $\frac{15}{20}$ **d** $\frac{2}{8}$ **e** $\frac{20}{20}$

2 Calculate

a $\frac{3}{4} + \frac{1}{4}$ **b** $\frac{7}{10} + \frac{3}{10}$

c $1 - \frac{7}{10}$ **d** $1 - \frac{3}{5}$

3 Calculate

a $1 - 0.1$ **b** $1 - 0.6$ **c** $1 - 0.15$

4 Convert these fractions into decimals.

a $\frac{1}{100}$ **b** $\frac{25}{100}$ **c** $\frac{35}{100}$ **d** $\frac{5}{100}$ **e** $\frac{36}{100}$

Orientation

What I should know		What I will learn		What this leads to
Key stage 3	→	■ Understand and use the probability scale ■ Identify different mutually exclusive outcomes ■ Understand and use measures of probability and relative frequency ■ Calculate probabilies with two events	→	Life choices involving uncertainty

Rich task

Inside a bag are three cards with the letters A, N and D written on them.
Pick one card from the bag at random (without looking at it).
Note the letter.
Replace the card in the bag.
How many cards will you have picked before you have all the letters to spell the word AND?

D1.1 Probability

This spread will show you how to:

- List all outcomes for single events and identify different mutually exclusive outcomes

Keywords
Equally likely
Event
Outcome
Probability
Systematically

To understand probability, you first need to learn what these words mean.

- A **trial** is an activity.
  Picking one ball from a bag is a trial.
- An **outcome** is one possible result of a trial.
  All the outcomes when picking a ball from the bag are red, red, red, red, red, red, red, red, green, green, green, green, green, green, green, green.
- An **event** is one or more outcomes of a trial.
  A red ball is an event, when picking a ball from the bag.

Each outcome is **equally likely** as the balls are identical in size and shape.

- **Probability** measures how likely it is that an event will happen.
- You can calculate probability using the formula:

$$\text{Probability of an event happening} = \frac{\text{Number of favourable outcomes}}{\text{Total number of all possible outcome}}$$

All probabilities have a value between 0 and 1.
The probability of an event can be written as P(event).

0 means impossible.
1 means certain.

Example

An ordinary dice is rolled.

a List the possible outcomes.
b Calculate the probability of choosing
 i a 5
 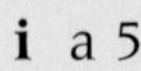
 ii an even number.

---

a

or 1, 2, 3, 4, 5, 6.

Draw the 6 outcomes in order or **systematically**.

b **i** There is one 5.
There are 6 possible equally likely outcomes.
$P(5) = \frac{1}{6}$

P(5) means the probability of a 5

ii There are 3 even numbers.
There are 6 possible outcomes.
$P(\text{even}) = \frac{3}{6} = \frac{1}{2}$

Exercise D1.1 Grade E/F

1 Copy these tables and put each outcome in the appropriate table.

The event is impossible
Probability is 0

The event is certain
Probability is 1

a Picking a blue ball from a bag of blue balls.
b Picking a red ball from a bag of blue balls.
c Next month will have 7 days.
d Next year will have 12 months.
e You will roll an 8 on an ordinary six-sided dice.

2 List all the possible outcomes for these trials.
a spinning a coin
b rolling a tetrahedron dice (4 faces, numbered 1, 2, 3, 4)
c picking a letter from C H A N G E
d spinning the spinner shown on the right
e picking a day from all the days of the week.

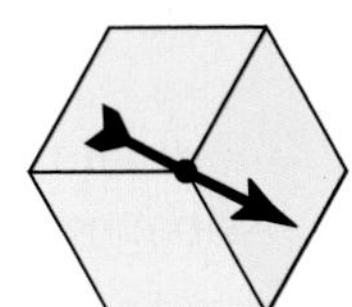

3 Answer each of these questions for each bag A to E.

A

B

C

D

E

a List the 4 possible outcomes, when a ball is taken from the bag.
b Calculate the probability of taking out a blue ball.
c Calculate the probability of taking out a red ball.
d Which colour ball is the most likely to be taken out?
e Which colour ball is the least likely to be taken out?

Functional Maths

A02

4 A raffle has only one prize. 250 tickets are sold.
Calculate the probability of winning the prize if you buy
a one ticket **b** ten tickets.

5 There are 48 boys and 72 girls in a year group at a school.
One student is selected at random.
Calculate the probability that the student is
a a boy **b** a girl.

D1.2 Probability scale

This spread will show you how to:

- Understand and use the probability scale

Keywords
Chance
Mutually exclusive
Outcome
Probability
Probability scale

The **chance** of an event happening is measured by the **probability**.

All probabilities have a value between 0 and 1 and can be marked on a **probability scale**.

You can use fractions or decimals on the probability scale.

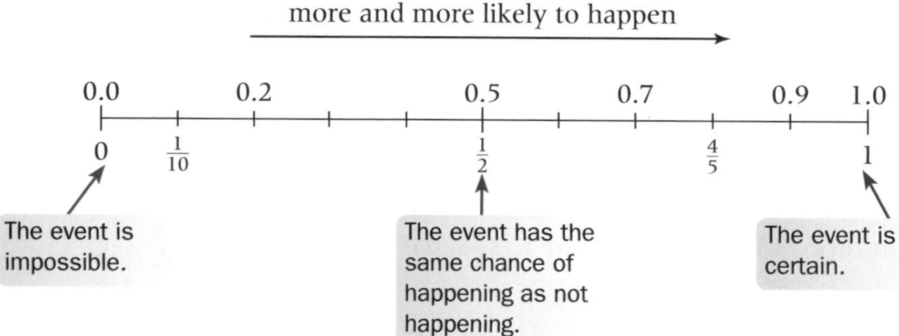

An equilateral triangle is made into a spinner as shown. The possible **outcomes** are Orange, Orange and Green.

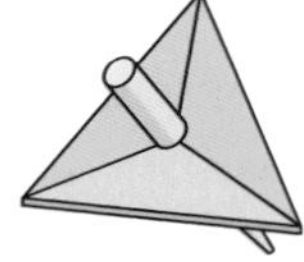

These outcomes are **mutually exclusive** because if you get one outcome you cannot get the other one.

Probability of spinning orange $= \frac{2}{3}$

Probability of **not** spinning orange $= \frac{1}{3}$

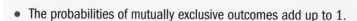

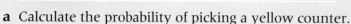

- The probabilities of mutually exclusive outcomes add up to 1.
- Probability of an event not happening = 1 − probability of the event happening

$\frac{2}{3} + \frac{1}{3} = 1$

$\frac{1}{3} = 1 - \frac{2}{3}$

Example

The probability of picking a coloured counter from the tin is shown.

Colour	Red	Orange	Yellow
Probability	0.4	0.25	

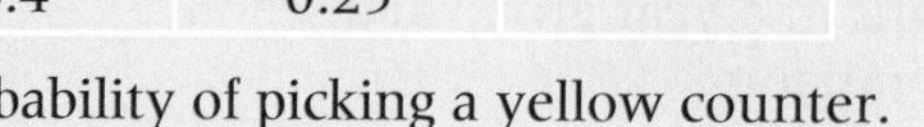

a Calculate the probability of picking a yellow counter.
b Which colour counter is the least likely to be picked?

a $0.4 + 0.25 = 0.65$
$1 - 0.65 = 0.35$
P(yellow) $= 0.35$

b Orange, as orange has the smallest probability.

Exercise D1.2 — Grade D

1 Draw a 10 cm line. Put a mark at every centimetre.
Label the marks 0.0, 0.1, 0.2, ..., 0.9, 1.0 as shown.

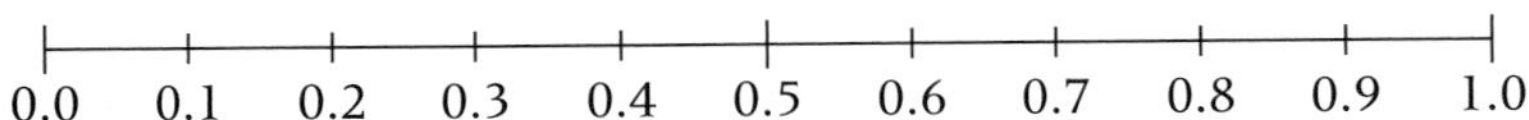

On your probability scale, mark the position of

a an impossible event
b an even chance event
c a certain event.

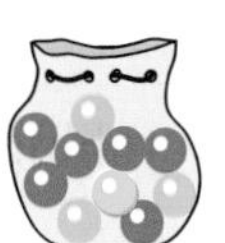

2 A bag contains 1 yellow, 3 green and 6 red balls.
One ball is taken out at random.

a Calculate the probability that the ball is
i yellow **ii** green **iii** red.
b Draw a probability scale as in question 1.
On your scale, mark the positions of P(yellow), P(green) and P(red).
c Which colour is the least likely to be picked?
d Which colour is the most likely to be picked?
e Add the answers P(yellow), P(green) and P(red).

3 A spinner is made from a regular octagon.
There are 6 pink and 2 green triangles.

a Calculate the probability that the arrow spins to
i a pink triangle
ii a green triangle.
b Draw a probability scale as in question 1.
On your scale, mark the positions of P(pink) and P(green).
c Which colour is the least likely?
d Which colour is the most likely?
e Add the answers P(pink) and P(green).

4 The probability of winning a raffle is 0.01.
What is the probability of not winning the raffle?

5 A bag contains red, yellow and green counters.
One counter is taken out at random.
The probability that the counter is a particular colour is shown in the table.

Colour	Red	Yellow	Green
Probability	0.3	0.1	

Calculate the probability of taking a green counter out of the bag.

D1.3 Mutually exclusive outcomes

This spread will show you how to:
- Identify different mutually exclusive outcomes
- Know that the sum of the probabilities of all the outcomes is 1

Keywords
Mutually exclusive
Or
Outcomes

The possible **outcomes** when a dice is rolled are 1, 2, 3, 4, 5, 6.

These outcomes are **mutually exclusive** because if you get one outcome, you cannot get another one.

The probability of rolling a 4 $= \frac{1}{6}$

The probability of rolling a 5 $= \frac{1}{6}$

The probability of rolling a 4 **or** a 5 $= \frac{2}{6}$

Notice that

P(4 or 5) = P(4) + P(5)

$$\frac{2}{6} = \frac{1}{6} + \frac{1}{6}$$

P(4) $= \frac{1}{6}$

P(5) $= \frac{1}{6}$

Or means either of the outcomes 4 or 5.

Example

A spinner is made from a regular pentagon and numbered from 1 to 5. Calculate

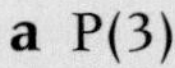

a P(3) **b** P(3 or 4) **c** P(3 or an odd number)

a There is one 3. There are 5 possible outcomes. P(3) $= \frac{1}{5}$

b P(3) $= \frac{1}{5}$ P(4) $= \frac{1}{5}$

The outcomes are mutually exclusive and so

$$\begin{aligned} P(3 \text{ or } 4) &= P(3) + P(4) \\ &= \frac{1}{5} + \frac{1}{5} \\ &= \frac{2}{5} \end{aligned}$$

c P(3) $= \frac{1}{5}$ P(odd) $= \frac{3}{5}$

The events are not mutually exclusive so you can't add the probabilities.

A list of the 5 possible outcomes is

$$\begin{pmatrix} 1 \\ \text{odd} \end{pmatrix} \quad \begin{pmatrix} 2 \\ \text{even} \end{pmatrix} \quad \begin{pmatrix} 3 \\ \text{odd} \end{pmatrix} \quad \begin{pmatrix} 4 \\ \text{even} \end{pmatrix} \quad \begin{pmatrix} 5 \\ \text{odd} \end{pmatrix}$$

P(3 or an odd number) $= \frac{3}{5}$

There are 3 outcomes that are OK.

Exercise D1.3 Grade D

1 Events are mutually exclusive if they cannot occur at the same time. State if these events are mutually exclusive.

a spinning a Head and spinning a Tail with a coin
b rolling a 2 and rolling a 3 with a dice
c rolling a 2 and rolling an even number with a dice
d rolling a 2 and rolling an odd number with a dice
e rolling a 2 and rolling a prime number with a dice
f winning and losing a game of chess
g sunny and rainy weather
h taking out a red ball and taking out a blue ball, when taking out one ball from a bag.

2 This is a net of a tetrahedral dice. The dice is made and rolled. What is the probability of rolling

a a 3 **b** a 2 **c** a 2 or a 3?

3 A bag contains 4 red discs, 5 blue discs and 1 white disc. One disc is taken out. Calculate the probability that the disc is

a red **b** blue **c** white
d red or white **e** blue or white **f** red or blue or white

4 Five names are written on cards and placed in a bag. One name is taken out of the bag at random. Calculate the probability that

a the first letter on the card is H
b the first letter on the card is G
c the first letter on the card is H or G
d the card has 5 letters written on it
e the card has 5 or 6 letters written on it.

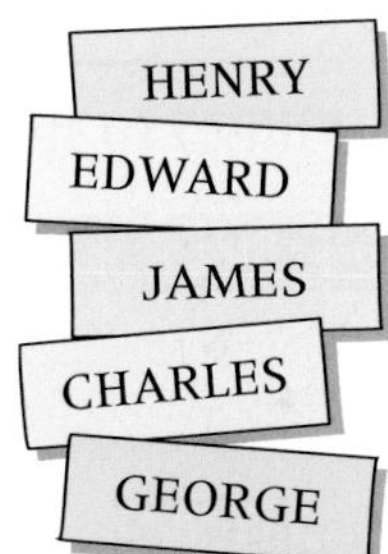

AO2 Functional Maths

5* A survey of vehicles passing the school gate is taken.

C C C C V L C C V B
C L C C C C B C C V
V V C C L C C B C C
L B C C C V L C C C
B V C V C C V C C V

C = Car
L = Lorry
B = Bus
V = Van

a Copy and complete the frequency table.
b Calculate the estimated probability that the next vehicle that passes will be
i a car **ii** a lorry **iii** a bus or a van

Vehicle	Tally	Frequency
Car (C)		
Lorry (L)		
Bus (B)		
Van (V)		

***Note:** You will learn more about estimated probability on page 110, so you may wish to leave this question until then.

D1.4 Two-way tables 1

This spread will show you how to:

- Understand two-way tables and use them to calculate probabilities

Keywords
Equally likely
Random
Two-way table

- A **two-way table** links two types of information.

p.144

23 children and adults attend a birthday party.
The two-way table shows this information.

	Male	Female
Adult	0	4
Child	7	12

There were no adult males.

$7 + 12 = 19$ children at the party.

$4 + 12 = 16$ females at the party.

You can use two-way tables to calculate probabilities.

Example

The shoe sizes of fifty Y10 students are shown in the two-way table.

	Size 6	Size 7	Size 8	Size 9
Boy	5	8	9	8
Girl	8	9	2	1

One of the students is selected at random.
Calculate the probability that the student is

a a boy

b a girl

c a girl who wears size 7 shoes

d a student who wears size 8 shoes.

a $5 + 8 + 9 + 8 = 30$ boys

$\text{P(boy)} = \frac{30}{50} = \frac{3}{5}$

b $\text{P(girl)} = 1 - \frac{3}{5} = \frac{2}{5}$

c $\text{P(girl with size 7 shoes)} = \frac{9}{50}$

d $9 + 2 = 11$

$\text{P(size 8)} = \frac{11}{50}.$

Exercise D1.4 Grade E

AO2 Functional Maths

1 The numbers of passengers in 50 cars are recorded.
The results are shown in the two-way table.

	Number of passengers			
	0	1	2	3
Number of cars	20	15	10	5

Calculate the probability that a car has

a 0 passengers
b 1 passenger
c 2 passengers
d 3 passengers.

2 A tray contains brown and white eggs. Some of the eggs are cracked.
The two-way table shows the number of eggs in each category.

	Cracked	Not cracked
Brown	2	6
White	4	12

a Calculate the number of eggs that are
i on the tray
ii brown
iii white
iv cracked
v not cracked.

One egg is selected at random.

b Calculate the probability that the egg is
i brown and cracked
ii white and not cracked
iii a brown egg
iv a white egg
v a cracked egg
vi an uncracked egg.

3 An athletic club enters 10 athletes in various races at a meeting.
Each athlete enters only one race.
The two-way table shows the number of athletes that won or didn't win for each race.

	Won	Didn't win
100 m	0	5
200 m	1	0
400 m	0	0
800 m	0	1
1500 m	1	2

One athlete is selected at random for a drugs test.

Calculate the probability that the selected athlete

a is the 200 m winner
b entered the 100 m race
c entered the 400 m race
d won a race
e didn't win a race.

D1.5 Expected frequency

This spread will show you how to:

- Understand and use estimates or measures of probability

Keywords
Expect
Expected frequency
Trial

If you know the probability of an event, you can calculate how many times you **expect** the outcomes to happen.

Example

A dice is rolled 60 times.
Calculate the number of

a fours

b even numbers you would expect.

a $P(4) = \frac{1}{6}$ or 1 four for every 6 rolls
or 10 fours for every 60 rolls.

b $P(\text{even}) = \frac{1}{2}$ $\frac{1}{2}$ of 60 = 30 times should be even.

- The **expected frequency** is the number of times you expect the outcomes to happen.
- Expected frequency = probability × number of trials.

Each roll of the dice is called a **trial**.

Example

Red, yellow and green balls are put in a bag.
The probability of taking out each colour of ball is given in the table.

Red	Yellow	Green
0.1	0.3	0

a Calculate the probability of taking out a green ball.
b Which colour is the most likely to be taken out?
c There are 60 balls in the bag.
How many of them are red, yellow and green?

a $0.1 + 0.3 = 0.4$
$1 - 0.4 = 0.6$
$P(\text{green}) = 0.6$

b Green is the most likely as 0.6 is the biggest probability.

c Red: $0.1 \times 60 = 6$ red balls
Yellow: $0.3 \times 60 = 18$ yellow balls
Green: $0.6 \times 60 = 36$ green balls

The outcomes of a red or a yellow or a green ball are mutually exclusive.

Exercise D1.5

Grade C

1 A crisp manufacturer claims that '3 out of every 4 people prefer Potayto Crisps'
If 100 people are asked, how many would you expect to prefer Potayto Crisps?

2 The probability of a drawing pin landing point up when dropped, is 0.8.
If 100 drawing pins are dropped, how many of them would you expect to land point up?

3 Research has shown that when you take a dog for a daily walk, the probability that you will have a conversation with someone is $\frac{3}{10}$.
If you walked a dog daily throughout September, how many times would you expect to have a conversation with someone?

'30 days has September, April, June and November.'

4 A spinner is made from a circle divided into 12 equal sectors, coloured green, yellow and pink.
If the spinner is spun 60 times, how many times would you expect the colour to be

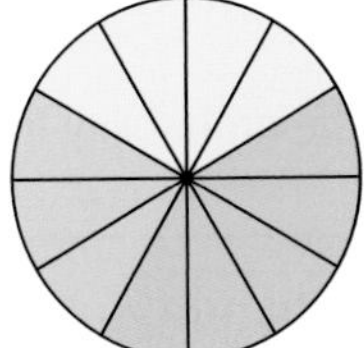

a green
b yellow
c pink?

5 The probability of rolling each number for this biased dice is shown in the table.

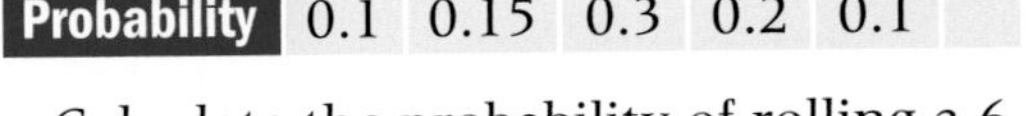

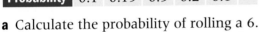

Number	1	2	3	4	5	6
Probability	0.1	0.15	0.3	0.2	0.1	

a Calculate the probability of rolling a 6.
b Calculate the expected frequencies for each number, if the dice is rolled
  i 100 times
  ii 500 times
  iii 1000 times.

A02 Functional Maths

6 In a 'roll a penny' game, a penny is rolled into the box.

To win you need to land the penny off any black lines.

It costs 1p to have a go and winners are given 10p back.

The probability of landing the penny off the black lines is $\frac{1}{20}$.

If 200 pennies are rolled into the box, how much profit would you expect the game to make?

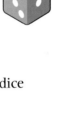

1p a go
Roll the penny off the black lines and get 10p back

D1.6 Relative frequency

This spread will show you how to:

- Understand and use estimates or measures of probability and relative frequency
- Compare experimental data and theoretical probabilities

Keywords
Biased
Equally likely
Estimate
Experiment
Fair
Relative frequency
Trial

- A dice is **fair** if the numbers are all **equally likely** to be rolled.
  You would normally expect a dice to be fair, as each face is identical.
- A spinner is **biased** if the colours are NOT all **equally likely to happen**.
  This spinner is not fair as the size and shape of each colour are not identical.

It is not always possible to calculate the theoretical probability.

- You can **estimate** the probability from experiments.

Example

Sam knows the probability of a Head when spinning a coin should be $\frac{1}{2}$ (or 0.5). She thinks the coin is biased and so she spins the coin 50 times. The results are shown in the frequency table.

	Frequency
Head	35
Tail	15

a Estimate the probability of getting a Head when spinning the coin.

b Do you think the coin is biased? Explain your answer.

a Sam got a Head on 35 out of 50 occasions.
Estimated probability of getting a Head $= \frac{35}{50} = \frac{7}{10} = 0.7$

b The spinner could be biased as 0.7 is significantly larger than 0.5. However, Sam needs to spin the coin a lot more times before she can make the decision.

- Estimated probability is called the **relative frequency**.

Each spin of the coin is called a **trial**.

In the example, if Sam calculated the relative frequency of getting a Head after each spin, she could graph the results.

Highest relative frequency is 1.

Lowest relative frequency is 0.

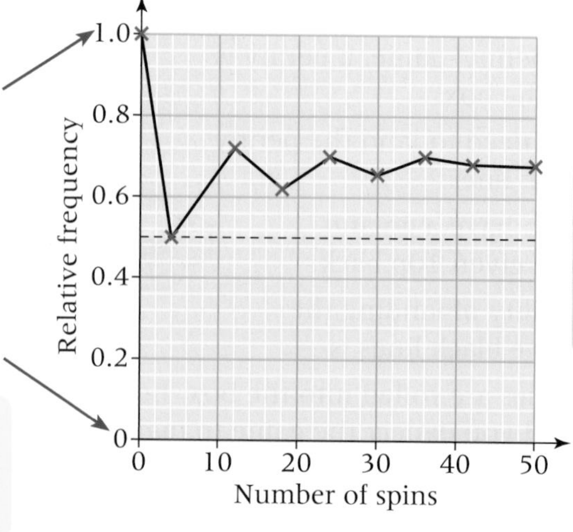

P(Head) $= \frac{1}{2} = 0.5$
This is the theoretical probability of spinning a Head.

- The estimated probability becomes more reliable as you increase the number of trials.

Exercise D1.6

Grade C

Functional Maths

A02

1 The colours of 50 cars are recorded. The colours are shown.

Blue	Red	Other	Silver	Blue	Red	Silver	Silver	Blue
Other	Red	Silver	Silver	Blue	Red	Red	Other	Silver
Silver	Red	Red	Silver	Silver	Blue	Blue	Silver	Silver
Red	Red	Other	Blue	Red	Red	Other	Red	Red
Red	Silver	Blue	Blue	Blue	Other	Silver	Other	Other
Other	Silver	Red	Red	Blue				

a Copy and complete the frequency chart to show the 50 colours.

b State the modal colour.

c Give an estimate of the probability that the next car will be

i blue **ii** red **iii** silver.

Colour	Tally	Frequency
Blue		
Red		
Silver		
Other		

2 A spinner is made from a regular pentagon.
The scores are recorded.

1	2	3	4	3	5	1	2
5	4	2	1	3	1	5	4
2	2	3	1	4	5	4	2
3	1	2	2	4	4	5	5
1	2	3	4	2	4	1	1

a Draw a frequency chart to show the scores.

b State the modal score.

c How many times is the spinner spun?

d Estimate the probability of scoring

i a 1 **ii** a 2 **iii** a 3 **iv** a 4 **v** a 5.

e If the spinner is fair, how many times would you expect to spin a 3 from 100 spins?

3 There are 10 coloured balls in a bag.
One ball is taken out and then replaced in the bag.
The colours of the balls are shown in the frequency table.

Colour	Red	Green	Blue
Frequency	9	14	27

a How many times was a ball taken out of the bag?

b Estimate the probability of taking out

i a red ball **ii** a green ball **iii** a blue ball.

c How many balls of each colour do you think are in the bag?

d How could you improve this guess?

D1.7 Two events

This spread will show you how to:

- List all of the outcomes for two successive events in a systematic way

Keywords
Event
Outcome
Successive
Systematic
Tree diagram

You can list the possible **outcomes** for two successive **events**.

Successive means following on, such as 3, 4, 5.

Example

A spinner has colours red, yellow and green.
A coin has Heads or Tails.
Julie spins the spinner and flips the coin.

a List all the possible outcomes.
b What is the probability that Julie gets yellow and a Tail?
c If the spinner is spun and coin is flipped 60 times, how many times would you expect to get a yellow and a Tail?

a There are several ways to illustrate the outcomes.

- You could produce a list:

Red – Head
Red – Tail
Yellow – Head
Yellow – Tail
Green – Head
Green – Tail

This list is **systematic** because it is in order.

- You could draw a **tree diagram**.

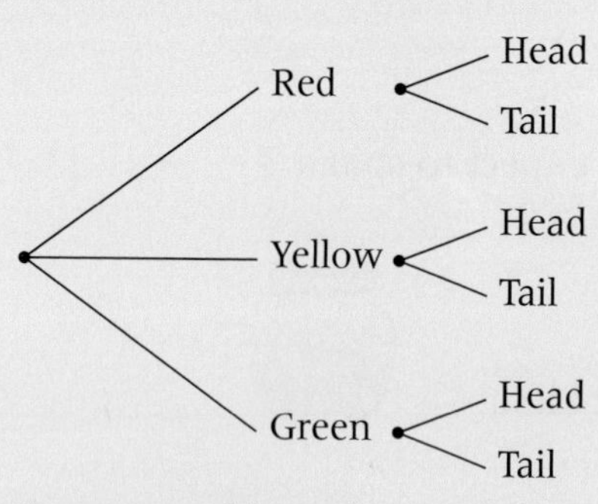

Outcomes
Red and Head
Red and Tail
Yellow and Head
Yellow and Tail
Green and Head
Green and Tail

- Or you could produce a table.

Colour on spinner	Red	Red	Yellow	Yellow	Green	Green
Head/Tail on coin	Head	Tail	Head	Tail	Head	Tail

b Yellow and Tail occurs once. There are 6 possible outcomes.

P(Yellow and Tail) $= \frac{1}{6}$

c Expected outcomes = P(Yellow and Tail) $\times$ 60

$= \frac{1}{6} \times 60$

$= 10$

Exercise D1.7

Grade C

Functional Maths

A02

1 Tamsin is going to hire a different DVD on Wednesday and Thursday.
She has a choice of 3 films: A, B or C.
Copy and complete the table to show her 6 possible choices.

Wednesday	Thursday
A	B
A	

2 A fair spinner is labelled A, B, C.
Another spinner is labelled D, E, F.
Both spinners are spun.

a List the 9 possible outcomes.

b Calculate the probability of getting an A and an E.

c Calculate the probability of not getting either an A or an E.

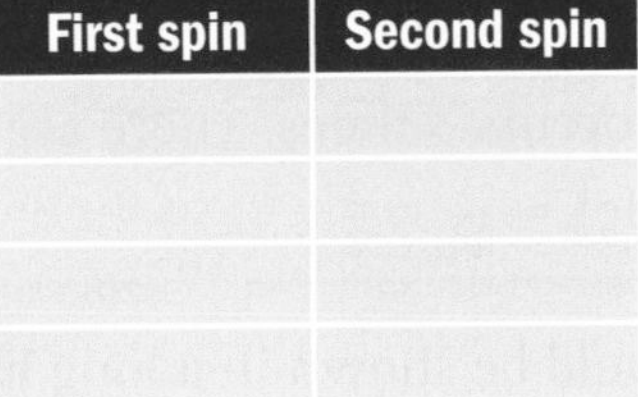

3 A coin has Heads or Tails. The coin is spun and then spun again.

a Copy and complete the table to show the four possible outcomes.

b Copy and complete the tree diagram to show the four outcomes.

	First spin	Second spin
Outcomes		

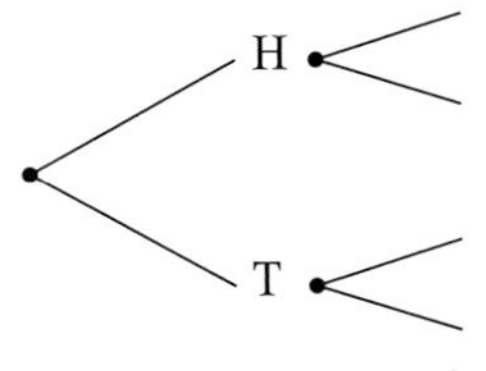

1st spin 2nd spin

c Calculate the probability of getting a Head and then a Head.

d Calculate the probability of not getting a Head and then a Head.

e If both coins are spun 100 times, how many times would you expect to get a Head and then a Head?

4 A pack of cards contains 26 red cards and 26 black cards. A card is taken out of the pack and replaced. Another card is taken out.

a Copy and complete the table to show the outcomes.

b Draw a tree diagram to show the same outcomes.

c Calculate the probability of getting a red card and a black card in any order.

First selection	Second selection
Red	

D1.8 Two events again

This spread will show you how to:

- List all of the outcomes for two successive events in a systematic way

Keywords
Equally likely
Sample space diagram

You can use a systematic list or a tree diagram for two or more events.
You can only use a **sample space diagram** if there are two events.

Example

A dice is numbered 1, 2, 3, 4, 5, 6. A spinner has colours red, blue, yellow and green.
Stephanie rolls the dice and spins the spinner.

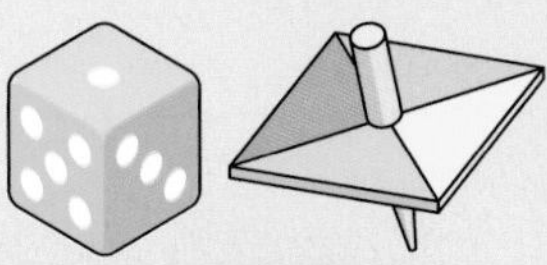

a Draw a sample space diagram to show the possible outcomes.
b What is the probability that she gets an even number and blue?

a

		Score on the dice					
		1	2	3	4	5	6
Colour on the spinner	Red	(1, R)	(2, R)	(3, R)	(4, R)	(5, R)	(6, R)
	Blue	(1, B)	(2, B)	(3, B)	(4, B)	(5, B)	(6, B)
	Yellow	(1, Y)	(2, Y)	(3, Y)	(4, Y)	(5, Y)	(6, Y)
	Green	(1, G)	(2, G)	(3, G)	(4, G)	(5, G)	(6, G)

b Even and Blue occurs 3 times. There are 24 possible outcomes.
P(Even and Blue) $= \frac{3}{24} = \frac{1}{8}$

The 24 outcomes could be shown in a long list or a complicated tree diagram.

- The sample space diagram shows the outcomes of two successive events clearly and concisely.

The sample space diagram can only be used for **equally likely** outcomes.

Example

Two spinners are numbered 1, 3, 5 and 2, 4, 6.
Each spinner is spun and the scores are added.

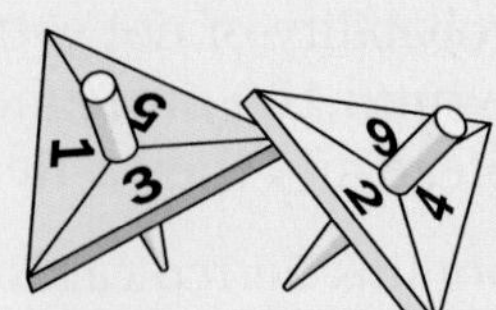

a Draw a sample space diagram to show the possible totals.
b What is the probability of getting a total of 7?

a

	1	3	5
2	3	5	7
4	5	7	9
6	7	9	11

b 7 occurs 3 times. There are 9 possible outcomes.
P(total of 7) $= \frac{3}{9} = \frac{1}{3}$

Exercise D1.8

Grade D

1 A spinner is made from a square and coloured red (R), yellow (Y), green (G) and pink (P). Another spinner is made from a regular pentagon and labelled A, B, C, D, E. Both spinners are spun.

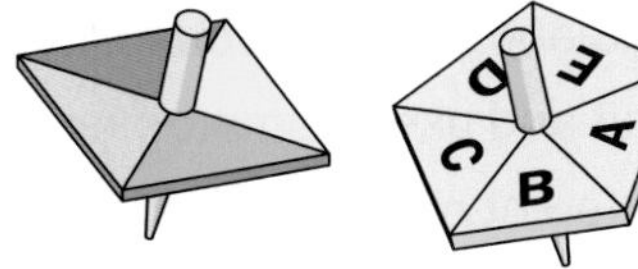

a List the 20 possible outcomes.

b Copy and complete the sample space diagram to show the outcomes.

colour spinner

Letter spinner	R	Y	G	P
A	(R, A)			
B				
C				
D				
E				

c Calculate the probability of getting Green and a C.

2 A dice is made from a tetrahedron, and numbered 1, 2, 3, 4. A coin has Heads or Tails. The dice is rolled and the coin is spun.

a Copy and complete the sample space diagram to show the possible outcomes.

Dice

Coin	1	2	3	4
Heads	(1, H)			
Tails				

b Calculate the probability of getting

i a 3 and a Head

ii an even number and a Head.

3 A 'fruit machine' has only two windows. Each window can show a Club (♣), a Diamond (♦), a Spade (♠) or a Heart (♥).

a Draw a sample space diagram to show the 16 possible outcomes.

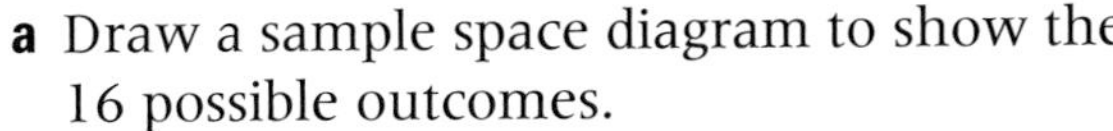

b Calculate the probability of getting two of the same symbols.

4 Two fair dice each numbered 1 to 6 are rolled. List all the possible outcomes.

a Calculate the probability of getting a double six.

b The scores on the top faces are added together. State what is the most likely number to get, giving a reason for your choice.

D1.9 Probability revision

This spread will show you how to:

- Understand and use the probability scale
- Understand and use estimates or measures of probability
- Identify different mutually exclusive outcomes

Keywords
Equally likely
Event
Expected frequency
Mutually exclusive
Outcome
Probability
Trial

The possible **outcomes** of spinning a coin are 'Heads' or 'Tails'.
An **event** is one or more outcomes.
A Head is an event, when spinning a single coin.

For the spinning coin:

- Each outcome is **equally likely**.
  The two sides of the coin are identical in size and shape.
- The outcomes are **mutually exclusive.**
  If you get one outcome you cannot get the other one.

The **probability** of an event is a measure of how likely it is that the event will happen.

0 means impossible.
1 means certain.

- You can calculate probability using
- Probability of an event happening $= \dfrac{\text{number of favourable outcomes}}{\text{total number of all possible outcomes}}$

The probability of an event can be written as P(event).

- The probabilities of mutually exclusive outcomes add up to 1.

- Probability of an event not happening = 1 − probability of the event happening

- The **expected frequency** is the number of times you expect the outcomes to happen.

- Expected frequency = probability × number of trials

Each spin of the coin is called a **trial**.

Example

40 red and 10 yellow balls are put into a bag.
One ball is taken out at random and then replaced.

a Decide whether the following statement is true or false.
Give a reason for your answer.
'The balls are either red or yellow, so the probability of picking a red is $\frac{1}{2}$.'

b How many red balls would you expect to have picked after picking and replacing a ball 20 times?

a False. There are 40 red balls out of a total of 50, so P(red) $= \frac{40}{50}$
$= 0.8$.

b Expected number of red balls = 0.8 × 20=16

Exercise D1.9 Grade E–C

1 **a** Give an example of an event with a probability of 0.
  b Give an example of an event with a probability of 1.

2 There are 12 boys and 18 girls in a class. One student is chosen at random. Calculate the probability that the student is
  a a boy **b** a girl.

3 **a** Arrange these probabilities in order of likelihood of happening, with the least likely first.
  $\frac{2}{5}$ $\frac{3}{8}$ 0.35 $\frac{3}{10}$ 45%
  b Draw a 10 cm line. Put a mark at every centimetre. Label the marks 0, 0.1, 0.2, ..., 0.9, 1 as shown.

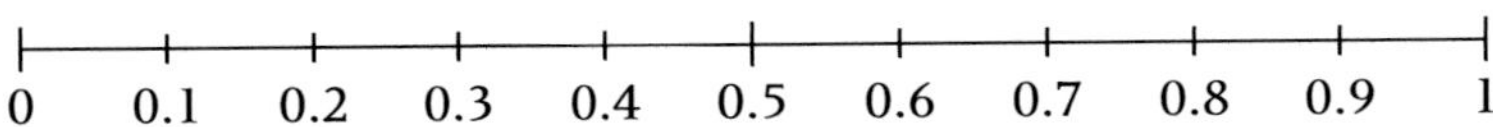

  On your probability scale, mark the positions of the probabilities in part **a**.

4 Red, blue and green cubes are put in a bag. The probability of taking out each colour of cube is shown in the table.

Red	Blue	Green
$\frac{1}{2}$	$\frac{1}{8}$	

  a Calculate the probability of taking out a green cube.
  b What colour is most likely to be taken out?
  c What colour is least likely to be taken out?
  d If a cube is taken out and then replaced 16 times, how many red, blue and green cubes would you expect to take out?

5 A spinner is made from a square. The spinner is spun 100 times. The results are shown in the table.

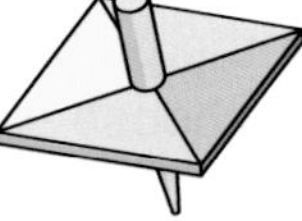

Colour	Green	Red	Blue	Yellow
Frequency	20	27	25	28

  a Calculate an estimate for the probability of each colour occurring.
  b How many times would you expect each colour to occur if the spinner is fair? Explain your reasoning.

D1 Summary

Check out

You should now be able to:

- Understand and use the vocabulary of probability scale
- Calculate probabilities of events, including equally likely outcomes, giving answers in their simplest form
- Identify different mutually exclusive events and know that the sum of the probabilities of these outcomes is 1
- Understand and use estimates or measures of probability and relative frequency
- Calculate the expected frequency of an event
- List all outcomes for single events and for two successive events in a systematic way
- Compare experimental data and theoretical probabilities

Worked exam question

A school snack bar offers a choice of four snacks.
The four snacks are burgers, pizza, pasta and salad.
Students can choose one of these four snacks.
The table shows the probability that a student will choose burger or pizza or salad.

Snack	burger	pizza	pasta	salad
Probability	0.35	0.15		0.2

One student is chosen at random from the students who use the snack bar.

a Work out the probability that the student

i did not choose salad,

ii chose pasta. (3)

300 students used the snack bar on Tuesday.

b Work out an estimate for the number of students who chose pizza. (2)

(Edexcel Limited 2005)

a

i $1 - 0.2 = 0.8$

ii
$$\begin{array}{r} 0.35 \\ 0.15 \\ 0.2\ + \\ \hline 0.70 \end{array}$$

$1 - 0.7 = 0.3$

Show the addition and subtraction calculations.

b $0.15 \times 300 = 45$ students

Show this multiplication calculation.

Exam questions

1 The two-way table gives some information about how 100 children travelled to school one day.

	Walk	Car	Other	Total
Boy	15		14	54
Girl		8	16	
Total	37		30	100

a Copy and complete the two-way table. (3)

One of the children is picked at random.

b Write down the probability that this child walked to school that day. (1)

One of the girls is picked at random.

c Work out the probability that this girl did not walk to school that day. (2)

(Edexcel Limited 2009)

2 The probability that a biased dice will land on a four is 0.2.
Pam is going to roll the dice 200 times.

Work out an estimate for the number of times the dice will land on a four. (2)

(Edexcel Limited 2004)

3 There are three beads in a bag.
One bead is blue, one bead is yellow and one bead is green.

Paul takes a bead at random from the bag.

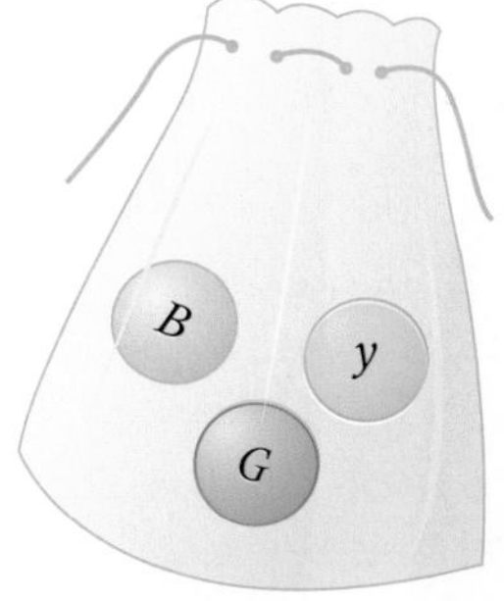

He notes its colour and leaves it out of the bag. He then takes another bead out at random and notes its colour.
List all the possible outcomes for the two beads. (2)

A2 Expressions

Introduction

Engineers and scientists use algebraic expressions to model and explain the behaviour of real events and activities. Without algebra there would be no aircraft, mobile phones or plasma TVs.

What's the point?

Algebra is an extension of arithmetic, but using letters instead of numbers. By using algebra, we can invent and use rules to explain real-life phenomena.

Check in

1 Follow the order of operations to work out these calculations.

a $3 \times 5 - 12 + 2$ **b** $4 + 2 \times 3 - 1$

c $6 \div 3 + 2$ **d** $3 \times 4 - 4 \div 2$

2 **a** Write all the factors of

i 18 **ii** 12 **iii** 24

b Write all the common factors of 18, 12 and 24.

Orientation

What I should know	What I will learn	What this leads to
Key stage 3 → N1 →	■ Use letters to represent numbers ■ Simplify expressions ■ Use index notation ■ Expand and factorise expressions	→ A5 → N5

Rich task

A square grid is numbered from 1 to 100. A 2×2 square is shaded in as shown on the grid.
The numbers in the opposite corners of the 2×2 square are multiplied together.
Investigate.

1	2	3	4	5	6	7	8	9	10
11	12	13	14	15	16	17	18	19	20
21	22	23	24	25	26	27	28	29	30
31	32	33	34	35	36	37	38	39	40
41	42	43	44	45	46	47	48	49	50
51	52	53	54	55	56	57	58	59	60
61	62	63	64	65	66	67	68	69	70
71	72	73	74	75	76	77	78	79	80
81	82	83	84	85	86	87	88	89	90
91	92	93	94	95	96	97	98	99	100

A2.1 Algebraic expressions

This spread will show you how to:

- Use letters to represent unknown numbers in algebraic expressions
- Simplify algebraic expressions by collecting like terms

Keywords
Expression
Like terms
Simplify
Term

You can describe everyday situations using algebra.

- In algebra, you use letters to represent unknown numbers.

You do not write the $\times$ sign. $n = 1 \times n$

These boxes hold n pens each.

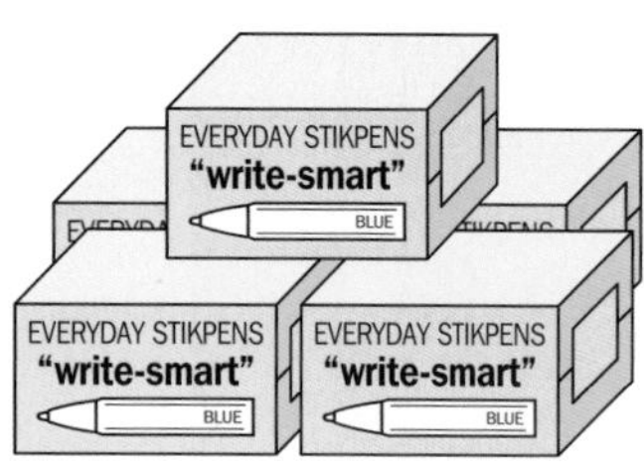

In 5 boxes there are
$n + n + n + n + n = 5 \times n = 5n$ pens

These boxes hold s pens each.

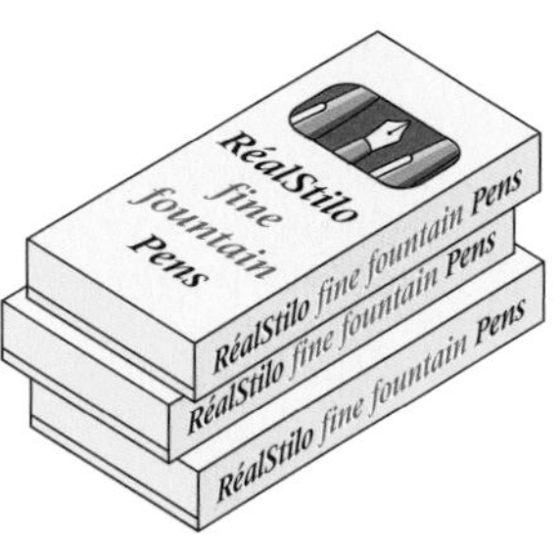

In 3 boxes there are $3s$ pens.

$5n$ and $3s$ are **terms**.

There are $5n + 3s$ pens in total.

$5n + 3s$ is an **expression**.

- You can **simplify** an algebraic expression by collecting **like terms**.
  Like terms have exactly the same letters.

Example

Simplify these expressions:

a $4x + 2y - 2x + 3y$ **b** $7p - 3q + 5q - p$ **c** $5c - 2b + 2c - 3b$

a $4x + 2y - 2x + 3y$
$= 4x - 2x + 2y + 3y$
$= 2x + 5y$

b $7p - 3q + 5q - p$
$= 7p - p + 5q - 3q$
$= 6p + 2q$

c $5c - 2b + 2c - 3b$
$= 5c + 2c - 2b - 3b$
$= 7c - 5b$

Rearrange, keeping terms and their signs together.

Example

In a fruit shop,
apples cost 20p each and
oranges cost 15p each.
Write an expression for the cost
of x apples and y oranges.

Cost of x apples: $x \times 20 = 20x$
Cost of y oranges: $y \times 15 = 15y$
Total cost: $20x + 15y$

Write numbers before letters.

Exercise A2.1 Grade E

1 Simplify these expressions.

a $b + b + b + b$ **b** $y + y + y - y$ **c** $a - a + a + a + a + a - a$

d $3p + 6p$ **e** $5x - 2x$ **f** $4z - z + 3z$

2 Simplify these expressions.

a $2p + 5q + 3p + q$ **b** $6x + 2y + 3x + 5y$

c $4m + 2n - 2m + 6n$ **d** $5x + 3y - 4x + 2y$

e $7r - 4s + r - 2s$ **f** $2f - 3g + 5g - 6f$

g $3a + 2b + 5c - a + 4b$ **h** $7u - 5v + 3w + 3v - 2u$

i $5x - 3y - 2x + 4z - y + z$ **j** $4r + 6s - 3t + 2r + 5t - s$

AO2 Functional Maths

3 **a** One guitar has 6 strings. How many strings are there on t guitars?

b One cookie has 3 peanuts on top. How many peanuts are needed for n cookies?

c One horse has 4 horseshoes. How many horseshoes are needed for x horses?

4 In one month, Dan sends x texts.

a Alix sends 4 times as many texts as Dan. How many is this?

b Kris sends 8 more texts than Alix. How many is this?

5 A factory makes bags.

a The factory makes m small bags. A small bag has 2 zips. How many zips do they need?

b The factory makes three times as many large bags as small bags. How many large bags do they make?

c Each large bag has 4 buttons. How many buttons do they need for the large bags?

6 In a pizza takeaway

- a medium pizza has 6 slices of tomato
- a large pizza has 10 slices of tomato.

How many slices of tomato are needed

a for c medium pizzas

b for d large pizzas?

c Write an expression for the total number of slices of tomato needed for c medium and d large pizzas.

7 Write algebraic expressions for the cost of

a f teas and g scones

b j fruit juices and k flapjacks

c x teas, y milks and z scones

d p milks, q fruit juices and r flapjacks.

Café price list	
Tea	50p
Fruit juice	80p
Milk	60p
Scone	30p
Flapjack	40p

A2.2 Indices

This spread will show you how to:

- Use index notation and simple instances of index laws

Keywords
Base
Index
Indices
Power
Simplify

- You can use **index** notation to write repeated multiplication.

$5 \times 5 = 5^2$ | $m \times m = m^2$ | You say 'm squared'

$5 \times 5 \times 5 = 5^3$ | $m \times m \times m = m^3$ | You say 'm cubed'

$5 \times 5 \times 5 \times 5 = 5^4$ | $m \times m \times m \times m = m^4$ | You say 'm to the **power** of 4'

5 is the **base**, 4 is the index.

'index 4' and 'power 4' mean the same.

You can simplify expressions with **indices** and numbers.

Indices is the plural of index.

Example

Simplify

a $y \times y \times y \times y \times y$ **b** $4 \times r \times r$

c $3 \times p \times p \times p \times q \times q$ **d** $2 \times s \times s \times 3 \times t \times t \times t$

---

a $y \times y \times y \times y \times y = y^5$ **b** $4 \times r \times r = 4 \times r^2 = 4r^2$

c $3 \times p \times p \times p \times q \times q$
$= 3 \times p^3 \times q^2$
$= 3p^3q^2$

d $2 \times s \times s \times 3 \times t \times t \times t$
$= 2 \times s^2 \times 3 \times t^3$
$= 2 \times 3 \times s^2 \times t^3$
$= 6s^2t^3$

y is multiplied by itself 5 times, so index is 5.

Rearrange so the numbers are together.

You can simplify expressions with powers of the same base.

$n^2 \times n^2$
$= n \times n \times n \times n = n^4$

$t^5 \div t^2 = \frac{t^5}{t^2} = \frac{{}^1\not{t} \times {}^1\not{t} \times t \times t \times t}{{}^1\not{t} \times {}^1\not{t}} = t^3$

- To multiply powers of the same base, add the indices.

$x^a \times x^b = x^{(a + b)}$

- To divide powers of the same base, subtract the indices.

$x^a \div x^b = x^{(a - b)}$

These are the **index laws**.

p.236

Example

Simplify

a $s^2 \times s \times s^3$ **b** $\frac{d^2 \times d^4}{d^3}$

---

a $s^2 \times s \times s^3 = s^{(2+1+3)} = s^6$ **b** $\frac{d^2 \times d^4}{d^3} = \frac{d^6}{d^3} = d^{(6-3)}$
$= d^3$

$s = s^1$

Exercise A2.2

Grade C

1 Write these expressions in the simplest form.

a $y \times y \times y \times y$ **b** $m \times m \times m \times m \times m \times m$

c $x \times x \times x$ **d** $p \times p$

2 Simplify

a $3 \times t \times t$ **b** $4 \times p \times q \times q$

c $6 \times v \times v \times w \times w \times w$ **d** $2 \times r \times r \times r \times r \times s$

3 Simplify

a $2 \times m \times m \times 3 \times n$ **b** $4 \times y \times y \times y \times 2 \times z \times z$

c $3 \times g \times 4 \times h \times h \times h$ **d** $5 \times x \times 2 \times y \times y \times y \times y$

4 Simplify

a $3m^2 \times 2$ **b** $3 \times 4p^3$ **c** $2x \times 3y^2$ **d** $5r^2 \times 2s^2$

5 Simplify

a $n^2 \times n^3$ **b** $s^3 \times s^4$ **c** $p^3 \times p$ **d** $t \times t^3$

6 Write each of these as a single power in the form x^n.

a $x^2 \times x^2 \times x^3$ **b** $x \times x^5 \times x^2$ **c** $x^3 \times x^2 \times x^4$ **d** $x^5 \times x \times x$

7 Write each of these as a single power in the form r^n.

a $r^4 \div r^2$ **b** $r^5 \div r^4$ **c** $r^7 \div r^2$ **d** $r^8 \div r^5$

8 Simplify

a $\dfrac{m^6}{m^2}$ **b** $\dfrac{x^4}{x^3}$ **c** $\dfrac{t^7}{t^5}$ **d** $\dfrac{y^4}{y}$

9 Simplify

a $\dfrac{x^2 \times x^3}{x^4}$ **b** $\dfrac{m^3 \times m}{m^2}$ **c** $\dfrac{s^2 \times s^4}{s^3}$ **d** $\dfrac{v \times v^3 \times v^3}{v^4}$

e $\dfrac{q^2 \times q^3 \times q^2}{q^4}$ **f** $\dfrac{t^3 \times t \times t^2}{t^2}$ **g** $\dfrac{p^4 \times p^2 \times p^2}{p^7}$ **h** $\dfrac{y^2 \times y^4 \times y}{y^3 \times y^2}$

Problem

AO3

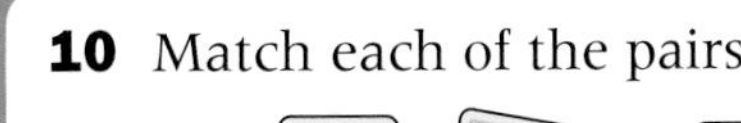

10 Match each of the pairs.

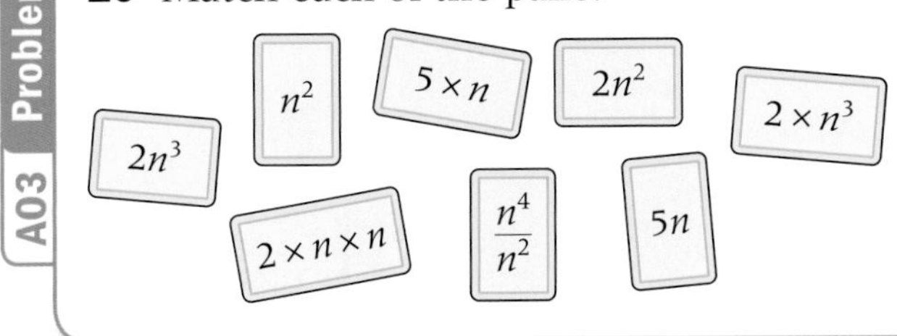

A2.3 Brackets in algebra

This spread will show you how to:

- Expand single brackets within algebraic expressions

Keywords
Brackets
Expand
Simplify

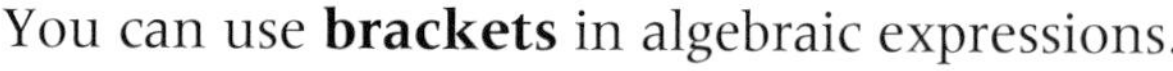

You can use **brackets** in algebraic expressions.

p.266

- You can multiply out brackets.
  - You multiply each term inside the bracket by the term outside.

$2(x+4) = 2 \times x + 2 \times 4 = 2x + 8$

$2 \times (x + 4) = 2(x + 4)$ You don't write the $\times$.

Example

Expand

a $2(3x + 1)$ **b** $n(n + 5)$

a $2(3x + 1) = 2 \times 3x + 2 \times 1$
$= 6x + 2$

b $n(n + 5) = n \times n + 5 \times n$
$= n^2 + 5n$

Expand means 'multiply out'.

$n \times n = n^2$

To **simplify** expressions with brackets, expand the brackets and collect like terms.

Example

Simplify

a $m(m + 2) + m$ **b** $3(x + 1) + 2(4x + 2)$

c $5y(2y - 3)$ **d** $-4(x - 6)$

a $m(m + 2) + m = m^2 + 2m + m$
$= m^2 + 3m$

b $3(x + 1) + 2(4x + 2)$
$= 3x + 3 + 8x + 4$
$= 11x + 7$

c $5y(2y - 3) = 5y \times 2y + 5y \times -3$
$= 10y^2 - 15y$

d $-4(x - 6) = -4 \times x + -4 \times -6$
$= -4x + 24$

Like terms have the same power of the same letter. m^2 and m are **not** like terms.

Exercise A2.3 Grade D

1 Expand the brackets in these expressions.

a $3(m + 2)$ **b** $4(p + 6)$ **c** $2(x + 4)$ **d** $5(q + 1)$
e $2(6 + n)$ **f** $3(2 + t)$ **g** $4(3 + s)$ **h** $2(4 + v)$

2 Expand these expressions.

a $3(2q + 1)$ **b** $2(4m + 2)$ **c** $3(4x + 3)$ **d** $2(3k + 1)$
e $5(2 + 2n)$ **f** $3(4 + 2p)$ **g** $4(1 + 3y)$ **h** $2(5 + 4z)$

3 Expand and simplify each of these expressions.

a $3(p + 3) + 2p$ **b** $2(m + 4) + 5m$ **c** $4(x + 1) - 2x$
d $2(5 + k) + 3k$ **e** $4(2t + 3) + t - 2$ **f** $3(2r + 1) - 2r + 4$

4 Expand and simplify each of these expressions.

a $2(n + 3) + 3(n + 2)$ **b** $4(p + 1) + 2(3 + p)$
c $4(2x + 1) + 2(x + 3)$ **d** $2(3n + 2) + 3(4n + 1)$

Functional Maths

AO2

5 At a pick-your-own fruit farm, Lucy picks n apples.
Mary picks 5 more apples than Lucy.
a Write down, in terms of n, the number of apples Mary picks.

Nat picks 3 times as many apples as Mary.
b Write down, in terms of n, the number of apples Nat picks.

6 On Monday a shop sells s DVDs.
On Tuesday the shop sells 6 more DVDs than on Monday.
a Write an expression for the number of DVDs it sells on Tuesday.

On Wednesday the shop sells twice as many DVDs as on Tuesday.
b Write an expression for the number of DVDs it sells on Wednesday.

On Thursday the shop sells 7 more DVDs than on Wednesday.
c Write an expression for the number of DVDs it sells on Thursday.

Give your answer in its simplest form.

7 A small box contains 12 toffees.
Sam buys y small boxes of toffees.
a Write an expression for the number of toffees Sam buys.

A large box contains 20 toffees.
Sam buys 2 more of the large boxes than the small ones.
b Write an expression for the number of large boxes of toffees he buys.
c Find, in terms of y, the total number of toffees in the large boxes that Sam buys.
d Find, in terms of y, the total number of toffees Sam buys.
Give your answer in its simplest form.

8 Expand

a $x(4x + 1)$ **b** $m(m^2 + 2)$ **c** $2t(t^2 + 4)$ **d** $3p(p^2 + 1)$

9 Expand and simplify

a $4m(m - 3)$ **b** $2p(p - 6)$ **c** $-3(x + 2)$ **d** $-5(2m - 4)$

A2.4 Simplifying expressions

This spread will show you how to:

- Transform algebraic expressions using the rules of arithmetic

Keywords
Brackets
Indices

You can add, subtract, multiply or divide algebraic terms.

$3n + 5n + 8n = 16n$ $\quad 4p - p = 3p$ $\quad 2 \times 6p = 12p$ $\quad 8r \div 4 = 2r$

- To simplify an expression, you follow the same order of operations as in arithmetic.

  Brackets ⇒ **I**ndices ⇒ **D**ivision or **M**ultiplication ⇒ **A**ddition or **S**ubtraction

You can use the acronym BIDMAS to remember the order.

Example

Simplify

a $4n + 2 \times 5n$ **b** $3r \times 2s$ **c** $4t^2 - 3 \times t^2 + t$

a $4n + 2 \times 5n = 4n + (2 \times 5n)$
$= 4n + 10n$
$= 14n$

b $3r \times 2s = 3 \times r \times 2 \times s$
$= 3 \times 2 \times r \times s$
$= 6rs$

Rearrange: numbers first, then letters.

c $4t^2 - 3 \times t^2 + t = 4t^2 - (3 \times t^2) + t$
$= 4t^2 - 3t^2 + t$
$= t^2 + t$

Collect like terms.

To simplify an expression with brackets, expand the brackets first.

$3(n - 2) = 3 \times n + 3 \times -2 = 3n - 6$

$3 \times -2 = -6$

When you expand brackets, keep each term with its sign.

$$4(x - 1) - 2(x + 3) = 4 \times x + 4 \times -1 + -2 \times x + -2 \times 3$$
$$= 4x \quad - 4 \quad - 2x \quad -6$$
$$= 4x - 2x - 4 - 6$$
$$= 2x - 10$$

Example

Expand and simplify

a $3(5y - 2)$ **b** $2(3p + 1) - 3(p + 2)$

a $3(5y - 2) = 3 \times 5y + 3 \times -2$
$= 15y - 6$

b $2(3p + 1) - 3(p + 2) = 6p + 2 - 3p - 6$
$= 3p - 4$

Exercise A2.4

Grade D

1 Simplify these expressions.

a $3r + 3 \times 2r$ **b** $2m^2 + 2m \times m$ **c** $6x \div 2 + x$

d $2t \times 4v$ **e** $5m \times 2n$ **f** $3x \times 2y^2$

g $x^2 + x^2 + x$ **h** $3 \times 3w - 2 \times 4$ **i** $z \times z^2 + 3z + 1$

2 Expand these expressions.

a $4(2y + 3)$ **b** $2(3x - 2)$ **c** $3(2k - 2)$ **d** $4(1 - n)$

3 Write these expressions in their simplest form.

a $3k^2 - 2 \times k^2 + k$ **b** $4m + 6m + 2 + m^2$ **c** $6t - (4 \times -t) + 5$

Did you know?

Renaissance mathematicians in Italy called algebra *'l'Arte Magiore'* (the greater art). Arithmetic was called *l' Arte Minore*.

4 Expand these expressions.

a $2m(m - 3)$ **b** $4p(2p - 1)$ **c** $r(r^2 + 3)$ **d** $2s(s^2 - 4)$

5 Expand and simplify each of these expressions.

a $3(r + 2) + 2(r - 1)$ **b** $4(s + 1) - 2(s + 2)$

c $3(2j + 3) - 2(j + 2)$ **d** $3(4t - 2) + 3(t - 1)$

6 Simplify these expressions.

a $3(4m + 1)(m - 1)$ **b** $2(3p - 1)(p - 2)$

c $-5(2q + 3)(q - 3)$ **d** $4(2v - 3)(v - 1)$

A03 Problem

7 Jake is n years old.
Jake's sister is 4 years older than Jake.
Jake's mother is 3 times older than his sister.
Jake's father is 4 times older than Jake.
Jake's uncle is 2 years younger than Jake's father.
Jake's grandmother is twice as old as Jake's uncle.

a Copy the table and write each person's age in terms of n.

Jake	Sister	Mother	Father	Uncle	Grandmother
n					

b Find, in terms of n, how much older Jake's grandmother is than his mother. Give your answer in its simplest form.

A2.5 Factorising

This spread will show you how to:

- Factorise an algebraic expression

Keywords
Common factor
Factor
Factorise

- Factorising is the 'opposite' of expanding brackets.

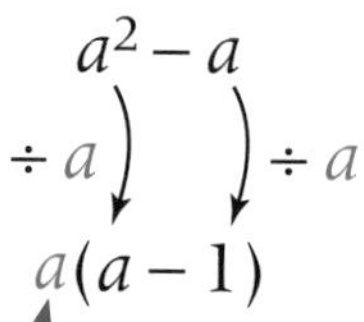

In number...
a factor is a number that exactly divides into another number.

2, 3 and 4 are factors of 12.

In algebra...
a factor is a number or letter that exactly divides into another term.

3 and $2x$ are factors of $6x$.

p.230

- To factorise an expression, look for a **common factor** for all the terms.

A common factor divides into all the terms.

$3x + 9$, $\div 3$, $\div 3$ → $3(x + 3)$

Write the common factor outside the bracket.

$a^2 - a$, $\div a$, $\div a$ → $a(a - 1)$

Sometimes the common factor is a letter.

a divides into a^2 and a.

Example

a Find the common factors of $12x$ and 8.
b Factorise: $12x + 8$.

a 2 and 4 are common factors of $12x$ and 8.
b $12x + 8 = 4 \times 3x + 4 \times 2$
$= 4(3x + 2)$

To factorise completely, use the highest common factor. The highest common factor of $12x$ and 8 is 4.

Example

Factorise

a $3y - 9$ **b** $x^2 - 3x$ **c** $12x^2 + 3x$

a $3y - 9 = 3 \times y - 3 \times 3 = 3(y - 3)$
b $x^2 - 3x = x \times x - 3 \times x = x(x - 3)$
c The highest common factor is $3x$,
so write $3x$ outside the bracket:
$3x(4x + 1)$

You can check your answer by expanding:
$x(x - 3) = x^2 - 3x$

Check:
$3x \times 4x = 12x^2$
$3x \times 1 = 3x$

Exercise A2.5 — Grade D

1 Find all the common factors of

a $2x$ and 6 **b** $4y$ and 12 **c** 10 and $20j$ **d** 6 and $12p$
e 9 and $6q$ **f** $6t$ and 4 **g** $4x$ and 10 **h** $24t$ and 8

2 Find the highest common factor of

a $3x$ and 9 **b** $12r$ and 10 **c** $6m$ and 8 **d** 4 and $4z$

3 Find the highest common factor of

a y^2 and y **b** $4s^2$ and s **c** $7m$ and m^3 **d** $2y^2$ and $2y$

4 Factorise

a $2x + 10$ **b** $3y + 15$ **c** $8p + 4$ **d** $6 + 3m$
e $5n + 5$ **f** $12 + 6t$ **g** $14 + 4k$ **h** $9z - 3$

5 Factorise

a $w^2 + w$ **b** $z - z^2$ **c** $4y + y^2$ **d** $2m^2 - 3m$
e $4p^2 + 5p$ **f** $7k - 2k^2$ **g** $3n^3 - 2n$ **h** $5r + 3r^2$

A03 Problem

6 The cards show expansions and factorisations.
Match the cards in pairs.

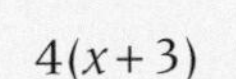

$4(x+3)$	$4x^2-3x$	$3(x-4)$	$4x+3x^2$
$3x-12$	$x(4+3x)$	$4x+12$	$x(4x-3)$

7 Factorise

a $4y - 12$ **b** $2x^2 + 3x$ **c** $3y^2 - 1$ **d** $15 + 5t^2$
e $3m + 9m^2$ **f** $2r^2 - 2r$ **g** $4v^3 + v$ **h** $3w^2 + 3w$

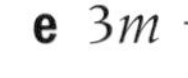

Check your answers by expanding.

A03 Problem

8 Debbie, Kate and Bryn factorise $16x^2 + 4x$.
Here are their answers.

Debbie	Kate	Bryn
$16x^2 + 4x = 2(x^2 + 2x)$	$16x^2 + 4x = 4x(4x + 1)$	$16x^2 + 4x = 2x(8x^2 + 2)$

a Who is correct?
b Explain where the other two have gone wrong.

A2 Summary

Check out

You should now be able to:

- Use letters to represent numbers in algebraic expressions
- Simplify algebraic expressions by collecting like terms
- Use index notation and simple laws of indices
- Multiply a single term over a bracket
- Factorise an algebraic expression using common factors
- Write expressions to solve problems

Worked exam question

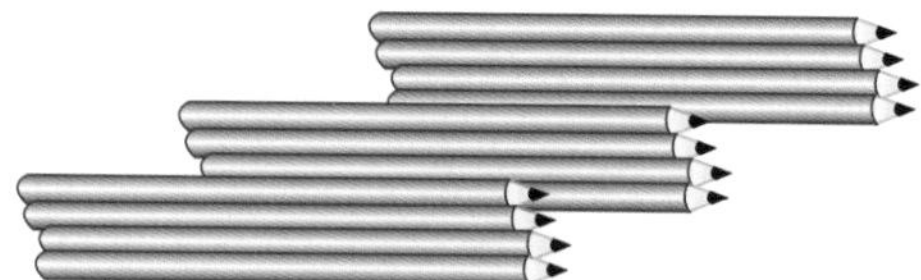

Lisa packs pencils in boxes.
She packs 12 pencils in each box.
Lisa packs x boxes of pencils.

a Write down an expression, in terms of x, for the number of pencils Lisa packs. (1)

Lisa also packs pens in boxes.
She packs 10 pens into each box.
Lisa packs y boxes of pens.

b Write down an expression, in terms of x and y, for the total number of pens and pencils Lisa packs. (2)

(Edexcel Limited 2003)

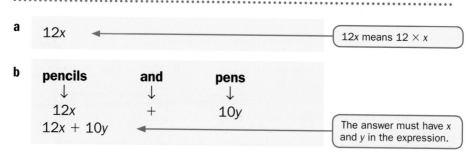

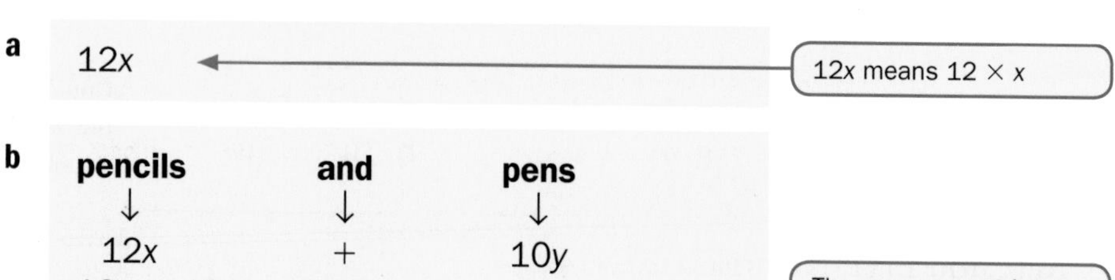

a
$12x$
$12x$ means $12 \times x$
b
pencils ↓ $12x$
and ↓ $+$
pens ↓ $10y$
$12x + 10y$
The answer must have x and y in the expression.

Exam questions

1 **a** Simplify $3p + 2q - p + 2q$ (2)
b Simplify $3y^2 - y^2$ (1)
c Simplify $5c + 7d - 2c - 3d$ (2)
d Simplify $4p \times 2q$ (1)
(Edexcel Limited 2005)

2 **a** Simplify $a + a + a + a$ (1)
b Expand $3(2b - 1)$ (2)
c Simplify $c^2 \times c$ (1)
d Simplify $d^3 \div d$ (1)

3 **a** Work out the value of $3x - 4y$ when $x = 3$ and $y = 2$ (2)
b Work out the value of $\frac{p(q - 3)}{4}$ when $p = 2$ and $q = -7$ (3)
(Edexcel Limited 2007)

4 **a** Factorise $x^2 - 5x$ (2)
b Expand $3(5x - 2)$ (1)
(Edexcel Limited 2007)

5 A cup of tea costs 80 pence.
a Write down an expression, in terms of x, for the cost, in pence, of x cups of tea. (1)
A cup of coffee costs 95 pence.
b Write down an expression, in terms of y, for the cost, in pence, of y cups of coffee. (1)
c Write down an expression, in terms of x and y, for the cost, in pence, of x cups of tea and y cups of coffee. (2)
(Edexcel Limited 2008)

A03

6 The area of a rectangle is $(4x + 12)$ cm^2.
Give two possible alternatives for the length and width of the rectangle.
Your answers should include x.

D2

Collecting data

Introduction

In the run-up to a general election, opinion polls are conducted to find out what people are likely to vote for. An opinion poll might consist of a sample of just 1000 people, and so it should be as representative of the entire population as possible. By conducting opinion polls, political parties can estimate how many people are likely to vote for them.

What's the point?

Statistics allow organisations to make sense of large amounts of data, so that they can appreciate opinions and trends and therefore make informed decisions.

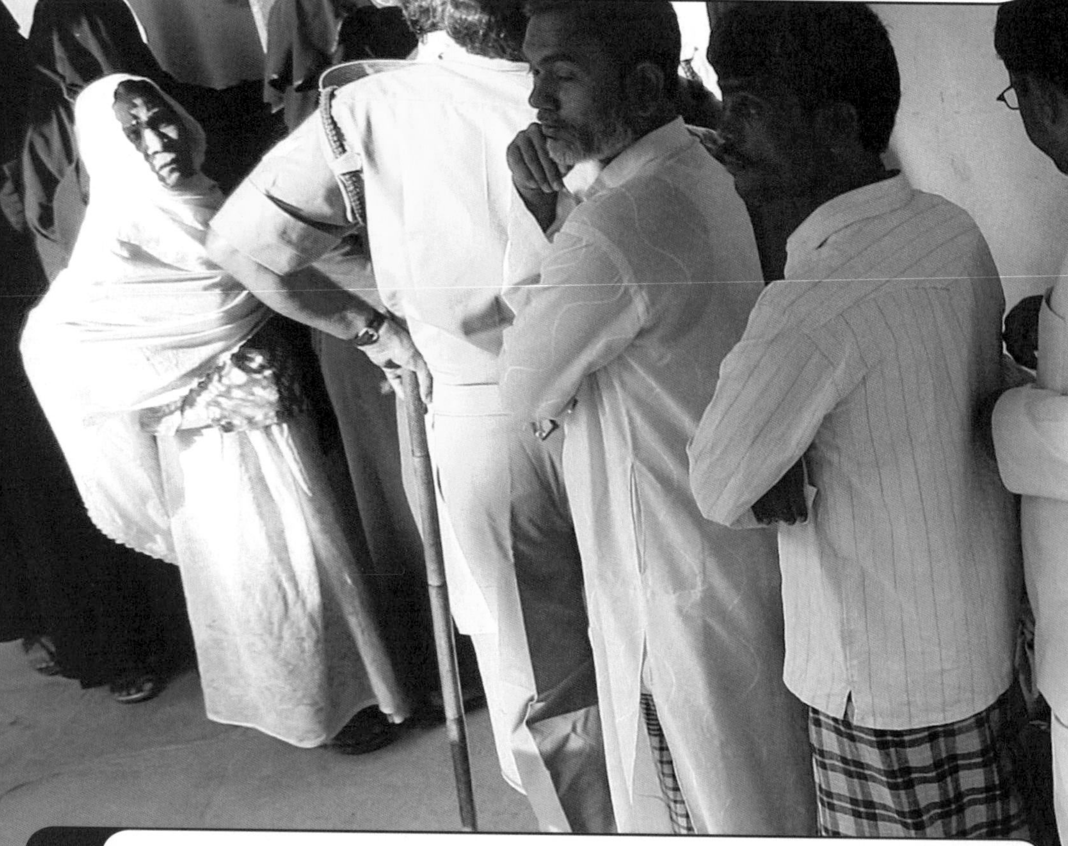

Check in

1 Put these numbers in order of size, smallest first.

- **a** 56, 47, 48, 55, 65, 44, 61, 59
- **b** 1.7, 2.5, 0.8, 2.1, 1.5, 0.5
- **c** 31.2, 32.1, 23.1, 13.2, 13.1, 21.3

2 Calculate

- **a** 36 + 45
- **b** 82 + 97
- **c** 36 + 45 + 24
- **d** 138 + 67
- **e** 325 + 116
- **f** 91 + 17
- **g** 148 − 13
- **h** 256 − 79
- **i** 345 − 126
- **j** 125 − 84

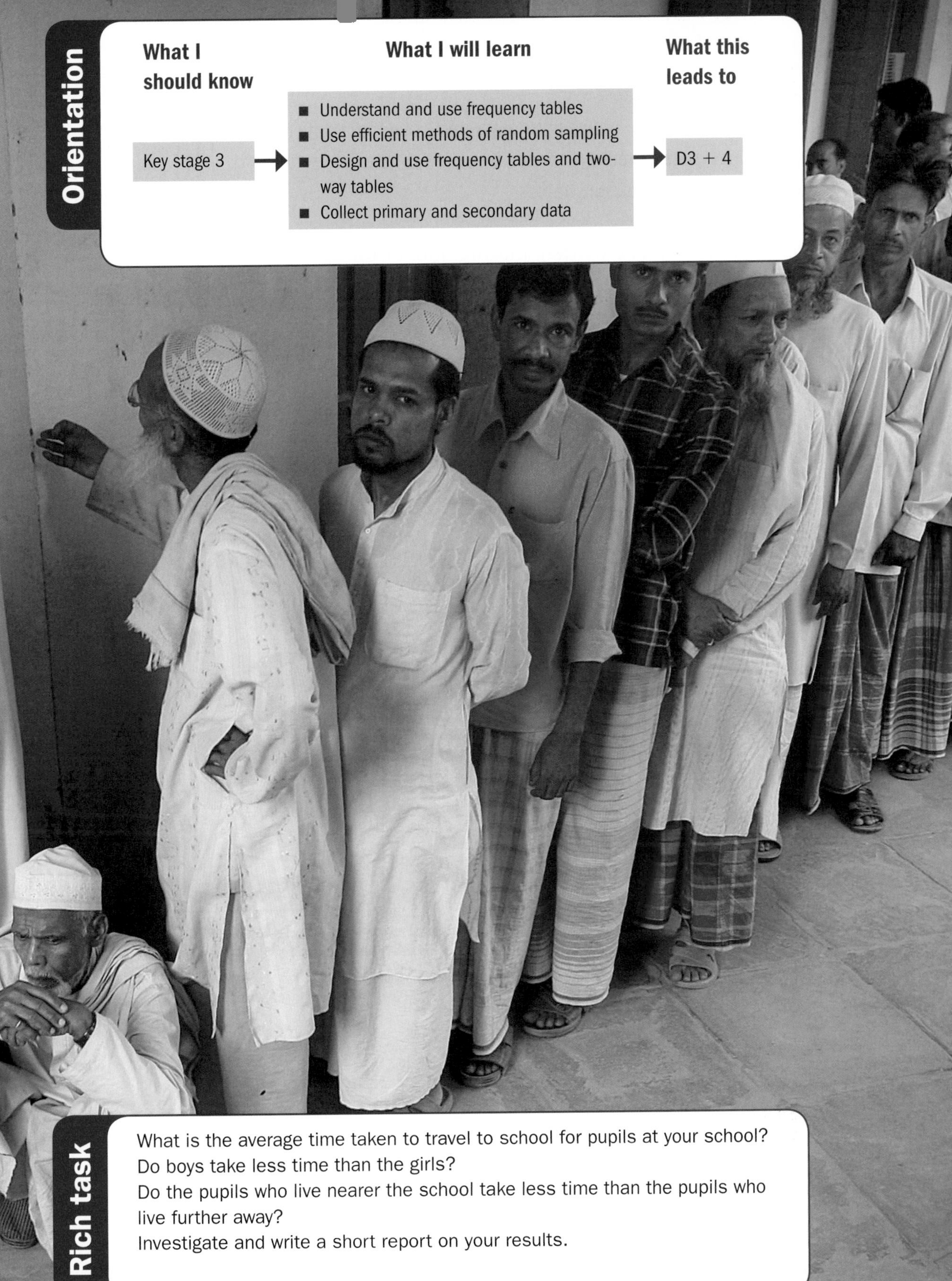

Orientation

What I should know		What I will learn		What this leads to
Key stage 3	→	■ Understand and use frequency tables ■ Use efficient methods of random sampling ■ Design and use frequency tables and two-way tables ■ Collect primary and secondary data	→	D3 + 4

Rich task

What is the average time taken to travel to school for pupils at your school?
Do boys take less time than the girls?
Do the pupils who live nearer the school take less time than the pupils who live further away?
Investigate and write a short report on your results.

D2.1 Frequency tables

This spread will show you how to:

- Recognise the difference between primary and secondary data
- Design and use data-collection sheets for discrete data
- Understand and use frequency tables

Keywords
Data
Data-collection sheet
Frequency table
Primary data
Secondary data
Tally chart

Before this headline could be written, information, or **data**, was collected.

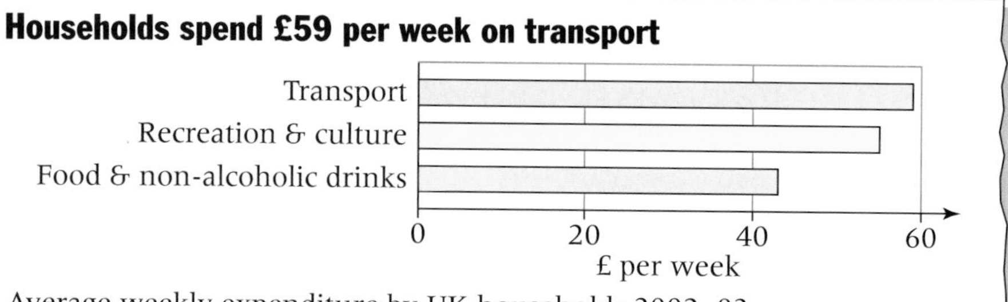

- **Primary data** is data you collect yourself.

  You count the scores when rolling a dice.

- **Secondary data** is data someone else has already collected.

  This includes information from newspapers or the internet.

- You can collect data using a **data-collection sheet**.

  This one is a **tally chart**.

Coin face	Tally	Frequency
Head	卌 卌 |||	13
Tail	卌 卌 ||	12

卌 = 5

The coin was spun 13 + 12 = 25 times.

Data can also be shown using a **frequency table**.

Example

The number of televisions in each house in Fern's street is shown in the frequency table.

a Calculate the number of houses in Fern's street.

b Calculate the total number of televisions in Fern's street.

Number of TVs	Number of houses
0	1
1	5
2	12
3	9
4	1

The numbers in the table are

0, 1, 1, 1, 1, 1, 2, 2, 2, 2, 2, 2, 2, 2, 2, 2, 2, 2, 3, 3, 3, 3, 3, 3, 3, 3, 3, 4

a $1 + 5 + 12 + 9 + 1 = 28$ houses

b $0 + 5 + 24 + 27 + 4 = 60$ televisions

TVs	Houses	TVs × Houses
0	1	$0 \times 1 = 0$
1	5	$1 \times 5 = 5$
2	12	$2 \times 12 = 24$
3	9	$3 \times 9 = 27$
4	1	$4 \times 1 = 4$

Exercise D2.1 — Grade F

1 **a** Copy and complete the tally chart to find the frequency of the vowels a, e, i, o, u in this sentence.

b Which vowel occurs the most often?

c Which vowel occurs the least often?

d Calculate the total number of vowels in the sentence.

e Find a paragraph of writing in a newspaper and complete a similar tally chart.

Vowel	Tally	Frequency
a		
e		
i		
o		
u		

A02 Functional Maths

2 Rainfall, measured in millimetres, is recorded daily for the month of April.

4 2 1 0 0 1 2 2 3 5
7 8 5 3 3 2 0 0 0 1
2 3 2 4 6 7 8 8 1 2

a Copy and complete the tally chart to show this information.

b State the number of completely dry days in April.

c Calculate the total amount of rain to fall throughout April. State the units of your answer.

Rainfall (mm)	Tally	Number of days
0		
1		
2		
3		
4		
5		
6		
7		
8		

3 Nails can be bought in bags.
There are approximately 20 nails in each bag.
The numbers of nails in 40 bags are recorded.

19 20 19 21 20 20 20 21
22 19 19 19 21 20 20 21
19 21 21 22 20 19 20 21
20 20 21 21 20 20 22 21
19 19 20 20 21 20 20 20

a Copy and complete the tally chart to show this information.

b Calculate the total number of nails in all 40 bags.

Number of nails	Tally	Number of bags
19		
20		
21		
22		

4 Sophie did a survey to find the number of CDs owned by the students in her class. The results are shown in the frequency table.

a Calculate the number of students in Sophie's class.

b Calculate the total number of CDs owned by the whole class.

Number of CDs	Number of students
0	1
1	8
2	6
3	8
4	2
5	3

D2.2 Observation, controlled experiment and sampling

This spread will show you how to:

- Collect primary and secondary data using a variety of methods
- Use efficient methods of random sampling
- Discuss how data relates to a problem, identifying and minimising possible sources of bias

Keywords
Biased
Data logging
Observation
Random sample

- You can collect data by **observation**.
  To find the average daily rainfall, you would have to measure the rainfall every day for a period of time.
- You can collect data by **controlled experiment**.
  To see if a Head or a Tail occurs more often, you would have to spin a coin a number of times.
- You can collect data by **data logging**.
  For example, your heart rate can be measured when exercising.

You will need a **data-collection sheet**, whichever method you use.

An observation usually involves watching.

An experiment usually involves setting up a test.
Data is usually collected automatically when data logging.

Example

Design a suitable data-collection sheet to find the number of cars in households in your street.

Number of cars	Tally	Frequency
0		
1		
2		
3		
4 or more		

Covers all possibilities

Sometimes it is impossible to collect data from all the population and so a **random sample** is used.

- In a random sample, each person or item must be equally likely to be chosen.

The sample must not be **biased**.
The sample is biased if each person or item is not equally likely to be chosen.

Example

Describe a method to choose a random sample of 30 students for a year group of 120 students.

- Number each student from 1 to 120.
- Put a different number on 120 pieces of paper.
- Place the pieces of paper in a bag.
- Pick out 30 numbers from the bag.

Taking every 4th student from an alphabetical or form list is biased.

Exercise D2.2 Grade D

1 Decide whether these data collections are an observation, a controlled experiment, or data logging.

a Spinning a spinner
b The types of drink bought from a vending machine at break
c Choosing a colour from a given set of colours
d Automatically measuring the temperature of ice as it is heated
e Measuring the 'bounce' of different rubber balls dropped from the same height
f The make of vehicles passing the school gates
g The number of passes a player makes during a game
h Automatically measuring the number of vehicles travelling on a road
i The usage of the slide, the swing and the roundabout in a playground
j Automatically measuring pulse rate on a jogging machine.

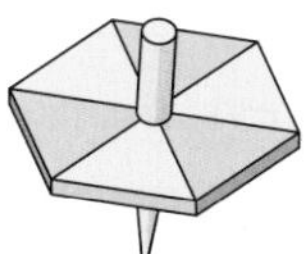

A spinner is an instrument for creating random outcomes, usually in probability experiments.

Functional Maths AO2

2 The number of occupants in passing cars are counted. The results are

1	2	1	4	3	1	2	1	5	4
1	1	1	2	1	3	1	4	1	1
1	2	1	1	1	2	1	1	4	2
2	2	1	2	1	3	2	1	2	1

a Is this data collection an observation, a controlled experiment or data logging?
b Construct a data-collection sheet to show this data.
c Calculate the total number of cars that passed.
d Calculate the total number of occupants of the cars that passed.

DID YOU KNOW?

So-called 'carpool lanes' are being considered on UK motorways. Cars would have to carry at least two people, in a bid to ease congestion.

Problem AO3

3 A dice, numbered 1 to 6, is rolled and the scores recorded.

a Is this data collection an observation, a controlled experiment or data logging?
b Construct a suitable data-collection sheet.

The scores are

1	5	6	2	1	4	2	1	2	5	6	1	3	2	2
2	1	2	1	2	2	1	6	5	4	3	2	1	1	1
5	5	6	1	2	2	1	4	3	3	2	2	1	4	6

c Complete your data-collection sheet with the data.
d Which score occurred the most often?
e Calculate the total number of rolls of the dice.
f Do you think the dice is biased? Explain your answer.
g How could you improve the reliability of your answer?

D2.3 Surveys and questionnaires

This spread will show you how to:

- Collect primary and secondary data using a variety of methods

Keywords
Data-collection sheet
Hypothesis
Questionnaire
Survey

Surveys are used to find people's opinions or to test a **hypothesis**.

- You can collect data by using a survey with
  - a **data-collection sheet**
  - a **questionnaire**.

A hypothesis is a predictive statement, for example 'boys are taller than girls'.

This data-collection sheet allows you to ask one question and collects all the data on one sheet.

Do you smoke?	Tally	Frequency
Yes	卌 卌 II	
No	卌	

A questionnaire gives you more data, but you need one questionnaire for each person in your survey.

You must be careful what questions you ask in a survey.

Male ☐ Female ☐
Age group: Under 20 ☐
20 or over ☐
Do you smoke? Yes ☐
No ☐

Never ask a leading question, such as: The speed of cars today, it's very bad, isn't it?	• Avoid giving your opinion. What do you think of the speed of cars today? Too slow ☐ About right ☐ Too fast ☐
Never ask a vague question, such as: Do you eat cereal?	• Ask for factual responses. Did you eat cereal for breakfast today?
Never ask a question that gives too many responses, such as: What do you like to eat?	• Limit the choice of responses. Meat ☐ Fish ☐ Vegetables ☐
Never ask a complicated, wordy question.	• Ask simple, straightforward questions.
Don't forget to allow for all possible responses.	• Use 'Don't know' or 'Other'.
Never use 'occasionally', 'regularly' or 'sometimes' as they mean different things to different people.	• Ask for numerical responses. 1–10 ☐ 11–20 ☐ 21–30 ☐

Example

Give two reasons why the response section of this questionnaire is unsatisfactory.

How much money are you carrying?
£0.01–£1 ☐ £1–£2 ☐ Over £2 ☐

- No response is possible for £0.
- £1 is in two categories.

Exercise D2.3 — Grade D

AO2 Functional Maths

1 Lauren wants to find out how often the students in her class eat 'Take-away' food.

a One of the questions in her questionnaire is shown. Write one criticism of this question.

Which 'Take-away' meals do you like?

[ ]

b Another question is shown. Write one criticism of this question.

Have you had a 'Take-away' meal recently?

Yes [ ] No [ ]

2 **a** Devise a question that could be used to give this frequency table.

b Calculate the number of people that completed this survey.

Fruit	Number of people
Apple	43
Banana	35
Pear	13
Other	9

3 Ross intends to survey shoppers about their shopping habits.

a One of the questions in his questionnaire is shown. Write two criticisms of the response section.

How old are you?

Under 20 [ ] 20–30 [ ] 30–40 [ ]

b Another question is shown. Write one criticism of the question and one criticism of the response section.

Do you shop often?

Seldom [ ] Rarely [ ] Sometimes [ ]

c Ross is going to use the questionnaire outside one shop. Write one criticism of his plan.

d Rewrite the questions in parts a and b.

4 **a** Devise a question that could produce this data-collection sheet.

b Calculate the total number of people that completed the survey.

c Write one criticism of the choice of categories for the channel.

Channel	Tally	Frequency
BBC1	~~||||~~ ||	7
BBC2	|||	3
1TV	~~||||~~ |	6
Channel 4	||	2
Five	|	1
Other	~~||||~~ ~~||||~~ |	11

5 One question in a questionnaire about reading habits is 'Do you read a newspaper regularly?'

a Write one criticism of this question.

b Rewrite the question, including a response section.

c Another question is:

When was the last time you bought a book?

1 year ago [ ] 2 years ago [ ] 3 or more years ago [ ]

Write two criticisms of the response section.

D2.4 Grouped data

This spread will show you how to:

- Design and use data-collection sheets for discrete and grouped data

Keywords
Class intervals
Continuous
Discrete
Group
Grouped frequency table

Some surveys produce data with many different values.

- You can **group** data into **class intervals** to avoid too many categories.

Example

The exam marks of class 10A are shown:

35	47	63	25	31	8	19	55	47	14
24	36	56	61	15	43	22	50	66	10
36	45	18	20	53	31	40	60	44	47

Complete the **grouped frequency table**.

Mark	Tally	Frequency
1–20		
21–40		
41–60		
61–80		

→

Mark	Tally	Frequency
1–20	𝍸 II	7
21–40	𝍸 IIII	9
41–60	𝍸 𝍸 I	11
61–80	III	3

𝍸 = 5

Check that the frequencies add to 30.

- **Discrete** data can only take exact values (usually collected by counting), for example the number of students in each class in a school.

- **Continuous** data can take any value (collected by measuring), for example the heights of the students in your class.

  Continuous data cannot be measured exactly.

- You can write class intervals for discrete data like this:

People
1–10
10–20
21–30

11–20 means between 11 and 20 including 11 and 20.

- You can write class intervals for continuous data like this:

Weight (w)
$50 \leq w < 55$
$55 \leq w < 60$
$60 \leq w < 65$

The first interval is between 50 and 55, including 50 but not including 55.

Exercise D2.4 — Grade D

1 Decide whether this data is discrete or continuous.

a The number of taxis waiting at a station
b The number of drinks in a machine
c The heights of people
d The number of magazines in a shop
e The weights of animals
f The number of people in an office
g The handspans of people
h The speed of cars
i Dress sizes
j Shoe sizes.

Functional Maths | A02

2 **a** Copy and complete the frequency table using these test marks.

8 14 21 4 15 22 25 24 15 11
10 17 24 20 13 16 12 9 3 14
20 10 16 15 7 23 23 14 15 16
8 2 9 19 12 10 10 20 13 13
15 17 11 14 19 20 23 23 24 5

Test mark	Tally	Frequency
1–5		
6–10		
11–15		
16–20		
21–25		

b Calculate the number of people who took the test.

3 **a** Copy and complete the frequency table using these weights of people, given to the nearest kilogram.

48 63 73 55 59 61 70 63 58 67
46 45 57 58 63 71 60 47 49 51
53 61 68 65 70 60 52 59 50 49
48 47 63 61 58 71 53 51 60 70

Weight (kg)	Tally	Number of people
$45 \leqslant w < 50$		
$50 \leqslant w < 55$		
$55 \leqslant w < 60$		
$60 \leqslant w < 65$		
$65 \leqslant w < 70$		
$70 \leqslant w < 75$		

b Calculate the number of people who took the test.

4 Every student in Emma's class threw a ball as far as possible. The lengths of the throws, to the nearest metre, are shown.

8 15 18 11 10 20 24 11 12
21 22 9 7 12 14 18 6 19
20 22 21 17 13 15 20

a Draw and complete a frequency table, using class intervals $0 \leqslant l < 5$, $5 \leqslant l < 10$, $10 \leqslant l < 15$, ...

b How many students are in Emma's class?

5 The masses of parcels, in kilograms, are shown.

1.8 1.9 2.3 2.0 0.7 1.9 3.4 1.8
2.1 1.2 3.2 3.1 1.5 1.7 2.9 2.7
3.7 0.9 2.5 3.3 0.2 2.7 2.8 3.5
1.9 1.8 0.3 0.8 2.5 1.7 0.5 1.0
0.5 2.4 3.0 3.6 1.3 3.3 3.2 1.9

a Draw and complete a frequency table, using class intervals $0 < m \leqslant 1.0$, $1.0 < m \leqslant 2.0$, ...

b Which class interval has the greatest number of parcels?

c Calculate the total number of parcels that were weighed.

D2.5 Two-way tables 2

This spread will show you how to:

- Design and use two-way tables

Keywords
Column
Frequency table
Row
Two-way table

- You can organise data in a table, such as a **frequency table**, using **rows** and **columns**.

p.106

Method of travel	Number of students
Car	14
Bus	11
Walk	5

11 students travelled by bus.

- A **two-way table** shows more detail and links two types of information, for example, method of travel and gender.

	Boys	Girls
Car	4	10
Bus	6	5
Walk	2	3

5 girls travelled by bus.

Example

Design a data-collection sheet, in the form of a two-way table, that could be used to survey the audience at a pantomime.
The survey must distinguish between children and adults.

	Child	Adult
Male		
Female		

or

	Male	Female
Child		
Adult		

Example

Katie and Marcus counted their music collection.
Complete the two-way table.

Type	Katie	Marcus	Totals
CD	6		
MP3		10	
Totals	15		28

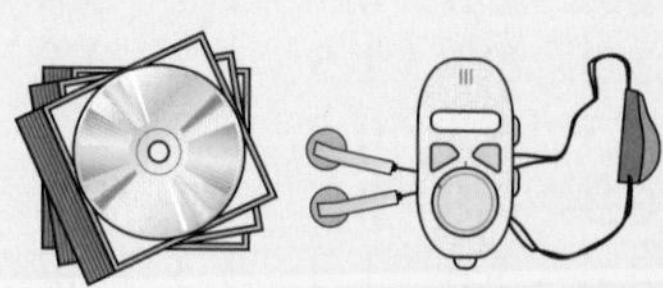

Calculate the missing values

15 − 6 = 9
9 + 10 = 19
28 − 19 = 9
9 − 6 = 3
3 + 10 = 13
Check: 15 + 13 = 28

Type	Katie	Marcus	Totals
CD	6	3	9
MP3	9	10	19
Totals	15	13	28

Exercise D2.5

Grade D

A02 Functional Maths

1 The two-way table shows the numbers of cars and vans that are crushed or saved for spare parts.

	Crushed	Spare parts
Cars	15	24
Vans	7	12

a State the number of
  i cars that are crushed
  ii vans that are saved for spare parts.

b Calculate the total number of
  i cars
  ii crushed vehicles.

c Calculate the total number of vehicles shown in the table.

2 A class of 32 students play either football or badminton.
There are 15 girls in the class, with 5 boys and 8 girls playing badminton.

a Copy and complete the two-way table.

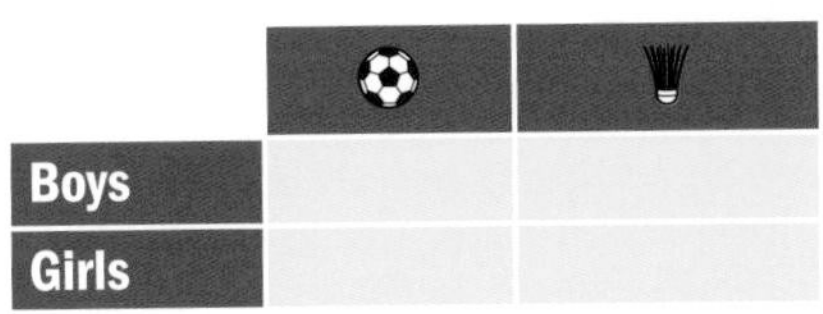

Boys		
Girls		

b How many boys play football?

3 One hundred mobile phones are surveyed for colour (either black or silver) and for the payment method (either pay as you go or contract).

a Devise a two-way table that would show this information.

b Choose four suitable numbers for your table.

4 A vending machine only sells tea and coffee.
Janice is carrying out a survey about the use of sugar in drinks.
Devise a two-way table that Janice could use to show this information.

5 A car salesperson sells vehicles that are either saloons or hatchbacks and are bought part-exchange or cash.
Devise a suitable two-way table to summarise their sales.

D2.6 Databases and random sampling

This spread will show you how to:

- Gather data from secondary sources
- Use effective methods for random sampling
- Identify sources of bias and plan to minimise it

Keywords
Biased
Database
Equally likely
RAN#
Random sample

- A **database** is an organised collection of data, especially in a form that can be used by a computer.

An example might be the records of the Year 11 students in a school.
You can sort a computer database

- alphabetically
- numerically.

You can sort using any or several of the columns (fields).

This database has been sorted by number.

Number	Surname	Forename	Form	Gender
0001	Smith	Thomas	10E	Male
0002	Jones	Michaela	10B	Female
0003	Chapham	Leah	10A	Female
0004	Clark	Alan	10B	Male

Sometimes there is too much data in a database to process all the data, and so a **random sample** is used.

- In a random sample, each person or item must be **equally likely** to be chosen.

If each person is not equally likely to be chosen, the sample is **biased**.

Example

Describe a method to choose a random sample of 30 students from a year group of 120 students.

- Number each student from 1 to 120.
- Generate 30 random numbers, by either
  - picking 30 numbers from a bag of 120, numbered 1 to 120, or
  - using the RAN# key on a calculator.
- You can generate random numbers on a calculator using the random function. RAN# generates random numbers from 0.000 to 0.999.

- You can generate a random number from, say, 1 to 120 by using 120 × RAN#.

Use the first three digits of the display.

Exercise D2.6

Grade D

A02 Functional Maths

1 Sanjit wants to buy a laptop. He creates a database of the 10 laptops he is considering buying.

Laptop number	Speed of processor	RAM memory	Size of hard drive	Screen size	Warranty	Cost
1	2.16 GHz	1 GB	120 GB	15.4″	No	£275
2	2.0 GHz	2 GB	160 GB	14.1″	1 year	£500
3	1.6 GHz	1 GB	120 GB	8.9″	1 year	£220
4	1.8 GHz	2 GB	120 GB	17″	1 year	£350
5	2.0 GHz	2 GB	64 GB	12.1″	3 years	£600
6	2.0 GHz	2 GB	160 GB	15.4″	2 years	£310
7	2.16 GHz	1 GB	120 GB	15.4″	3 years	£345
8	2.0 GHz	4 GB	320 GB	15.4″	3 years	£437
9	1.8 GHz	2 GB	160 GB	15.4″	1 year	£402
10	2.53 GHz	5 GB	500 GB	15.6″	No	£549

a Write down the costs of the laptops in order of price, smallest first.

b Write down the speeds of the processors in order of size, smallest first.

c Which laptop has the smallest processor speed?

d Which laptop has the largest RAM memory?

e List the laptops that have

  i a screen size of 15″ or more

  ii at least 160 GB of hard drive memory

  iii a 2-year or 3-year warranty.

f Sanjit wants a laptop with a screen size of 15″ or more, at least 160 GB of hard drive memory and one with a 2- or 3-year warranty. Which laptop is the cheapest option?

2 A class of 30 students decide to elect a class representative by a random process. State whether these methods of selection are random or biased. Give a reason for each answer.

a Arrange the class list into alphabetical order and select the first name on the list.

b Arrange the class list into alphabetical order and select the last name on the list.

c Put the names of the students on cards of equal size. Put the cards into a bag and pick out one card.

d Arrange the students in order of height and select the smallest student.

e Hide a gold star in the classroom, and select the student who finds the star.

f Number the students from 1 to 30. Roll a dice and select the student with that number.

g Number the students from 1 to 30. Use a calculator to find 30 × RAN# and take the first two digits on the display.

D2 Summary

Check out

You should now be able to:

- Design and use data collection sheets for discrete and grouped data
- Understand and use frequency tables
- Collect data using a variety of methods
- Collect data from a variety of sources
- Identify possible sources of bias
- Design and use two-way tables
- Extract data from a database

Worked exam question

The manager of a school canteen has made some changes.
She wants to find out what students think of these changes.
She uses this question on a questionnaire.

"What do you think of the changes in the canteen?"

☐ Excellent ☐ Very good ☐ Good

a Write down what is wrong about this question. (1)

This is another question on the questionnaire.

"How much money do you normally spend in the canteen"

☐ A lot ☐ Not much

b **i** Write down one thing that is wrong with this question. (1)

ii Design a better question for the canteen manager to use. You should include some response boxes. (2)

(Edexcel Limited 2004)

---

a The choice of responses is biased.
'Poor' and 'Very poor' are needed.

b **i** 'A lot' and 'Not much' are vague and will be misunderstood.
ii How much money did you spend in the canteen yesterday?

£0	£0.01–£1	£1.01–£2	£2.01–£3	over £3
☐	☐	☐	☐	☐

Other answers for **b i** could be: -
No mention of money
No mention of time
The small number of possible responses.

There is no overlap of amounts of money in the response boxes.

The response boxes cover all possibilities.

Exam questions

1 Emma went into town to buy a new bed.
The table gives the price of different types of beds.

Bed size	Non storage	2-drawer	4-drawer	Mattress only
Single	£340	£390	—	£270
Double	£500	£540	£590	£335
King	£570	£615	£650	£380
Super King	£600	£595	£700	£430

Emma buys a Double 2-drawer bed.

a What price is this bed? (1)

Steve only wants to buy a mattress.

b How much is the cheapest mattress? (1)

c Which bed size will this mattress fit? (1)

A03

2 The two-way table gives some information about the lunch arrangements of 85 students.

	School lunch	Packed lunch	Other	Total
Male	21		13	47
Female		5		
Total	40			85

Copy and complete the two-way table. (3)

(Edexcel Limited 2006)

A02

3 Kavic wants to collect some information about the different makes of cars in a car park.

Design a suitable data collection sheet that Kavic could use to collect this information. (3)

(Edexcel Limited 2007)

Functional Maths 3: Recycling

The focus on protecting the environment from further damage is now stronger than ever. Recycling and reusing waste materials have become an important part of everyday life both for manufacturers and consumers.

This time-series chart shows the total waste per person produced by households in the UK and the proportion of this waste that was recycled between 1983/4 and 2007/8.

What can you say in general about the amount of waste produced and recycled by households in the UK during this time? Justify your response by referring to the data.

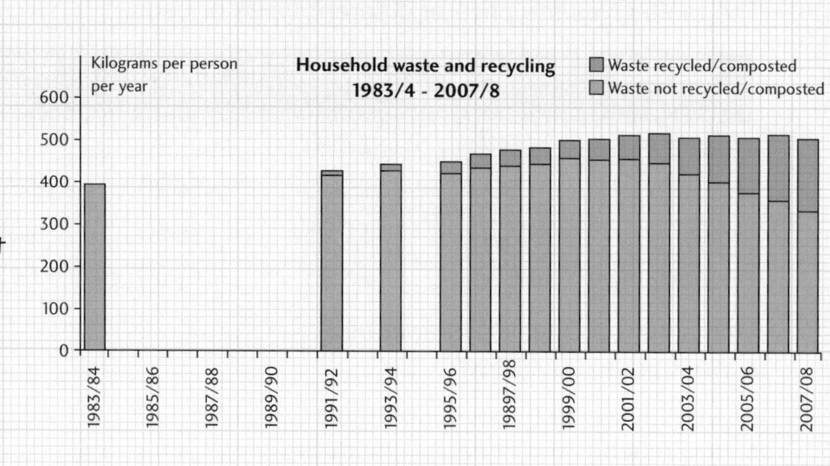

Copy and complete this table giving the values shown in the time-series chart.

Year	1983/84	1991/92	1993/94	1995/96	1996/97	1997/98	1998/99	1999/00	2000/01	2001/02	2002/03	2003/04	2004/05	2005/06	2006/07	2007/08
Waste not recycled/ composted	394	417		423	438	441	443	457	455	456	449	425		376	359	
Waste recycled/ composted	3	11	15	27	32	36			52	60	71	87	113	135	157	173
Total waste	397	427	445		469	477	483	505	507		521	512	517	511		507

The data shows that less than 0.8% of UK household waste was recycled in the year 1983/4. Work out what percentage of UK household waste (to the nearest 0.01%) was recycled each year until 2007/8. Add this information to your table.

Can you think of any reason for the trend shown by this data?

By what percentage has the amount of

a) household waste

b) waste recycled by households

changed during this time in the UK?

What realistic predictions do you think the government could have made about household waste for the year 2008/09?

Manufacturers are responsible for designing packaging that is as environmentally friendly as possible while also protecting the product.

A drinks company sells its brand of Cola in 500ml plastic (PET) bottles. The company has reduced the weight of these bottles by a third since the 1970s. The bottles weighed 39g in the 1970s.
What is the weight of a new bottle?
The company plans to start using bottles that weigh 24g.
What further reduction in weight (%) would this be?

Glass milk bottles are 50% lighter than they were 50 years ago.

As well as reducing the consumption of raw materials, lighter packaging also saves money in other ways such as transport costs.

A supermarket sells tomatoes in packs of six. The packaging consists of a plastic tray with a lid as shown. How much lighter (as a %) would each package be if it were made with no lid?

Do you think that not having lids would risk the quality of the tomatoes?

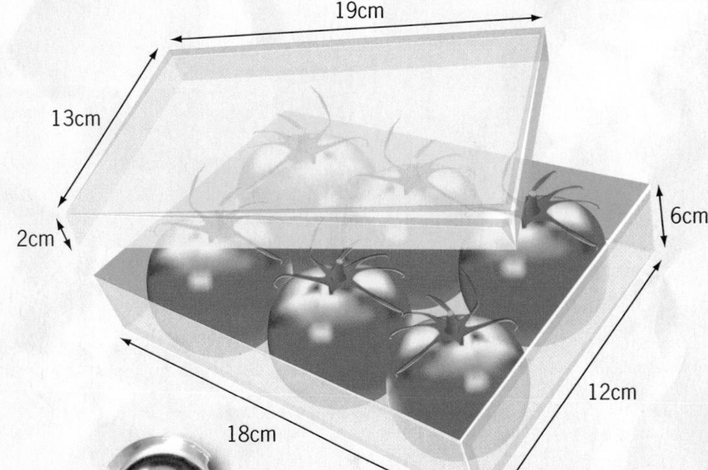

The product/pack ratio compares the weight of the packaging with the weight of the product it contains. Companies use this ratio to assess the suitability of the packaging used for each of their products. They often express it as a percentage to show how much of the overall weight is contributed by the packaging.

Look at some of the packaging you have at home. Could it be adapted to use less material without increasing the risk of damage to the product? If so, how?

How does the packaging used for perishable goods (e.g. food) differ from that used for non-perishable goods (e.g. electrical items)?

Research some well-known manufacturing companies on the Internet to find out about their packaging guidelines. Do they have different rules for different products (e.g. perishable/non-perishable goods)?

Introduction

Many of the man-made shapes we see in everyday life are cuboids, particularly in packaging.

What's the point?

Cuboids are easy to assemble, and most importantly they stack up without leaving any gaps. This makes them more economical and practical for packaging and transporting goods.

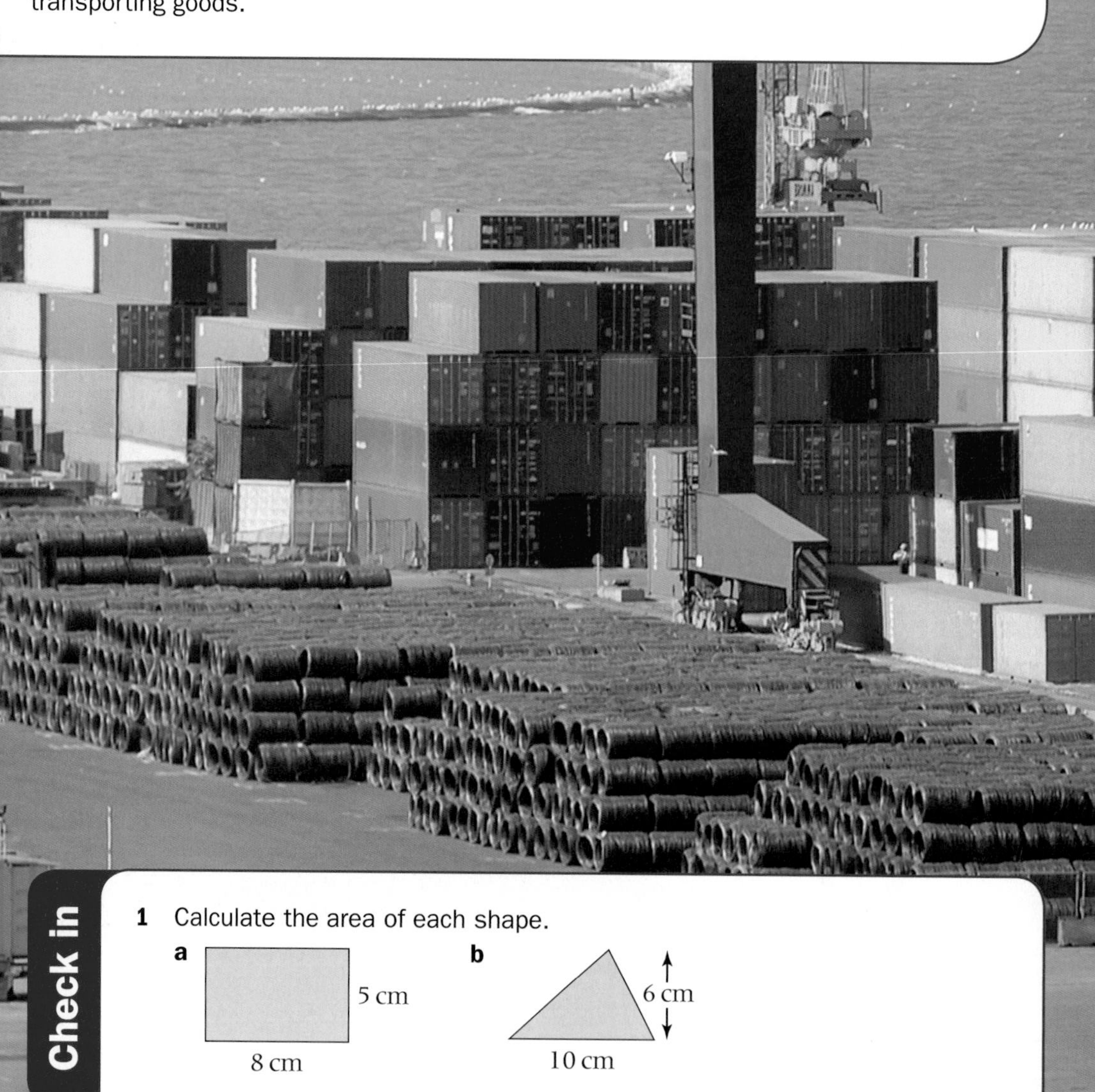

Check in

1 Calculate the area of each shape.

a Rectangle: 8 cm by 5 cm

b Triangle: base 10 cm, height 6 cm

2 Evaluate

a 25×10

b 63×100

c 4.1×10

d 2.5×100

e 3.5×1000

f $40 \div 10$

g $56 \div 10$

h $4000 \div 100$

i $410 \div 100$

j $5200 \div 1000$

Orientation

What I should know	What I will learn	What this leads to
G1 →	■ Investigate 3-D shapes made from cuboids ■ Calculate the volume of cuboids and prisms	→ G5

Rich task

Here are the front and side views of a 3D shape made from cubes.
Draw the 3D shape on isometric dotty paper.
Are you sure - are there any other alternatives?
Investigate.

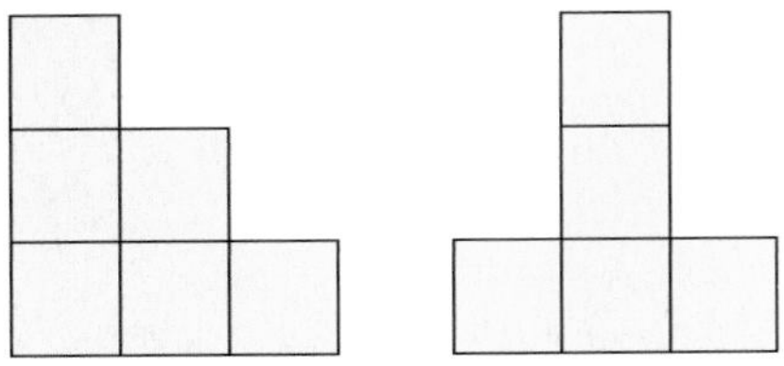

Left

Front

G3.1 3-D shapes

This spread will show you how to:

- Investigate 3-D shapes made from cuboids, using 2-D representations of 3-D shapes

Keywords
Cube
Cuboid
Edge
Face
Net
Prism
Pyramid
Solid
Three-dimensional (3-D)
Vertex

- A **solid** is a **three-dimensional (3-D)** shape.

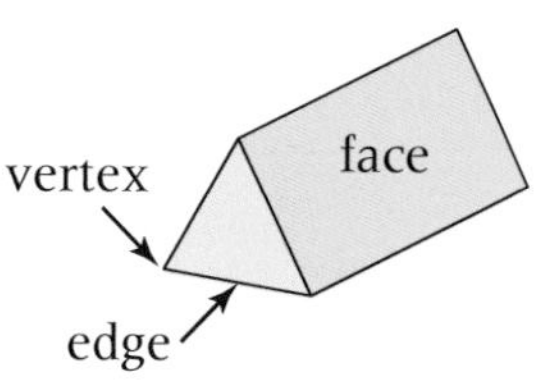

A **face** is a flat surface of a solid.
An **edge** is the line where two faces meet.
A **vertex** is a point at which three or more edges meet.

You need to know the names of these 3-D shapes.

The plural of vertex is vertices.

A **cube** has 6 square faces
12 equal edges
8 vertices

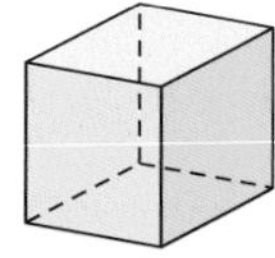

A **cuboid** has 6 rectangular faces
12 edges
8 vertices

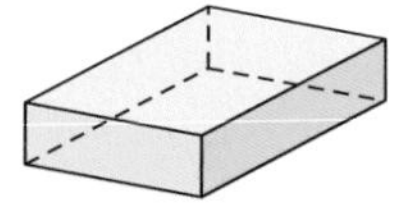

A **prism** has a constant cross-section.

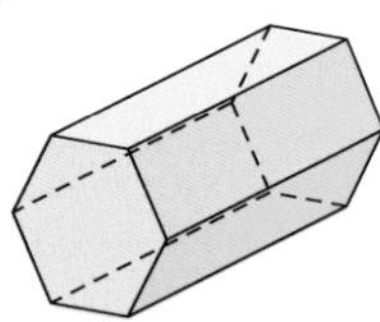

hexagonal prism

A **pyramid** has faces that taper to a common point.

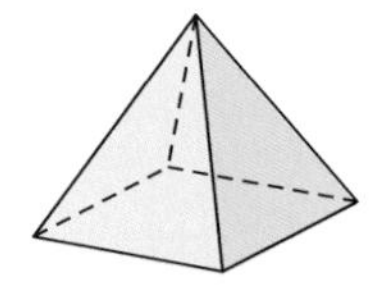

square-based pyramid

You name a prism by the shape of its cross-section.

You name a pyramid by the shape of its base.

- A **net** is a 2-D shape that can be folded to form a **3-D** shape.

p.280

Example

The nets of four solids are shown. Name the solid that can be made from each net.

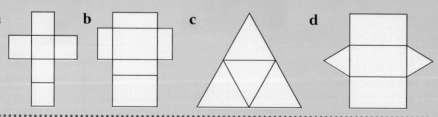

a **b** **c** **d**

---

a cube
b cuboid
c tetrahedron
d triangular prism

A tetrahedron has 4 faces – all equilateral triangles.

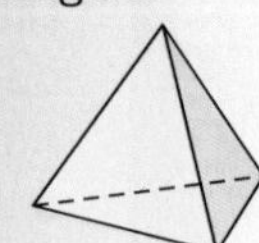

Exercise G3.1

Grade E/F

1 Give the mathematical name of each of these solids.

a 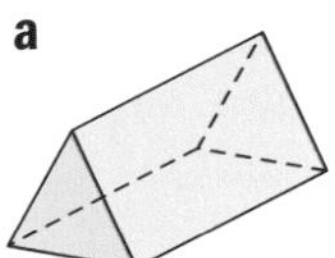

b 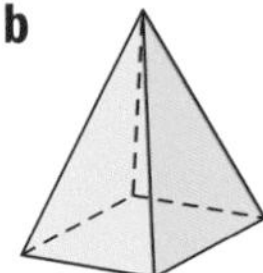

c 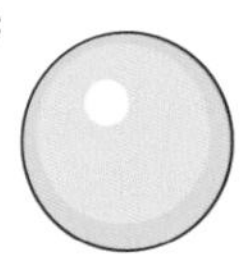

d 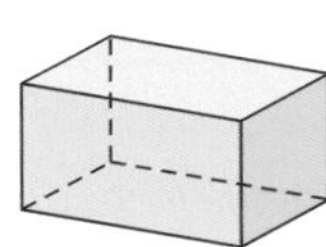

e 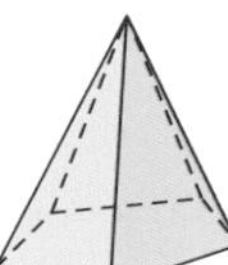

f 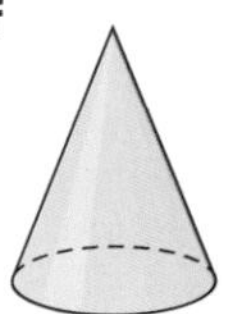

g 

h 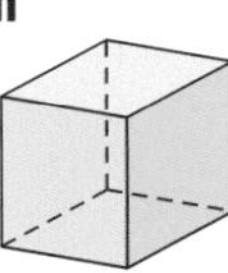

i 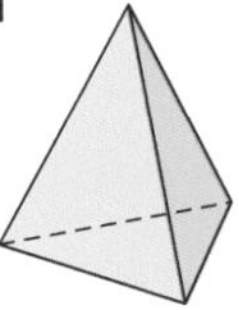

j 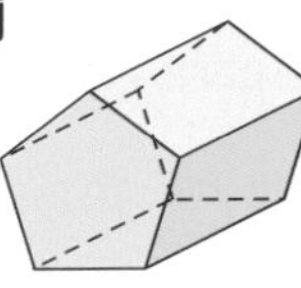

2 Draw

a a prism with a square cross-section

b a pyramid with a hexagonal base

c a tetrahedron.

3 This solid consist of eight triangles.
It is called an octahedron.
Write

a the number of faces

b the number of edges

c the number of vertices of this solid.

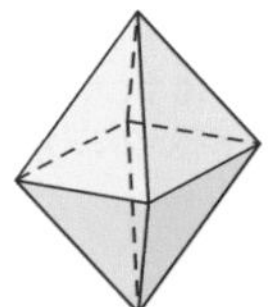

DID YOU KNOW?

In Science, a glass triangular prism is used to separate white light into rainbow colours.

AO3 Problems

4 a Copy and complete this table.

Name of solid	Number of faces (f)	Number of edges (e)	Number of vertices (v)
Cuboid	6	12	8
Triangular prism			
Square-based pyramid			
Tetrahedron			
Pentagonal prism			
Square-based prism			
Cube			
Hexagonal pyramid			
Octagonal prism			
Pentagonal pyramid			

b Write a relationship between f, e and v.

5 Sketch **six** different nets of a cube.

G3.2 Volume of a cuboid

This spread will show you how to:

- Calculate the volume of cuboids and shapes made from cuboids

Keywords
Cube
Cuboid
Cubic centimetre (cm^3)
Cubic metre (m^3)
Volume

- The **volume** of a 3-D shape is the amount of space it takes up.

You measure volume using **cubes**.

One **cubic centimetre** is 1 cm^3.

One **cubic metre** is 1 m^3.

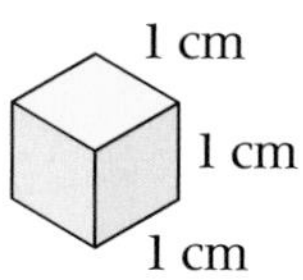

The ^{3} in cm^3 shows there are 3 dimensions in the cube: length, width and height.

You can find the volume of a **cuboid** by counting cubes.

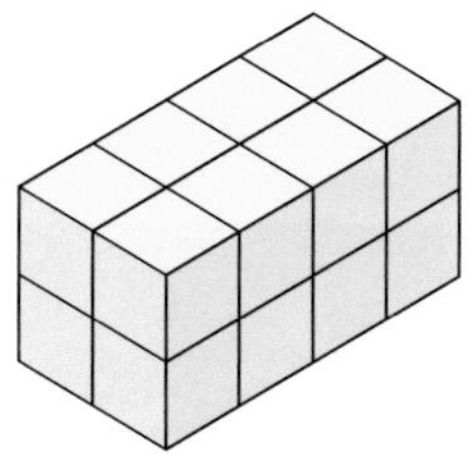

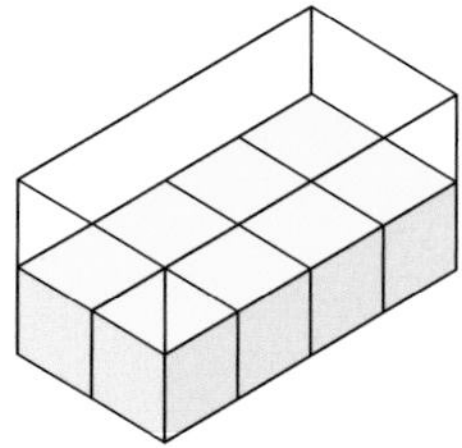

On the bottom layer there are 4 × 2 = 8 cubes.

For 2 layers, there are 2 × 8 = 16 cubes.

- Volume of cuboid = length × width × height.

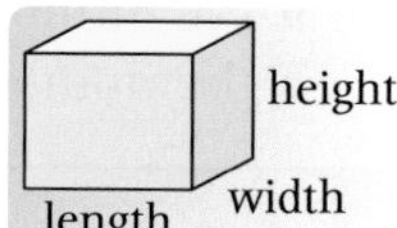

Example

Calculate the volume of each shape. State the units in your answers.

a

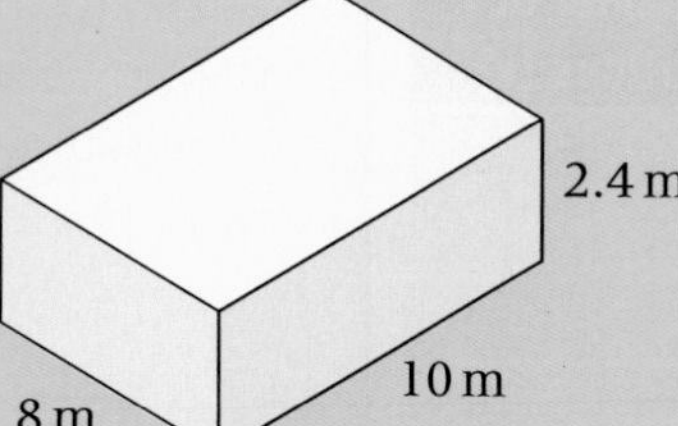

b

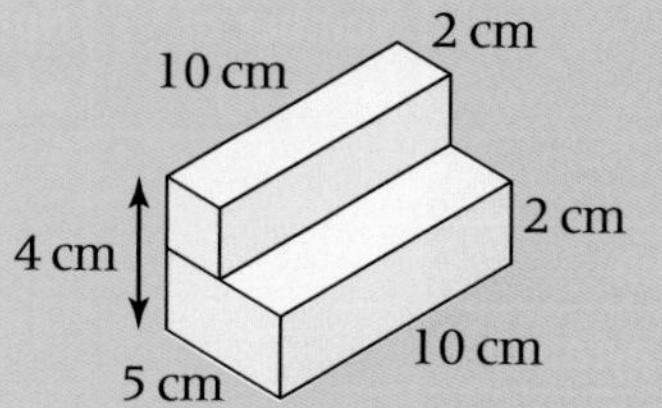

a Volume = length × width × height
$= 8 \times 10 \times 2.4 = 192\,m^3$

b Volume of yellow cuboid = length × width × height
$= 2 \times 2 \times 10$
$= 40\,cm^3$

2 cm
2 cm
10 cm

Volume of green cuboid = length × width × height
$= 5 \times 10 \times 2$
$= 100\,cm^3$

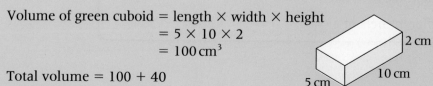

2 cm
5 cm
10 cm

Total volume = 100 + 40
$= 140\,cm^3$

Exercise G3.2 Grade E

1 Calculate the volume of each cuboid. State the units of each answer.

a

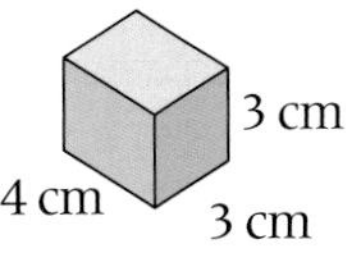

b

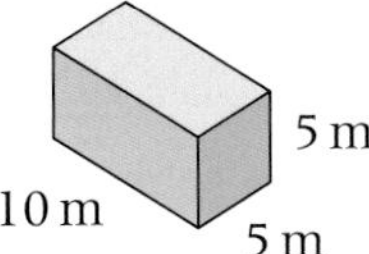

c

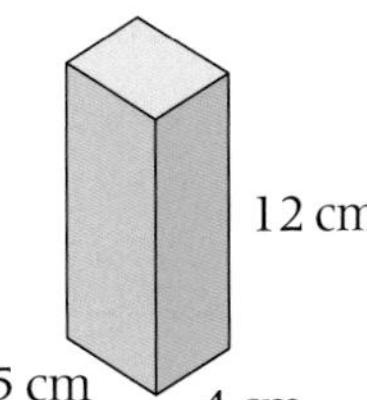

2 How many 1 cm cubes will fit into this box?

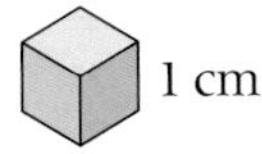

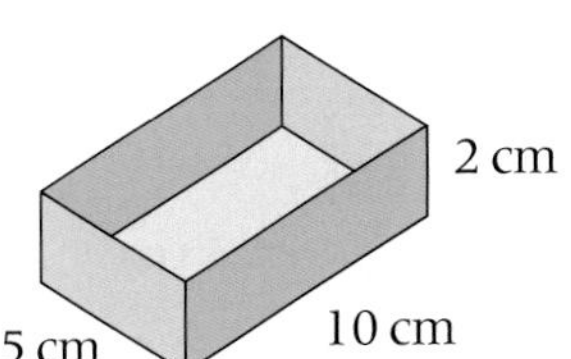

3 Calculate the volume of these cuboids. Give each answer to a suitable degree of accuracy.

a

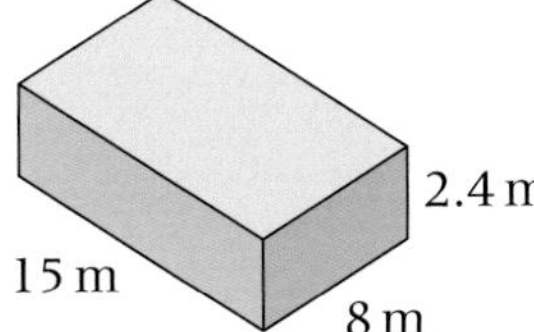

b

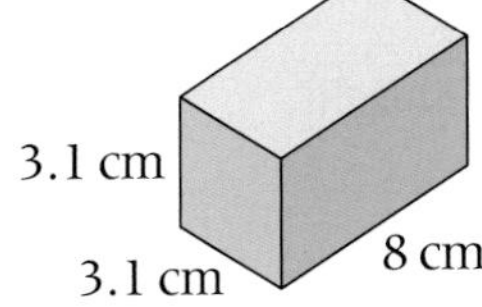

c

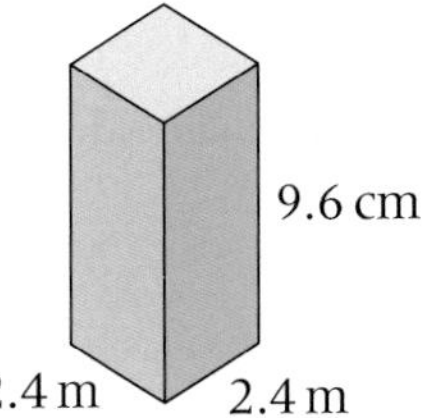

4 This cuboid has a square base.
The square measures 15 cm by 15 cm.
The volume of the cuboid is $1350\,\text{cm}^3$.
Calculate its height, in centimetres.

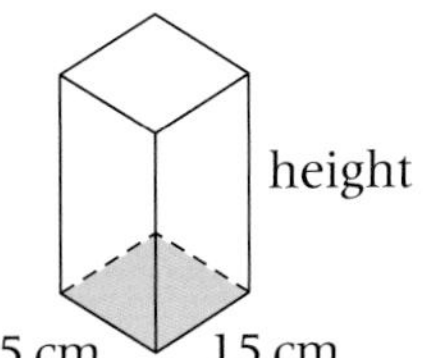

Volume = $15 \times 15 \times$ height
so
1350 = $15 \times 15 \times$ height

5 Calculate each unknown length. Give your answers to a suitable degree of accuracy.

a

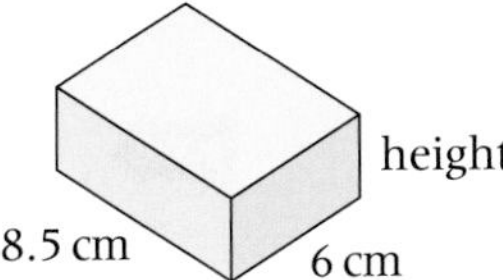
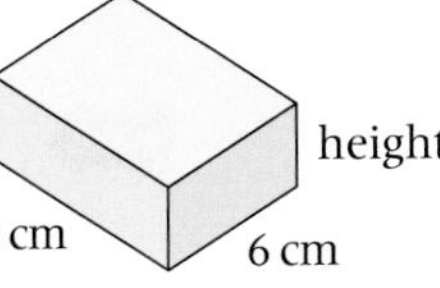

Volume = $153\,\text{cm}^3$

b

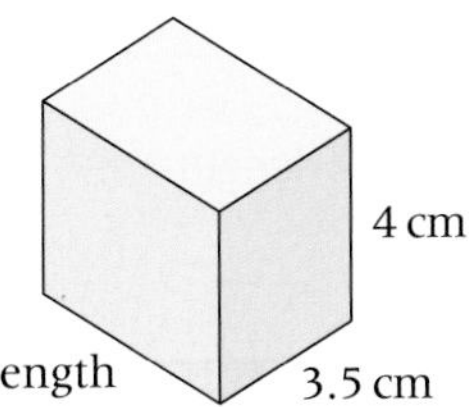

Volume = $80\,\text{cm}^3$

c

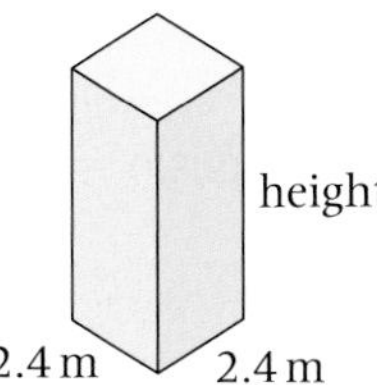

Volume = $50\,\text{m}^3$

6 Calculate the volume of each shape. State the units of your answers.

a

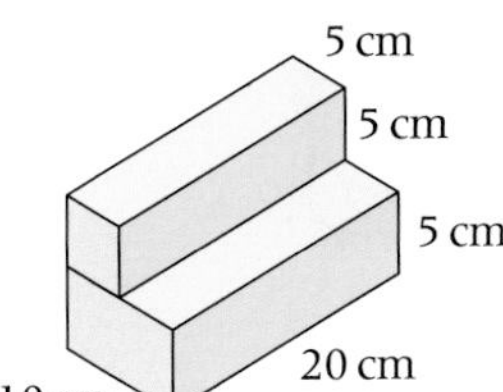

b

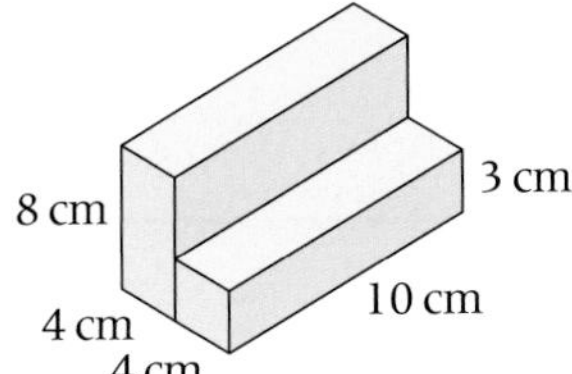

c

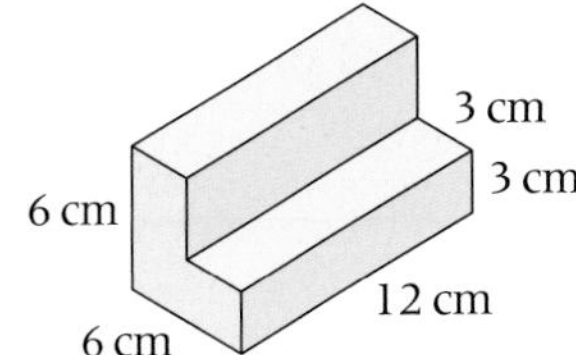

G3.3 Volume of a prism 1

This spread will show you how to:
- Calculate the volume of right prisms

Keywords
Cross-section
Cubic centimetre (cm^3)
Cubic metre (m^3)
Prism
Volume

The **volume** of a 3-D shape is the amount of space it takes up.

Volume is measured in cubic units: cubic centimetres (cm^3), cubic metres (m^3).

The ^{3} in cm^3 shows there are 3 dimensions in a cube: length, width and height.

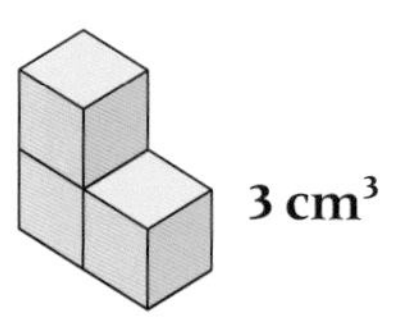

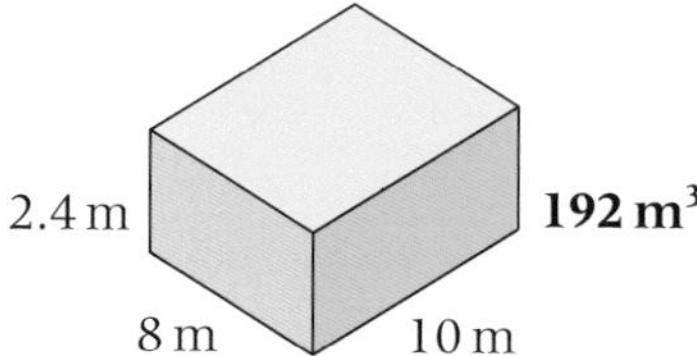

- Volume of a cuboid = length × width × height

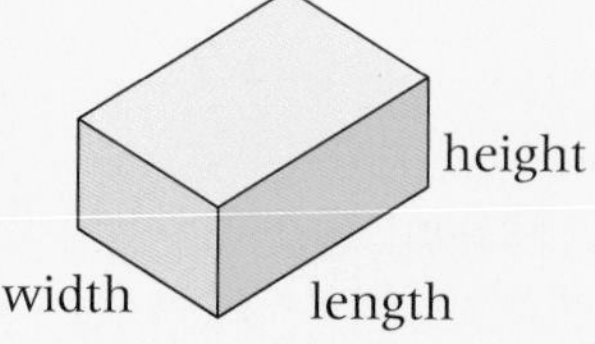

A **prism** is a 3-D shape with the same **cross-section** throughout its length.

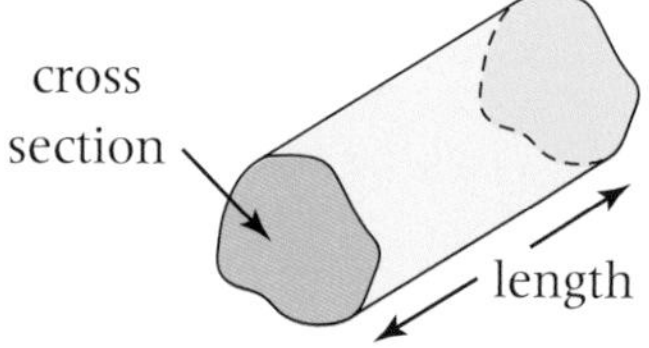

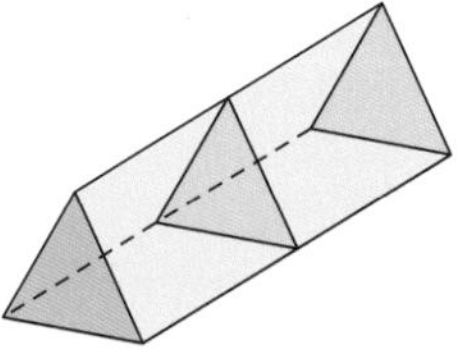

A cuboid is a prism.

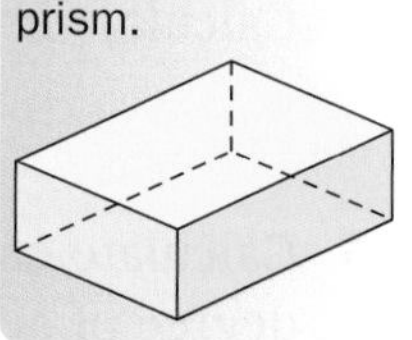

- Volume of a prism = area of cross-section × length

Example

Calculate the volume of this triangular prism. State the units of your answer.

Area of triangle $= \frac{1}{2} \times 4 \times 2 = 4\,m^2$
Volume of prism = area of triangle × 8
$= 4 \times 8 = 32\,m^3$

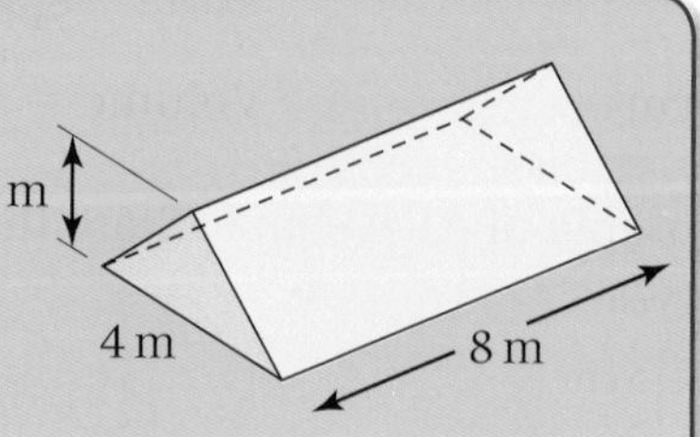

Exercise G3.3

Grade C

1 Calculate the volume of these cuboids.

a

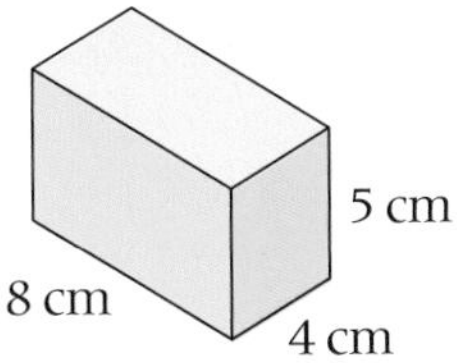

b

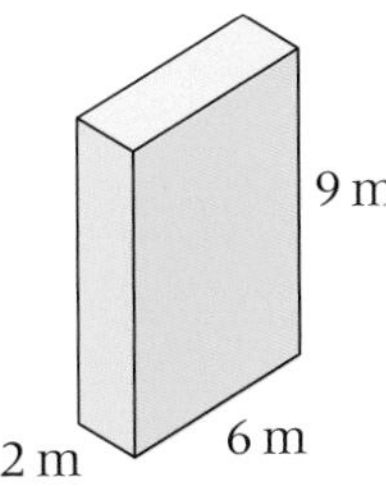

c

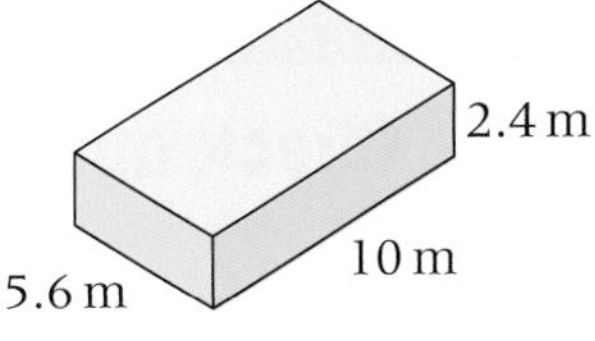

Give the units of your answers.

2 Calculate the volume of these cuboids.

a

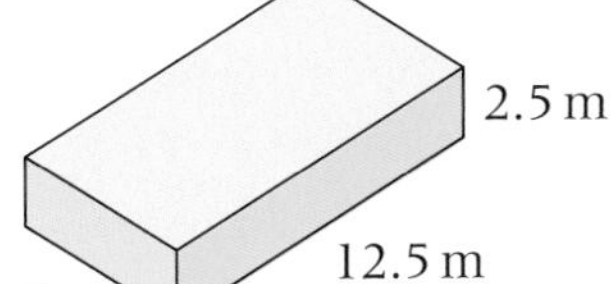

b

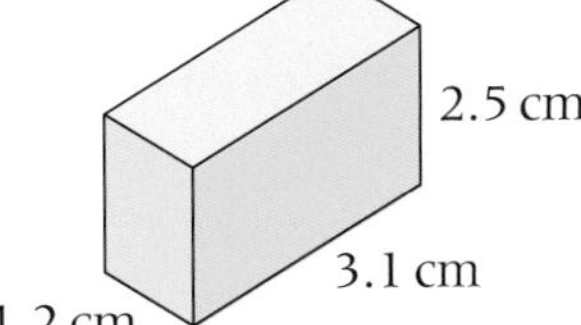

c

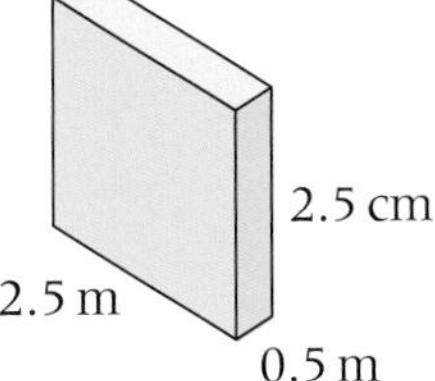

3 Calculate the area of cross-section and the volume for each prism.

a

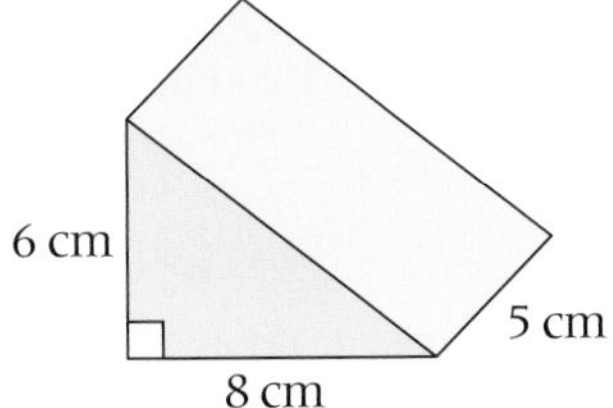

b

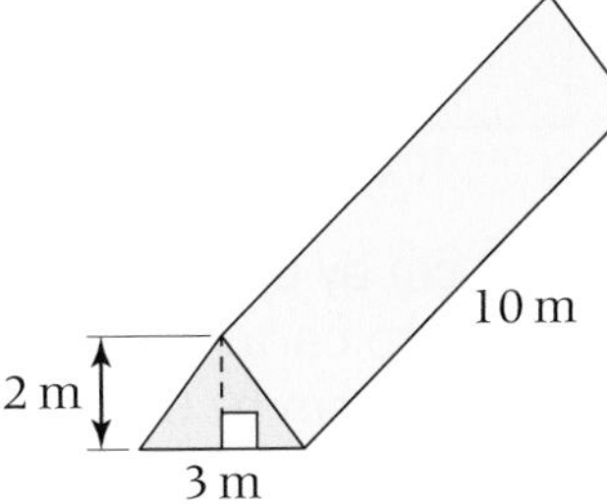

c

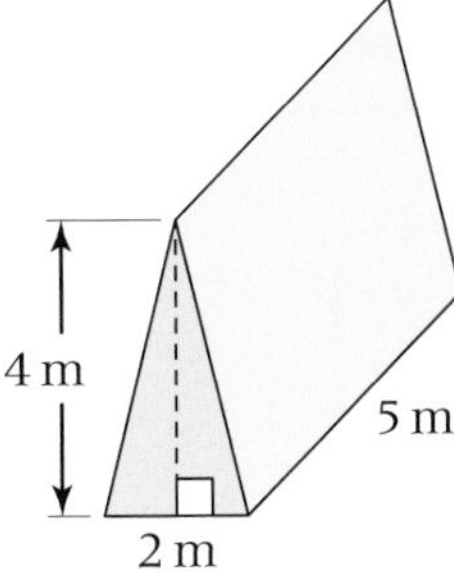

d

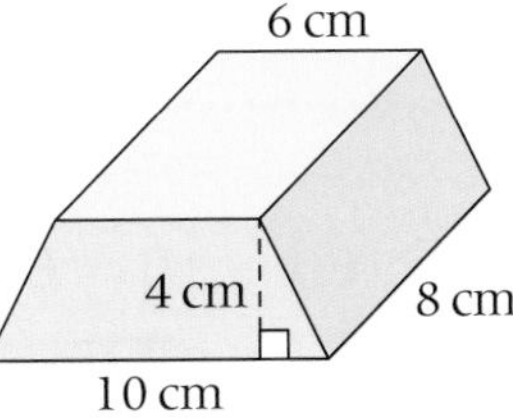

Functional Maths

A02

4 Marcus is planning to go camping, but requires a tent with a capacity greater than $5\,\text{m}^3$. He can borrow the tent shown. Does it fulfil Marcus' needs?

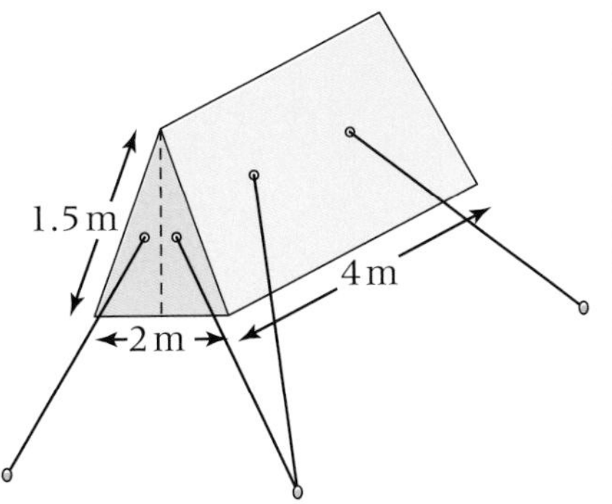

Summary

Check out

You should now be able to:

- Use 2-D representations of 3-D shapes
- Know the terms face, edge and vertex
- Draw nets and show how they fold to make a solid
- Calculate the volume of cuboids and shapes made from cuboids

Worked exam question

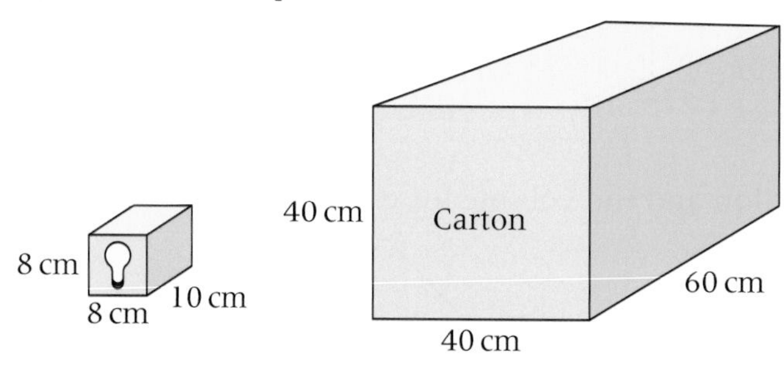

Diagram NOT accurately drawn

A light bulb box measures 8 cm by 8 cm by 10 cm.
Light bulb boxes are packed into cartons.
A carton measures 40 cm by 40 cm by 60 cm.

Work out the number of light bulb boxes which can completely fill one carton. (4)

(Edexcel Limited 2007)

$40 \div 8 = 5 \quad 40 \div 8 = 5 \quad 60 \div 10 = 6$
Number of boxes $= 5 \times 5 \times 6$
$= 150$ boxes

Show each division and the final multiplication calculations.

OR

Volume of the carton $= 40 \times 40 \times 60$
$= 96\,000 \text{ cm}^3$
Volume of a box $= 8 \times 8 \times 10 = 640 \text{ cm}^3$
Number of boxes $= 96\,000 \div 640$
$= 150$ boxes

Show each multiplication and the final division calculations.

Exam questions

1

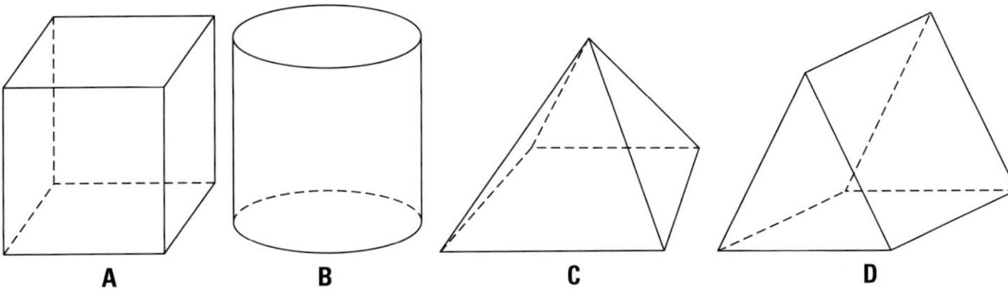

The diagram shows four 3-D solid shapes.

a Write down the number of vertices of shape **A**. (1)

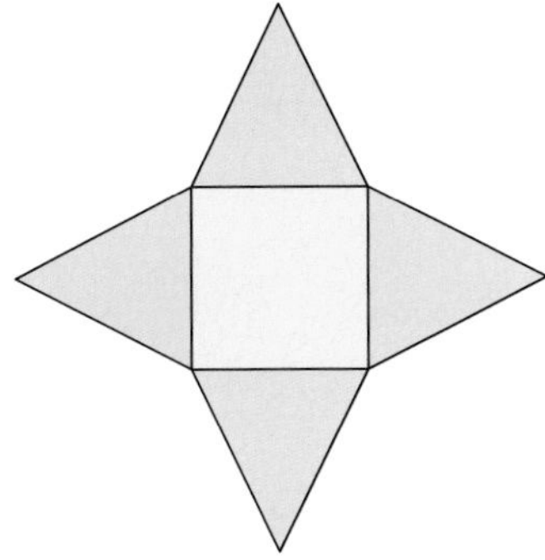

Here is the net of one of the shapes, **A**, **B**, **C** or **D**.

b Which shape? (1)

(Edexcel Limited 2009)

A02 + 3

2 Tasmin and Katie plan to go to a festival, and they need a tent like the one shown. They want to be able to stand up in it (they are both 5 feet 6 inches), and they both need to be able to lie down lengthways.

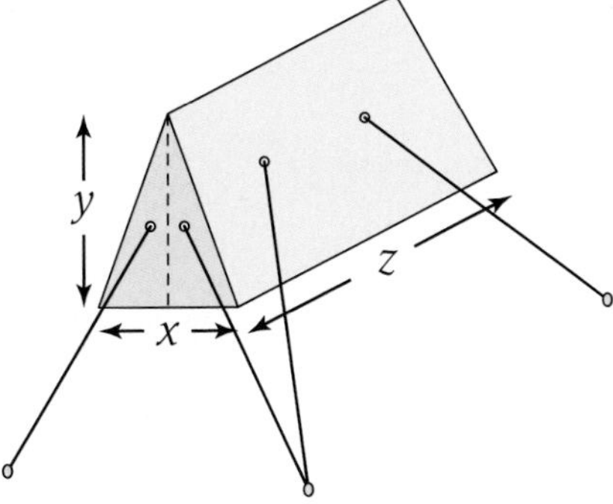

a Suggest suitable dimensions x, y and z for the tent, in centimetres. Give reasons for your choices. (4)

b Using your answer to part **a**, find the capacity of the tent in m^3. (2)

A3

Real-life graphs

Introduction

When sky divers jump out of an aircraft they immediately accelerate towards the earth under the force of gravity, until they reach terminal velocity at about 55m/s. When they pull their ripcord, they will decelerate before reaching a new constant velocity.

What's the point?

When a skydiver falls at terminal velocity the relationship between the distance travelled and the time taken is linear. This means that every second the skydiver is falling the same distance. The skydiver is then able to calculate the height at which to jump and for how long they can freefall safely.

Check in

1 Plot these points on a coordinate grid.

a (3, 6) **b** (−4, 2)

c (5, −3) **d** (−3, −1)

2 Copy and complete this table of values for the equation $y = 2x + 5$

x	−2	−1	0	1	2
y					

Orientation

What I should know	What I will learn	What this leads to
A1 →	■ Plot straight line graphs ■ Use graphs to find solutions ■ Draw and interpret graphs arising from real-life situations	→ A7

Rich task

In a store there are a range of different mobile phone packages available.

Package 1 Pay as you go 10p per minute
Package 2 £5 per month and then all calls at 5p per minute
Package 3 £12 per month, with 100 minutes of free calls, and then all calls at 3p per minute
Package 4 £25 per month, with 600 minutes of free calls, and then all calls at 2p per minute.

Which package is the best value for money?

A3.1 Drawing linear graphs 2

This spread will show you how to:

- Plot straight line graphs

Keywords
Explicit
Implicit

- To plot a graph of a function:
  - Draw up a table of values
  - Calculate the value of y for each value of x
  - Draw a suitable grid
  - Plot the (x, y) pairs and join them with a straight line.

p.32

This lesson revises the work done in A1.

Example

Draw the graph of $y = 3x - 4$.

First construct a table of values.

x	-2	-1	0	1	2
y	-10	-7	-4	-1	2

Choose four or five values, including negative values and zero.

Then plot the points and draw the line.

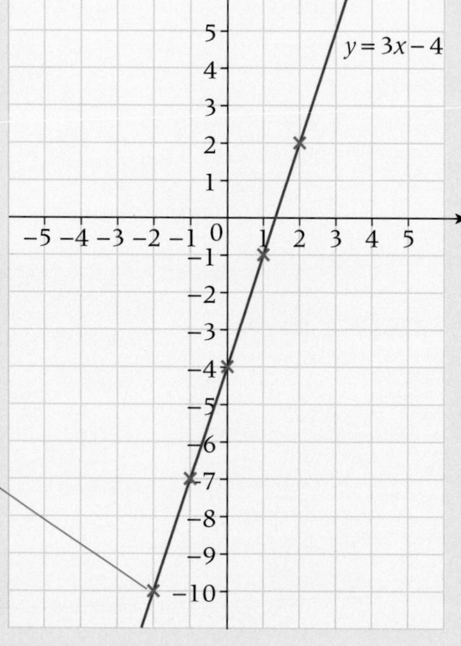

The smallest y-value is -10. Make sure your grid includes this value.

The equation $y = 3x - 4$ gives y **explicitly** in terms of x.
The equation $2x + 3y = 6$ gives y **implicitly** in terms of x.

An **explicit** function has the variables separated by the = sign.
An **implicit** function can have the variables on the same side of the = sign.

- To draw a graph of an implicit function:
  - Draw up a table of values for $x = 0$ and $y = 0$ **or**
  - Rearrange the equation to make y the subject.

For $2x + 3y = 6$:

x	0	$2x = 6$ $x = 3$
y	$3y = 6$ $y = 2$	0

For $2x + 3y = 6$:

$3x = 6 - 2y$

$y = \dfrac{6 - 2x}{3}$

x	-2	-1	0	1	2
y	$\frac{10}{3}$	$\frac{8}{3}$	2	$\frac{4}{3}$	$\frac{2}{3}$

Exercise A3.1

Grade C

1 **a** Copy and complete the table of values for $y = 2x + 5$.

x	-3	-1	0	1	3
y	-1			7	

b Draw the graph of $y = 2x + 5$ on a copy of the grid.

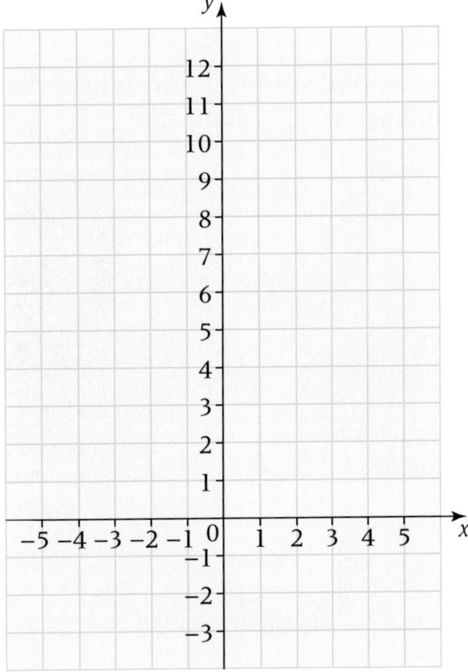

2 Draw the graphs of these functions.

a $y = 3x - 2$ **b** $y = -2x + 4$ **c** $y = \frac{1}{2}x + 3$ **d** $y = 5 - x$

3 Draw the graphs of these functions.

a $x + y = 4$ **b** $2x - y = 3$ **c** $2y + y = 4$ **d** $3y + 6y = 9$

4 Draw the graphs of these functions.

a $y = 5x - 3$ **b** $4y - y = 2$ **c** $y = 3 - 4x$ **d** $2x - 3y = 6$

AO3 Problem

5 Rearrange these equations to make y the subject. Which is the odd one out?

$y = 2x + \frac{1}{2}$ | $2y - 4x = 1$ | $4x + 2y = 1$ | $8x - 4y = -2$

6 **a** Draw the graph of $y = 3x + 4$.

b Use your graph to find

i the value of y when $x = \frac{1}{2}$ **ii** the value of x when $y = -\frac{1}{2}$.

AO3 Problem

7 Draw the graphs of these functions on the same axes.

a $y = 2x + 1$ **b** $y = 2x - 2$ **c** $y = 2x + 5$ **d** $y = 2x$

What do you notice?

8 Draw the graphs of these functions on the same axes.

a $y = -x$ **b** $y = -x + 3$ **c** $y = -x - 2$

What do you notice?

Where do you think the graph of $y = -x + 1$ would be on your grid?

Real-life graphs 1

This spread will show you how to:

- Draw and interpret graphs modelling real-life situations

Keyword
Model

You can use graphs to **model** the depth of water flowing in or out of a container at a constant rate.

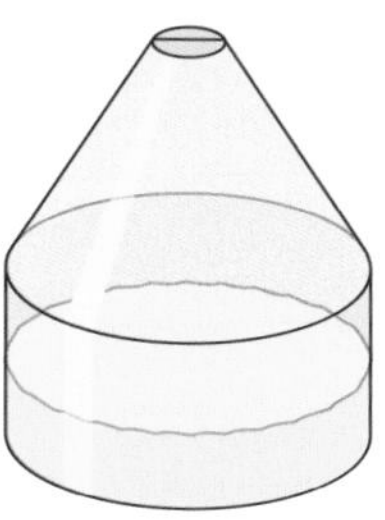

Imagine water filling this container.

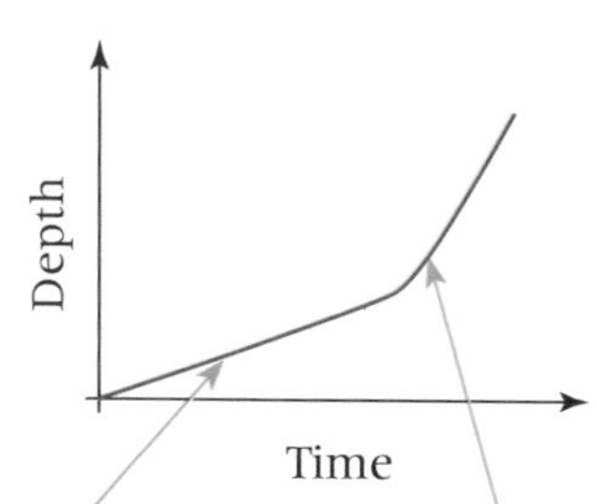

The bottom part of the container has the same diameter, so fills at a steady rate

The top part starts wide then narrows. As the container gets narrower, it fills faster.

- In a real-life graph involving time, time is usually represented by the x-axis.

Example

Sketch a graph to show what happens as

1. Sam fills a bath with both taps running
2. He realises it is too hot so turns off the hot tap
3. He turns off the cold tap
4. He gets in
5. Has a long soak
6. Gets out
7. Pulls out the plug.

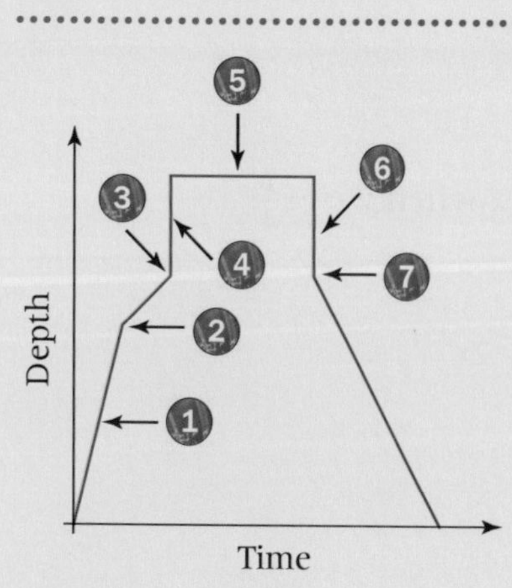

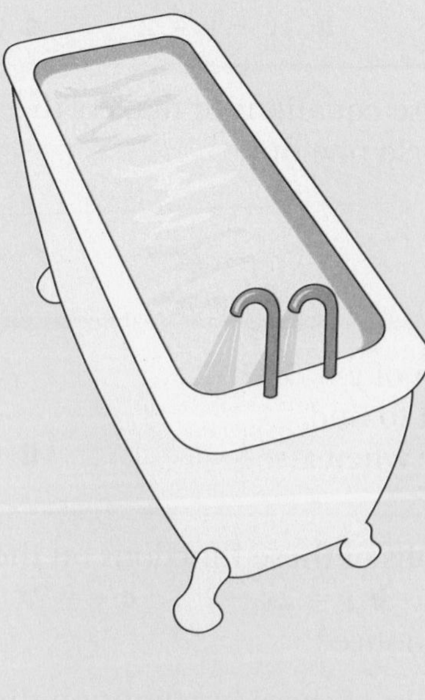

Label the axes with the quantities they represent.
A scale is not needed for a sketch graph.

Exercise A3.2 — Grade C

1 Match the four sketch graphs with the containers.

A

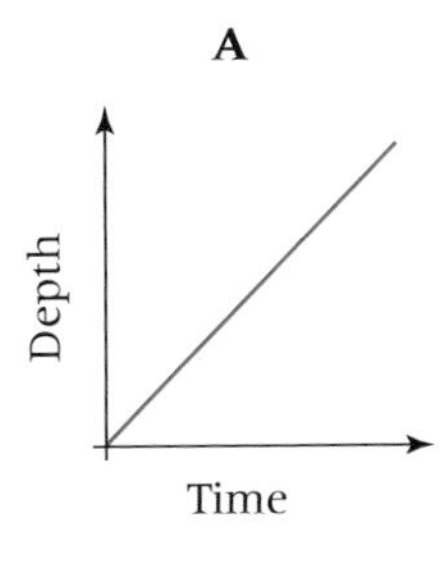

B

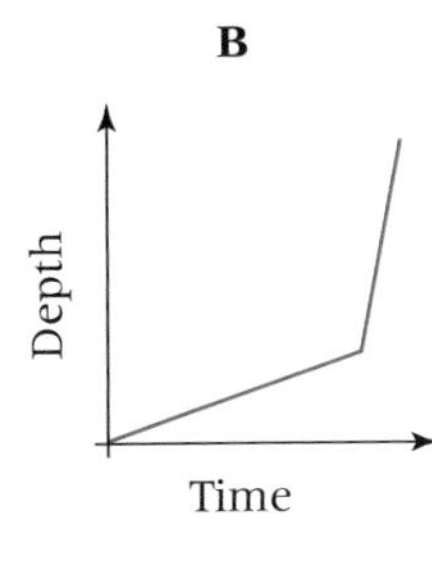

C

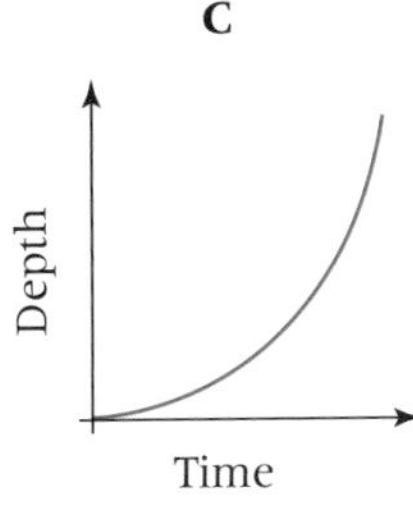

D

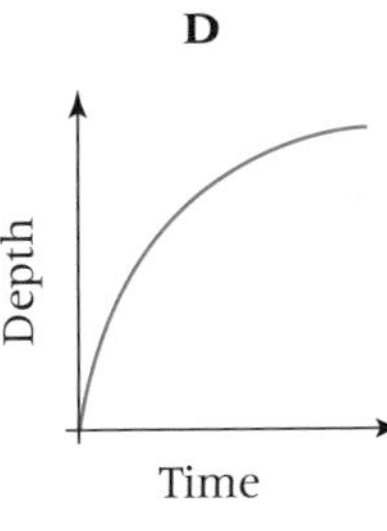

1

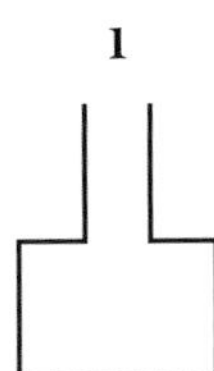

2

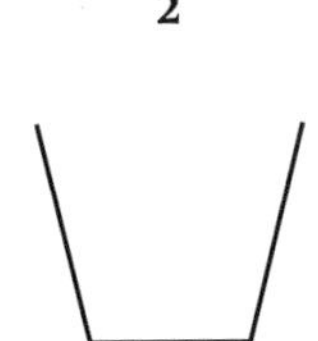

3

4

2 The sketch graph shows Andrew's height from 3 to 23 years of age. Explain what the graph shows at each stage and explain why this might be.

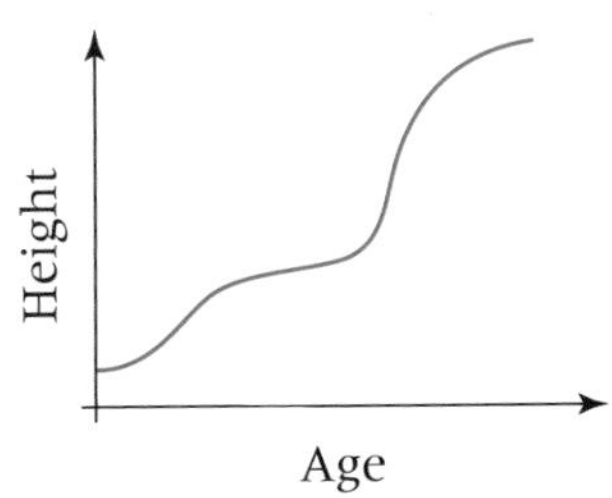

3 Sketch a graph of depth against time as this container is filled.

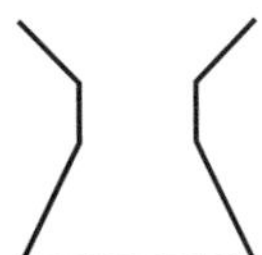

A02 Functional Maths

4 Construct sketch graphs to represent these situations.

a A woman is pregnant and puts on weight. When her baby arrives, she finds it difficult to lose any of the weight for six months, but then joins an exercise class and eats healthily. She is back to her natural weight a year and a half after becoming pregnant. (Graph is weight against time.)

b A frozen chicken is taken out of the freezer and left to defrost. Two hours later it is put in the microwave briefly to speed up and finish off the process. The chicken is then put in the oven to roast for Sunday lunch. (Graph is temperature against time.)

5 A skateboarder at a skate park uses a ramp, as shown. For one go on the ramp, construct a sketch graph of

a speed against time

b acceleration against time.

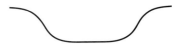

A3.3 Conversion graphs

This spread will show you how to:
- Draw and use conversion graphs

Keywords
Convert
Scale
Units

You can use a conversion graph to **convert**
- a distance in miles to a distance in kilometres
- a distance in kilometres to a distance in miles.

Example

Use the conversion graph to convert these distances.
a 2.5 miles to kilometres
b 6 km to miles

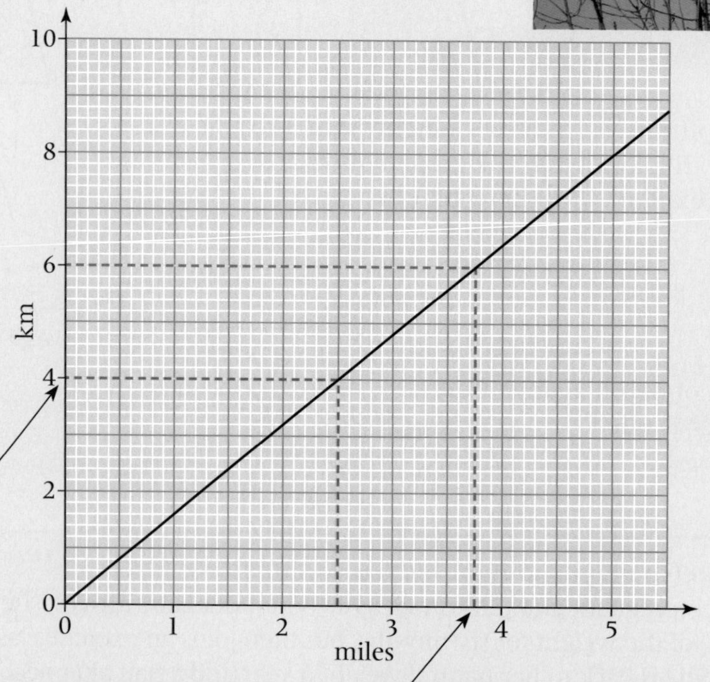

Read the **scale** on the axes carefully. The vertical axis goes up in 2s.

a To convert 2.5 miles to kilometres:
- Find 2.5 miles on the 'miles' axis
- Draw a vertical line up to the graph
- Draw a horizontal line across to the 'kilometres' axis
- Read off the value: 4 km.

b To convert 6 km to miles:
- Find 6 km on the 'kilometres' axis
- Draw a horizontal line across to the graph
- Draw a vertical line down to the 'miles' axis
- Read off the value: 3.75 miles.

- You can use a conversion graph to convert between units:
  - distance (miles ↔ km)
  - weight (pounds ↔ kg)
  - temperature (°C ↔ °F)
  - currency (£ ↔ €)

Exercise A3.3

Grade E

1 Use the conversion graph on page 168 to convert

a 3 miles to kilometres **b** 10 km to miles

c 4.5 miles to km **d** 2 km to miles.

Which is longer: 1 mile or 1 km?

2 Use this kilograms to pounds (lb) conversion graph to convert

a 6 lbs to kg

b 10 lbs to kg

c 4 kg to lbs

d 1.8 kg to lbs

e 7 lbs to kg

f 2.2 kg to lbs

g 12 lbs to kg

h 5 kg to lbs.

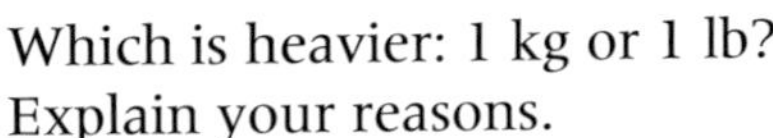

Which is heavier: 1 kg or 1 lb?
Explain your reasons.

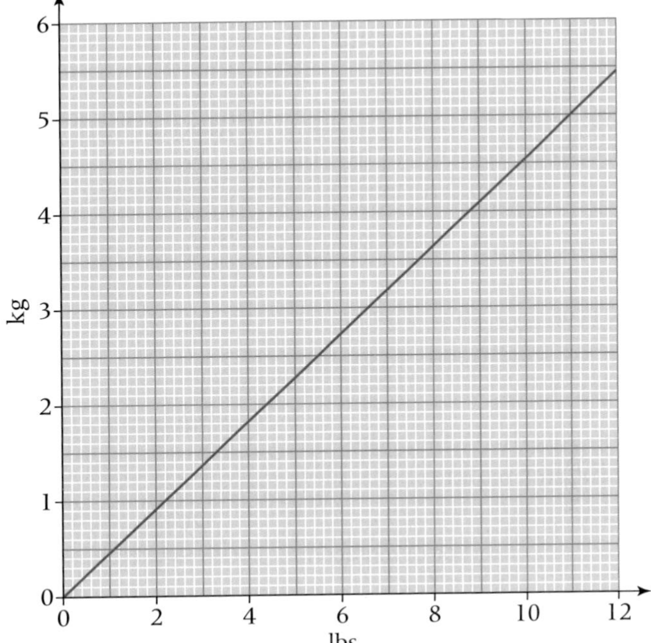

3 **a** Use this °C to °F conversion graph to convert these temperatures.

i 20 °C to °F

ii 58 °F to °C

iii 30 °C to °F

iv 20 °F to °C

b The freezing point of water is 0 °C.
What is the freezing point of water in °F?

c Copy this table.
Use the graph to convert the temperatures in this table to °F.

Reykjavik	Oslo	Paris	Madrid	Sydney
−2 °C	2 °C	6 °C	12 °C	24 °C
□ °F	□ °F	□ °F	□ °F	□ °F

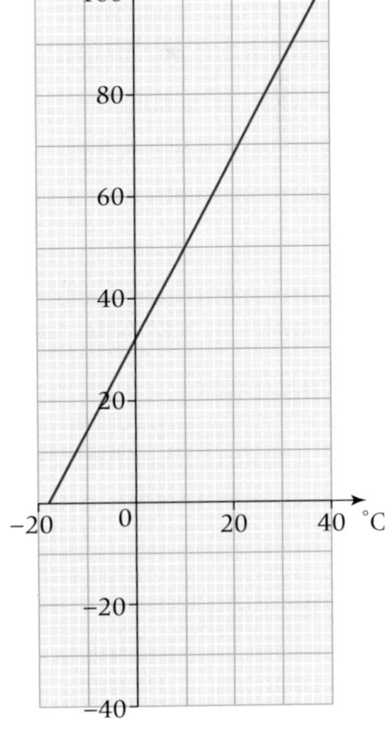

A3.4 Drawing conversion graphs

This spread will show you how to:

- Draw, discuss and interpret graphs arising from real-life situations

Keywords
Conversions
Exchange rate

Davina buys some euros for a trip to France.
The **exchange rate** is £1 = €1.20.

She draws a conversion graph to help her convert prices.

First she works out some simple **conversions** to plot on the graph:

Two points is enough to plot a straight line. The third point checks the line is accurate.

She wants to include prices up to £40.
£20 = €24, so £40 = €48.
The euros scale needs to go up to at least €50.

She chooses the scale so her graph fits her paper.

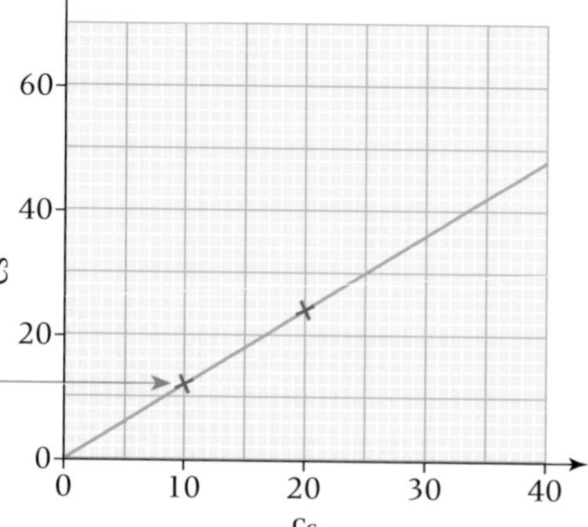

The graph has £s on the horizontal axis and euros on the vertical axis. You could use either axis for either currency.

To draw a conversion graph:

Work out three simple conversions

Decide on a suitable scale

Plot your three points

Join the points with a straight line, right to the edge of the grid.

Example

The conversion rate for miles to kilometres is
5 miles = 8 kilometres

a Work out two simple conversions you could plot for a miles to kilometres conversion graph.

b The graph needs to convert distances up to 50 miles. What is the highest value needed on the km scale?

a You know: 5 miles = 8 km
Try the zero value
0 miles = 0 km
Use doubling: 10 miles = 16 km.

b 5 miles = 8 km
So 5×10 miles = 8×10 km
50 miles = 80 km
The highest value needed on the km scale is 80 km.

Try the zero value – what is 0 miles in km?

Use doubling.

Exercise A3.4 Grade D

1 The conversion rate for millimetres to centimetres is

1 cm = 10 mm

a Work out two simple conversions you could plot for a millimetres to centimetres conversion graph.

b The graph needs to convert distances up to 10 cm. What is the highest value needed on the mm scale?

2 The conversion rate for pounds (lb) to kilograms (kg) is

1 kg = 2.2 lbs

a Copy and complete these conversions.

0 kg = ____ lbs

10 kg =____ lbs

5 kg = ____ lbs

b Copy the axes on to graph paper.

c Complete the labelling of the axes.

d Use your conversions from part **a** to draw a conversion graph from pounds to kilograms on your grid.

e Use your graph to convert

i 10 lbs to kg **ii** 5 lbs to kg

iii 3 kg to lbs **iv** 2.5 kg to lbs.

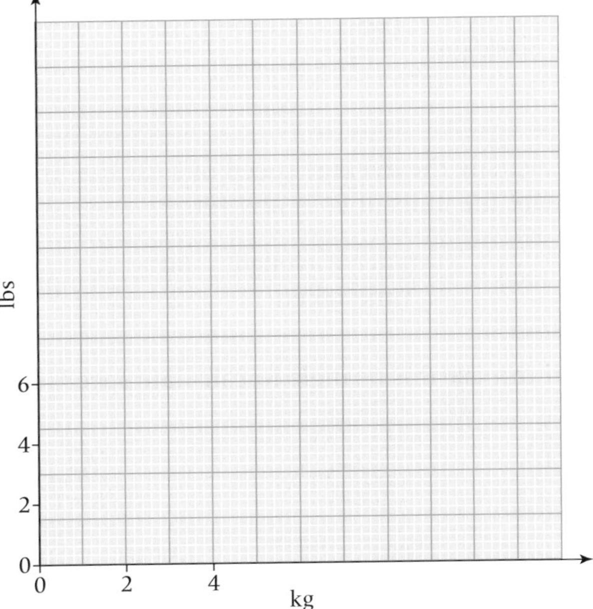

AO2 Functional Maths

3 One day the exchange rate for pounds (£) to US dollars ($) is

£1 = $1.70

a Work out three simple conversions you could plot for a pounds to dollars conversion graph.

b Max needs a graph to convert amounts up to £30 to dollars. What is the highest value needed on the dollars scale?

c Draw a conversion graph for pounds to dollars.

d Use your graph to find

i £5 in dollars **ii** $30 in pounds.

AO2 Functional Maths

4 The exchange rate for pounds to New Zealand dollars (NZ$) is

£1 = NZ$2.40

a Draw a conversion graph to convert amounts up to £20 to New Zealand dollars.

b Use your graph to decide which cap is cheapest.

A3.5 Compound measures

This spread will show you how to:

- Understand and use compound measures including speed

Keywords
Density
Distance
Mass
Speed
Time
Volume

Speed measures how fast something is moving.
Speed can be measured in metres per second (m/s), miles per hour (mph) or kilometres per hour (km/h).

- Speed (s) $= \dfrac{\text{Distance travelled } (D)}{\text{Time taken } (T)}$

Example

Calculate the average speed of a car that travels 50 miles in 2 hours.
State the units of your answer.

$$\text{Speed} = \frac{\text{Distance travelled}}{\text{Time taken}} = \frac{50}{2} = 25\,\text{mph}$$

25 mph is the average speed of the car.

You can use this triangle to calculate speed, distance or time.

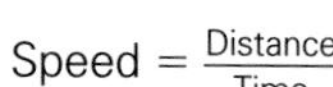

Speed $= \dfrac{\text{Distance}}{\text{Time}}$

Distance = Speed × Time

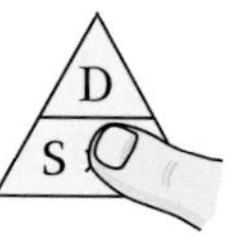

Time $= \dfrac{\text{Distance}}{\text{Speed}}$

Cover up the quantity you want to calculate.

Example

James walks at 4 km per hour for 30 minutes. How far does he walk?
State the units of your answer.

Distance = Speed × Time

$= 4 \times \frac{1}{2} = 2\,\text{km}$

Notice the different units of minutes and hours.

30 minutes $= \frac{1}{2}$ hour

Example

Priti's car uses 35 litres of petrol to travel 310 miles.
What is the rate of petrol consumption?

The rate of petrol consumption = 310 miles for every 35 litres
$= \frac{310}{35}$ for every 1 litre
= 8.857 14... miles for every litre
= 8.9 miles per litre (1 decimal place)

This means that for every 1 litre of petrol used the car travels 8.9 miles.

310 miles (÷ 8.9) 35 litres (× 8.9)

Exercise A3.5

Grade C

A02 Functional Maths

1 Cheryl takes 4 hours to walk 10 miles. Calculate her average speed, giving the units of your answer.

2 Copy and complete this table.

	Distance (m)	Time (s)	Speed (M/s)
a	40	5	
b	120	8	
c	3000	20	
d	480	12	
e	12.5	5	

3 A cyclist travels at 15 mph for $2\frac{1}{2}$ hours. How many miles is the journey?

4 Copy and complete this table.

	Distance (miles)	Time (hours)	Speed (mph)
a		4	80
b		7	25
c		6	45
d		2.5	20
e		2 hr 30 mins	50

5 I can usually drive at an average speed of 60 mph on the motorway. How long will a 150-mile journey take?

6 Copy and complete this table.

	Distance (km)	Time (h)	Speed (km/h)
a	160		80
b	20		8
c	70		20
d	27		6
e	100		30

7 A 420-km journey by car takes 6 hours and uses 30 litres of petrol. Calculate

a the average speed **b** the petrol consumption in km per litre.

8 An athlete runs 1500 m in 4.5 mins. Calculate the athlete's speed in

a metres per minute **b** metres per second.

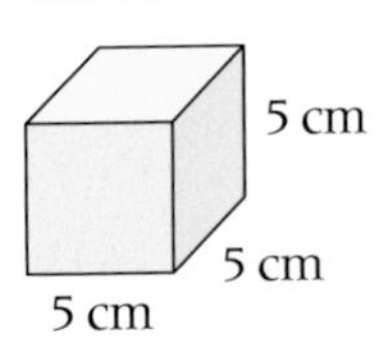

Did you know?

Hybrid vehicles combine an internal combustion engine with an electric motor and battery to reduce fuel consumption. Some use half as much fuel as a normal car over the same distance.

A3.6 Distance–time graphs

This spread will show you how to:

- Draw, discuss and interpret distance–time graphs

Keywords
Distance
Time

- A distance–time graph represents a journey.
- It shows how the **distance** from the starting point changes over **time**.

This distance–time graph illustrates Ayesha's shopping trip to Birmingham.

The vertical axis represents the distance from home.

The horizontal axis represents the time from when the trip starts.

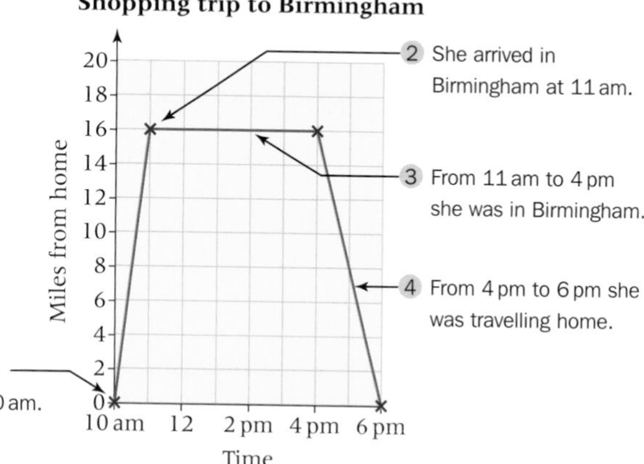

- On a distance–time graph, a horizontal line represents a stay in one place.

Example

The Smith family were going on holiday. The distance–time graph shows the first part of their journey.

a What time did they set off?
b How far did they drive before they stopped for a break?
c How long did they stop for?
d The journey to Sunshine-on-Sea is 240 km. The Smiths arrived at 4 pm. Copy and complete the graph to show the last part of their journey.

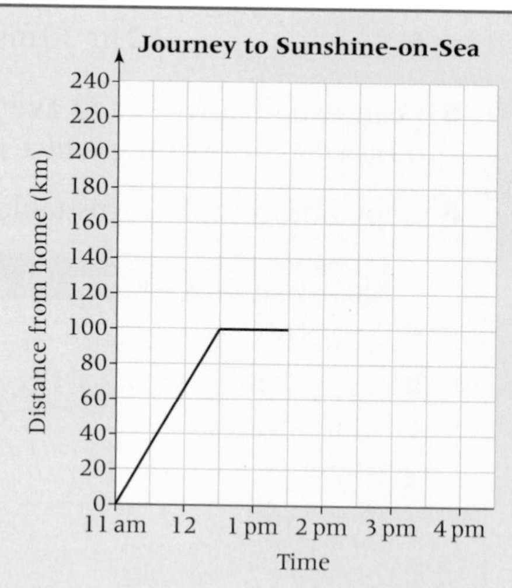

a They set off at 11 am.
b They drove 100 km before stopping.
c 12.30 to 1.30 = 1 hour
d Journey ends at 4 pm, 240 km.

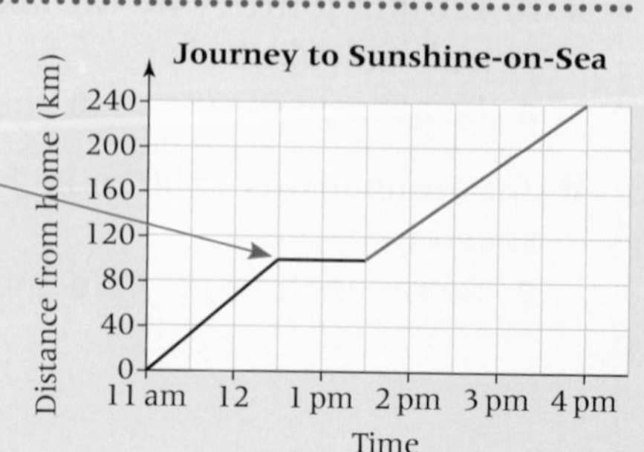

Exercise A3.6

Grade E

1 The distance–time graph illustrates the first part of a coach tour.

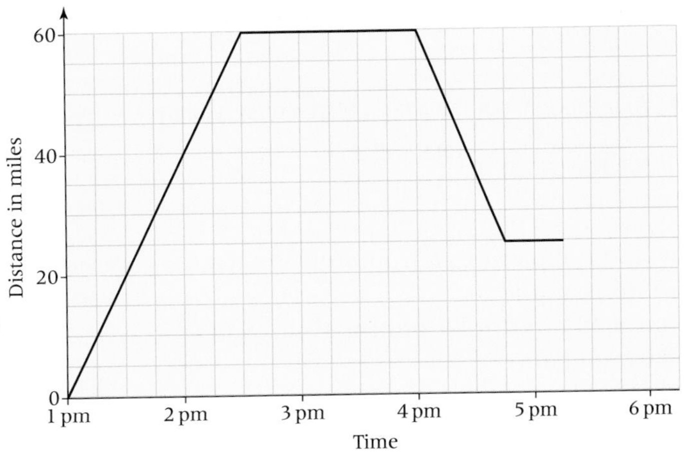

a What time did the coach tour set off?

b The coach arrived at Kinross Castle at 2.30 pm. How many miles did the coach drive to the castle?

c How long did the coach stop at the castle?

d The tour stopped for a tea break at 4.45 pm. How far from home were they?

e The tea break lasted $\frac{1}{2}$ hour. Then the coach drove home, arriving at 6 pm. Copy the graph and complete it to show the whole tour.

2 The graph illustrates a cycle ride. Match each section of the graph to a part of the description below.

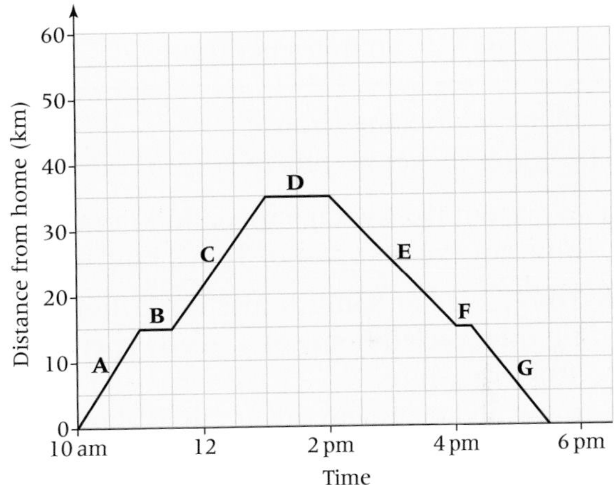

a 15 minute tea break

b Cycle 20 km in $1\frac{1}{2}$ hours

c 1 hour lunch break

d Cycle 15 km in 1 hour

e Cycle 15 km in $1\frac{1}{4}$ hours

f $\frac{1}{2}$ hour rest

g Cycle 20 km in 2 hours

3 The graph represents Karim's car journey to Cornwall.

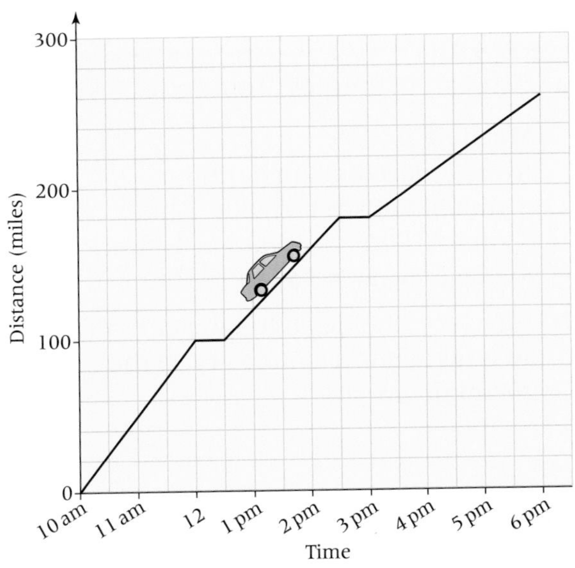

a How long did the journey take him altogether?

b How many miles was the journey altogether?

c How long did it take him to drive the first 100 miles?

d How long did he stop for at 12 pm?

e After his break at 12 pm, he drove another 80 miles before he stopped again. How long did it take him to drive this 80 miles?

A3.7 Average speed

This spread will show you how to:
- Work out an average speed from a distance–time graph

Keywords
Average speed

- You can work out the **average speed** for a journey from a distance–time graph.

$$\text{Average speed} = \frac{\text{total distance}}{\text{total time}}$$

The graph illustrates a train journey from York to Banbury.
From 8.30 pm until 9 pm the train waits at Birmingham.
The whole journey is 200 miles.
The whole journey takes 4 hours.
The average speed for the whole journey is

$$\text{Average speed} = \frac{\text{total distance}}{\text{total time}}$$
$$= \frac{200}{4} = 200 \div 4$$
$$= 50 \text{ miles per hour}$$

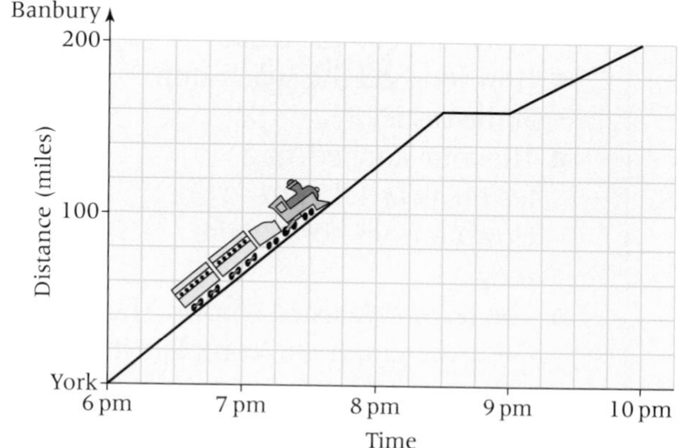

Example

Tom cycled to Sam's house.
The graph shows his journey.

a Work out the average speed in km per hour for the first part of Tom's journey.

b Tom stayed at Sam's house for $1\frac{1}{2}$ hours.
He then cycled home at a steady speed of 20 km per hour.
Copy and complete the graph to show this information.

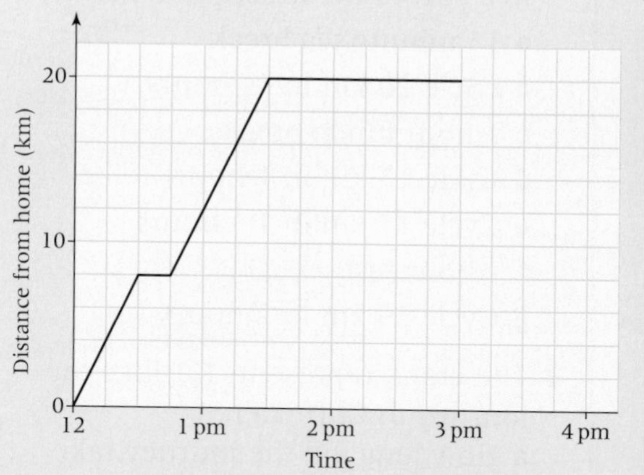

---

a First part of journey, Tom cycles 8 km in $\frac{1}{2}$ hour.

Method 1
Average speed in km per hour
= number of km cycled in 1 hour
8 km in $\frac{1}{2}$ hour → 16 km in 1 hour
Average speed = 16 km per hour

Method 2
Using the formula:
Average speed = $8 \div \frac{1}{2}$
= 16 km per hour

For speeds in km per hour, use distances in km and times in hours.

b Tom cycles home at 20 km per hour.
So it takes him 1 hour to cycle the 20 km home.

Exercise A3.7

Grade C

Functional Maths

A02

1 The graph shows Shani's journey to her grandmother's house.

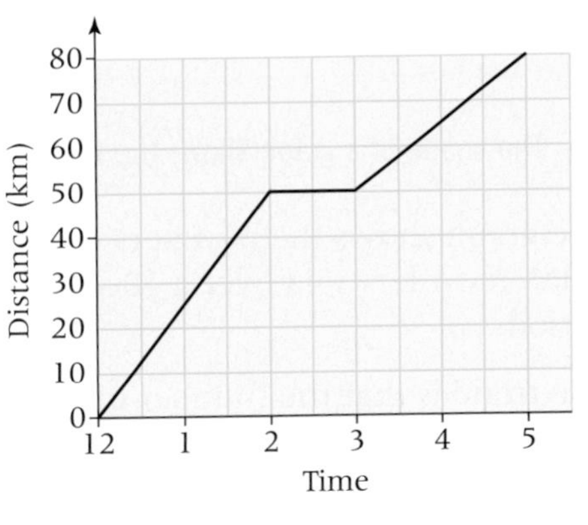

a What was the total distance she travelled?

b What was the total time for the journey?

c Work out the average speed for the complete journey using the formula

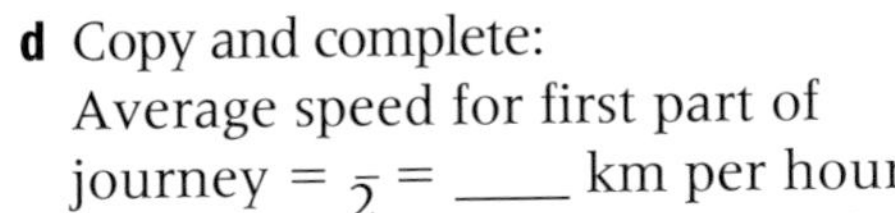

$$\text{Average speed} = \frac{\text{total distance}}{\text{total time}}$$

d Copy and complete:
Average speed for first part of journey $= \frac{\_}{2} =$ ____ km per hour

e Work out the average speed for the second part of her journey.

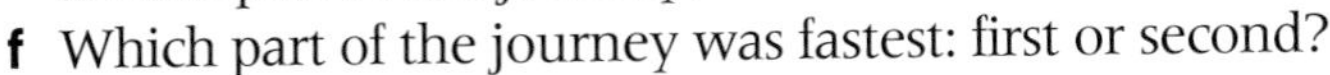

f Which part of the journey was fastest: first or second?

g Copy and complete:
The steeper the graph, the ________ the speed.

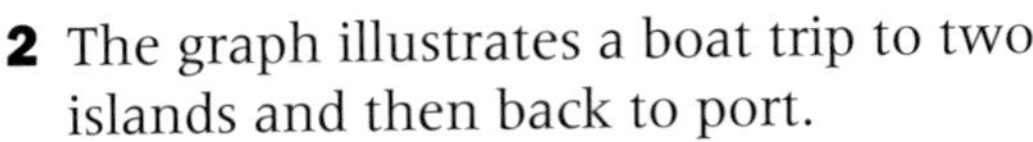

2 The graph illustrates a boat trip to two islands and then back to port.

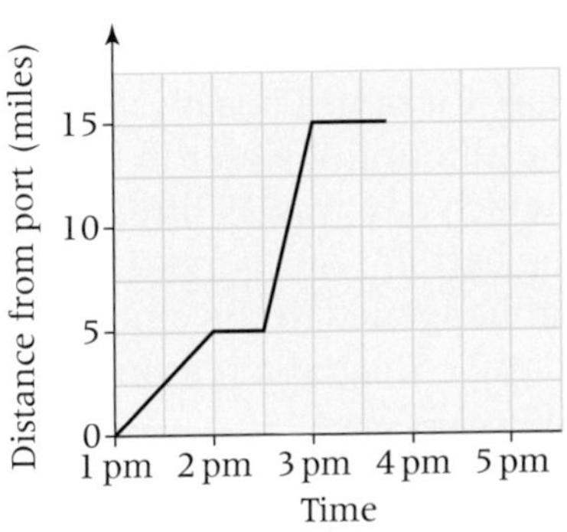

a How far from port was the first island?

b How long did the boat stop at the first island?

c From the graph, on which part of the trip was the boat travelling fastest? Explain how you know.

d Work out the average speed for the trip to the first island.

e How many miles is it from the first island to the second?

f How long did it take to travel from the first island to the second?

Use your answers to parts **e** and **f**.

g Work out the average speed for the second part of the trip, to the second island.

h How far is the second island from the port?

i The boat waited for $\frac{3}{4}$ hour at the second island and then sailed back to port at a steady speed of 15 miles per hour.
Copy and complete the graph for the trip.

j What time did the boat arrive back in port?

3 Here is a graph showing part of Dave's trip to the dentist.

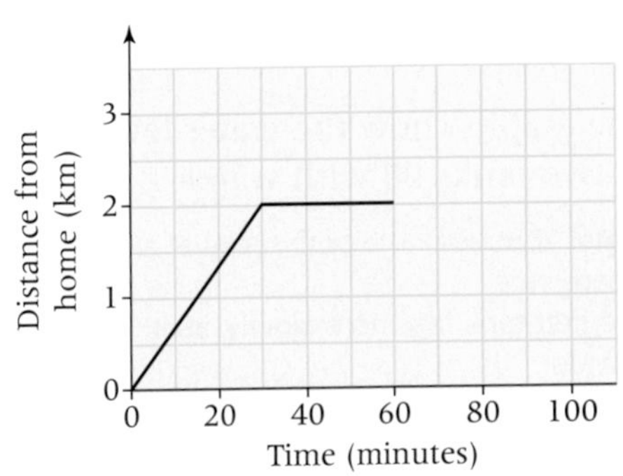

a How far is the dentist's from Dave's home?

b Dave took 30 minutes to walk to the dentist's.
Work out his walking speed in km/h.

c Dave was at the dentist's for 30 minutes.
Then he jogged home at 6 km/h.
Copy and complete the travel graph.

A3.8 Real-life graphs 2

This spread will show you how to:
- Interpret real-life graphs

Keywords
Decrease
Increase
Trend

- The shape of a graph shows the **trend**.

The graph shows the numbers of video recorders sold over a 10 year period.

The trend is that the number of video recorders sold is **decreasing**.

You can read information from a graph, but read the axis labels and scale carefully.

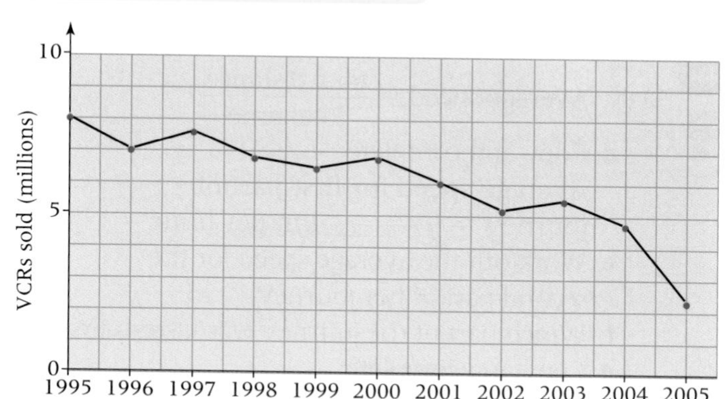

Example

The graph shows the amount of rainwater in a barrel over a few days.

a On day 1 it rained heavily. What happened to the amount of water in the barrel?
b On which day was 25 litres poured out of the barrel?
c What happened to the amount of water on day 2? Suggest a reason for this.

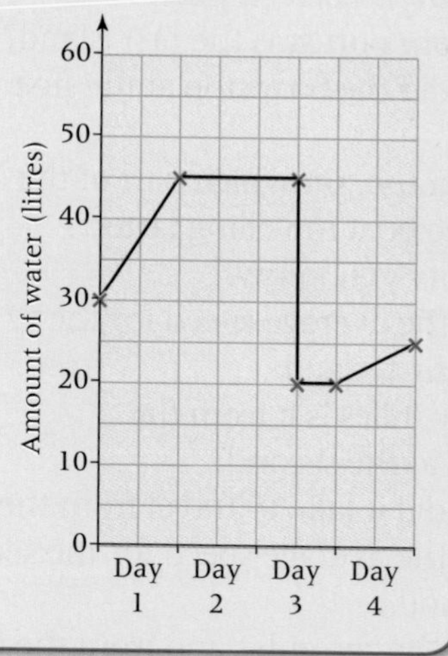

a The amount of water increased.
b Day 3, as the amount suddenly reduced by 25 litres.
c Amount of water stayed the same. It probably did not rain on day 2 and no water was poured out.

Think what could affect the amount of water.

- A straight line shows that a quantity is changing at a steady rate.
The steeper the slope, the faster the change.

quantity **increasing** | no change | quantity **decreasing**

p.166

The graphs show the water level as two tanks fill with water.

Water is poured into both tanks at a steady rate.
The first tank fills more slowly, as it is wider.
The second tank fills more quickly, as it is narrower.

The steeper the slope, the faster the change in water level.

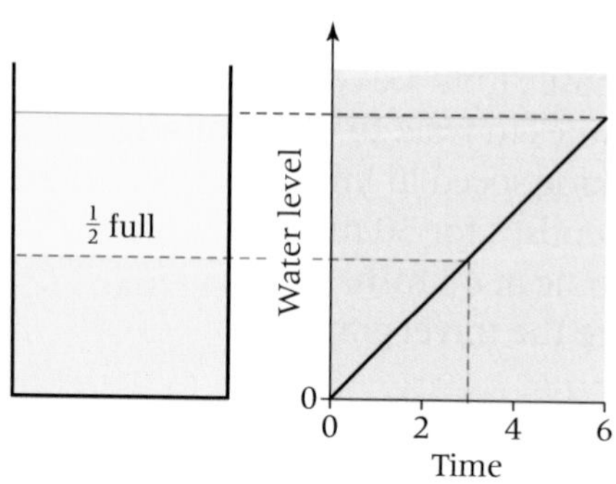

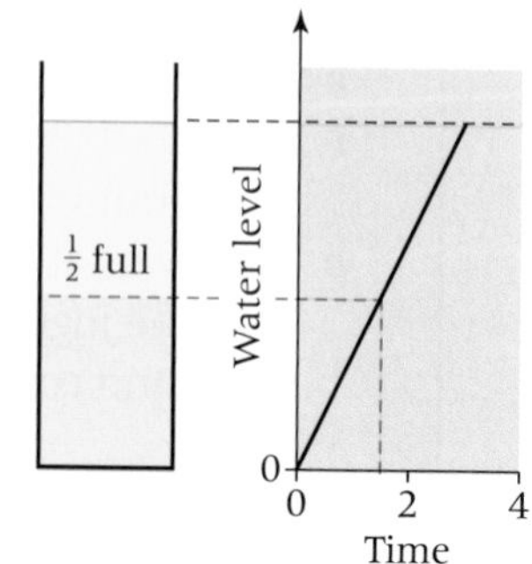

Exercise A3.8

Grade C

Functional Maths

AO2

1 The graph shows sales of 'Time 2 Chat' mobile phones.

a How many phones were sold in March?

b How many phones were sold in June?

c How many more phones were sold in June than in January?

d Here are the sales figures for the next three months.

Month	October	November	December
Number of phones sold	400	325	400

Copy the graph and complete it for this information.

e What happened to sales in November and December? Suggest a reason for this.

f What overall trend does the graph show?

2 The graph shows how a bean plant grew from a seed over several weeks.

a How tall was the plant after 6 weeks?

b How much did the plant grow between weeks 8 and 10?

c How tall did the plant grow in total?

d How much did the plant grow between 15 and 20 weeks.

e Is the plant likely to reach a height of 3 metres? Explain your answer.

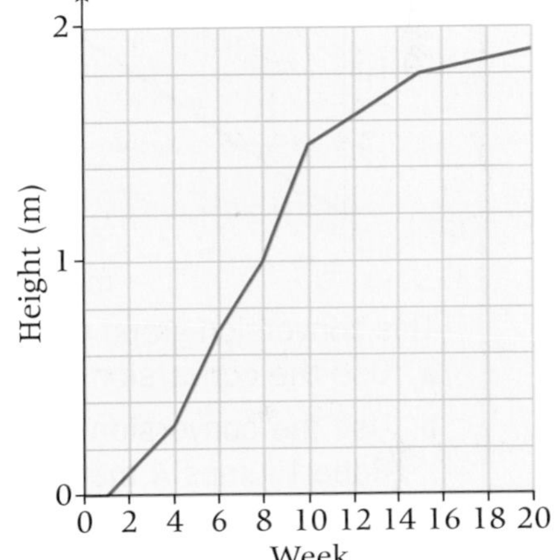

3 Rain rushes into these rain barrels at a steady rate.
The graphs show how the water level changes.
Match each graph to a rain barrel.

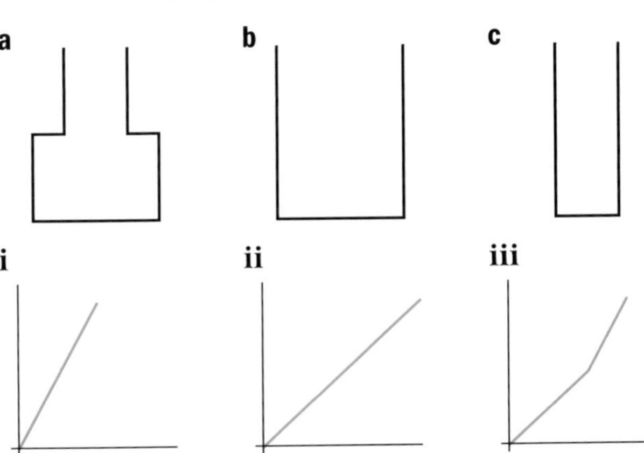

Summary

Check out

You should now be able to:

- Plot straight line graphs of functions in which y is or is not the subject
- Draw, discuss and interpret graphs arising from real-life situations
- Draw and interpret conversion graphs
- Read values from a graph

Worked exam question

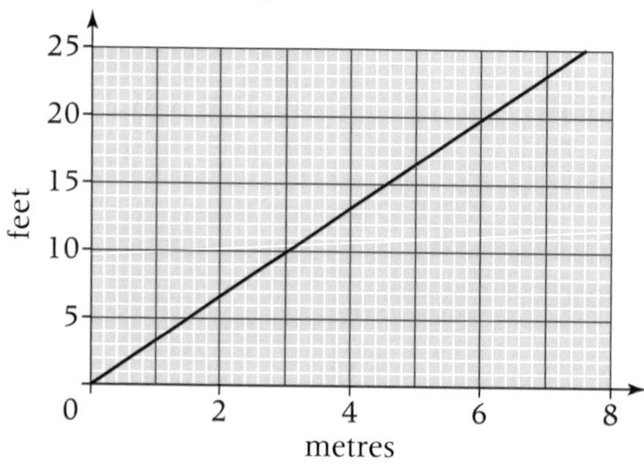

This conversion graph can be used to change between metres and feet.

a Use the conversion graph to change 6 metres to feet. (1)

b Use the conversion graph to change 8 feet to metres. (1)

Robert jumps 4 metres.

James jumps 12 feet.

c **i** Who jumps furthest, Robert or James?

ii How did you get your answer? (2)

(Edexcel Limited 2008)

---

a 20 feet ← Make sure you use the correct scale for each conversion.

b 2.4 metres

c **i** Robert
ii Using the graph, 4 metres is 13 feet. ← You need to convert 4 metres to feet.

OR

c **i** Robert
ii Using the graph, 12 feet is 3.6 metres. ← You need to convert 12 feet to metres.

Exam questions

1 Here are six temperature/time graphs.

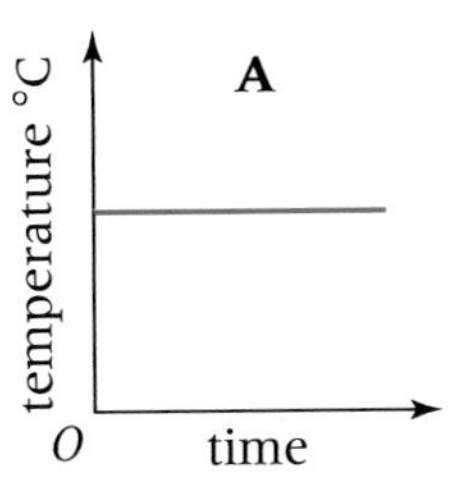

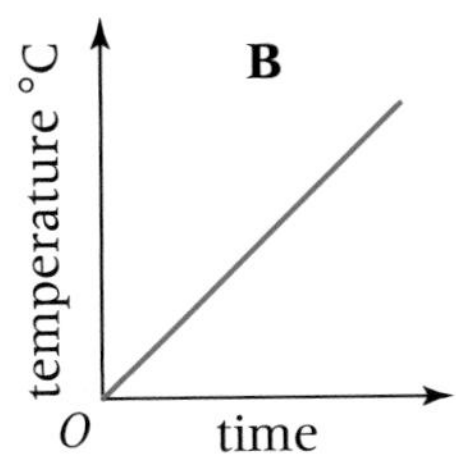

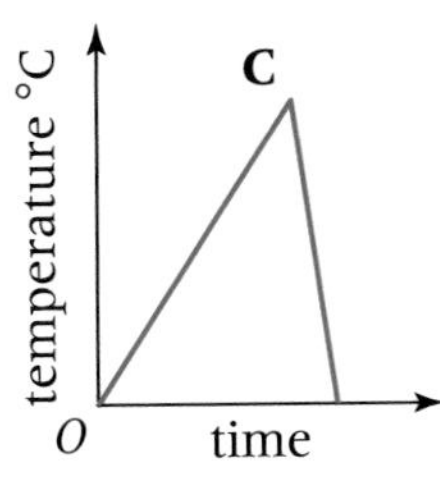

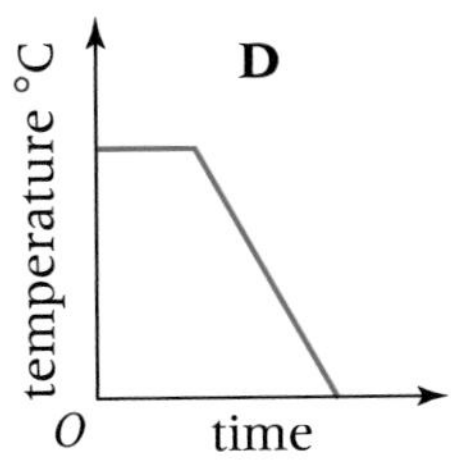

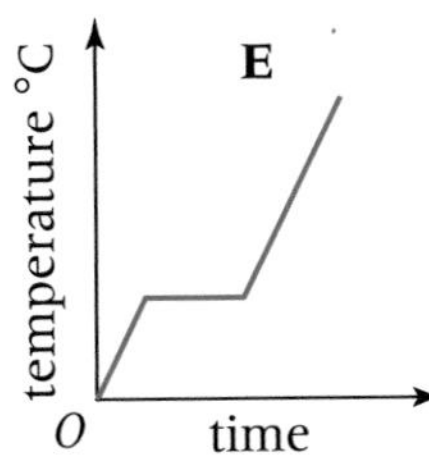

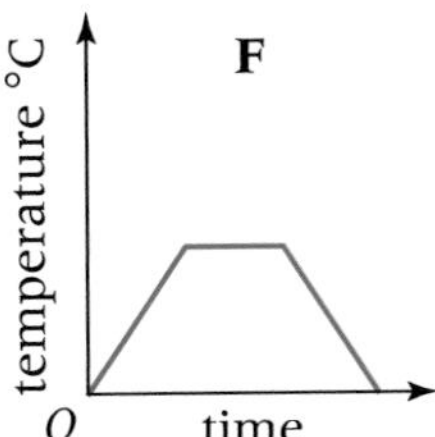

Each sentence in the table describes one of the graphs.
Write the letter of the correct graph next to each sentence.

The first one has been done for you.

The temperature starts at 0°C and keeps rising.	**B**
The temperature stays the same for a time and then falls.	
The temperature rises and then falls quickly.	
The temperature is always the same.	
The temperature rises, stays the same for a time and then falls.	
The temperature rises, stays the same for a time and then rises again.	

(3)

(Edexcel Limited 2008)

N4 Ratio and calculator methods

Introduction

The concepts of ratio and proportion are vital to art and architecture. The Golden Ratio, *phi*, is a quantity appears commonly in the natural world (for example in human proportions), and has been used through millennia to create aesthetic shapes, such as in buildings and in paintings, that look natural and balanced.

What's the point?

Art and design often draw inspiration from the natural world – an understanding of the mathematical proportions that are inherent in nature can yield results that are pleasing to the eye.

Check in

1. A car has a fuel consumption of 30 miles per gallon. How many miles will it travel on 8 gallons of petrol?
2. Gavin is running at 5 mph. He runs for 3 hours. How far does he travel?
3. Convert
   - **a** 23 cm into metres
   - **b** 2.4 km into centimetres.

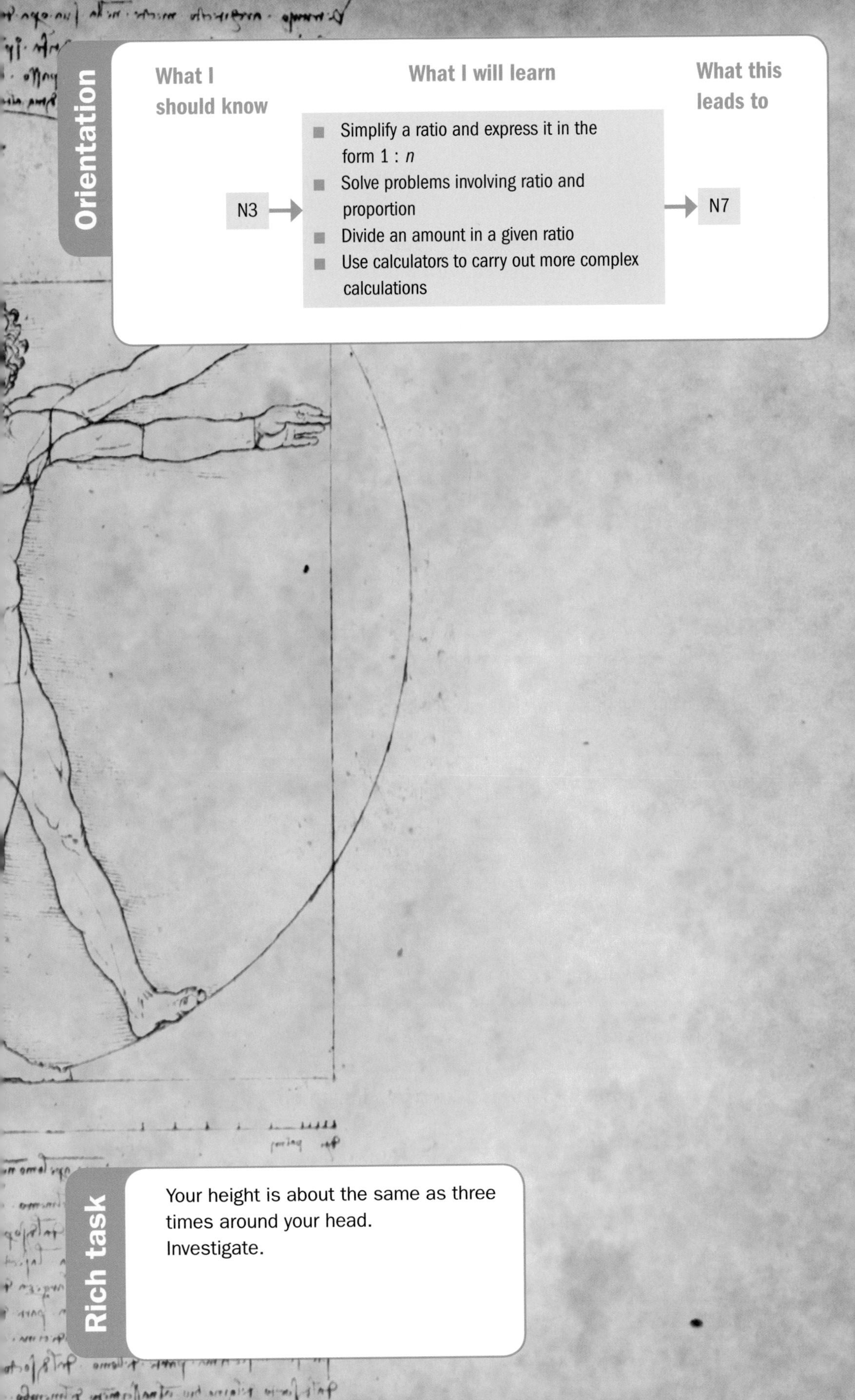

Orientation

What I should know	What I will learn	What this leads to
N3 →	Simplify a ratio and express it in the form 1 : n Solve problems involving ratio and proportion Divide an amount in a given ratio Use calculators to carry out more complex calculations	→ N7

Rich task

Your height is about the same as three times around your head.
Investigate.

N4.1 Introducing ratio

This spread will show you how to:

- Simplify a ratio and express it in the form 1 : n
- Solve simple problems involving ratio

Keywords
Ratio
Scale
Simplest form
Unitary form

You can compare the size of two quantities using a **ratio**.
2 : 3 means '2 parts of one quantity, compared with 3 parts of another.'

- You can simplify a ratio by dividing both parts by the same number. When a ratio cannot be simplified any further it is in its **simplest form**.

Example

Express each of these ratios in its simplest form.

a 55 : 65 **b** 3 m : 120 cm **c** 2.5 : 4.5

a 55 : 65

55 : 65 (÷5) → 11 : 13

Answer 11 : 13

b 3 m : 120 cm

300 : 120 (÷10) → 30 : 12 (÷6) → 5 : 2

Answer 5 : 2

c 2.5 : 4.5

2.5 : 4.5 (×10) → 25 : 45 (÷5) → 5 : 9

Answer 5 : 9

In part **b**, convert the measurements to the same unit.

Convert decimals to whole numbers by multiplying everything by the same number.

- A ratio can be expressed in the form 1 : n. This is called the **unitary form**.

Example

Write these ratios in the form 1 : n.

a 6 cm : 9 cm **b** 4 cm : 2 m

a 6 cm : 9 cm

6 : 9 (÷6) → 1 : 1.5

Answer 1 : 1.5

b 4 cm : 2 m Change 2 m into 200 cm

4 : 200 (÷4) → 1 : 50

Answer 1 : 50

A simplified ratio does not contain any units in the final answer.

Maps and plans are drawn to **scale**.

Example

On a plan, a real-life measurement of 4 m is drawn as a length of 25 cm. What is the scale of the plan?

Ratio of plan : real life
= 25 cm : 4 m

Change 4 m into 400 cm

25 : 400 (÷25) → 1 : 16

The scale of the plan is 1 : 16.

Exercise N4.1

Grade D

1 Write each of these ratios in its simplest form.
a 4 : 8 **b** 16 : 10 **c** 40 : 25 **d** 36 : 24
e 95 : 45 **f** 28 : 168 **g** 4 : 8 : 6 **h** 20 : 25 : 40

2 Write each of these ratios in its simplest form.
a 40 cm : 1 m **b** 55 mm : 8 cm **c** 3 km : 1200 m
d 4 m : 240 cm **e** 700 mm : 42 cm **f** 12 mins : 450 secs

AO2 Functional Maths

3 Express each of these pairs of measurements as a ratio in its simplest form.
a A table width of 40 cm to a table length of 1.2 m. What is the ratio of width to length?
b A lorry is 8.4 m long. A van is 360 cm long. What is the ratio of the lorry length to the van length?
c An alloy contains 24 kg of tin and 3.2 kg of zinc. What is the ratio of tin to zinc in the alloy?
d A bag of newly dug potatoes contains 6.4 kg of potatoes and 576 g of earth. What is the ratio of earth to potatoes in the bag?

Did you know?

Ratio plays a very important part in photography. The focal ratio (or f-number) of a lens is dependent on the focal length and the lens diameter.

4 Write each of these ratios in its simplest form.
a 1.5 : 4.5 **b** 2.25 : 1.5 **c** $\frac{1}{2} : \frac{1}{4}$ **d** $\frac{3}{8} : \frac{1}{2}$

5 Write each of these ratios in the form 1 : n.
a 4 : 10 **b** 39 : 150 **c** 30 : 125 **d** 720 g : 30 kg
e 95p : £22.50 **f** 3.2 : 480 **g** 0.36 : 4.5

6 In each of these questions, work out the scale of the map, plan or model. This is a ratio expressed in the form 1 : n.
a On a plan, a length of 4 cm represents a real-life measurement of 2 m. What is the scale of the plan?
b On a map, a length of 3.2 cm represents a real-life measurement of 640 m. What is the scale of the map?
c On a plan, a length of 7.2 cm represents a real-life measurement of 2.592 m. What is the scale of the plan?

AO2 Functional Maths

7 Solve each of these problems.
a In a batch of concrete the ratio of sand to cement is 5 : 3. How much sand is needed to mix with 21 kg of cement?
b In a metal alloy the ratio of aluminium to zinc is 7 : 2.5. How much aluminium is needed to mix with 10 kg of zinc?

N4.2 Calculating with ratio

This spread will show you how to:

- Solve problems involving ratio and proportion
- Divide an amount in a given ratio

Keywords
Ratio
Scale

A **ratio** tells you how many times bigger one number is compared to another number.

Example

a A pencil is 150 mm long. A pen is 165 mm long. How many times longer than the pencil is the pen?

b An alloy is made from zinc and copper in the ratio 3 : 8. How much zinc would you need to mix with 43 kg of copper? Give your answer to an appropriate degree of accuracy.

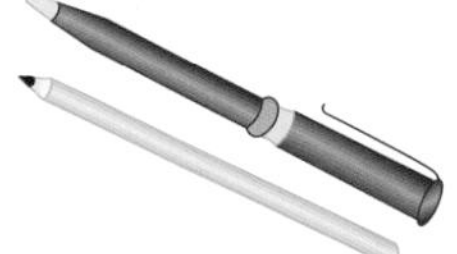

a Pencil length : Pen length

$150 : 165 = 10 : 11$

Pen $= \frac{11}{10}$ of length of pencil

Pen $= \frac{11}{10} \times$ length of pencil

b Amount of zinc $= \frac{3}{8} \times$ amount of copper

$= \frac{3}{8} \times 43\,\text{kg} = 0.375 \times 43\,\text{kg}$

$= 16.125\,\text{kg} = 16\,\text{kg}$ (nearest kg)

Example

A map has a **scale** of 1 : 2500. A distance in real life is 50 m. What is this distance on the map?

Distance on map $= \frac{1}{2500} \times$ distance in real life

$= \frac{1}{2500} \times 50\,\text{m}$

$= \frac{1 \times 5000}{2500}\,\text{cm}$

$= 2\,\text{cm}$

$50\,\text{m} = 50 \times 100\,\text{cm}$
$= 5000\,\text{cm}$

You can divide a quantity in a given ratio.

Example

Sean and Patrick share £355 in the ratio 3 : 7. How much money do they each receive?

Sean receives 3 parts for every 7 parts that Patrick receives.

Total number of parts = 3 + 7 = 10 parts
Each part = £355 ÷ 10 = £35.50

Sean will receive 3 parts = 3 × £35.50 = £106.50
Patrick will receive 7 parts = 7 × £35.50 = £248.50

Check your answer by adding up the two parts. They should add up to the amount being shared! £106.50 + £248.50 = £355

Exercise N4.2 Grade D

1 In each question, simplify the ratio, draw a diagram and write two statements. The first one is done for you.

a A length of 50 cm : length of 80 cm

50 : 80

5 : 8

$\times\frac{8}{5}$: 50 cm → 80 cm; $\times\frac{5}{8}$: 80 cm → 50 cm

a length of 80 cm $= \frac{8}{5} \times$ a length of 50 cm

a length of 50 cm $= \frac{5}{8} \times$ a length of 80 cm

b Andrew's height of 144 cm : Andrew's width of 48 cm

c A limousine of length 6.4 m : a car of length 280 cm

d A can containing 330 ml : a can containing 0.44 litres

AO2 Functional Maths

2 Solve each of these problems.

a The ratio of boys to girls in a class is 4 : 5. There are 12 boys in the class. How many girls are there?

b In a metal alloy the ratio of aluminium to tin is 8 : 5. How much aluminium is needed to mix with 55 kg of tin?

c The ratio of the number of purple flowers to the number of white flowers in a garden is 5 : 11. There are 132 white flowers. How many purple flowers are there?

d The ratio of KS3 students to KS4 students in a school is 7 : 6. There are 588 KS3 students. How many KS4 students are there at the school?

3 a A map has a scale of 1 : 400. A distance in real life is 4.8 m. What is this distance on the map?

b In a school the ratio of teachers to students is 1 : 22.5. If there are 990 students at the school, how many teachers are there?

c The model of an aircraft is in the scale 1 : 32. If the real aircraft is 12.48 m long, how long is the model?

4 A map has a scale of 1 : 5000.

a What is the distance in real life of a measurement of 6.5 cm on the map?

b What is the distance on the map of a measurement of 30 m in real life?

5 Solve each of these problems.

a Divide £90 in the ratio 3 : 7.

b Divide 369 kg in the ratio 7 : 2.

c Divide 103.2 tonnes in the ratio 5 : 3.

d Divide 35.1 litres in the ratio 5 : 4.

e Divide £36 in the ratio 1 : 2 : 3.

More ratio problems

This spread will show you how to:

- Express a ratio as a fraction, a decimal or a percentage
- Divide an amount in a given ratio
- Recognise the inaccuracy of model measurements

Keywords
Ratio
Scale

A **ratio** compares the size of two or more objects. You can express a ratio as a fraction, a decimal or a percentage.

Wing span of model : Wing span of enlargement
2 : 5

Model wing span is
$\frac{2}{5}$ of enlargement wing span
$\frac{2}{5} \times$ enlargement wing span
$0.4 \times$ enlargement wing span
40% of enlargement wing span

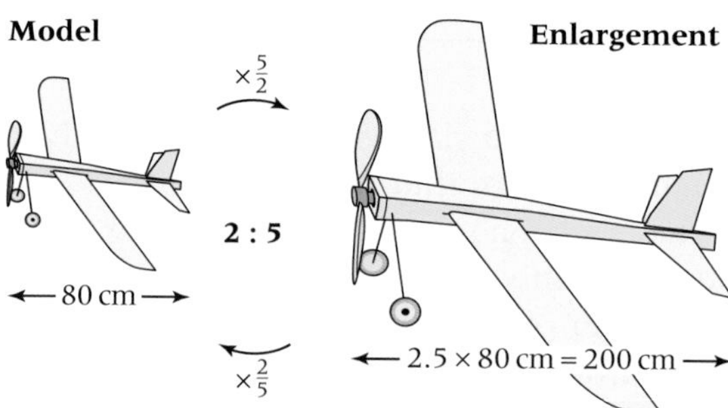

Enlargement wing span is
$\frac{5}{2}$ of model wing span
$\frac{5}{2} \times$ model wing span
$2.5 \times$ model wing span
250% of model wing span

You will study enlargements in the next chapter.

Some **multi-step** calculations involving ratio and **scale** need to be broken down into smaller steps.

Example

A model is made of a truck. The length of the model is 28 centimetres. The length of the real truck is 6.3 metres. Work out the ratio of the length of the model to the length of the real truck. Write your answer in the form 1 : *n*.

Step 1
Express the ratio in equal units.

Length of model : length of truck

28 cm : 6.3 m ⇒ 28 cm : 630 cm ⇒ 28 : 630

Step 2
Express the ratio in the form 1 : *n*.

28 : 630 (÷ 28 on both sides)
1 : 22.5

The scale is 1 : 22.5.

When a ratio is expressed in different units, convert the measurements to the same unit.

- When a measurement is written down, it is always written to a given degree of accuracy. The real measurement can be anywhere within ± half a unit.

Example

A man walks 23 km (to the nearest km). Write the maximum and minimum distance he could have walked.

Because the real measurement has been rounded, it can lie anywhere between 22.5 km (minimum) and 23.5 km (maximum).

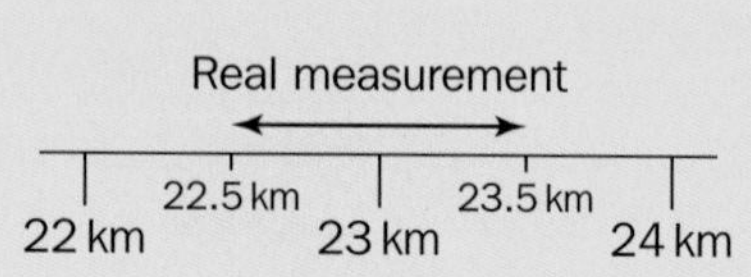

Exercise N4.3

Grade D

1 Solve each of these problems. Give your answers to 2 decimal places where appropriate.

a Divide £75 in the ratio 8 : 7.

b Divide £1000 in the ratio 7 : 13.

c Divide 364 days in the ratio 5 : 2.

d Divide 500 g in the ratio 2 : 5.

e Divide 600 m in the ratio 5 : 9.

A02 Functional Maths

2 a The ratio of men to women in a club is 3 : 7. There are 18 men who are members of the club. How many women are members of the club?

b In a recipe the ratio of butter to flour is 3 : 2. How much flour is needed to mix with 360 g of butter?

c The heights of two buildings are in the ratio 8 : 9. The smaller building has a height of 56 feet. What is the height of the larger building?

d Marlene reads two books on holiday. The first book is a travel book with 258 pages. The second book is a science fiction novel, with more pages than the travel book. The number of pages in the two books is in the ratio 3 : 5. How many pages are there in the science fiction novel?

3 a The ratio of the length of a car to the length of a van is 2 : 3. The car has a length of 240 cm.

i Express the length of the car as a percentage of the length of the van.

ii Calculate the length of the van.

b The ratio of the weight of Dave to Morgan is 6 : 5. Morgan has a weight of 85 kg.

i Express the weight of Dave as a percentage of the weight of Morgan.

ii Calculate the weight of Dave.

4 Work out these problems. For each problem show all the steps in your working out.

a A metal alloy is made from copper and aluminium. The ratio of the weight of copper to the weight of aluminium is 5 : 3.

i What weight of the metal alloy contains 45 grams of copper?

ii Work out the weight of copper and the weight of aluminium in 184 grams of the metal alloy.

b Siobhan and Ralph shared £700 in the ratio 2 : 3.
Siobhan gave a quarter of her share to Karen.
Ralph gave a fifth of his share to Karen.
What fraction of the £700 did Karen receive?

5 The length of a car is 2.6 m correct to 1 decimal place.

a Write the maximum value that the length could be.

b Write the minimum value that the length could be.

N4.4 Calculator methods 1

This spread will show you how to:

- Use calculators to carry out more complex calculations
- Use checking procedures, including approximation to estimate the answer to multiplication and division problems
- Give answers to an appropriate degree of accuracy

Keywords
Appropriate degree of accuracy
Brackets
Order of perations

You can use the bracket keys on a scientific calculator to do calculations where the **order of operations** is not obvious.

Example

a Use a calculator to work out the value of

$$\frac{21.42 \times (12.4 - 6.35)}{(63.4 + 18.9) \times 2.83}$$

Write all the figures on the calculator display.

b Put brackets in this expression so that its value is 45.908.
$8.2 + 3.4 \times 2.7 - 4.3$

---

a Rewrite the calculation as $(21.42 \times (12.4 - 6.35)) \div ((63.4 + 18.9) \times 2.83)$
Type this into the calculator:

`(21.42×(12.4-6.35))÷((63.4+18.9)×2.83)` → `(21.42×(12.4-` `0.556401856`

So the answer is 0.556 401 856.

Estimate:
$\frac{20 \times (12 - 6)}{(60 + 20) \times 3} = \frac{120}{240} = 0.5$

b By inserting a pair of brackets: $(1.4 + 3.9 \times 2.2) \times 4.6$
The calculator should display 45.908. ☒ This is the correct answer.

You can solve multi-step problems using a calculator. You will need to give your answer to an **appropriate degree of accuracy**.

Example

The diagram shows a box in the shape of a cuboid.

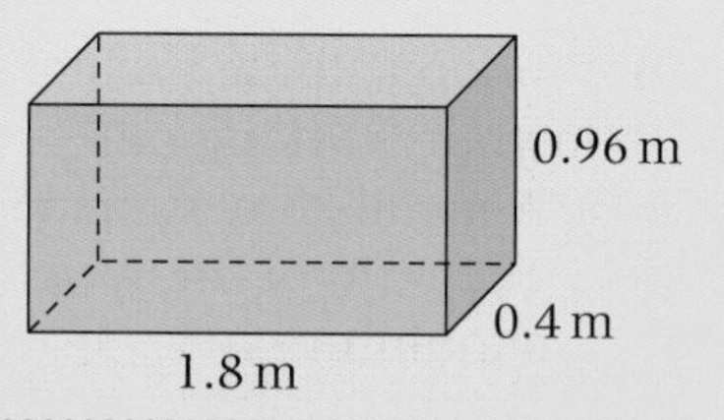

a Work out the volume, in m³, of the box.
b Saleem builds boxes of different sizes.
He charges £7.89 for each m³ of a box's volume.
Work out Saleem's charge for building this box.

---

a Volume of a cuboid
= length × width × height
Volume $\approx 2 \times 1 \times 0.4 = 0.8$ m³
Volume $= 1.8 \times 0.4 \times 0.96$
$= 0.6912$ m³
$= 0.7$ m³

b Saleem's charge
= cost for each m³ × number of m³
Estimate: Saleem's charge ≈ £8 × 0.8
= £6.40
Type: Saleem's charge = £7.89 × 0.6912
= £5.453 568
= £5.45

Exercise N4.4 Grade D

1 Put brackets into each of these expressions to make them correct.

a $2.4 \times 4.3 + 3.7 = 19.2$ b $6.8 \times 3.75 - 2.64 = 7.548$

c $3.7 + 2.9 \div 1.2 = 5.5$ d $2.3 + 3.4^2 \times 2.7 = 37.422$

e $5.3 + 3.9 \times 3.2 + 1.6 = 24.02$ f $3.2 + 6.4 \times 4.3 + 2.5 = 46.72$

2 Use your calculator to work out each of these. Write all the figures on your calculator.

a $\dfrac{165.4 \times 27.4}{(0.72 + 4.32)^2}$ b $\dfrac{(32.6 + 43.1) \times 2.3^2}{173.7 \times (13.5 - 1.78)}$

c $\dfrac{24.67 \times (35.3 - 8.29)}{(28.2 + 34.7) \times 3.3}$ d $\dfrac{1.45^2 \times 3.64 + 2.9}{3.47 - 0.32}$

e $\dfrac{12.93 \times (33.2 - 8.34)}{(61.3 + 34.5) \times 2.9}$ f $\dfrac{24.7 - (3.2 + 1.09)^2}{2.78^2 + 12.9 \times 3}$

Functional Maths

A02

3 Work out each of these using your calculator. In each case give your answer to an appropriate degree of accuracy.

a Véronique puts carpet in her bedroom. The bedroom is in the shape of a rectangle with a length of 4.23 m and a width of 3.6 m. The carpet costs £6.79 per m^2.

i Calculate the floor area of the bedroom.

ii Calculate the cost of the carpet which is required to cover the floor.

b Calculate $\frac{1}{3}$ of £200.

4 Barry sees a mobile phone offer.

Vericheep Fone OFFER

Monthly fee £12.99

FREE - 200 texts every month

FREE - 200 voice minutes every month

Extra text messages 3.2p each

Extra voice minutes 5.5p each

Barry decides to see if the offer is a good idea for him.
His current mobile phone offers him unlimited texts and voice minutes for £22.99 per month.

a In February, Barry used 189 texts and 348 voice minutes. Calculate his bill using the new offer.

b In March, Barry used 273 texts and 219 voice minutes. Calculate his bill using the new offer.

c Explain if the new offer is a good idea for Barry.

5 Sezer has 110.5 hours of music downloaded on her computer. She accidentally deletes 80.15 hours of her music!
How much music does Sezer have remaining on her computer hard drive?
Give your answer

a in hours and minutes b in minutes

Luckily Sezer has backed up her music library!

N4 Summary

Check out

You should now be able to:

- Use ratio notation and express a ratio in its simplest form
- Divide a quantity in a given ratio
- Express a ratio as a fraction, decimal or percentage
- Solve problems involving ratio
- Carry out calculations using the functions of a calculator
- Be aware of possible rounding errors during multi-step calculations

Worked exam question

There are some sweets in a bag.

18 of the sweets are toffees.
12 of the sweets are mints.

a Write down the ratio of the number of toffees to the number of mints.
Give your ratio in its simplest form. (2)

There are some oranges and apples in a box.

The total number of oranges and apples is 54
The ratio of the number of oranges to the number of apples is 1 : 5

b Work out the number of apples in the box. (2)

(Edexcel Limited 2009)

a

number of toffees : number of mints
18 : 12
3 : 2

The ratio must be in this order.

Write the ratio before simplifying.

b

Total number of parts = 1 + 5 = 6 parts
Each part is 54 ÷ 6 = 9 pieces of fruit

Number of apples = 5 × 9 = 45 apples

Show this divide sum.

Exam questions

1 The length of a coach is 15 metres.

Jonathan makes a model of the coach.
He uses a scale of 1:24

Work out the length, in centimetres, of the model coach. (2)

(Edexcel Limited 2005)

2 Work out $\dfrac{3.28 + 2.4}{7.1 - 1.8^2}$

Write down all the numbers on your calculator display. (2)

A02

3

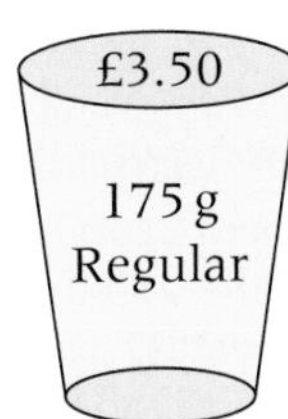

A Large tub of popcorn costs £3.80 and holds 200 g.
A Regular tub of popcorn costs £3.50 and holds 175 g.

Rob says that the 200 g Large tub is better value for money.
Linda says that the 175 g Regular tub is the better value for money.

Who is correct?

Explain the reasons for your answer.
You must show all your working. (2)

(Edexcel Limited 2006)

Functional Maths 4: Holiday

Mathematics can help you to plan and budget for a holiday, as well as to understand currency, temperature and other units of measure at your destination.

holiday

Paris

LOUISE'S family are planning to go on holiday. Her parents will pay for the trip, but she must raise her own spending money.

1 How much money could Louise save in the three months from March to May if she hired a DVD once a week instead of going to the cinema?

Screen 13
29/11/09
17:50
A GOOD NIGHT £4.50

Hire charge £1.99 per film! SIGN UP NOW!!

2 A neighbour offers to pay Louise £10 per week if she takes her dog for a 30-minute walk every weekday before school. What hourly rate of pay does this represent? How much would Louise earn if she walked the dog every weekday throughout March, April and May?

3 Louise's brother sold 18 of his CDs for £45. How much did he sell each CD for? He then sold another two CDs and 11 DVDs for £43.50. How much did he charge for each DVD?'

How could you raise money towards a holiday fund or to buy a new item? How long would it take you to reach your target amount?

If you are going on holiday outside of the UK, then you will need to convert your money from £ Sterling to the local currency of your destination. Many European countries now use the Euro, €.

In 2005, the average £ Sterling : Euro exchange rate was 1 : 1.46.

In that year, how many

a) Euros would you receive in exchange for £150

b) £ Sterling would you receive in exchange for 120EUR?

Suppose that you are charged £70 (with no commission) to buy 91.7EUR.

What is the exchange rate? Give your answer as a ratio £ Sterling : Euro.

Some companies charge a commission fee to exchange currency. With an added charge of 1%, how many Euros would you now receive (at the same exchange rate) for £70?

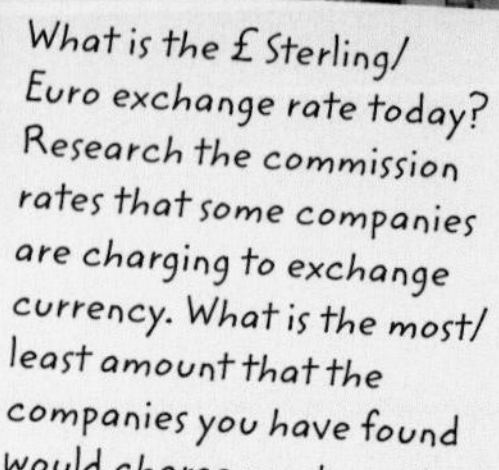

What is the £ Sterling/Euro exchange rate today? Research the commission rates that some companies are charging to exchange currency. What is the most/least amount that the companies you have found would charge you to exchange £150 into Euros?

Deciding on your method of transport is an important part of planning a holiday.

Some travel options between Oxford and Paris are shown.

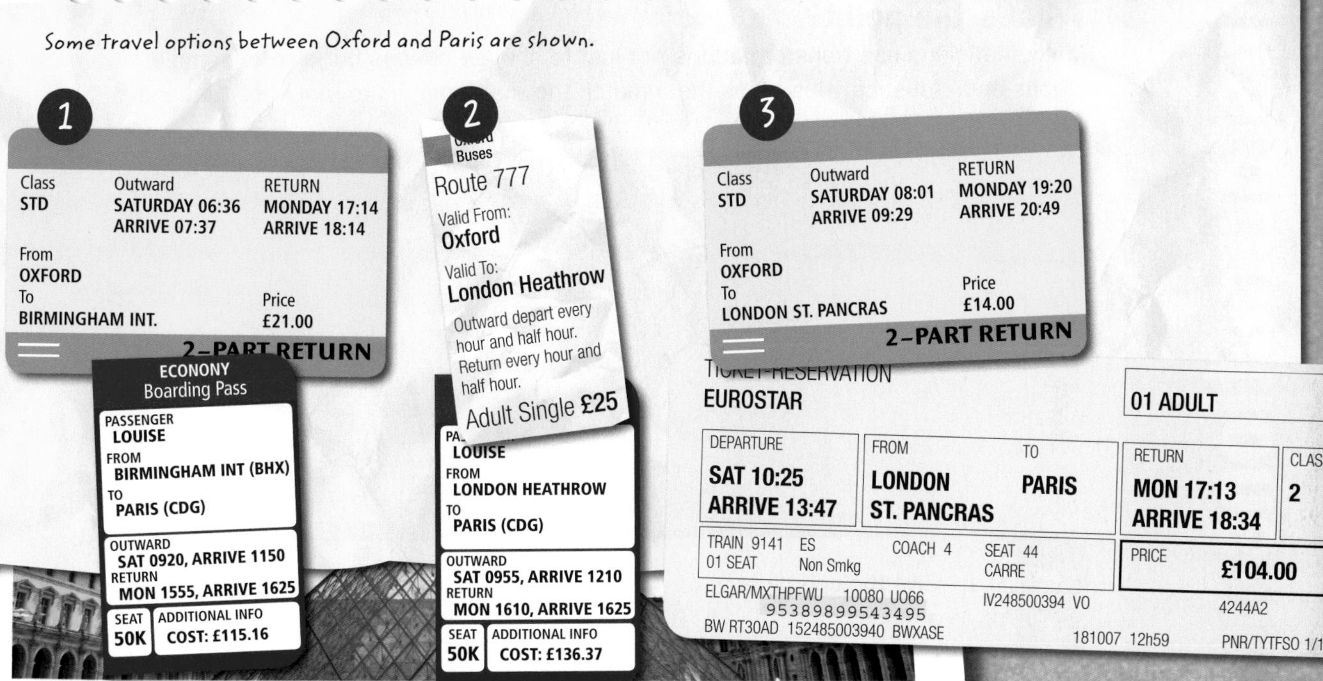

1
Class STD
Outward SATURDAY 06:36 ARRIVE 07:37
RETURN MONDAY 17:14 ARRIVE 18:14
From OXFORD
To BIRMINGHAM INT.
Price £21.00
2-PART RETURN
ECONOMY Boarding Pass
PASSENGER LOUISE
FROM BIRMINGHAM INT (BHX)
TO PARIS (CDG)
OUTWARD SAT 0920, ARRIVE 1150
RETURN MON 1555, ARRIVE 1625
SEAT 50K
ADDITIONAL INFO COST: £115.16
2
Buses
Route 777
Valid From: Oxford
Valid To: London Heathrow
Outward depart every hour and half hour. Return every hour and half hour.
Adult Single £25
LOUISE
FROM LONDON HEATHROW
TO PARIS (CDG)
OUTWARD SAT 0955, ARRIVE 1210
RETURN MON 1610, ARRIVE 1625
SEAT 50K
ADDITIONAL INFO COST: £136.37
3
Class STD
Outward SATURDAY 08:01 ARRIVE 09:29
RETURN MONDAY 19:20 ARRIVE 20:49
From OXFORD
To LONDON ST. PANCRAS
Price £14.00
2-PART RETURN
EUROSTAR
01 ADULT
DEPARTURE SAT 10:25 ARRIVE 13:47
FROM LONDON ST. PANCRAS
TO PARIS
RETURN MON 17:13 ARRIVE 18:34
2
TRAIN 9141 ES 01 SEAT
Non Smkg
COACH 4
SEAT 44 CARRE
PRICE £104.00
ELGAR/MXTHPFWU 10080 U066
95389899543495
IV248500394 VO
4244A2
BW RT30AD 152485003940 BWXASE
181007 12h59
PNR/TYTFSO 1/1

WHICH travel option would you choose? Explain your response with reference to the travel times and costs. All times given are local. Paris is in the time zone GMT + 1 hour.

The foreign travel legs of the same journey options can be paid for in Euros for the following prices:

Return flight BHX to Paris CDG 151.49€; return Eurostar journey 130€, return flight London Heathrow to Paris CDG 162.82€.

How does each of the prices in Euros compare with the corresponding price in GBP?

Explore travel options from your hometown to different destinations. Be careful, there are some times hidden costs such as additional taxes and fees.

■ Different countries often use different units of measure for quantities such as temperature.

An Internet site states that the maximum and minimum temperatures in Rome on a particular day are 99°F and 63°F respectively.

A formula that can be used to convert between °C and °F is temp(°C) = 5(temp(°F) – 32)/9

What are the corresponding maximum and minimum temperatures in Rome?

The maximum and minimum temperatures in London on the same day were 25°C and 16°C. What are these temperatures in °F?

What are the maximum and minimum temperatures in your home town today? Use the formula in the example to convert the temperatures you have found from °C to °F.

G4 Transformations

Introduction

Transformations change points and shapes by moving them from one place to another. When you play a computer game your character is able to move around the screen because of mathematical transformations. Combinations of these transformations, often taking place in 3D worlds, allow the characters to move in many different ways.

What's the point?

Mathematicians use transformations not just to change shapes but also to change graphs and statistics. This helps them match the mathematics to real life situations.

Check in

1 Give the coordinates of

a A **b** B

c C **d** D

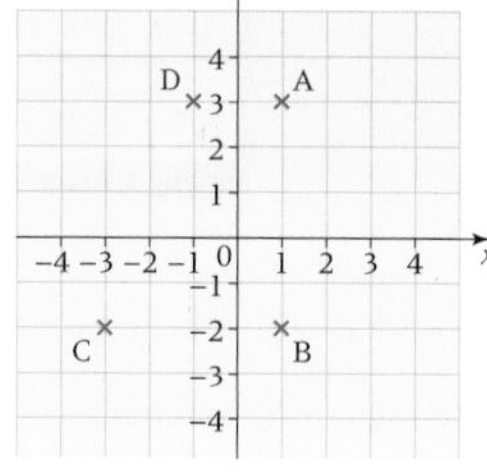

2 Give the equation of each straight line.

a

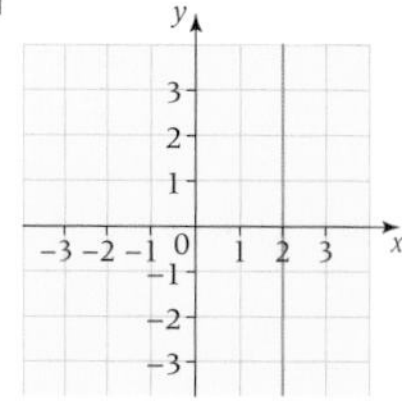

b

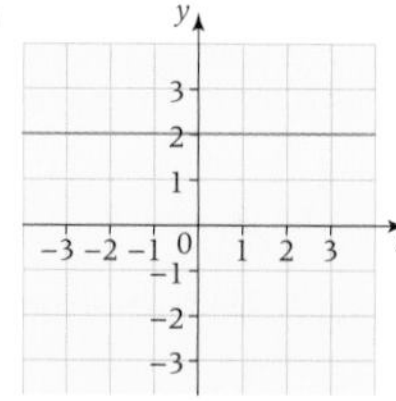

c

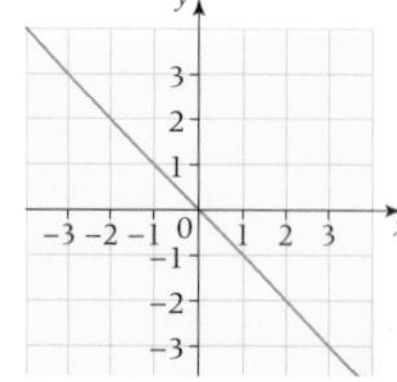

d

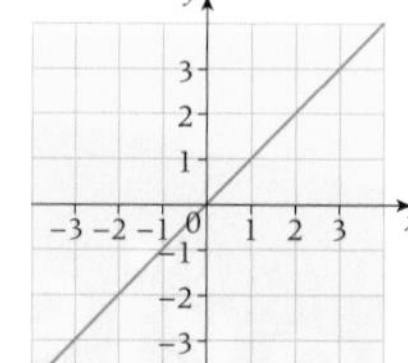

Orientation

What I should know	What I will learn	What this leads to
Key stage 3 →	■ Understand, recognise and describe reflections, rotations, translations and enlargements ■ Understand congruence	→ G5

Rich task

A shape (object) is reflected in the line $y = x$.
To find the new coordinates of each vertex of the shape (image), simply swap the x and y coordinates around.
Investigate rules for finding the image coordinates for this and other transformations.

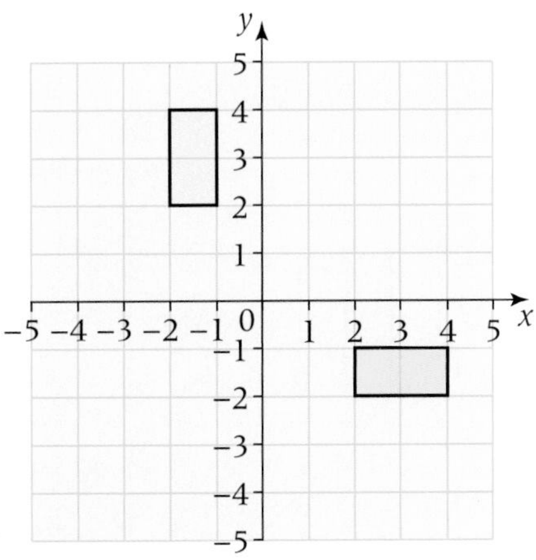

G4.1 Reflections

This spread will show you how to:

- Transform 2-D shapes using reflections

Keywords
Equation
Equidistant
Mirror line
Reflection

A reflection flips a shape over.

- You describe a **reflection** using the **mirror line** or reflection line.

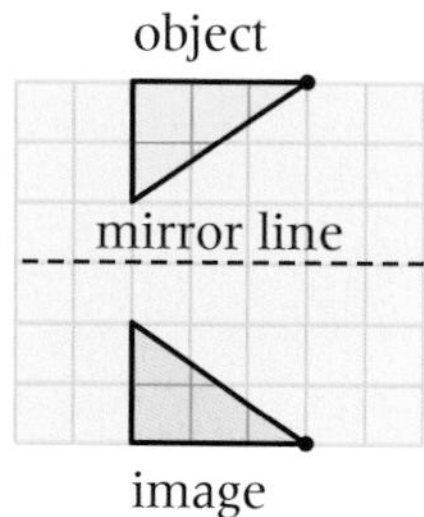

Choose a point on the object to find the corresponding point on the image.

Corresponding points are **equidistant** from the mirror line.

Each dot is 3 units from the mirror line.

Example

a Draw a mirror line so that shape B is a reflection of shape A.
b Give the **equation** of the mirror line.

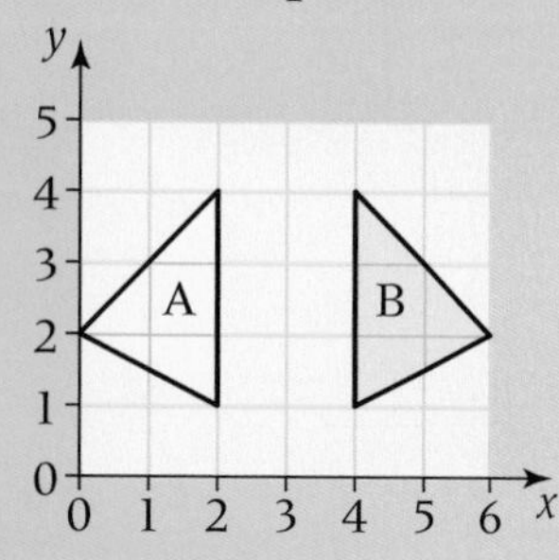

a

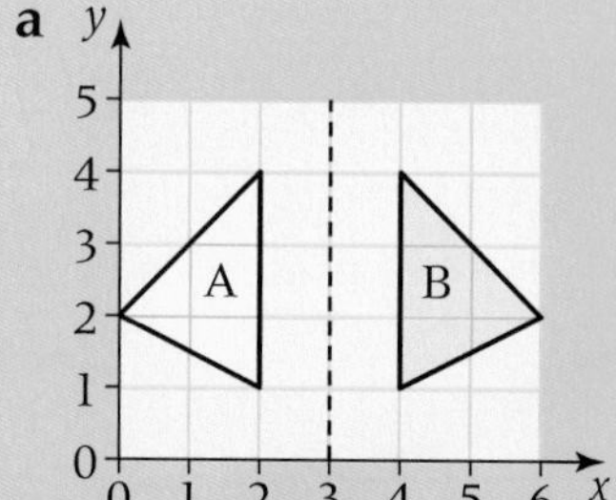

b Choose some coordinates on the line: (3, 0) (3, 1) (3, 2).
The x-coordinates are all 3.
The line is $x = 3$.

Example

a Draw the reflection of the shaded shape in the mirror line.
b Give the equation of the mirror line.

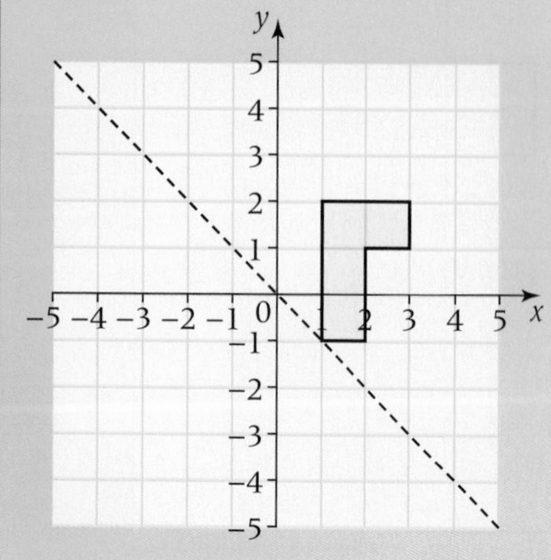

a

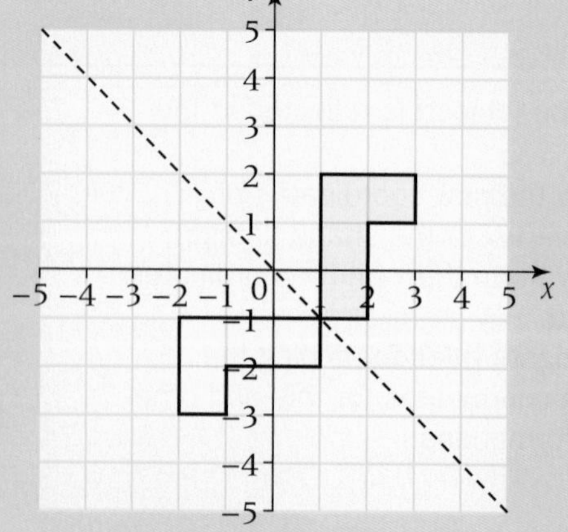

b Choose some coordinates on the line: $(-2, 2)$, $(3, -3)$, $(5, -5)$
The line is $y = -x$

Exercise G4.1

Grade D

1 Copy and complete the diagrams to show the reflections of the triangles in the mirror line $x = 2$.

a

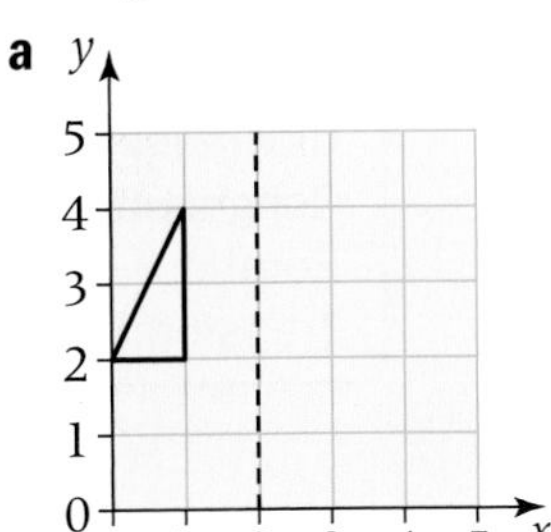

b

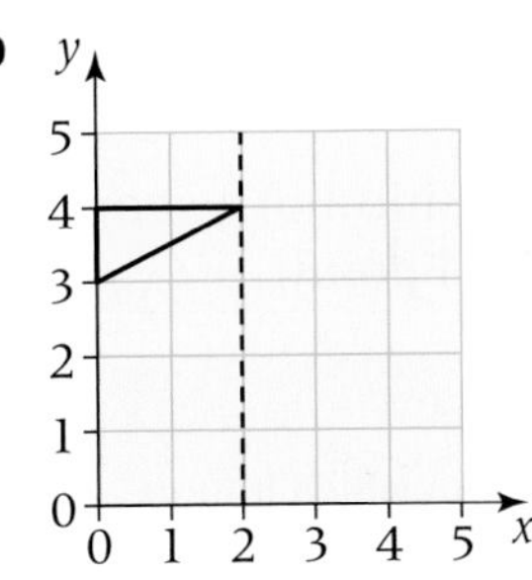

c

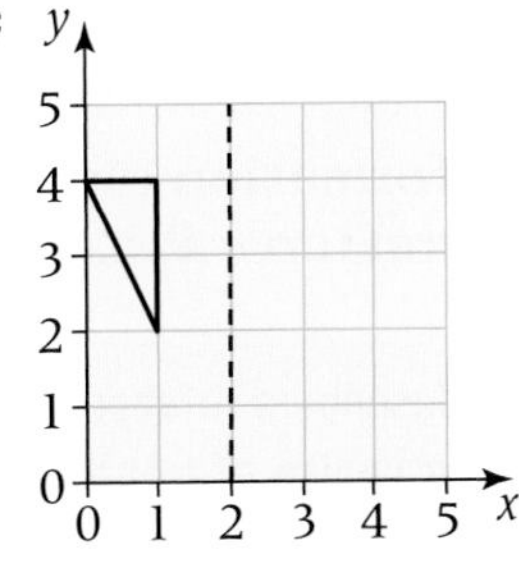

2 Give the equation of the mirror line for each reflection.

a

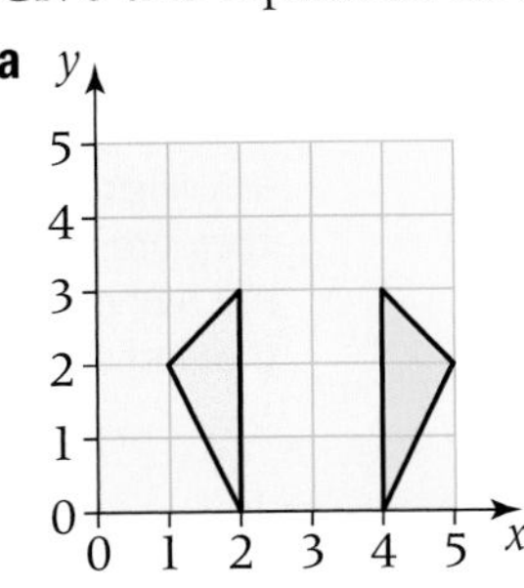

b

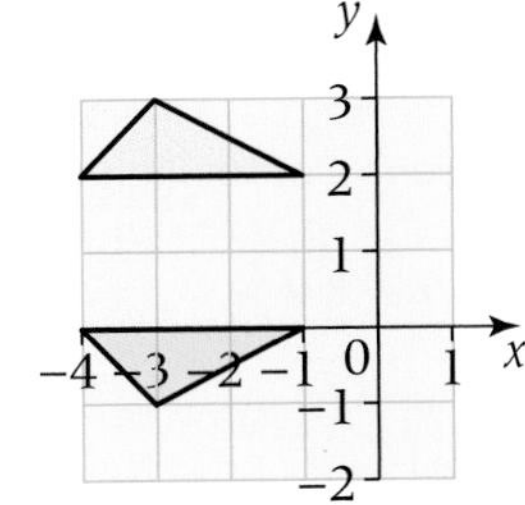

c

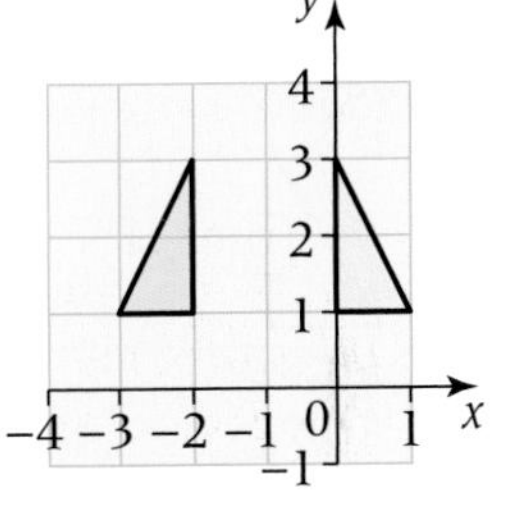

3 **a** Copy the diagram.

b Reflect the triangle in the mirror line.

c Give the equation of the mirror line.

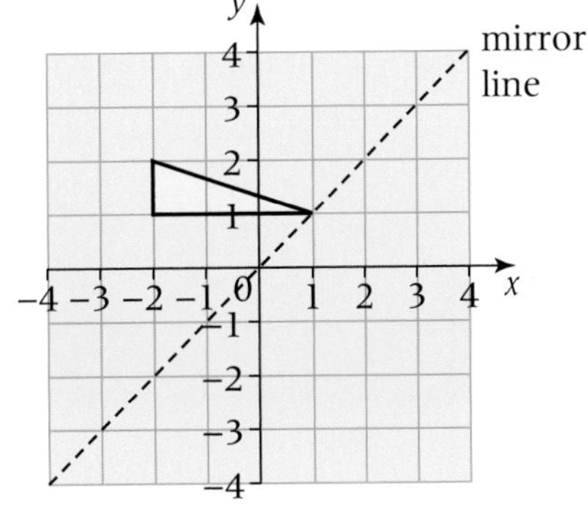

4 **a** Copy the diagram.

b Plot the points (0, 1) (3, 1) (3, 2) to form a triangle.

c Reflect the triangle in the mirror line.

d Give the coordinates of the reflected points.

e Give the equation of the mirror line.

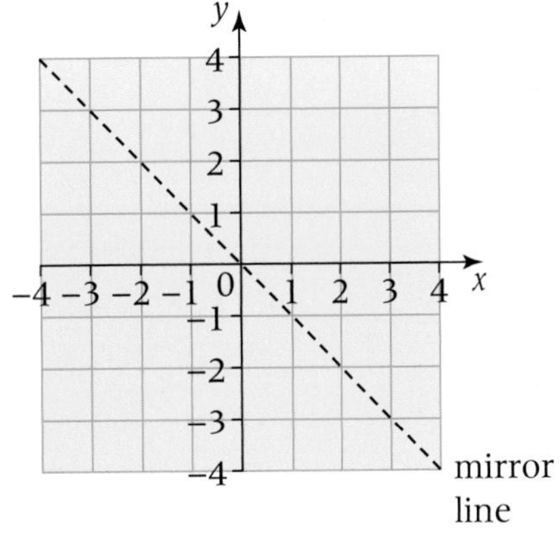

G4.2 Rotations

This spread will show you how to:

- Transform triangles and other 2-D shapes by reflection, rotation, translation and a combination of these transformations

Keywords
Anticlockwise
Centre of rotation
Clockwise
Congruent
Rotation
Transformation

A **transformation** can change the position of a shape.
A **rotation** turns a shape about a fixed point.

- You describe a rotation by giving:
  - the **centre of rotation** – the point about which it turns
  - the angle of turn
  - the direction of turn – either **clockwise** or **anticlockwise**.

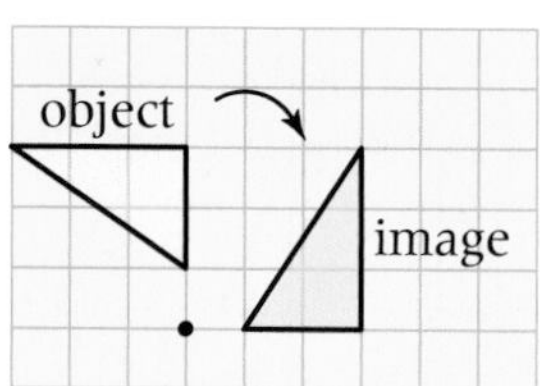

The dot is the centre of rotation.
The turn is 90°.
The direction is clockwise.

The two shapes are **congruent**. They are exactly the same size and the same shape.

Example

a Draw the position of the red triangle after a rotation of 90° clockwise about the origin.
b Give the coordinates of the point A **after** the rotation.

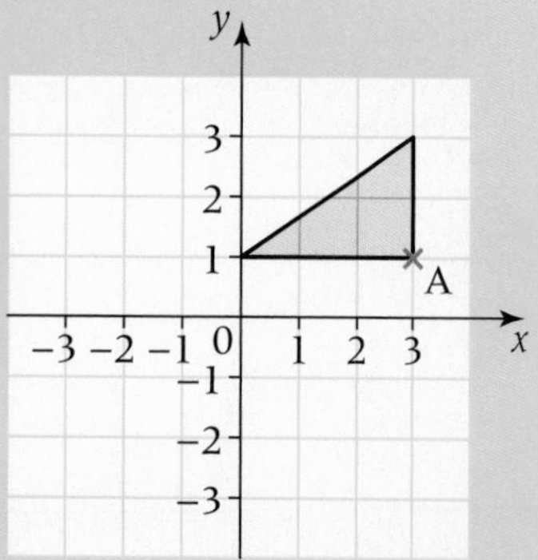

a

centre of rotation

b (1, −3)

The origin is the point (0, 0).

Use tracing paper to find the position of the blue triangle.

Example

A regular pentagon is divided into five isosceles triangles.
The centre of the pentagon is marked with a dot (•).
The green triangle is rotated about the dot onto the yellow triangle.

a State whether the green and yellow triangles are congruent or similar.
b Calculate the angle and direction of the rotation.

a Congruent – same size and same shape.
b The five angles at the dot total 360°.
One angle at the dot is 360° ÷ 5 = 72°.
Rotation is 72° clockwise about the dot.

Exercise G4.2 Grade D

1 State the angle and direction of turn for each of these rotations about the dot (•), green shape to blue shape:

2 The diagram shows the pattern made by repeated 90° rotations of a right-angled triangle about the dot (•).
Draw a similar pattern using repeated 45° rotations about the dot (•).

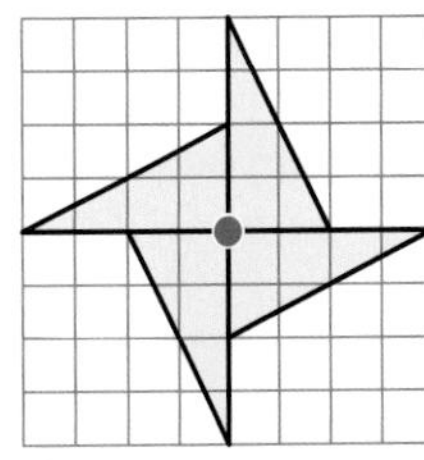

3 Copy this grid.

a Plot and join the points O (0, 0), A (2, 1), B (3, 0) and C (2, −1).

b Give the mathematical name of this shape.

c Rotate the shape through 90° anticlockwise about the origin.

d Give the coordinates of the point A after the rotation.

e Are the two shapes congruent?

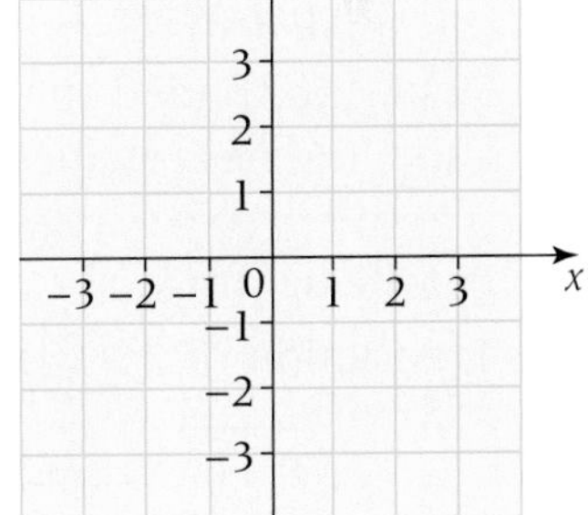

4 **a** Copy the shape and axes on square grid paper.

b Rotate the triangle by 90° anticlockwise about the point (1, 2).

c Give the coordinates of the vertices of the triangle after the rotation.

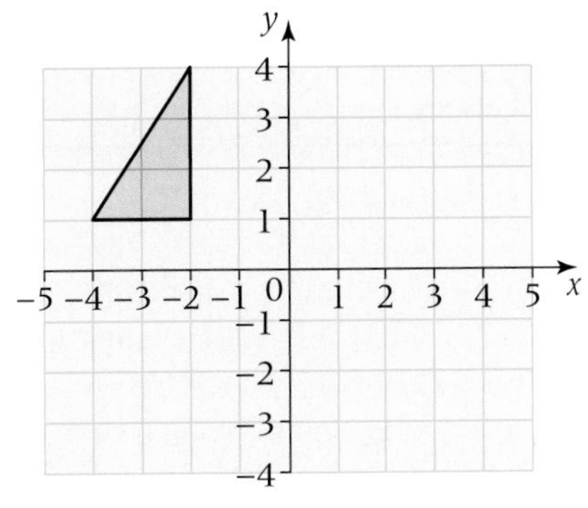

G4.3 Translations

This spread will show you how to:

- Understand, recognise and describe translations

Keywords
Congruent
Slide
Translation
Vector

A **translation** is a **sliding** movement.

To get from the green shape to the blue shape, you translate the object 1 unit right and 3 units down.

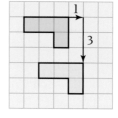

You can write this translation as a **vector**, $\begin{pmatrix} 1 \\ -3 \end{pmatrix}$.

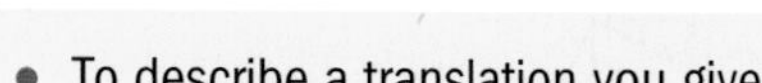

- To describe a translation you give
  - the distance moved left or right, then
  - the distance moved up or down.
- You can use a **vector** to describe the translation.

You can **transform** an object into a **congruent** image using a translation.

Congruent shapes are the same size and shape.

The two shapes are **congruent**.

Choose a point on the object to locate the corresponding point on the image.

This is a translation of $\begin{pmatrix} 3 \\ 1 \end{pmatrix}$.

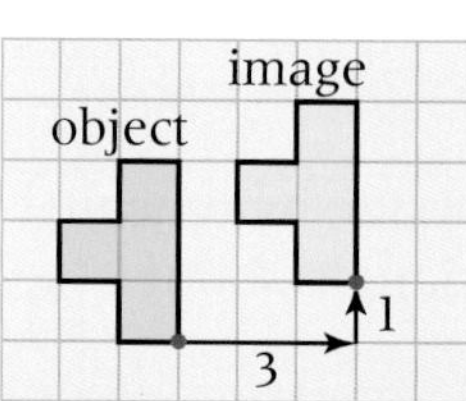

Example

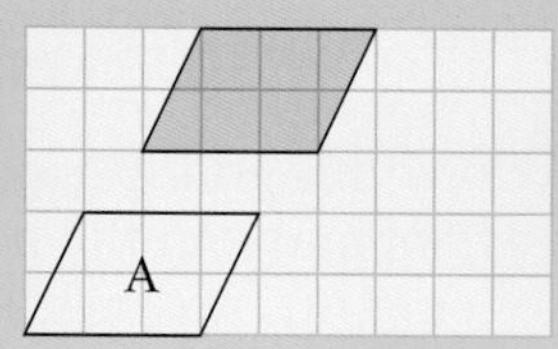

a Give the mathematical name of the shaded shape.
b Describe fully the transformation that moves the shaded shape to shape A.
c Draw the shaded shape after a translation of $\begin{pmatrix} 3 \\ -1 \end{pmatrix}$. Label the new shape B.

a Parallelogram
b Translation of $\begin{pmatrix} -2 \\ -3 \end{pmatrix}$.
c

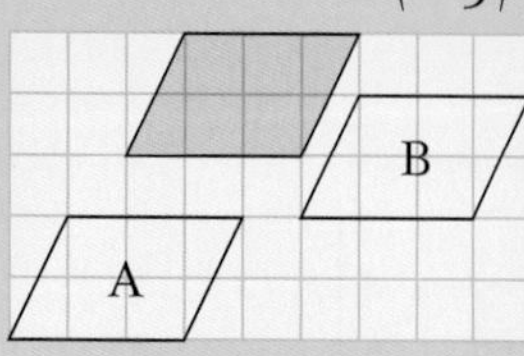

Exercise G4.3 Grade D

1 Which shapes are translations of the green shape?

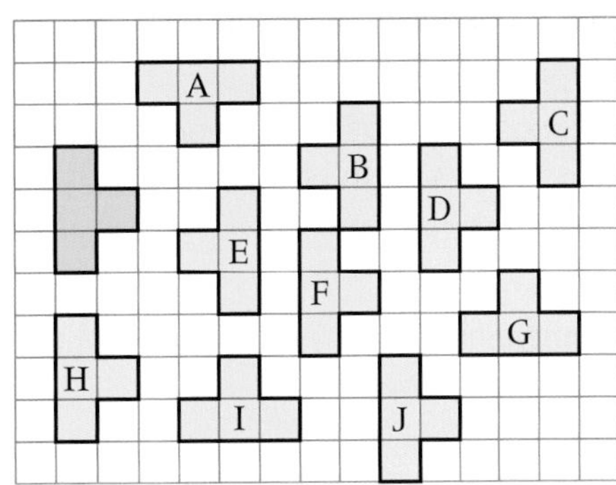

2 Describe the translation that moves the green triangle to the other triangles.

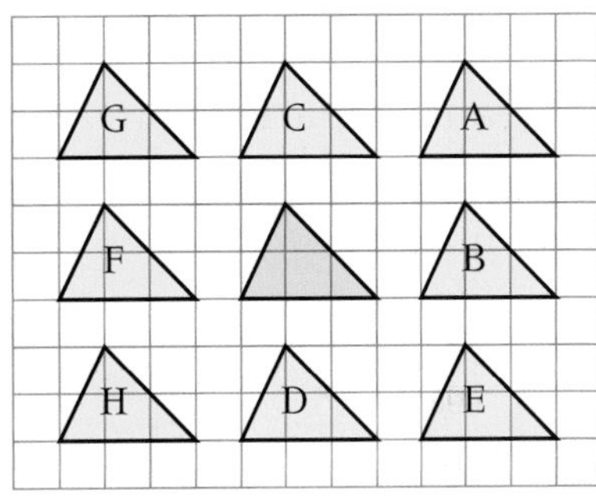

3 Describe these translations.

a A to B **b** D to B
c B to D **d** A to C
e C to D **f** D to A
g C to A **h** B to A
i B to C **j** A to D

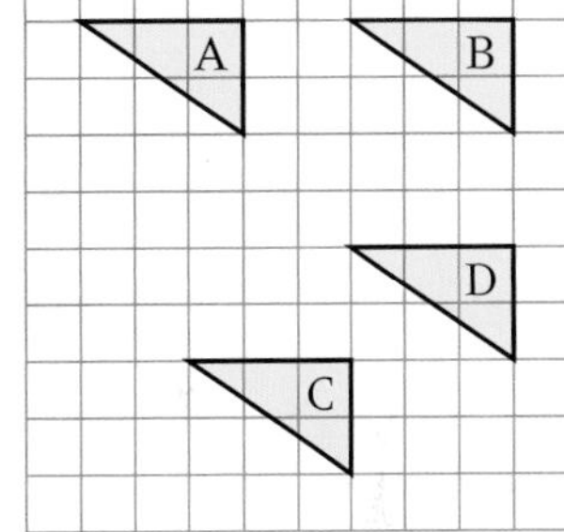

4 **a** State the coordinates of point A.
b What is the mathematical name of the shape?
c Draw the shape after a translation of $\begin{pmatrix} 5 \\ -2 \end{pmatrix}$.
d State whether the two shapes are congruent.
e Give the coordinates of the point A after the translation.

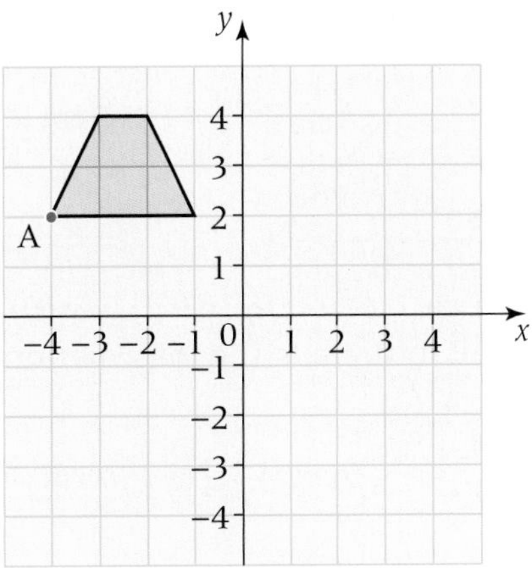

G4.4 Congruence

This spread will show you how to:
- Understand congruence
- Recognise that translations, rotations and reflections preserve length and-angle

Keywords
Congruent
Reflection
Rotation
Transformation
Translation

- **Congruent** shapes are exactly the same size and the same shape.

Congruent shapes fit exactly on top of each other.

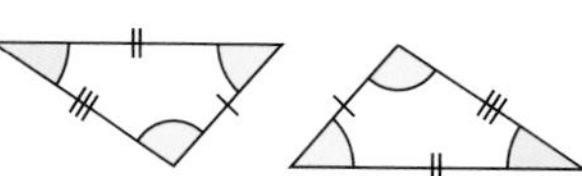

Corresponding angles are equal and corresponding sides are equal.

A rotation moves one triangle to the other triangle.

These **transformations** produce congruent shapes.

reflection

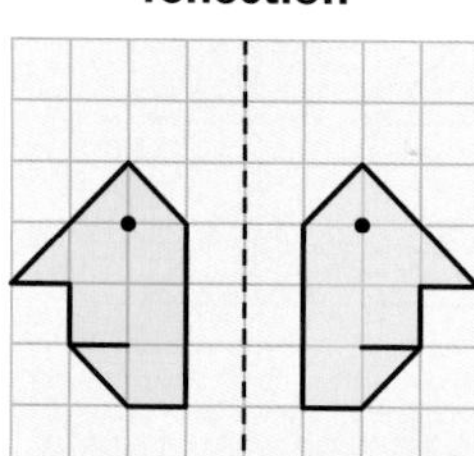

rotation

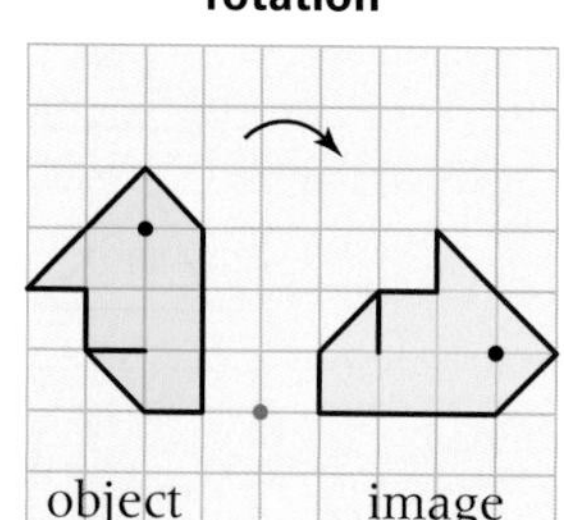

translation

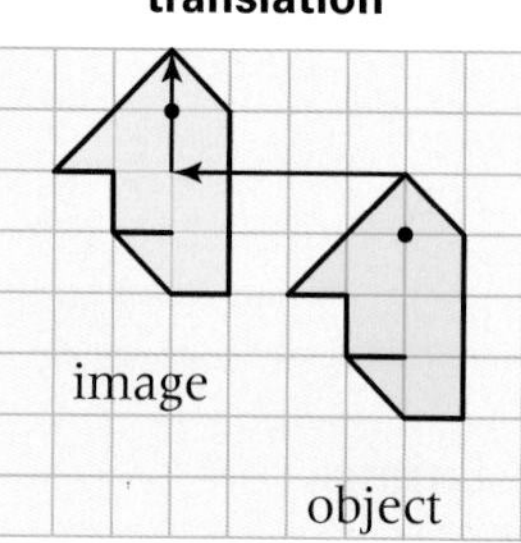

Example

This is triangle A.

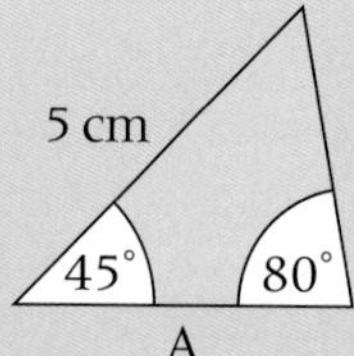

Which of these triangles are congruent to triangle A?

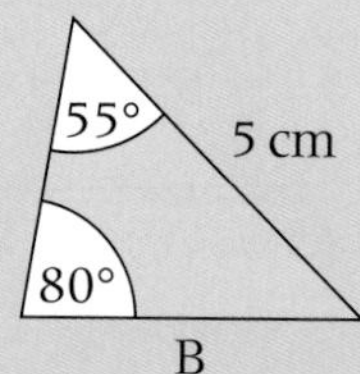

5 cm 60° 80° C

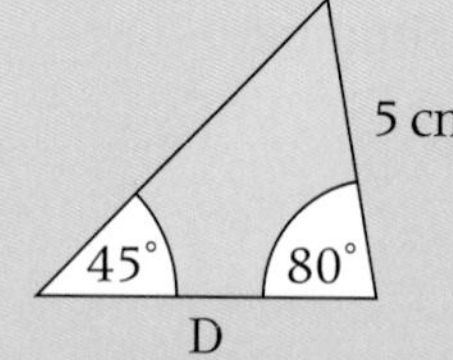

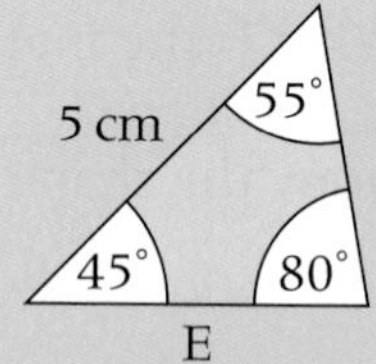

Fill in the missing information (angles in a triangle add to 180°).

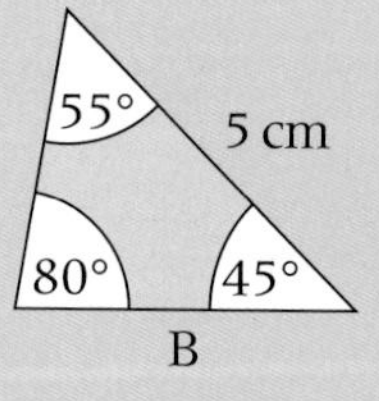

Yes, congruent to A

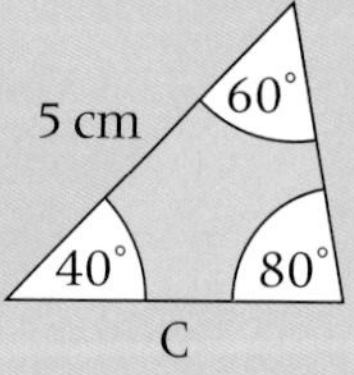

No, 40° is wrong

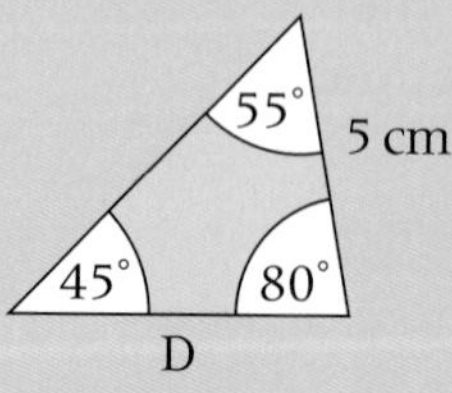

No, 5 cm is wrong

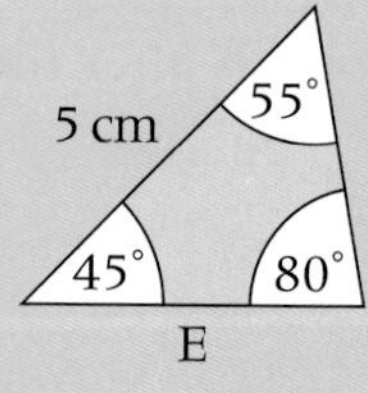

Yes, congruent to A

Exercise G4.4 Grade D

1 How many pairs of congruent triangles are there in this kite?

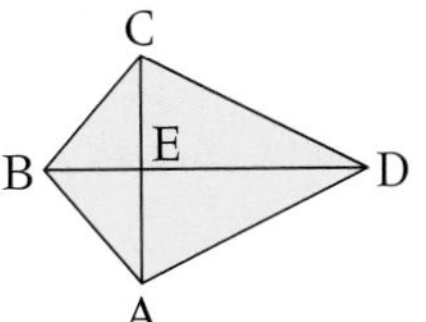

2 Which of these triangles are congruent to triangle A?

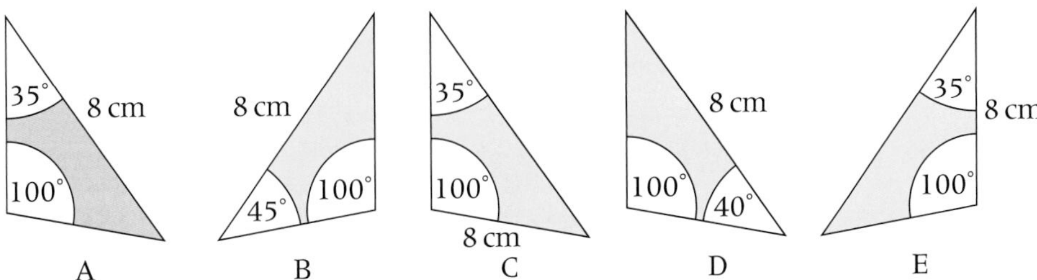

3 **a** Copy this shape and grid.
Translate triangle A by $\begin{pmatrix} 3 \\ 0 \end{pmatrix}$.
Label the image B.

b Translate triangle A by $\begin{pmatrix} 2 \\ -4 \end{pmatrix}$.
Label the image C.

c Describe the transformation of triangle C to triangle B.

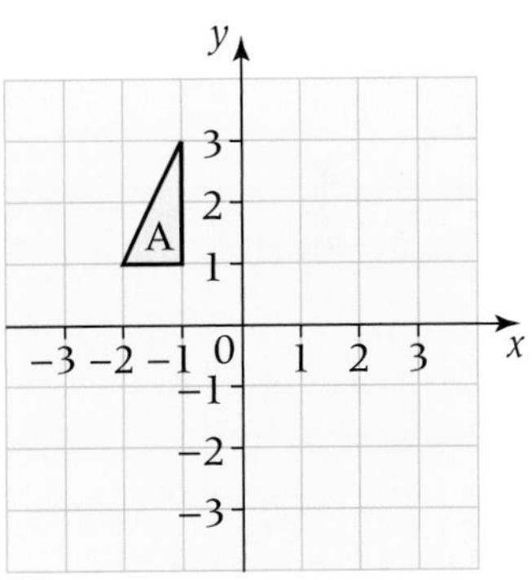

4 **a** Copy this shape and grid.
Rotate triangle A through 90° anticlockwise about the origin.
Label the image B.

b Rotate triangle A through 180° about the origin.
Label the image C.

c Describe the transformation of triangle C to triangle B.

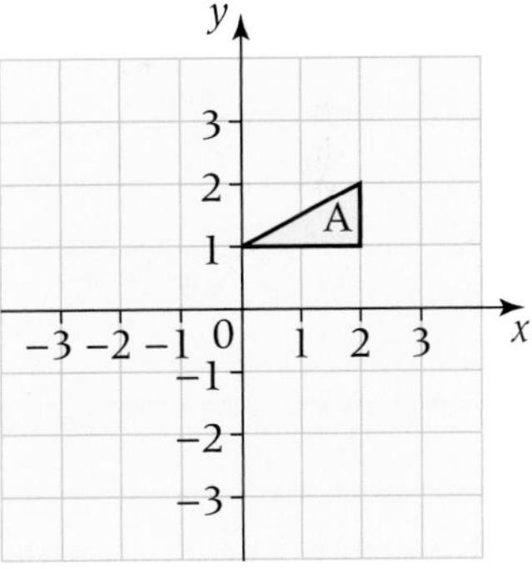

5 **a** Copy this shape and grid. Reflect triangle A in the x-axis.
Label the image B.

b Reflect triangle A in the y-axis.
Label the image C.

c Describe the transformation of triangle C to triangle B.

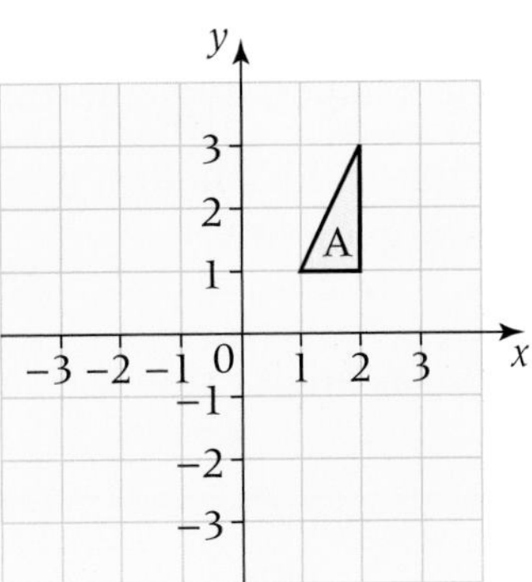

G4.5 Enlargements

This spread will show you how to:

- Recognise, visualise and construct enlargements of objects

Keywords
Enlargement
Multiplier
Scale factor
Similar
Transformation

To enlarge a shape, multiply corresponding lengths by the same scale factor.

- The scale factor is the **multiplier** in the **enlargement**.

p.284

The green trapezium is an enlargement of the yellow trapezium.

Corresponding lengths are multiplied by 2, $1 \times 2 = 2$, $2 \times 2 = 4$.

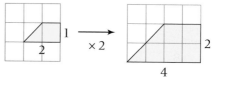

The scale factor of this enlargement is 2.

The two trapeziums are **similar** – same shape but different size.

Example

The green shape is an enlargement of the yellow shape.

Calculate the scale factor for each enlargement.

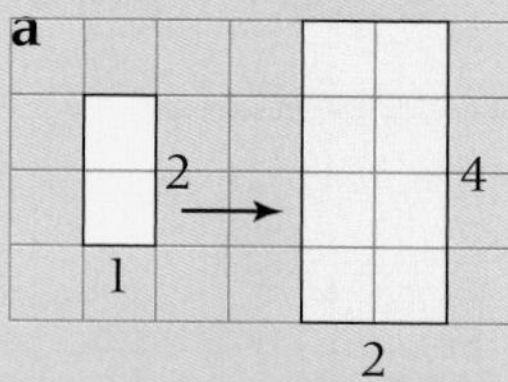

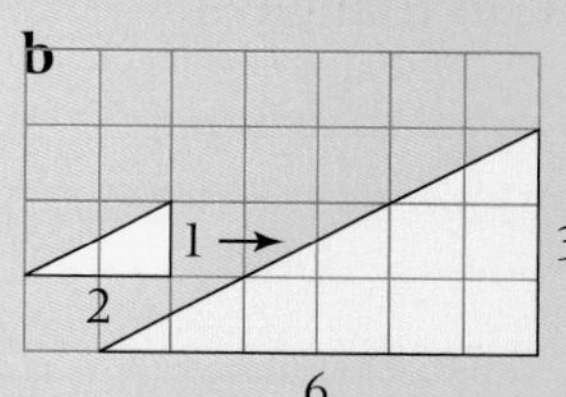

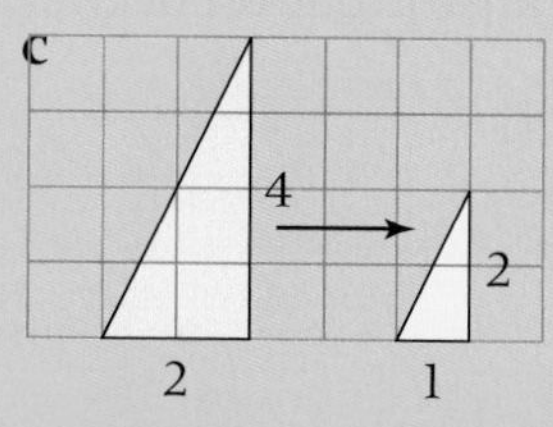

The scale factor is less than 1 as the shape actually reduces during the enlargement.

a Scale factor $= 4 \div 2$
$= 2$
Check: $1 \times 2 = 2$

b Scale factor $= 6 \div 2$
$= 3$
Check: $1 \times 3 = 3$

c Scale factor
$= 2 \div 4 = \frac{1}{2}$
Check: $2 \times \frac{1}{2} = 1$

Example

The green kite is an enlargement of the yellow kite by scale factor 3.

The smallest angle in the yellow kite is 53°.

What is the smallest angle in the enlargement?

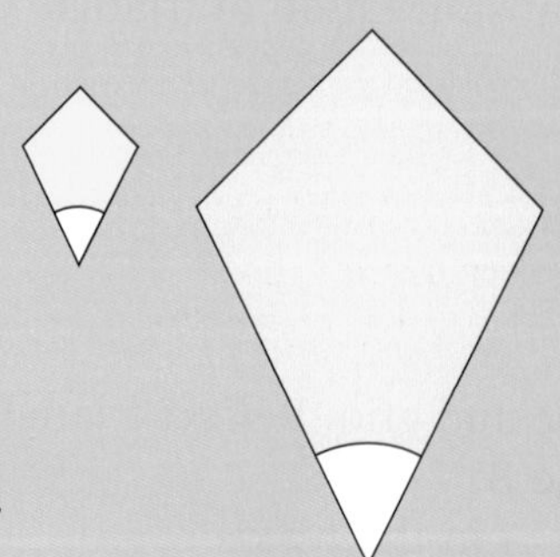

53°, as angles stay the same in enlargements.

Each length is multiplied by 3.

Exercise G4.5 Grade E

1 Calculate the scale factor of these enlargements.

a

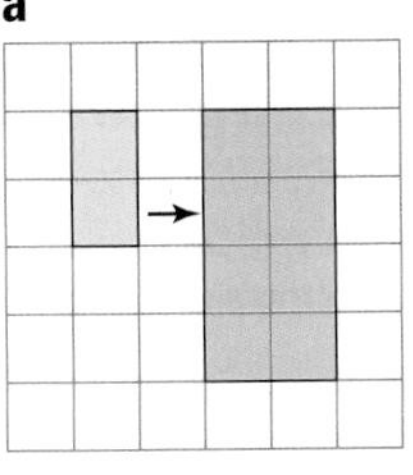

b

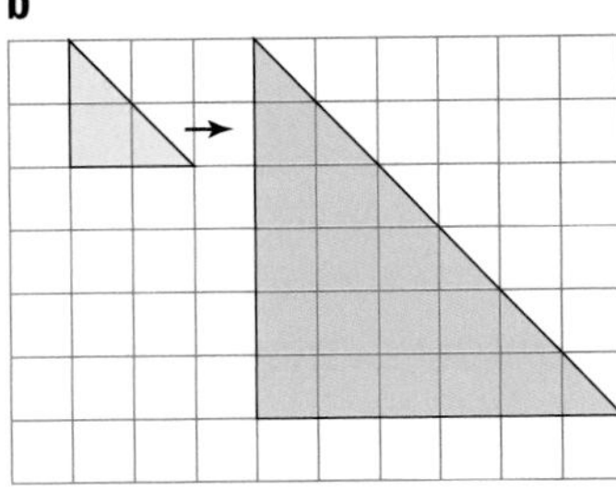

c

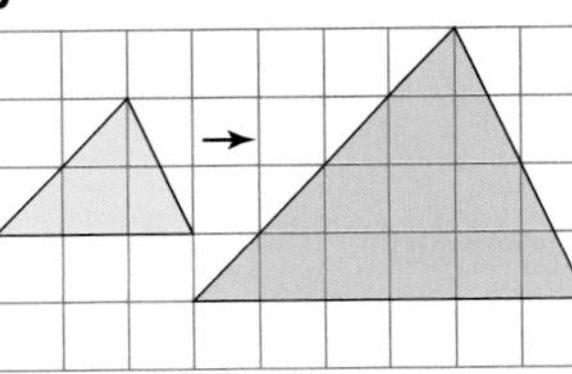

d

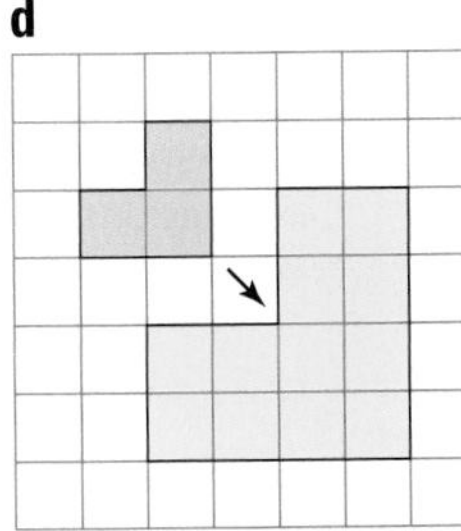

e

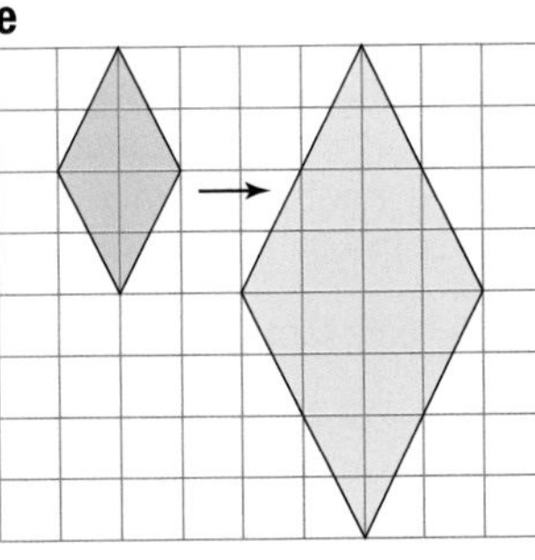

f

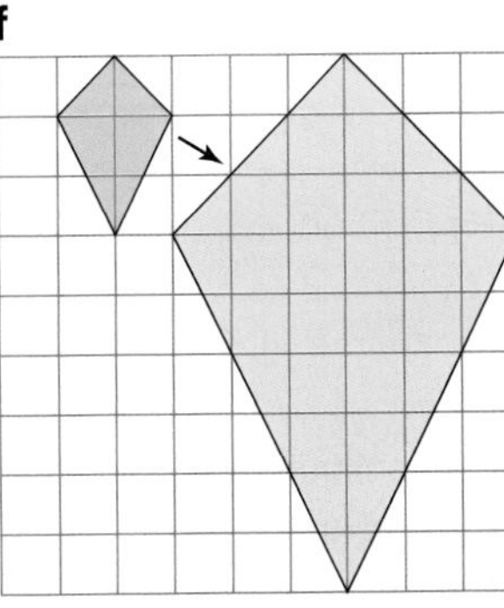

g

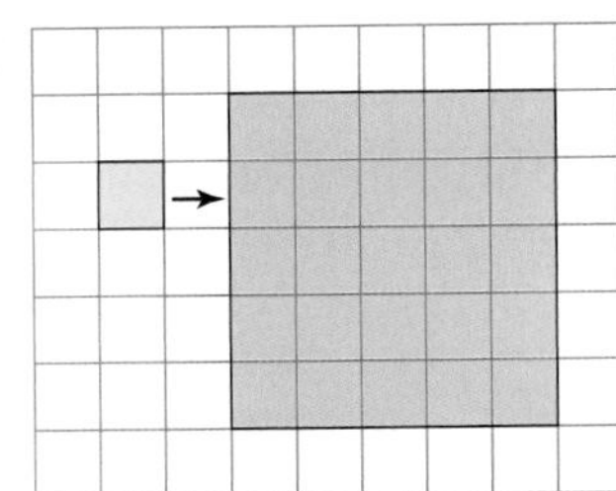

h

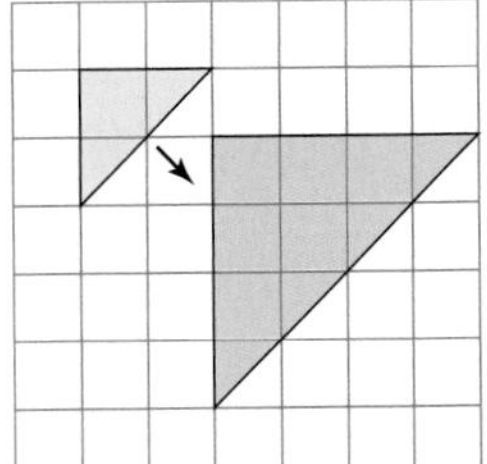

2 a Decide if these rectangles are enlargements of the yellow rectangle. If so, calculate the scale factor.

b List the rectangles that are similar to the yellow rectangle.

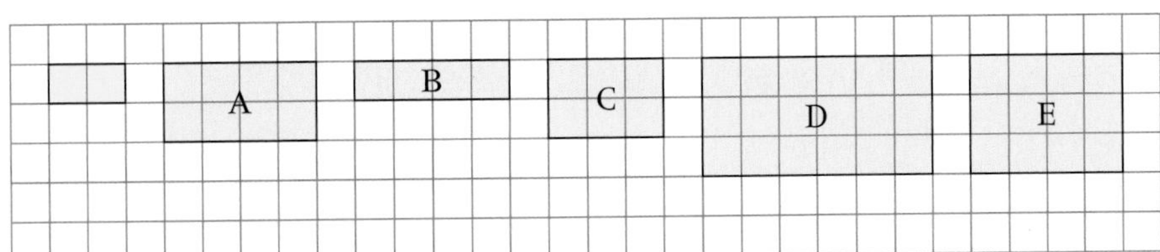

3 a Decide if these triangles are enlargements of the yellow triangle. If so, calculate the scale factor.

b List the triangles that are similar to the yellow triangle.

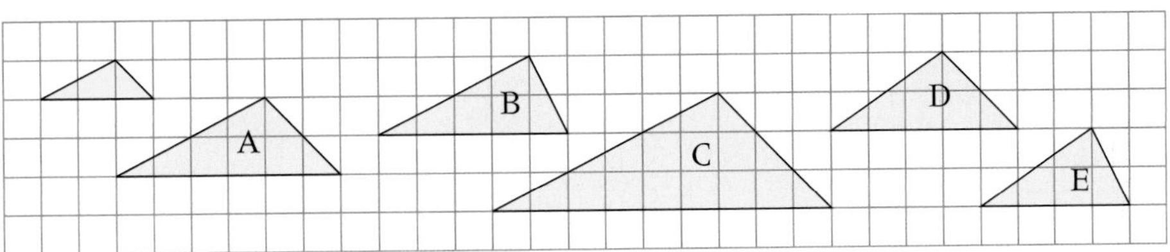

G4.6 More enlargements

This spread will show you how to:

- Understand that enlargements are specified by a centre and positive scale-factor

Keywords
Centre of enlargement
Enlargement
Scale factor
Vertices

- In an **enlargement**
  - the angles stay the same
  - the lengths increase in proportion.

The position of an enlargement is fixed by the **centre of enlargement**.

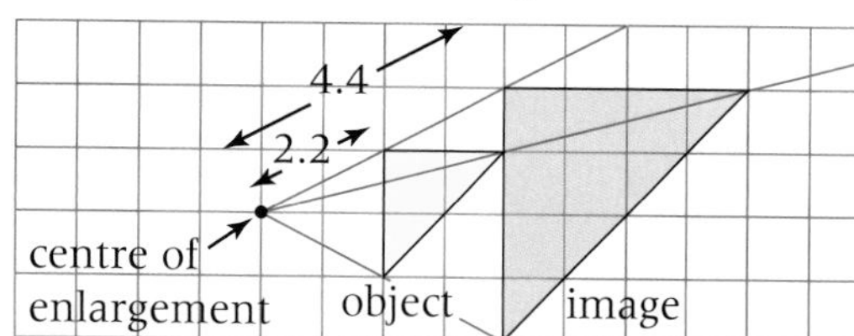

You multiply the distance from the centre to the object by the **scale factor**. This gives the distance to the image along the same extended line.

The scale factor of the enlargement is 2.

The red lines start from the centre and pass through corresponding **vertices** of the two shapes.

- To describe an enlargement, you give
  - the scale factor
  - the centre of enlargement.

Example

Find the centre of enlargement and calculate the scale factor of the enlargement from A to B.

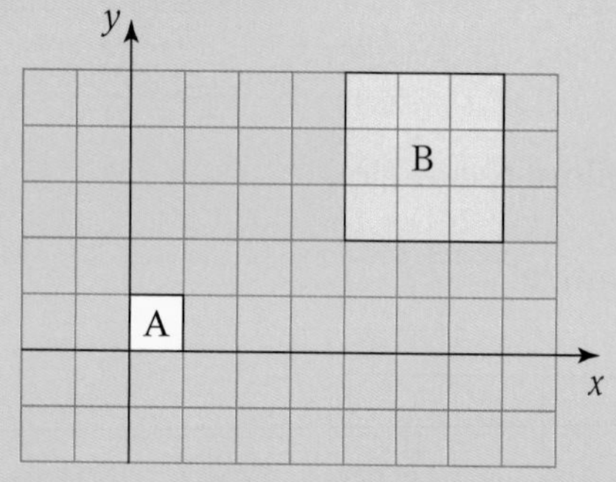

Draw the red lines to find the centre of enlargement.
Centre of enlargement is $(-2, -1)$
Scale factor $= 3 \div 1 = 3$

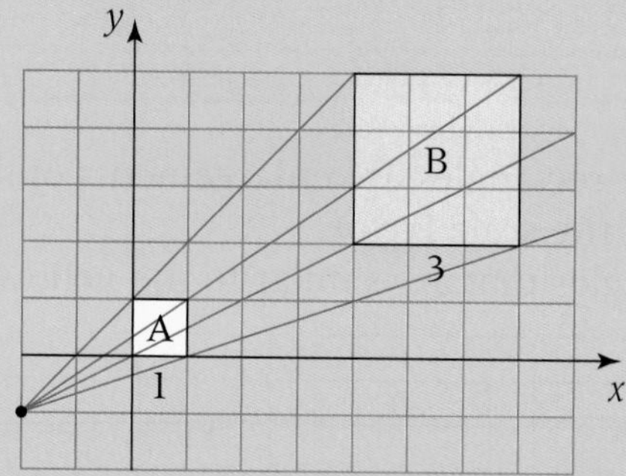

Example

Draw the enlargement of the yellow shape, using scale factor 2 and P as the centre of enlargement.

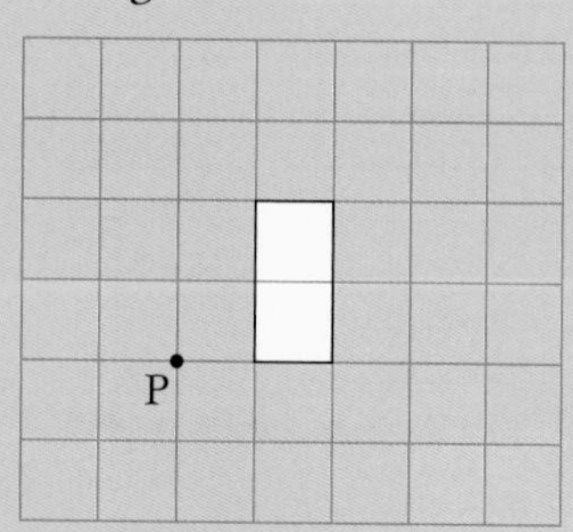

Draw lines from P to each vertex.
Multiply the distances from the centre by 2.

$2 \times 2 = 4 \quad 2.2 \times 2 = 4.4$

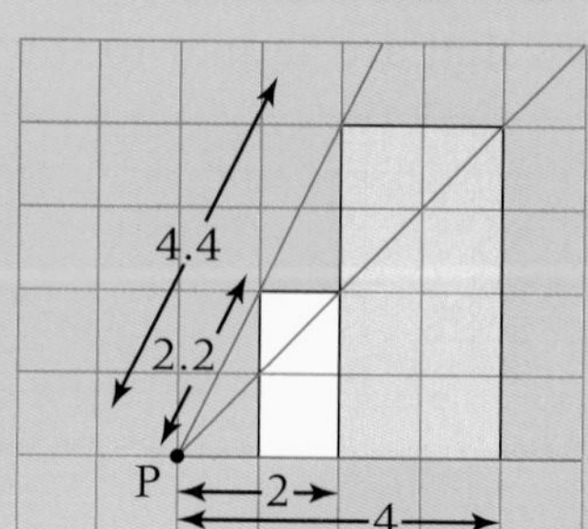

Exercise G4.6 Grade D

1 Copy each diagram on square grid paper. Find the centre of enlargement and calculate the scale factor for these enlargements.

a

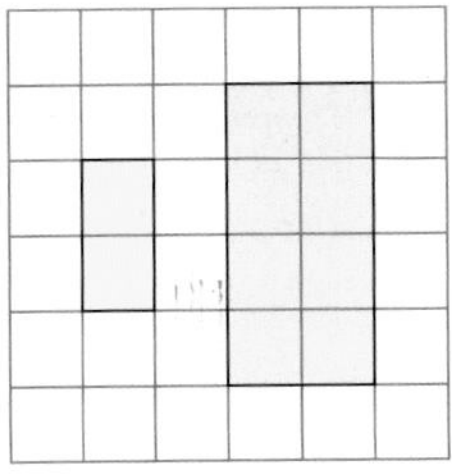

b

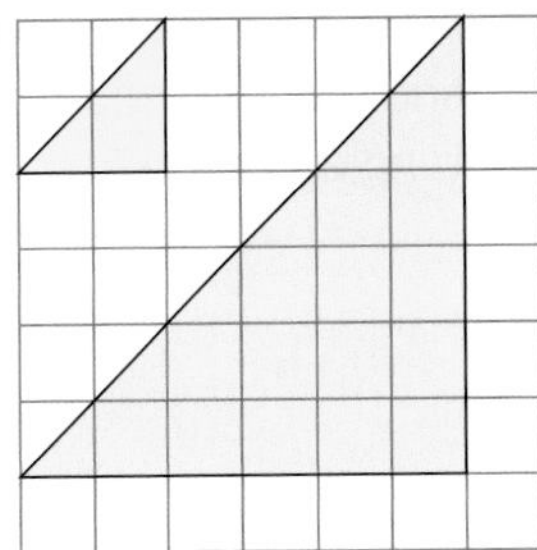

c

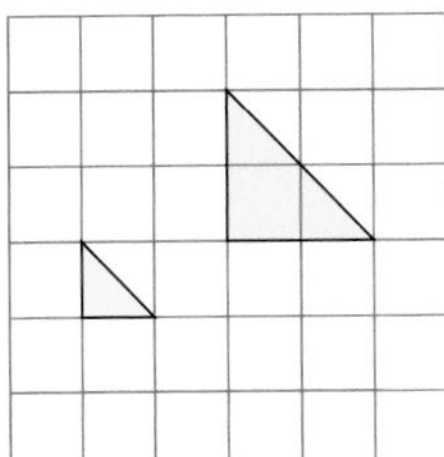

d

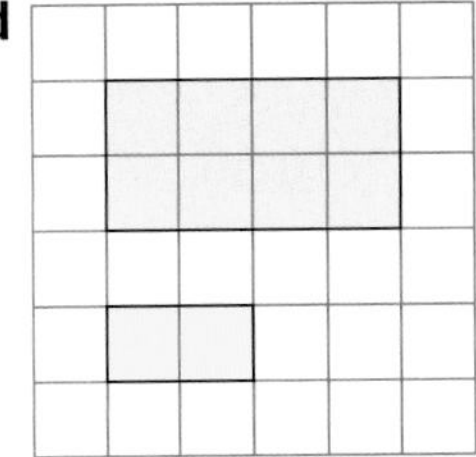

2 Copy each diagram on square grid paper.
Enlarge each shape by the given scale factor using the given centre of enlargement.

a

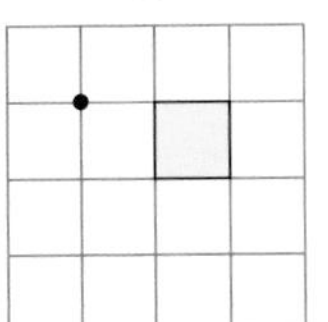

Scale factor 3

b

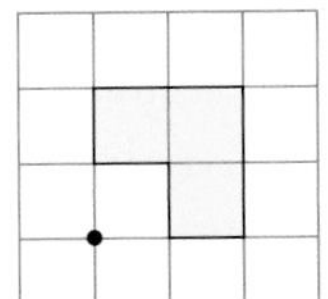

Scale factor 2

c

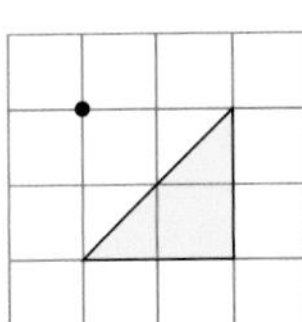

Scale factor 2

d

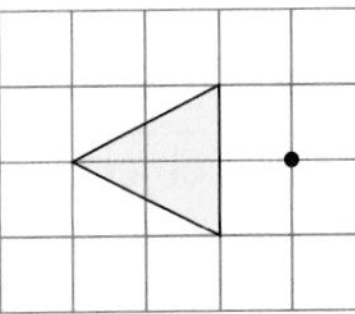

Scale factor 3

e

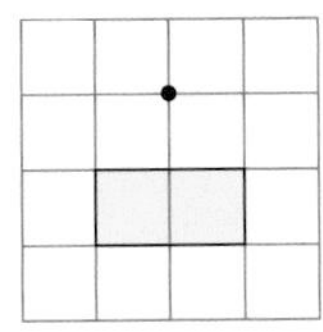

Scale factor 3

f

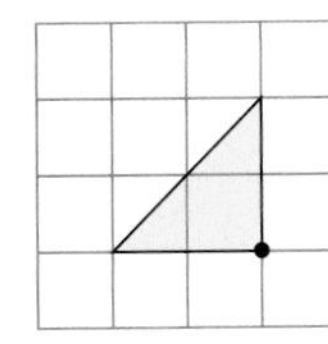

Scale factor 2

g

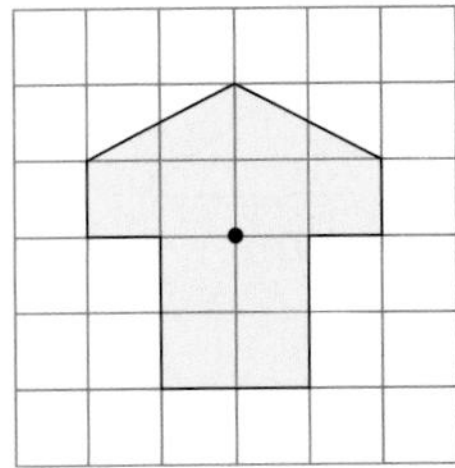

Scale factor 2

h

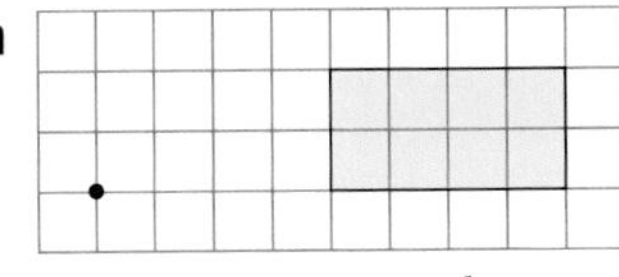

Scale factor $\frac{1}{2}$

i

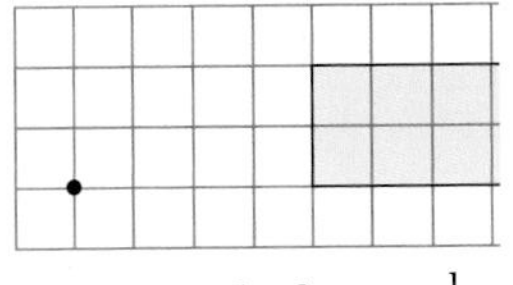

Scale factor $\frac{1}{2}$

j

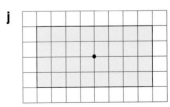

Scale factor $\frac{1}{2}$

G4.7 Similar shapes

This spread will show you how to:

- Identify the scale factor of an enlargement as the ratio of the lengths of any two corresponding line segments and apply this to triangles
- Understand that any two circles and any two squares are mathematically similar, while in general, two rectangles are not

Keywords
Enlargement
Scale factor
Similar

- In an **enlargement**, the object and the image are **similar**,
  - the angles stay the same
  - the lengths increase in proportion.

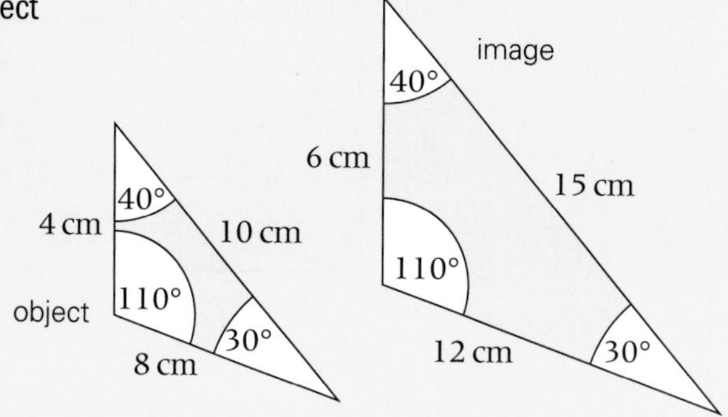

You use corresponding lengths to find the **scale factor**.

- Scale factor $= \dfrac{\text{length of image}}{\text{length of object}}$.

Example

These triangles are similar.
Find the length x.

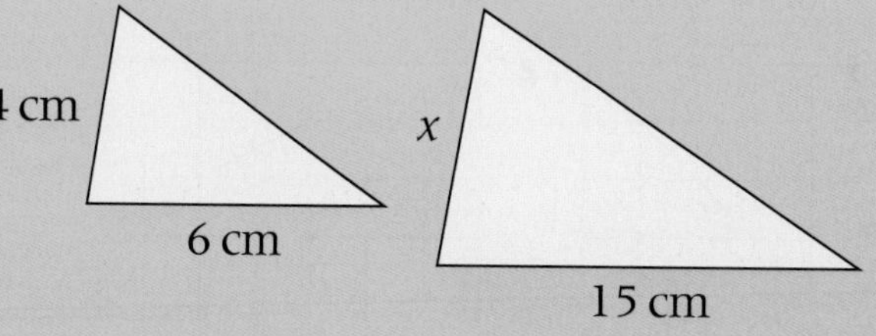

p.354

The scale factor is $\frac{15}{6} = 15 \div 6$
$= 2.5$

$x = 4\,\text{cm} \times 2.5$
$= 10\,\text{cm}$

Exercise G4.7 — Grade C

1 In each question, the two triangles are similar.
Find the value of the unknown angles.

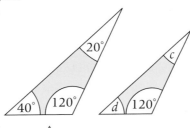

> Angles in a triangle add to 180°.

a

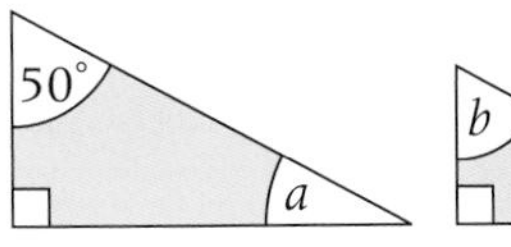

b

20°
40°
120°
c
d
120°

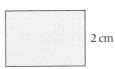

c

d

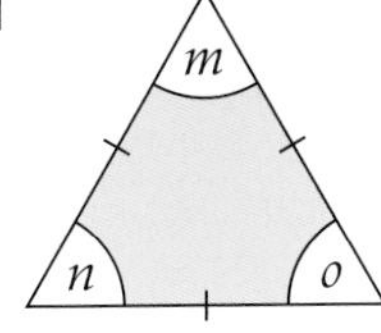

p
q
r

2 Which of these rectangles are similar to the green rectangle?

For the ones that are similar, give the scale factor of the enlargement.

2 cm
3 cm

a

b

c

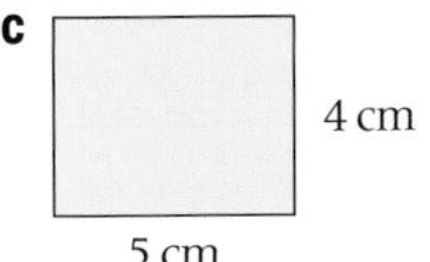

d

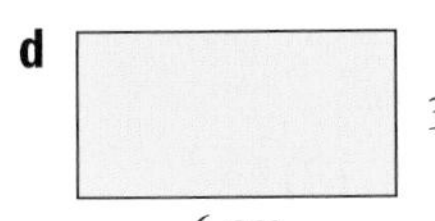

e

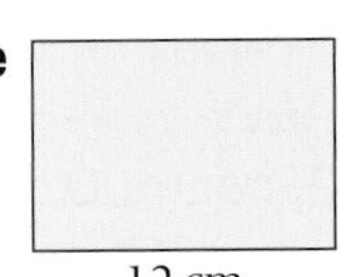

f

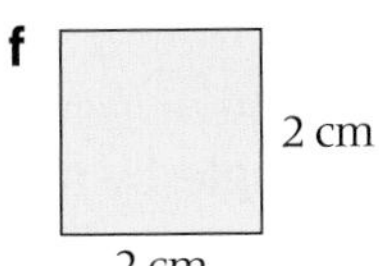

3 In each question, the two triangles are similar. Calculate the scale factor of the enlargement and the unknown length.

a

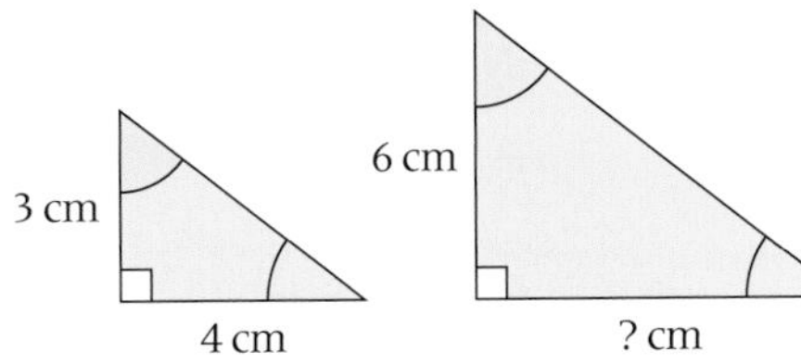

b

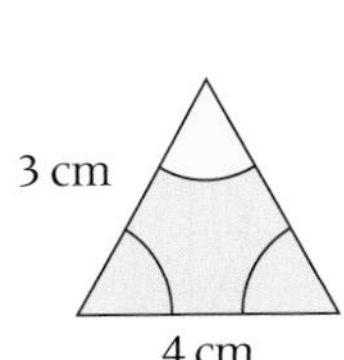

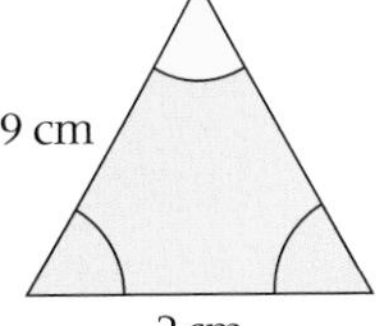

AO3 Problem

4 Which of these types of shapes will **always** be similar, no matter what their size?

Give reasons for your answers.

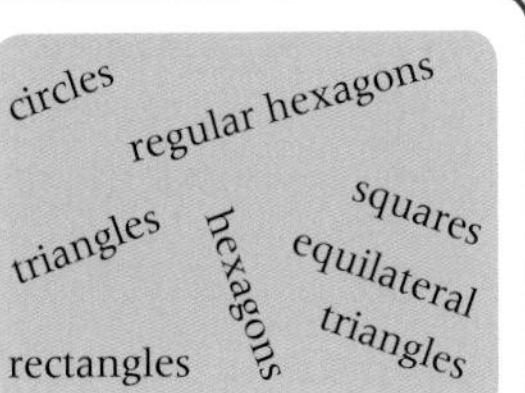

circles
regular hexagons
squares
triangles
hexagons
equilateral triangles
rectangles

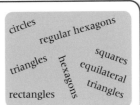

Summary

Check out

You should now be able to:

- Recognise and visualise reflections, rotations and translations
- Describe and transform 2-D shapes using reflections, rotations, translations and a combination of these transformations
- Understand congruence and identify congruent shapes
- Describe and transform 2-D shapes using enlargements

Worked exam question

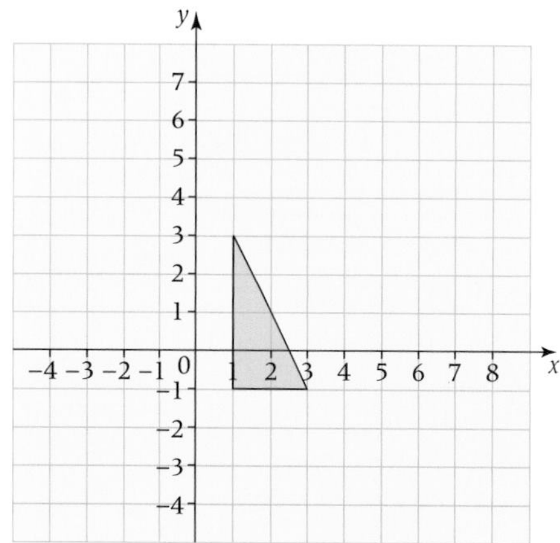

Enlarge the shaded triangle by scale factor 2, centre O. (3)

(Edexcel Limited 2004)

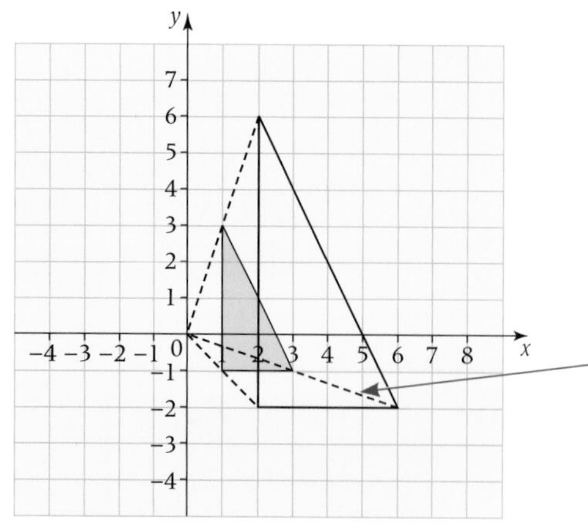

You can show the lines radiating from the centre of enlargement.

(3)

(Edexcel Limited 2004)

Exam questions

1

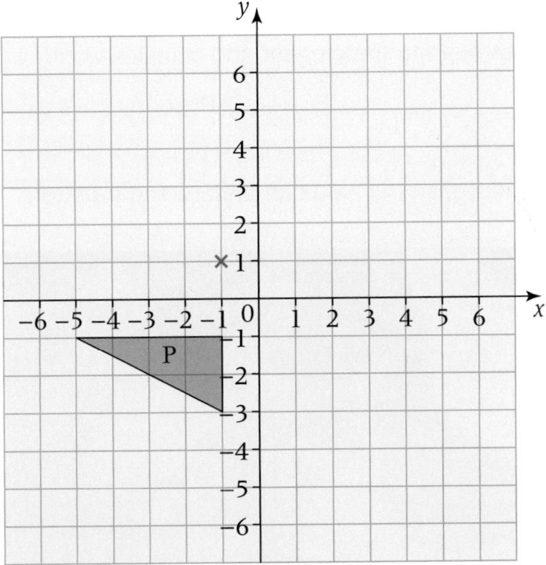

a Rotate triangle **P** 180° about the point (−1, 1).
Label the new triangle **A**. (2)

b Translate triangle **P** by the vector $\begin{pmatrix} 6 \\ -1 \end{pmatrix}$

Label the new triangle **B**. (1)

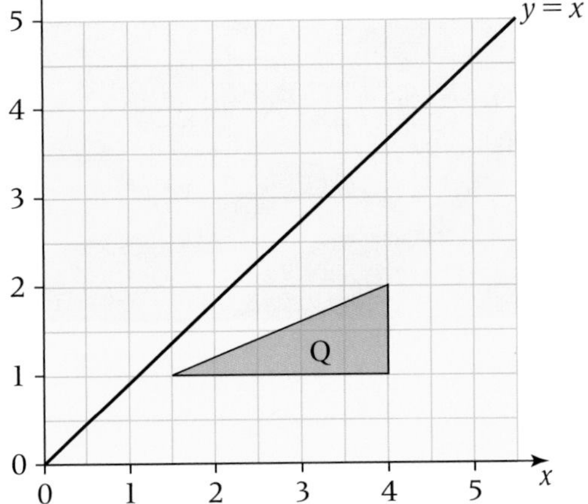

c Reflect triangle **Q** in the line $y = x$.
Label the new triangle **C**. (2)

(Edexcel Limited 2008)

Introduction

There are lots of different types of sequences in mathematics: from the most basic arithmetic sequences such as the set of even numbers, to the curious Fibonacci sequence used to describe plant growth, through to the elegant and complex world of iterative sequences used in chaos theory.

What's the point?

Sequences allow you to find patterns in nature, so that you can understand it better.

Check in

1 Work out the difference between

a 5 and 8 **b** 3 and 9
c 6 and 11 **d** -4 and $+2$

2 Find the difference between

a 10 and 7 **b** 9 and 5
c 12 and 7 **d** 3 and -1

3 Write down the first six multiples of

a 4 **b** 3
c 5 **d** 6

Orientation

What I should know		What I will learn		What this leads to
N1	→	■ Generate and describe sequences using a term-to-term and position-to-term rule ■ Describe and find the general term of a linear sequence	→	Careers in finance and computing
Key stage 3	→			

Rich task

You have 15 circles. Here is a sequence of patterns that you can make.

Devise the first three terms of a different sequence using all 15 circles. Find the *n*th term of your sequence.

Can you find another sequence that uses all 15 circles?
Investigate finding the first three terms of sequences for different numbers of circles.

A4.1 Term-to-term rules

This spread will show you how to:

- Generate and describe sequences using a term-to-term rule

Keywords
Common difference
Decreasing
Increasing
Linear
Rule
Sequence
Term

You can describe a **sequence** by giving the first **term** and the term-to-term **rule**.
The rule tells you how to work out each term from the one before.

Example

Write the first five terms in the sequence with first term 4 and term-to-term rule 'add 3'.

4, 7, 10, 13, 16

Start with 4; add 3 each time.

- In an **increasing** sequence, the terms are getting larger.
  For example 5, 9, 13, 17, 21, ...
- In a **decreasing** sequence, the terms are getting smaller.
  For example 12, 10, 8, 6, 4, ...

You can work out the term-to-term rule for a sequence and use it to find more terms.

Example

For each sequence, work out the two missing terms.
Describe the sequence in words.

a 19, 9, −1, −11, ... **b** 2, ___, 14, ___, 26, 32

a 19, 9, −1, −11, ___, ___
The first term is 19 and the terms decrease by 10 each time.
The next two terms are −21 and −31.

b From 26 to 32 is an increase of 6.
The sequence is 2, 8, 14, 20, 26, 32.
The first term is 2 and the terms increase by 6 each time.

A **linear** sequence increases or decreases in equal-sized steps.
The size of the 'step' is called the **common difference**.
For example: 7, 3, −1, −5, −9 Common difference = 4

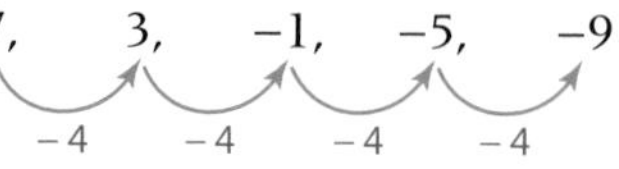

In some sequences, the 'steps' from one term to another are not equal.

Example

Describe how this sequence is increasing: 3, 4, 7, 12, 19, ...
Work out the next two terms in the sequence.

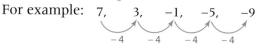

3, 4, 7, 12, 19, ...
+1 +3 +5 +7

The first difference is 1 and the difference increases by 2 each time.
The next two terms are 28 and 39.

To find the next term, +9:
19 + 9 = 28
To find the one after, +11:
28 + 11 = 39

Exercise A4.1 Grade E

1 Write out the first five terms of these sequences.

1st term	Rule
6	Increase by 4 each time
26	Increase by 5 each time
10	Decrease by 3 each time
−6	Decrease by 2 each time
−23	Decrease by 7 each time

2 Write down the first five terms in each of these sequences.

a Even numbers
b Odd numbers larger than 16
c Multiples of 4
d Multiples of 6 greater than 20
e Two more than the 5 times table
f Square numbers
g One more than square numbers
h Powers of 2.

3 Write out the first five terms of these sequences.

a 2nd term 7, increases by 3 each time.
b 2nd term 19, decreases by 6 each time.
c 3rd term 12, increases by 4 each time.
d 3rd term 14, decreases by 8 each time.
e 5th term is 8, increases by 6 each time.

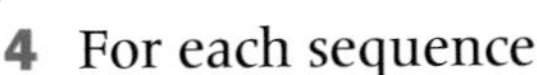

4 For each sequence

i work out the two missing terms
ii describe the sequence.

a 3, 10, 17, 24, ___, ___
b −7, 1, 9, 17, ___, ___
c −19, −16, −13, −10, ___, ___
d 7, ___, 15, 19, 23, ___
e 3, ___, ___, 27, 35, 43
f 16, 11, 6, ___, ___, −9
g ___, −8, −5, −2, ___, 4
h ___, 6, ___, −8, −15

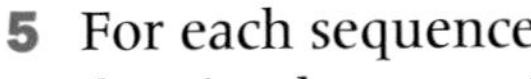

5 For each sequence

i write the terms in order from smallest to largest
ii describe the sequence.

a 8, 3, 5, 12, 2
b 25, 18, 27, 22, 28
c −3, 0, −6, 4, −5
d 20, 8, 6, 15, 11
e −21, −9, −23, −17, −24
f −1, 5, −15, −7, 3

AO3 Problem

6 Challenge

In each set of numbers there are two sequences mixed together. Write out each pair of sequences.

a 1, 3, 4, 5, 7, 7, 9, 10, 11, 13
b 2, 4, 7, 8, 11, 15, 16, 19, 23, 32

A4.2 The general term

This spread will show you how to:

- Generate and describe sequences using a position-to-term rule

Keywords
General term
*n*th term
Position-to-term

- A **position-to-term** rule links a term with its position in the sequence.

For example, the 4 times table: 4, 8, 12, 16, 20, 24, ... can be written as

1st term = T(1)	2nd term = T(2)	3rd term = T(3)	4th term = T(4)	5th term = T(5)	6th term = T(6)
4	8	12	16	20	24

$T(1) = 1 \times 4$ $T(3) = 3 \times 4$
$T(2) = 2 \times 4$ $T(10) = 10 \times 4$

The **general term** or ***n*th term** of the 4 times table is $T(n) = n \times 4$ or $4n$.

You can generate a sequence from the general term.

Example

Find the first three terms and the 10th term of the sequence with general term $3n + 2$.

1st term $3 \times 1 + 2 \rightarrow 5$
2nd $3 \times 2 + 2 \rightarrow 8$
3rd $3 \times 3 + 2 \rightarrow 11$
10th $3 \times 10 + 2 \rightarrow 32$

'Substitute' means swap a number for a letter.

To find a term, **substitute** its position number for *n*.

Example

The *n*th term of a sequence is $n^2 - 8$.
Copy and complete the table of results.

Term number	Term
1	
2	
3	
4	
10	
n	$n^2 - 8$

Term number	Term
1	$1^2 - 8 = 1 - 8 = -7$
2	$2^2 - 8 = 4 - 8 = -4$
3	$3^2 - 8 = 9 - 8 = 1$
4	$4^2 - 8 = 16 - 8 = 8$
10	$10^2 - 8 = 100 - 8 = 92$
n	$n^2 - 8$

Squared comes first then subtract 8.

Exercise A4.2 — Grade C

1 Find the first three terms and the 10th term of these sequences.

a $5n + 1$ **b** $3n + 8$ **c** $8n - 4$ **d** $6n - 8$

e $24 - 2n$ **f** $15 - 5n$ **g** $7n - 20$ **h** $4n - 6$

2 Copy and complete the table of results for each sequence.

a $3n + 8$

Term number	Term
1	11
2	
3	
4	
10	
n	$3n + 8$

b $6n - 15$

Term number	Term
1	−9
2	
3	
4	
10	
n	$6n - 15$

3 Write the first five terms of the sequences with nth term

a $n^2 + 4$ **b** $n^2 - 2$ **c** $2n^2$ **d** $12 - n^2$

4 Find the 2nd, 5th and 10th terms of the sequences with nth term

a $n^2 + 8$ **b** $n^2 - 6$ **c** $2n^2 + 7$

5 The general term of a sequence is given by $4n + 1$.

a Find the first three terms.

b Copy and complete:

Each term is ___ more than a multiple of ___

c Is 222 in the sequence? Explain.

6 The general term of a sequence is $2n^2 + 1$.

a Find the first three terms.

b Manjit worked out that the 5th term was 101.

Explain why he was wrong.

AO3 Problem

7 The general term of the sequence of square numbers is n^2.

a Write the first five terms of this sequence.

b Work out the differences between consecutive terms.

c Copy and complete this table.

1st square number	1	1
2nd square number	4	1 + 3
3rd square number	9	1 + 3 + 5
4th square number		
5th square number		
6th square number		

d What square number is equal to

$1 + 3 + 5 + 7 + 9 + 11 + 13 + 15 + 17 + 19$?

Do not work out the addition!

A4.3 Finding the *n*th term

This spread will show you how to:

- Describe and find the general term of a linear sequence

Keywords
Arithmetic sequence
Coefficient
Common difference
Linear

In some *n*th terms, the **coefficient** of n is negative.
For example, $5 - 3n$. The coefficient of n is -3.

Example

Write the first five terms of the sequence whose nth term is $5 - 3n$.

1st term: $5 - 3 \times 1 = 2$
2nd term: $5 - 3 \times 2 = -1$
3rd term: $5 - 3 \times 3 = -4$
4th term: $5 - 3 \times 4 = -7$
5th term: $5 - 3 \times 5 = -10$

The coefficient of n is the number that n is multiplied by.
In this example, the coefficient of n is -3.

Here are some linear sequences you have met before.

Name of sequence	General term	Sequence	Common difference
Multiple of 2	$2n$	2, 4, 6, 8, 10, …	+2
Multiple of 3	$3n$	3, 6, 9, 12, 15, …	+3
Multiple of 4	$4n$	4, 8, 12, 16, 20, …	+4
Multiple of 5	$5n$	5, 10, 15, 20, 25, …	+5
Multiple of −3	$-3n$	−3, −6, −9, −12, −15, …	−3

- For a **linear** sequence, the **common difference** tells you the multiple of n in the general form.

Another name for a linear sequence is an **arithmetic sequence.**

Example

Find the general term of the sequence
5, 8, 11, 14, 17 …

The common difference is +3.
The *n*th term contains the term $3n$.
Compare the sequence to the multiples of 3:

$3n$	3	6	9	12	15
Term	5	8	11	14	17

Each term is 2 more than a multiple of 3.
The general term is $3n + 2$.

Check:
$n = 1 \rightarrow 3 + 2 = 5$
$n = 2 \rightarrow 6 + 2 = 8$
$n = 3 \rightarrow 9 + 2 = 11$
…

- To find the general term of a linear sequence
  - work out the common difference
  - write the common difference as the coefficient of n
  - compare the terms in the sequence to the multiples of n

Exercise A4.3 — Grade C

1 Write the first five terms for the sequence with nth term

a $10 - 2n$ **b** $2 - n$ **c** $18 - 4n$ **d** $20 - 7n$
e $16 - 3n$ **f** $6 - 5n$ **g** $-2n - 5$ **h** $30 - 5n$
i $8 - 3n$ **j** $14 - 10n$ **k** $6 - n^2$ **l** $2n^2 - 10$

2 **a** Find the common difference for the series 5, 9, 13, 17, 21, ...

b Copy and complete:
The nth term contains the term □n.

c Copy and complete this table to show the sequence and the multiples of n.

Sequence					
□n					

d Compare the terms in the sequence to the multiples of n and write the general term for the sequence.

3 Follow the steps in question **2** to find the general terms for these sequences.

a 11, 17, 23, 29, 35, ... **b** 1, 10, 19, 28, 37, ...
c 15, 22, 29, 36, 43, ... **d** −10, −6, −2, 2, 6, ...
e 20, 17, 14, 11, 8, ... **f** 15, 11, 7, 3, −1, ...
g 16, 8, 0, −8, −16, ... **h** 31, 23, 15, 7, −1, ...

4 Find the nth term for each of these arithmetic sequences.

a 7, 11, 15, 19, 23, ... **b** −6, −2, 2, 6, 10, ...
c 32, 23, 14, 5, −4, ... **d** 15, 9, 3, −3, −9, ...

5 Copy and complete these tables for linear sequences.

a

Term number	Term
1	7
2	10
3	
4	16
5	19
n	

b

Term number	Term
1	−4
2	2
3	8
4	
5	20
10	
n	

A4.4 Pattern sequences

This spread will show you how to:

- Explain how the formula for the general term of a linear expression works

Keywords
Common difference
*n*th term
Pattern

You can find the ***n*th term** for a sequence of **patterns**.

Here is a pattern made of pencils: The next pattern in the sequence is:

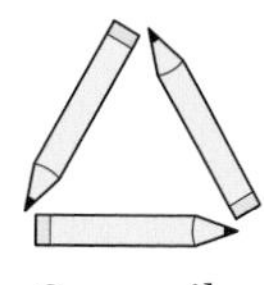

3 pencils

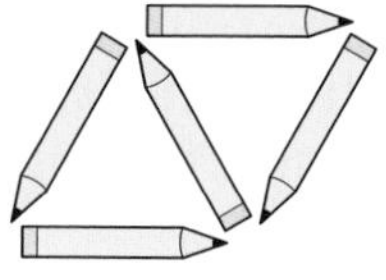

5 pencils

You add 2 pencils each time.

The nth term is an expression for the number of pencils in the nth pattern. To find the nth term, write the numbers of pencils in a table.

Pattern number	1	2	3	4	5
Number of pencils	3	5	7	9	11

You can work out the number of pencils in pattern 5 by continuing the number sequence.

The number sequence 3, 5, 7, 9, 11 has **common difference** 2. So the nth term contains the term $2n$.

$2n$	2	4	6	8	10
Sequence	3	5	7	9	11

Each term is 1 more than a multiple of 2.
The nth term is $2n + 1$.

Example

Here are some patterns made up of dots.

○ ○
○ ○ ○
Pattern number 1

○ ○ ○
○ ○ ○ ○
Pattern number 2

○ ○ ○ ○
○ ○ ○ ○ ○
Pattern number 3

Pattern number	1	2	3	4	5
Number of dots	5	7			

a Draw the next pattern in the sequence.
b Copy and complete the table for the first five terms.
c How many dots will there be in pattern number 10?

a ○ ○ ○ ○ ○
○ ○ ○ ○ ○ ○
Pattern number 4

b

Pattern number	1	2	3	4	5
Number of dots	5	7	9	11	13

Each time you add 2 dots – one to each row.

c The number sequence continues:

Pattern number	6	7	8	9	10
Number of dots	15	17	19	21	23

There will be 23 dots in the 10th pattern.

Exercise A4.4

Grade C

1 Here is a sequence of patterns made from squares.

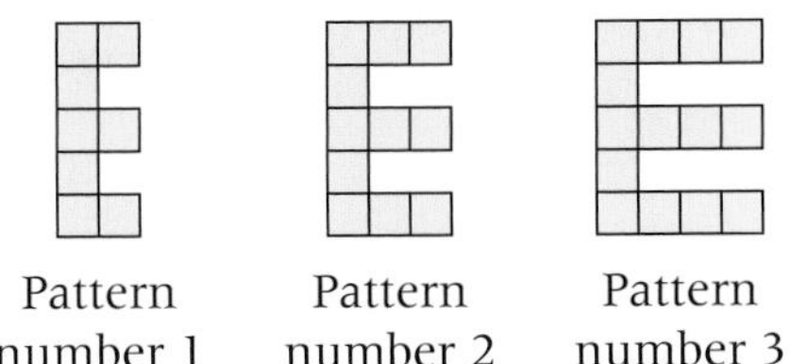

Pattern number	1	2	3	4	5
Number of squares					

a Draw the next pattern in the sequence.
b Copy and complete the table for the first five terms.
c How many squares will there be in pattern number 10?

2 Here are some patterns made from crosses.

Pattern number	1	2	3	4	5
Number of crosses					

a Draw the next pattern in the sequence.
b Copy and complete the table for the first five terms.
c Describe in words how the sequence grows.
d Work out the common difference for the number sequence.
e Find the nth term for the number sequence.

3 Here is a sequence of patterns of squares.

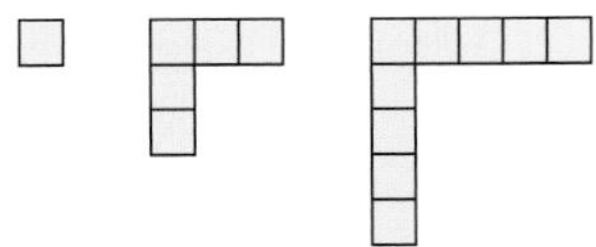

a Write the number of squares in the next two patterns.
Explain how you worked them out.
b Find, in terms of n, an expression for the number of dots in the nth pattern.
c Find the number of squares in the 50th pattern.

4 Repeat question **3** for these sequences of patterns.

a

b

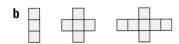

c

A4.5 More pattern sequences

This spread will show you how to:

- Explain how the formula for the general term of a linear expression works

Keywords
Justify

A farmer uses hurdles to build pens for his sheep. For the first pen he needs four hurdles.

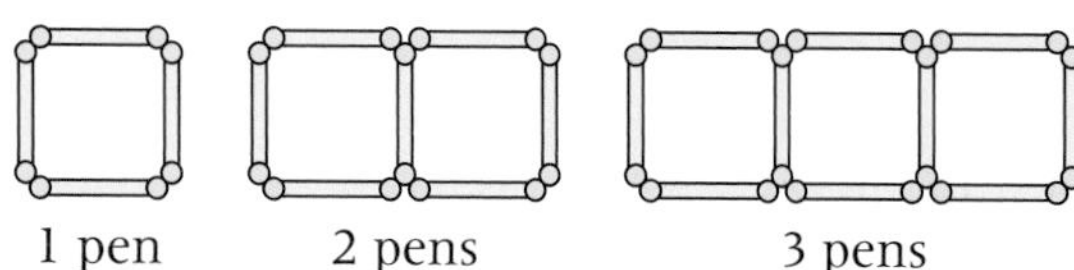

To make each new pen, he adds three more hurdles. The sequence for the number of hurdles is

4, 7, 10, 13, 16, ...

Common difference = 3

nth term = $3n + 1$

n	1	2	3	4	5
$2n$	3	6	9	12	15
Sequence	4	7	10	13	16

You can **justify** the nth term by looking at the pattern it comes from.

Justify means explain why it is correct.

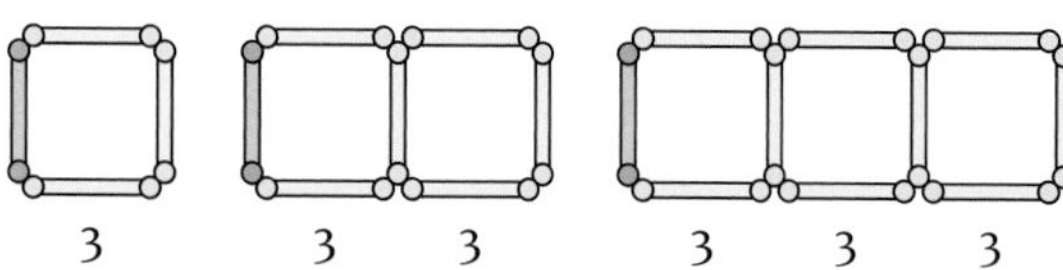

The nth pattern will have n lots of three hurdles (or $3n$), plus the one on the left-hand side.

Example

Here is a sequence of patterns of dots.

a Write the number of dots in the first five patterns.

b Find, in terms of n, an expression for the number of dots in the nth pattern.

c Justify your expression in n by comparing it with the dot patterns.

a 5, 7, 9, 11, 13

b Common difference = 2
Number of dots in nth pattern is $2n + 3$.

n	1	2	3	4	5
$2n$	2	4	6	8	10
Sequence	5	7	9	11	13

Each term is 3 more than a multiple of 2.

c The nth pattern will have $2 \times n$ dots, arranged with n above and n below the horizontal row, plus the horizontal row of three dots.

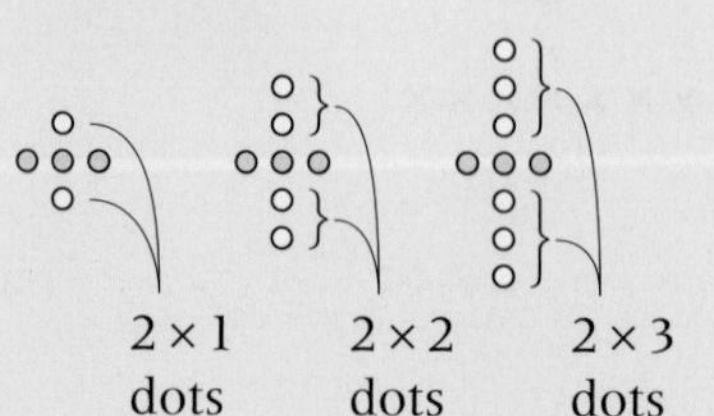

Look for what changes (the $2n$ term) and what stays the same (the +3 term).

Exercise A4.5 — Grade C

1 Here is a sequence of patterns of dots.

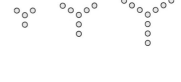

a Write the number of dots in the first five patterns.

b Find, in terms of n, an expression for the number of dots in the nth pattern.

c Justify your expression in n by comparing it with the dot patterns.

2 Kim is designing bead patterns for different-sized cushions. Here are her patterns for the first three sizes.

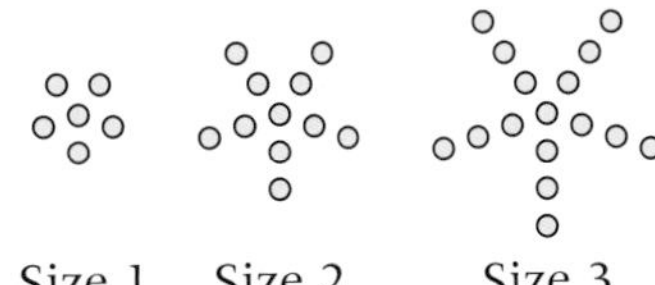

Size 1 Size 2 Size 3

a Write the numbers of beads in the patterns for the first five sizes.

b Find, in terms of n, an expression for the number of beads for the nth size pattern.

c Justify your expression in n by comparing it with the bead patterns.

3 Jas is building a house of cards.

Stage 1 Stage 2 Stage 3

a How many cards does he add each time?

b Write down the number of cards for the first five stages.

c Find, in terms of n, an expression for the number of cards in the nth stage.

d Justify your expression in n by comparing it with the diagrams.

e There are 52 cards in a pack. If Jas continues his pattern, can he use them all? Explain your answer.

4 Dave is building a fence from vertical and horizontal posts.
The fence grows like this:

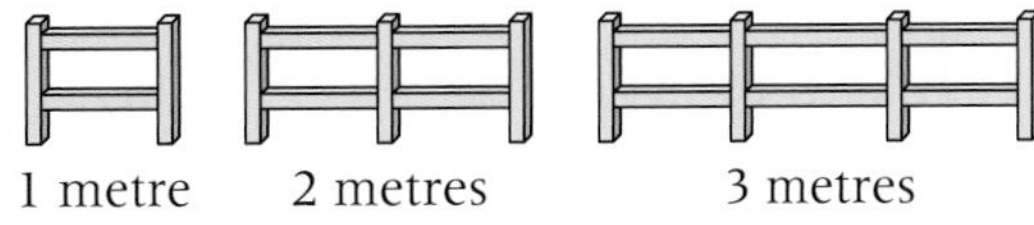

a Describe in words how the fence grows.

b How many posts will he need for 5 metres of fence?

c Find an expression in n for the number of posts for an n metre fence.

d Justify your expression in n by comparing it with the fence diagrams.

e Dave's garden is 26 metres long. How many posts will he need?

5 A car hire company charges these rates.

> Small car = £20 per day + £50 Medium car = £25 per day + £60
> Large car = £30 per day + £70

a Copy and complete this table of charges for 1 to 7 days.

b How would you work out the charge for a

i large car for 10 days

ii medium car for 14 days

iii small car for n days?

		Number of days						
		1	2	3	4	5	6	7
Type of car	Small							
	Medium							
	Large							

A4

Summary

Check out

You should now be able to:

- Generate sequences of numbers using a term-to-term rule
- Generate sequences of numbers using a position-to-term rule
- Generate and describe sequences derived from diagrams
- Find and use the *n*th term of a linear sequence
- Identify which terms cannot be in a sequence

Worked exam question

Here are the first five terms of a number sequence.

3 7 11 15 19

a Work out the 8th term of the number sequence. (1)

b Write down an expression, in terms of *n*, for the *n*th term of the number sequence. (2)

(Edexcel Limited 2006)

a

3 7 11 15 19 23 27 31

+4 +4 +4 +4 +4 +4 +4

The 8th term is 31.

b The *n*th term is $4n + ?$

You should write this stage of your working.

n	1	2	3	4
$4n$	4	8	12	16
term	3	7	11	15

The *n*th term is $4n - 1$.

Exam questions

1 **a** The first odd number is 1.

i Find the 3rd odd number.

ii Find the 12th odd number. (2)

b Write down a method you could use to find the 100th odd number. (1)

Here are some patterns made with dots.

Pattern Number 1 Pattern Number 2 Pattern Number 3

c Copy the pattern and complete Pattern Number 4.

Pattern Number 4 (1)

The table shows the number of dots used to make each pattern.

d Complete the table.

Pattern number	1	2	3	4	5
Number of dots	5	8	11		

(2)

(Edexcel Limited 2005)

2 Here are the first 5 terms of an arithmetic sequence.

6 11 16 21 26

Find an expression, in terms of n, for the nth term of the sequence. (2)

(Edexcel Limited 2003)

A03

3 Here are the first three terms of a sequence.

1 2 4 □ □

Suggest what the next two terms could be.
Give **two** possible alternatives. (2)

N5

Integers, powers and roots

Introduction

When you use the internet to pay for goods you need to know that your financial details are safe. To make these details secure they are turned into a secret code (encrypted). The message can be encrypted using the product of two very large prime numbers – the person receiving the message has to know both of these prime numbers so that they can decrypt the message.

What's the point?

The problems involved in identifying very large prime numbers make it very difficult for someone intercepting an encrypted message to crack the code.

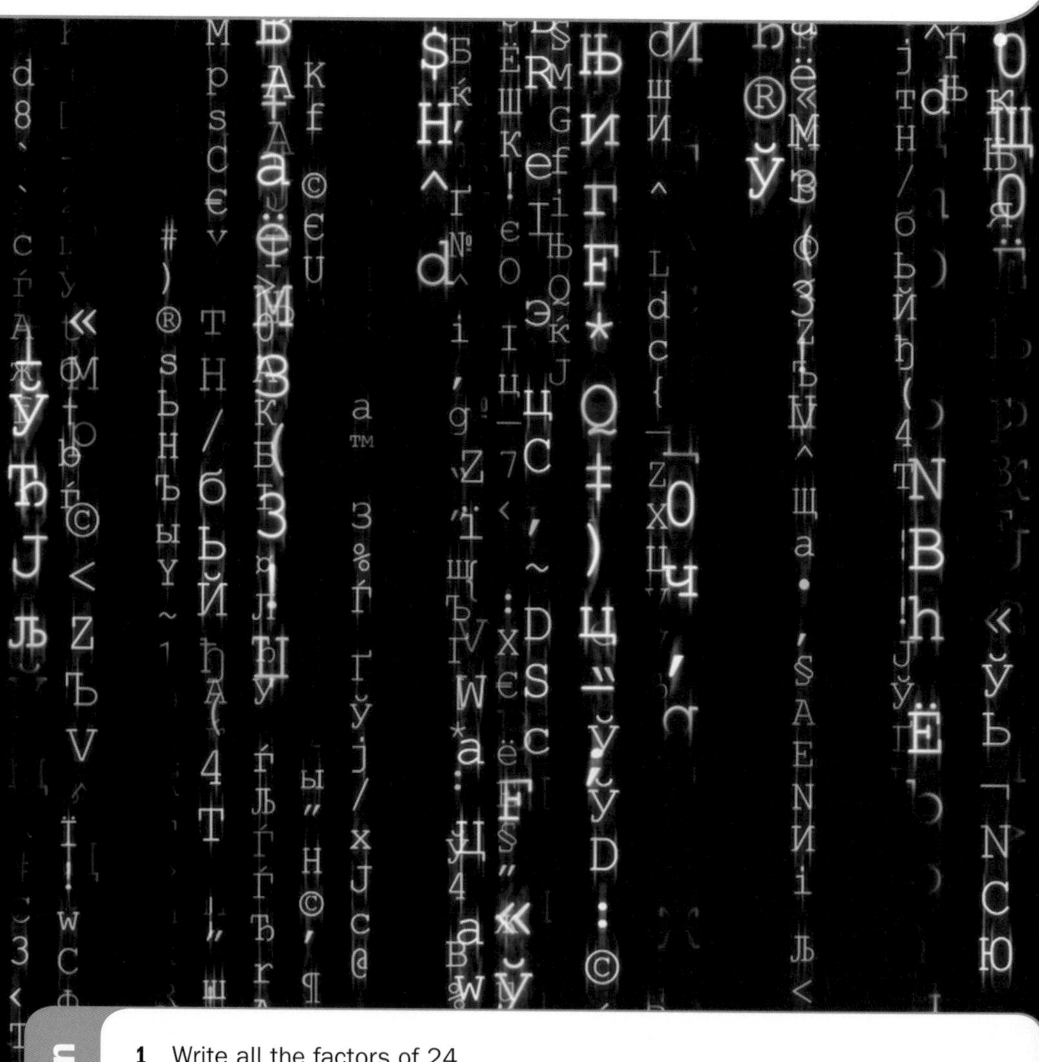

Check in

1. Write all the factors of 24.
2. Write the first 6 prime numbers.
3. Work out the value of each of these expressions.
   a $3^2 \times 5$ **b** $2^2 \times 5^2$

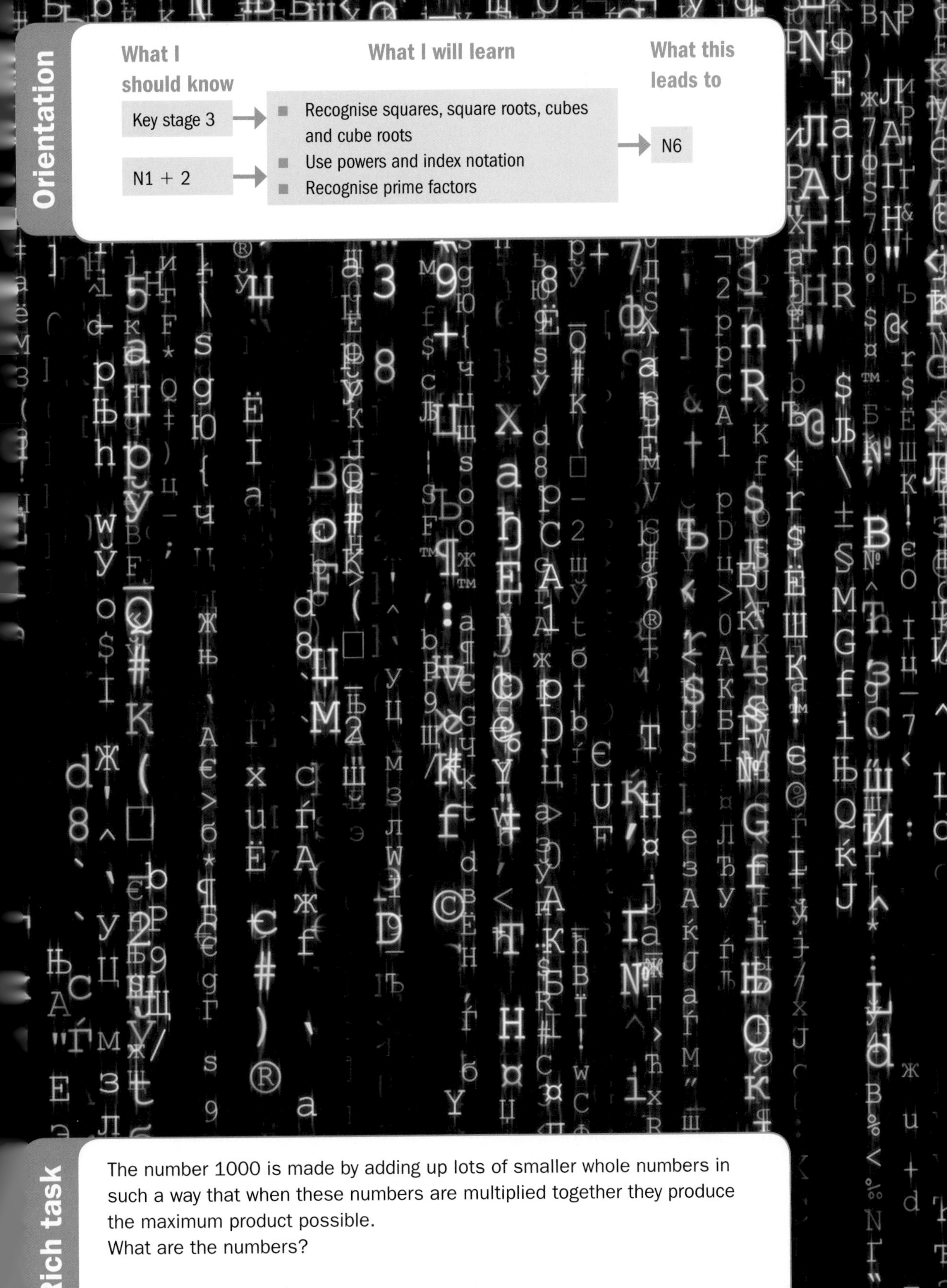

Orientation

What I should know	What I will learn	What this leads to
Key stage 3 N1 + 2	■ Recognise squares, square roots, cubes and cube roots ■ Use powers and index notation ■ Recognise prime factors	N6

Rich task

The number 1000 is made by adding up lots of smaller whole numbers in such a way that when these numbers are multiplied together they produce the maximum product possible.
What are the numbers?

N5.1 Factors and multiples

This spread will show you how to:

- Express a whole number as a product of its factors
- Understand and use simple divisibility tests
- Find the highest common factor and least common multiple of two numbers

Keywords
Factor
Highest common factor
Least common multiple
Multiple
Product

- Any whole number can be written as the **product** of two factors.

48 = 4 × 12 so 4 and 12 are **factors** of 48.

You can use simple divisibility tests to find the factors of a number.

A **factor** divides into a number exactly, with no remainder.

Here are some simple tests:

Factor	Test	120
2	the number ends in a 0, 2, 4, 6 or 8	120
3	the sum of the digits is divisible by 3	1 + 2 + 0 = 3
4	the last two digits of the number are divisible by 4	20 ÷ 5 = 4
5	the number ends in 0 or 5	120
6	the number is divisible by 2 *and* by 3	60, 40
7	there is no simple check for divisibility by 7	
8	half of the number is divisible by 4	15
9	the sum of the digits is divisible by 9	–
10	the number ends in 0	120

Factors of 120:
1 × 120
2 × 60
3 × 40
4 × 30
5 × 24
6 × 20
8 × 15
10 × 12

The **multiples** of 15 are 15, 30, 45, 60, ...

- You can find the **highest common factor** (HCF) of two numbers by listing all the factors of both numbers.
- You can find the **least common multiple** (LCM) of two numbers by listing the first few multiples of each number.

The **multiples** of a number can be divided exactly by the number, leaving no remainder.

Example

Find the HCF and LCM of 10 and 15.

The factors of 10 are: 1 2 5 10
The factors of 15 are: 1 3 5 15

1 and 5 are **common factors** of 10 and 15.
5 is the highest common factor of 10 and 15.

The first six multiples of 10 are: 10 20 30 40 50 60
The first six multiples of 15 are: 15 30 45 60 75 90

30 and 60 are **common multiples** of 10 and 15.
30 is the least common multiple of 10 and 15.

Exercise N5.1 Grade E

1 Look at this list of numbers.

2	3	4	5	6	8	10
12	15	16	17	18	19	20

a Write all the numbers that are factors of 20.
b Write all the numbers that are factors of 192.
c Write all the numbers that are multiples of 5.
d Write all the numbers that are **prime numbers**.

Remember:
A **prime number** has only two factors, 1 and itself.

2 Write all the factor pairs of each of these numbers.

a 24 **b** 45 **c** 66 **d** 100 **e** 120
f 132 **g** 160 **h** 180 **i** 360 **j** 324
k 224 **l** 264 **m** 312 **n** 325 **o** 432

3 Write the first three multiples of each of these numbers.

a 17 **b** 29 **c** 42 **d** 25 **e** 47
f 35 **g** 90 **h** 120 **i** 95 **j** 208

4 Find a number between 300 and 400 that has exactly 15 factors.

5 Find the highest common factor of

a 6 and 4 **b** 25 and 40 **c** 18 and 30 **d** 24 and 56
e 30 and 75 **f** 36 and 54 **g** 50 and 125 **h** 24, 36 and 72
i 30, 75 and 105

6 Find the least common multiple of

a 6 and 4 **b** 5 and 8 **c** 12 and 18
d 15 and 25 **e** 14 and 21 **f** 30 and 75

AO3 Problem

7 a Two hands move around a dial. The faster hand moves around in 24 seconds, and the slower hand in 30 seconds. If the two hands start together at the top of the dial, how many seconds does it take before they are next together at the top?

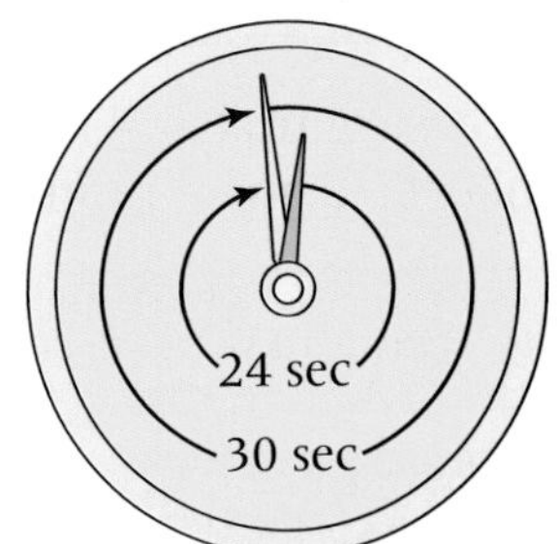

b A wall measures 234 cm by 432 cm.
What is the largest size of square tile that can be used to cover the wall, without needing to cut any of the tiles?

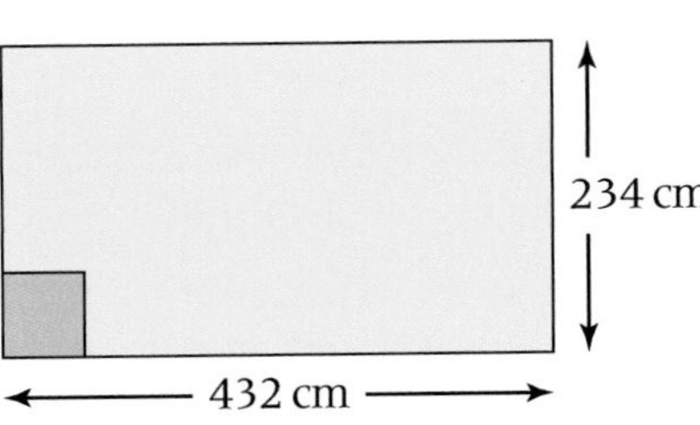

Squares and square roots

This spread will show you how to:

- Use powers and index notation for small positive integer powers
- Use the square and square root functions of a scientific calculator

Keywords
Index
Power
Square number
Square root

- A **square number** is the result of multiplying a whole number by itself.

Your calculator should have an x^2 function key.

Square numbers can be written using **index** notation.

$1^2 = 1 \times 1 = 1$ $\quad 2^2 = 2 \times 2 = 4$ $\quad 3^2 = 3 \times 3 = 9$

- A **square root** is a number that when multiplied by itself it is equal to a given number. Square roots are written using $\sqrt{\ }$ notation.

$\sqrt{225} = 15$ and -15 because $15 \times 15 = 225$ and $-15 \times -15 = 225$
You can write $\sqrt{225} = \pm 15$

Example

a Calculate the value of $\sqrt{300}$ using a calculator.
b Find $\sqrt{900}$ using a calculator.

a Using the calculator you would type

$\boxed{\sqrt{x}}\ \boxed{3}\ \boxed{0}\ \boxed{0}\ \boxed{=}$ $\quad$ √300 17.32050808

So $\sqrt{300} = 17.32$ (2 dp)

Check: $17.32^2 = 17^2$
$17^2 < 20^2 = 400$
$17^2 > 15^2 = 225$
17.32^2 is greater than 225 but less than 400.

b $\sqrt{900} = \sqrt{9 \times 100}$
$= \sqrt{9} \times \sqrt{100}$
$= 3 \times 10$
$= 30$

Use a calculator to find a square root using the $\sqrt{x}$ function key.

You can use trial and improvement to **estimate** the square root of a number to a given number of decimal places.

Example

Use trial and improvement to find $\sqrt{30}$ to 1 decimal place.

Estimate	Check (square of estimate)	Answer	Result
5	5^2	25	Too small
6	6^2	36	Too big
5.5	5.5^2	30.25	Too big
5.4	5.4^2	29.16	Too small
5.45	5.45^2	29.7025	Too small

So $\sqrt{30} = 5.5$ (1 decimal place)

In Paper 1 you will not be allowed to use a calculator.

p.388

Exercise N5.2 Grade E/D

1 Write

a the 5th square number **b** the 11th square number

c the 15th square number **d** the 17th square number.

2 In each of these lists of numbers, identify the square numbers.

a 8, 16, 24, 30, 36 **b** 49, 59, 69, 79, 99

c 140, 121, 135, 144, 136 **d** 214, 218, 223, 225, 222

3 Use your calculator to work out each of these squares. Give your answer to 2 decimal places as appropriate.

a 16^2 **b** 3.7^2 **c** 50^2 **d** 6.7^2

e 17.8^2 **f** $(-4.2)^2$ **g** 1.9^2 **h** 0.1^2

i $(-3.9)^2$ **j** 2.1^2 **k** $(-0.7)^2$ **l** 13.25^2

4 Calculate each of these using a calculator, giving your answer to 2 dp as appropriate. Remember to give your answer as both a positive and a negative square root.

a $\sqrt{529}$ **b** $\sqrt{157}$ **c** $\sqrt{41}$ **d** $\sqrt{0.16}$

e $\sqrt{6.46}$ **f** $\sqrt{800}$ **g** $\sqrt{1345}$ **h** $\sqrt{38.6}$

i $\sqrt{7093}$ **j** $\sqrt{234.652}$

5 Without a calculator, write the whole number that is closest in value to

a $\sqrt{50}$ **b** $\sqrt{80}$ **c** $\sqrt{30}$ **d** $\sqrt{40}$

e $\sqrt{120}$ **f** $\sqrt{150}$ **g** $\sqrt{8}$ **h** $\sqrt{5}$

AO3 Problem

6 Use your calculator to work out these problems.

a $\sqrt{7} = 2.645751$

Calculate $(2.645751)^2$.

Explain why the answer is not 7.

b Two consecutive numbers are multiplied together.

The answer is 3192.

What are the two numbers?

7 **a** Use a trial and improvement method to find the square root of 20 to 1 decimal place.

Estimate	Check	Answer	Result
4	4^2	16	Too small
5	5^2	25	
4.5			

b Use a similar method to find

i $\sqrt{40}$ **ii** $\sqrt{60}$ **iii** $\sqrt{95}$

N5.3 Cubes and cube roots

This spread will show you how to:

- Use powers and index notation for small positive integer powers
- Use the cube and cube root functions of a scientific calculator

Keywords
Cube number
Cube root
Index
Power

- A **cube number** is the result of multiplying a whole number by itself and then multiplying by that number again.

Your calculator should have a x^3 function key.

Cubes of numbers are written using **index** notation.

$1^3 = 1 \times 1 \times 1 = 1$ $\quad 2^3 = 2 \times 2 \times 2 = 8$ $\quad 3^3 = 3 \times 3 \times 3 = 27$

- A **cube root** is a number that when multiplied by itself and then multiplied by itself again is equal to a given number. Cube roots are written using $\sqrt[3]{\ }$ notation.

$\sqrt[3]{4913} = 17$ because $17^3 = 17 \times 17 \times 17 = 4913$

- A positive number has a positive cube root and a negative number has a negative cube root.

$\sqrt[3]{-125} = -5$ because $(-5)^3 = -5 \times -5 \times -5 = -125$

Example

Calculate the value of $\sqrt[3]{200}$.

Using a calculator you might type

$\sqrt[3]{x}$ 2 0 0 =

Display: $\sqrt[3]{200}$ 5.848035476

So $\sqrt[3]{200} = 5.85$ (2 dp)

Check: $5.85^3 \approx 6^3$
$5.85^3 < 6^3 = 216$
$5.85^3 > 5^3 = 125$
5.85^3 is greater than 125 but less than 216.

Use a calculator to find a cube root using the $\sqrt[3]{x}$ function key.

You can use trial and improvement to estimate cube roots.

In your Paper 1 assessment you will not be allowed to use a calculator.

Example

Use trial and improvement to find $\sqrt[3]{18}$ to 1 decimal place.

Estimate	Check (cube of estimate)	Answer	Result
2	2^3	8	Too small
3	3^3	27	Too big
2.5	2.5^3	15.625	Too small
2.6	2.6^3	17.576	Too small
2.7	2.7^3	19.683	Too big
2.65	2.65^3	18.609 625	Too big

So $\sqrt[3]{18} = 2.6$ (1 decimal place)

p.388

Exercise N5.3 — Grade C

1 Write

a the 7th cube number **b** the 10th cube number
c the 13th cube number **d** the 19th cube number.

2 In each of these lists of numbers, identify the square and cube numbers.

a 4, 11, 16, 27, 35 **b** 24, 44, 64, 84, 124, 144
c 156, 196, 216, 256, 286 **d** 700, 800, 900, 1000, 1200

3 Use your calculator to work out each of these. Give your answer to 2 decimal places as appropriate.

a 8^3 **b** 2.4^3 **c** 20^3 **d** 3.9^3
e 11.7^3 **f** $(-2.8)^3$ **g** 8.9^3 **h** 0.5^3
i $(-5.4)^3$ **j** 9.9^3 **k** $(-0.1)^3$ **l** 16.85^3

4 Calculate these using a calculator, giving your answers to 2 dp as appropriate.

a $\sqrt[3]{729}$ **b** $\sqrt[3]{100}$ **c** $\sqrt[3]{64}$ **d** $\sqrt[3]{86}$
e $\sqrt[3]{7.6}$ **f** $\sqrt[3]{2.7}$ **g** $\sqrt[3]{1.331}$ **h** $\sqrt[3]{56.3}$
i $\sqrt[3]{12\,167}$ **j** $\sqrt[3]{-216}$ **k** $\sqrt[3]{-70}$ **l** $\sqrt[3]{0.015\,625}$

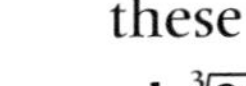

5 **a** Use a trial and improvement method to find the cube root of each of these numbers to 1 decimal place.

i $\sqrt[3]{20}$

Estimate	Check (cube of estimate)	Answer	Result
2	2^3	8	Too small
3	3^3	27	
2.5			

ii $\sqrt[3]{50}$

Estimate	Check (cube of estimate)	Answer	Result
3	3^3	27	Too small
4	4^3		

iii $\sqrt[3]{80}$ **iv** $\sqrt[3]{150}$ **v** $\sqrt[3]{300}$ **vi** $\sqrt[3]{500}$ **vii** $\sqrt[3]{900}$ **viii** $\sqrt[3]{1500}$

b Use the cube root key on your calculator to check your answers.

Powers

This spread will show you how to:

- Use powers and index notation for small positive integer powers
- Multiply and divide by powers of 10

Keywords
Index
Power
Powers of 10

- You can use **index** notation to describe **powers** of any number.
  $4.6^5 = 4.6 \times 4.6 \times 4.6 \times 4.6 \times 4.6$

To work out 4.6^5 you might type: [4] [·] [6] [y^x] [5] [=]

The calculator display should read 2059.62976.

Some calculators may have a different key, for example [x^y] or

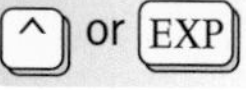

[^] or [EXP].

- Powers of the same number can be multiplied and divided.
  When multiplying, you add the indices.

p.124

$5^3 \times 5^4 = (5 \times 5 \times 5) \times (5 \times 5 \times 5 \times 5) = 5^7 \Rightarrow 5^{3+4} = 5^7$

When dividing, you subtract the indices.

$3^5 \div 3^2 = \frac{3 \times 3 \times 3 \times \cancel{3} \times \cancel{3}}{\cancel{3} \times \cancel{3}} = 3 \times 3 \times 3 = 3^3 \Rightarrow 3^{5-2} = 3^3$

The decimal system is based upon **powers of 10**.

Example

Calculate **a** 6.3×10^3 **b** $120 \div 10^4$.

a

Thousands	Hundreds	Tens	Units	•	tenths	hundredths	
			6	•	3		$\times 10^3$
6	3	0	0	•			

$6.3 \times 10^3 = 6300$

b

Hundreds	Tens	Units	•	tenths	hundredths	thousandths	
1	2	0	•				$\div 10^4$
			•	0	1	2	

$120 \div 10^4 = 0.012$

When you multiply by 10^3, all the digits move **three** places to the left.

When you divide by 10^4, all the digits move **four** places to the right.

Example

Simplify each quantity, leaving your answer as a single power.

a $3^2 \times 3^3$ **b** $8^5 \div 8^2$ **c** $x^7 \div x^3$

a $3^2 \times 3^3$
$= 3^{2+3}$
$= 3^5$

b $8^5 \div 8^2$
$= 8^{5-2}$
$= 8^3$

c $x^7 \div x^3$
$= x^{7-3}$
$= x^4$

Exercise N5.4 — Grade C

1 Calculate these without using a calculator.
a 4^2 **b** 2^5 **c** 5^3
d 7^4 **e** 9^3

2 Use the x^y function key on your calculator to work out these, giving your answers to 2 decimal places where appropriate.
a 15^3 **b** 3^6 **c** 2^{10}
d 21.6^4 **e** 13^3

3 Use your calculator to work out each of these.
a $2^4 + 3^2$ **b** $10^3 \div 5^2$ **c** $8^6 - 13^3$
d $10^6 \div 5^3$ **e** $\left(\frac{1}{4}\right)^4 + \left(\frac{1}{8}\right)^2$

4 Use the x^y function key on your calculator to find the value of x.
a $3^x = 27$ **b** $5^x = 625$ **c** $10^x = 10\,000$
d $4^x = 16\,384$ **e** $x^2 = 529$

5 Calculate these.
a 3.4×10^2

Thousands	Hundreds	Tens	Units	•	tenths	hundredths	
			3	•	4		$\times 10^2$

b 76.6×10^3 **c** $85 \div 10^3$ **d** 2.3×10^4
e 0.312×10^6 **f** 5.62×10^4 **g** $2960 \div 1000$

6 Simplify each of these, leaving your answer as a single power of the number.
a $3^2 \times 3^2$ **b** $7^3 \times 7^2$ **c** $2^7 \times 2^5$
d $10^7 \div 10^4$ **e** $3^{10} \div 3^6$ **f** $4^2 \times 4^3 \times 4^2$
g $10^5 \times 10^2 \times 10^3$ **h** $7^4 \times 7^1 \times 7$
i $\dfrac{2^3 \times 2^5}{2^2}$ **j** $\dfrac{10^3 \times 10^4}{10^2}$ **k** $\dfrac{4^2 \times 4^2 \times 4^2}{4^6}$

7 Copy these and fill in the missing numbers.
a $540 \div 10^2 =$ ___ **b** $6850 \div 10^? = 6.85$
c $3.12 \times$ ___ $= 31\,200$ **d** $1.73 \times 10^6 =$ ___

8 Simplify each of these, leaving your answer as a single power of the number or letter where appropriate.
a $y^2 \times y^3$ **b** $4^8 \times 4^2$ **c** $w^{12} \div w^7$
d $4^y \div 4^2$ **e** $\dfrac{g^6 \times g^3}{g^5}$ **f** $3^2 \times 4^3$

N5.5 Prime factor decomposition

This spread will show you how to:

- Recognise prime factors and express a number as a product of its prime factors
- Find the HCF and LCM of two numbers

Keywords
Factor
HCF
LCM
Prime factor
Prime number

- A **prime factor** is a factor of a number which is also prime.

Factors of 28 are {1, 2, 4, 7, 14, 28}.
Prime factors of 28 are {2, 7

- Every whole number can be written as the product of its **prime factors**.

There are two common methods to find the prime factors.

Factor trees

Split the number into a **factor** pair.
Continue splitting until you reach a prime factor.

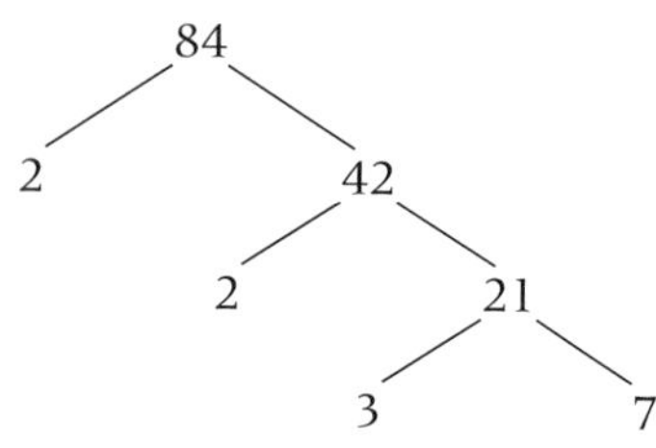

$84 = 2 \times 2 \times 3 \times 7$

Division by prime numbers

Divide the number by the smallest **prime number**.
Repeat dividing by larger prime numbers until you reach a prime number.

2	84
2	42
3	21
	7

$84 = 2 \times 2 \times 3 \times 7$

- You can find the **highest common factor (HCF)** by using prime factors.
  For example, the HCF of 30 and 135:

$30 = 2 \times 3 \times 5 \quad = 2 \times 3 \times 5$

2	30
3	15
	5

$135 = 3 \times 3 \times 3 \times 5 = 3 \times 3 \times 3 \times 5$

3	135
3	45
3	15
	5

HCF $= 3 \times 5 = 15$

- Write each number as the product of its prime factors.
- Pick out the common factors 3 and 5.
- Multiply these together to get the HCF.

- You can find the **least common multiple (LCM)** by using prime factors.

For example, the LCM of 28 and 126:

$28 = 2^2 \times 7 = 2 \times 2 \times 7$

2	28
2	14
	7

$126 = 2 \times 3^2 \times 7 = 2 \times 3 \times 3 \times 7$

2	126
3	63
3	21
	7

HCF $= 2 \times 7 = 14$
LCM $= 2 \times 3 \times 3 \times 14 = 252$

- Write each number as the product of its prime factors.
- Pick out the common factors 2 and 7.
- Multiply these together to get the HCF (14).
- Multiply the HCF by the remaining factors – the remaining factors are 2, 3 and 3.

Exercise N5.5

Grade C

1 Work out the value of each of these expressions.

a 3×5^2 **b** $2^3 \times 5$ **c** $3^2 \times 7$

d $2^2 \times 3^2 \times 5$ **e** $3^2 \times 7^2$

2 Express these numbers as products of their prime factors.

a 18 **b** 24 **c** 40 **d** 39

e 48 **f** 82 **g** 100 **h** 144

i 180 **j** 315 **k** 444 **l** 1350

3 In each of these questions, Jack has been asked to write each of the numbers as the product of its prime factors.

i Mark his work and identify any errors he has made.

ii Correct any of Jack's mistakes.

a 126

2	126
3	63
3	21
	7

Answer: $126 = 2 \times 3^2$

b 210

2	210
3	105
3	21
	7

Answer: $2 \times 3^2 \times 7$

c 221

	221

Answer: 221

A03 Problem

4 The number 18 can be written as $2 \times 3 \times 3$.
You can say that 18 has three prime factors.

a Find three numbers with exactly three prime factors.

b Find five numbers with exactly four prime factors.

c Find four numbers between 100 and 300 with exactly five prime factors.

d Find a two-digit number with exactly six prime factors.

5 Find the HCF of

a 9 and 24 **b** 15 and 40 **c** 18 and 24

d 96 and 144 **e** 12, 15 and 18 **f** 425 and 816.

6 Find the LCM of

a 9 and 24 **b** 15 and 40 **c** 18 and 24

d 20 and 30 **e** 12, 15 and 18 **f** 48, 54 and 72.

7 Cancel these fractions to their simplest forms using the HCF of the numerator and denominator to help.

a $\frac{6}{8}$ **b** $\frac{12}{18}$ **c** $\frac{60}{96}$

d $\frac{36}{54}$ **e** $\frac{117}{169}$ **f** $\frac{26}{65}$

N5 Summary

Check out

You should now be able to:

- Use powers and index notation for small positive integer powers
- Use the square, square root, cube and cube root functions of a calculator
- Multiply and divide by powers of 10
- Use index laws for multiplication and division of positive integer powers
- Identify factors, multiples and prime numbers from a list of numbers
- Find the highest common factor and the least common multiple of two or three numbers
- Express a number as a product of prime factors

Worked exam question

Write as a power of 7

a $7^8 \div 7^3$

b $\dfrac{7^2 \times 7^3}{7}$

(3)

(Edexcel Limited 2007)

a $7^8 \div 7^3 = 7^5$ ← Subtract the indices: $8 - 3 = 5$

b $\dfrac{7^2 \times 7^3}{7}$

$7^2 \times 7^3 = 7^5$

$7^5 \div 7 = 7^4$ ← Write the answer as a power of 7

Exam questions

1 Here is a list of 8 numbers.

5 6 12 20 25 26 28 33

a From the list write down

i a square number (1)

ii a number that is a multiple of 7 (1)

iii two numbers that are factors of 40 (1)

iv two numbers with a sum of 59 (1)

b Tony says that "6 is a cube number because $2^3 = 6$".
Tony is wrong. Explain why. (1)

(Edexcel Limited 2004)

2 Work out the value of

a 4^3

b $\sqrt{81}$

c $5^2 \times 2^3$ (3)

3 Use your calculator to work out the value of $\sqrt{20.25} + 1.65^2$

a Write down all the figures on your calculator display. (2)

b Write your answer to part **a** correct to one significant figure. (1)

(Edexcel Limited 2007)

4 Find the Least Common Multiple (LCM) of 45 and 60. (2)

5 a Express 56 as the product of its prime factors. (2)

b Find the Highest Common Factor (HCF) of 56 and 98. (1)

(Edexcel Limited 2006)

6 Express 264 as a product of its prime factors. (3)

A02 + 3

7 A large rectangular play area measures 36 metres by 42 metres.
The council wants to lay the play area with square concrete tiles.
Tiles are available with lengths of whole numbers of metres.
If the tiles are to be as large as possible, how many tiles will be needed?

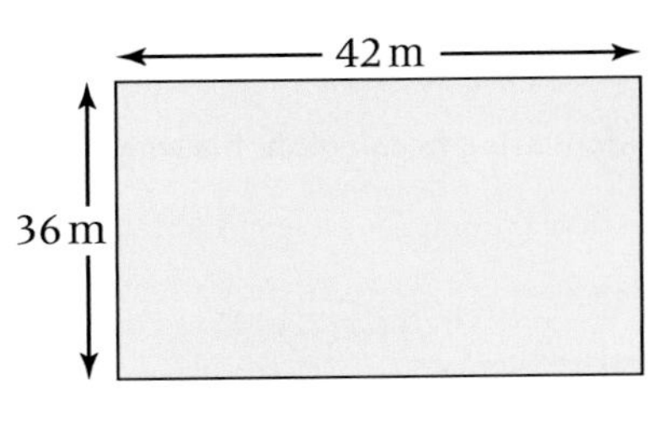

(4)

Functional Maths 5: Business

One out of every two small businesses goes bust within its first two years of trading. Mathematics can be applied to reduce the risk of failure for a business as well as to maximise its profits.

A manager needs to know how much cash is coming into and going out of the business. Accountants must set a suitable budget that includes realistic performance targets, and limits expenditure to what the business can afford.

Example

Annie sells hand made cards at a monthly craft fair.

The production costs and selling price per card are:

Cost of materials used	Production time	Wages paid	Selling price	Profit
£0.30	15 minutes	£1.00	£2.55	£1.25

This is Annie's cash flow budget for her first three craft fairs (some of the information is missing):

	January (£)	February (£)	March (£)
TOTAL SALES INCOME	56.10	71.40	63.75
Materials used	6.60	8.40	7.50
Wages			
Craft fair fees	10.00	10.00	10.00
Advertising	5.00	5.00	5.00
TOTAL EXPENDITURE	43.60		
NET CASH SURPLUS/DEFICIT	12.50		
CASH BALANCE BROUGHT FORWARD	-	12.50	
CASH BALANCE TO CARRY FORWARD	12.50		

How many cards did Annie sell in each of the three months?

Use this information to calculate the wages paid for each month.

Calculate the total expenditure for each month. During which month were Annie's expenses highest?

The net surplus (profit) or net deficit (loss) is calculated using the formula Balance = Income − Expenditure

Copy the table and complete the missing values.

On separate copies of the table template, show how the cash flow could change if

a) the craft fair fees were increased to £15

b) the cost of the materials used per card increased to £0.40

c) the selling price per card was increased to £2.75.

Investigate how other changes to costs/income might affect Annie's cash flow.

The breakeven point is when a company's expenditure is equal to its income. If the company can operate at levels above the breakeven point, it will make a profit. If sales fall below this point, the company will make a loss.

For Annie's cards:

Fixed costs = craft fair fees (£10) + advertising (£5) = £15;

Variable cost per card = material costs (£0.30) + wages (£1) = £1.30 per card;

Total costs = fixed costs + variable costs

To calculate total variable cost, multiply: variable cost per card × number of cards

To calculate revenue, multiply: sales price per card × number of cards

If 20 cards are sold, revenue = £2.55 × 20 = £51

Variable costs and revenue increase in direct proportion with the number of cards produced.

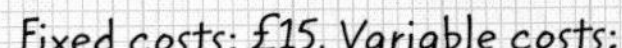

Fixed costs: £15, Variable costs: £1.30 per card, Sales price: £2.55 per card

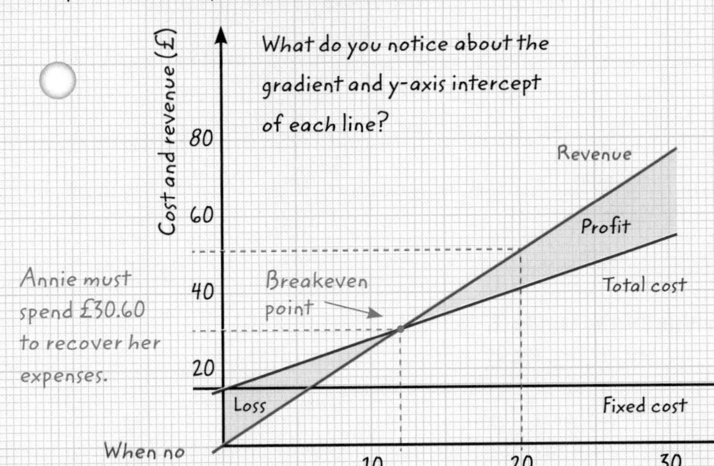

Cost and revenue (£)
80
60
40
20
10
20
30
Number of cards
What do you notice about the gradient and y-axis intercept of each line?
Revenue
Profit
Total cost
Breakeven point
Loss
Fixed cost
Annie must spend £30.60 to recover her expenses.
When no cards are sold the revenue is £0.
Annie would need to sell 12 cards at this price to break even.

Make sure you understand where the plotted values come from. You may find it useful to draw up a table of values (showing number of cards, fixed costs, variable costs, total costs and revenue).

The fixed cost line is horizontal because the fixed costs do not change regardless of the number of cards produced.

Plot your own charts to show the breakeven point if

a) the craft fair fees were increased to £15

b) the cost of the materials used per card increased to £0.40

c) the selling price per card was increased to £2.75.

Investigate how other changes to costs/income could affect Annie's profit/loss.

D3 Displaying and interpreting data

Introduction

Statistics are vital in medicine as they are used to test the safety and performance of new drugs. Tests are performed on large groups of people and the analysis of the results is used to evaluate the safety and reliability of the new drug.

What's the point?

When data is analysed it is essential for that analysis to be correct. Statisticians use a range of techniques to analyse and compare large data sets. It is the use of statistical techniques that ensures a drug is safe to be on sale to the general public.

Check in

1 Calculate the value of the angle *x*.

a

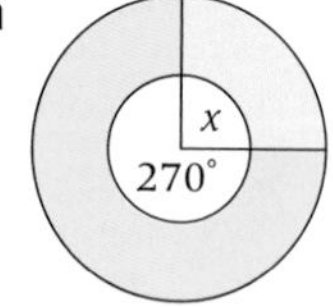

b

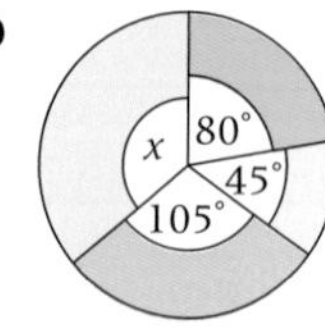

2 Calculate mentally:

a $360 \div 3$ **b** $360 \div 8$ **c** $360 \div 6$

d $360 \div 5$ **e** $360 \div 60$ **f** $360 \div 18$

g $360 \div 12$ **h** $360 \div 20$ **i** $360 \div 36$

Orientation

What I should know	What I will learn	What this leads to
D2 →	■ Draw and produce relevant diagrams and charts ■ Draw and use frequency diagrams ■ Draw and use stem-and-leaf diagrams ■ Draw and use line graphs ■ Draw and use scatter graphs, and understand correlation	→ D4

Rich task

The taller you are the heavier you are.
Investigate if this statement is true.

D3.1 Diagrams and charts 1

This spread will show you how to:

- Draw and produce relevant diagrams and charts to display data

Keywords
Bar chart
Bar-line chart
Category
Pictogram
Pie chart
Sector

You can use a variety of diagrams and charts to display data.

Pictograms use symbols to represent the size of each category.

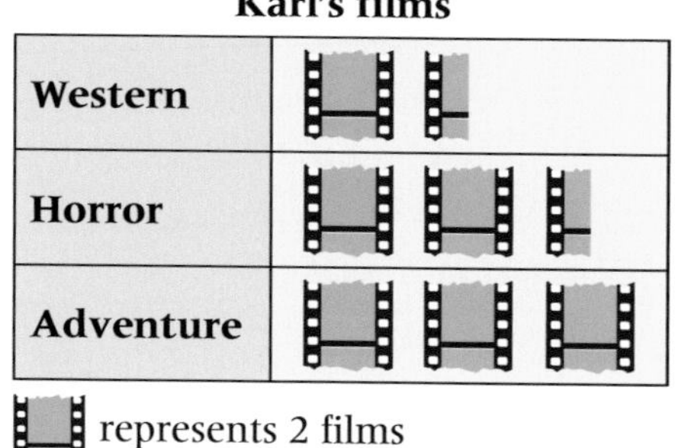

Bar charts use bars to represent frequencies.

Vowels in sentence

Frequency (0, 5, 10); Vowel: A E I O U

Notice the gaps between the bars.

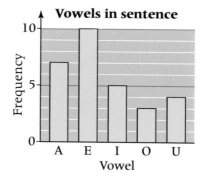

Bar-line charts use vertical lines to represent numerical data.

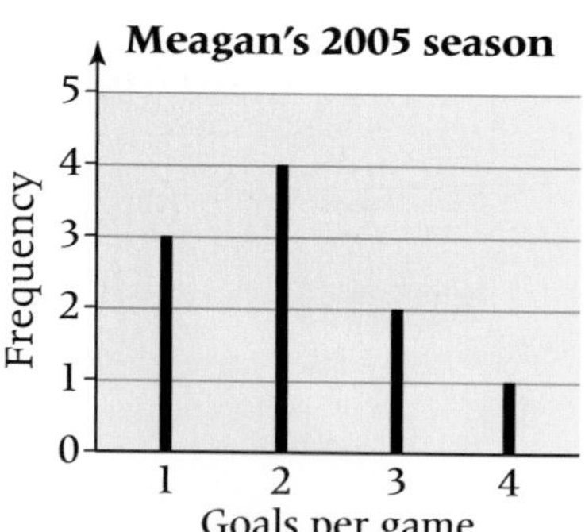

Pie charts use sectors of a circle to represent the size of each category.

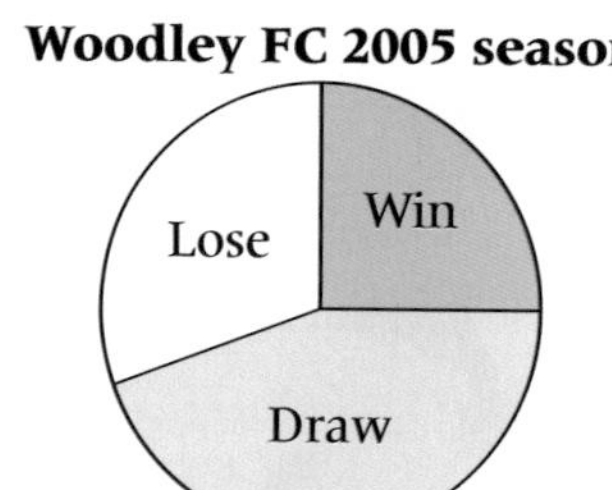

The size of the **sector** angle is proportional to the frequency.

Example

240 people are asked to name their favourite fruit.
The results are shown.

Fruit	Apple	Banana	Orange	Other
Number of people	50	80	72	38

Draw a pie chart to illustrate the information.

Calculate the angle for one person:

$360° \div 240 = 1.5°$

Calculate the angles for each category:

Apple	$50 \times 1.5° = 75°$
Banana	$80 \times 1.5° = 120°$
Orange	$72 \times 1.5° = 108°$
Other	$38 \times 1.5° = 57°$
Add to Check:	$360°$

Measure, colour and label the sectors.

Favourite fruits

Other, Apple, Orange, Banana

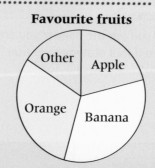

Check by adding the angles of the sectors.

Exercise D3.1

Grade E–F

A02 Functional Maths

1 The pictogram shows the results for the 'Best Live Band' survey.

U2	🎸🎸🎸🎸🎸
The White Stripes	🎸🎸🎸½🎸
Kings of Leon	
Arcade Fire	
Radiohead	

🎸 represents 100 votes

The votes were as follows:

U2	The White Stripes	Kings of Leon	Arcade Fire	Radiohead
500	350	300	250	150

a Calculate the total number of votes made.

b Copy and complete the pictogram.

2 A football team plays 36 matches in the season. The results are

Win	Draw	Lose
15	8	?

a Calculate the number of matches that were lost.

b Calculate the angle one match represents in a pie chart.

c Calculate the angle of each category in the pie chart.

d Draw a pie chart to show the information.

DID YOU KNOW?

Florence Nightingale was a celebrated statistician as well as a nurse. She used pie charts and diagrams to show the need for improved hygiene conditions.

3 The weather record for 60 days is shown in the frequency table.

a Calculate the angle one day represents in a pie chart.

b Calculate the angle of each category in the pie chart.

c Draw a pie chart to show the data.

Weather	Number of days
Sunny	15
Cloudy	18
Rainy	14
Snowy	3
Windy	10

4 A fishing catch consisted of 480 fish. The frequency table shows the amount of each type.

a Calculate each angle of a pie chart to illustrate this information.

b Draw the pie chart.

Fish	Frequency
Cod	120
Plaice	100
Haddock	96
Sardines	116
Mackerel	48

Grouped frequency diagrams

This spread will show you how to:

- Recognise the difference between discrete and continuous data, using appropriate diagrams and charts

Keywords
Bar chart
Continuous
Discrete
Frequency polygon
Grouped
Histogram

- **Discrete** data can only take exact values (usually collected by counting).
- **Continuous** data can take any value (collected by measuring).

You must be careful if the data is **grouped**.

You can use a **bar chart** to display grouped discrete data.

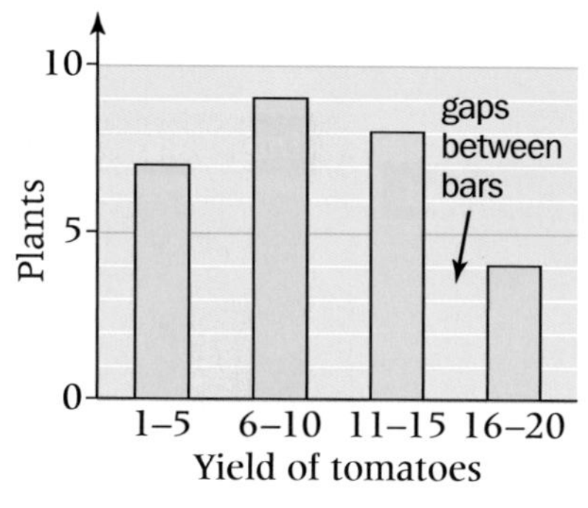

You can use a **histogram** to display grouped continuous data.

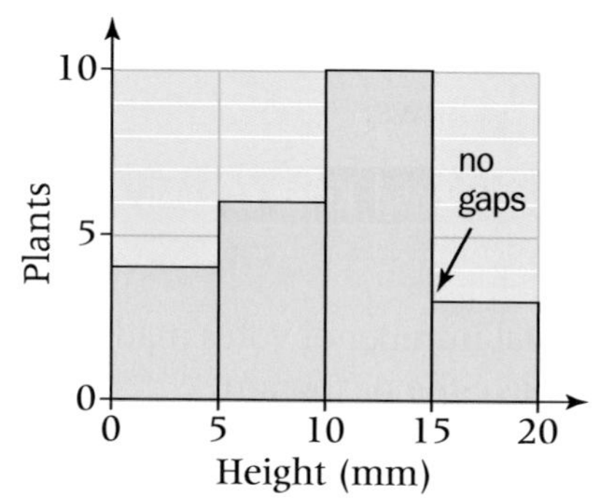

- You can use a **frequency polygon** to display grouped **continuous** data.

Frequency polygons use straight lines drawn from the top centre of each bar.

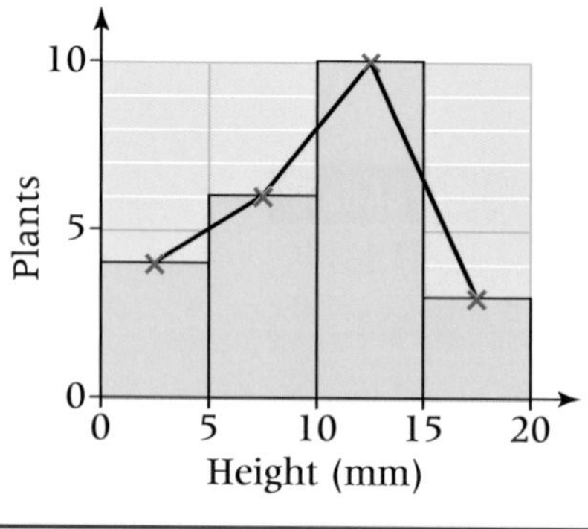

→

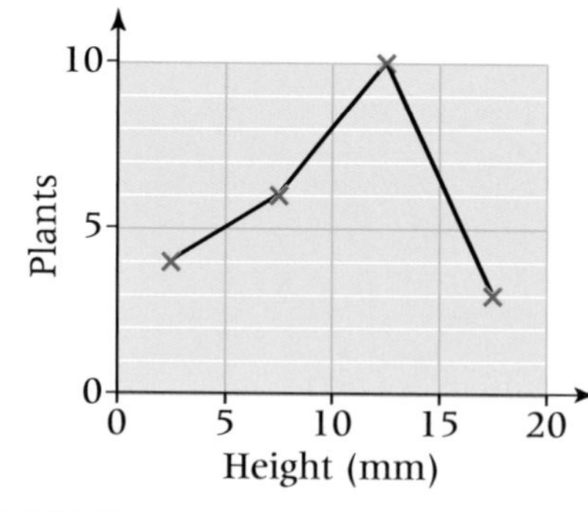

Plot the points at the midpoints of the class intervals.

Example

The times taken, in seconds, to run 100 m are shown in the table.

Time (seconds)	Number of people
$0 < t \leqslant 10$	0
$10 < t \leqslant 20$	4
$20 < t \leqslant 30$	6
$30 < t \leqslant 40$	3

Draw a frequency diagram to illustrate this information.

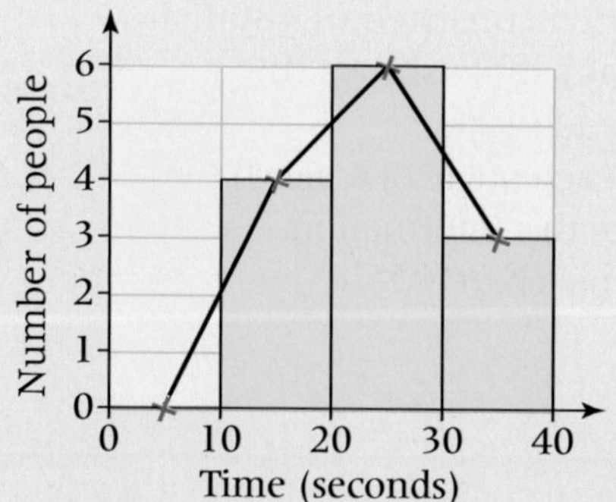

Don't draw both diagrams.

Either the histogram or the frequency polygon answers this question.

Exercise D3.2

Grade D

Functional Maths

A02

1 **a** Copy and complete the frequency table using these heights of people.

153 134 155 142 140 163 150 135
170 156 171 161 141 153 144 163
140 160 172 157 136 160 134 154
176 154 173 179 160 152 170 148
151 165 138 143 147 144 156 139

Height (cm)	Tally	Number of people
$130 < h \leqslant 140$		
$140 < h \leqslant 150$		
$150 < h \leqslant 160$		
$160 < h \leqslant 170$		
$170 < h \leqslant 180$		

b Copy and complete the histogram on graph paper.

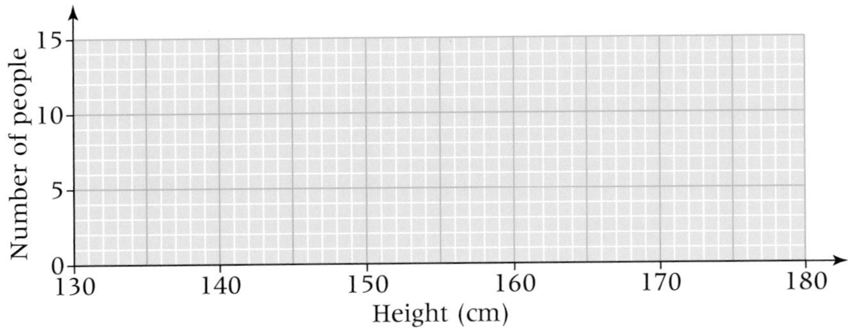

c Draw a frequency polygon on the same axes and graph paper.

2 The depth, in centimetres, of a reservoir is measured daily throughout April. Draw a histogram to show the depths.

Depth (cm)	Number of days
$0 < d \leqslant 5$	1
$5 < d \leqslant 10$	5
$10 < d \leqslant 15$	14
$15 < d \leqslant 20$	8
$20 < d \leqslant 25$	2

3 The exam marks of 40 students are shown in the frequency table. Draw a bar chart to show the exam marks.

Exam mark (%)	Number of students
1 to 20	4
21 to 40	9
41 to 60	13
61 to 80	11
81 to 100	3

4 The times taken for 50 runners of the London Marathon are shown in the frequency table.

a Draw a histogram to show the times.

b Draw the frequency polygon on the same diagram.

Time (hours)	Number of runners
$0 < t \leqslant 1$	0
$1 < t \leqslant 2$	1
$2 < t \leqslant 3$	23
$3 < t \leqslant 4$	18
$4 < t \leqslant 5$	8

D3.3 Stem-and-leaf diagrams 1

This spread will show you how to:

- Draw and use stem-and-leaf diagrams

Keywords
Ordered
Stem-and-leaf diagram

- You can use a **stem-and-leaf diagram** to display numerical data.

A stem-and-leaf diagram shows

- the shape of the distribution
- each individual value of the data.

This stem-and-leaf diagram is **ordered**, as the data is in numerical order.

stem	leaf
130	5
120	0 6 9
110	2 2 6 8
100	3 7

This means 135.

This means 120.

Key: | 110 | 2 | means 112

Always give a key.

Example

The weights, in kilograms, of 10 parcels are shown:

4.2 3.7 3.5 2.8 1.5
0.9 2.4 1.4 1.0 2.4

Show this data in an ordered stem-and-leaf diagram.

First choose the stem.
Go up in ones.

0.0	
1.0	
2.0	
3.0	
4.0	

You can order the data before you draw the diagram if you want.

Then write in the leaves.

0.0	9
1.0	5 4 0
2.0	8 4 4
3.0	7 5
4.0	2

order

Finally, order the leaves.

0.0	9
1.0	0 4 5
2.0	4 4 8
3.0	5 7
4.0	2

Key: | 1.0 | 5 | means 1.5 kg

Examiner's tip: The key is essential to gain full marks.

Exercise D3.3 Grade D

A02 Functional Maths

1 The times, in seconds, for a sample of 30 students to guess 2 minutes are

112 110 108 131 125 130
120 121 117 135 116 110
140 108 142 126 125 136
119 126 137 108 144 119
120 134 117 111 121 138

Copy and complete the ordered stem-and-leaf diagram.

100	
110	
120	
130	
140	

Key:

120	3

means 123 seconds

2 The times taken, in seconds, for 25 athletes to run 400 metres are given.

44.3 44.4 43.3 43.2 44.0
45.2 45.0 44.5 45.6 43.9
46.5 46.3 46.0 46.5 44.7
46.9 44.1 43.8 45.0 46.9
43.0 46.1 45.1 43.8 45.9

Draw an ordered stem-and-leaf diagram, using stems of 43.0, 44.0, 45.0 and 46.0. Remember to give the key.

3 **a** Use the temperatures in °C to draw an ordered stem-and-leaf diagram. Choose suitable stems.

	°C	°F
Athens	20	68
Berlin	31	88
Brussels	25	77
Cairo	34	93
Cape Town	17	63
Corfu	26	79
Dublin	14	57
Edinburgh	14	57
Faro	24	75
Guernsey	14	57

	°C	°F
Hong Kong	32	90
London	19	66
Los Angeles	20	68
Malaga	23	73
Malta	26	79
Miami	29	84
Moscow	22	72
Nairobi	20	68
New York	21	70
Oslo	10	50

	°C	°F
Paris	26	79
Perth	27	81
Rome	26	79
Sydney	19	66
Tel Aviv	28	82
Tenerife	23	73
Tokyo	23	73
Toronto	19	66
Vancouver	22	72
Vienna	29	84

b Use the temperatures in °F to draw another ordered stem-and-leaf diagram.

D3.4 Time series graphs

This spread will show you how to:

- Draw and use line graphs for time series, recognising data trends

Keywords
Horizontal
Line graph
Time series graph
Trend

You can use a **line graph** to show how data changes as time passes.

The data can be discrete or continuous.

The temperature of a liquid is measured every minute.

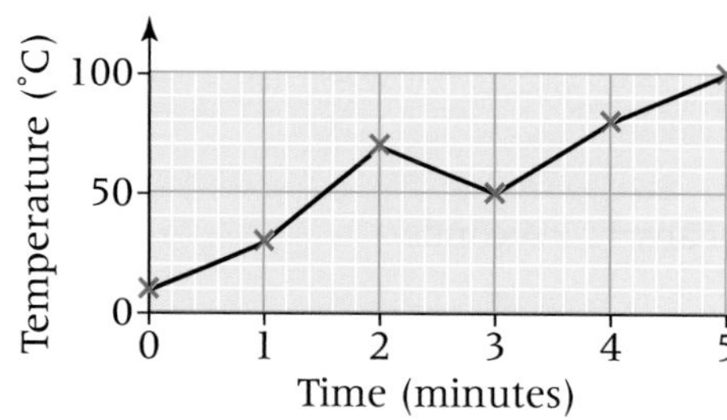

This is an example of a **time series graph**.

- A time series graph shows
  - how the data changes over time, or the **trend**
  - each individual value of the data.

Examiner's tip
Time series graphs should not appear in your assessment.

Time is always the **horizontal** axis.

Time could be seconds, minutes, hours, days, weeks, months or years.

Example

The table shows the average monthly rainfall, in centimetres, in Sheffield over the last 30 years.

Month	Jan	Feb	Mar	Apr	May	Jun	Jul	Aug	Sep	Oct	Nov	Dec
Rainfall (cm)	8.7	6.3	6.8	6.3	5.6	6.7	5.1	6.4	6.4	7.4	7.8	9.2

Draw a line graph to show this information.

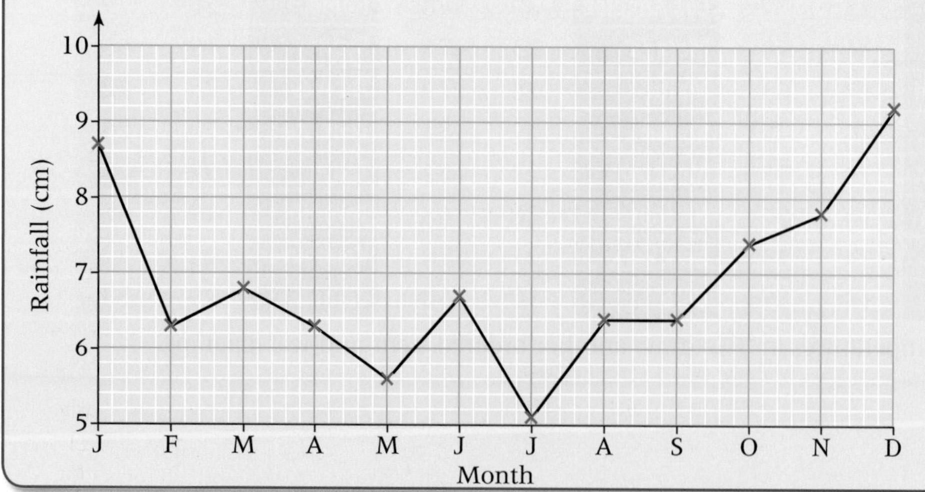

Each division on the vertical axis is 0.2 cm.

The vertical scale doesn't have to start at zero.

Exercise D3.4 Grade D

Functional Maths
A02

1 The numbers of DVDs rented from a shop during a week are shown.

Sunday	Monday	Tuesday	Wednesday	Thursday	Friday	Saturday
18	9	7	11	15	35	36

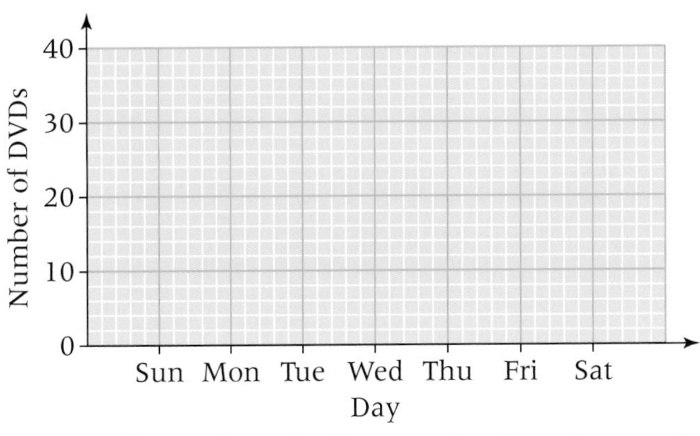

Copy and complete the line graph, choosing a suitable vertical scale.

2 Every year on his birthday, Peter's weight in kilograms is measured.

Age	2	3	4	5	6	7	8	9	10	11	12	13
Weight (kg)	14	16	18	20	22	25	28	31	34	38.5	40	45

Draw a line graph to show the weights.

3 The hours of sunshine each month are shown in the table.

Jan	Feb	Mar	Apr	May	Jun	Jul	Aug	Sep	Oct	Nov	Dec
43	57	105	131	185	176	194	183	131	87	53	35

Draw a line graph to show the hours of sunshine.

4 The daily viewing figures, in millions, for a reality TV show are shown.

Day	Sat	Sun	Mon	Tue	Wed	Thu	Fri
Viewers (in millions)	3.2	3.8	4.3	4.5	3.1	5.2	7.1

Draw a line graph to show the viewing figures.

5 Some of the men's world record times for running 100 m are shown.

Draw a line graph to show the world record times.

Comment on the results.

Year	Athlete	Time (sec)
1968	Jim Hines (USA)	9.95
1983	Calvin Smith (USA)	9.93
1988	Carl Lewis (USA)	9.92
1991	Leroy Burrell (USA)	9.90
1991	Carl Lewis (USA)	9.86
1994	Leroy Burrell (USA)	9.85
1996	Donovan Bailey (Can)	9.84
1999	Maurice Greene (USA)	9.79
2002	Tim Montgomery (USA)	9.78
2005	Asafa Powell (Jam)	9.77
2009	Usain Bolt (Jam)	9.58

Ben Johnson's world records of 9.83 secs in 1987 and 9.79 secs in 1988 were both annulled after he tested positive for drugs at the Seoul Olympics.

Be careful with the horizontal axis (don't miss out the 1970s!)

D3.5 Scatter graphs 1

This spread will show you how to:

- Draw and use scatter graphs, and compare two data sets
- Understand correlation and use lines of best fit

Keywords
Correlation
Line of best fit
Relationship
Scatter graph
Variables

You can use a **scatter graph** to compare two sets of data, for example, height and weight.

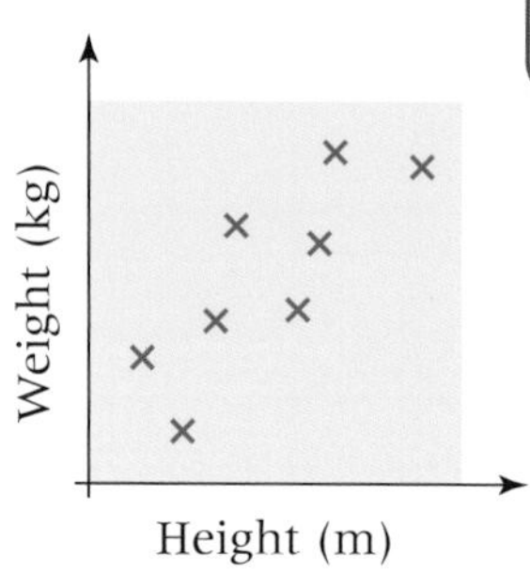

The data can be discrete or continuous.

- The data is collected in pairs and plotted as coordinates.
- If the points lie roughly in a straight line, there is a linear **relationship** or **correlation** between the two **variables**.

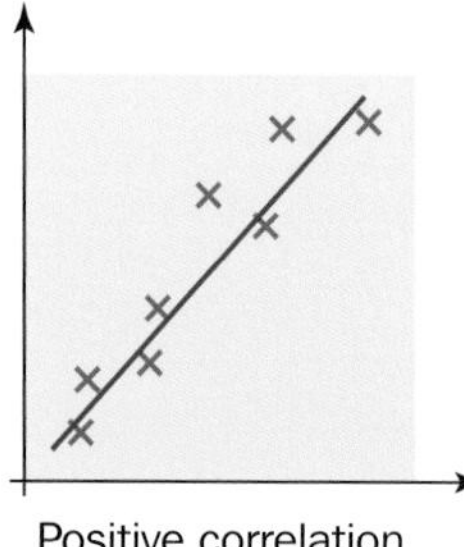
Positive correlation

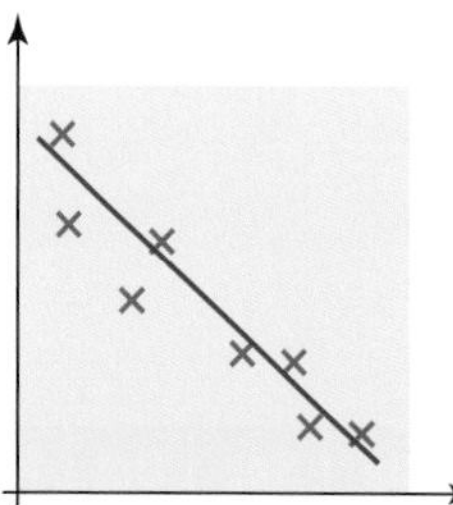
Negative correlation

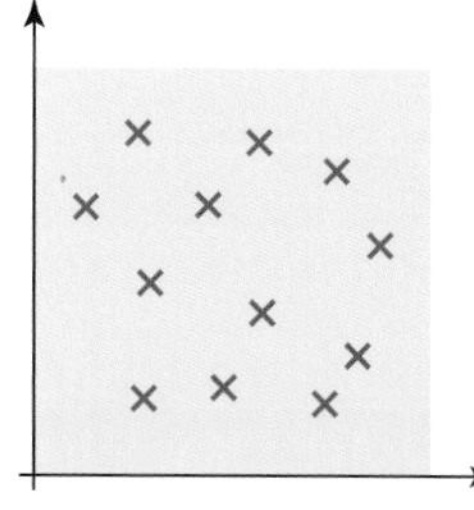
No correlation

Plotted points are not joined on a scatter diagram.

The straight line is the **line of best fit.**

Example

The exam results (%) for Paper 1 and Paper 2 for 10 students are shown.

Paper 1	56	72	50	24	44	80	68	48	60	36
Paper 2	44	64	40	20	36	64	56	36	50	24

a Draw a scatter graph and line of best fit.

b Describe the relationship between the Paper 1 results and Paper 2 results.

a Plot the exam marks as coordinates. The line of best fit should be close to all the points, with approximately the same number of crosses on either side of the line.

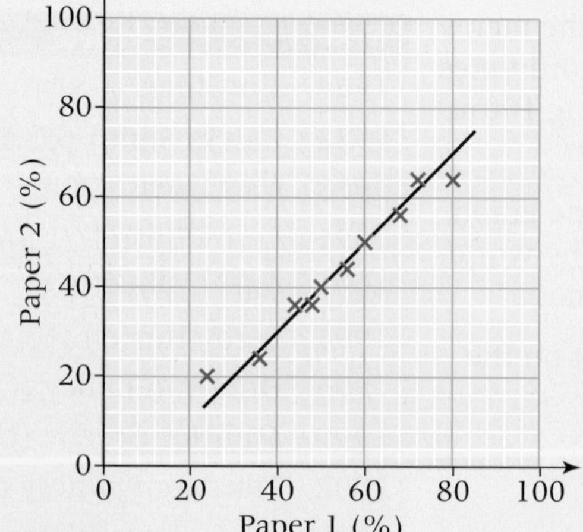

b Students who did well on Paper 1 did well on Paper 2. Students who did not do well on Paper 1 did not do well on Paper 2 either.

The line of best fit does not have to pass through (0, 0).

Exercise D3.5 Grade C

Functional Maths

AO2

1 Describe the type of correlation for each scatter graph.

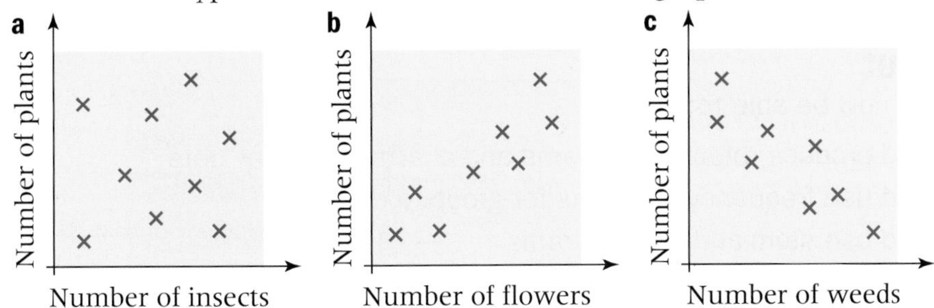

2 The table shows the amount of water used to water plants and the daily maximum temperature.

Water (litres)	25	26	31	24	45	40	5	13	18	28
Maximum temperature (°C)	24	21	25	19	30	28	15	18	20	27

a Copy and complete the scatter graph for this information.

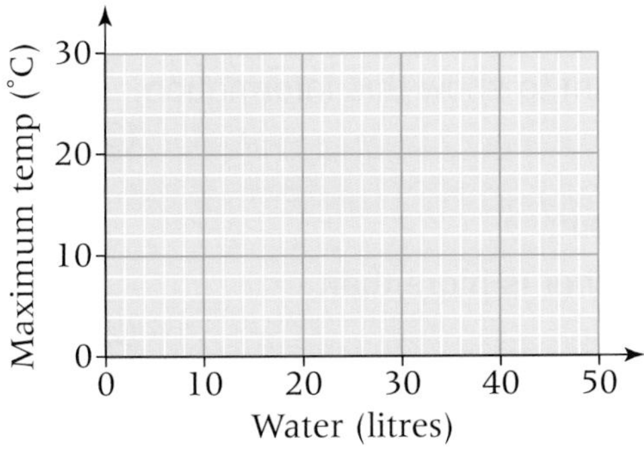

b State the type of correlation shown in the scatter graph.

c Copy and complete these sentences:

i As the temperatures increases, the amount of water used _____.

ii As the temperature decreases, the amount of water used _____.

3 The times taken, in minutes, to run a mile and the shoe sizes of ten athletes are shown in the table.

Shoe size	10	$7\frac{1}{2}$	5	9	6	$8\frac{1}{2}$	$7\frac{1}{2}$	$6\frac{1}{2}$	8	7
Time (mins)	9	8	8	7	5	13	15	12	5	6

a Draw a scatter graph to show this information.
Use 2 cm to represent 1 shoe size on the horizontal axis.
Use 2 cm to represent 5 minutes on the vertical axis.

b State the type of correlation shown in the scatter graph.

c Describe, in words, any relationship that the graph shows.

D3 Summary

Check out

You should now be able to:

- Draw and produce relevant diagrams and charts to display data
- Draw and use frequency diagrams for grouped data
- Draw and use stem-and-leaf diagrams
- Draw and use line graphs
- Interpret scatter diagrams and distinguish between positive, negative and zero correlation

Worked exam question

Here are the ages, in years, of 15 teachers.

35	52	42	27	36
23	31	41	50	34
44	28	45	45	53

a Draw an ordered stem and leaf diagram to show this information. You must include a key. (3)

One of these teachers is picked at random.

b Work out the probability that this teacher is more than 40 years old. (2)

(Edexcel Limited 2008)

a

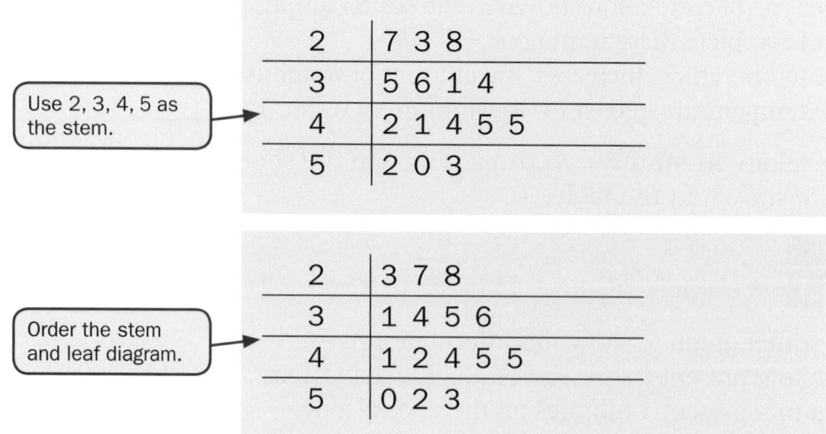

b

There are 8 teachers over 40 years old.

$\frac{8}{15}$

Write the probability as a fraction.

Exam questions

1 The table gives information about the numbers of birds in a garden one morning.

Fish	Frequency	
Blue tit	36	
Chaffinch	32	
Redpoll	22	

Draw an accurate pie chart to show this information. (4)

2 60 students take a science test.
The test is marked out of 50.
This table shows information about the students' marks.

Science mark	0–10	11–20	21–30	31–40	41–50
Frequency	4	13	17	19	7

On a copy of the grid, draw a frequency polygon to show this information.

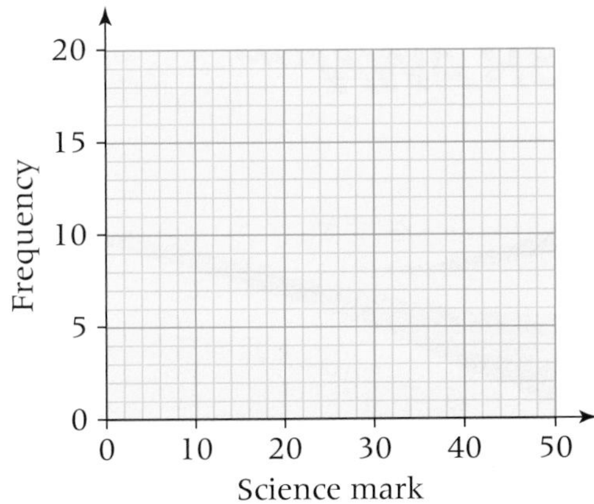

(2)
(Edexcel Limited 2008)

AO3

3 Here is a scatter diagram with four data entries showing.
Copy the diagram and insert a further 6 crosses to show negative correlation.

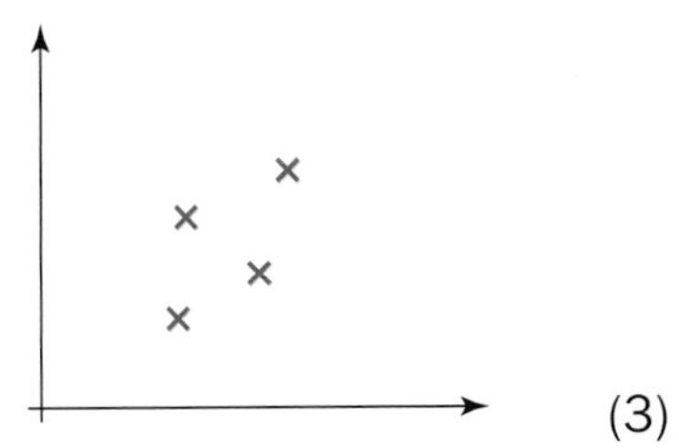

(3)

A5 Equations

Introduction

Formula 1 engineers use complex mathematical equations to predict the effect on performance of their cars when they make technical modifications. Mathematicians turn problems in the real world into mathematical equations which they know how to solve.

What's the point?

Learning how to solve equations allows complicated real life problems to be solved.

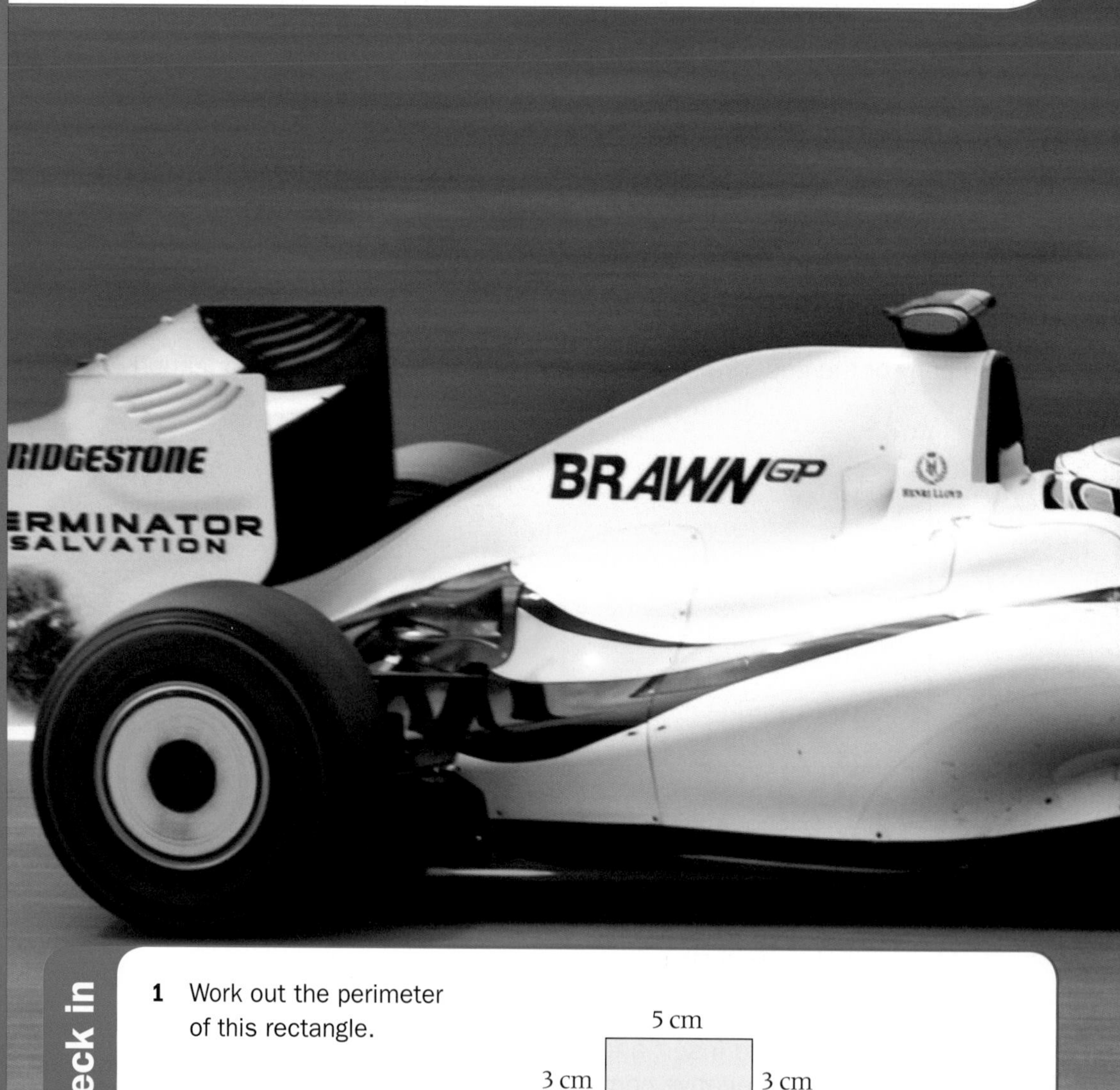

Check in

1 Work out the perimeter of this rectangle.

5 cm

3 cm   3 cm

5 cm

2 Work out

a $4x \div 4$ **b** $3m \div 3$

c $6n \div 2$ **d** $8p \div 4$

Orientation

What I should know	What I will learn	What this leads to
A2 →	■ Solve simple equations, using inverse operations and the balance method ■ Construct and solve equations from real-life problems	→ A7

Rich task

In this diagram, the equation $3x + 2 = 17$ has been changed in different ways, but all of these ways still give the same solution of $x = 5$.
Describe each change to the equation.
Continue each change for at least one more step.
Invent some changes of your own.

Centre: $3x + 2 = 17$

Arrows lead from $3x + 2 = 17$ to each of:

- $6x + 4 = 34$
- $3x + 3 = 18$
- $4x + 2 = x + 17$
- $1.5x + 1 = 8.5$
- $2x + 2 = 17 - x$
- $3x + 1 = 16$

A5.1 Solving equations using function machines

This spread will show you how to:

- Set up simple equations from written problems
- Solve simple equations using inverse operations

Keywords
Equation
Function machine
Inverse operation

You can solve simple 'think of a number' problems mentally.

I think of a number,
I add 7 and my answer is 27.
What is my number?

In your head, you subtract the 7 that was added.

You can write the problem as an **equation**, using x for the unknown number: $x + 7 = 27$

You can solve the equation to find x, using a **function machine**.

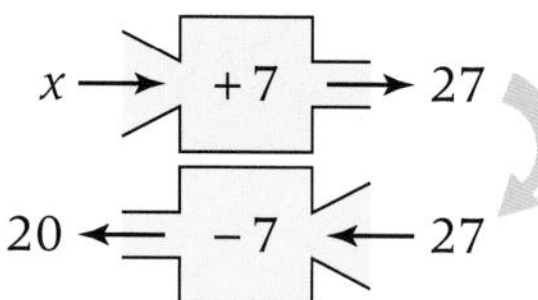

An equation includes letter and number terms and an = sign.
$x + 2 = 5$ is an equation.

- To solve an equation you can
  - write it as a function machine
  - work backwards through the function machine, using the **inverse operation**.

Example

Complete these function machines.

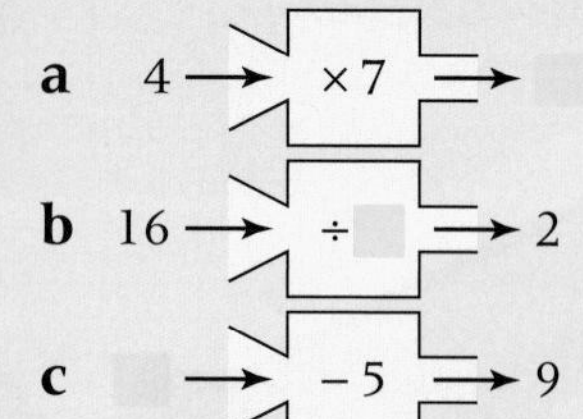

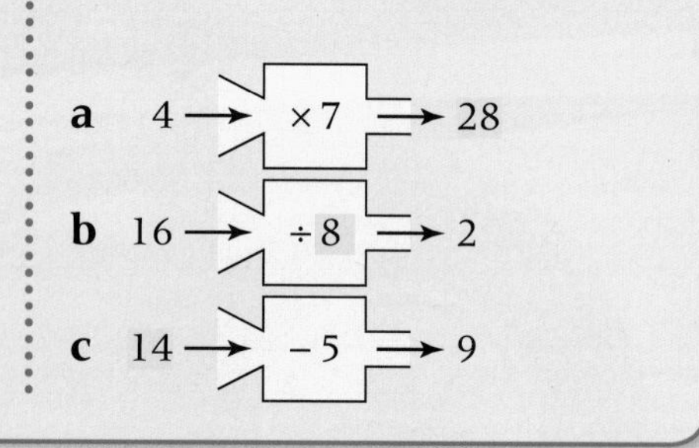

In part **c**, work backwards using the inverse: $9 + 5 = 14$

You can write equations with division and multiplication using function machines.

Example

Write each equation as a function machine. Then solve it using inverse operations.

a $y - 6 = 15$ **b** $4x = 12$ **c** $\frac{z}{3} = 5$

$\frac{z}{3}$ means $z \div 3$.

a

y → −6 → 15
21 ← +6 ← 15

$y = 21$

Check: $21 - 6 = 15$ ✓

b

x → ×4 → 12
3 ← ÷4 ← 12

$x = 3$

Check: $3 \times 4 = 12$ ✓

c

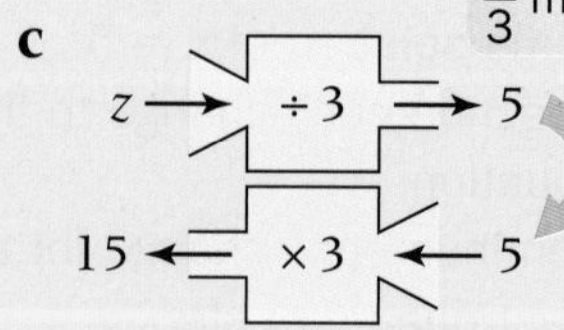

$z = 15$

Check: $15 \div 3 = 5$ ✓

Exercise A5.1 Grade F

AO3 Problem

1 For each 'think of a number' problem

i find the number

ii explain how you worked out the answer.

a I double a number: the answer is 28.

b I add 7 to a number: the answer is 33.

c I subtract 12 from a number: the answer is 9.

d I divide a number by 6: the answer is 7.

2 Copy and complete these function machines.

a 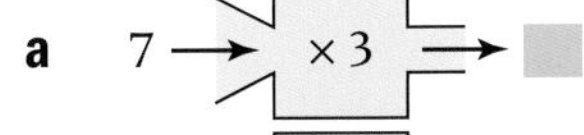

b 35 → ÷ 5 → ☐

c 27 → ☐ → 19

d 6 → × ☐ → 36

e ☐ → + 12 → 40

f ☐ → × 4 → 28

g ☐ → − 7 → 36

h ☐ → ÷ 4 → 13

3 Draw the inverse function machine for each machine in question **2**.

4 Write each equation as a function machine.
Then solve it using inverse operations.

a $a + 9 = 23$ **b** $b - 8 = 17$ **c** $c + 18 = 34$

d $d - 15 = 41$ **e** $3x = 24$ **f** $\frac{f}{5} = 8$

g $6g = 48$ **h** $\frac{h}{7} = 28$ **i** $i - 17 = 14$

j $j + 28 = 53$ **k** $5k = 95$ **l** $\frac{m}{8} = 7$

Use x for the unknown number.

5 Solve these equations.

a $c + 13 = 21$ **b** $d - 6 = 35$ **c** $7f = 63$

d $\frac{g}{4} = 6$ **e** $5h = 100$ **f** $\frac{i}{7} = 6$

g $6j = 54$ **h** $k - 7 = 15$ **i** $l + 9 = 24$

j $8m = 48$ **k** $\frac{n}{4} = 12$ **l** $8q = 56$

m $4r = 128$ **n** $\frac{u}{18} = 4$

AO3 Problem

6 Write each 'think of a number' problem as an equation.
Solve the equation to find the number.

a I think of a number and subtract 12. The answer is 11.

b I think of a number and divide by 5. The answer is 8.

A5.2 Solving two-step equations

This spread will show you how to:

- Solve simple equations using inverse operations
- Solve two-step problems using inverse operations

Keywords
Inverse operations
Two-step problem

This 'think of a number' problem has two steps:

I think of a number, multiply by 4 and add 5. The answer is 13.

For a **two-step problem**, use two function machines:

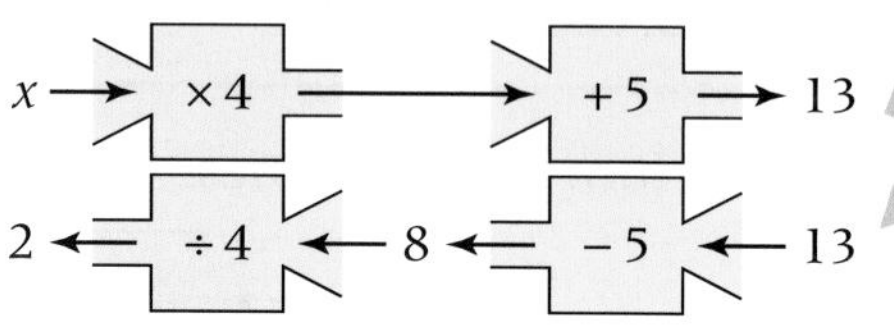

Step 1: add 4
Step 2: multiply by 5

You can write this two-step problem as an equation:
$x \times 4 + 5 = 13$ or $4x + 5 = 13$

In algebra:
- leave out the ×
- write numbers before letters.

Example

Use inverse function machines to work out the value of n.

a

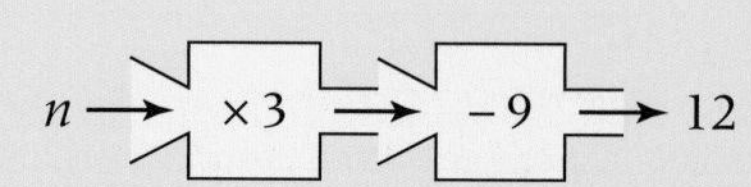

b

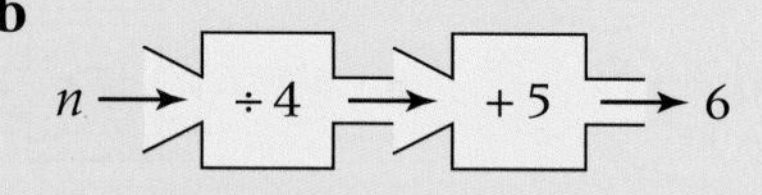

---

a

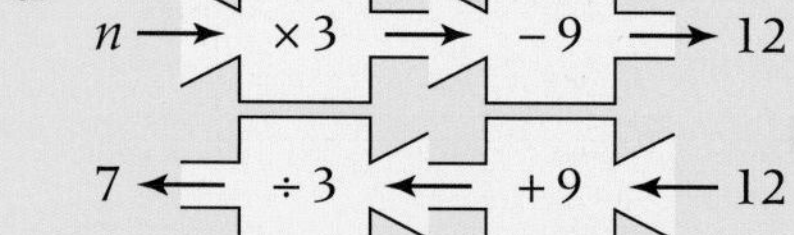

b

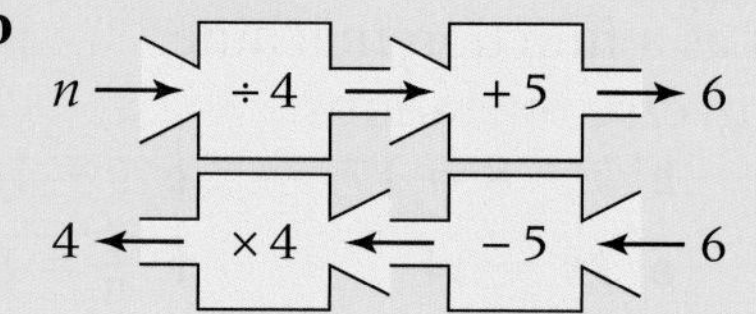

In part **a** the inverse functions are:
12 + **9** = 21
21 ÷ **3** = 7

Example

Copy and complete the table for this two-step function.

	×6	−2
1		
2		
x		
		46

	×6	−2
1	6	4
2	12	10
x	$6x$	$6x - 2$
8	48	46

You can solve an equation using **inverse operations**.

Example

Solve these equations.

a $3m + 5 = 17$

b $\frac{n}{2} - 4 = 16$

---

a

m → ×3 → +5 → 17
4 ← ÷3 ← 12 ← −5 ← 17

$m = 4$
Check: $3 \times 4 + 5 = 12 + 5 = 17$ ✓

b

n → ÷2 → −4 → 16
40 ← ×2 ← +4 ← 16

$n = 40$
Check: $40 \div 2 - 4 = 20 - 4 = 16$ ✓

Exercise A5.2 Grade E

1 Copy and complete these two-step function machines.

a $3 \rightarrow \times 2 \rightarrow -1 \rightarrow ?$ **b** $6 \rightarrow \times 4 \rightarrow +8 \rightarrow ?$

c $18 \rightarrow \div 3 \rightarrow +4 \rightarrow ?$ **d** $28 \rightarrow \div 4 \rightarrow -6 \rightarrow ?$

e $12 \rightarrow \div 2 \rightarrow \square \rightarrow 11$ **f** $5 \rightarrow \square \rightarrow -3 \rightarrow 22$

2 Use inverse function machines to solve each of these.

a $a \rightarrow \times 4 \rightarrow -5 \rightarrow 19$ **b** $b \rightarrow \times 3 \rightarrow +8 \rightarrow 35$

c $e \rightarrow \div 4 \rightarrow -5 \rightarrow 2$ **d** $f \rightarrow \div 3 \rightarrow +11 \rightarrow 17$

e $g \rightarrow \div 5 \rightarrow +3 \rightarrow 9$ **f** $h \rightarrow \div 8 \rightarrow -3 \rightarrow -1$

3 Copy and complete the tables for these two-step functions.

a

	×4	+3
1		
2		
x		
		43

b

	÷3	−1
12		
9		
x		
		7

c

	×5	−3
1		
2		
x		
		52

4 Solve these equations.

a $3a - 5 = 25$ **b** $2b + 9 = 27$ **c** $6e + 11 = 23$

d $\frac{f}{5} + 3 = 6$ **e** $\frac{g}{7} - 8 = 2$ **f** $\frac{i}{6} + 4 = 9$

g $\frac{j}{5} - 8 = 4$ **h** $3k - 20 = -5$ **i** $8m - 5 = 7$

j $3p - 8 = -14$

5 Write these function machines as equations.

a $x \rightarrow \times 3 \rightarrow -1 \rightarrow 11$ **b** $n \rightarrow \times 4 \rightarrow +7 \rightarrow 27$

c $q \rightarrow \times 5 \rightarrow +3 \rightarrow 33$ **d** $r \rightarrow \div 3 \rightarrow +15 \rightarrow 22$

AO3 Problem

6 For each of these 'think of a number' problems

i write an equation **ii** solve your equation to find the number.

a I double a number and add 7. The answer is 15.

b I multiply a number by 4 and subtract 5. The answer is 13.

c I divide a number by 5 and add 3. The answer is 11.

A5.3 Solving equations using the balance method

This spread will show you how to:

- Solve simple equations using the balance method

Keywords
Inverse operation

You can solve simple equations using the balance method.
You change both sides in the same way.

$5x + 12 = 32$
$5x + 12 - 12 = 32 - 12$
$5x = 20$
$5x \div 5 = 20 \div 5$
$x = 4$

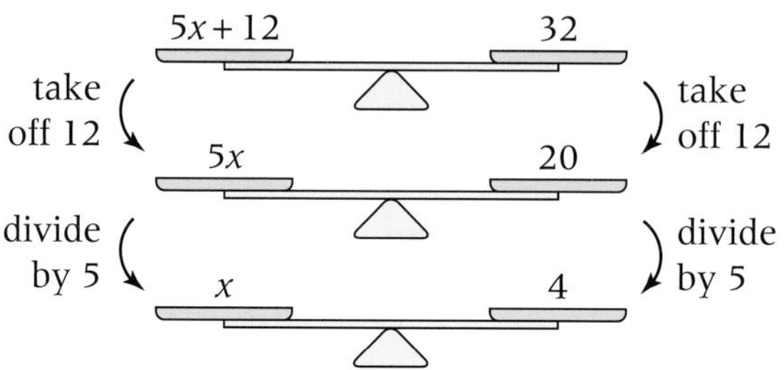

Subtract 12 from both sides.

Divide both sides by 5.

You can use **inverse operations** to transform the equation.

$3x - 10 = 11$
$3x - 10 + 10 = 11 + 10$
$3x = 21$
$3x \div 3 = 21 \div 3$
$x = 7$

+10 is the inverse of −10.

÷3 is the inverse of ×3.

Example

Solve these equations using the balance method.

a $\frac{t}{3} - 5 = -3$ **b** $18 - 4m = 6$

a $\frac{t}{3} - 5 = -3$
$\frac{t}{3} - 5 + 5 = -3 + 5$
$\frac{t}{3} = 2$
$\frac{t}{3} \times 3 = 2 \times 3$
$t = 6$

b $18 - 4m = 6$
$18 - 4m + 4m = 6 + 4m$
$18 = 6 + 4m$
$18 - 6 = 6 - 6 + 4m$
$12 = 4m$
$3 = m$
$m = 3$

To avoid having $-4m$, add $4m$ to both sides of the equation.

Example

The perimeter of this rectangle is 24 cm.

4 cm
x cm

a Write an equation for the perimeter of the rectangle.
b Hence find x, the length of the rectangle.

a Perimeter $= 4 + x + 4 + x = 24$
$2x + 8 = 24$

b $2x + 8 = 24$
$2x = 16$ Subtract 8 from both sides.
$x = 8$ cm

Exercise A5.3 **Grade D**

1 Solve these equations using the balance method.

a $3x + 9 = 24$ **b** $5 + 7x = 40$ **c** $4x - 8 = 24$

d $5x - 17 = 13$ **e** $2x + 7 = 18$ **f** $\frac{x}{10} + 6 = 11$

g $\frac{y}{3} - 2 = 4$ **h** $\frac{z}{4} - 4 = 60$ **i** $15 - 4y = 3$

j $22 - 6p = 10$

2 Solve these equations using the method you prefer.

a $5m - 6 = 29$ **b** $18 + 2p = 4$ **c** $10 - 3n = 4$

d $14 = 6q - 16$ **e** $7 = 29 + 2r$ **f** $4k - 36 = -12$

g $-11 = 6m - 41$ **h** $\frac{a}{2} + 2 = 6$

AO3 Problem

3 One of these equations has a different solution to the other two. Which is it?

$\frac{m}{2} + 12 = 16$ $6p + 12 = 16$ $\frac{n}{4} + 11 = 13$

4 In each wall, add two bricks to find the number on the brick above.
Write and solve equations to find the unknown letter in each wall.

a

36

$2n + 3$ | $4n + 3$

$2n$ | 3 | $4n$

b

54

$4m - 3$ | $m - 3$

$4m$ | -3 | m

5 The perimeter of this rectangle is 36 cm.

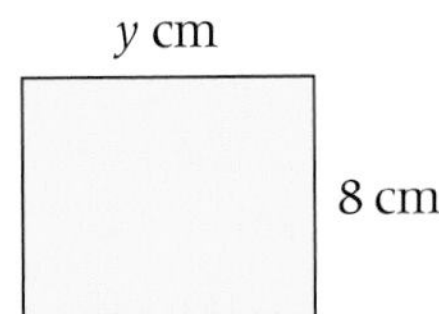

a Write an equation for the perimeter in terms of y.
b Solve your equation to find y, the width of the rectangle.

6 Find the missing side length for each shape.

a

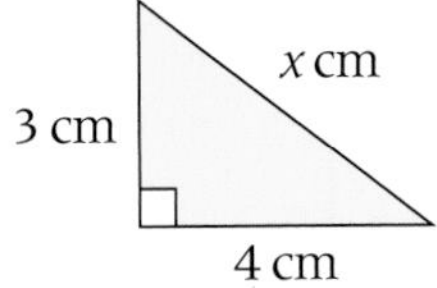

Perimeter = 12 cm

b

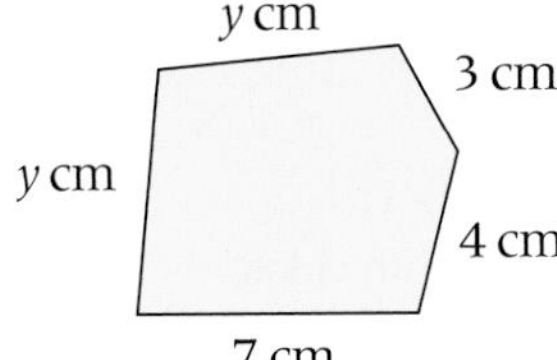

Perimeter = 26 cm

c

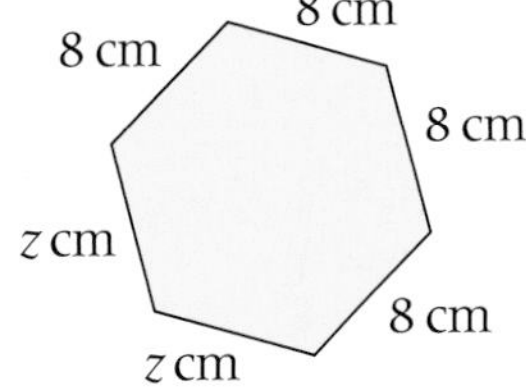

Perimeter = 48 cm

What do you notice about shape **c**?

A5.4 Solving equations with brackets

This spread will show you how to:
- Solve equations involving brackets

Keywords
Brackets
Expand
Solve

- You can **expand brackets** in an algebraic expression.
  - You multiply each term inside the bracket by the term outside.

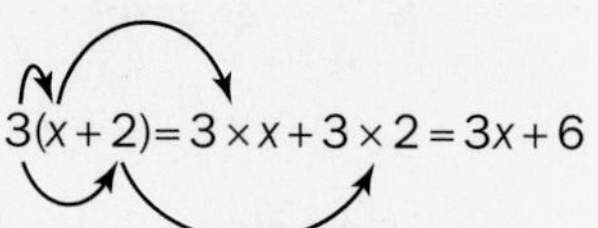

- To solve an equation with brackets:
  - Expand the brackets
  - Solve using the balance method.

Example

Solve

a $4(x + 1) = 12$ **b** $3(y - 3) = 6$

a
$4(x + 1) = 12$ Expand the brackets.
$4 \times x + 4 \times 1 = 12$
$4x + 4 = 12$
$4x + 4 - 4 = 12 - 4$
$4x = 8$ Divide both sides by 4.
$x = 2$

b
$3(y - 3) = 6$
$3 \times y + 3 \times -3 = 6$ Keep each term with its sign.
$3y - 9 = 6$ $3 \times -3 = -9$
$3y - 9 + 9 = 6 + 9$
$3y = 15$ Divide both sides by 3.
$y = 5$

Solutions may be negative numbers or fractions.

Example

Solve the equations.

a $5(a + 3) = 10$ **b** $2(z - 2) = 1$

a
$5(a + 3) = 10$
$5a + 15 = 10$
$5a + 15 - 15 = 10 - 15$
$5a = -5$ Divide both sides by 5.
$a = -1$

b
$2(z - 2) = 1$
$2z - 4 = 1$ Add 4 to both sides.
$2z = 5$ Divide both sides by 2.
$z = \frac{5}{2}$ or $2\frac{1}{2}$

Exercise A5.4 Grade D

1 Expand the brackets in these expressions.

a $4(x+3)$ **b** $2(y-4)$

c $5(3-a)$ **d** $3(-b+2)$

2 Expand the brackets and solve these equations.

a $3(x+1)=15$ **b** $4(s-2)=16$

c $2(t-3)=0$ **d** $4(-v+1)=-8$

3 Expand the brackets in these expressions.

a $-2(c+4)$ **b** $-3(d-3)$

c $2(4m-1)$ **d** $-4(2n-3)$

4 Expand and solve

a $3(a+4)=-6$ **b** $2(b-5)=-12$

c $-4(6-c)=-16$ **d** $3(2d-3)=26$

5 Solve

a $4(e+1)=10$ **b** $3(f-2)=-4$

c $8(2-g)=10$ **d** $-4(h-6)=26$

6 Solve these equations.

a $-2(x+3)=11$ **b** $-10(y-4)=15$

c $12(z-5)=-30$

Which is the odd one out?

7 The diagram shows an equilateral triangle.
Each side has length $x-2$.

a Copy and complete this expression for the perimeter of the triangle:
Perimeter = 3(   )

b The perimeter of the triangle is 12 cm.
Use your expression from part **a** to find the value of x.

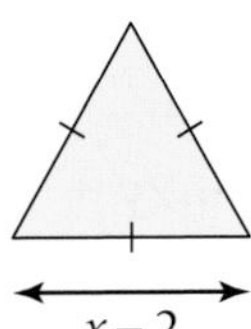

AO3 Problem

8 The diagram shows a square with sides $2y+5$ cm.

a Write an expression for the perimeter of the square.

b The perimeter of the square is 28 cm.
Find the value of y.

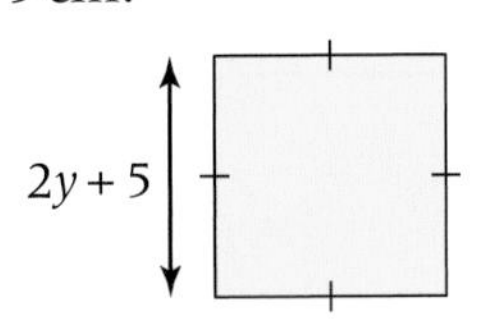

Perimeter = 4(   )

9 Write an expression for the area of this rectangle.
The area of the rectangle is 8 cm^2.
Find the value of z.

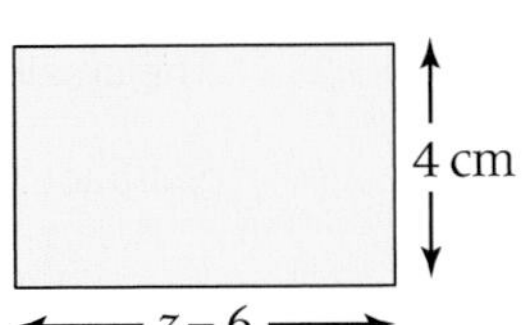

A5.5 Equations with the unknown on both sides

This spread will show you how to:

- Solve linear equations using the balance method, including equations with fractional or negative solutions

Keywords
Solve
Unknown

When you **solve** an equation, you find the value of the letter term or **unknown**.

In some equations the unknown is on both sides of the equals sign.

- You can solve equations with the unknown on both sides using the balance method.

Here is an example

$4x + 2 = 3x + 5$	The $3x$ term has the smallest number of x.
$4x - 3x + 2 = 3x - 3x + 5$	Subtract $3x$ from both sides.
$x + 2 = 5$	
$x - 2 = 5 - 2$	Subtract 2 from both sides.
$x = 3$	

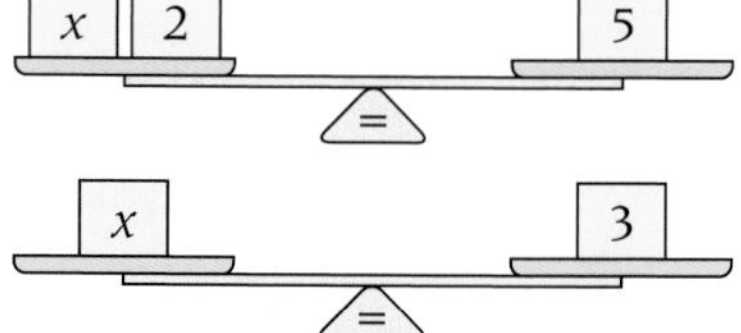

Example

Solve the equation
$3y - 7 = 2y + 3$

$3y - 2y - 7 = 2y - 2y + 3$	The smallest term in y is $2y$.
$y - 7 = 3$	Subtract $2y$ from both sides.
$y = 3 + 7 = 10$	Add 7 to both sides.

Example

Here is an equation
$4t + 10 = 2t + 4$
Find the value of t.

$4t - 2t + 10 = 2t - 2t + 4$	The smallest term in t is $2t$.
$2t + 10 = 4$	Subtract $2t$ from both sides.
$2t + 10 - 10 = 4 - 10$	
$2t = -6$	
$t = -3$	Divide both sides by 2.

Exercise A5.5

Grade D

1 Solve these equations.

a $4m + 2 = 3m + 7$
b $6p - 5 = 5p - 2$
c $3t + 2 = 2t + 5$
d $3n - 11 = 2n - 4$
e $4q + 2 = 5q - 6$
f $5s - 2 = 4s + 6$

2 Solve these equations.

a $2s + 5 = 3s + 8$
b $4t - 2 = 5t + 2$
c $6u + 10 = 5u + 8$
d $4v - 6 = -15 - 5v$

3 Find the value of the unknown in each of these equations.

a $2a + 14 = 6a - 6$
b $4b - 2 = 6b + 6$
c $3c - 4 = c + 1$
d $5d + 15 = -6 - 2d$

4 Solve these equations.

a $4x + 3 = 18 + 2x$
b $4x + 10 = 2x + 4$
c $8x + 15 = 12x + 14$
d $6x - 4 = 10x + 2$

AO3 Problem

5 Mae doubles a number and adds 5 to get 21.

a Write an expression for Mae's calculation.
Use n to represent the number.

21 = □n + □

b Tim multiplies the same number by 4 and subtracts 11 to get 21.
Write an expression for Tim's calculation, using n to represent the number.

□n − □ = 21

c Write your expressions from parts **a** and **b** as an equation.

expression **a** = 21, expression **b** = 21
→ expression **a** = expression **b**

d Solve your equation to find the value of n.

6 Write equations for these 'think of a number' problems as you did in question **5**.
Solve them to find the value of the number.

a I think of a number, multiply by 2 and add 7.
I get the same answer when I multiply the number by 4 and subtract 13.

$2n + 7 = 4n - 13$

b I think of a number, multiply by 5 and subtract 8.
I get the same answer when I double the number and add 10.

c I think of a number, multiply by 3 and add 4.
I get the same answer when I multiply by 5 and add 12.

□n − □ = □n + □

A5 Summary

Check out

You should now be able to:

- Set up simple equations
- Solve simple equations using inverse operations
- Solve simple equations using the balance method
- Solve linear equations requiring simplification of brackets
- Solve equations involving negative signs and negative solutions
- Solve linear equations where the unknown appears on either side or on both sides of the equation
- Check a solution is correct by substituting it back into the equation

Worked exam question

a Solve $4y + 3 = 2y + 9$ (2)

b Solve $5(t - 3) = 8$ (2)

(Edexcel Limited 2007)

a

$$4y + 3 = 2y + 9$$
$$4y - 2y + 3 = 2y - 2y + 9$$
$$2y + 3 = 9$$
$$2y + 3 - 3 = 9 - 3$$
$$2y = 6$$
$$y = 3$$

Subtract $2y$ from both sides.

Subtract 3 from both sides.

Check in the original equation.
$4 \times y + 3 = 2 \times y + 9$
$4 \times 3 + 3 = 2 \times 3 + 9$
$15 = 15$

b

$$5(t - 3) = 8$$
$$5t - 15 = 8$$
$$5t - 15 + 15 = 8 + 15$$
$$5t = 23$$
$$t = 4.6$$

First expand the brackets.

Check in the original equation.
$5 \times (t - 3) = 8$
$5 \times (4.6 - 3) = 8$
$8 = 8$

Exam questions

1 a Solve $2x = 8$ (1)

b Solve $y - 5 = 10$ (1)

c Solve $3z - 2 = 19$ (2)

A03

2

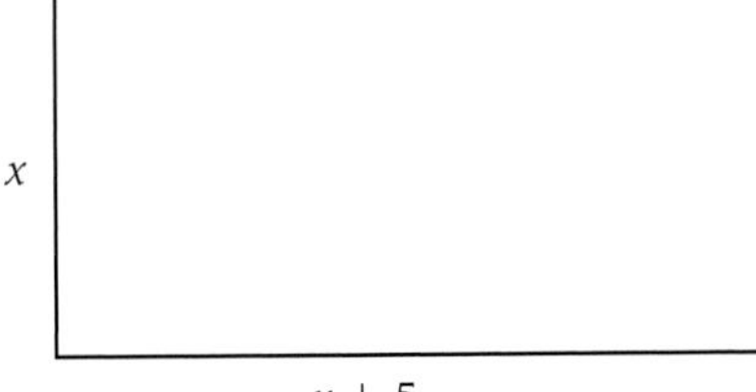

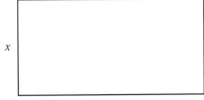

Diagram NOT accurately drawn

The diagram shows a rectangle.
All the measurements are in centimetres.
By finding x, work out the perimeter of the rectangle. (5)

3

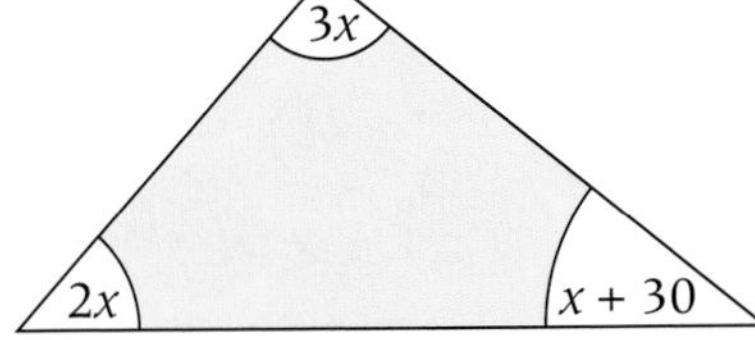

Diagram NOT accurately drawn

The diagram shows a triangle.
The sizes of the angles, in degrees, are

$3x$
$2x$
$x + 30$

Work out the value of x. (3)

(Edexcel Limited 2008)

Introduction

Some of the most basic shapes that we work with in graphic art and design are polygons. Understanding their angles enables us to understand how polygons fit together.

What's the point?

Tiling patterns rely on an understanding of angles in polygons. In the natural world, honeycombs are created using a tessellation of hexagons.

Check in

1. Using a protractor, draw angles of size
   a 30° **b** 50° **c** 105°
2. Using a ruler and protractor, construct these triangles.
   a

   7 cm
   60°
   5 cm

   b

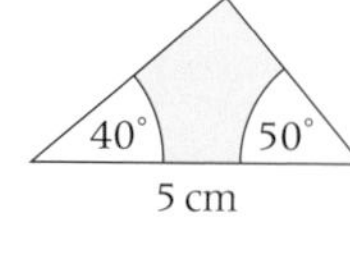

Orientation

What I should know	What I will learn	What this leads to
G 2 + 3 →	■ Calculate and use interior and exterior angles of polygons ■ Draw plans and elevations ■ Convert between measures of length, area and volume ■ Understand the effects of enlargement on the properties of shapes	→ Careers in graphic design and technical drawing

Rich task

Look at the photograph. You can see some lines which are parallel and some which seem to converge at a point called the vanishing point.
Investigate the heights of the **objects in the photograph** and their distances from the vanishing point.
Investigate with other perspective photographs.

G5.1 Interior angles of a polygon

This spread will show you how to:
- Calculate and use interior angles of polygons

Keywords
Diagonal
Interior
Polygon
Regular
Vertices

A **polygon** is a 2-D shape with three or more straight sides.

- A **regular** shape has equal sides and equal angles.

A regular hexagon has 6 equal sides and 6 equal angles.

You should know the names of these polygons:

Sides	Name	Sides	Name
3	triangle	7	heptagon
4	quadrilateral	8	octagon
5	pentagon	9	nonagon
6	hexagon	10	decagon

- The angles inside a shape are called **interior** angles.

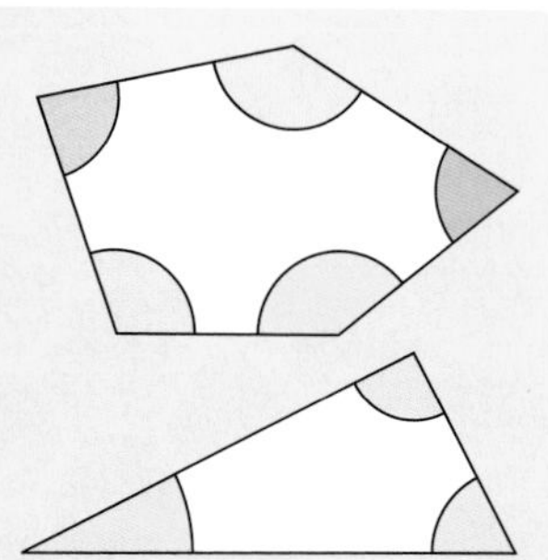

'interior' means inside.

p.66

- The interior angles in a triangle add to 180°.

You can split a polygon into triangles by drawing diagonals from the same vertices.

A **diagonal** joins two vertices, but is not a side.

Example

Calculate the sum of the interior angles for a pentagon.

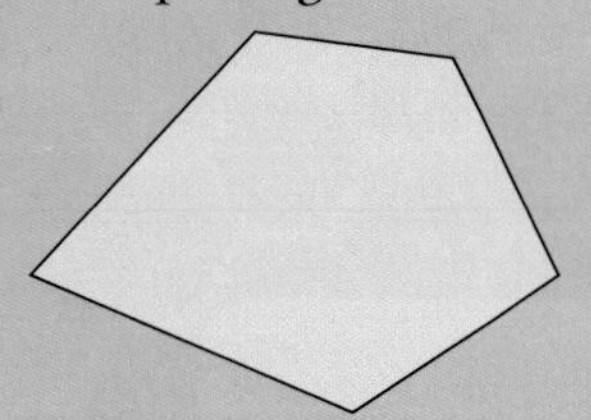

Draw in the two diagonals.
Three triangles formed: $3 \times 180° = 540°$
Sum of interior angles = 540°

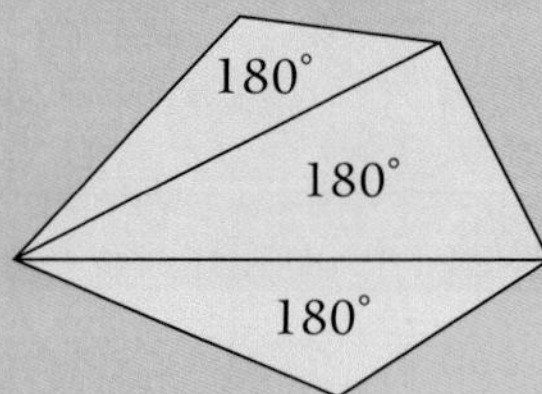

Example

Calculate the value of x in this regular hexagon.

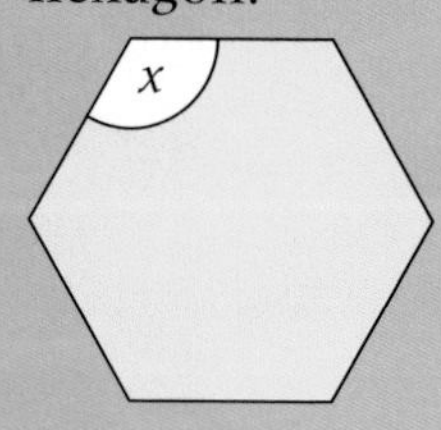

4 triangles
$4 \times 180° = 720°$
Sum of interior angles = 720°
There are 6 interior angles, so:
One interior angle, $x = 720° \div 6 = 120°$

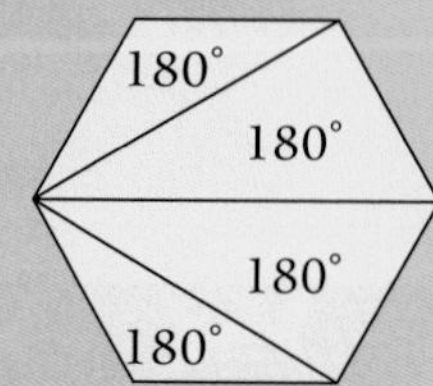

Exercise G5.1 — Grade C

1 **a** Calculate the value of one interior angle of an equilateral triangle.

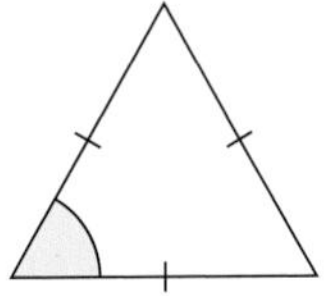

Two equilateral triangles are placed together to form a rhombus.

b Calculate the value of each interior angle of this rhombus.

c Calculate the sum of the interior angles of a rhombus.

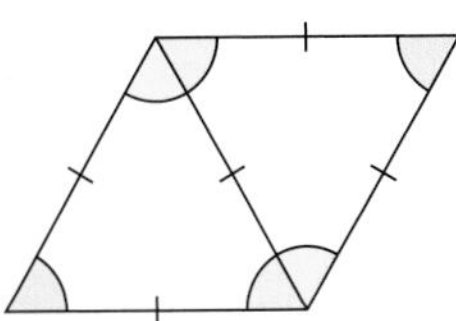

A03 Problem

2 Draw these polygons. Draw diagonals from **one** vertex.
(The quadrilateral is done for you.)

a Copy and complete this table of results.

Number of sides n	Number of triangles	Sum of the interior angles
3	1	180°
4	2	
5		
6		
7		
8		
9		
10		

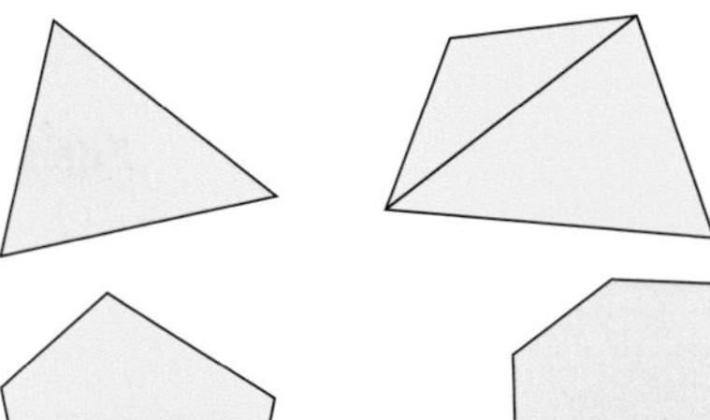

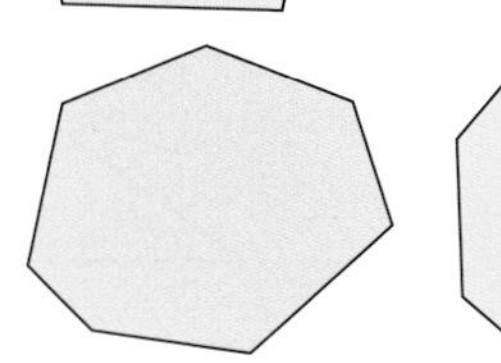

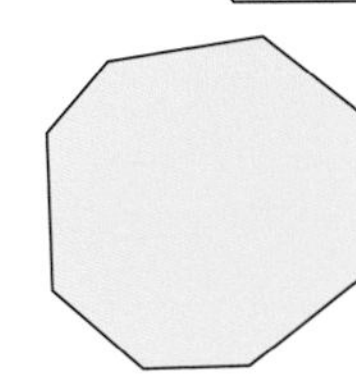

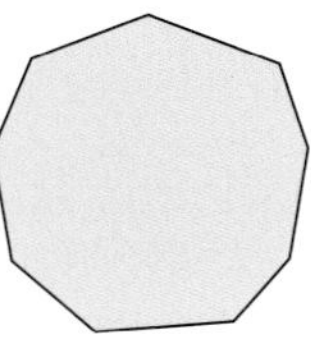

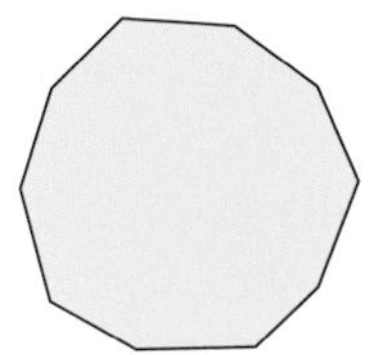

b Try to find a rule linking the number of sides n to the sum of the interior angles.

c Without drawing, what would the sum of the interior angles of a 15-sided polygon be?

3 **a** Calculate the sum of the interior angles for a regular octagon.

b Calculate the value of one interior angle of a regular octagon.

c Copy and complete this table for regular polygons.

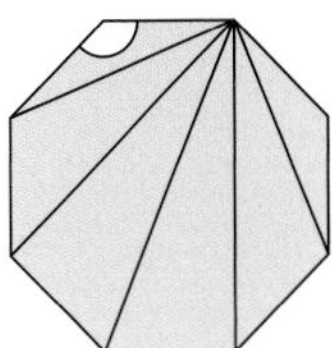

Number of sides	Name	Number of triangles	Sum of the interior angles	One interior anlges
3	Equilateral triangle	1	180°	60°
4	Square	2	360°	90°
5				
6				
7				
8	Regular octagon			
9				
10				

G5.2 Exterior angles of a polygon

This spread will show you how to:

- Calculate and use interior and exterior angles of polygons

Keywords
Exterior
Interior
Polygon
Regular

The angles inside a shape are called interior angles.

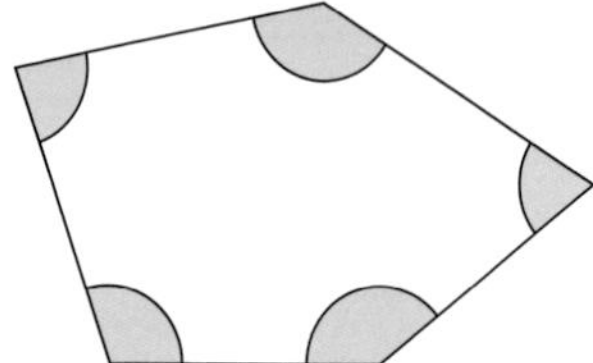

Interior = inside

You find the **exterior angles** of a polygon by extending each side of the shape in the same direction.

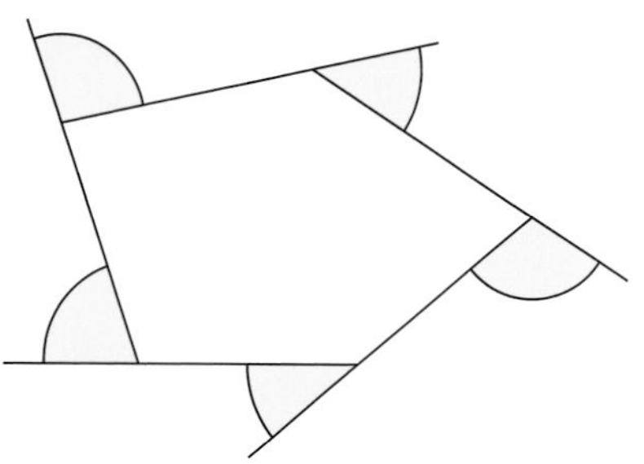

Exterior = outside

- The exterior angles of any polygon add to 360°.

- Interior angle + exterior angle = 180°
- (angles on a straight line add to 180°)

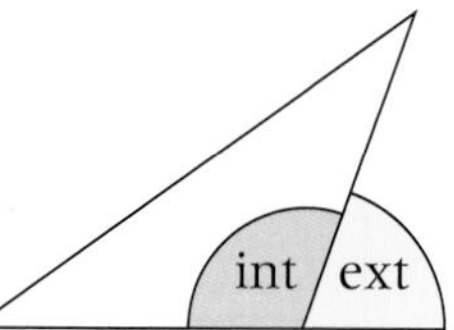

Example

Calculate the values of x and y in this regular hexagon.

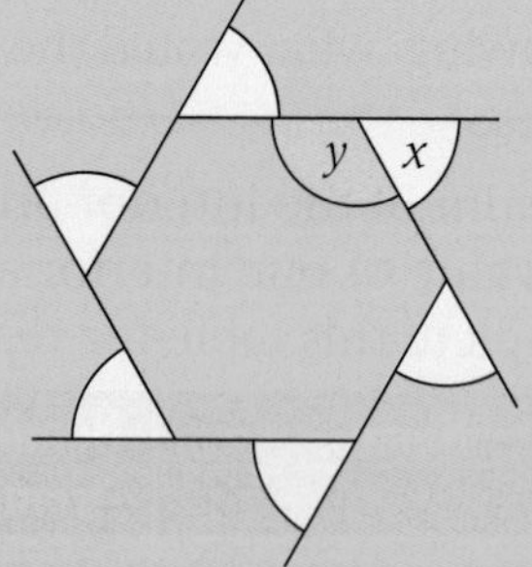

The six exterior angles add to 360°.

$x = 360° \div 6 = 60°$

$180° - 60° = 120°$ (angles on a straight line add to 180°)

$y = 120°$

Exercise G5.2 — Grade C

1 **a** State the total of the exterior angles of this regular octagon.
b Calculate the value of one of the exterior angles.
c Copy and complete this table of results for regular polygons.

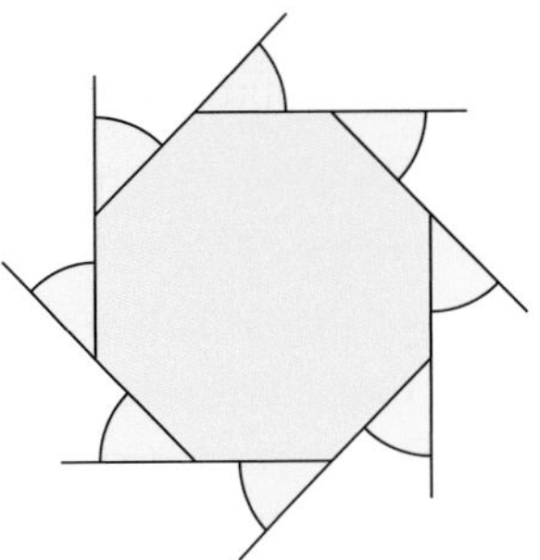

Number of sides	Name	Sum of exterior angles	One exterior anlges
3	Equilateral triangle		
4	Square		
5			
6			
7			
8	Regular octagon		
9			
10			

2 The interior angle of a regular polygon is 162°.
a Calculate the value of an exterior angle.
b State the sum of the exterior angles of the polygon.
c Calculate the number of exterior angles in the polygon.
d State the number of sides of the regular polygon.

3 A regular polygon has 15 sides.
a Calculate the value of an exterior angle.
b Calculate the value of an interior angle.

4 Calculate the size of the angles marked with letters in these polygons.

a

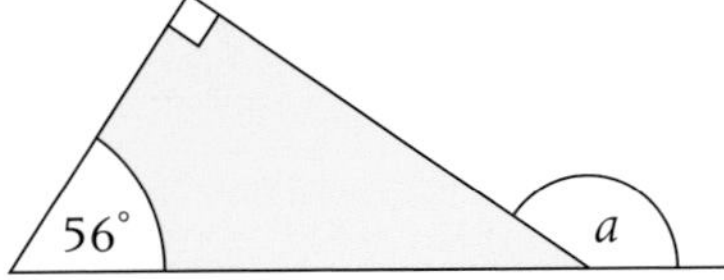

b

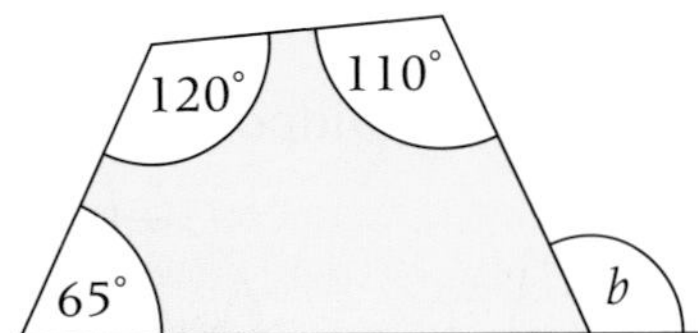

AO3 Problem

5 An interior angle of a regular polygon is three times the exterior angle.
a Calculate the value of each exterior angle.
b Calculate the value of each interior angle.
c Give the name of the regular polygon.

G5.3 Tessellations

This spread will show you how to:

- Use rotations and translations to make tessellations
- Recognise congruent polygons

Keywords
Congruent
Regular
Rotate
Tessellation
Translate

A **tessellation** is a tiling pattern with no gaps or overlaps.
You can rotate, **translate** and repeat shapes to make a tessellation.

Example

a Give the mathematical name of this shape.

b Show how the shape tessellates.

a It has 6 sides. It is a hexagon. **b**

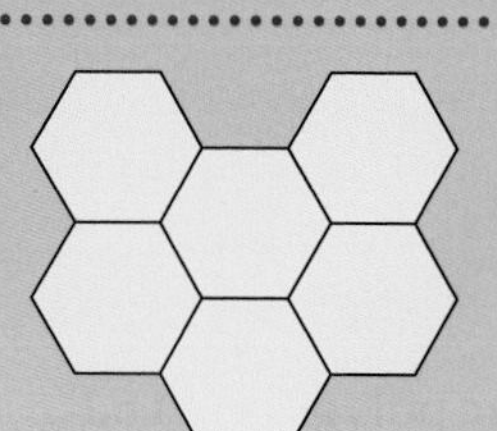

These shapes are **congruent** – they are the same size and shape.

- Any triangle tessellates.
  Rotate the triangle about the midpoint of a side.

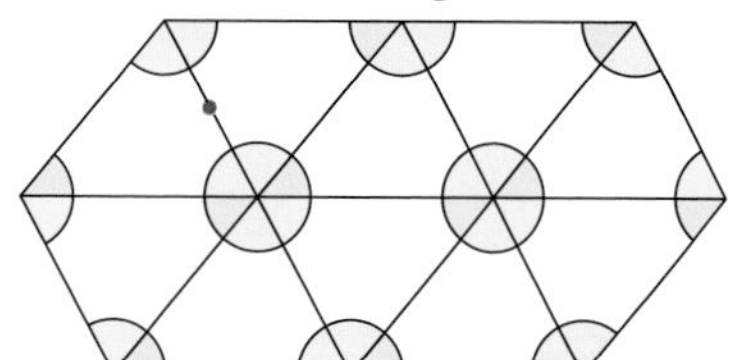

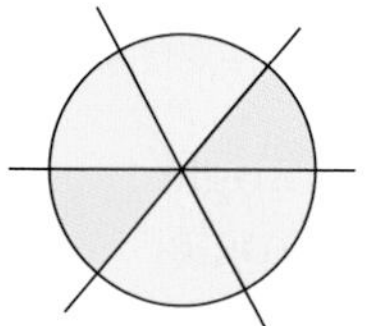

The six angles add to 360°.

- Any quadrilateral tessellates.
  Rotate the quadrilateral about the midpoint of a side.

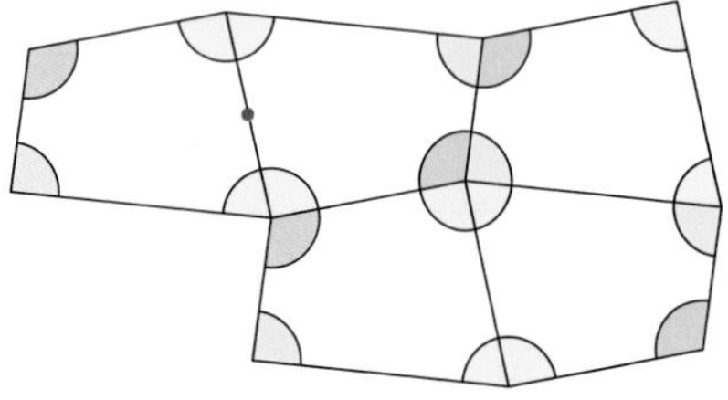

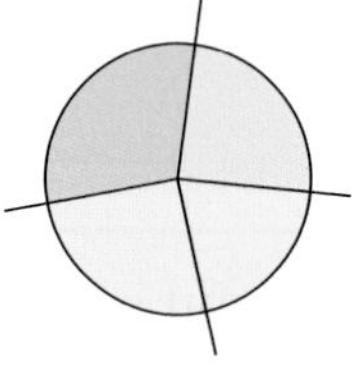

The four angles add to 360°.

- Only three regular shapes tessellate.

Equilateral triangles

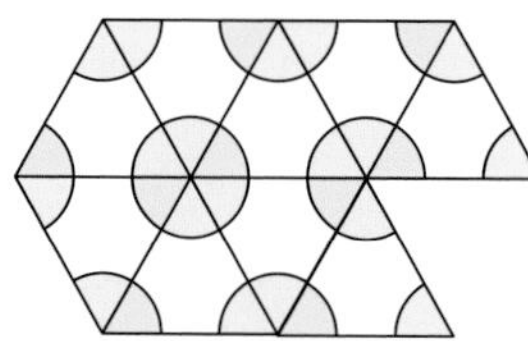

Squares

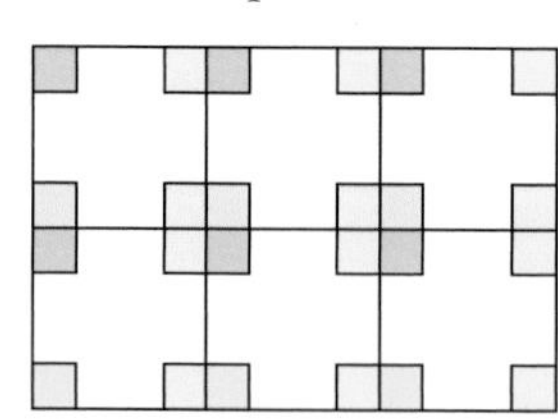

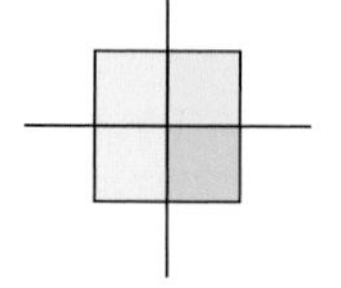

Hexagons

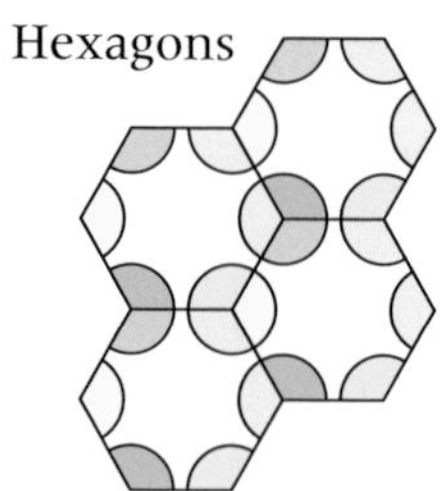

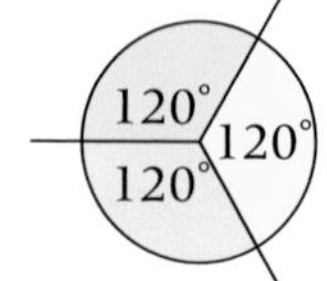

A **regular** shape has equal sides and equal angles.

The angles at a point add to 360°.

Exercise G5.3 Grade C

1 **a** Calculate the interior angle of a regular hexagon.
b Explain why a regular hexagon tessellates.

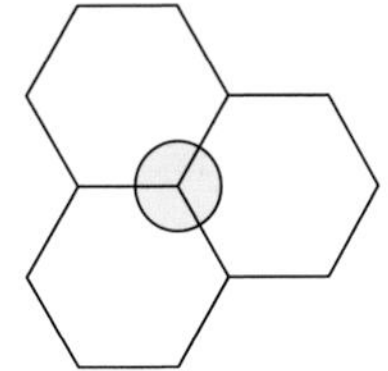

2 Calculate the interior angle of a regular octagon. Show your working.

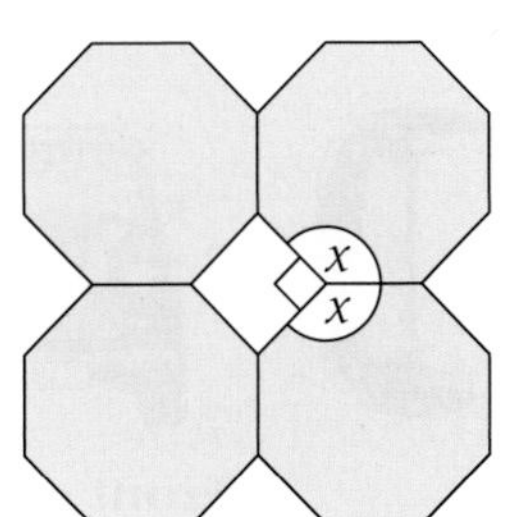

See page 274 to remind yourself about interior angles.

3 Six kites fit together as shown. Calculate the values of a and b

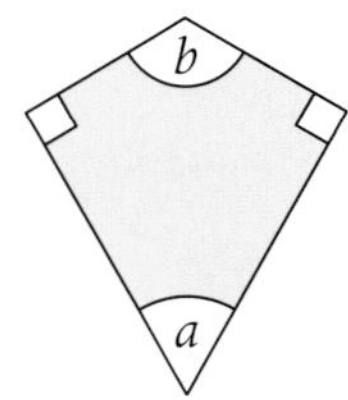

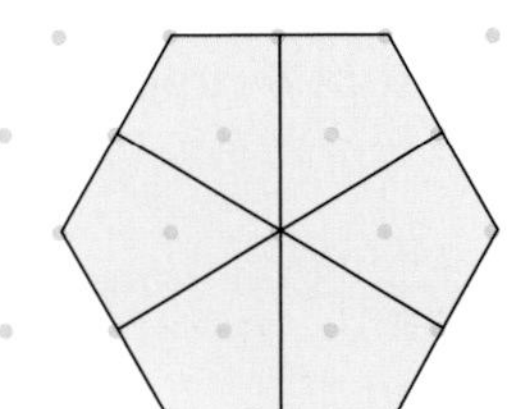

4 Twelve right-angled triangles fit together as shown. Calculate the values of a and b.

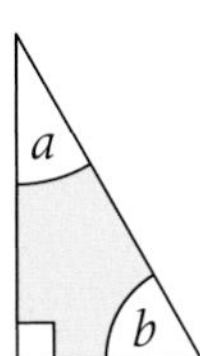

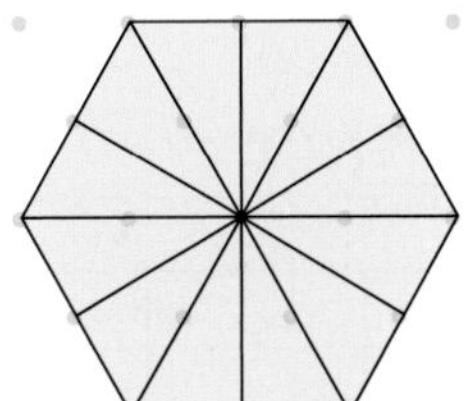

5 This pattern uses congruent equilateral triangles, rectangles and a hexagon.
a Calculate the interior angle of the hexagon.
b Show that the hexagon is regular.

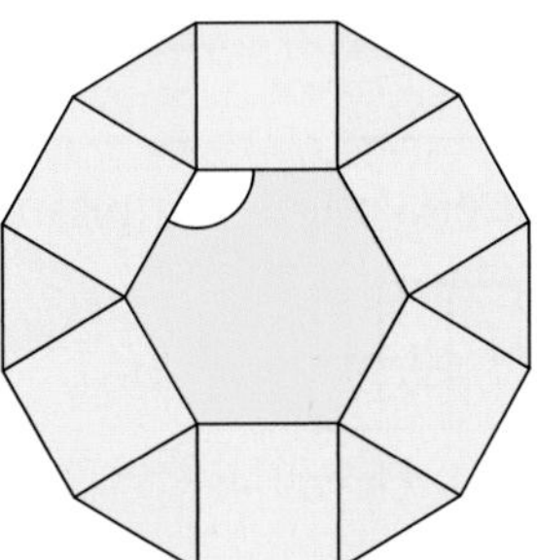

AO3 Problem

6 Does a regular pentagon tessellate? Explain your answer.

G5.4 Plans and elevations

This spread will show you how to:

- Analyse 3-D shapes through plans and elevations

Keywords
3-D
Front elevation
Plan
Side elevation

You can look at this car from different directions.

from above, … from the front, … and from the side.

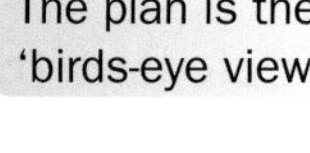

The plan is the 'birds-eye view'.

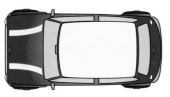

Plan

Front elevation

Side elevation

Example

This solid is made from 8 cubes.
Draw

a the plan
b the side elevation
c the front elevation

on square grid paper.

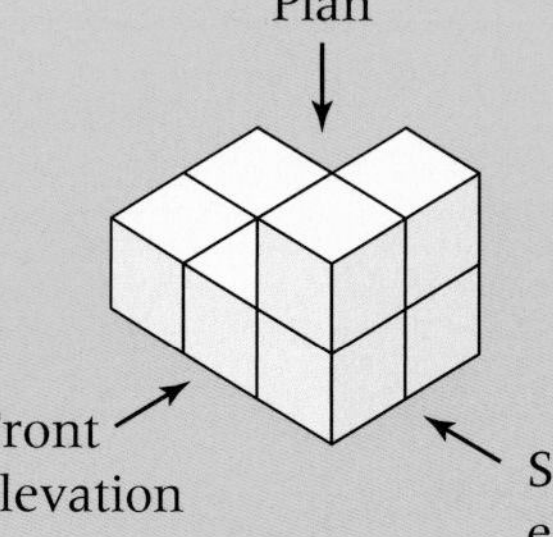

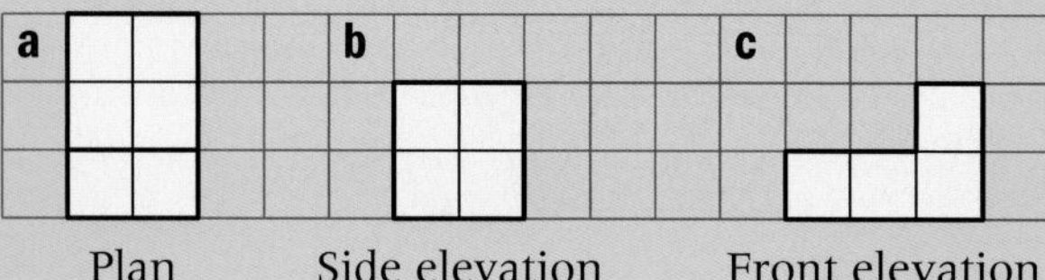

Plan Side elevation Front elevation

Notice the extra bold line in the plan, when the level of the cubes alters.

Example

The plan and front elevation of a prism are shown.

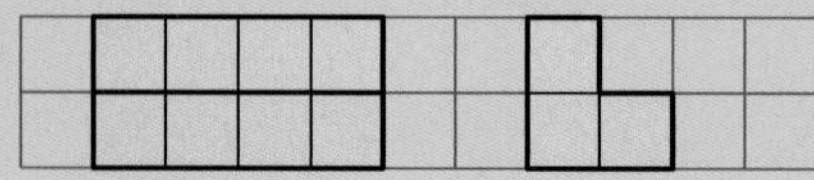

Plan Front elevation

a Draw a 3-D sketch of the prism.
b Draw the side elevation on square grid paper.

a

b

Side elevation

Exercise G5.4

Grade D

1 On square grid paper, draw the plan (P), the front elevation (F) and the side elevation (S) for each solid.

a

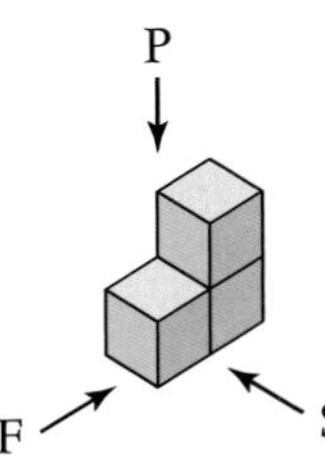

b

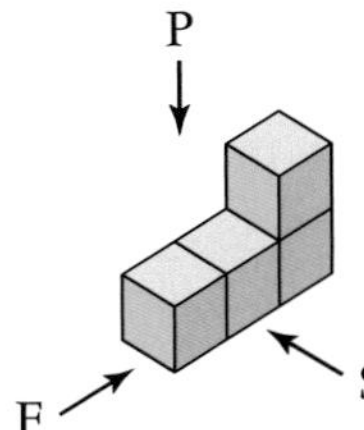

c

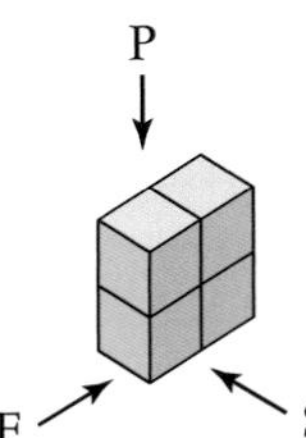

d

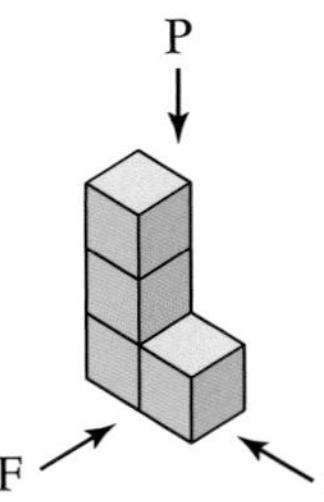

e

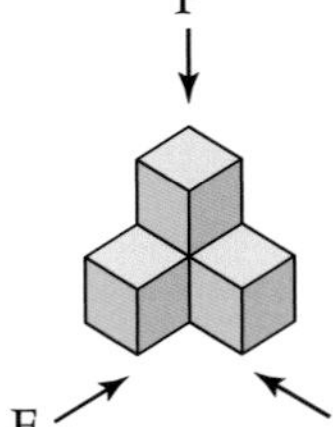

f

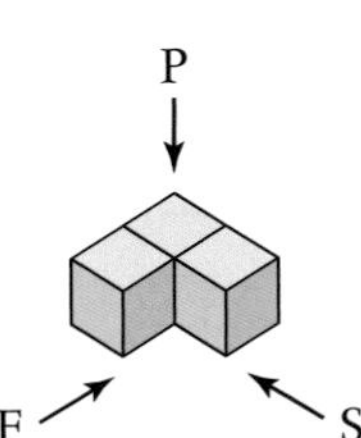

2 The plan, front elevation and side elevation are given for these solids made from cubes. Draw a 3-D sketch of each solid and state the number of cubes needed to make it.

a

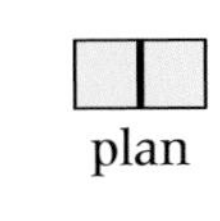

plan

front elevation

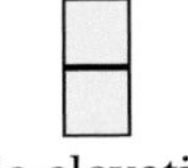

side elevation

b

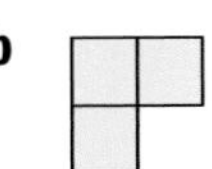

plan

front elevation

side elevation

c

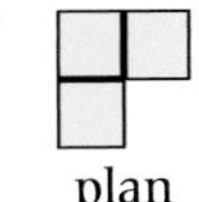

plan

front elevation

side elevation

3 Sketch the plan (P), the front elevation (F) and the side elevation (S) for each solid.

These solids are drawn on an **isometric grid.**

a

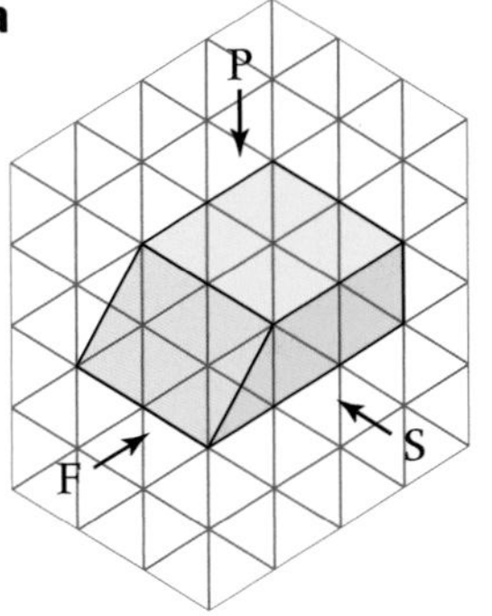

b

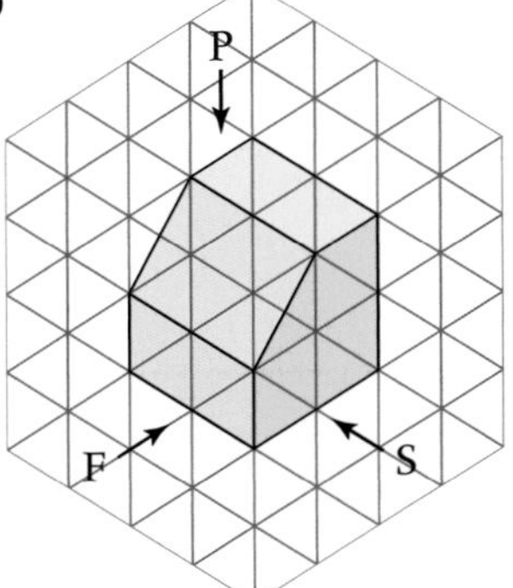

c

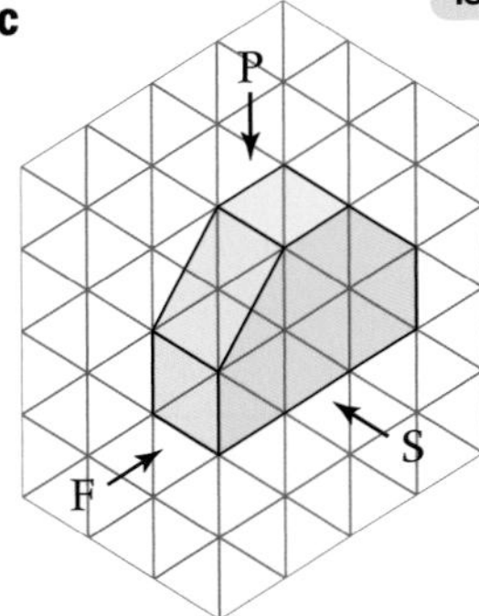

G5.5 2-D and 3-D measures

This spread will show you how to:

- Convert between length measures, area measures including cm^2 and m^2, and volume measures including cm^3 and m^3

Keywords
Area
Cubic centimetre
Cubic metre
Litre
Square centimetre
Square metre
Volume

You should know these relationships between the metric units of length:

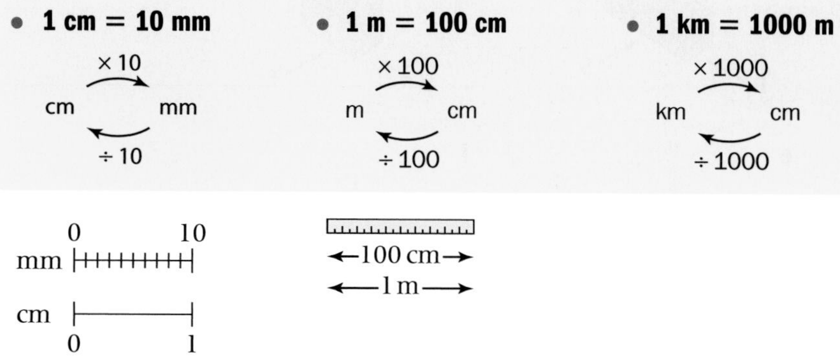

The relationships between the metric units of area are:

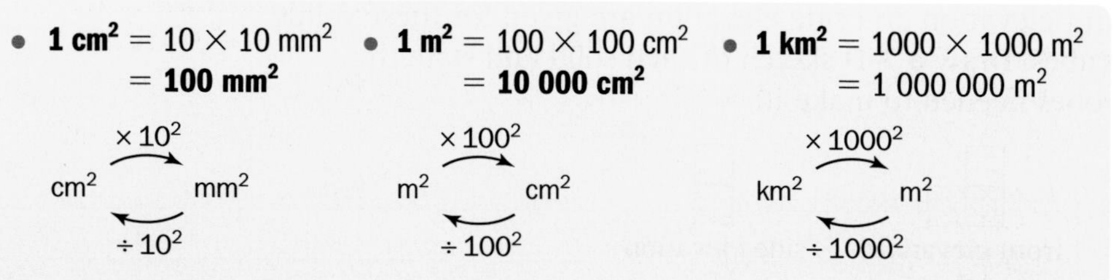

You don't need to learn these, but you should be able to work them out for yourself.

Example

Change 5 m^2 to cm^2.

$5\ m^2 = 5 \times 10\,000\ cm^2$
$= 50\,000\ cm^2$

You expect a larger number, so multiply.

The relationship between metric units of **volume** are

- **1 cm^3** $= 10 \times 10 \times 10\ mm^3$ $=$ **1000 mm^3**

  $cm^3 \xrightarrow{\times 10^3} mm^3$, $mm^3 \xrightarrow{\div 10^3} cm^3$

- **1 m^3** $= 100 \times 100 \times 100\ cm^2$ $=$ **1 000 000 cm^3**

  $m^3 \xrightarrow{\times 100^3} cm^3$, $cm^3 \xrightarrow{\div 100^3} m^3$

Vol = 1 m^3
$= 100 \times 100 \times 100\ cm^3$
$= 1\,000\,000\ cm^3$

1 m = 100 cm

1 m = 100 cm

1 m = 100 cm

Example

Change 6 000 000 cm^3 to cubic metres (m^3).

$6\,000\,000\ cm^3 = 6\,000\,000 \div 1\,000\,000\ m^3$
$= 6\ m^3$

You expect a smaller number, so divide.

Exercise G5.5 — Grade C

1 Convert these metric measurements of length.

a 180 cm to mm **b** 45 mm to cm **c** 350 cm to m
d 2000 m to km **e** 3500 m to km **f** 4500 mm to m
g 85 cm to m **h** 2500 mm to cm **i** 2500 mm to m
j 800 m to km

2 Here are two identical rectangles, A and B.

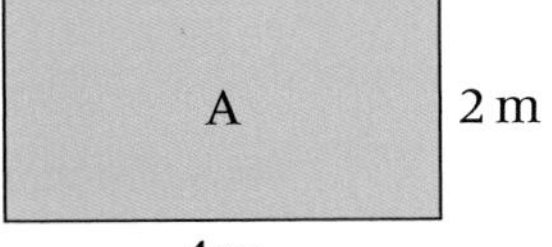

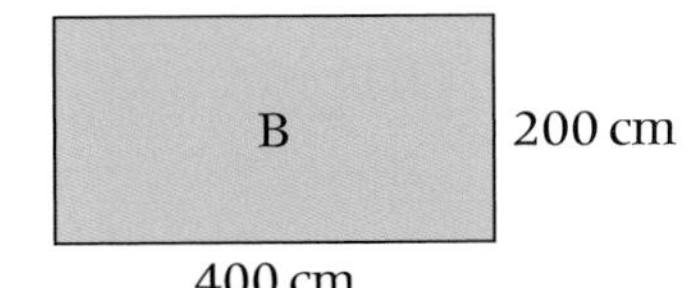

a Calculate the area of rectangle A in m^2.
b Calculate the area of rectangle B in cm^2.

3 **a** Calculate the area of this rectangle in m^2.
b Convert your answer to cm^2.

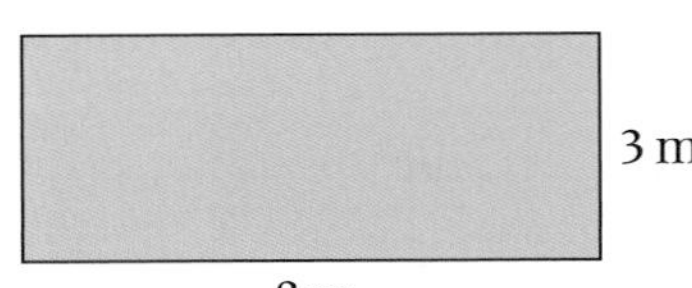

4 Convert these areas to mm^2.

a 4 cm^2 **b** 7.3 cm^2 **c** 10.9 cm^2
d 2.5 cm^2 **e** 400 cm^2

$cm^2 \xrightarrow{\times 10^2} mm^2$, $mm^2 \xrightarrow{\div 10^2} cm^2$

$10^2 = 100$

5 Convert these areas to cm^2.

a 600 mm^2 **b** 1200 mm^2 **c** 850 mm^2
d 6500 mm^2 **e** 10 000 mm^2

6 Convert these areas to m^2.

a 40 000 cm^2 **b** 85 000 cm^2 **c** 1 000 000 cm^2
d 125 000 cm^2 **e** 5000 cm^2

$m^2 \xrightarrow{\times 100^2} cm^2$, $cm^2 \xrightarrow{\div 100^2} m^2$

$100^2 = 10\,000$

7 Convert these areas to cm^2.

a 5 m^2 **b** 10 m^2 **c** 6.5 m^2
d 7.75 m^2 **e** 0.6 m^2

8 Convert these areas to km^2.

a 4 000 000 m^2 **b** 18 000 000 m^2
c 500 000 m^2 **d** 1 500 000 m^2

$km^2 \xrightarrow{\times 1000^2} m^2$, $m^2 \xrightarrow{\div 1000^2} km^2$

$1000^2 = 1$ million

9 Convert these volumes to litres.

a 1 m^3 **b** 6 m^3 **c** 7.5 m^3

1 m^3 = 1000 litres

G5.6 Scale factors

This spread will show you how to:

- Understand the effects of enlargement on the angles, perimeter, area and volume of shapes and solids

Keywords
Area
Enlargement
Multiplier
Perimeter
Scale factor
Volume

In this **enlargement**, corresponding lengths are multiplied by 2, so the **scale factor** is 2.

p.206

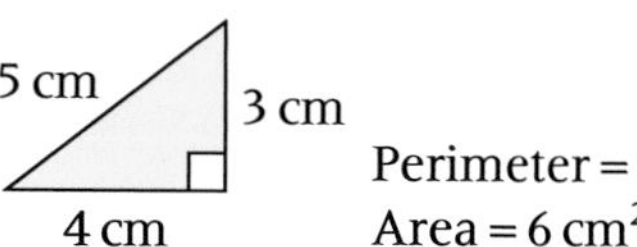

Perimeter = 12 cm
Area = 6 cm²

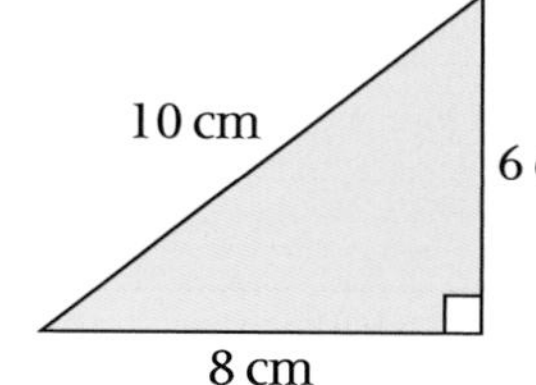

Perimeter = 24 cm
Area = 24 cm²

Area of a triangle $= \frac{1}{2} \times$ base $\times$ height.

If scale factor for length is 2 then scale factor for **area** is $2 \times 2 = 4$.

Scale factor is 2 but area is ×4.

In this enlargement, corresponding lengths are multiplied by 2, so the scale factor is 2.

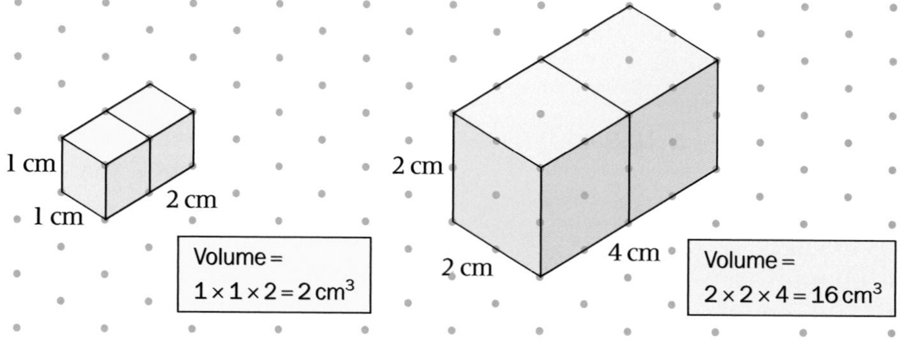

Volume of a cuboid = length × width × height.

If scale factor for length is 2, then scale factor for **volume** is $2 \times 2 \times 2 = 8$.

Scale factor is 2 but volume is ×8.

- If scale factor for length is L then scale factor for area is $L \times L = L^2$ and scale factor for volume is $L \times L \times L = L^3$.

Example

A 2 cm by 3 cm by 4 cm cuboid is shown. Calculate

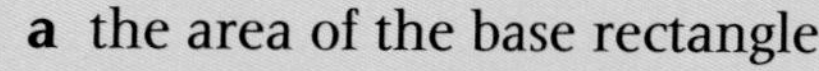

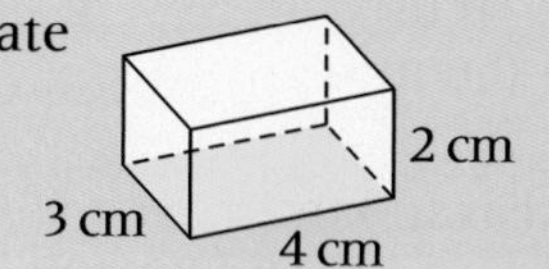

a the area of the base rectangle
b the volume of the cuboid.
The cuboid is enlarged by scale factor 3.
c Calculate the area of the new base rectangle.

a Area $= 3 \times 4 = 12$ cm²
b Volume $= 2 \times 3 \times 4 = 24$ cm³
c Scale factor is 3, so new lengths are
$3 \times 3 = 9$ cm, $4 \times 3 = 12$ cm,
$2 \times 3 = 6$ cm
Area $= 9 \times 12 = 108$ cm²

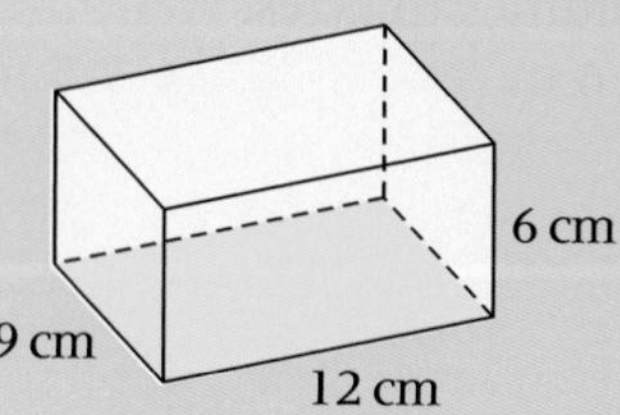

Note that enlarged volume $= 6 \times 9 \times 12$
$= 648$ cm³

Scale factor is 3 but area is ×9.

Scale factor is 3 but volume is ×27.

Exercise G5.6 — Grade C

1 **a** Calculate the perimeter of this rectangle. State the units of your answer.

b Find the area of the rectangle. State the units of your answer.

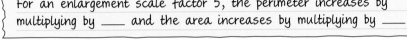

2 cm

6 cm

The rectangle is enlarged by scale factor 5.

c Calculate the length and width of the enlarged rectangle.

d Calculate the perimeter of the enlarged rectangle.

e Calculate the area of the enlarged rectangle.

f Copy and complete this sentence:

> For an enlargement scale factor 5, the perimeter increases by multiplying by ___ and the area increases by multiplying by ___.

2 **a** Calculate the volume of this cuboid. State the units of your answer.

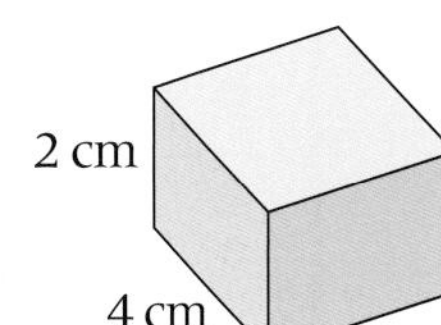

The cuboid is enlarged by scale factor 3.

b Calculate the dimensions of the new cuboid.

c Calculate the volume of the new cuboid.

d Copy and complete this sentence:

> For an enlargement scale factor 3, the volume increase by multiplying by ___.

3 **a** Calculate the area of this triangle. State the units of your answer.

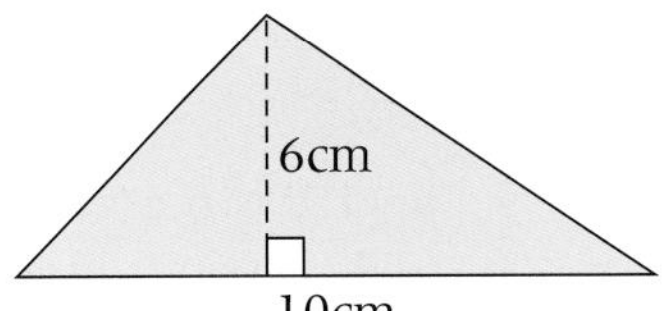

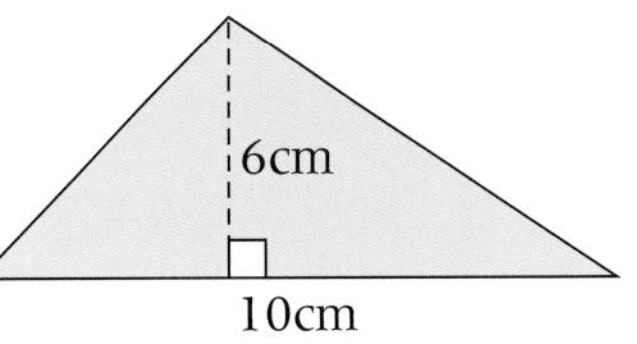

The triangle is enlarged by scale factor 2.

b Calculate the area of the enlarged triangle.

4 **a** Calculate the volume of this cuboid. State the units of your answer.

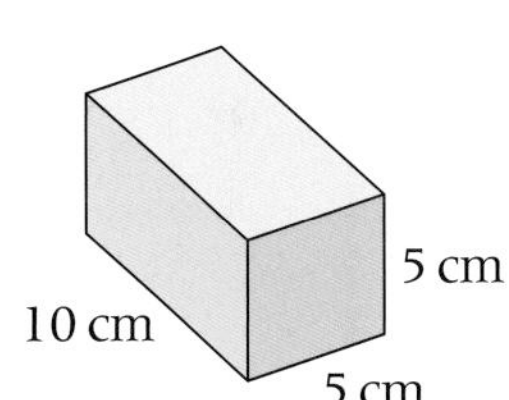

The cuboid is enlarged by scale factor 2.

b Calculate the volume of the enlarged cuboid.

5 Copy and complete this table for enlargements.

Scale factor	Multiplier for length	Multiplier for area	Multiplier for volume
2	2	4	8
3	3	9	27
4			
5			
6			
7			

6 A shape has a perimeter of 14 cm and an area of 10 cm^2. Calculate the perimeter and area of the shape after an enlargement of scale factor 4.

G5 Summary

Check out

You should now be able to:

- Recall and use properties of angles at a point, on a straight line and of opposite angles at a vertex
- Use the properties of right-angled, equilateral, isosceles and scalene triangles
- Describe and transform 2-D shapes using enlargements
- Enlarge 2-D shapes using a centre of enlargement and a positive scale factor
- Identify shapes that are similar

Worked exam question

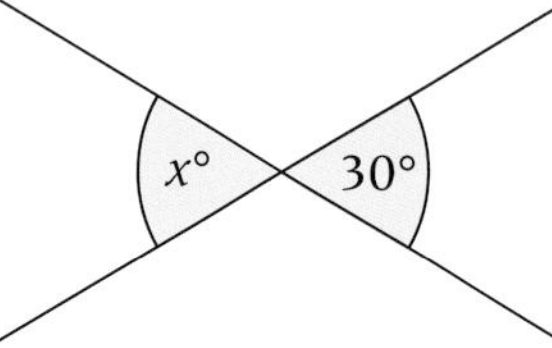

Diagram NOT accurately drawn

a **i** Write down the value of x.
ii Give a reason for your answer. (2)

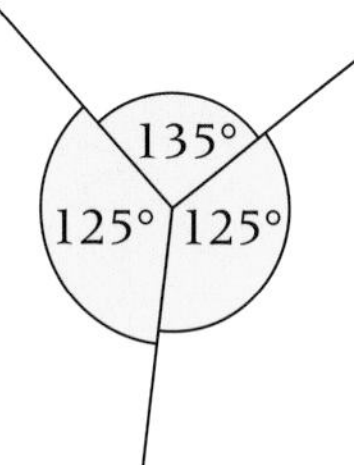

Diagram NOT accurately drawn

This diagram is wrong.

b Explain why. (1)

(Edexcel Limited 2008)

---

a

i $x = 30°$
ii Vertically opposite angles are equal.

b

135
125
125 +
385 The angles at a point should add to 360°

Write the addition sum to show that the three angles add to 385°.

Exam questions

1 Here are the front elevation, side elevation and the plan of a 3-D shape.

Front elevation

Side elevation

Plan

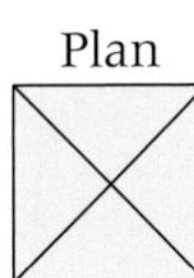

Draw a sketch of the 3-D shape. (2)

(Edexcel Limited 2008)

2 Change 7 m^2 to cm^2. (2)

(Edexcel Limited 2005)

A02 + 3

3 Cheryl wants to make a tessellating pattern of regular octagons.
Will she be able to do this, without any gaps?
Give reasons for your answer.

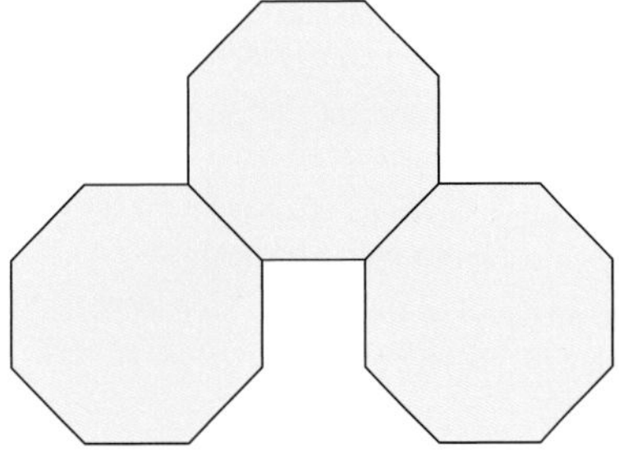

(4)

Functional Maths 6: Radio maths

Mathematics can be used to explain how radio transmission works.

Radio transmitters use continuous sine waves to send and receive information such as music or speech.

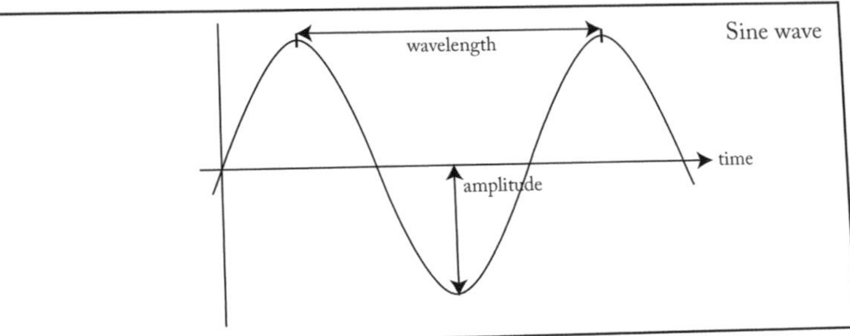

The frequency is the number of waves transmitted per second, measured in hertz (Hz).

1 kilohertz	= 1 kHz	= 1,000 Hz
1 megahertz	= 1 MHz	= 1,000,000 Hz
1 gigahertz	= 1 GHz	= 1,000,000,000 Hz

Express a. 2,000 Hz in kilohertz
b. 2 GHz in megahertz.

For a sound wave, the larger the amplitude, the louder the sound.
A higher frequency gives a sound with a higher pitch.

Compare the sound produced by these waves. Comment on their pitch and volume, referring to the diagrams.

a.

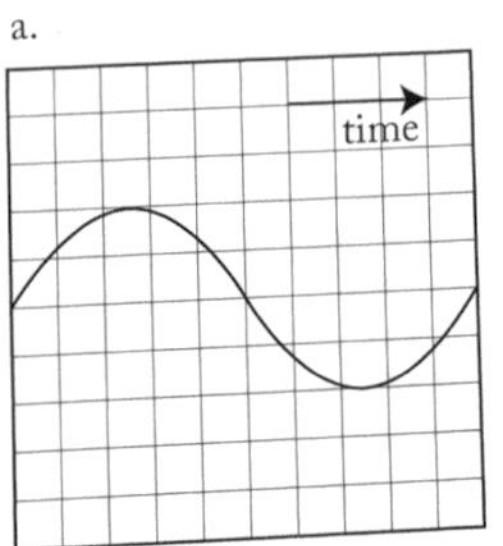

b.

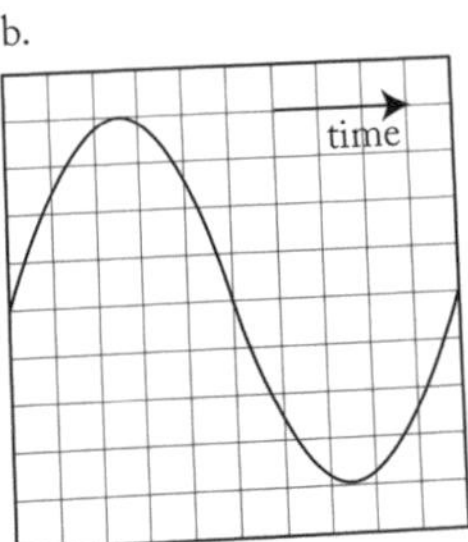

c.

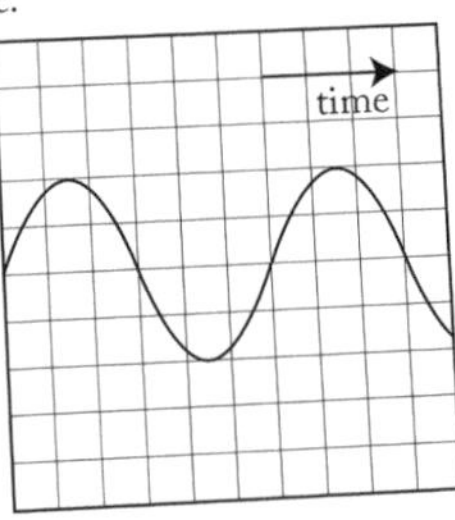

The original sound wave carrying the music or speech is not a sine wave.
The radio transmitter must encode the information on to a sine wave before it can be sent.
Two ways of doing this are by varying the sine waves amplitude (AM radio) or its frequency (FM radio).

AM radio stations transmit on frequencies between 535 kHz and 1700 kHz.

FM radio stations transmit on frequencies between 88 mHz and 108 mHz.

640 on the AM dial stands for 640 kHz.

88.7 FM stands for 88,700,000 Hz.

Wave speed (m/s) = frequency (Hz) × wavelength (m)

Maths FM transmits on the frequency 100.0 FM with a wavelength of 3m.

a. What is the frequency of the radio station in
   i. mHz ii. Hz?
b. Use the formula at the top of the page to calculate the speed of the waves that are being transmitted.
c. Rearrange the formula to give an equation for frequency in terms of wave speed and wavelength.
d. Use your answers from parts b and c to calculate the frequency (in Hz) of a radio station that transmits waves of wavelength 2.80m.
e. Is the radio station in part d on the AM or FM dial? Justify your answer and write down its AM or FM frequency.

Investigate the frequency and wavelengths used by the radio stations that you and your friends and family listen to.

Mathematics can also be applied to plan and produce radio programmes.

DJ Cool uses this wheel diagram to plan his hour-long show:

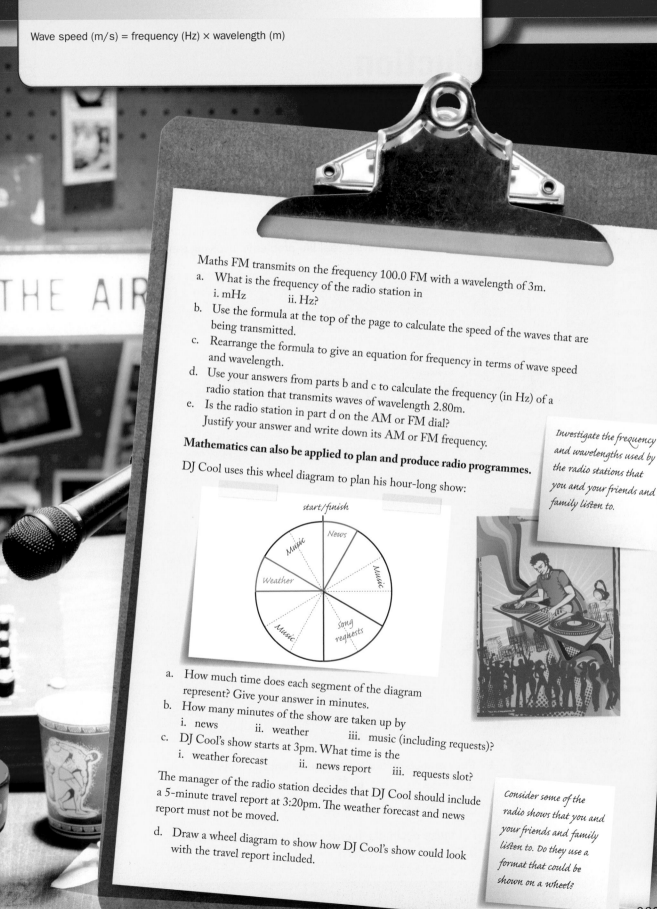

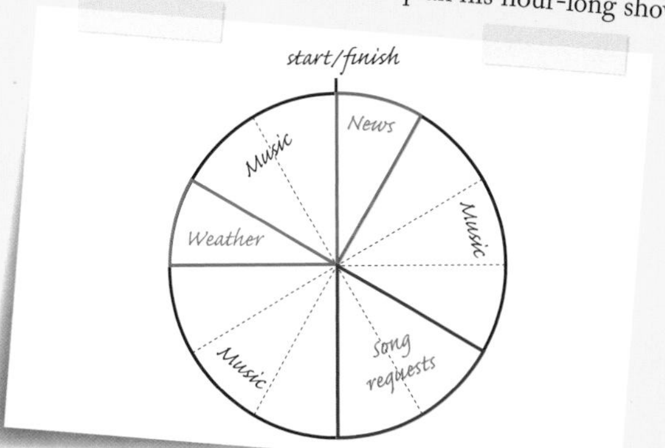

start/finish

News

Music

Song requests

Music

Weather

Music

a. How much time does each segment of the diagram represent? Give your answer in minutes.
b. How many minutes of the show are taken up by
   i. news ii. weather iii. music (including requests)?
c. DJ Cool's show starts at 3pm. What time is the
   i. weather forecast ii. news report iii. requests slot?

The manager of the radio station decides that DJ Cool should include a 5-minute travel report at 3:20pm. The weather forecast and news report must not be moved.

d. Draw a wheel diagram to show how DJ Cool's show could look with the travel report included.

Consider some of the radio shows that you and your friends and family listen to. Do they use a format that could be shown on a wheel?

N6 More fractions and decimals

Introduction

The very first fractions can be traced back to the ancient Egyptians.
They wrote all their fractions as unit fractions (such as $\frac{1}{2} + \frac{1}{3}$ to mean the fraction $\frac{5}{6}$). Since then, fractions have been expressed in different ways by different cultures over the centuries.
It was not until the 17th century that fractions as we know them today existed in Europe.

What's the point?

Understanding how fractions work enables us to make a lot of connections in mathematics, for instance in solving real life problems involving ratio and proportion.

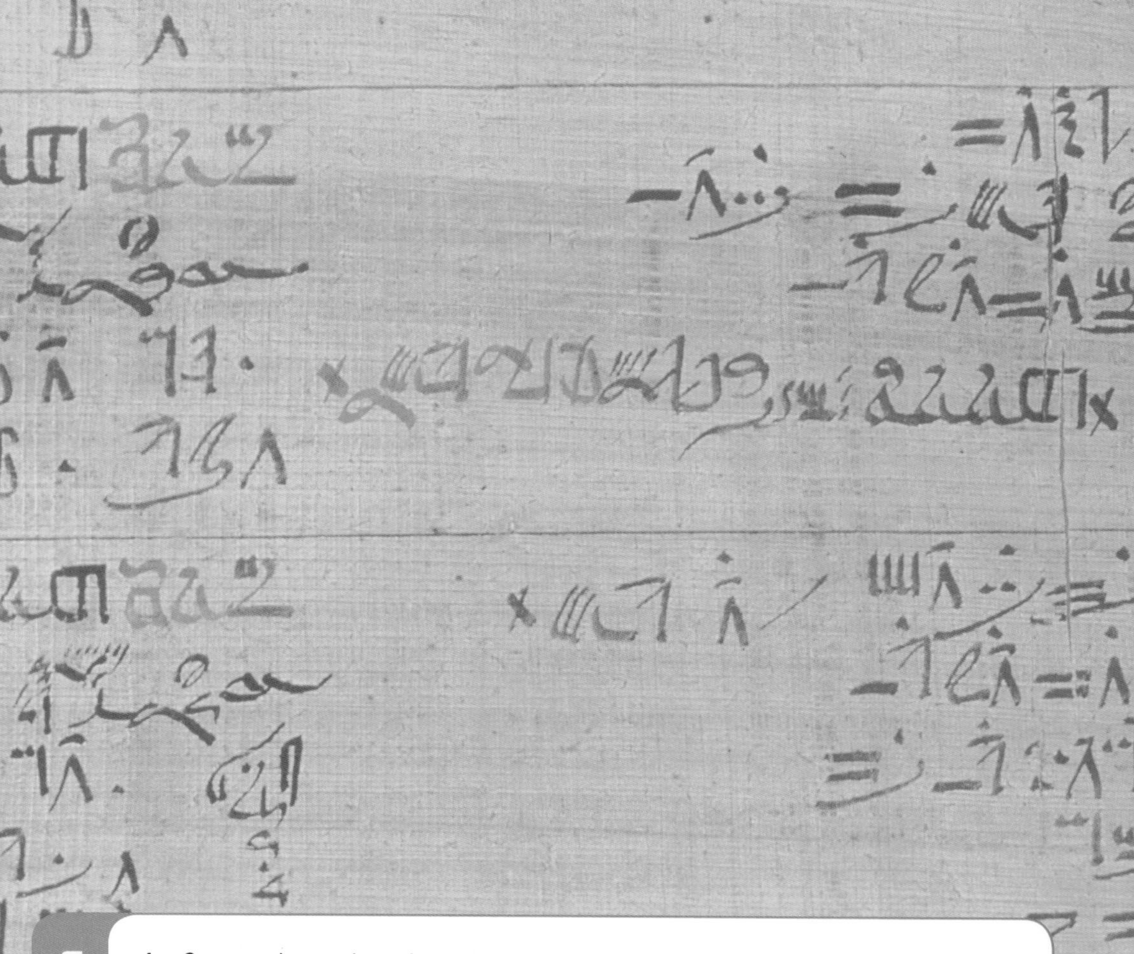

Check in

1 Copy and complete these equivalent fractions.

a $\frac{2}{3} = \frac{\square}{15}$ **b** $\frac{45}{60} = \frac{3}{\square}$

2 Calculate $12 \times \frac{1}{4}$.

3 Put these decimals in order from smallest to largest.

0.75 0.8 0.7 0.875

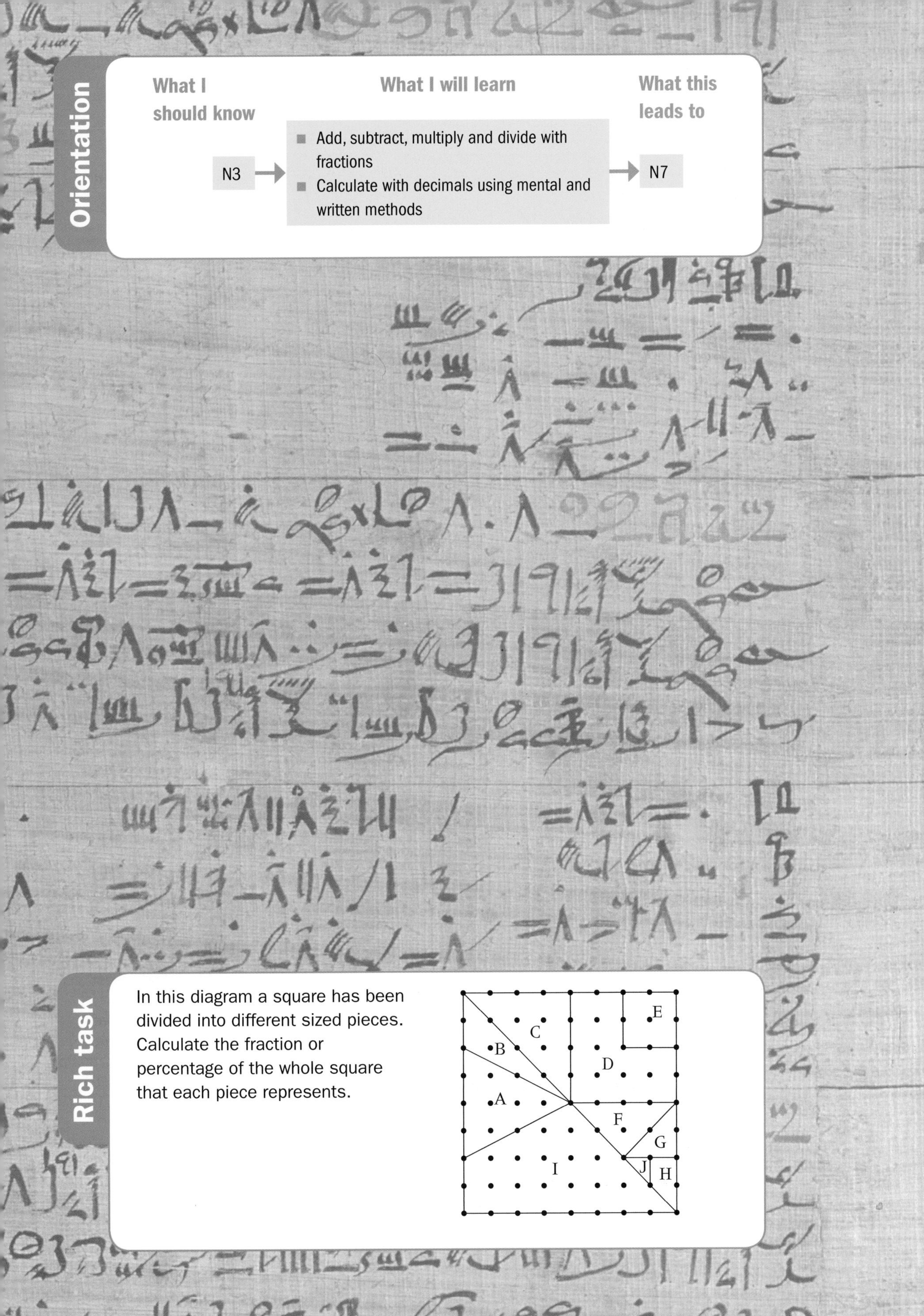

Orientation

What I should know	What I will learn	What this leads to
N3 →	■ Add, subtract, multiply and divide with fractions ■ Calculate with decimals using mental and written methods	→ N7

Rich task

In this diagram a square has been divided into different sized pieces. Calculate the fraction or percentage of the whole square that each piece represents.

N6.1 Adding and subtracting fractions

This spread will show you how to:

- Add, subtract, multiply and divide with fractions

Keywords
Common denominator
Equivalent
Fraction

It is easy to add or subtract **fractions** when they have the same denominator.

 +  = 

$\frac{3}{8} + \frac{1}{8} = \frac{4}{8}$

- You can add or subtract fractions with different denominators by first writing them as **equivalent** fractions with the same denominator.

Example

Calculate **a** $\frac{3}{5} + \frac{1}{3}$ **b** $1\frac{3}{4} - \frac{5}{7}$ **c** $1\frac{7}{10} + 2\frac{3}{5}$

a $\frac{3}{5} + \frac{1}{3}$

$$\frac{3}{5} + \frac{1}{3} = \frac{9}{15} + \frac{5}{15} = \frac{9+5}{15} = \frac{14}{15}$$

$\frac{3}{5} \xrightarrow{\times 3} \frac{9}{15}$ $\frac{1}{3} \xrightarrow{\times 5} \frac{5}{15}$

The lowest **common denominator** is the lowest common multiple of 5 and 3, which is 15.

b $1\frac{3}{4} - \frac{5}{7}$

Change the mixed numbers to improper fractions:

$1\frac{3}{4} = \frac{7}{4}$

$$1\frac{3}{4} - \frac{5}{7} = \frac{7}{4} - \frac{5}{7} = \frac{49}{28} - \frac{20}{28} = \frac{49-20}{28} = \frac{29}{28} = 1\frac{1}{28}$$

$\frac{7}{4} \xrightarrow{\times 7} \frac{49}{28}$ $\frac{5}{7} \xrightarrow{\times 4} \frac{20}{28}$

The lowest common denominator is the lowest common multiple of 4 and 7, which is 28.

c $1\frac{7}{10} + 2\frac{3}{5}$

Change the mixed numbers to improper fractions:

$1\frac{7}{10} = \frac{17}{10}$ $2\frac{3}{5} = \frac{13}{5}$

$$1\frac{7}{10} + 2\frac{3}{5} = \frac{17}{10} + \frac{13}{5} = \frac{17}{10} + \frac{26}{10} = \frac{17+26}{10} = \frac{43}{10} = 4\frac{3}{10}$$

$\frac{13}{5} \xrightarrow{\times 2} \frac{26}{10}$

An alternative method is to write:
$1 + \frac{7}{10} + 2 + \frac{3}{5}$
$= 3 + \frac{7}{10} + \frac{3}{5}$
$= \ldots$

The lowest common denominator is the lowest common multiple of 5 and 10, which is 10.

Exercise N6.1 — Grade D

1 Work out

a $\frac{1}{3}+\frac{1}{3}$ **b** $\frac{3}{8}+\frac{2}{8}$ **c** $\frac{8}{11}-\frac{3}{11}$ **d** $\frac{8}{17}+\frac{5}{17}$

e $\frac{14}{23}-\frac{11}{23}$ **f** $\frac{5}{27}+\frac{8}{27}$

2 Work out each of these, leaving your answer in its simplest form.

a $\frac{2}{3}+\frac{1}{3}$ **b** $\frac{8}{9}-\frac{2}{9}$ **c** $\frac{8}{11}+\frac{5}{11}$ **d** $\frac{15}{13}-\frac{8}{13}$

e $\frac{14}{9}+\frac{1}{9}$ **f** $\frac{17}{12}-\frac{9}{12}$ **g** $1\frac{2}{3}+\frac{2}{3}$ **h** $4\frac{2}{7}-\frac{5}{7}$

3 Work out

a $\frac{1}{3}+\frac{1}{2}$ **b** $\frac{1}{4}+\frac{3}{5}$ **c** $\frac{3}{5}-\frac{1}{3}$ **d** $\frac{4}{5}-\frac{2}{7}$

e $\frac{5}{8}+\frac{1}{3}$ **f** $\frac{4}{9}+\frac{2}{5}$ **g** $\frac{7}{9}-\frac{2}{11}$ **h** $\frac{7}{15}+\frac{3}{7}$

Write both fractions as equivalent fractions with the same denominator.

4 Work out each of these, leaving your answer in its simplest form as appropriate.

a $\frac{2}{5}-\frac{1}{15}$ **b** $\frac{1}{2}-\frac{1}{3}$ **c** $\frac{2}{5}+\frac{7}{20}$ **d** $\frac{1}{2}-\frac{1}{6}$

5 Work out each of these, leaving your answer in its simplest form.

a $\frac{4}{5}+\frac{2}{3}$ **b** $1\frac{1}{2}+\frac{3}{5}$ **c** $1\frac{1}{3}+1\frac{1}{4}$ **d** $1\frac{2}{7}+\frac{3}{5}$

e $2\frac{2}{5}-\frac{1}{3}$ **f** $3\frac{3}{8}-1\frac{1}{2}$ **g** $4\frac{1}{3}-2\frac{3}{4}$ **h** $3\frac{4}{7}-2\frac{8}{9}$

A02 Functional Maths

6 Work out each of these, leaving your answer in its simplest form.

a Pete walked $3\frac{2}{3}$ miles before lunch and then a further $2\frac{1}{4}$ miles after lunch. How far did he walk altogether?

b A bag weighs $2\frac{3}{16}$ lb when it is full. When empty the bag weighs $\frac{3}{8}$ lb. What is the weight of the contents of the bag?

c Henry and Paula are eating peanuts. Henry has a full bag weighing $1\frac{3}{16}$ kg. Paula has a bag that weighs $\frac{4}{5}$ kg. What is the total mass of their two bags of peanuts?

d Simon spent $\frac{2}{3}$ of his pocket money on a computer game. He spent $\frac{1}{5}$ of his pocket money on a ticket to the cinema. Work out the fraction of his pocket money that he had left.

e Calculate the perimeter of each of these swimming pools.

i $2\frac{2}{7}$ feet, $12\frac{3}{8}$ feet

ii

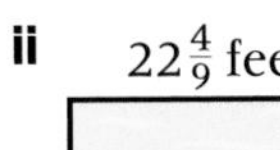

iii

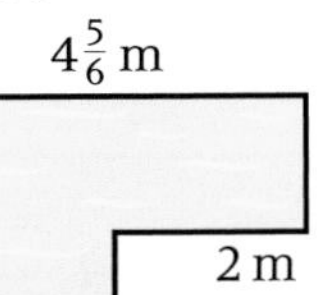

N6.2 Multiplying and dividing fractions

This spread will show you how to:

- Add, subtract, multiply and divide with fractions
- Recognise and use a unit fraction as a multiplicative inverse

Keywords
Equivalent
Integer
Fraction
Multiplicative inverse
Unit fraction

You can multiply a **unit fraction** by an integer using a number line.

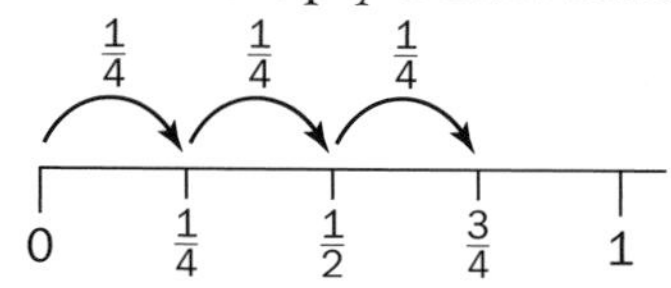

$\frac{1}{4} \times 3 = \frac{3}{4}$

A unit fraction has numerator 1: $\frac{1}{2}, \frac{1}{3}, \frac{1}{4}, \ldots$

Multiplying by $\frac{1}{4}$ is the same as dividing by 4.

$3 \times \frac{1}{4} = \frac{3}{4} \longleftrightarrow 3 \div 4 = \frac{3}{4}$

- You can multiply any fraction by an **integer** using unit fractions.

$$4 \times \frac{3}{8} = 4 \times 3 \times \frac{1}{8} = \frac{12}{8} = 1\frac{4}{8} = 1\frac{1}{2}$$

You can divide an integer by a unit fraction.

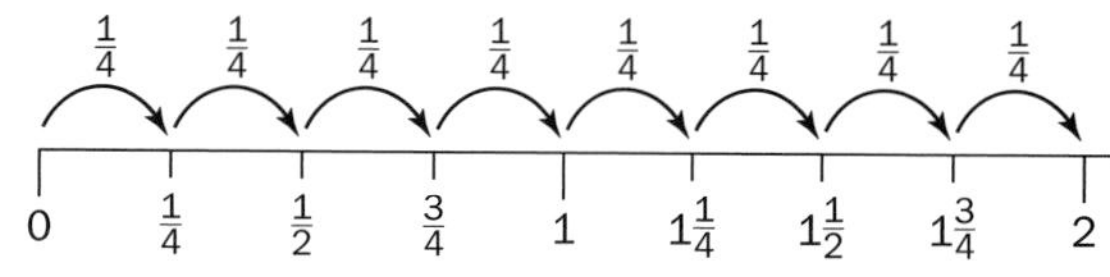

$2 \div \frac{1}{4} = 8$

Think how many $\frac{1}{4}$s are there in 2 wholes?

1	2	5	6
3	4	7	8

- You can divide an **integer** by any fraction using unit fractions.

$$4 \div \frac{2}{3} = 4 \div 2 \div \frac{1}{3} = 2 \div \frac{1}{3} = 2 \times 3 = 6$$

- You can multiply a fraction by another fraction by multiplying the numerators together and multiplying the denominators together.

$$\frac{3}{5} \times \frac{5}{8} = \frac{3 \times 5}{5 \times 8} = \frac{15}{40} = \frac{3}{8}$$

You can use the relationship between multiplication and division.

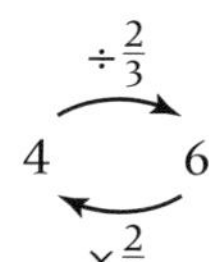

Dividing by $\frac{2}{3}$ is the same as multiplying by $\frac{3}{2}$.

Multiplying by $\frac{2}{3}$ is the same as dividing by $\frac{3}{2}$.

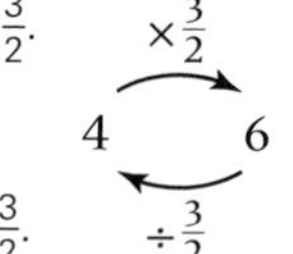

$\times\frac{3}{2}$ is the **multiplicative inverse** of $\div\frac{3}{2}$.

Example

Calculate

a $4 \div \frac{3}{5}$ **b** $\frac{3}{8} \div \frac{5}{6}$ **c** $2\frac{2}{5} \div 4\frac{1}{4}$

a $4 \div \frac{3}{5} = 4 \times \frac{5}{3} = \frac{20}{3} = 6\frac{2}{3}$

b $\frac{3}{8} \div \frac{5}{6} = \frac{3}{8} \times \frac{6}{5} = \frac{3 \times 6}{8 \times 5} = \frac{18}{40} = \frac{9}{20}$

c $2\frac{2}{5} \div 1\frac{1}{4} = \frac{12}{5} \div \frac{5}{4} = \frac{12}{5} \times \frac{4}{5} = \frac{12 \times 4}{5 \times 5} = \frac{48}{25} = 1\frac{23}{25}$

Exercise N6.2 Grade D

1 Calculate each of these, leaving your answer in its simplest form.

a $3 \times \frac{1}{2}$ **b** $6 \times \frac{1}{3}$ **c** $10 \times \frac{1}{3}$
d $15 \times \frac{1}{7}$ **e** $\frac{1}{10} \times 25$ **f** $\frac{1}{3} \times 13$

2 Calculate each of these, leaving your answer in its simplest form.

a $3 \times \frac{2}{3}$ **b** $6 \times \frac{2}{3}$ **c** $5 \times \frac{2}{3}$ **d** $2 \times \frac{7}{24}$
e $4 \times \frac{3}{20}$ **f** $\frac{4}{5} \times 20$ **g** $\frac{3}{5} \times 10$ **h** $\frac{11}{8} \times 17$

3 Calculate each of these, leaving your answer in its simplest form.

a $4 \div \frac{1}{2}$ **b** $2 \div \frac{1}{5}$ **c** $2 \div \frac{1}{7}$
d $10 \div \frac{1}{2}$ **e** $12 \div \frac{1}{4}$ **f** $22 \div \frac{1}{10}$

AO2 Functional Maths

4 Calculate each of these, leaving your answer in its simplest form.

a What is the total weight of 7 boxes that each weigh $\frac{2}{5}$ kg?
b What is the total length of 5 pieces of wood that are each $\frac{3}{7}$ of a metre long?

5 Calculate each of these, leaving your answer in its simplest form.

a $4 \div \frac{2}{3}$ **b** $7 \div \frac{2}{5}$ **c** $2 \div \frac{5}{6}$ **d** $12 \div \frac{6}{7}$
e $20 \div \frac{5}{12}$ **f** $5 \div \frac{7}{9}$ **g** $3 \div 1\frac{1}{2}$ **h** $3 \div 1\frac{2}{5}$

6 Calculate each of these, leaving your answer in its simplest form.

a $\frac{2}{5} \times \frac{3}{4}$ **b** $\frac{3}{5} \times \frac{3}{4}$ **c** $\frac{5}{7} \times \frac{3}{4}$ **d** $\frac{4}{7} \times \frac{3}{5}$
e $\frac{5}{6} \times \frac{4}{5}$ **f** $\frac{3}{8} \times \frac{7}{9}$ **g** $\frac{3}{5} \times \frac{10}{9}$ **h** $\frac{15}{16} \times \frac{12}{5}$
i $(\frac{3}{7})^2$ **j** $1\frac{3}{4} \times \frac{2}{7}$ **k** $3\frac{2}{3} \times \frac{7}{11}$ **l** $1\frac{3}{8} \times 1\frac{2}{5}$

7 Calculate each of these, leaving your answer in its simplest form.

a $4 \div \frac{2}{5}$ **b** $\frac{2}{3} \div \frac{4}{5}$ **c** $\frac{4}{5} \div \frac{3}{4}$ **d** $\frac{4}{7} \div \frac{2}{3}$
e $\frac{3}{7} \div \frac{4}{9}$ **f** $\frac{3}{5} \div \frac{1}{3}$ **g** $\frac{3}{4} \div 3$ **h** $\frac{4}{7} \div 5$
i $\frac{4}{11} \div 5$ **j** $\frac{7}{4} \div \frac{2}{3}$ **k** $\frac{7}{4} \div \frac{3}{2}$ **l** $\frac{9}{5} \div \frac{5}{3}$
m $1\frac{1}{2} \div \frac{3}{4}$ **n** $2\frac{1}{4} \div \frac{2}{3}$ **o** $2\frac{2}{5} \div \frac{9}{7}$

AO2 Functional Maths

8 Calculate each of these, rounding your answer as appropriate.

a A plank of wood is $4\frac{3}{5}$ metres long. How many pieces of wood of length $1\frac{1}{4}$ metres can be cut from the piece of wood?
b A paint pot can hold $2\frac{3}{4}$ litres of paint. Hector buys $11\frac{1}{5}$ litres of emulsion paint. How many times can Hector **fill** the paint pot with emulsion paint?

N6.3 Mental methods with decimals

This spread will show you how to:

- Use a range of mental and written methods for calculations with whole numbers and decimals

Keywords
Compensation
Mental method
Multiple
Partitioning
Place value

There are lots of **mental methods** you can use to help you work out calculations in your head.

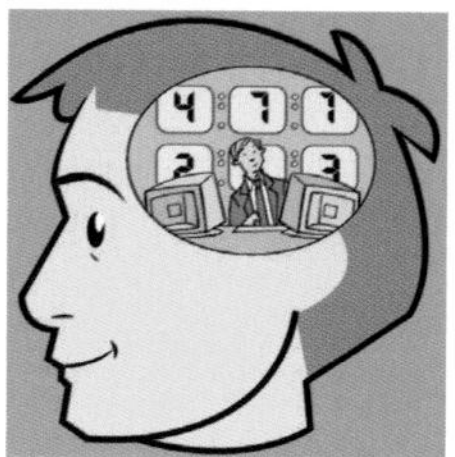

You can use **place value**.

Example

Use the fact that $35 \times 147 = 5145$ to write the value of

a 3.5×1.47 **b** $0.35 \times 147\,000$ **c** $51.45 \div 3.5$

a $3.5 \times 1.47 = (35 \div 10) \times (147 \div 100)$
$= 35 \times 147 \div 1000$
$= 5145 \div 1000$
$= 5.145$

b $0.35 \times 147\,000 = (35 \div 100) \times (147 \times 1000)$
$= 35 \times 147 \times 10$
$= 5145 \times 10$
$= 51\,450$

c $51.45 \div 3.5 = \dfrac{51.45}{3.5} = \dfrac{514.5}{35}$
$= \dfrac{(5145 \div 10)}{35}$
$= 147 \div 10$
$= 14.7$

You can use **partitioning**.

Example

a Calculate $18.5 - 7.7$. **b** Calculate 6.3×12.

a $18.5 - 7.7 = 18.5 - 7 - 0.7$
$= 11.5 - 0.7$
$= 10.8$

b $12 = 10 + 2$
$6.3 \times 12 = (6.3 \times 10) + (6.3 \times 2)$
$= 63 + 12.6$
$= 75.6$

Split **12** into **10** + **2**. Then work out **10** × 6.3 and **2** × 6.3. Add your two answers together.

You can use **compensation**.

Example

a Calculate **a** $12.4 - 4.9$ **b** 23.2×1.9

a $12.4 - 4.9 = 12.4 - 5 + 0.1$
$= 7.4 + 0.1$
$= 7.5$

b $1.9 = 2 - 0.1$
$23.2 \times 1.9 = (23.2 \times 2) + (23.2 \times 0.1)$
$= 46.4 - 2.32$
$= 44.08$

Rewrite **1.9** as **2** − **0.1**. Work out **2** × 23.2 and **0.1** × 23.2. Subtract your two answers.

Exercise N6.3 Grade E

1 Calculate

a 9×7 **b** $121 \div 10$ **c** 2×2.7 **d** $48.4 \div 2$
e 3.6×100 **f** $430 \div 100$ **g** 23.6×10 **h** $0.78 \div 100$

2 Use an appropriate mental method to calculate these.
Show the method you have used.

a 1.4×11 **b** 21×9 **c** 5.3×11 **d** 41×2.8
e 19×7 **f** 12×5.3 **g** $147 \div 3$ **h** $276 \div 4$
i 3.2×11 **j** 31×5.6 **k** 14.9×9 **l** 25.3×31
m 14×8 **n** $51 \div 1.5$ **o** $81 \div 4.5$ **p** 4.4×4.5

3 Use the mental method of partitioning to work out each of these.

a $19.5 - 7.6$ **b** $45.3 + 12.6 + 7.2$ **c** $132.6 - 21.4$
d 7.2×13 **e** 8.4×12 **f** 11×19.2
g $129 \div 3$ **h** $292 \div 4$

4 Use the mental method of compensation to work out each of these.

a $19.5 - 7.9$ **b** $48.4 - 12.8$ **c** $164.5 - 15.9$
d 8.1×19 **e** 36×3.9 **f** 17×5.9

5 Use an appropriate mental method to calculate each of these.

a $27.6 + 21.7$ **b** $1623 - 897$ **c** 32×2.1 **d** 2.9×23
e 19×1.4 **f** 9×7.5 **g** $2.4 \div 0.2$ **h** $\dfrac{30 \times 0.2}{0.15}$

6 **a** Using the information that $69 \times 147 = 10\,143$, write the value of each of these.

i 69×1470 **ii** 690×1470 **iii** 6.9×147 **iv** 0.69×14.7
v 6.9×0.147 **vi** 690×1.47 **vii** 0.069×14.7 **viii** 0.69×0.147

b Using the information that $37 \times 177 = 6549$, write the value of each of these.

i 3.7×17.7 **ii** 0.37×1770 **iii** $654.9 \div 177$ **iv** $65.49 \div 3.7$

7 **a** Using the information that $43 \times 217 = 9331$, write the value of each of these.

i 4.3×2170 **ii** 0.43×2.17 **iii** $933.1 \div 4.3$ **iv** $93.31 \div 0.217$

b Using the information that $48 \times 164 = 7872$, write the value of each of these.

i 4.8×16.4 **ii** $0.48 \times 16\,400$ **iii** $787.2 \div 1640$ **iv** $78.72 \div 4.8$

N6.4 Written methods with decimals

This spread will show you how to:

- Use a range of mental and written methods for calculations with whole numbers and decimals
- Use checking procedures, including approximation to estimate the answer to multiplication and division problems

Keywords
Dividend
Divisor
Estimate
Grid method
Standard method
Whole number

You can multiply decimals by replacing them with an equivalent **whole-number** calculation that is easier to work out.

Example

Carol is working out the area of carpet she needs for her floor. The floor is in a rectangle with a length of 4.8 m and a width of 3.12 m. What is the area of Carol's floor?

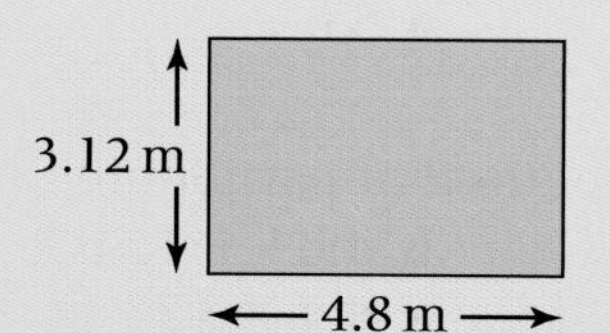

p.54

$4.8 \times 3.12 = (48 \div 10) \times (312 \div 100)$
$= 48 \times 312 \div 1000$

×	300	10	2
40	40 × 300 = 12 000	40 × 10 = 400	40 × 2 = 80
8	8 × 300 = 2400	8 × 10 = 80	8 × 2 = 16

48 × 312 = 12 000 + 400 + 80 + 2400 + 80 + 16 = 14 976
The area of Carol's floor is 4.8 × 3.12 = 48 × 312 ÷ 1000
= 14 976 ÷ 1000
= 14.98 m^2 (2 decimal places)

Estimate the answer first.
4.8 × 3.12 ≈ 5 × 3
= 15 m^2

You can divide a number by a decimal by rewriting the calculation as an equivalent whole-number division.

Example

Mandy has a floor with an area of 91 m^2. She fills the floor with carpet tiles which have an area of 2.8 m^2.
How many tiles does she need to cover the floor?

91 ÷ 2.8 = 910 ÷ 28

```
28)910
  −840      28 × 30
    70
   −56      28 × 2
    14.0
   −14.0    28 × 0.5      30 + 2 + 0.5 = 32.5
     0
```

910 ÷ 28 = 91 ÷ 2.8 = 32.5

Mandy needs 91 ÷ 2.8 = 32.5 tiles.

Estimate the answer first.
91 ÷ 2.8 ≈ 90 ÷ 3
= 30

Exercise N6.4 Grade E

1 Use a written method for each of these calculations.

a $16.4 + 9.68$ **b** $27.3 + 5.41$ **c** $9.51 - 6.7$
d $24.3 + 7.69$ **e** $34.76 - 8.29$ **f** $38.29 - 24.8$
g $16.5 - 12.67 + 5.34$ **h** $78.7 - 14.92 + 16.66 - 12.9$

2 Use an appropriate method of calculation to work out

a 15×3.4 **b** 5.6×18 **c** 8.4×13
d 23×7.6 **e** 28×4.2 **f** 9.7×49

3 Use an appropriate method of calculation to work out

a $27.3 \div 7$ **b** $36.6 \div 6$ **c** $70.4 \div 8$
d $73.8 \div 6$ **e** $119.7 \div 9$ **f** $119.2 \div 8$

AO2 Functional Maths

4 Use a mental or written method to solve each of these problems.

a Oliver sells tomatoes at the market. On Thursday he sells 78.6 kg; on Saturday he sells 83.38 kg. What mass of tomatoes has he sold during the two days?

b A mobile phone without a battery weighs 188.16 g. When the battery is inserted the combined mass of the mobile phone and battery is 207.38 g. What is the mass of the battery?

c A recycling box is full of things to be recycled.
The empty box weighs 1.073 kg.

Bottles	12.45 kg
Cans	1.675 kg
Paper	8.7 kg
Plastic objects	? kg

The total weight of the box and all the objects to be recycled is exactly 25 kg. What is the weight of the plastic objects?

At least half the household waste produced in the UK each year could be recycled. Unfortunately in 2005 only 12% was recycled!

5 Use an appropriate method of calculation to work out

a 2.3×1.74 **b** 1.6×2.75 **c** 1.7×44.3
d 2.5×5.88 **e** 8.7×4.79 **f** 38×4.78
g 3.4×4.45 **h** 0.54×8.28 **i** 0.93×3.87

AO2 Functional Maths

6 a Scooby buys 1.8 m of carpet. Each metre costs £1.85.
How much does this cost in total?

b Shaggy buys 7.8 kg of apples. Each kilogram of apples costs £1.45.
How much money does Shaggy pay for the apples?

c Brian is a gardener. He plants trees at a rate of 11.8 trees per hour.
How many trees does he plant in 6.4 hours?

d Clarke works as a car mechanic. He charges £31.70 per hour for his work.
How much does he charge for working 2.5 hours?

Calculator methods 2

This spread will show you how to:

- Know how to use function keys for squares, powers and reciprocals

Keywords
Power
Square
Square root
Reciprocal

There are some key presses on a standard scientific calculator that you should become familar with.

Reciprocal key

Find the reciprocal of 5.

Type:

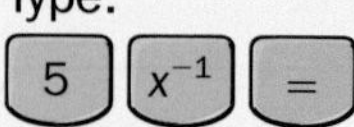

Answer: 0.2

(Hint: the reciprocal of 5 is $5^{-1} = \frac{1}{5} = 0.2$)

Square and square root keys

Find a) the square of 25, b) the square root of 30

a) Type:

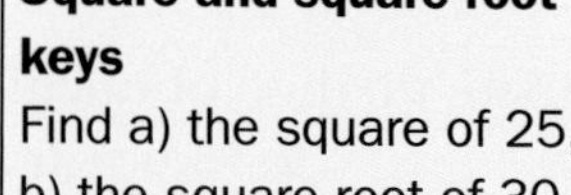

=

Answer: 625

b) Type:

=

Answer: 5.47722 = 5.48 (3 sf)

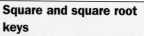

Fraction key

Find $3\frac{1}{2} + 2\frac{3}{5}$

Type:

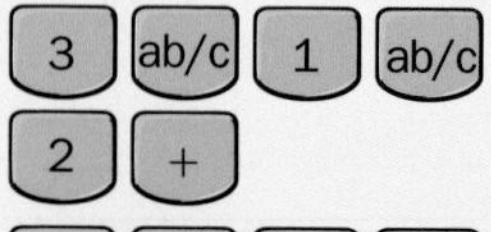

Answer: $6\frac{1}{10}$

Power key

Find 8^4

Type:

8 ^ 4 =

Answer: 4096

Check by finding the 4th root of 4096:

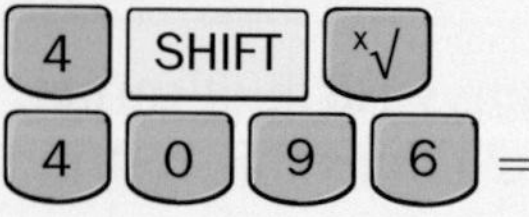

=

Answer: 8

You should also be familiar with:

The **memory keys** – these can be useful when working with multi-step calculations

Statistical keys – these allow you to input a set of data and work out statistics like the mean

Exercise N6.5

Grade C

1 Using a calculator, find the reciprocal of each of these numbers.

a 6 **b** $\frac{5}{2}$ **c** $3\frac{1}{3}$

d 0.75 **e** 1.2

2 Using the square and square root keys, find these quantities. Give your answer to 2 dp where appropriate.

a 29^2 **b** 0.4^2 **c** $\left(\frac{3}{5}\right)^2$

d $\sqrt{5}$ **e** $\sqrt{0.75}$

3 Use a calculator to calculate these fraction sums.

a $2\frac{2}{9} + 4\frac{2}{5}$ **b** $6\frac{2}{7} - 3\frac{3}{4}$ **c** $\left(2\frac{1}{5}\right)^2$

4 Calculate these quantities.

a 7^4 **b** 10^6 **c** $\sqrt[3]{27}$ **d** $\sqrt[5]{32}$

5 **a** James says that when you square a number the answer always gets bigger.
Give two examples to show that this is not always true.

b Lauren says that when you find the square root of a number the answer always gets smaller.
Give two examples to show that this is not always true.

c Describe in your own words what happens to the size of a number when you find the square or the square root of it.

Problem A03

6 Saira is solving a puzzle.
She must use each of the numbers 1, 2 and 3 once and only once to make this calculation correct.

$$\frac{\sqrt{\square\square^2 + \square 7}}{7} = 2$$

Help Saira by copying and completing the calculation so that it is correct.

N6

Summary

Check out

You should now be able to:

- Add, subtract, multiply and divide fractions
- Recognise the equivalence of fractions and decimals
- Use mental and written methods for calculations with whole numbers and decimals
- Use one calculation to find the answer to another
- Use calculator methods to find powers and reciprocals

Worked exam question

Here are two fractions, $\frac{3}{4}$ and $\frac{4}{5}$.

Which is the larger fraction?

You must show your working to explain your answer.

You may use the grids to help with your explanation.

(3)

(Edexcel Limited 2007)

$\frac{3}{4} = 0.75$

$\frac{4}{5} = 0.8$

$\frac{4}{5}$ is the larger fraction

Write each decimal equivalent.

OR

Write each fraction in $\frac{1}{20}$s.

$\frac{3}{4} = \frac{15}{20}$

$\frac{4}{5} = \frac{16}{20}$

$\frac{4}{5}$ is the larger fraction

OR

You must write the answer "$\frac{4}{5}$ is the larger fraction."

$\frac{3}{4}$ of 20 squares = 15 squares

$\frac{4}{5}$ of 20 squares = 16 squares

$\frac{4}{5}$ is the larger fraction

You could shade 15 squares and 16 squares in the grids.

Exam questions

AO2

1 Fatima bought 48 teddy bears at £9.55 each.

a Work out the total amount she paid. (3)

Fatima sold all the teddy bears for a total of £696.
She sold each teddy bear for the same price.

b Work out the price at which Fatima sold each teddy bear. (3)

(Edexcel Limited 2003)

2 **a** Work out $\frac{1}{4} + \frac{1}{12}$ (2)

b Work out $\frac{3}{4} \times \frac{1}{6}$ (1)

AO2

3 The cost of 1.5 kg of peaches is £0.84
The total cost of 3 kg of peaches and 2 kg of apples is £2.34
Work out the cost of 1 kg of apples. (3)

(Edexcel Limited 2007)

AO2

4 A full glass of water holds $\frac{1}{6}$ of a bottle of water.

How many glasses of water can be filled from $2\frac{1}{2}$ bottles of water? (3)

(Edexcel Limited 2007)

5 Using the information that
$2.7 \times 58 = 156.6$
write the value of

a 27×58 (1)

b 27×5.8 (1)

c 2.7×5.8 (1)

A6

Formulae and inequalities

Introduction

Businesses try to maximise profits, by maximising productivity and minimising costs. However, there are factors, or constraints, such as the number of workers, the capacity of factories, cost of materials etc., which affect these things. The solution is often found by representing the different constraints as straight line graphs and using a process called linear programming to find the optimal solution.

What's the point?

Many real-life decisions are about obtaining the best results within given constraints - from comparing the price plans of different mobile phones to choosing the most cost-effective way of spending your time. Plotting linear functions and solving equations lie at the heart of many real-life decision making situations.

Check in

1 Work out the value of each expression when $y = 3$.

a $2y$ **b** $4y - 1$

c y^2 **d** $4y \div 2$

2 Multiply out

a $3(x + 1)$ **b** $2(x - 1)$

c $4(2x + 3)$ **d** $3(4x - 2)$

3 Solve, using the balance method

a $2x + 3 = 11$ **b** $3y - 4 = 14$

4 Factorise

a $4x + 8$ **b** $6x + 2$ **c** $3y - 9$

Orientation

What I should know	What I will learn	What this leads to
A1 + 2 + 5 →	■ Understand algebraic terminology ■ Substitute values into formulae ■ Write formulae to represent everyday situations ■ Change the subject of simple formulae ■ Solve simple one-sided and two-sided inequalities	→ Courses and careers in business and finance

Rich task

This L-shape is drawn on a 10×10 grid numbered from 1 to 100.
It has 5 numbers inside it.
We can call the shape L_{35} because the largest number inside it is 35.
The total of the numbers inside L_{35} is 138.
Find a connection between the L-number and the total of the numbers inside the L-shape.
What happens if you work on a 9×9 grid, or an 8×8 grid.
What about an $n \times n$ grid?

1	2	3	4	5	6	7	8	9	10
11	12	13	14	15	16	17	18	19	20
21	22	23	24	25	26	27	28	29	30
31	32	33	34	35	36	37	38	39	40
41	42	43	44	45	46	47	48	49	50
51	52	53	54	55	56	57	58	59	60
61	62	63	64	65	66	67	68	69	70
71	72	73	74	75	76	77	78	79	80
81	82	83	84	85	86	87	88	89	90
91	92	93	94	95	96	97	98	99	100

A6.1 Formulae, equations and identities

This spread will show you how to:

- Understand and use the words equation, formula, identity, and expression

Keywords
Equation
Expression
Formula
Function
Identity
Substitute

In algebra you use letters to represent numbers.

- An **expression** is made up of algebraic terms. It has no equals sign.

$2x + 3b$ and $2(l + w)$ are expressions.

- A **function** links two variables. When you know one, you can work out the other.

$x \rightarrow 3x + 2$ or $y = 3x + 2$ is a function.

- A **formula** is a rule linking two or more variables.

$P = 2l + 2w$ is a formula for the perimeter of a rectangle.

- An **equation** is only true for particular values of a variable. You can solve the equation to find the solution.

$x + 4 = 10$ is an equation. Its solution is $x = 6$.

- An **identity** is true for any values of the variables.

$a + a + a + a \equiv 4a$ is an identity.

The sign $\equiv$ means identically equal to.

You can **substitute** values into expressions, functions and formulae.

Formulae is the plural of formula.

Example

Work out the value of each expression when $x = 2, y = 4, z = 3$.

a $xy - z$ **b** $3x + 5y$ **c** $\frac{x + y}{z}$

$xy = x \times y$

a $xy - z = 2 \times 4 - 3$
$= 8 - 3 = 5$

b $3x + 5y = 3 \times 2 + 5 \times 4$
$= 6 + 20 = 26$

c $\frac{x + y}{z} = \frac{2 + 4}{3} = \frac{6}{3} = 2$

Write in the multiplication sign.

You can solve equations using the balance method.

Example

Solve $3x + 5 = 17$.

$3x + 5 = 17$
$3x + 5 - 5 = 17 - 5$ Subtract 5 from both sides.
$3x = 12$
$3x \div 3 = 12 \div 3$ Divide both sides by 3.
$x = 4$

Do the same to both sides.

Exercise A6.1

Grade E

1 Work out the value of each expression when
$a = 6$, $b = 3$, $c = \frac{1}{2}$, $d = 4$.

a ad **b** $2b$ **c** ab **d** $a + cd$
e $ad + b$ **f** $3b - d$ **g** $2dc - a$ **h** $ab - dc$

2 Work out the value of each expression when $e = -2, f = 3, g = -6$.

a $ef + g$ **b** $eg + f$ **c** $2e^2 - g$ **d** $\frac{fg}{e}$

3 For each function, work out the value of y
i when $x = 4$
ii when $x = -2$.

a $y = 4x + 3$ **b** $y = 2x - 6$ **c** $y = \frac{1}{2}x + 10$
d $y = 6x - 1$ **e** $y = x^2$ **f** $y = 2x^2 + 4$

4 Solve these equations.

a $2x + 3 = 15$ **b** $2y - 5 = 17$ **c** $4x + 15 = 7$
d $3y - 13 = -10$ **e** $23 = 6b + 5$ **f** $7 = 19 + 3c$
g $15 - 7f = 1$ **h** $60 - 3g = 72$

5 Multiply out the brackets and write each of these as an identity.
The first one has been done for you.

a $7(x + 4) \equiv 7 \times x + 7 \times 4 \equiv 7x + 28$
b $3(x - 2)$ **c** $2(3 + x)$ **d** $5(2 - x)$

6 Copy and complete these identities by factorising.

a $8m + 4 \equiv 4\ (\quad)$ **b** $12n - 9 \equiv \square\ (\quad)$ **c** $15p + 55 \equiv \square\ (\quad)$
d $q^2 + 2q \equiv q\ (\quad)$ **e** $16r - 28 \equiv \square\ (\quad)$ **f** $4pq - 10q \equiv \square\ (\quad)$

7 Copy the table.

Expressions	Equations	Functions	Formulae	Identities

Write these under the correct heading in your table.

a $a + bc = bc + a$ **b** $y = 3x + 2$ **c** $a + bc = d$
d $3a + 5 = -4$ **e** $4xy + 3x - z$ **f** $E = mc^2$
g $s = ut$ **h** $x - 1 = y$

A6.2 Substituting into formulae

This spread will show you how to:

- Substitute values into formulae

Keywords
Formula
Substitute

- You can **substitute** numbers into a **formula** written in words.

The formula for the perimeter of a regular hexagon is

Perimeter = $6 \times$ length of one side

This regular hexagon has sides of length 3 cm.
Its perimeter = 6×3 cm = 18 cm.

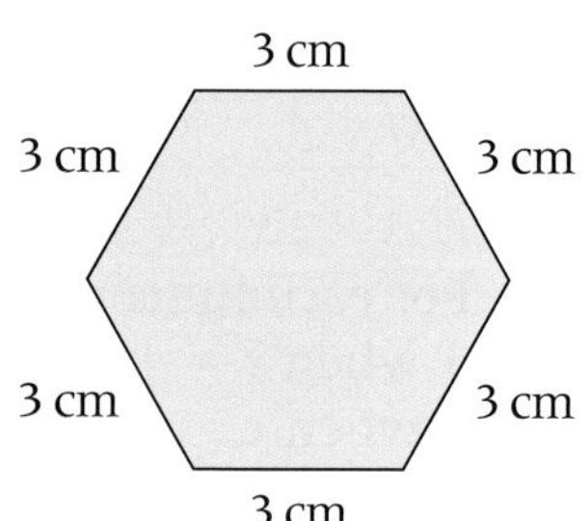

- You can substitute numbers into a formula written using letters.

Example

Apples cost 20p each and bananas cost 25p each.

The formula for the cost (in pence) of a apples and b bananas is

cost = $20a + 25b$

Find the cost of 8 apples and 3 bananas.

Cost = $20 \times 8 + 25 \times 3$
= $160 + 75$
= 235 pence or £2.35

a apples cost $a \times 20$p.
b bananas cost $b \times 25$p.

Substitute $a = 8$ and $b = 3$

- You can solve an equation to find a value from a formula.

Example

In the formula $v = u + at$

a find v when $u = 2$, $a = 5$, $t = 20$ **b** find u when $v = 50$, $a = 2$, $t = 15$

a $v = u + at$
$v = 2 + 5 \times 20$
$= 2 + 100 = 102$

b $v = u + at$
$50 = u + 2 \times 15$
$50 = u + 30$
$50 - 30 = u + 30 - 30$
$20 = u$

Subtract 30 from both sides.

Exercise A6.2 Grade E

1 The area of card needed to make an open cube-shaped box is calculated by

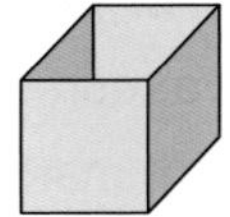

Area of card = 5 × area of one side of box

Use this formula to work out the area of card needed for a box with

a area of one side $12\,\text{cm}^2$ **b** area of one side $20\,\text{cm}^2$
c area of one side $1\,\text{m}^2$ **d** area of one side $2.3\,\text{m}^2$

Functional Maths A02

2 The bill for a mobile phone is calculated using the formula

Cost in pounds = 0.05 × number of texts + 0.10 × minutes of calls

a Use the formula to work out the bills for
- **i** Nadia: 40 texts and 20 minutes of calls
- **ii** Saleem: 5 texts and 70 minutes of calls
- **iii** Marcus: 32 texts and 15 minutes of calls.

b What is the cost for a call lasting 1 minute? Give your answer in pence.

3 The cost of hiring a van is given by the formula $C = 25d + 40$ where C is the cost in pounds and d is the number of days.
Work out the cost of

a hiring the van for 3 days **b** hiring the van for 10 days.

4 In the formula $v = u + at$ find v when
a $u = 3, a = 5, t = 2$ **b** $u = 12, a = 4, t = 9$

5 In the formula $V = lwh$ find V when $l = 3, w = 6, h = 8$.

6 Use the formula $s = ut + \frac{1}{2}at^2$ to find the value of s when
a $u = 2, a = 3, t = 5$ **b** $u = -3, t = 4, a = 12$

7 Use the formula $t = \dfrac{v - u}{a}$ to find t when
a $v = 35, u = 27, a = 4$ **b** $v = 12, u = 16, a = -2$

8 In the formula $A = 2b + c$, find c if $A = 14$ and $b = 5$.

9 $P = 2l + 2w$

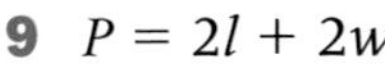

a Find w when $P = 18, l = 6$. **b** Find l when $P = 20, w = 8$.

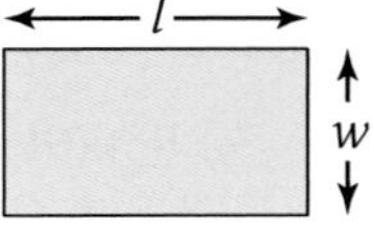

10 Using the simple interest formula, $I = \dfrac{PRT}{100}$
a find P when $I = 12, R = 20, T = 30$.
b find R when $I = 3.6, T = 18, P = 10$.

Problem A03

11 Gemma and Paul evaluated $5x^2$ when $x = 6$.
Who was right? Explain why.

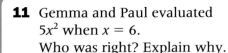

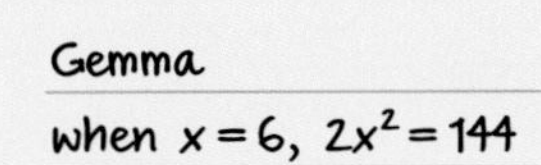

Paul
when $x = 6$, $2x^2 = 72$

Writing formulae

This spread will show you how to:

- Write formulae to represent everyday situations
- Use formulae from mathematics and other subjects

Keywords
Formula

A **formula** can save time when you have to work out similar calculations over and over again.

- You can write a formula to represent an everyday situation.
  - Write the formula in words and then using letters.
  - Explain what the letters represent.

Example

A plumber charges £25 for a callout and £30 per hour of work. Write a formula for the plumber's charge.

Charge in pounds = 25 + 30 × number of hours of work

$C = 25 + 30h$

where C = charge in pounds, h = number of hours of work.

Example

A bus ticket to town costs £3 for an adult and 90p for a child.

a Write a formula to work out the cost in pounds of bus tickets for different numbers of adults and children.
b Use your formula to work out the cost of tickets for 3 adults and 5 children.
c Mr and Mrs Karim and their children paid £8.70 for bus tickets. How many children bought tickets?

a Cost in pounds = 3 × number of adults + 0.90 × number of children

$C = 3n + 0.90m$

where C = cost in pounds, n = number of adults, m = number of children.

90p = 0.90

b $C = 3n + 0.90m$
$= 3 \times 3 + 0.90 \times 5$
$= 9 + 4.50 = £13.50$

$n = 3$, $m = 5$

Write the answer in pounds.

c $C = 3n + 0.90m$
$8.70 = 3 \times 2 + 0.90m = 6 + 0.90m$
$8.70 - 6 = 6 - 6 + 0.90m$
$2.70 = 0.90m$
$2.70 \div 0.90 = 0.90m \div 0.90$
$3 = m$
3 children bought tickets.

Substitute $C = 8.70$ and $n = 2$.

Exercise A6.3 Grade D

Functional Maths A02

1 An electrician charges £35 for each job + £20 per hour.

a Write a formula for the electrician's charge in pounds.

b Use your formula to find the charge of a job that takes 3 hours.

2 The cost of a taxi is £2 for a callout + 60p for each mile.

a Write a formula for the cost of a taxi in pounds.

b Work out the cost for a journey of

i 5 miles **ii** 15 miles.

3 In Spain a hire car costs €75 plus €35 a day.

a Write a formula for the cost of hiring a car in euros.

b How much does it cost to hire a car for 7 days?

c Louise paid €495 to hire a car.
How many days did she hire it for?

4 Pencils are arranged in rectangles.
The number of pencils needed to make a rectangle is

2 × number of pencils along the bottom + 2

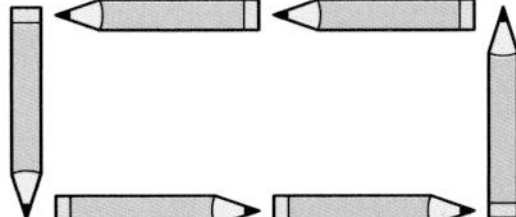

a Write this formula using letters.

b Check that your formula gives the correct answer for a rectangle of length 5.

c Work out how many pencils are needed for a rectangle of length 8.

d A rectangle uses 48 pencils. What is its length?

5 Cinema tickets cost £6.80 for adults and £4.50 for children.
5 adults took a group of children to the cinema.
The tickets cost £97 in total.
How many children went to the cinema?

Write a formula first.

6 The cost of hiring a steam cleaner is

- £32.50 for the first day
- £24.75 for each extra day.

Tariq paid £131.50 to hire the steam cleaner.
How many days did he hire it for?

7 Tickets for a fun day cost £3 for adults and £1.50 for children.
The total cost of tickets for a group of adults and children was £54.

a Write a formula for the cost for n adults and m children.
In the group there were 4 children for every adult.

b Write this information using algebra: $m = 4 \times$ ...

c Substitute your expression from part **b** into your formula from part **a**.

d Use your formula from part **c** to work out the number of adults in the group.

Changing the subject of a formula

This spread will show you how to:
- Change the subject of simple formulae

Keywords
Subject

- The **subject** of a formula is the letter on its own on one side of the equals sign.

The formula for the number of slabs in a rectangular patio is

$N = lw$

where l is the number of slabs along the length and w is the number along the width.

N is the subject of the formula. You can substitute values for l and w to find N.

Rick has 24 slabs. He is trying to decide on the dimensions for a patio. For a patio 6 slabs long, he substitutes $N = 24$ and $l = 6$ into the formula:

$24 = 6w$

He solves to find w

$24 \div 6 = 6w \div 6$, so $w = 4$.

To work out w for different values of l, each time he has to:

substitute for N and l
solve the equation.

To save time, Rick can rearrange the formula to make w the subject.

- You can change the subject of a formula using the balance method.

$$N = lw$$
$$\frac{N}{l} = \frac{lw}{l}$$
$$\frac{N}{l} = w$$

w is multiplied by l.

To get w on its own, use the inverse operation 'divide by l'.

Do the same to both sides.

Example

Rearrange these formulae to make x the subject.

a $y = x - a$ **b** $y = mx + c$ **c** $y = \frac{x}{2} - b$

a
$$y = x - a$$
$$y + a = x - a + a$$
$$x = y + a$$

b
$$y = mx + c$$
$$y - c = mx + c - c$$
$$y - c = mx$$
$$\frac{y - c}{m} = \frac{mx}{m}$$
$$\frac{y - c}{m} = x$$

c
$$y = \frac{x}{2} - b$$
$$y + b = \frac{x}{2}$$
$$2(y + b) = x$$

Exercise A6.4 — Grade C

1 $v = u + at$
Find u when
a $v = 20, a = 2, t = 6$ **b** $v = 8, a = 5, t = 2$

2 $y = mx + c$
Find c when
a $y = 10, m = 2, x = 3$ **b** $y = 8, m = 3, x = -2$

3 $3y = 2x - 4$
Find x when
a $y = 6$ **b** $y = 3$

4 $R = \frac{V}{I}$. Find V when
a $R = 6, I = 10$ **b** $R = 7.2, I = 20$

5 $s = \frac{D}{T}$. Find t when
a $s = 70, d = 35$ **b** $s = 13, d = 52$

> **DID YOU KNOW?**
>
> Ohm's law is a formula used by electrical engineers and is usually written
> V = IR (V = voltage,
> I = current,
> R = resistance).
> The law was discovered by the German physicist Georg Ohm in 1827.

6 Rearrange each formula
a $y = mx + c$, make x the subject **b** $v = u + at$, make t the subject
c $y = \frac{x}{2} + d$, make x the subject **d** $x + 3y = 4$, make y the subject

7 For each of these formulae make t the subject.
a $s = 3t - 6$ **b** $2x = 5t + 9$ **c** $12 + 2t = 3x$

8 Rearrange each formula to make y the subject.
a $4x + 6y = 2$ **b** $3y - 2x = 6$ **c** $3x - 5y = z$

9 These patterns are made with pencils. The formula to work out the number of pencils (P) in a row of n huts is

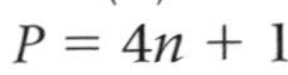
$P = 4n + 1$

5 pencils

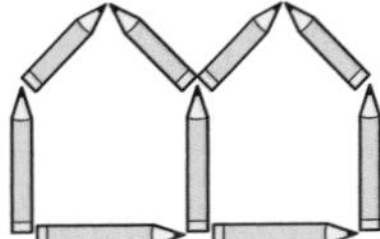
9 pencils

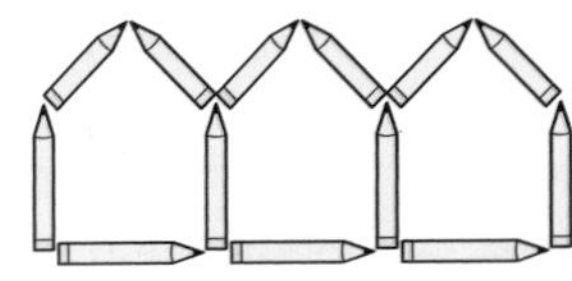
13 pencils

a Rearrange this formula to make n the subject.
b Use your formula to work out the number of huts you can make with
i 37 pencils **ii** 53 pencils **iii** 229 pencils.

AO2 Functional Maths

10 The formula for calculating the cost in pounds of an electricity bill is

$C = 17.5 + 0.1u$ where u is the number of units used.

By rearranging the formula, work out the numbers of units used when the cost is
a £37.50 **b** £32.50 **c** £74.50

A6.5 Inequalities

This spread will show you how to:

- Solve simple one-sided and two-sided inequalities, representing the solution on a number line

Keywords
Greater than
Inequality
Less than
Solution set

- In an **equation**, the left-hand side equals the right-hand side.
  - In an **inequality**, the left-hand and right-hand sides are not necessarily equal.
  - An inequality usually has a range of values.

You use one of these signs to show the relationship between the two sides of an inequality:

$<$	**less than**	$>$	**greater than**
$\leqslant$	less than or equal to	$\geqslant$	greater than or equal to

You can show inequalities on a number line.

$x<2$	x is less than 2	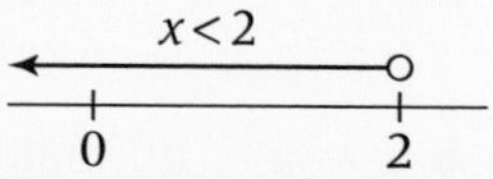
$x>2$	x is greater than 2	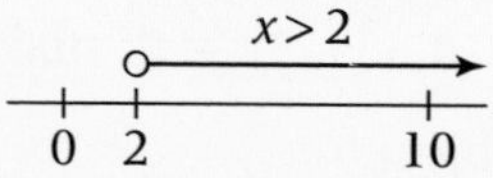
$y\leqslant 4$	y is less than or equal to 4	
$y\geqslant 4$	y is greater than or equal to 4	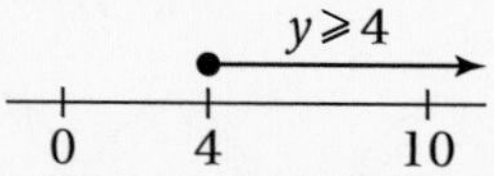

The open circle shows that 2 is not included.

The filled-in circle shows that 4 is included.

Example

a Show the inequality $x > -1$ on a number line.
b If $x < 4$, what can you say about $2x$?

a

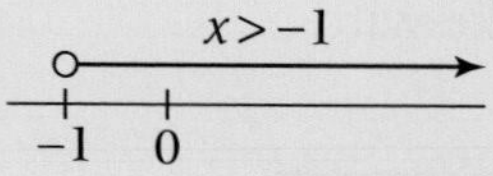

b If $x < 4$, then $2x$ must be less than $2 \times 4 = 8$.
So $2x < 8$.

Values greater than −1 are in the **solution set**.

Inequalities can have more than one term, for example $3x + 4 < 19$.
You can solve an inequality to find a set of values for x.
Just use the balance method, as for solving an equation, by treating the inequality sign like an equals sign.

Example

a Solve the inequality $3x + 4 < 19$
b Show the solution set on a number line.

a Using the balance method:

$$3x + 4 < 19$$
$$3x + 4 - 4 < 19 - 4$$
$$3x < 15$$
$$x < 5$$

b

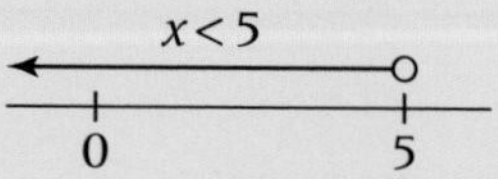

The solution set is $x < 5$.

Exercise A6.5 — Grade C

1 Show these inequalities on a number line.

a $x < 1$ **b** $x \geqslant 1$ **c** $x \geqslant 5$ **d** $x < -2$

e $x < 1.5$ **f** $x > -4$ **g** $x \leqslant 3$ **h** $x \leqslant -1.5$

2 **a** If $x > 5$, what can you say about **i** $2x$ **ii** $4x$?

b If $y \leqslant 6$, write an inequality for **i** $3y$ **ii** $5y$.

c If $x \geqslant -4$, write an inequality for $5x$.

d If $m < -3$, write an inequality for $6m$.

3 Solve these inequalities and show the solution sets on number lines.

a $2x \leqslant 4$ **b** $2x < 10$ **c** $3x > -6$ **d** $4x \geqslant -16$

4 Copy and complete these.

a If $3x + 2 > 11$ then $3x > \square$ and $x > \square$

b If $7x - 4 > 31$ then $7x > \square$ and $x > \square$

c If $2x + 9 \leqslant 11$ then $2x \leqslant \square$ and $x \leqslant \square$

d If $5x - 3 \geqslant 12$ then $5x \geqslant \square$ and $x \geqslant \square$

5 Solve each of these inequalities.
Show each solution on a number line.

a $x + 7 \leqslant 12$ **b** $x - 2 \geqslant 4$ **c** $3x + 5 \geqslant 11$ **d** $2x - 5 < 3$

e $5x + 1 \geqslant -4$ **f** $6x - 2 \leqslant 16$ **g** $3x + 2 > 11$ **h** $2x - 9 \leqslant -5$

6 Solve these inequalities.

a $5x - 4 \geqslant 11$ **b** $4x + 7 > 15$ **c** $3x + 5 \geqslant 5$ **d** $4x + 7 > 3$

e $5x + 6 \geqslant -4$ **f** $3x - 8 \leqslant 4$ **g** $4x + 20 \geqslant 10$ **h** $2x + 23 < 8$

7 Match each inequality to a number line.

a
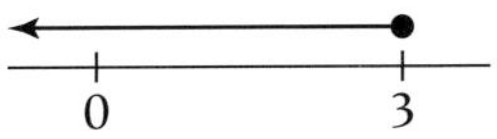

b
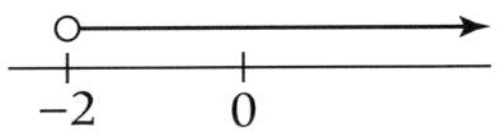

c
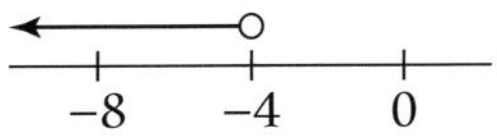

d
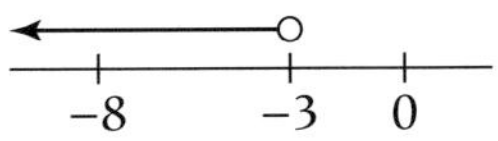

e
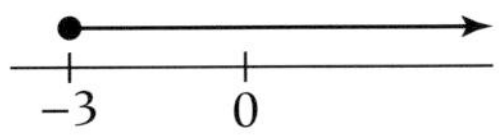

f
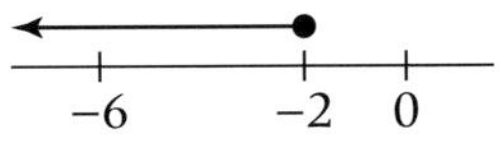

i $x < -3$

ii $x \leqslant 3$

iii $x - 1 \leqslant -3$

iv $x \geqslant -3$

v $x - 1 > -3$

vi $x + 2 < -2$

A6.6 Two-sided inequalities

This spread will show you how to:

- Solve simple one-sided and two-sided inequalities, representing the solution on a number line

Keywords
Greater than
Inequality
Integer
Less than
Solution set

You can read inequalities in two directions.

If $x > 5$, then $5 < x$ If $y \leqslant -2$, then $-2 \geqslant y$

You can use two-sided inequalities to show upper and lower limits.

$2 < x < 5$ means that x is greater than 2 and less than 5.

On a number line:

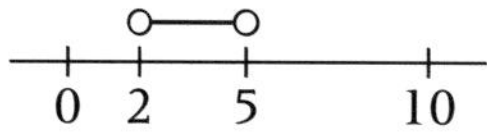

$x > 2$ and $x < 5$.

You can combine two inequalities to show a range of values:

$y > 3$ and $y < 10$
combine to give $3 < y < 10$

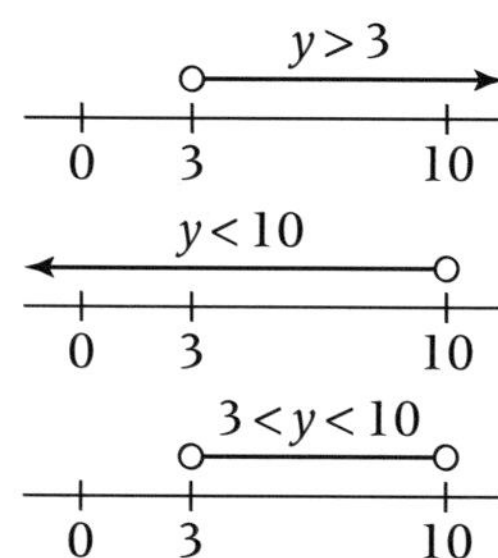

Example

Split each two-sided inequality into two single inequalities.

a $-3 < x \leqslant 1$ **b** $8 > y \geqslant 2$

a $x > -3, x \leqslant 1$ **b** $y < 8, y \geqslant 2$

- You can solve two-sided inequalities to find the solution set.
  - You can give the **integer** values in the solution set.

An integer is a whole number such as -1, 4, 10.

Example

If $-4 < 2n \leqslant 6$
n is an integer.

a Show all the possible values of n on a number line.
b Write all the possible values of n.

a $-4 < 2n$, so $2n > -4$ $2n \leqslant 6$
$n > -2$ $n \leqslant 3$

The solution is $-2 < n \leqslant 3$:

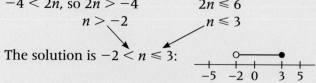

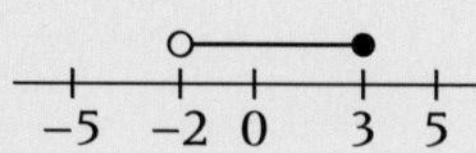

b The possible integer values of n are -1, 0, 1, 2, 3.

Divide both sides by 2 to get n on its own.

-2 is not included.
3 is included.

Exercise A6.6 — Grade C

1 If $7 < x$ (7 is less than x) then you can say x is greater than 7 or $x > 7$.
Write each of these in another way.

a $5 > x$ **b** $6 \leqslant y$ **c** $4 \geqslant y$ **d** $9 < r$
e $15 \geqslant w$ **f** $2 < s$ **g** $-12 > u$ **h** $-4 \leqslant v$

2 Split each two-sided inequality into two single inequalities.

a $1 < x < 5$ **b** $-1 < x < -5$ **c** $-2 < x < 4$
d $-6 \leqslant x \leqslant -1$ **e** $2 < x < 7$ **f** $2 \geqslant x \geqslant -1$

3 Write the inequalities shown by these number lines.

a
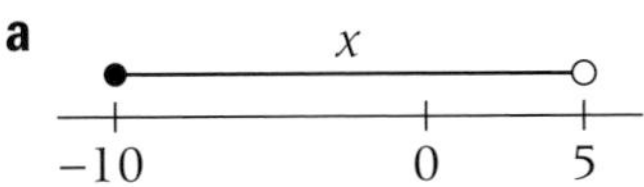

b
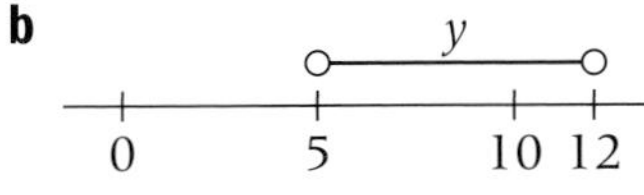

c
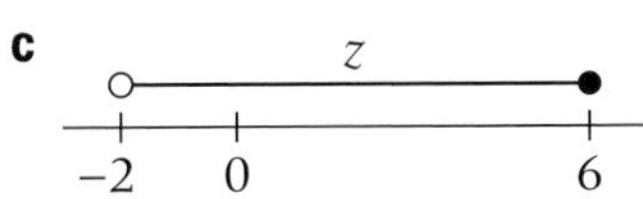

d
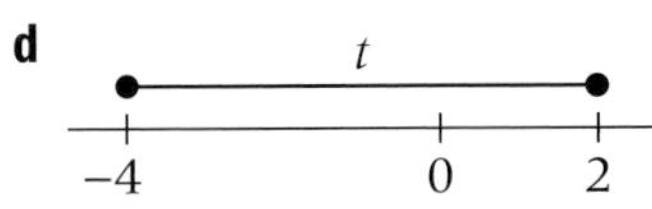

4 Show these inequalities on number lines like this.

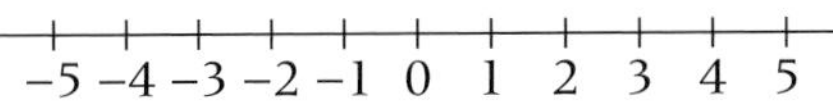

a $-3 \leqslant x < 2$ **b** $4 \geqslant n > -1$ **c** $1 < y \leqslant 3$ **d** $-4 \leqslant m < 0$

5 For each of the inequalities in question 4, list the integer values.

6 If x can take the possible integer values $-1, 0, 1, 2, 3$, which of these could be true?

a $x > -2$ **b** $-1 \leqslant x \leqslant 3$ **c** $-2 < x < 4$
d $-1 \leqslant x < 3$ **e** $-2 < x \leqslant 3$

7 n is an integer.
$-4 \leqslant n < 5$

a Show all the possible values of n on a number line.
b Write all the possible values of n.

Using a number line may be helpful.

8 $2 \leqslant 2x < 10$
x is an integer.
Write all the possible values of x.

9 In these inequalities, y is an integer.
For each inequality, write all the possible values of y.

a $-6 < 2y \leqslant 4$
b $-3 \leqslant 3y < 15$
c $3 < 2y \leqslant 10$

A6.7 Graphs of quadratic functions

This spread will show you how to:

- Recognise the form of and plot simple quadratic graphs

Keywords
Quadratic
Solution

A **quadratic** function includes a 'squared' term, for example x^2.
These are all quadratic functions:

x^2 $\quad$ $x^2 + 3$ $\quad$ $x^2 + 3x - 1$ $\quad$ $2x - x^2$

- To draw a graph of a quadratic function:
  - Draw a table of values
  - Calculate the value of y for each value of x
  - Draw a suitable grid
  - Plot the (x, y) pairs and join them with a smooth curve.

Example

Draw the graph of $y = x^2 + 1$.

Draw a table of values.
$y = x^2 + 1$

x	-3	-1	0	1	3
y	10	2	1	2	10

Draw a suitable grid.
Then plot the coordinate pairs and join the points.

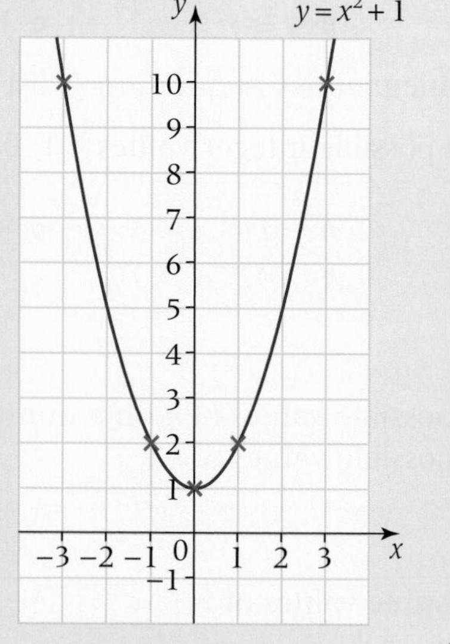

Graphs of quadratic functions have a distinctive shape.

- The graph of a quadratic function
  - is always a U-shaped curve
  - is symmetrical about a vertical line
  - always has a maximum point or a minimum point.

Quadratic graphs can be upside down:

y
Maximum point
0
x

Exercise A6.7 — Grade C

1 **a** Copy and complete the table of values for $y = x^2$.

x	-3	-1	0	1	3
y					

b Draw a pair of axes from 0 to 10 on the y-axis and from -5 to $+5$ on the x-axis.

c Plot the coordinate pairs on the grid.

d Join the points with a smooth curve.

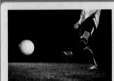

Did you know?

The path traced out by a ball that is kicked or thrown in the air can be modelled by a quadratic function.

2 Draw the graphs of $y = x^2 + 2$ and $y = x^2 + 3$ on the same axes as your graph from question **1**.
What do you notice?

3 Draw the graphs of $y = x^2 - 1$ and $y = x^2 - 3$ on the same pair of axes.
What do you notice?

4 Match these graphs to their equations.

a $y = x^2 + 1$

b $y = x^2 - 2$

c $y = 2 + x^2$

d $y = x^2 - 1$

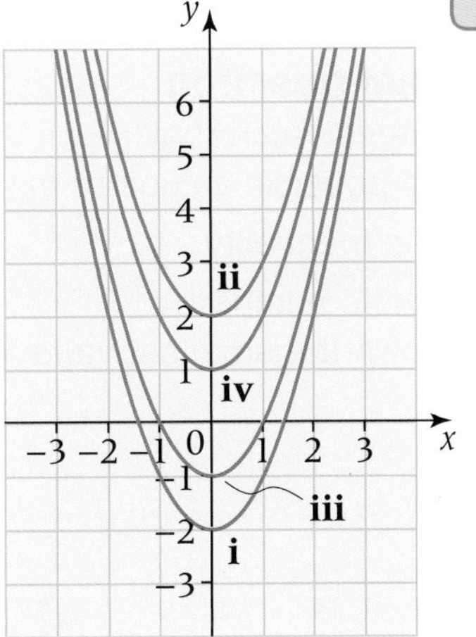

5 **a** Draw the graph of $y = x^2$ on square grid paper.

b Draw the line $y = 9$ on your graph.
Write down the coordinates of the points where the graphs cross.

c Your two pairs of coordinates from part **b** both give **solutions** to the equation $x^2 = 9$.
What are the two x-values that satisfy this equation?

d Draw the line $y = 6$ on your graph.

e Use the line $y = 6$ to help you to find two solutions to the equation $x^2 = 6$.

f What horizontal line would you draw on the graph of $y = x^2$ to find the solutions to $x^2 = 3$?

g Can you find a solution to the equation $x^2 = -9$?
Explain your answer.

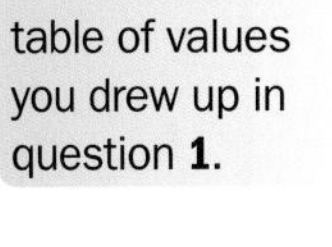

You can use the table of values you drew up in question **1**.

A6

Summary

Check out

You should now be able to:

- Understand and use the words equation, formula, identity and expression
- Substitute numbers into expressions, functions and formulae
- Use formulae from mathematics and other subjects
- Write formulae to represent everyday situations
- Change the subject of a simple formula
- Solve simple linear inequalities and represent the solution set on a number line
- Plot simple quadratic graphs

Worked exam question

a m is an integer such that $-1 \leq m < 4$
List all the possible values of m. (2)

b **i** Solve the inequality $3x \geq x + 7$

ii x is a whole number.
Write down the smallest value of x that satisfies

$3x \geq x + 7$ (3)

(Edexcel Limited 2007)

a $-1, 0, 1, 2, 3$

$-4 \quad -3 \quad -2 \quad -1 \quad 0 \quad 1 \quad 2 \quad 3 \quad 4$

b

$$\begin{aligned} 3x &\geq x + 7 \\ 3x - x &\geq x - x + 7 \\ 2x &\geq 7 \\ x &\geq \tfrac{7}{2} \\ x &\geq 3\tfrac{1}{2} \end{aligned}$$

Show this working out.

c 4

Use your inequality from part **b** to answer part **c**.

$3 \times 4 \geq 4 + 7$
$12 \geq 11$ is a check that the answer $x = 4$ is correct.

Exam questions

AO2

1 Tom the plumber charges £35 for each hour he works at a job, plus £50.
The amount Tom charges, in pounds, can be worked out using

> Multiply the number of hours he works by 35
> Add 50 to your answer

Tom works for 3 hours at a job.
a Work out how much Tom charged. (2)

At his next job Tom charged the customer £260.
b How many hours did Tom work? (3)

Tom works h hours at a job.
He charges P pounds.
c Write down a formula for P in terms of h. (3)
(Edexcel Limited 2007)

2 $v = u + 10t$
Work out the value of v when
a $u = 10$ and $t = 7$ (2)
b $u = -2.5$ and $t = 3.2$ (2)
(Edexcel Limited 2006)

3 **a** Solve $4(x + 3) = 6$ (3)
b Make t the subject of the formula $v = u + 5t$ (2)
(Edexcel Limited 2005)

4 **a** $-3 \leq n < 2$
n is an integer.
Write down all the possible values of n. (2)
b Solve the inequality $5x < 2x - 6$ (2)
(Edexcel Limited 2006)

G6

Constructions and loci

Introduction

When a company grow in size and opens new branches in different towns, they often need to find a suitable location for their distribution warehouse. In an effort to save transport costs, they will often try to choose a site which has good transport links and which is as close as possible to each branch.

What's the point?

Mathematicians can use constructions to find all the places on a map that are an equal distance (equidistant) from two towns. By applying some basic geometry, companies can make their operations more efficient, thereby saving themselves a lot of money.

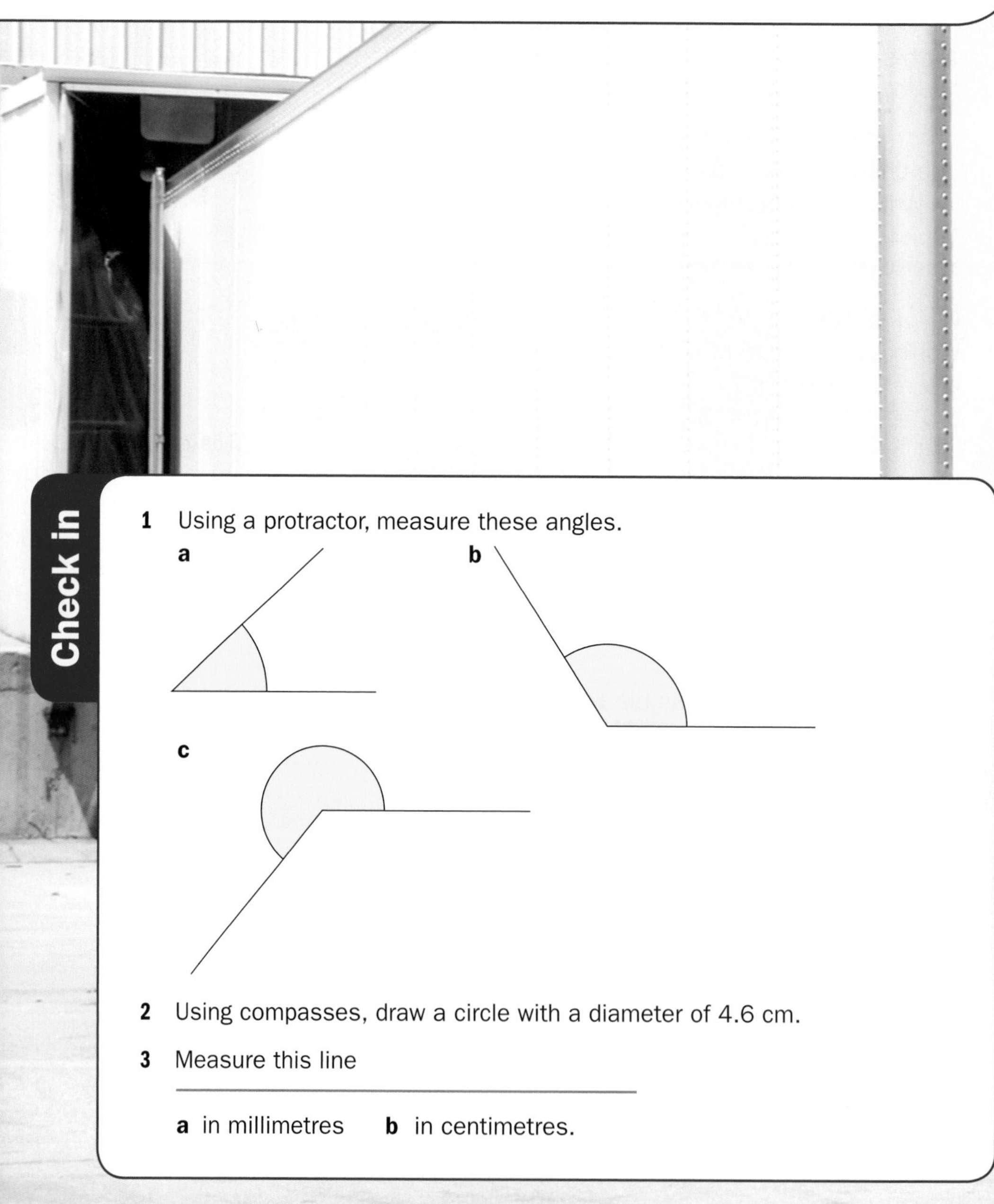

Check in

1 Using a protractor, measure these angles.

a

b

c

2 Using compasses, draw a circle with a diameter of 4.6 cm.

3 Measure this line

a in millimetres **b** in centimetres.

Orientation

What I should know		What I will learn		What this leads to
G2	→	■ Understand and use bearings ■ Construct triangles using protractor and compasses ■ Construct perpendiculars and angle bisectors ■ Construct loci ■ Use and interpret maps and scale drawings	→	Careers in: ● architecture ● technical drawing ● graphic design

Rich task

Two ships, on the same line of latitude, are both travelling at a speed of 10km/h. The first ship is on a bearing of 030° (angle *a*) and the second ship is on a bearing of 330° (angle *b*).

Construct a scale diagram to show where the two ships meet.
On the same diagram, show clearly where the ships would have met if the first ship increased its bearing by 10° and the second ship decreased its bearing by 10°.

Investigate.

G6.1 Bearings

This spread will show you how to:
- Understand angle measure using the associated language

Keywords
Bearing
Direction
Scale
Three-figure bearing

North, East, South or West are not enough to give an accurate direction on most occasions.

- A **bearing** is an angle measured clockwise from North.

To give a **direction** accurately, you need to find an angle measured on a 360° **scale**.

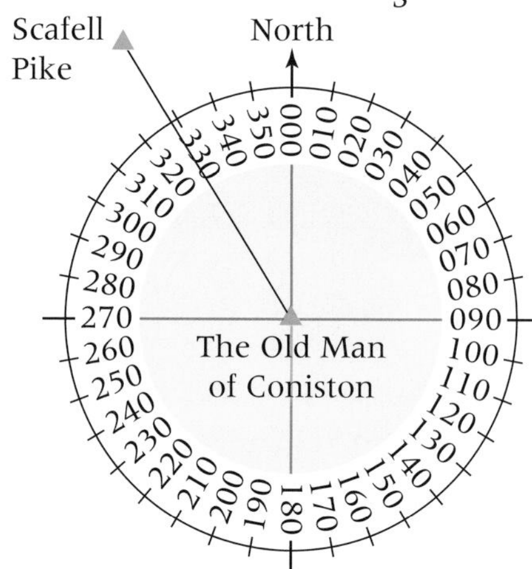

000° = North.

- To specify a direction with a bearing:
  - measure from North
  - measure clockwise
  - use three figures.

The bearing of Scafell Pike from the Old Man of Coniston is 328°

Example

A boat is sinking.

The bearing of the boat from Dawlish Warren is 168°.

The bearing of the boat from Holcombe is 085°.

a Mark the position of the boat on the map.

b How far is the boat from Dawlish?

c What is the bearing of the boat from Dawlish?

a See map.

b 2 cm represents 1 km.
5 cm represents 2.5 km.
The boat is 2.5 km from Dawlish.

c 125°

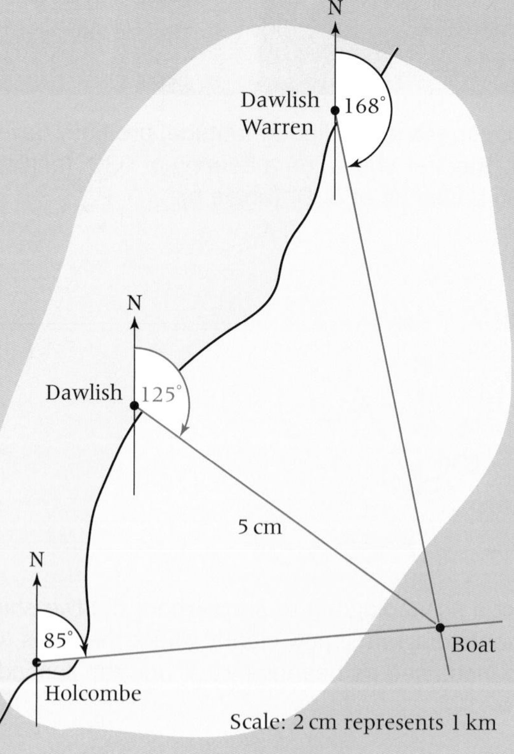

From Dawlish Warren means centre the protractor **at** Dawlish Warren.

Do not rub out the construction lines.

Exercise G6.1 Grade E

1 For each question, put a cross on your page.
Plot the points and join them to form a quadrilateral.
Name the shape, then measure and calculate the perimeter.

a

Bearing from the cross	060°	120°	240°	300°
Distance from the cross	5 cm	5 cm	5 cm	5 cm

b

Bearing from the cross	000°	090°	180°	270°
Distance from the cross	2.5 cm	5 cm	2.5 cm	5 cm

c

Bearing from the cross	035°	145°	215°	325°
Distance from the cross	5 cm	5 cm	5 cm	5 cm

A02 Functional Maths

2 Measure and write the bearing of

a Leeds from Manchester
b Sheffield from Leeds
c Manchester from Leeds
d Manchester from Sheffield
e Leeds from Sheffield.

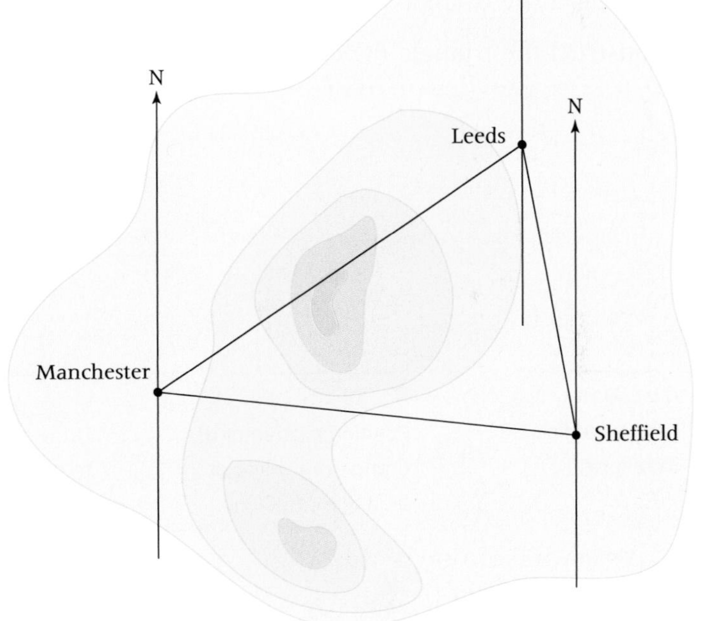

3 Copy the diagram.
The distance from Truro to Falmouth is 14 km.
The bearing of St. Mawes from Falmouth is 080°.
The bearing of St. Mawes from Truro is 170°.

a Mark the position of St. Mawes on your diagram.
b Calculate the distance from Falmouth to St. Mawes.
c Calculate the distance from Truro to St. Mawes.

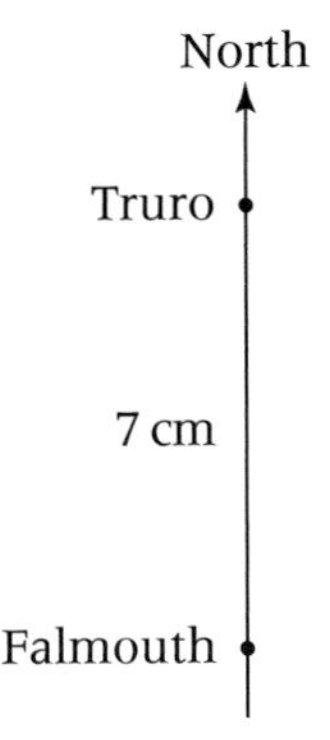

Scale: 1cm represents 2km

G6.2 Constructing triangles

This spread will show you how to:

- Construct triangles using a straight edge, protractor and compasses

Keywords
Construct
Hypotenuse
Right-angled

You will always **construct** identical triangles if you know

Two sides and the angle between them (SAS) or Two angles and a side (ASA) or Right angle, the hypotenuse and a side (RHS) or Three sides (SSS)

5cm
30°
6cm

60°
30°
7cm

5cm
3cm

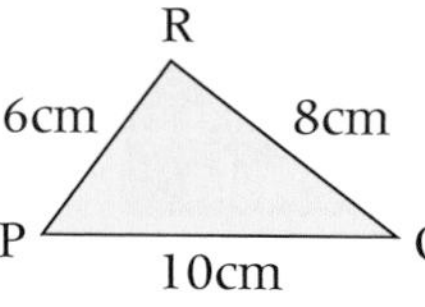

The longest side of a **right-angled** triangle is called the **hypotenuse.**

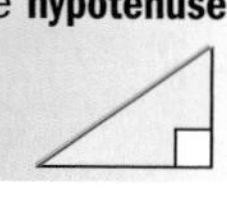

You will need a ruler and a protractor for SAS, ASA and RHS triangles.

You will need a ruler and compasses for SSS triangles.

Example

a Construct the triangle ABC so that angle C = 90°, AB = 6 cm and BC = 3 cm.

b Construct the triangle PQR with lengths PR = 6 cm, QR = 8 cm and PQ = 10 cm.

a

B 3 cm C

Draw base line BC 3 cm long.

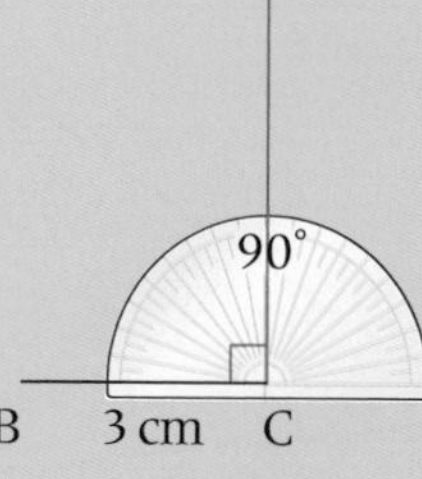

Position protractor at C and draw a line at an angle of 90˚.

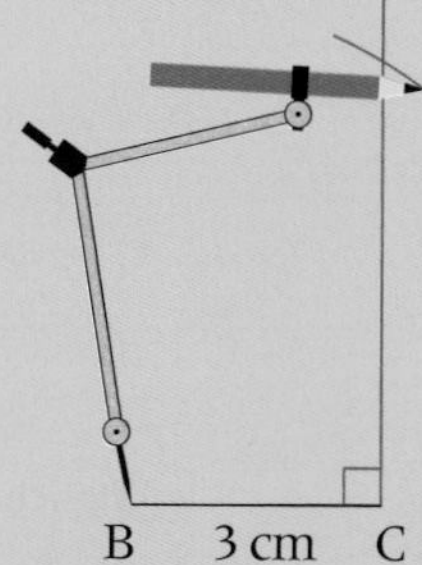

Draw an arc from B to cross the vertical line at C.

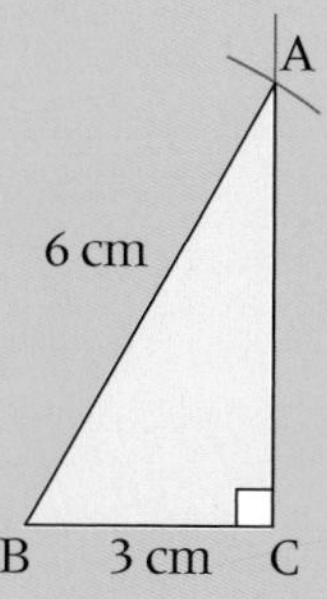

Draw the line AB.

Examiner's tip
Construction lines can earn marks.

b

P 10 cm Q

Using a straight edge, draw a base line PQ 10 cm long.

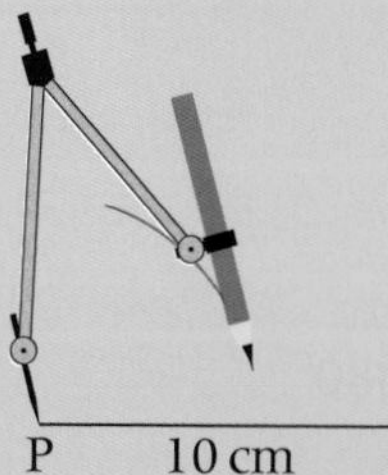

Open your compasses to 6 cm. Draw an arc from P.

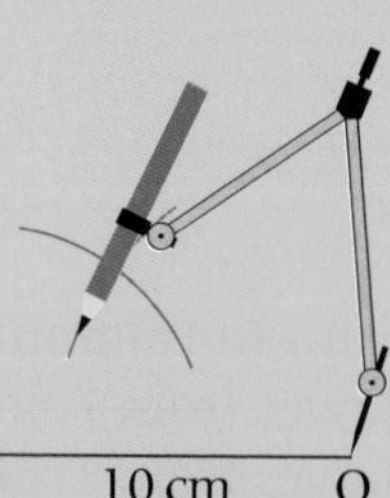

Open your compasses to 8 cm. Draw an arc from Q.

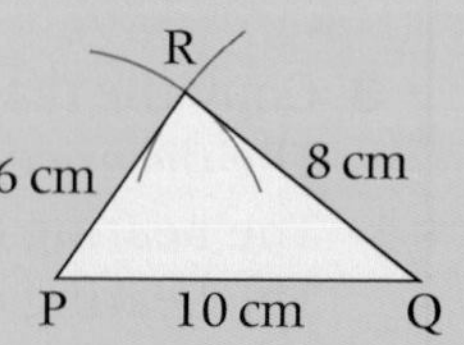

Label the intersection R and join up the lines.

Exercise G6.2 — Grade C/D

The triangles in this exercise have been sketched by hand.
Draw them accurately using the measurements given.

Leave your **construction lines** on your drawing to show your method.

1 Make accurate drawings of these triangles (SAS).
Measure the unknown length in each triangle.

a

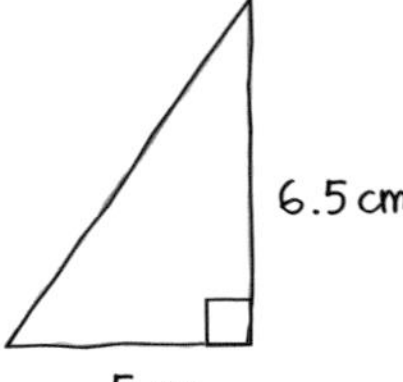

b

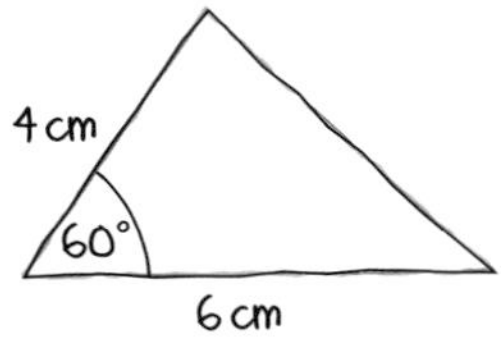

c

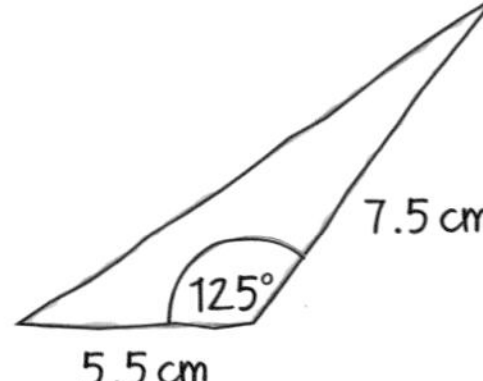

2 Make accurate drawings of these triangles (ASA).
Measure the two unknown lengths in each triangle. State the units of your answers.

a

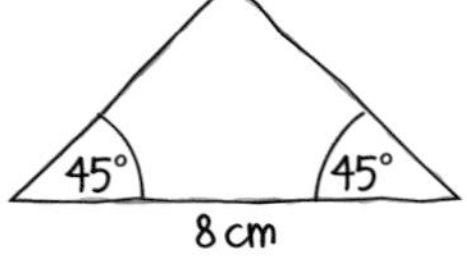

b

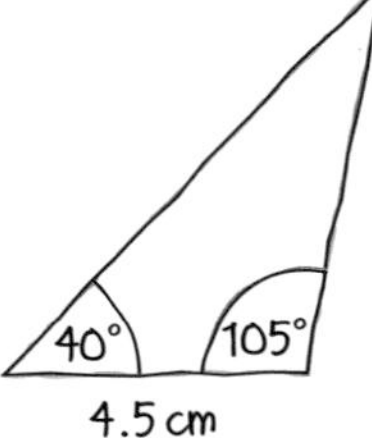

c

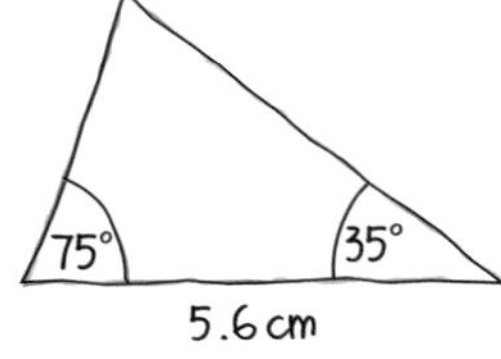

3 Make accurate drawings of these triangles (SSS).
Measure the marked angle in each triangle.

a

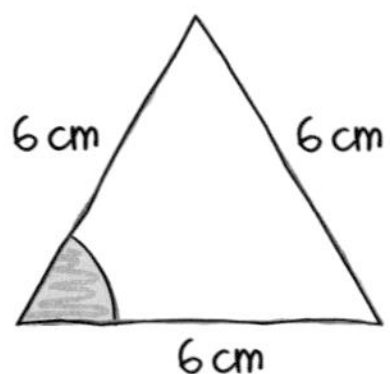

b

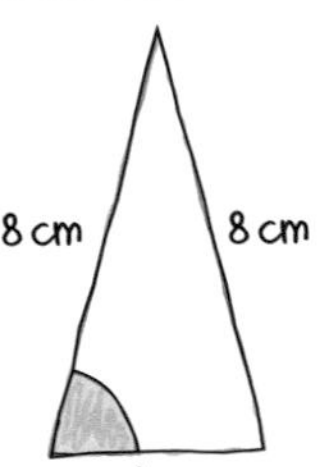

c

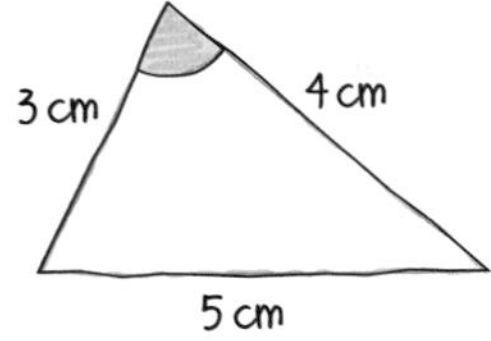

4 Make accurate drawings of these triangles (RHS).
Measure the unknown length and the marked angle in each triangle.

a

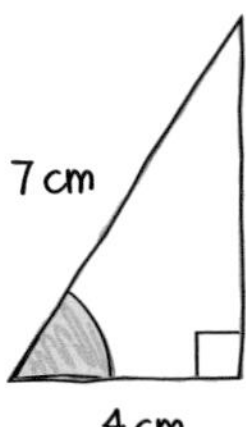

b

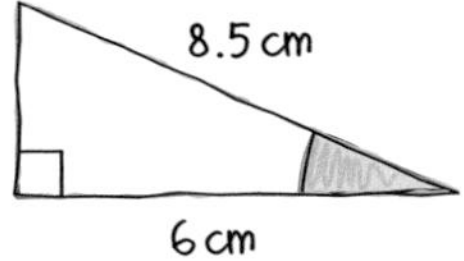

c

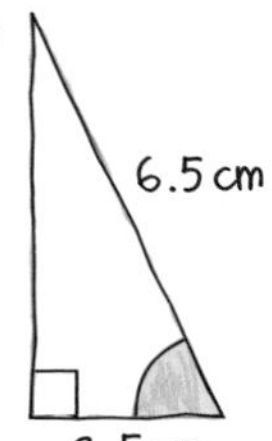

G6.3 Perpendicular lines

This spread will show you how to:

- Use a straight edge and compasses to construct the perpendicular from a point to a line and the perpendicular from a point on the line

Keywords
Arc
Compasses
Construct
Midpoint
Perpendicular
Perpendicular bisector

The shortest distance from a point to a line is the **perpendicular** distance.

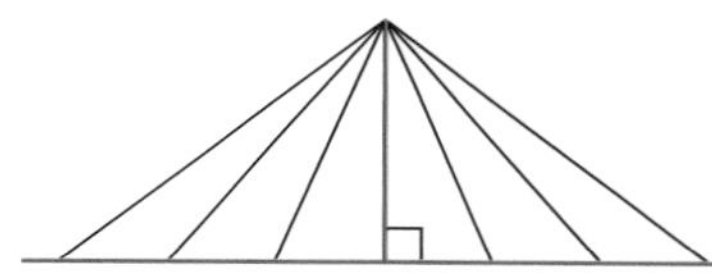

The perpendicular meets the line at right angles.

You construct a perpendicular from a point P to a line like this.

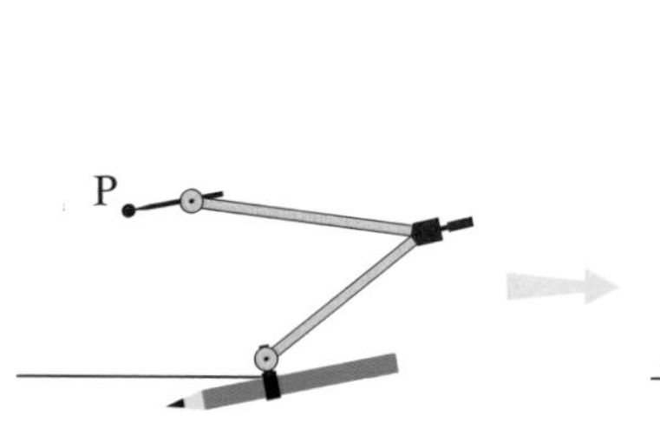

Open your compasses so that the distance is longer than the distance from the point to the line.

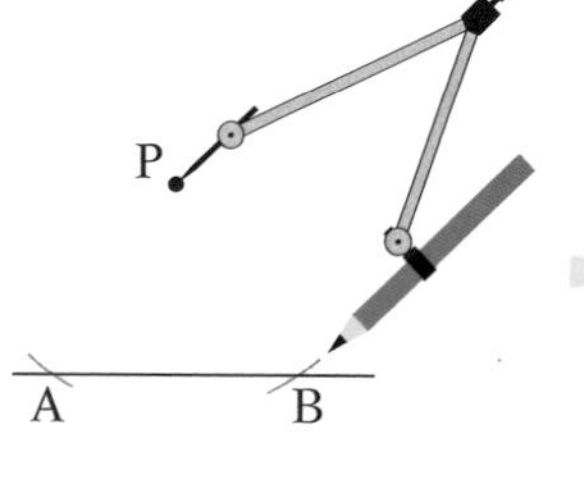

Construct two arcs from the point to the line.

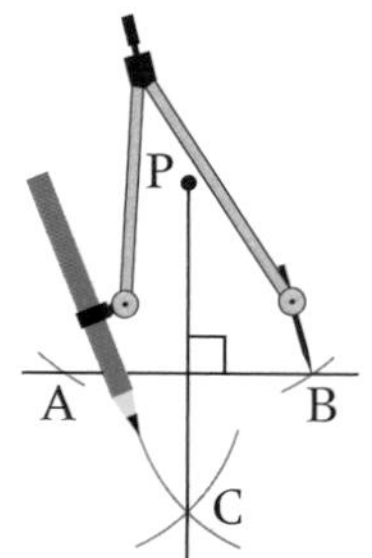

Keep the compasses the same width and construct an arc from A and from B to meet at C. Join point P to C.

Construct means use compasses.

You construct the perpendicular from a point P on the line like this.

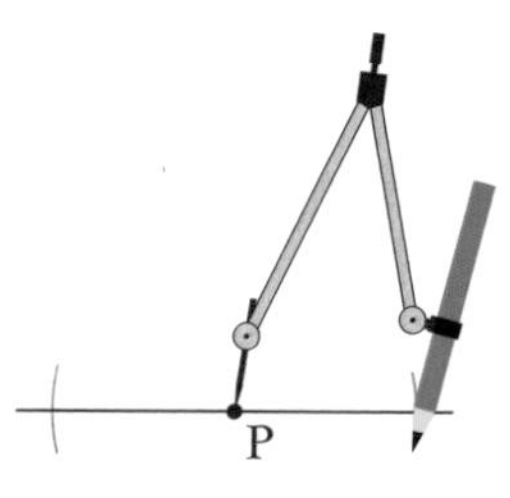

Construct two arcs on the line equidistant from point P.

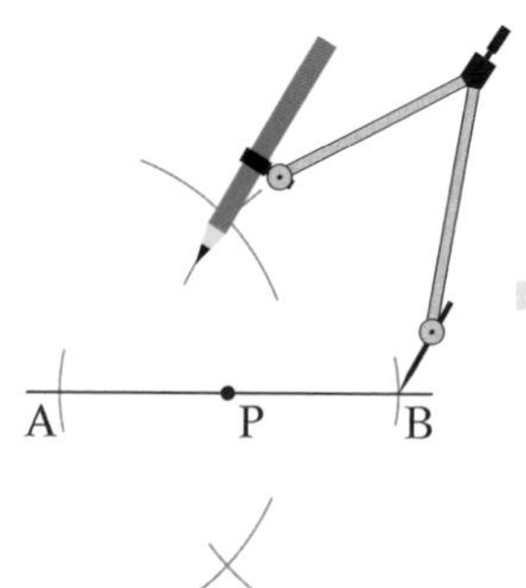

Keep the compasses the same width apart. Construct arcs above and below the line from point A and from point B.

A P B

Draw the perpendicular bisector of AB.

P is the **midpoint** of AB.

- A **perpendicular bisector** divides a straight line into two equal parts at right angles.

A B

This line is the perpendicular bisector of AB.

Exercise G6.3

Grade C

For all constructions use a pencil and do not rub out your construction lines.

1 **a** Draw a line AB, so that AB = 8 cm.
b Using compasses, construct the perpendicular bisector of AB.
c Label the midpoint of AB as M.
d Measure the length AM.

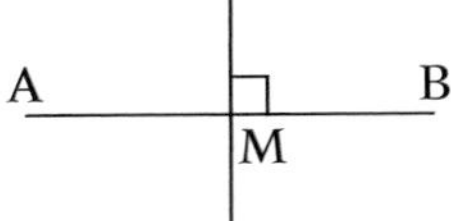

2 **a** Draw a line of length 64 mm.
b Construct the perpendicular bisector of the line.
c Check by measuring that the perpendicular bisector passes through the midpoint of the line.

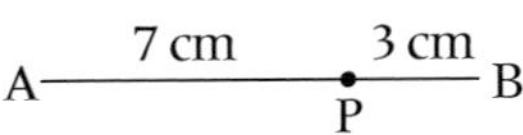

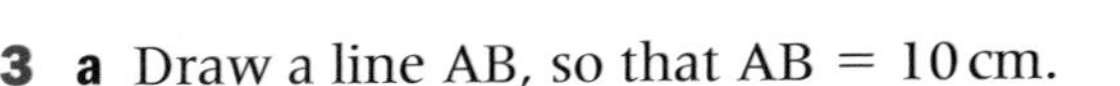

3 **a** Draw a line AB, so that AB = 10 cm.
b Mark the point P, so that AP = 7 cm.
c Construct the perpendicular to AB that passes through the point P.

4 **a** Draw a line AB, with a point P above the line.
b Using compasses, construct the perpendicular to AB that passes through the point P.
c Measure the angle between the line AB and the perpendicular from P.

A03 Problem

5 Construct these rhombuses using compasses and ruler.

a

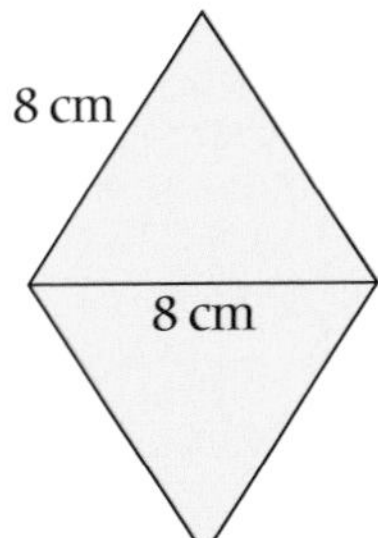

b

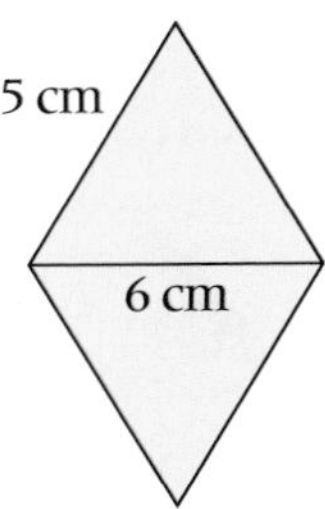

c

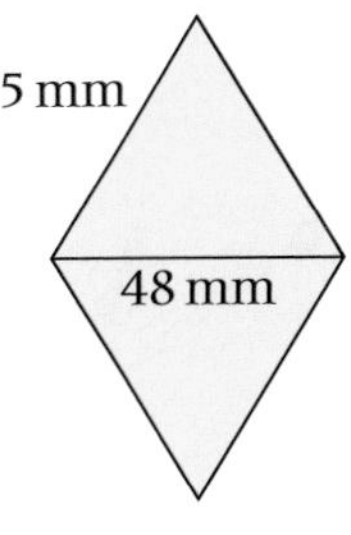

Draw the vertical diagonals on your diagrams.
For each rhombus, check that each diagonal is a perpendicular bisector of the other.

Angle bisectors

This spread will show you how to:

- Use straight edge and compasses to do standard constructions, including the bisector of an angle

Keywords
Angle bisector
Arc
Bisect
Compasses
Construct

- To **bisect** an angle, you cut the angle exactly in half.

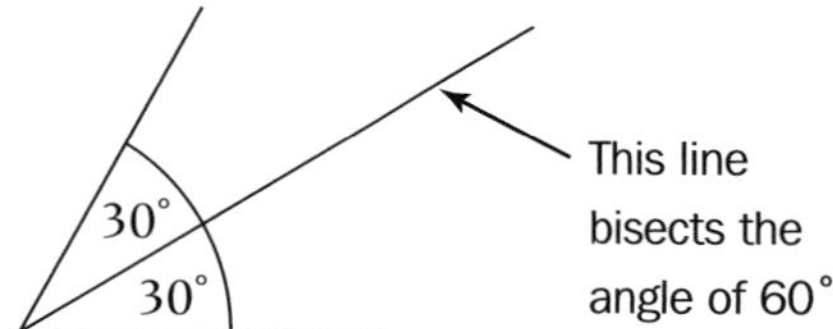

Construct means use compasses, not a protractor.

You use **compasses** to construct an **angle bisector**.

Angle AOC = angle BOC

Use compasses to draw equal arcs on each arm.

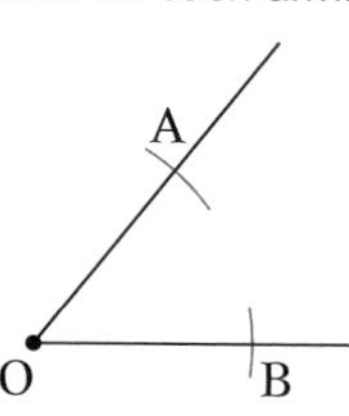

Draw equal arcs from these arcs that intersect at C.

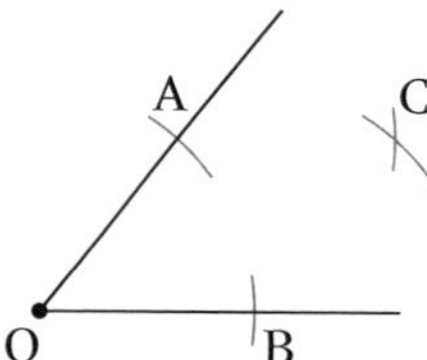

Join O to C, the vertex of the angle

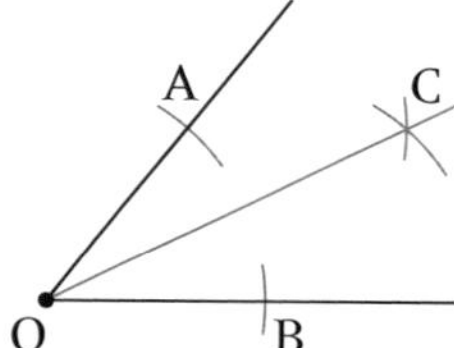

OACB is a rhombus.

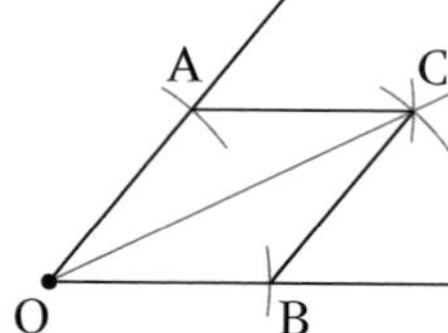

Example

Using compasses, construct

a an angle of 60°
b an angle of 30°.

a

A

Draw a line.

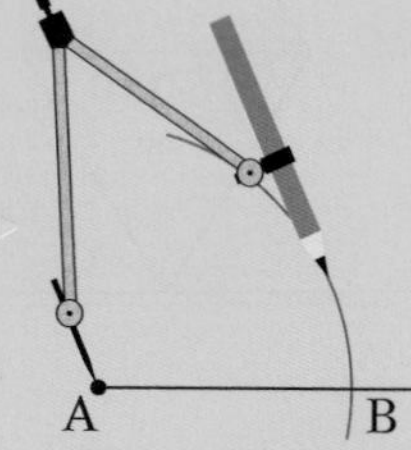

Draw an arc from A crossing the line at B.

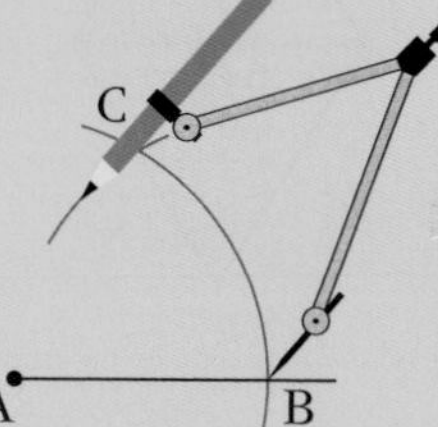

Draw an arc from B crossing the first arc at C.

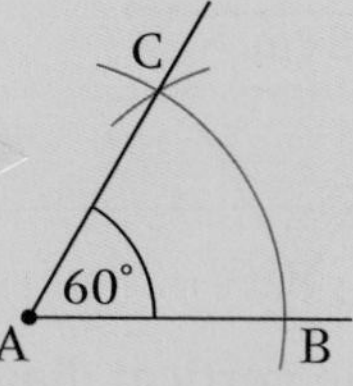

Draw a line from A to C.

b

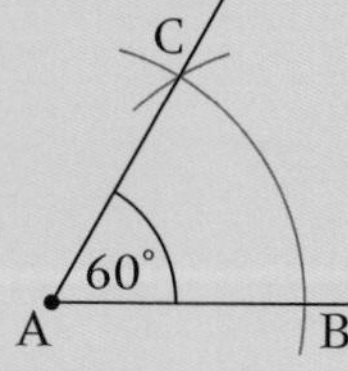

Use the angle of 60°.

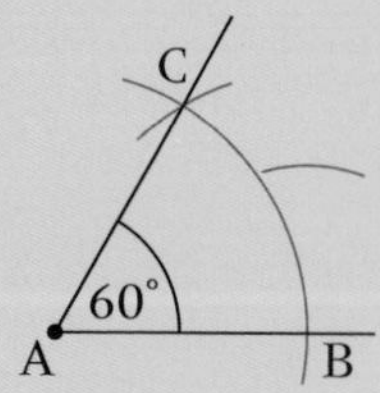

Draw an arc from B.

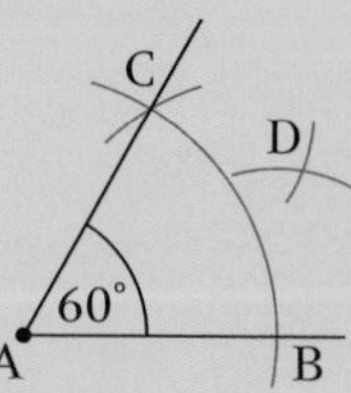

Draw an arc from C crossing the previous arc at D.

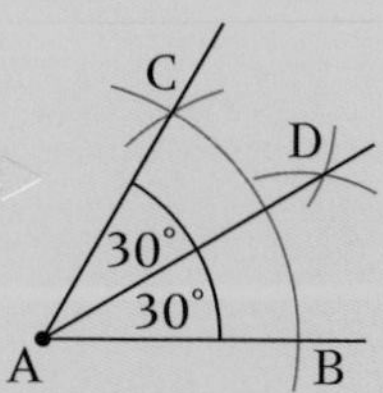

Draw a line from A to D.

Exercise G6.4

Grade C

1 Use a protractor to draw these angles.
a 70° **b** 110° **c** 90° **d** 130° **e** 50°
Using compasses, construct the angle bisectors for each angle.
Use a protractor to check each angle bisector.

2 **a** Using compasses, construct an angle of 60°.
b Use a protractor to check the angle.

3 Construct a triangle that is similar to this equilateral triangle.

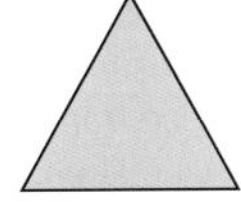

Similar shapes are the same in shape but different in size.

4 **a** Using compasses and ruler, construct an equilateral triangle with sides of length 5 cm.
b Use a protractor to check the angles.

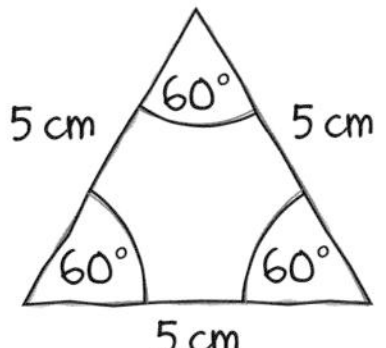

5 Using compasses, construct an angle of

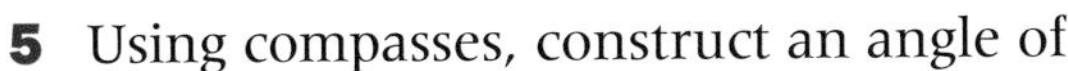

a 30° **b** 120°.
Hint: To construct a 30° angle, bisect a 60° angle.
Use a protractor to check your answers.

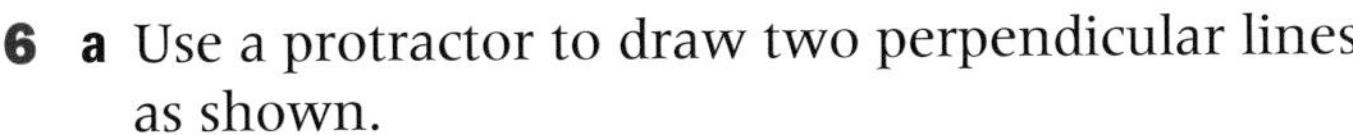

6 **a** Use a protractor to draw two perpendicular lines as shown.
b Using compasses, construct the bisectors of the right angles.
c Label the lines with N, NE, E, SE, S, SW, W, NW.

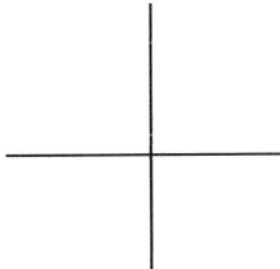

7 **a** Draw any two intersecting lines.
b Construct the angle bisectors for the acute angles.
c Construct the angle bisectors for the obtuse angles.
d Copy and complete this sentence:
The bisector of the acute angles is ______ to the bisector of the obtuse angles.

e Explain why the sentence is true for any two intersecting lines.

8 **a** Using compasses, construct the triangle PQR.
b Construct the angle bisectors for angle P, angle Q and angle R.
c Label the point of intersection of the angle bisectors as O.
d Draw a circle, centre O, that just touches the lines PQ, QR and PR.
e State the radius of this circle.

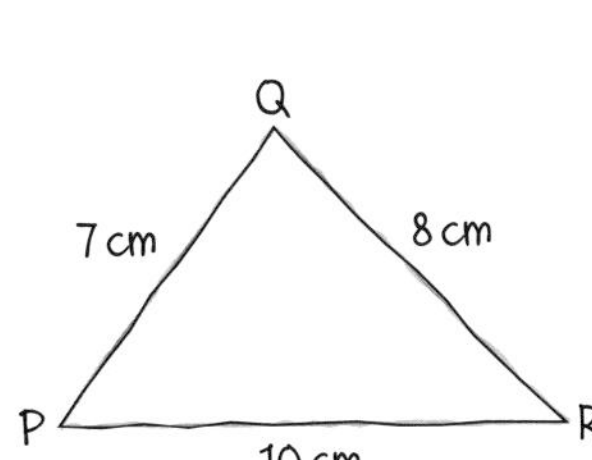

A03 Problem

9 Constuct a regular hexagon that fits exactly inside a circle.

G6.5 Loci

This spread will show you how to:

- Find loci, both by reasoning and by using ICT to produce shapes and paths

Keywords
Arc
Compasses
Construct
Equidistant
Loci
Locus
Perpendicular bisector

- The **locus** of an object is its path.
- A locus is a set of points that move according to a rule.

Loci is the plural of locus.

The red counters are all the same distance from the blue counter.

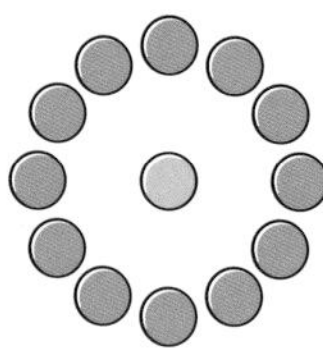

The locus is a circle.

The red counters are the same distance from the two blue lines.

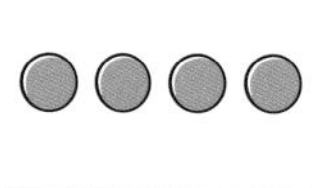

The locus is a straight line.

The red counters are the same distance from the two blue lines.

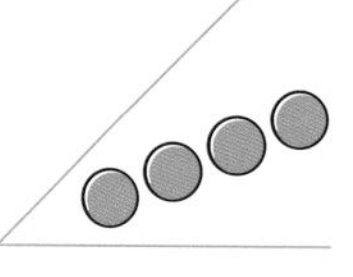

The locus is the angle bisector of the angle between the two blue lines.

The red counters are the same distance from the two blue counters.

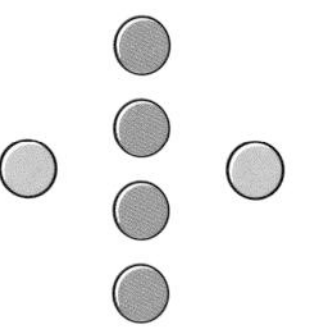

The locus is the perpendicular bisector of the line joining the two blue counters.

Example

Some treasure is positioned 2 m from C, but **equidistant** from A and B.
Using ruler and compasses only, mark the possible positions of the treasure.

×C

A× ×B

Draw a circle, centre C, radius 2 m.
Join A and B.
Construct the perpendicular bisector of AB.
Mark where the line crosses the circle.

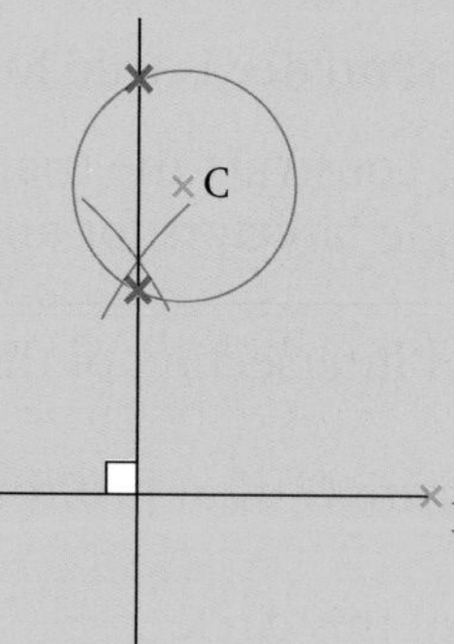

You can use LOGO to plot the path of a turtle.
You specify distance in mm and angles in degrees.

These commands ... produce this path.

FORWARD 100
LEFT 90
FORWARD 100

The plan view is

100 mm

100 mm

Exercise G6.5 — Grade C

1 a Using a protractor, draw and label an angle of 50°.
  b Draw the locus of the points that are the same distance from AB and BC.

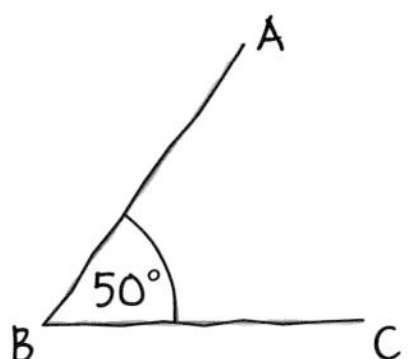

2 a Using compasses, construct and label an angle of 60°.
  b Construct the locus of the points that are equidistant from AB and BC.

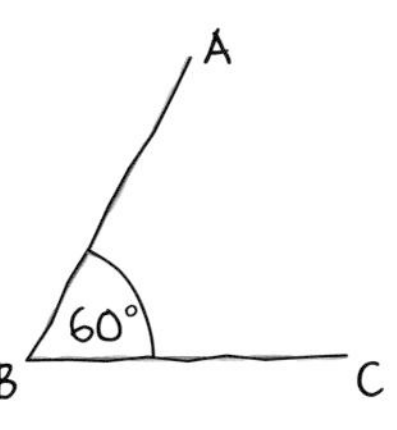

3 a Draw a line AB so that AB = 7 cm.
  b Construct the locus of the points that are equidistant from A and B.

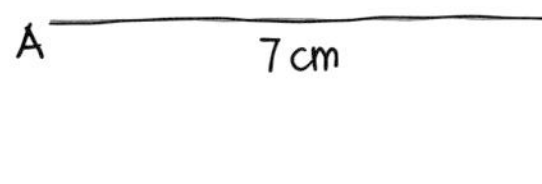

4 Draw a point and label it O.
Construct the locus of the points that are 3 cm from the point O.

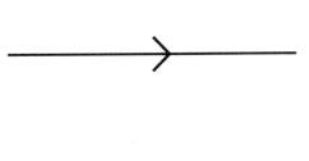

5 Draw two parallel lines.
Draw the locus of the points that are equidistant from the two lines.

Functional Maths **A02**

6 A 2 metre length of rope is used to tether a goat to a fixed point on a fence.

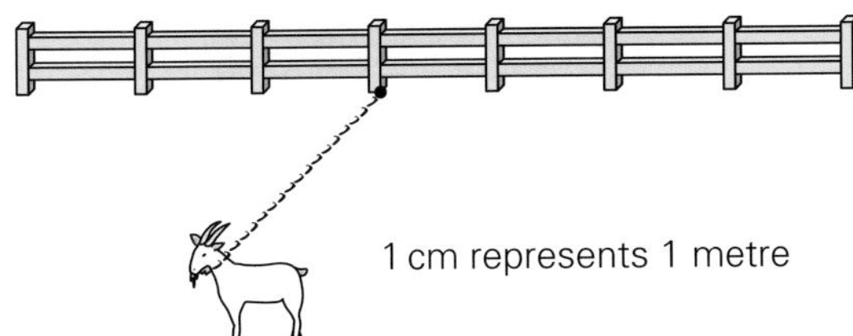

Draw a diagram to show the extent to which the goat can move while tethered.

7 a Draw a line AB so that AB = 8 cm.
  b Construct the locus of the points that are equidistant from A and B.
  c On your diagram, indicate the region that has points that are nearer to A than B.

G6.6 Maps and scale drawings

This spread will show you how to:

- Use and interpret maps and scale drawings

Keywords
Enlarged
Reduced
Scale drawing
Scale factor

In **scale drawings**, lines and shapes are **reduced** or **enlarged**.

Corresponding lengths are multiplied by the same **scale factor**.
You can write the scale factor as a ratio.

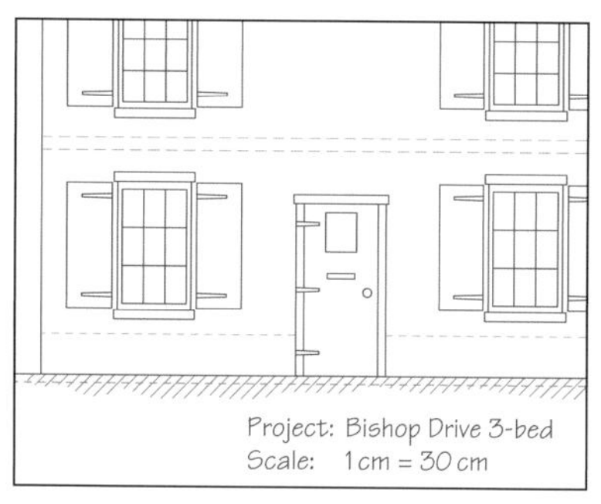

1 cm on the architect's plan = 30 cm of the actual house.

You can write this scale factor as 1 cm represents 30 cm
or 1 : 30.

Maps are scale drawings.

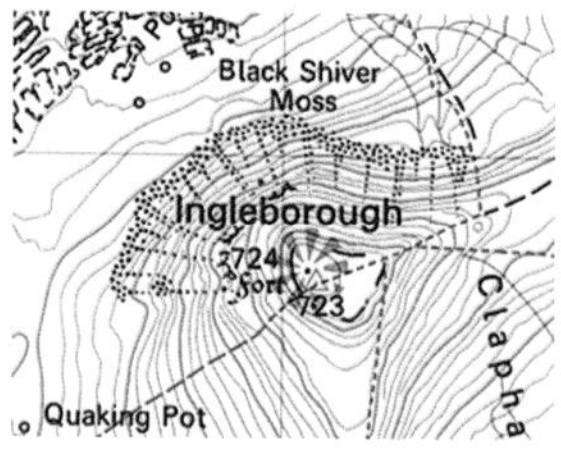

This is an enlargement of scale factor 50 000.

The map scale can be written 1 : 50 000.

You write the scale as 1 cm represents 50 000 cm
or 1 cm represents 500 m.

Example

In this scale drawing 1 cm represents 3 m.

a Calculate the height of the building.
b Calculate the length of the building.
c Calculate the area of the front.
State your units.
d There are 26 windows in the scale drawing.
How many windows are there on the front of the real house?

3 cm

7 cm

a 1 cm represents 3 m
3 cm represents $3 \times 3 = 9$ m
Height of building = 9 m

b 7 cm represents $7 \times 3 = 21$ m
Length of building = 21 m

c Area of front = $9\text{m} \times 21\text{m}$
$= 189\text{m}^2$

d 26 windows

The number of windows is the same on the scale drawing as on the real house.

Exercise G6.6 Grade E

1 The scale on a drawing is 1 cm represents 10 cm.
Calculate the distance represented by

0 10 20 cm

a 4 cm **b** 10 cm **c** 0.5 cm
d 6.5 cm **e** 12.5 cm

Functional Maths A02

2 This is an accurate scale drawing of a Dalek.
For the real Dalek, calculate
a the height
b the width of the base.

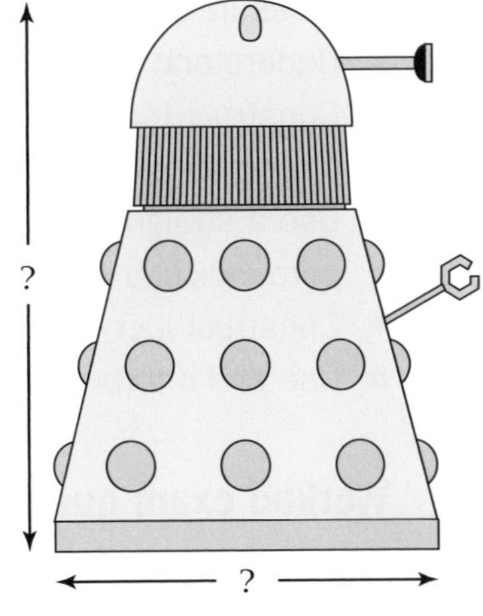

Scale: 1 cm represents 20 cm

3 On the plan of a house, a door measures 3 cm by 8 cm.
If the plan scale is 1 cm represents 25 cm, calculate the dimensions of the real door.

4 This is a scale drawing of a volleyball court.

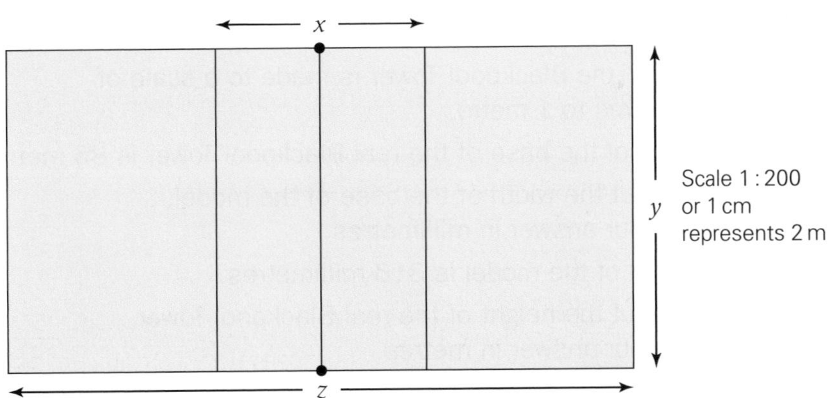

Calculate
a the actual distances marked x, y and z
b the area of the court. State the units of your answer.

5 A map has a scale of 1 : 50 000 or 1 cm represents 50 000 cm.
Calculate in metres the actual distance represented on the map by
a 2 cm **b** 8 cm **c** 10 cm
d 0.5 cm **e** 14.5 cm.

G6 Summary

Check out

You should now be able to:

- Measure and draw lines and angles
- Understand and use bearings
- Construct triangles and other 2-D shapes using a ruler, protractor and compasses
- Use a straight edge and compasses to construct perpendicular lines and bisectors
- Construct loci
- Use and interpret maps and scale drawings

Worked exam question

A model of the Blackpool Tower is made to a scale of 2 millimetres to 1 metre.

The width of the base of the real Blackpool Tower is 85 metres.

a Work out the width of the base of the model.
Give your answer in millimetres. (2)

The height of the model is 316 millimetres.

b Work out the height of the real Blackpool Tower.
Give your answer in metres. (2)

(Edexcel Limited 2008)

a

$85 \times 2 = 170$
170 mm

The answer must be given in millimetres.

b

$316 \div 2 = 158$
158 metres

The answer must be given in metres.

Show the multiplication and division calculations.

Exam questions

1 The diagram shows the position of two airports, A and B.
A plane flies from airport A to airport B.

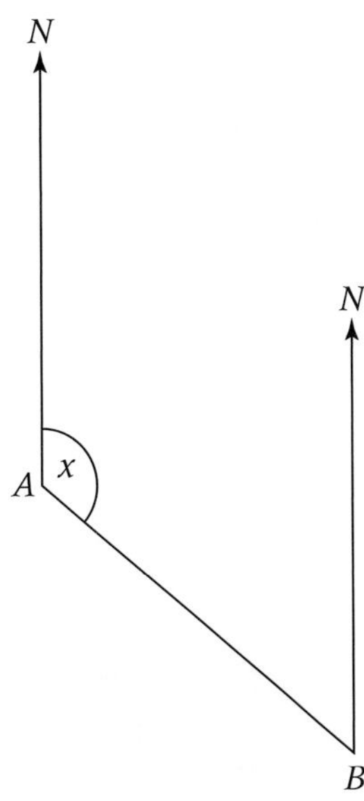

Scale: 1 cm represents 50 km

a Measure the size of the angle marked x. (1)

b Work out the real distance between airport A and airport B.
Use the scale 1 cm represents 50 km. (2)

Airport C is 350 km on a bearing of 060° from airport B.

c On a copy of the diagram, mark airport C with a cross (×).
Label it C. (2)

(Edexcel Limited 2008)

2 Use ruler and compasses to construct an equilateral triangle with sides of length 5 centimetres.
You must show all your construction lines.

3 Copy the diagram. Draw the locus of all points which are equidistant from the points P and Q.

P ×   × Q (2)

Functional Maths 7: Art

Graffiti artists often sketch their designs before projecting them onto the surface. They sometimes use grids or parts of their body as measuring tools to help them copy the proportions accurately.

1. A graffiti artist projects an image from a sketchpad of length 20cm and height 14.8cm onto a wall of length 6m.
   a. What scale factor is being used?
   b. What is the height of the graffiti wall?

   The artist's hand-span is 150mm.

   c. What are the dimensions of the wall in terms of hands?

Grid method

★★★★

The T is made up of a trapezium and a scalene triangle. The coordinates of its vertices are

(-4, -1), (-4, 4.6), (-6, 4), (-4, 6), (4, 7), (-2.6, 5) and (-2.6, -1).

2. Describe
   a. the shapes used to make up i. the A ii. the G
   b. the coordinates of the vertices of i. the A ii. the G.
3. The dimensions of the sketch are 12cm × 10cm.
   a. What scale factor would you use to project this image onto a surface of dimensions 24cm × 20cm?
   b. What would the effect be on the area of the image?
   c. Calculate the area of
      i. the original sketch ii. the enlarged image.
   d. Use a 2cm square grid to draw the enlarged image.

When a grid is being used, it is the shapes that make up the design and their borders that are important.

Here is a sketch of the word TAG drawn on a 1cm square grid. The artist's 'starting position', O, is the reference point (origin):

0

Sketch your own graffiti tags using geometric shapes. Use the grid method to create enlarged copies of your images.

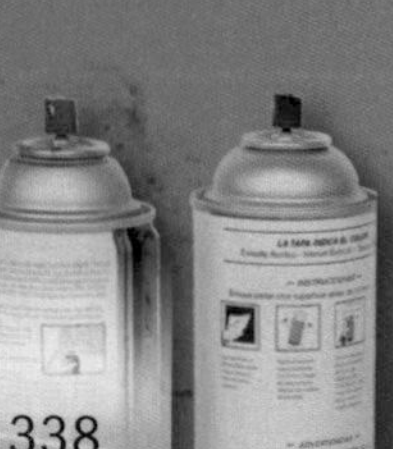

Crop circles are geometric patterns that are displayed in crop fields.

CROP CIRCLES

This crop circle was found in Wiltshire in 2008. The design is based on an equilateral triangle.

You can recreate the pattern using these steps:

1. Use your compasses to draw a circle
2. Choose a point on your circle. Use your compasses (do not alter them) to step round the circle. Mark at each point your pencil touches the circle
3. Join three of the marks to form an equilateral triangle
4. Join the other three marks to form an equilateral triangle in the reverse direction
5. Alter your compasses. Draw a circle, with the same centre, passing through the six intersections of the two triangles
6. Alter your compasses again. Draw a circle, centred at a point of one of the triangles, so that it touches the second circle you drew
7. Construct two more circles as in step 6 at the other two points of that triangle
8. Erase your construction lines.

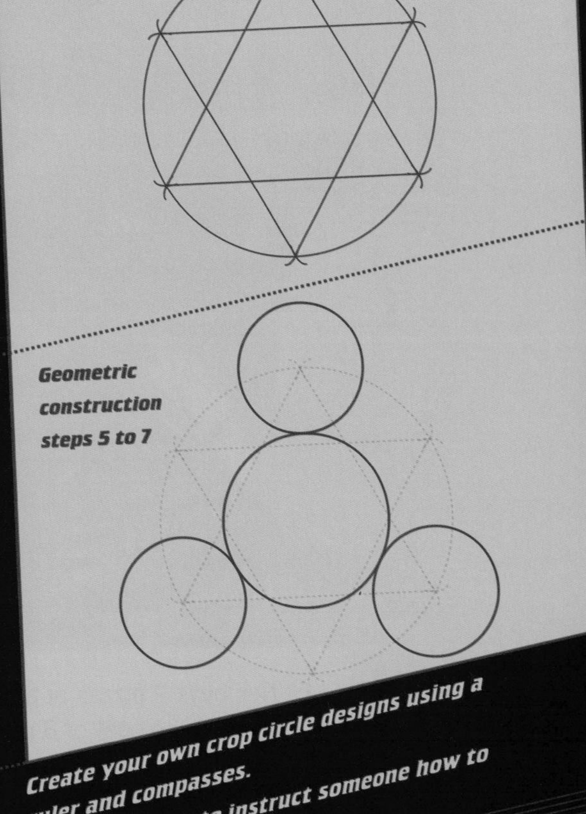

Create your own crop circle designs using a ruler and compasses.

Write the steps to instruct someone how to recreate your pattern.

N7

Proportionality

Introduction

Ergonomics is the study of how well technology suits the human body. When a new car seat is designed, its height from the floor, inclination, and movement are all designed in proportion to the average human body.

What's the point?

A car designer is able to use mathematics to calculate the precise dimensions of a scale model on which tests can be carried out, at far less expense than building a full size car.

Check in

1. Neil buys 2 pizzas at a cost of £7.00.
   What is the cost of 8 pizzas?
2. John weighs 50 kg. Kevin weighs 75 kg.
   How many times heavier than John is Kevin?
3. Krishna earns £8.50 per hour.
   How much does he get paid for 8 hours work?

Orientation

What I should know		What I will learn		What this leads to
N4	→	■ Use proportions to make simple comparisons ■ Understand and use proportion in problem solving ■ Solve problems involving exchange rates	→	Aspects of everyday life involving financial management

Rich task

A ship can sail at a steady speed of 30 km/h.
There is enough fuel to last for ten hours.
When the ship leaves port, there is a strong current of 6km/h which increases the speed of the ship to 36km/h.
Assuming the captain intends to use all the fuel, at what distance from port will she have to turn the ship around and head home?
(Remember on the return journey the strong current will be slowing down the speed of the ship to $30 - 6 = 24$km/h)

N7.1 Proportion

This spread will show you how to:

- Use decimals, fractions and percentages to describe proportions
- Use proportions to make simple comparisons

Keywords
Decimal
Equivalent
Fraction
Percentage
Proportion

- A **proportion** is a part of the whole.
  You can use **percentages**, **fractions** and **decimals** to describe proportions.

Example

p.88

a What proportion of this shape is shaded?

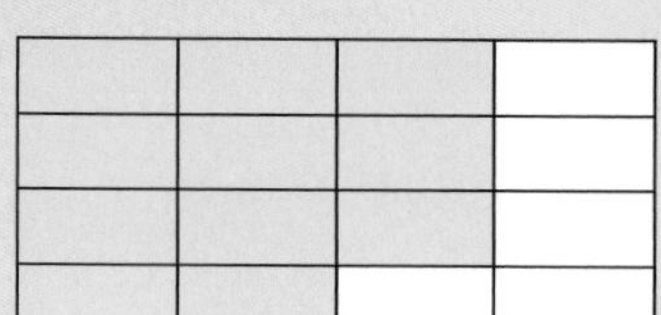

b What proportion of cars are blue?

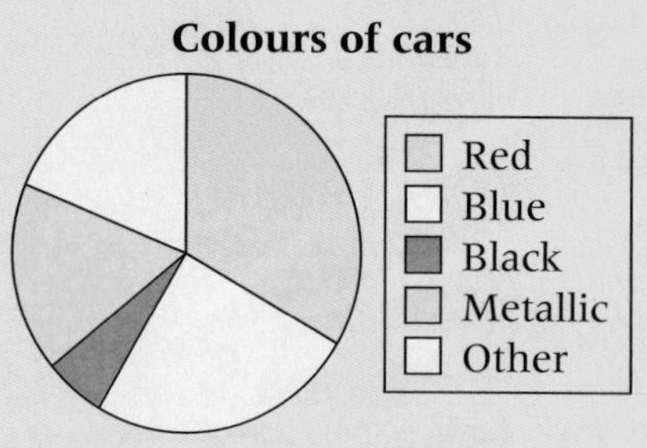

a The proportion shaded is $\frac{11}{16}$
$= 11 \div 16$
$= 0.6875$
$= 68.75\%$

b The sector representing blue cars is 90 degrees.
Fraction of blue cars $= \frac{90}{360} = \frac{1}{4}$
$= 1 \div 4$
$= 0.25$
$= 25\%$

- Change fraction to a decimal by division.
- Change decimal to a percentage by multiplying by 100.

- You can use proportions to make simple comparisons.

Example

John scores $\frac{26}{40}$ in his Maths exam and 63% in his English exam.
In which exam does he score the highest mark?

Change the Maths mark into a percentage:
$\frac{26}{40} = 26 \div 40$
$= 0.65$
$= 0.65 \times 100\%$
$= 65\%$
Maths mark = 65%   English mark = 63%
John scores a higher mark in his Maths exam.

It is easier to compare proportions by converting them to percentages.

Exercise N7.1 Grade E

1 Write the proportion of each of these shapes that is shaded.
Write each of your answers as
i a fraction in its simplest form
ii a percentage (to 1 decimal place as appropriate).

a
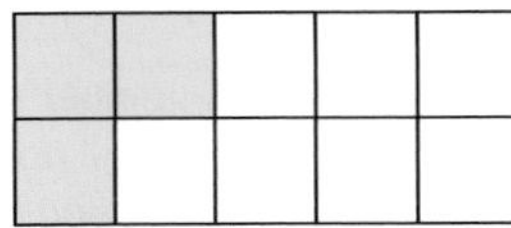

b
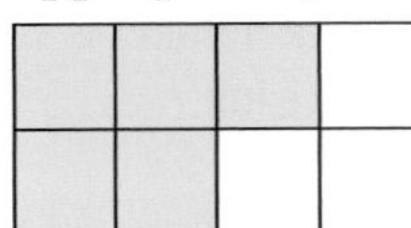

c
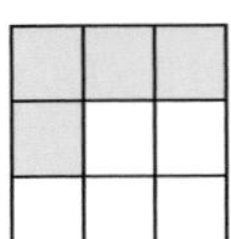

d
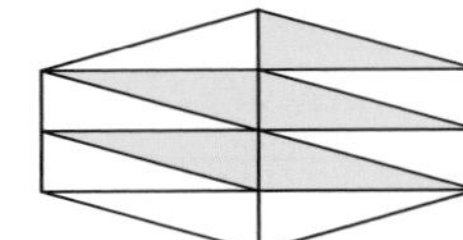

e
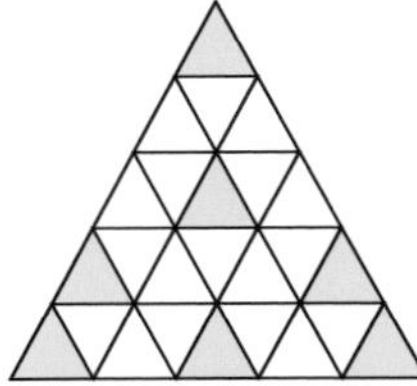

2 Put these fractions, decimals and percentages in order from lowest to highest.

Order these quantities without a calculator.

a $\frac{3}{5}$, 61%, 0.63 **b** $\frac{7}{10}$, $\frac{17}{25}$, 69%, 0.71 **c** $\frac{7}{20}$, $\frac{2}{5}$, $\frac{3}{8}$, 0.36, 34%

Order these quantities with a calculator.

d $\frac{3}{7}$, 42%, $\frac{2}{5}$ **e** 15%, $\frac{3}{19}$, 0.14, $\frac{1}{5}$ **f** 81%, $\frac{8}{9}$, 0.93, 0.9, $\frac{19}{20}$

A02 Functional Maths

3 Solve each of these problems without using a calculator.
Express each of your answers
i as a fraction in its lowest form
ii as a percentage.

a Brian's mark in a Geography test was 42 out of 70.
What proportion of the test did he answer correctly?

b Hannah collects dolls. She has 25 dolls altogether.
13 of the 25 dolls are from Russia.
What proportion of Hannah's dolls are from Russia?

c A restaurant makes a service charge of 3p in every 20p.
Work out 3p as a proportion of 20p.

d Class 11 X 2 has 30 students.
21 of these students are boys.
What proportion of the class are boys?

e Sakarako makes cakes. On Friday she makes 60 cakes.
Sakarako puts icing on 48 of the cakes.
What proportion of the cakes have icing on them?

N7.2 Unitary method

This spread will show you how to:

- Calculate missing amounts when two quantities are in direct proportion

Keywords
Direct proportion
Ratio
Unitary method

- A **ratio** tells you how many times bigger one number is compared to another number. You can calculate a ratio using division.

Examiner's tip: You will not be assessed on direct proportion in the foundation tier, but it is useful for solving real-life problems.

- Numbers or quantities are in **direct proportion** when the ratio of each pair of corresponding values is the same.

Example

Here is a price list for the cost of different-sized tins of paint.

Number of litres	Total cost (£)
2	9.00
3	13.50
5	22.50
10	45.00

a Are the number of litres of paint in proportion to the total cost?
b What is the ratio between the number of litres and the total cost?

For 2 tins of paint — Ratio of 'number of litres' to 'total cost' $= \frac{9}{2} = 4.5$
For 3 tins of paint — Ratio of 'number of litres' to 'total cost' $= \frac{13.5}{5} = 4.5$
For 5 tins of paint — Ratio of 'number of litres' to 'total cost' $= \frac{22.5}{5} = 4.5$
For 10 tins of paint — Ratio of 'number of litres' to 'total cost' $= \frac{45}{10} = 4.5$

a The ratio is the same, so the numbers are in direct proportion.
b The total cost is always 4.5 times bigger than the number of litres.

Remember: to find the ratio of two numbers you divide them.

- You can use the **unitary method** to solve problems involving direct proportion. In this method you always find the value of one unit of a quantity.

Example

Here is a recipe for mushroom soup. Work out the number of grams of mushrooms needed to make mushroom soup for eight people.

Mushroom Soup
(for 3 people)
270 g of button mushrooms
45 ml of white wine
450 ml of vegetable stock
3 tbsp of olive oil
3 garlic cloves

Number of people	Grams of mushrooms
3	270
÷ 3 → 1	÷ 3 → 90
× 8 → 8	× 8 → 720

You need 720 g of mushrooms for **eight** people.

The number of grams of mushrooms is in direct proportion to the number of people.

Exercise N7.2 Grade C

1 How many times bigger than

a 12 is 60 **b** 3 is 24 **c** 12 is 84
d 20 is 90 **e** 18 is 27 **f** 9 m is 30 m
g 16 km is 50 km **h** £10 is £72 **i** 36 kg is 240 kg
j \$25 is \$215 **k** 10 mm is 18 mm **l** 220p is 300p?

(Give your answers to 1 dp as appropriate.)

2 What proportion of

a 15 is 5 **b** 20 is 10 **c** 10 cm is 3 cm
d 12 kg is 3 kg **e** 4 cm is 15 mm **f** £30 is £12
g 3 m is 50 cm **h** 40 km is 60 km **i** £8 is £16?

A02 Functional Maths

3 Sven works as a manager.
He is paid by the hour.
Copy and complete this table to help him work out his pay.

Hours worked	6	1	3	30	38	48
Pay (£)	£120					

4 In each of these questions the items are all the same price.

a 2 pizzas cost £7.50. What is the cost of 5 pizzas?
b 4 sweets cost £1.40. What is the cost of 17 sweets?
c 11 packets of seeds cost £17.49. What is the cost of 7 packets of seeds?
d 5 tennis balls cost £2.60. What is the cost of 12 tennis balls?
e 5 kg of apples cost £3.95. What is the cost of 12 kg of apples?
f There are 2640 megabytes of memory on 11 identical memory sticks. How much memory is there on 3 memory sticks?
g 30 protractors cost £3.30. What is the cost of 17 protractors?
h Del needs 10 litres of lemon drink to fill 25 cups. Work out how many litres of lemon drink are needed to fill 30 cups.
i Three 1 litre tins of paint cost a total of £23.85. Find the cost of seven of the 1 litre tins of paint.

Ratio and proportion

This spread will show you how to:

- Calculate missing amounts when two quantities are in direct proportion

Keywords
Direct proportion
Multiplicative inverse
Ratio

- You can calculate a **ratio** using division.

Example

Morgan is 150 cm tall. Peter is 180 cm tall.

a How many times taller than Morgan is Peter?
b What fraction of Peter's height is Morgan?

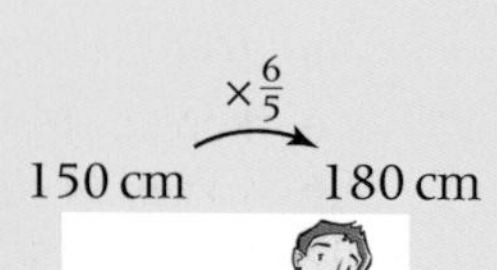

$\times\frac{5}{6}$

p.186

a Ratio of Peter's height to Morgan's height $= \frac{180}{150} = \frac{18}{15} = \frac{6}{5}$

Peter is $\frac{6}{5}$ or 1.2 times taller than Morgan.

b Ratio of Morgan's height to Peter's height $= \frac{150}{180} = \frac{15}{18} = \frac{5}{6}$

Morgan is $\frac{5}{6}$ of the height of Peter.

- When a problem involves two sets of numbers which are in **direct proportion** you can use ratios to solve it.

Example

Rio buys 144 cakes for a party with £80.
Gabby buys £150 of cakes at the same price.
How many cakes does Gabby buy?

Ratio of Gabby's money: Rio's money $= \frac{150}{80} = \frac{15}{8}$

Multiply Rio's number of cakes by this ratio:

$\times\frac{15}{8}$ (£80 buys 144 cakes) $\times\frac{15}{8}$
£150 buys 270 cakes

This is sometimes called the scaling method.

Exercise N7.3 — Grade C

In questions 1 and 2, give your answers to 2 dp as appropriate.

1 How many times bigger than
 a 15 is 30 **b** 10 m is 35 m
 c £6 is £21 **d** 12 km is 40 km?

2 What proportion of
 a 30 is 15 **b** 35 m is 10 m
 c £21 is £6 **d** 40 km is 12 km?

A02 Functional Maths

3 Stefan is looking at the vegetables he has planted in his garden. The broad beans are 50 cm tall. The sweetcorn is 100 cm tall.
 a How many times taller than the broad beans is the sweetcorn?
 b What proportion of the height of the sweetcorn are the broad beans?

4 Bobby and Wendy are comparing their weights. Bobby is 60 kg. Wendy is 48 kg.
 a How many times heavier than Wendy is Bobby?
 b What proportion of the weight of Bobby is Wendy?

5 Rudi and Colin are comparing their wages. Rudi earns £250 per week. Colin earns £400 per week.
 a How many times bigger is Colin's wage compared to Rudi's wage?
 b What proportion of Colin's wage does Rudi earn?

6 Copy and complete each of these direct proportion problems using the scaling method.
 a Trevor buys 4 kg of apples for £3.20. Gerry buys 7 kg of the same apples. How much does Gerry have to pay for his apples?

$\times\frac{7}{4}$ 4 kg costs £3.20 $\times\frac{7}{4}$
7 kg costs ______

 b Jermaine owns a sports equipment shop. He sells five tennis balls for £1.90. What is the cost of seven tennis balls?

×___ 5 tennis balls cost £1.90 ×___
7 tennis balls cost ______

 c Horace works for 9 hours a day. He is paid £76.05. He is paid the same amount for each hour he works. How much will he earn if he works for 20 hours?
 d 12 cans of tomato soup weigh 5040 g. What is the weight of 15 cans?

N7.4 Exchange rates

This spread will show you how to:

- Calculate exchange rates and solve problems involving exchange rates

Keywords
Rate
Ratio
Scale

- **A rate** is a way of comparing two quantities. It tells you how many units of one quantity there are compared to one unit of another quantity.

Example

Tariq is paid £374 a week. Each week he works for 44 hours.
What is his hourly rate of pay?

The rate of pay = £374 for every 44 hours

$= \frac{£374}{44}$ for every 1 hour

= £8.50 for every hour

= £8.50 per hour

- An exchange rate is a way of comparing two currencies. It tells you how many units of one currency there are compared to one unit of another currency.

Example

Katherine went to France. She changed £300 into €336.

a What was the exchange rate of euros to the pound?
b What was the exchange rate of pounds to the euro?

a Rate of euros to pounds $= \frac{€336}{£300}$

= 336 ÷ 300 euros for every pound

= 1.12 euros for every pound

Exchange rate is £1 = €1.12 (£1 will buy you €1.12).

b Rate of pounds to euros $= \frac{£300}{€336}$

= 300 ÷ 336 pounds for every euro

= 0.893 pounds for every euro

Exchange rate is €1 = £0.893 (€1 will buy you £0.893 or 89.3p).

Exercise N7.4 Grade D

Functional Maths

AO2

1 Work out the hourly rate of pay for each person.

Person	Money earned (£)	Hours worked (hours)	Hourly rate of pay (£ per hour)
Leonard	£210	30	
Pavel	£216	32	
Andy	£554.40	48	

2 Work out the rate for each of these.

a Wendy works for 3 hours. She gets paid £22.26.
What is her hourly rate of pay?

b Brian is a bricklayer. On average, he lays 680 bricks in 4 hours.
What is his hourly rate of laying bricks?

c Gustav travels in his car for 6 hours. He travels 330 km.
What is his average speed?

How far does he travel each hour?

3 Work out the exchange rate into pounds for each of these currencies.

Country	Number of pounds (£)	Number of other currency	Exchange rate(= £1)
Lithuania	£13	65 litas	£1 = ? litas
Namibia	£260	3003 dollars	£1 = ? dollars
Qatar	£82.40	519.12 riyals	£1 = ? riyals

4 Each of these people change amounts of money from pounds into euros. The exchange rate is £1 = €1.12.
Work out the number of euros each person receives.

Person	Amount (£)	Exchange rate (£1 = €1.12)	Amount (€)
Bernice	£240	£1 = €1.12	
Ingeborg	£720	£1 = €1.12	
Andrew	£6300	£1 = €1.12	

5 Each of these people change amounts of money from euros into pounds. The exchange rate is £1 = €1.12.
Work out the number of pounds each person receives.

Person	Amount (€)	Exchange rate (£1 = €1.12)	Amount (€)
Ann	€360	£1 = €1.12	
Raul	€768	£1 = €1.12	
Nicolas	€2448	£1 = €1.12	

You need to work out the exchange rate of pounds to the euro first.

N7.5 Percentage problems

This spread will show you how to:

- Calculate percentage increase and decrease using a range of methods
- Solve percentge problems

Keywords
Decrease
Increase
Percentage
Profit

You will often encounter percentages in real life.

p.92

- VAT (Value Added Tax) is a tax which is added to bills for services and purchases. VAT is always given as a **percentage**.

Example

Helen has a contract for her home phone.
She pays £38.29 for calls and a quarterly charge of £19.60.
VAT has to be added at 15%.
Calculate the cost of Helen's bill + VAT.

Estimate:

Bill = £40 + £20 = £60 VAT = 20% of £60 $= \frac{20}{100} \times 60$
$= 0.2 \times 60$
$= £12$

Bill + VAT = £60 + £12
= £72 estimated

Bill = £38.29 + £19.60
= £57.89

VAT = 15% of £57.89 $= \frac{15}{100} \times 57.89$
$= 0.15 \times 57.89$
$= 8.6835$
$= £8.68$

Bill + VAT = £57.89 + £8.68
= £66.57

The VAT rate in the UK in 2009 was 15%. It is subject to change by the Treasury.

You should always estimate your answers when working with a calculator to solve percentage problems.

Calculate VAT at 15% of the amount.
Add this to the original amount.

When people buy and sell things they try to sell for more than they paid.

- The difference between the selling price and cost price is called the **profit**
  A profit is normally written as a percentage of the cost price.

Example

Danii buys and sells protractors. She buys each protractor for 12p and sells them for 15p. What is her percentage profit?

Profit = 15p − 12p
= 3p

Calculate the profit.

Percentage profit $= \frac{3\text{p}}{12\text{p}}$

Write the profit as a fraction of the cost price.

$= \frac{3}{12}$
$= 0.25$
$= 25\%$

Express this fraction as a percentage.

Exercise N7.5

Grade C/D

Functional Maths

AO2

1 Calculate the selling price of each of these items. In each case give the answer to 2 decimal places.

Item	Cost price	% profit or % loss	Selling price
DVD	£8.50	Profit 20%	
DVD Player	£29.50	Loss 20%	
Pack 5 CD-RW	£4.60	Profit 73%	
USB hub 4-way	£21.30	Profit 32%	
TFT monitor	£185	Loss 4.6%	

2 Here are the prices of various objects without VAT. Calculate the real price of each item including VAT at a rate of 15%.

a

b

c

d

3 For each of these questions

i make an estimate

ii work out your answer using a suitable method

iii give your answer to an appropriate degree of accuracy.

a A carton of milk contains 580 ml. The size of the carton is increased by 28%. How much milk does it now contain?

b A piece of wood is 7.8 m long. It is reduced in length by 37%. What is the new length of the piece of wood?

c A lorry carries a load of sand that weighs 2.8 tonnes. The lorry loses 2.3% of its load as it travels. What mass of sand does the lorry now carry?

d A kitten weighs 300 g. After a month the kitten has grown by 73.2%. What is the new mass of the kitten?

4 Samir can buy a Games Console for one cash payment of £189, or pay a deposit of 24% and then 12 equal monthly payments of £12.
Which is the better option?
Explain and justify your answer.

Did you know?

Some things are exempt from VAT. This includes books bought by schools, as well as charity fundraising events.

N7.6 Interest

This spread will show you how to:

- Calculate percentage increase and decrease using a range of methods
- Calculate simple interest

Keywords
Appreciation
Decrease
Depreciation
Increase
Percentage
Simple interest

When you borrow money from a bank or building society you have to pay interest. When you save money, you earn interest.

People sometimes choose to have the interest they earn at the end of each year taken out of their bank account. This is called **simple interest**.

- To calculate simple interest, you multiply the interest earned at the end of the year by the number of years.

Example

Calculate the simple interest on investing £7650 for 3 years at an interest rate of 4.3%.

Interest each year = 4.3% of £7650 = $\frac{4.3}{100} \times 7650$
= 0.043×7650
= £328.95

Total amount of simple interest after 3 years = $3 \times$ £328.95
= £986.85

Don't forget to estimate:
4.3% of £7650
= 5% of £7000
= 10% of £7000 ÷ 2
= £700 ÷ 2
= £350

- Some items grow in value over time. This is called appreciation.
- Other items reduce in value over time. This is called depreciation.

Example

A company buys a van at a cost of £15 000.
Each year the van depreciates in value by 17%.
Work out the value of the van after 1 year.

End of Year 1 amount = (100 − 17)% of £15 000
= 83% × £15 000
= 0.83 × £15 000
= £12 450

Exercise N7.6 Grade C

A02 Functional Maths

1 **a** Louise puts £8750 into a bank account.
The bank pays interest of 7% on any money she keeps in the account for 1 year.
Calculate the interest received by Louise at the end of the year.

b Jermaine puts £45 800 into a savings account.
The account pays interest of 5.1% on any money he keeps in the account for 1 year. Calculate the interest received by Jermaine at the end of the year.

c Vicky takes out a loan of £24 800 for 1 year from a building society.
The building society charges interest on the loan of 7.6% for 1 year.
Calculate the total amount of money that Vicky must pay back at the end of the year.

2 Calculate the simple interest paid on £13 582

a at an interest rate of 5% for 2 years

b at an interest rate of 13% for 5 years

c at an interest rate of 4.9% for 7 years

d at an interest rate of 4.85% for 4 years.

3 Calculate the simple interest paid on

a an amount of £3950 at an interest rate of 10% for 2 years

b an amount of £6525 at an interest rate of 8.5% for 2 years

c an amount of £325 at an interest rate of 2.4% for 7 years

d an amount of £239.70 at an interest rate of 4.25% for 13 years.

A02 Functional Maths

4 **a** Nanette buys an antique wall covering for £430.
At the end of the year the wall covering has risen in value by 11%.
Calculate the new value of the wall covering.

b A new car costs £15 500.
After 1 year the car depreciates in value by 9%.
What is the value of the car after 1 year?

c A house is bought for £128 950.
After 1 year, the house increases in value by 16%.
What is the new value of the house?

N7.7 Proportional problems

This spread will show you how to:
- Calculate missing amounts when two quantities are in proportion
- Solve percentge problems

Keywords
Proportion
Ratio

You can use **ratio** and **proportion** to solve many problems.

Example

Here are the results of a survey to show the favourite colours chosen by students in a Reception class.

Draw a pie chart to show this information.

Colour	Frequency
Green	5
Red	6
Blue	7

p.246

The total number of people in the survey = 5 + 6 + 7 = 18 students.

$360 \div 18 = 20$

One person is represented by 20° on the pie chart.
The angle for green = 20 × 5 = 100°
The angle for red = 20 × 6 = 120°
The angle for blue = 20 × 7 = 140°

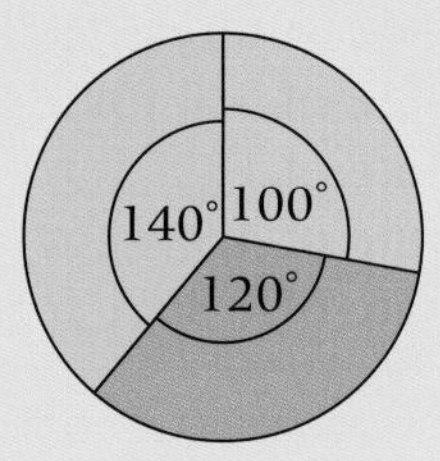

- You can calculate missing lengths when two objects are similar.

This means one object is an enlargement of the other object.

Example

These two triangles are similar. Calculate the length of XY.

p.210

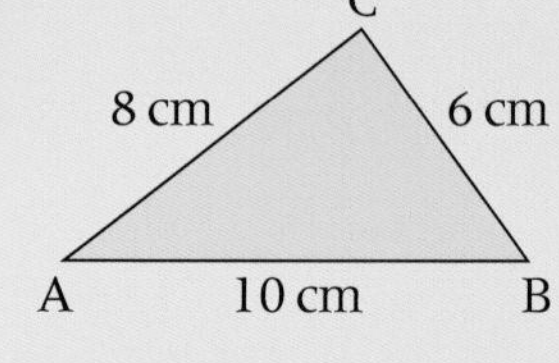

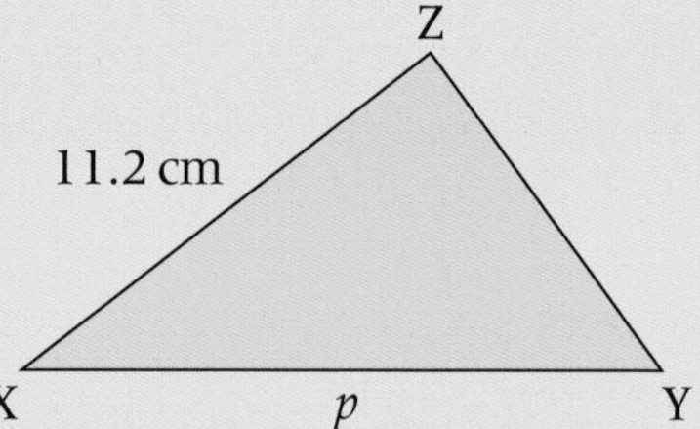

The corresponding sides of similar triangles are in proportion.
This means that the ratio of the corresponding sides is the same.

So

$$XY = AB \times \frac{11.2}{8}$$
$$= AB \times 1.4$$
$$= 10\,\text{cm} \times 1.4$$
$$= 14\,\text{cm}$$

AC $\xrightarrow{\times \frac{11.2}{8}}$ XZ
8 → 11.2

AB $\xrightarrow{\times \frac{11.2}{8}}$ XY
10 → p

Exercise N7.7 Grade C

AO2 Functional Maths

1 Work out each of these proportion problems.

a Alain buys 8 kg of apples for £4.40. Bernice buys 13 kg of the same apples. How much does Bernice have to pay for her apples?

b Material for stair carpets costs £45.16 for 4 metres. How much would 11 metres cost?

c 12 pencils cost £7.08. What is the cost of 18 pencils?

d 9 litres of super unleaded petrol cost £8.64. What is the cost of 35 litres of the petrol?

2 a Here are the results of a survey to show the favourite bands chosen by students in a class.
Draw a pie chart to show this information.

Colour	Frequency
Maximo Park	8
Red Hot Chili Peppers	3
Kaiser Chiefs	13

b Here are the results of a class survey to find how students in Class 11B travel to school.
Draw a pie chart to show this information.

Transport	Frequency
Walk	18
Bus	5
Cycle	2
Taxi/minibus	4
Car	1

3 a Change 360 cm into metres.

b Change 20 km into miles.

c Use the facts that 1 hour = 60 minutes; 1 minute = 60 seconds; 1 km = 1000 m; to change 50 km/h into metres per second.

d Use the facts that 1 hour = 60 minutes; 1 minute = 60 seconds; 1 km = 1000 m; 1 mile = 1.6 km; to change a speed of 8 m/s (metres per second) into miles per hour.

e Change 140 cm^2 into m^2.

4 For this pair of similar triangles, calculate the length of XY and YZ.

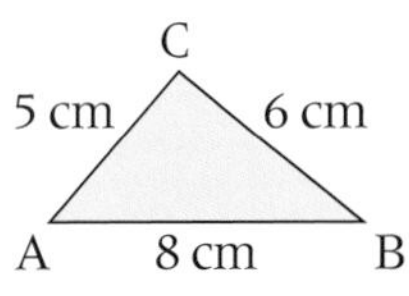

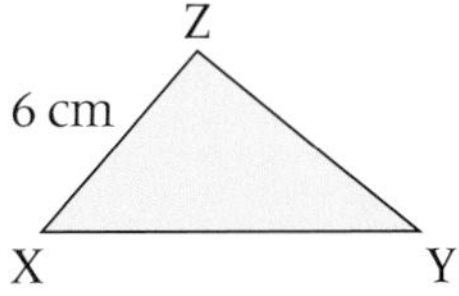

Challenge

5 a In a sale all prices are reduced by 20%. Germaine buys a book for £5.60 in the sale. What was the original price of the book?

b Monique has a pay rise of 6%. Her new wage is £371 per week. What was her original wage before the pay rise?

Find the percentage of the original price, then the value of 1%, then the value of 100%.

N7

Summary

Check out

You should now be able to:

- Express a proportion as a fraction, decimal or percentage
- Solve problems involving ratio and proportion
- Solve problems involving percentages

Worked exam question

Here are the ingredients for making cheese pie for 6 people.

Cheese pie for 6 people

180 g flour
240 g cheese
80 g butter
4 eggs
160 ml milk

Bill makes a cheese pie for 3 people.

a Work out how much flour he needs. (2)

Jenny makes a cheese pie for 15 people.

b Work out how much milk she needs. (2)

(Edexcel Limited 2008)

a

$180\text{ g} \div 2 = 90\text{ g}$

OR

$180\text{ g} \div 6 = 30\text{ g}$
$30\text{ g} \times 3 = 90\text{ g}$

You should show your calculation whichever method you use.

b

$160\text{ ml} \div 6 \times 15 = 400\text{ ml}$

OR

$160\text{ ml} \div 2 \times 5 = 400\text{ ml}$

OR

$160\text{ ml} \times 2.5 = 400\text{ ml}$

Exam questions

A02

1 Michael buys 3 files.

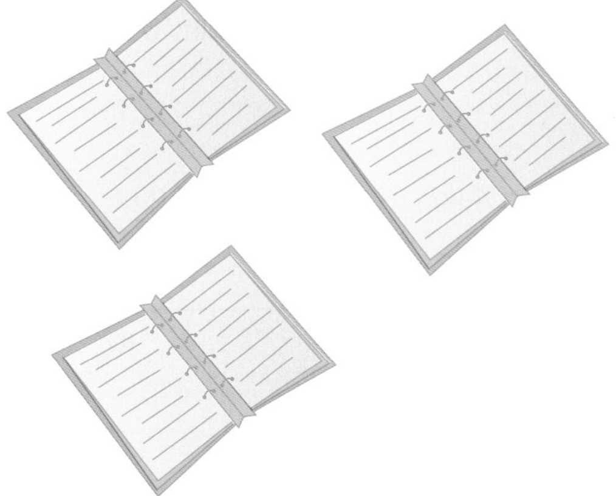

The total cost of these 3 files is £5.40
Work out the total cost of 7 of these files. (3)

(Edexcel Limited 2005)

A02

2 A garage sells British cars and foreign cars.
The ratio of the number of British cars sold to the number of foreign cars sold is 2 : 7
The garage sells 45 cars in one week.

a Work out the number of British cars the garage sold that week. (2)

A car tyre costs £80 plus VAT at $17\frac{1}{2}$%.

b Work out the total cost of the tyre. (3)

(Edexcel Limited 2008)

A02

3 Jamie goes on holiday to Florida.
The exchange rate is £1 = 1.70 dollars.

He changes £900 into dollars.

a How many dollars should he get? (2)

After his holiday Jamie changes 160 dollars back to pounds.
The exchange rate is still £1 = 1.70 dollars.

b How much money should he get?
Give your answer to the nearest penny. (2)

(Edexcel Limited 2007)

D4 Averages and charts

Introduction

Over 30% of the numbers in everyday use begin with the digit 1.
'Benford's law', as it is called, makes it possible to detect when a list of numbers has been falsified. This is particularly useful in fraud investigations for detecting 'made-up' entries on claim forms and expense accounts, and it has also been used in investigating the 2009 Iranian elections.

What's the point?

Recognising patterns in numbers and measures helps us to understand them, and also helps us to make sense of a world that is increasingly swamped with data.

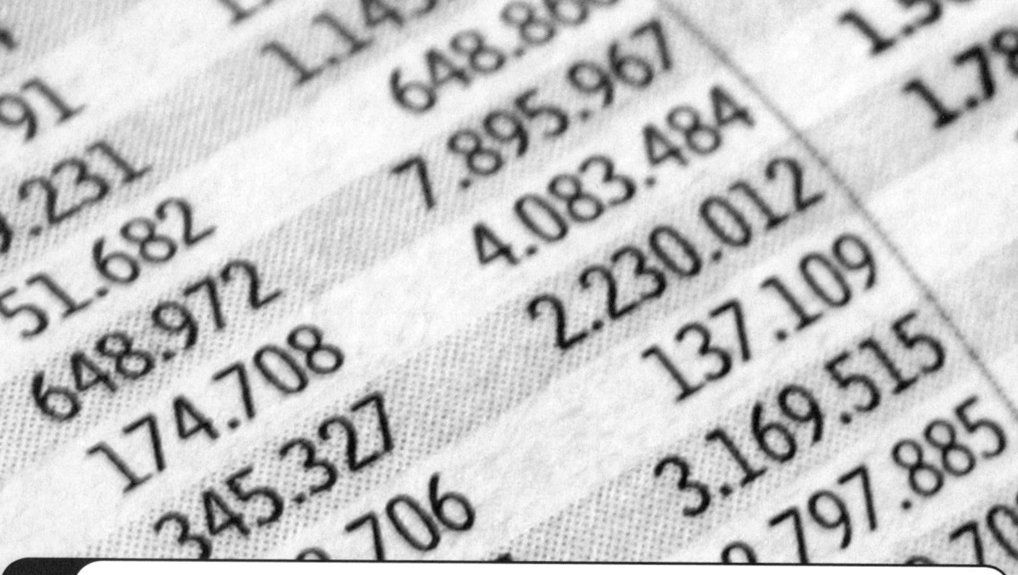

Check in

1 Order these numbers in size, smallest first.

a 6.5, 8, 4, 5.5, 7

b 3.2, 2.3, 3.4, 4.3, 4.2, 2.4

c 8.6, 7.5, 9.1, 7.9, 8.3

2 List the ten numbers recorded in each frequency table.

a

Number	Frequency
5	0
6	2
7	1
8	2
9	5

b

Number	Frequency
100	2
101	1
102	2
103	0
104	5

3 Find the missing angles.

a

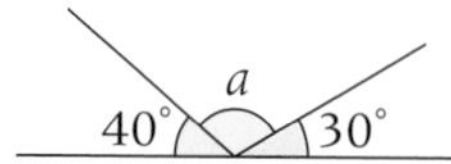

b

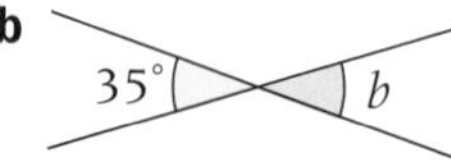

Orientation

What I should know		What I will learn		What this leads to
D2 + 3	→	- Distinguish between discrete and continuous data - Calculate the mean, median, mode and range - Estimate statistics for grouped data - Compare distributions and make inferences - Interpret a wide range of graphs and diagrams, including scatter graphs	→	Careers involving statistics include environmental statistics, medical statistics, social policy, actuarial science ...

Rich task

What is the most likely time during a football game for a team to score a goal? It is frequently stated by football commentators that teams are most likely to concede a goal within five minutes of scoring a goal themselves. Is this true? Investigate and write a report on your results.

Alternatively, ...

Investigate scoring patterns in a sport of your choice.

D4.1 Types of data and the range

This spread will show you how to:

- Recognise the difference between discrete and continuous data

Keywords

Continuous data
Discrete data
Range
Spread

- Numerical data can be discrete or continuous.

- **Discrete data** can only take exact values.

The shoe size $7\frac{1}{4}$ does not exist.

Shoe sizes (in the UK) could be 7, $7\frac{1}{2}$, 8, $8\frac{1}{2}$, 9.
There are no values between them.

- **Continuous data** can take any value within a given range.

The values of continuous data depend on the accuracy of the measurement.

Temperature can take any value between 21°C and 22°C.

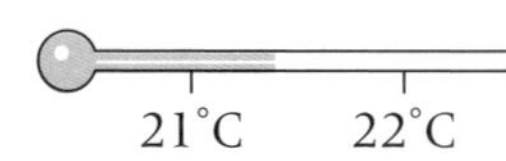

Continuous data cannot be measured exactly.

A height of 171 cm has been given to the nearest centimetre.

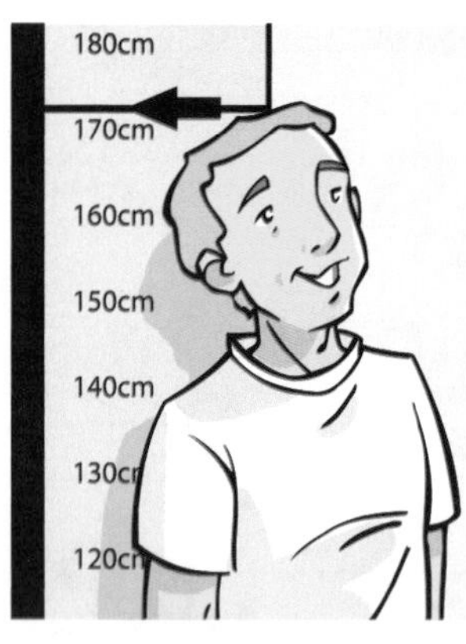

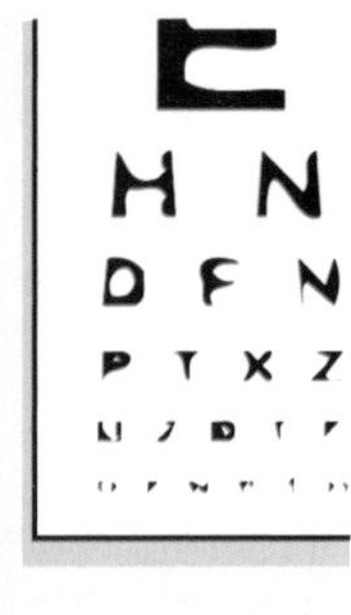

- You can measure the **spread** of a set of data by calculating the **range**.
- The **range** is the highest value minus the lowest value.

Example

There are eight classes in Year 10 of a school. The numbers of students that were absent from each class were 3, 1, 4, 8, 4, 2, 5, 1.

a Calculate the range of absences.
b State whether the data is discrete or continuous.

a Range = highest value − lowest value
= 8 − 1
= 7

b Discrete − you cannot have $7\frac{1}{2}$ students.

Exercise D4.1

Grade F

1 Decide whether each of these are discrete or continuous data.

a number of people in a room
b number of cars in a car park
c length of a piece of wood
d thickness of a piece of wood
e amount of water in a pan
f cost of buying a DVD
g time taken to walk to the shops
h weight of a piece of cheese
i number of tomatoes on a plant
j temperature in a fridge
k score on a dice
l your age

2 Calculate the range for each set of numbers.

a 0, 0, 1, 2, 2, 2, 3, 4, 4, 5, 5
b 6, 7, 8, 8, 8, 9, 9, 9, 10
c 32, 32, 33, 35, 41
d 48, 48, 48, 49, 49
e 85, 86, 87, 88, 89, 90, 91, 92
f 5, 6, 8, 4, 7, 9, 5, 6, 7
g 31, 34, 18, 25, 31, 26, 35, 27
h 17, 17, 15, 16, 21, 22, 20, 20
i $3\frac{1}{2}$, $3\frac{1}{2}$, $4\frac{1}{2}$, $4\frac{1}{2}$, $3\frac{1}{2}$, 5, 3, $3\frac{1}{2}$
j £3.00, £1.25, £4.70, £2.52, 85p

3 Calculate the range of these sets of numbers.

a

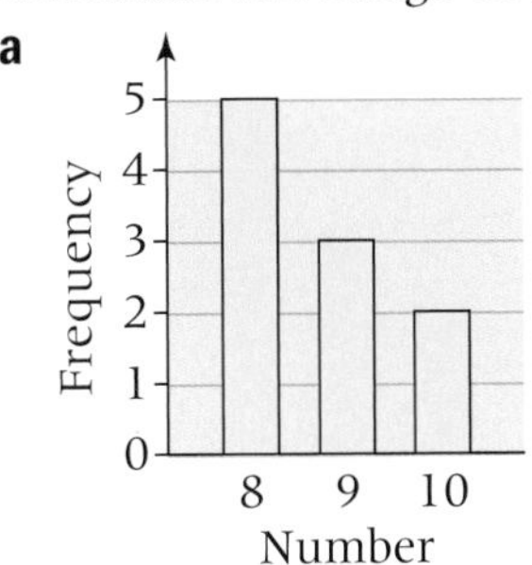

b

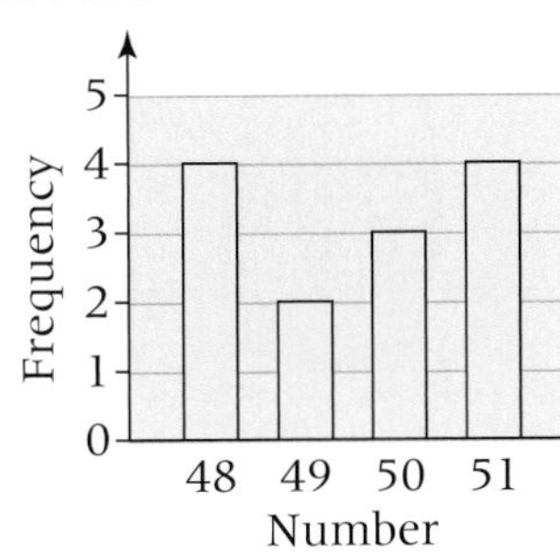

c

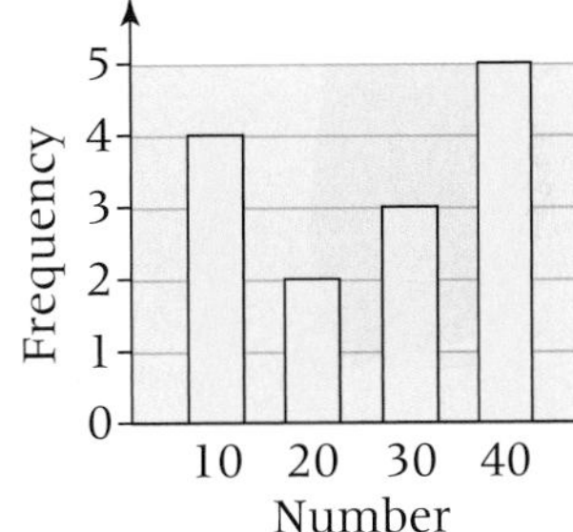

4 The weights, in kilograms, of 10 students are

[illegible]

Calculate the range of the weights. State the units of your answer.

Functional Maths AO2

5 The mean monthly temperature, in °F, is shown for Athens and Madrid.

	Jan	Feb	Mar	Apr	May	Jun	Jul	Aug	Sep	Oct	Nov	Dec
Athens	50	50	54	59	67	75	81	81	75	67	59	53
Madrid	42	45	49	53	60	69	76	76	69	58	49	44

a Calculate the range of temperatures for Athens.
b Calculate the range of temperatures for Madrid.
c Use your results to compare the temperatures in the two cities.

Problem AO3

6 The range of these numbers is 17.
Find two possible values for the unknown number.

34	40	25	?

D4.2 Averages

This spread will show you how to:

- Calculate the mean, median, and mode for sets of data

Keywords
Average
Mean
Median
Modal value
Mode
Representative value

The **average** 15-year-old boy in the UK is 172 cm tall.
This does not suggest that every boy's height is 172 cm, but that 172 cm is used to represent the height of all the 15-year-old boys in the UK.

- You can represent a set of data with one number, called the average.

There are three different ways to find a typical or **representative value** for a set of data.

- The mean of a set of data is the total of all the values divided by the number of values.
- The mode is the value that occurs most often.
- The median is the middle value when the data is arranged in order.

The mode is sometimes called the **modal value**.

Example

Calculate the mean, mode and median of
8, 3, 8, 7, 5

Mean $= (8 + 3 + 8 + 7 + 5) \div 5$
$= 31 \div 5$
$= 6.2$

Mode $= 8$ as 8 occurs most often

For the median, first arrange the numbers in numerical order:

3 5 7 8 8
↑
middle

Median $= 7$

To calculate the median of 7, 7, 8, 9, 10, 14: The middle numbers are 8 and 9. Median $= (8 + 9) \div 2 = 8.5$

Exercise D4.2 Grade F

1 **a** Calculate the mean of these five numbers.
3, 3, 8, 1, 5
b Copy the bar chart to illustrate the five numbers.
c Mark the mean on your diagram with a horizontal line.
d Show how the rectangles above the mean can be moved to give five bars with equal heights.

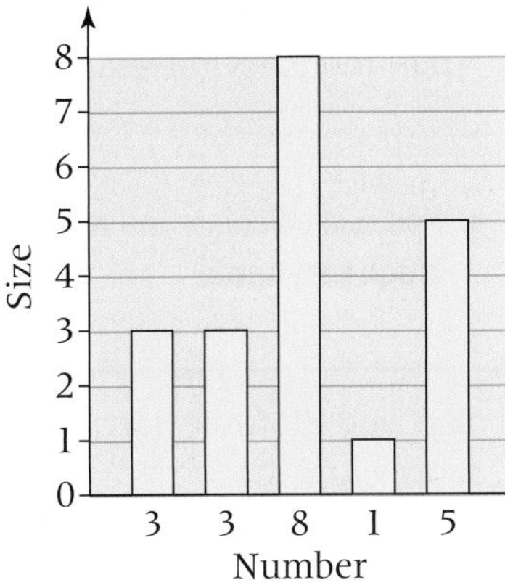

Functional Maths AO2

2 Forty vehicles are recorded as they pass, and their type is noted.

C C C T B B C C B C
T B B B C C C C C B
B C C C C T C B B C
C C B C C C C T C C

B = Bus
T = Tram
C = Car

a Copy and complete the frequency table for the vehicles.

Vehicle	Tally	Frequency
Bus (B)		
Tram (T)		
Car (C)		

The mode is sometimes called the modal value.

b State the modal vehicle.

3 Five men were asked to count the loose change in their pockets.
The results were
£2.47 £1.12 38p £2.15 85p
a Arrange the amounts in order, smallest first.
b Find the median amount of money. State the units of your answer.

4 The seven-day weather forecast for a warm week in August is shown.

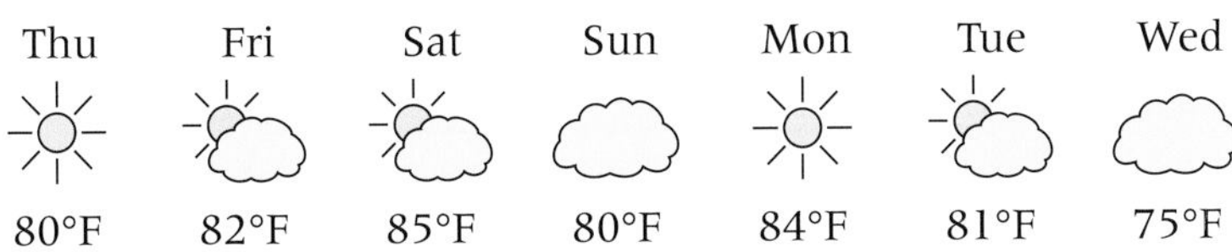

Temperatures are here given in degrees Fahrenheit (°F). Nowadays, temperatures are mostly quoted in degrees centigrade (°C).

Calculate
a the mean temperature
b the modal temperature
c the median temperature.

Problem AO3

5 Six numbers are arranged in order.
The median of these numbers is 5.5.
a Calculate the unknown number.
b Calculate the mean of the six numbers.

3.2	4.5	?	6.0	7.6	8.5

D4.3 Charts and tables

This spread will show you how to:

Use frequency tables for discrete and grouped data

Keywords
Frequency table
Mean
Median
Mode
Range

- You can calculate the **mean**, **mode**, **median** and **range** for discrete data from a **frequency table**.

Example

Ten people took part in a golf competition. Their scores are shown in the frequency table.

Calculate the mean, mode, median and range of the scores.

Score	Frequency
67	1
68	(4)
69	3
70	1
71	(1)

4 people scored 68.

1 person scored 71.

The results can be written in numerical order.

67, 68, 68, 68, 68, 69, 69, 69, 70, 71

Mean = 687 ÷ 10 = 68.7
Median = (68 + 69) ÷ 2 = 68.5
Mode = 68 (occurs 4 times)
Range = 71 − 67 = 4

Note:
You can use a scientific calculator to work out the mean of a small data set. You should work out how to do this on your own calculator.

Alternatively, you can calculate the mean, mode, median and range directly from the frequency table without rewriting the numbers.

Score	Frequency	Score × Frequency
67	1	67
68	4	(272)
69	3	207
70	1	70
71	1	71
	10	(687)

272: 68 + 68 + 68 + 68 or 68 × 4.

687: The total of all the scores of the 10 golfers.

Mean = 687 ÷ 10 = 68.7
Median = (5th value + 6th value) ÷ 2 = (68 + 69) ÷ 2 = 68.5
Mode = 68 as 68 occurs the most often.
Range = 71 − 67 = 4

The mode is 68, not 4.

Exercise D4.3

Grade E/F

Functional Maths AO2

1 The numbers of flowers on eight rose plants are shown in the frequency table.

a List the eight numbers in order of size, smallest first.

b Calculate the mean, mode, median and range of the eight numbers.

Number of flowers	Tally	Frequency
3	||||	4
4	||	2
5	||	2

2 The number of days that 25 students were present at school in a week are shown in the frequency table.

a List the 25 numbers in order of size, smallest first.

b How many students were present for 5 days of the week?

c Calculate the mean, mode, median and range of the 25 numbers.

Number of days	Tally	Frequency
0		0
1	||||	4
2	𝍸 |	6
3	||	2
4	𝍸	5
5	𝍸 |||	8

3 Twenty people decide to buy some raffle tickets.
Some of the people buy more than one ticket.
The table gives the information.
Calculate the

a mean **b** mode

c median **d** range.

Number of tickets	Tally	Number of people
1	𝍸 |	6
2	𝍸	5
3	||||	4
4	𝍸	5

4 This tetrahedral dice is rolled 50 times.
The scores are shown in the frequency table.

Calculate the

a mean **b** mode

c median **d** range.

Score	Tally	Frequency
1	𝍸 𝍸	10
2	𝍸 𝍸 |	11
3	𝍸 𝍸 |||	13
4	𝍸 𝍸 𝍸 |	16

Functional Maths AO2

5 The test results are shown for a class of 20 students.

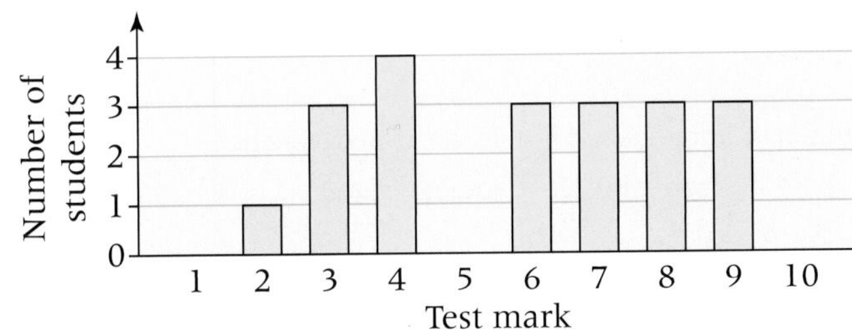

a Copy and complete the frequency table to illustrate these results.

Mark	1	2	3	4	5	6	7	8	9	10
Number of students	0	1								

b Calculate the mean, mode, median and range for the 20 marks.

D4.4 Comparing data

This spread will show you how to:

Compare distributions and make inferences

Keywords
Compare
Mean
Median
Mode
Range
Spread

- You can **compare** sets of data using the mean, mode, median and range.

Example

A team of 7 girls and a team of 8 boys do a sponsored run for charity. The distances the girls and boys ran are shown.

Girls

Distance (km)	Frequency
1	3
2	2
3	1
4	1
5	0

Boys

3, 5, 5, 3, 4, 4, 5, 5

all distances in kilometres

a Construct a similar frequency table for the boys' distance.

b By calculating the mean, median and range, compare each set of data.

a Boys

Distance (km)	Tally	Frequency	Distance × Frequency
1		0	0
2		0	0
3	||	2	6
4	||	2	8
5	||||	4	20
		8	37

b Girls

Mean $= (3 + 4 + 3 + 4 + 0) \div 7 = 14 \div 7 = 2$

Median $= 2$ (the 4th distance)

Range $= 4 - 1 = 3$ (highest value – lowest value)

Boys

Mean $= 34 \div 8 = 4.25$

Median $= (4 + 5) \div 2 = 9 \div 2 = 4.5$ (the mean of the 4th and 5th distances)

Range $= 5 - 3 = 2$ (highest value – lowest value)

The mean and median show the boys ran further on average than the girls.

The range shows that the girls' distances were more **spread** out than the boys' distances.

Exercise D4.4

Grade E

Functional Maths

A02

1 The number of bottles of milk delivered to two houses is shown in the table.

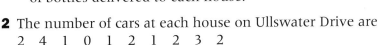

	Sat	Sun	Mon	Tues	Wed	Thur	Fri
Number 45	2	0	1	1	1	1	1
Number 47	4	0	2	2	2	2	2

a Calculate the range for Number 45 and Number 47.

b Use your answers for the range to compare the number of bottles delivered to each house.

2 The number of cars at each house on Ullswater Drive are

2 4 1 0 1 2 1 2 3 2

a Copy and complete the frequency table.

Number of cars	Tally	Number of houses
0		
1		
2		
3		
4		

b Calculate the mean, mode and median number of cars for Ullswater Drive. The mean, mode and median number of cars at each house on Ambleside Close are

Mean	Mode	Median
0.7	0	1

c Use the mean, mode and median to compare the number of cars on Ullswater Drive and Ambleside Close.

3 The number of days of rain each month in a particular year in Ireland and Spain is recorded.

	Jan	Feb	Mar	Apr	May	Jun	Jul	Aug	Sep	Oct	Nov	Dec
Ireland	27	22	27	24	23	24	25	24	26	26	26	28
Spain	11	10	10	11	10	7	2	5	6	11	11	12

a List each set of numbers in order, smallest first.

b Calculate the median days of rain for Ireland and for Spain.

c Using your answers for the median, compare the two sets of data.

d Calculate the range for each set of data.

e Using your answers for the range, compare the number of rainy days in Ireland and Spain.

D4.5 Grouped data

This spread will show you how to:

Estimate the mean for grouped data

Keywords
Class interval
Continuous data
Estimated mean
Grouped data
Mid-values
Modal class

The number of students in a class and their absences are shown.

Score	Frequency
0 to 4	9
5 to 9	8
10 to 14	(5)
15 to 19	6
20 to 24	2

5 students had either 10, 11, 12, 13 or 14 absences.

You cannot tell the **exact** number of absences in this frequency table.

Therefore you cannot calculate the exact mean, mode or median.

- For grouped data in a frequency table, you can calculate
  - the **estimated mean**
  - the **modal class**
  - the **class interval** in which the median lies.

Example

The times taken for 10 people to run a race are shown.
Use the frequency table to find
the estimated mean,
the modal class
and the class interval in which the median lies.

Time (t miutes)	Mid-value	Frequency	Mid-value × Frequency
$40 < t \leqslant 50$	45	1	45
$50 < t \leqslant 60$	55	2	110
$60 < t \leqslant 70$	65	5	325
$70 < t \leqslant 80$	75	2	150
	Total	10	630

Use $< \leqslant$ for **continuous data**. $40 < t \leqslant 50$ means more than 40, but less than or equal to 50.

By using the **mid-values**, the 10 times are taken as
45, 55, 55, 65, 65, 65, 65, 65, 75, 75.

Estimated mean = 630 ÷ 10
= 63 minutes

Modal class = $60 < t \leqslant 70$ as this class has the highest frequency

The median is given by the times of the 5th and 6th runners, which are within the class interval $60 < t \leqslant 70$.

45 + 55 + 55 + 65 + 65 + 65 + 65 + 65 + 75 + 75 = 630

Exercise D4.5 Grade C

Functional Maths

A02

1 The weights, to the nearest kilogram, of 25 men are shown.

69 82 75 66 72
73 79 70 74 68
84 63 69 88 81
73 86 71 74 67
80 86 68 71 75

a Copy and complete the frequency table.

Weight (kg)	Tally	Number of men
60 to 64		
65 to 69		
70 to 74		
75 to 79		
80 to 84		
85 to 89		

Note:
You can use a scientific calculator to work out the mean of grouped general data. You should find out how to do this on your calculator.

b State the modal class.
c Find the class interval in which the median lies.

2 The speeds of 10 cars in a 20 mph zone are shown in the frequency table.

Speed (mph)	Mid-value	Number of cars	Mid-value × Number of cars
11 to 15		1	
16 to 20		6	
21 to 25		2	
26 to 30		1	

a Calculate the number of cars that are breaking the speed limit.
b Copy the frequency table and calculate the mid-values for each class interval.
c Complete the last column of your table and find an estimate of the mean speed.

3 The heights, in centimetres, of some students are shown in the frequency table.

Height (cm)	Number of students
$140 < h \leqslant 150$	3
$150 < h \leqslant 160$	9
$160 < h \leqslant 170$	8
$170 < h \leqslant 180$	10

a Calculate the total number of students shown in the table.
b Find the class interval in which the median lies.
c State the modal class.
d Find an estimate for the mean height.

D4.6 Diagrams and charts 2

This spread will show you how to:

Interpret a wide range of graphs and diagrams and draw conclusions

Keywords

Bar chart
Bar-line chart
Pictogram
Pie chart
Sector

You can interpret data from a variety of diagrams.

Pictograms use symbols to represent the size of each category.

p.246

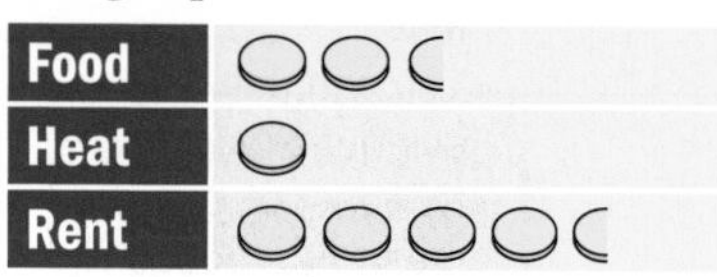

Key: ◯ represents £10

Bar charts use horizontal or vertical bars to represent the frequencies.

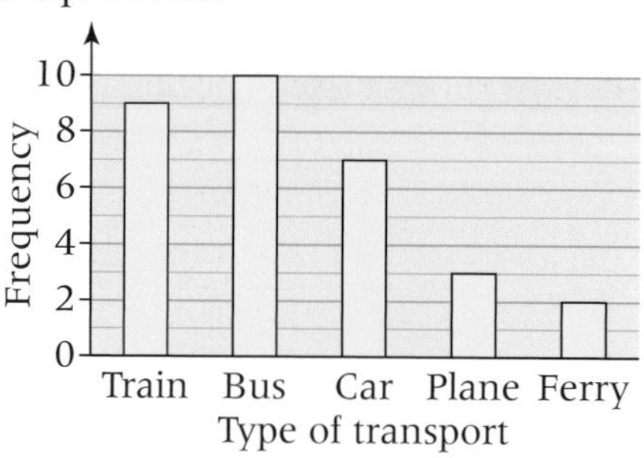

Notice the gaps between the bars.

Bar-line charts use vertical lines to represent numerical data.

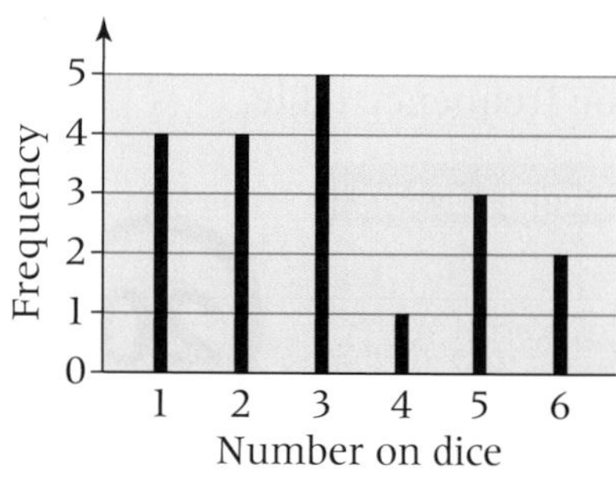

Pie charts use sectors of a circle to represent the size of each category.

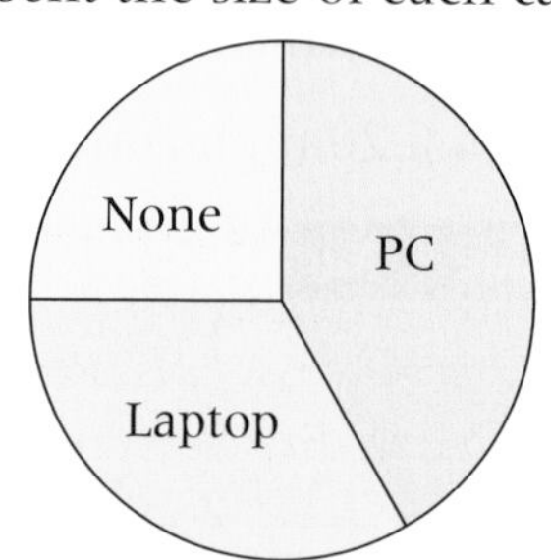

The size of the **sector** angle is proportional to the frequency.

Example

The pie chart shows 24 hours in the life of a Y11 student. The student spends 8 hours sleeping.
Calculate

a the value of x

b the fraction of time spent sleeping

c the percentage of time spent watching TV

d the number of hours for each category.

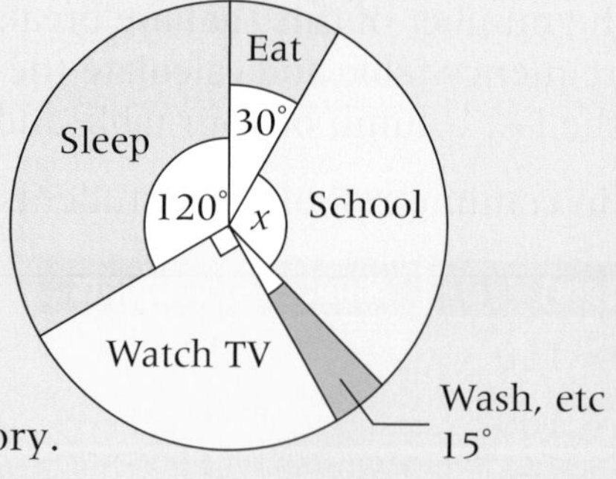

a $360° - (120° + 30° + 15° + 90°) = 105°$

b $\frac{120}{360} = \frac{1}{3}$

c $\frac{90}{360} = \frac{1}{4} = 25\%$

d 8 hours represent 120°
1 hour represents 15°

Eat	$30 \div 15 = 2$ hours
School	$105 \div 15 = 7$ hours
Wash etc	$15 \div 15 = 1$ hour
Watch TV	$90 \div 15 = 6$ hours

The angles at a point add to 360°.

Check:
$2 + 7 + 1 + 6 + 8 = 24$ hours

Exercise D4.6 — Grade E

Functional Maths — A02

1 A survey of the number of lorries passing through four villages each day is shown in the pictogram.

a Calculate the number of lorries passing daily through

i Abbey **ii** Batty **iii** Cotton

iv Ditty **v** all four villages taken together.

b Which village should be considered for a bypass?

Abbey	
Batty	
Cotton	
Ditty	

Key: represents 8 lorries

2 Travel insurance prices are shown on the bar chart.

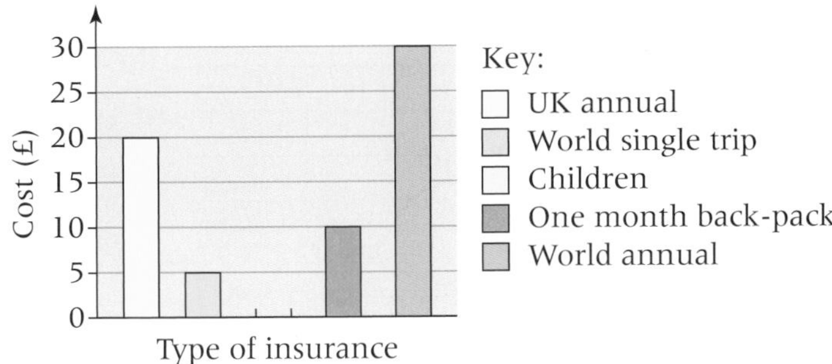

Did you know?

The greater the risks to yourself, the more expensive the travel insurance. This includes sporting holidays and travel to war zones.

a State the cost of

i annual insurance in the UK

ii one month back-packing insurance.

b Who is offered free travel insurance?

c Suzie plans to make four trips abroad during the year.
She can either buy World Single Trip insurance each time or World Annual insurance.
Which is her cheaper option? Show your working.

3 The bar-line chart shows the number of tickets bought by 10 people.

a State the number of people who bought

i 5 tickets **ii** 4 tickets.

b Calculate the total number of tickets that were bought by the 10 people.

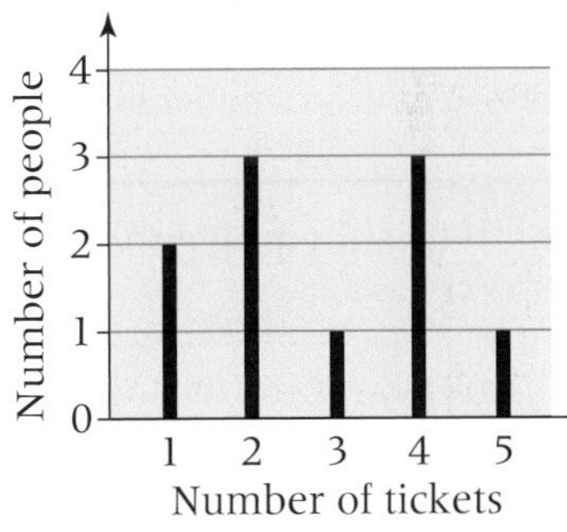

Problem — A03

4 The pie chart shows the year groups for 120 children.
Calculate

a the value of x

b the angle that represents one child

c the number of children in

i Year 4 **ii** Year 5 **iii** Year 6.

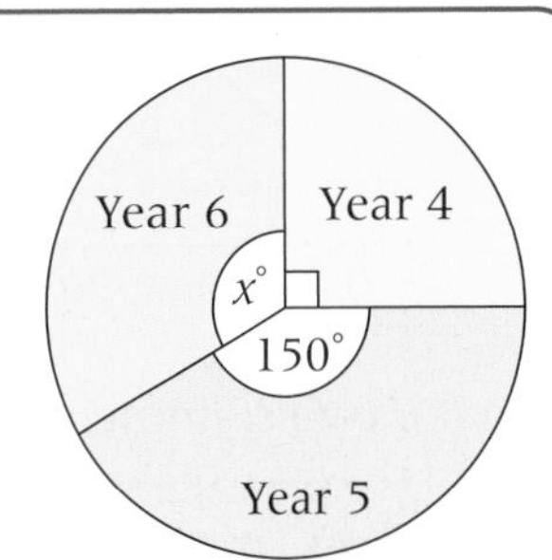

Diagrams and charts 3

This spread will show you how to:

- Interpret a wide range of graphs and diagrams and draw conclusions
- Compare distributions and make inferences
- Look at data to find patterns and exceptions

Keywords
Comparative bar chart
Frequency polygon
Grouped
Histogram
Modal

p.248

You can interpret **grouped** continuous data from a **histogram** and a **frequency polygon**.

The lengths of eight pieces of string are shown in the histogram.

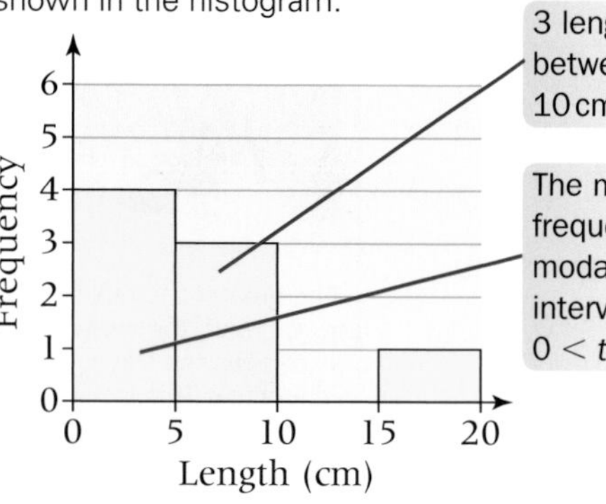

3 lengths are between 5 and 10 cm.

The most frequent or modal class interval is $0 < t \leqslant 5$.

The same eight lengths are shown in a frequency polygon.

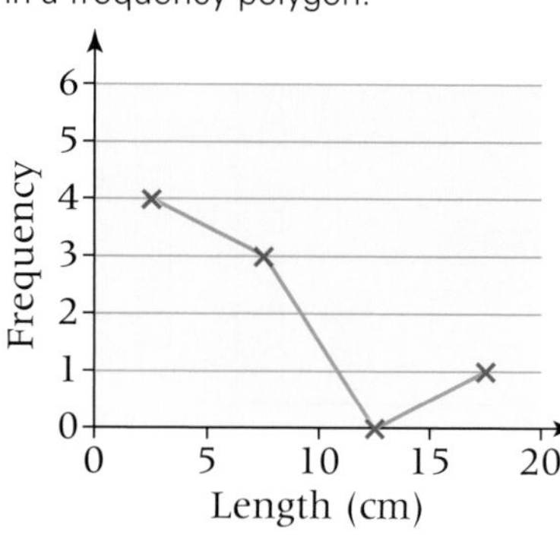

The points are plotted at the midpoints of the class intervals.

- You can interpret two sets of data from a **comparative bar chart**.

This shows the attendances of boys and girls on Wednesday and Friday.

Overall attendance is the same on both days.
Girls' attendance is better than boys'.

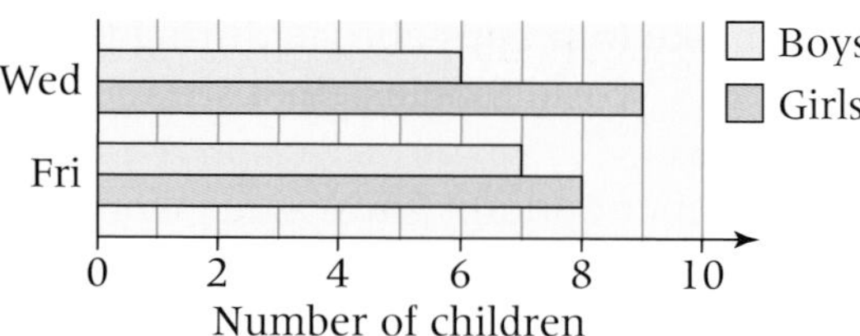

Example

The frequency polygons show the age distribution for the population of two villages.

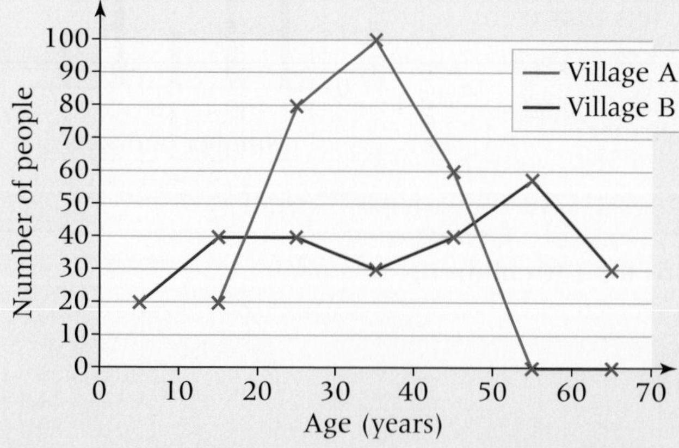

Make two statements to compare the distribution of ages in the two villages.

The ages in village B are more spread out.
The modal age is younger in village A than in village B.
Village A: 35 years   Village B: 55 years

Exercise D4.7 Grade D

Functional Maths

A02

1 The bar chart shows the number of minutes per day that men and women spent on household chores in 2000/01.
Which household chore did

a men and **b** women spend

i the most time doing

ii the least time doing?

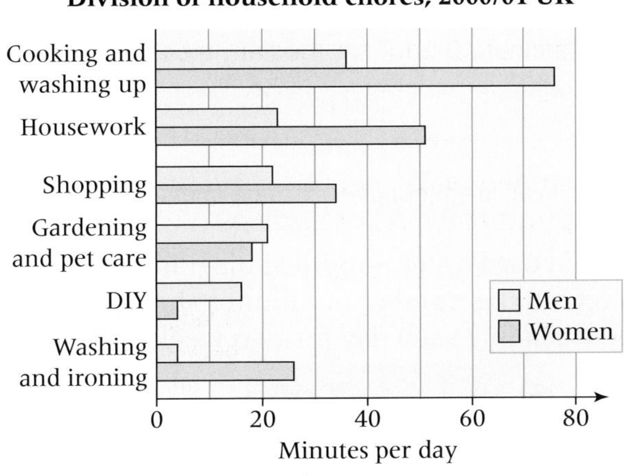

2 The populations of four countries in 1994 and 2004 are shown in the bar chart.

a State the population of

i Bangladesh in 1994

ii India in 2004.

b Which country shows the largest increase from 1994 to 2004?

c Which country's population is approximately the same in 1994 and 2004?

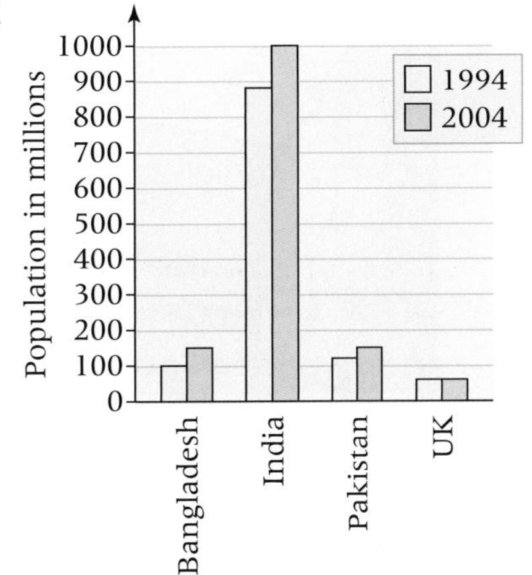

3 The histogram shows the best distances, in metres, that athletes threw a javelin in a competition.

a State the number of athletes who threw the javelin

i between 65 and 70 metres

ii between 80 and 85 metres.

b In which class interval was the winner?

c What is the modal class interval?

d Calculate the total number of athletes who threw a javelin.

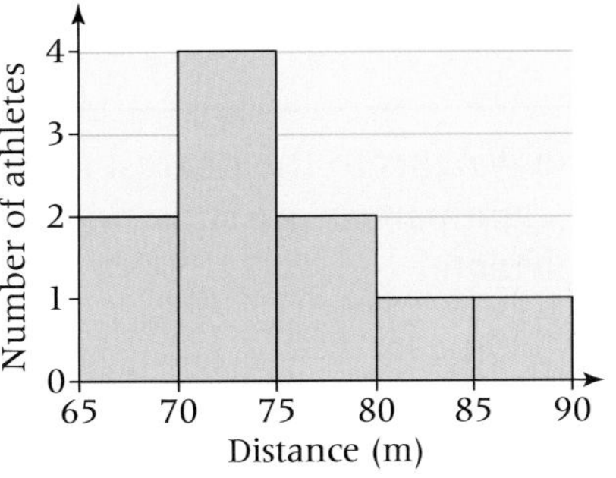

4 The lengths of the long jumps for men and women are shown in the frequency polygon.
Make two statements to compare the distributions of the length of long jumps for the men and women.

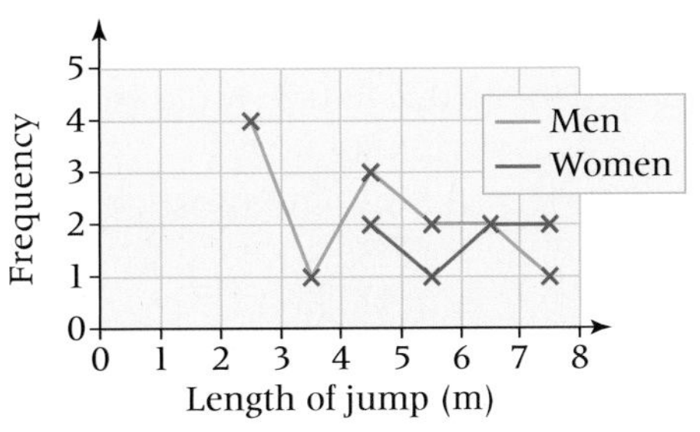

D4.8 Stem-and-leaf diagrams 2

This spread will show you how to:

- Interpret a wide range of graphs and diagrams and draw conclusions
- Calculate the mean, median, mode and range of small sets of discrete data.

Keywords
Ordered
Stem-and-leaf diagram

- You can interpret numerical data from a **stem-and-leaf diagram**.

Maggie used a stem-and-leaf diagram to record the number of minutes she spent reading each day for two weeks.

This stem-and-leaf diagram is **ordered** as the data is in numerical order.

stem	leaf
90	7
80	3 4 9
70	0 4 8
60	3 3 6
50	6 9
40	3 8

This means 97. (90 | 7)

This means 70. (70 | 0)

Key: | 80 | 7 | means 87

Always give the key.

The numbers in this stem-and-leaf diagram are

43, 48, 56, 59, 63, 63, 66, 70, 74, 78, 83, 84, 89, 97.

- You can calculate the mean, mode, median and range from a stem-and-leaf diagram.

Example

The weights to the nearest tenth of a kilogram, of eight parcels are shown in the diagram.
Calculate

a the mean
b the mode
c the median
d the range.

3.0	0
2.0	5
1.0	3 4 9
0.0	7 8 8

Key: | 1.0 | 3 | means 1.3 kg

a Mean = $(0.7 + 0.8 + 0.8 + 1.3 + 1.4 + 1.9 + 2.5 + 3.0) \div 8$
$= 1.55$ kg

b Mode = 0.8 kg, the most common weight

c Median = $(1.3 + 1.4) \div 2$ (2 middle numbers)
$= 1.35$ kg

d Range = $3.0 - 0.7$ (highest value − lowest value)
$= 2.3$

Exercise D4.8

Grade D

Functional Maths

AO2

1 The attendances of the nine Year 11 classes one Friday afternoon are shown in the stem-and-leaf diagram.

10	0 6
20	2 2 4 6 8 9
30	0

Key:

20	4

means 24 students

a Write out the nine attendances in numerical order, smallest first.

b Calculate

i the mean **ii** the mode

iii the median **iv** the range.

2 The test marks of 20 students are shown.

31 17 43 19 25 12 7 40 25 21

11 32 37 25 15 9 18 41 23 17

0	
10	
20	
30	
40	

Key:

20	5

means 25 marks

a Copy and complete the stem-and-leaf diagram.

b Redraw the diagram to give an ordered stem-and-leaf diagram.

c Calculate

i the mean **ii** the mode

iii the median **iv** the range.

3 The times, to the nearest second, for 15 athletes to run 800 m are shown in the stem-and-leaf diagram.

110	4 6 9
120	0 0 4 5 6 7
130	1 5 6
140	0 2 5

Key:

120	5

means 125 seconds

Calculate

a the mean

b the mode

c the median

d the range.

4 The speedway scores of a team during one season are shown in the stem-and-leaf diagram.

30	3 4
40	1 1 4 4 5 6 7 9 9 9
50	0 2 7
60	0

Key:

40	5

means 45 points

a Calculate the modal score.

b Calculate the number of scores shown in the diagram.

c If one score is chosen at random, calculate the probability that it is 50 or over.

5 Ten competitors achieve the following distances, measured in centimetres, in the High Jump and the Long Jump.

High Jump

180	1 3 2 5
190	1 6 7 7
200	3 7

Key:

190	6

means 196 cm

Long Jump

730	7 8
740	0 3 6 7 9
750	0 2

Key:

740	3

means 743 cm

a One competitor was injured and could not take part in one of the events. Which event did he miss?

b By calculating the range for each event, make a comparison between the two different events.

D4.9 Scatter graphs 2

This spread will show you how to:

- Have a basic understanding of correlation, including lines of best fit

Keywords
Correlation
Line of best fit
Relationship
Scatter graph
Variable

- You can interpret two sets of data that have been drawn on a **scatter graph**.

If the points are roughly in a straight line, there is a **relationship** or **correlation** between the two **variables**.

Positive correlation

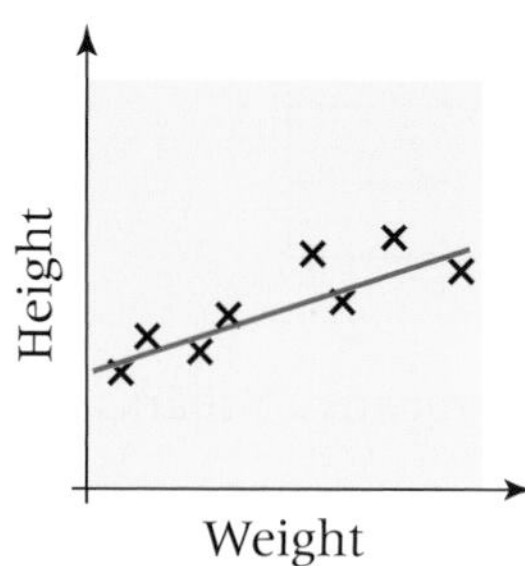

As height increases, weight also increases.

Negative correlation

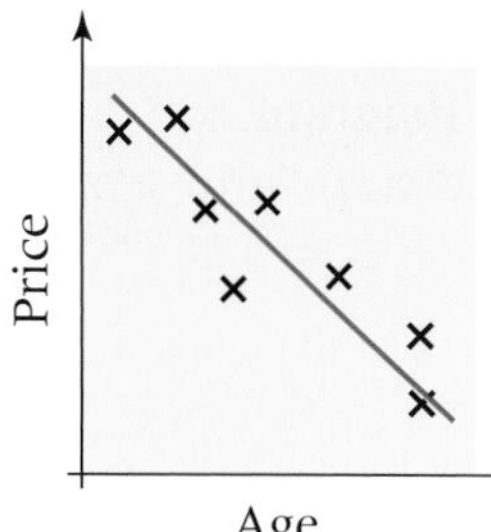

As the age of a car increases, the price decreases.

No correlation

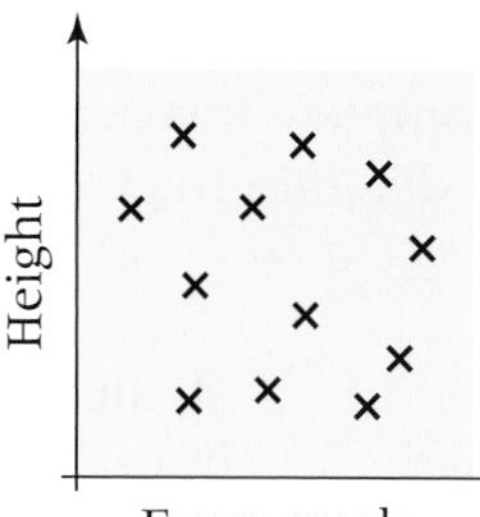

There is no linear relationship between height and exam mark.

The red straight line is the **line of best fit.**

You cannot draw a line of best fit for no correlation.

If the points lie close to the line of best fit, the correlation is strong.

Example

The scatter graph shows the number of goals scored by 21 football teams in a season plotted against the number of points gained.

a Describe the relationship between the goals scored and the number of points.

b Describe the goals and points for team A.

c If a team scored 45 goals, how many points would you expect it to have?

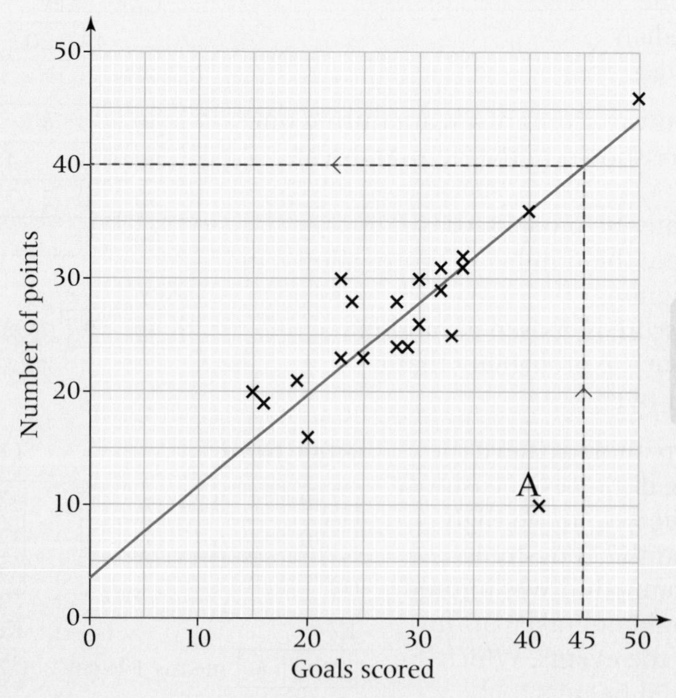

A line of best fit does not have to pass through (0, 0).

a Positive correlation or the more goals scored the more points gained.

b Scored lots of goals, but has gained very few points.

c See the graph: 45 goals gives 40 points.

Exercise D4.9 Grade C

1 Describe the type of correlation for each scatter graph.

a

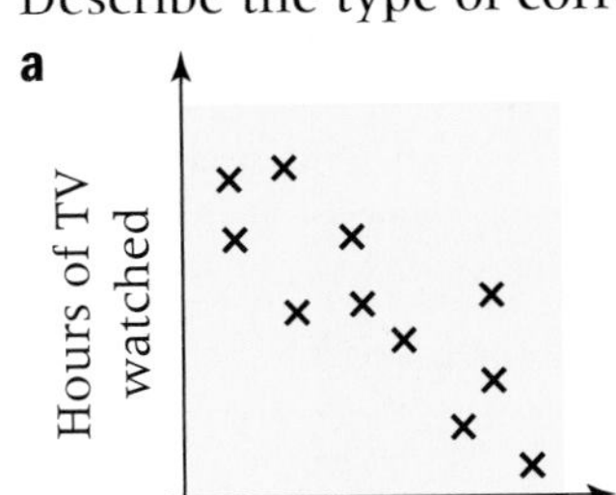

b

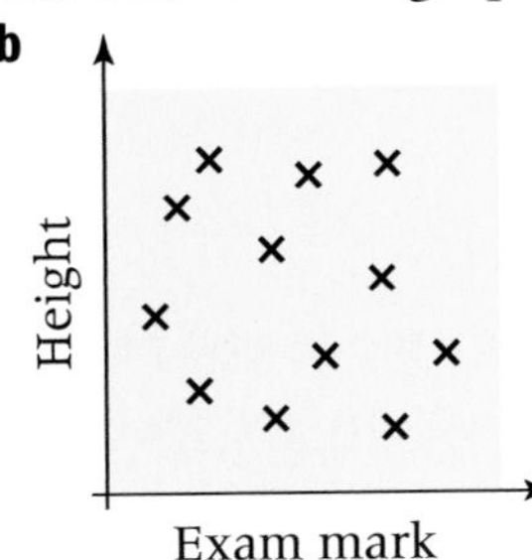

c

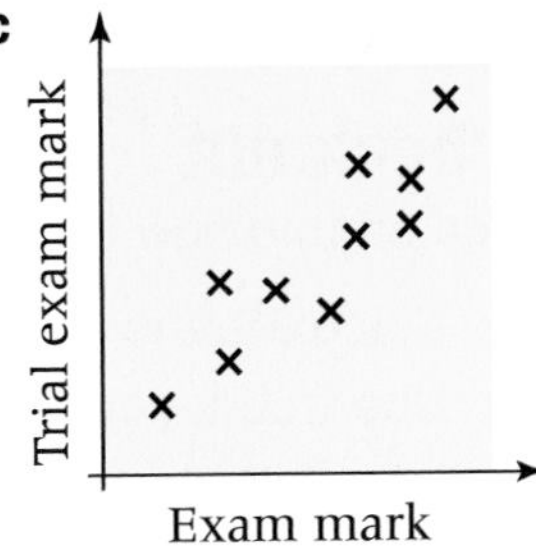

2 Describe the points A, B, C, D and E on each scatter graph.

a

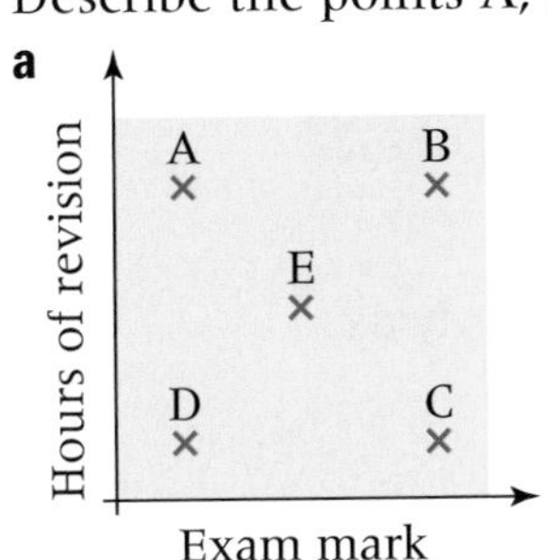

b

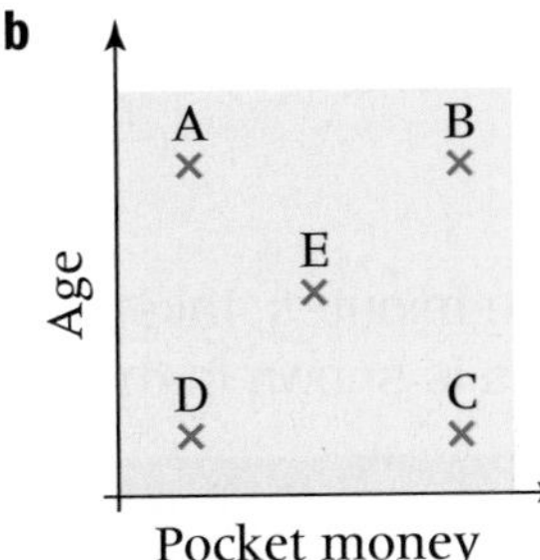

c

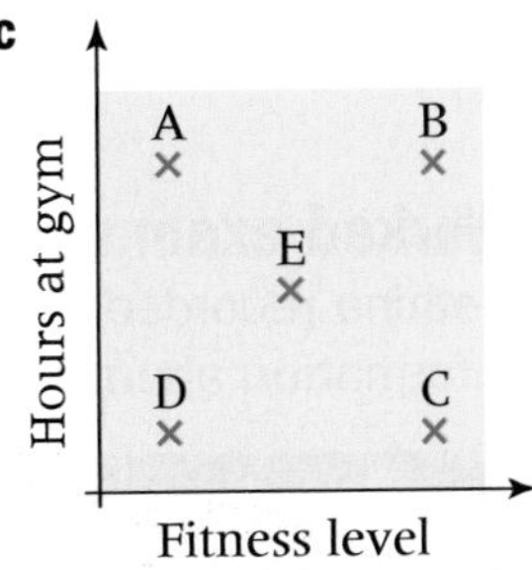

Functional Maths

AO2

3 The graph shows the marks in two papers achieved by nine students.
Use the line of best fit to estimate

a the Paper 2 mark for a student who scored 13 in Paper 1

b the Paper 1 mark for a student who scored 23 in Paper 2.

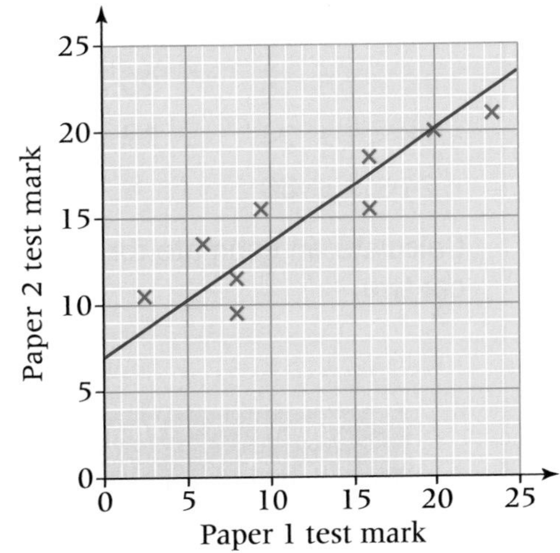

4 The table shows the age and diameter, in centimetres, of trees in a forest.

Age (years)	10	27	6	22	15	25	11	16	21	19
Diameter (cm)	20	78	9	65	38	74	25	44	59	50

a Draw a scatter diagram to show the information.

b State the type of correlation between the age and diameter of the trees.

c Draw a line of best fit.

d If the diameter of a tree is 55 cm, estimate the age of the tree.

Use 2 cm to represent 10 centimetres on the horizontal axis, numbered 0 to 80.
Use 2 cm to represent 5 years on the vertical axis, numbered 0 to 30.

D4 Summary

Check out

You should now be able to:

- Calculate the mean, median, mode and range for sets of data
- Use frequency tables for discrete and grouped data
- Interpret a range of graphs and diagrams
- Compare distributions and make inferences
- Look at data to find patterns and exceptions
- Understand correlation, including lines of best fit

Worked exam question

Sethina recorded the times, in minutes, taken to repair 80 car tyres. Information about these times is shown in the table.

Time (t minutes)	Frequency		
$0 < t \leq 6$	15		
$6 < t \leq 12$	25		
$12 < t \leq 18$	20		
$18 < t \leq 24$	12		
$24 < t \leq 30$	8		

Calculate an estimate for the mean time taken to repair each car tyre. (4)

(Edexcel Limited 2009)

Time (t minutes)	Frequency	Mid-value	F × Mv
$0 < t \leq 6$	15	3	45
$6 < t \leq 12$	25	9	225
$12 < t \leq 18$	20	15	300
$18 < t \leq 24$	12	21	252
$24 < t \leq 30$	8	27	216
	80		1038

Frequency × mid-value

Use consistent mid-values.

An estimate of the mean = $1038 \div 80 = 12.975$ minutes
$= 13.0$ minutes (to 1 d.p.)

Show this division calculation.

Exam questions

1 20 students scored goals for the school hockey team last month.
The table gives information about the number of goals they scored.

Goals scored	Number of students	
1	9	
2	3	
3	5	
4	3	

a Write down the modal number of goals scored. (1)
b Work out the range of the number of goals scored. (1)
c Work out the mean number of goals scored. (3)

(Edexcel Limited 2004)

A02

2 The scatter graph shows the Science mark and the Maths mark for 15 students.

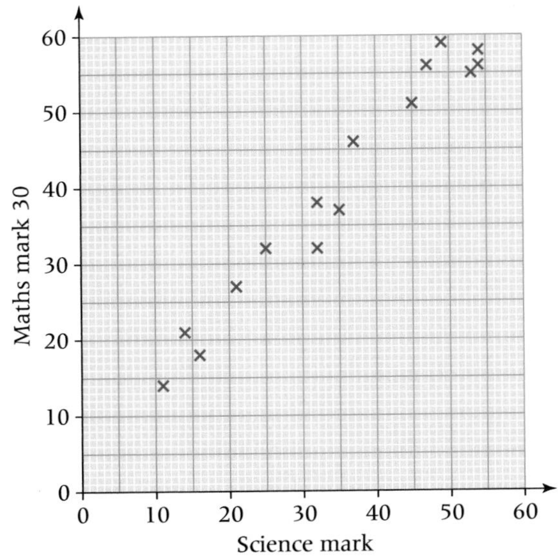

Natalie took her tests late.
Her Science mark was 42.
Estimate her Maths mark.
Give a reason for your answer. (3)

A7

Equations 2

Introduction

Scientists are currently trying to understand and respond to the effects of global warming on the environment. These effects are modelled by complex mathematical functions, and involve a large amount of data on a wide range of variables.

What's the point?

If we can understand the causes and effects of global warming, we can predict more accurately what is likely to happen, and begin to take steps to reduce its harmful effects. None of this would be possible without algebra.

Check in

1 Using values of x from -2 to 2, draw the graph of $y = 2x - 3$. (Remember to complete a table of values first).

2 Substitute the following values into the expression $x^3 - 2x$.

a 2 **b** 2.1 **c** -3.2

3 Solve the equations

a $2x + 3 = 17$ **b** $3(x - 4) = 18$

Orientation

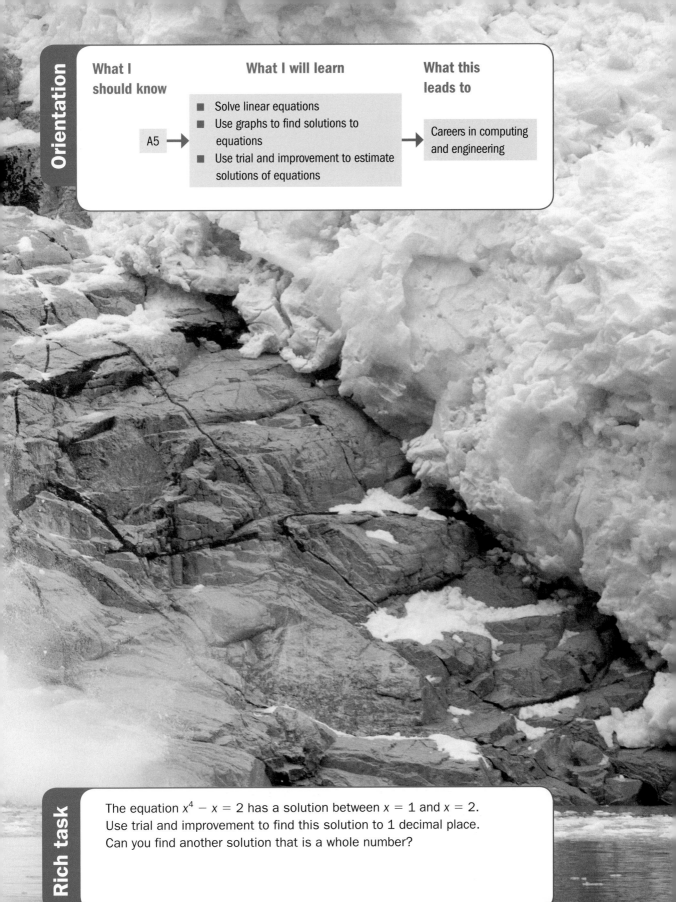

What I should know		What I will learn		What this leads to
A5	→	■ Solve linear equations ■ Use graphs to find solutions to equations ■ Use trial and improvement to estimate solutions of equations	→	Careers in computing and engineering

Rich task

The equation $x^4 - x = 2$ has a solution between $x = 1$ and $x = 2$.
Use trial and improvement to find this solution to 1 decimal place.
Can you find another solution that is a whole number?

A7.1 More equations with brackets

This spread will show you how to:

- Solve equations involving brackets

Keywords
Brackets
Expand

This square pattern is made from rectangular tiles.
Each tile has length $x + 3$ and width x.

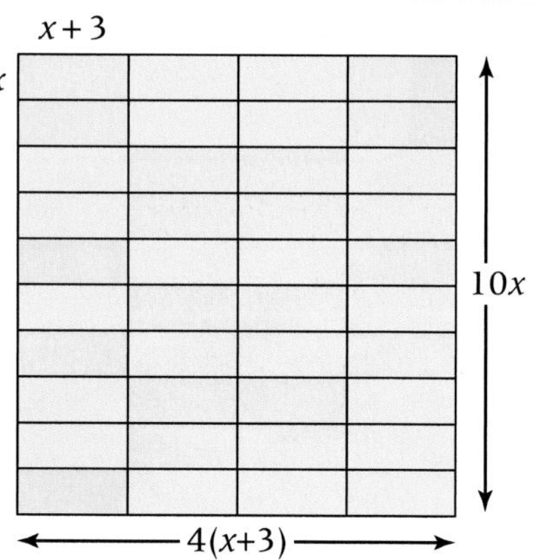

The pattern is 10 tiles wide: $10x$
The pattern is 4 tiles long: $4(x + 3)$

The pattern is a square, so length = width: $4(x + 3) = 10x$

Expand the **brackets**: $4x + 12 = 10x$

Subtract $4x$ from both sides: $12 = 10x - 4x$
$12 = 6x$

Divide both sides by 6: $2 = x$
So $x = 2$.

The dimensions of the square are 20 units long by 20 units wide.

p.266

- To solve equations with the unknown on both sides and brackets:
  - Expand the brackets
  - Use the balance method.

Example

Solve

a $2(y + 4) = 4y$

b $6r - 2 = 4(r + 3)$

a $2(y + 4) = 4y$ Expand the brackets.
$2y + 8 = 4y$ Subtract 2y from both sides.
$8 = 4y - 2y$
$8 = 2y$ Divide both sides by 2.
$4 = y$

b $6r - 2 = 4(r + 3)$
$6r - 2 = 4r + 12$ Subtract $4r$ from both sides.
$6r - 4r - 2 = 4r - 4r + 12$
$2r - 2 = 12$ Add 2 to both sides.
$2r = 12 + 2$
$2r = 14$ Divide both sides by 2.
$r = 7$

Exercise A7.1

Grade C/D

1 Solve these equations.

a $2(r+6)=5r$ **b** $6(s-3)=12s$

c $4(2t+8)=24t$ **d** $5(v-1)=6v$

2 Solve these equations.

a $2(a+5)=7a-5$ **b** $3(b-2)=5b-2$

c $2(c+6)=5c-3$ **d** $3d+8=2(d+2)$

3 Solve these equations.

a $3(2x-4)=7x-18$ **b** $2(3y+2)=5y-2$

c $4(2z+1)=6z+15$ **d** $-4(6m+1)=-17m-18$

4 Solve these equations.

a $2(e+3)=4e-1$ **b** $4f+3=2(f+2)$

c $4(2g+1)=6g+1$ **d** $3(2h+3)=5h+8$

AO3 Problems

5 **a** Choose one expression from each set of cards.

b Write them as an equation:
Expression from set 1 = expression from set 2

c Solve your equation to find the value of x.

d Repeat for different pairs of expressions.

Set 1

$2(x+3)$	$4(2x-1)$	$3(4x+1)$

Set 2

$3x-2$	$4x+1$	$8x-3$

6 The triangle and the square have equal perimeter.

a Write an expression for the perimeter of the triangle.

b Write an expression for the perimeter of the square.

c Use your two expressions to write an equation.

d Solve your equation to find the value of x.

7 **a** Write an expression for the area of square A.

b Square B and square A have equal area.
Write an equation in x to show this.

c Solve your equation to find the value of x.

AO2 Functional Maths

8 A blouse has m buttons. A shirt has $m+2$ buttons.

a Write an expression for the number of buttons on four blouses.

b Write an expression for the number of buttons on three shirts.

c Three shirts have the same number of buttons in total as four blouses.
Write an equation and solve it to find the value of m.

d How many buttons are there on a shirt?

A7.2 Equations with simple fractions

This spread will show you how to:

- Solve equations involving fractions and negative signs

Keywords
Fraction

Problems in algebra often contain fractions.

Tom and Jas share a packet of sweets.
Tom has half the sweets.
He counts them.
There are 15.

How many sweets were there in the packet?

To solve this problem, you multiply 15×2 to get 30.

You can write the problem in algebra like this: $\frac{x}{2} = 15$

Using the balance method, you do the same to both sides: $\frac{x}{2} \times 2 = 15 \times 2$

$x = 30$

$x \div 2 = \frac{x}{2}$

The inverse of $\div$ is $\times$

- You can solve equations involving **fractions** using the balance method.

Example

Solve

a $\frac{x}{4} = -3$ **b** $\frac{x}{3} + 2 = 7$ **c** $\frac{x+3}{2} = 5$ **d** $\frac{5-2x}{3} = 7$

a
$$\frac{x}{4} = -3$$
$$4 \times \frac{x}{4} = -3 \times 4$$
$$x = -12$$

b
$$\frac{x}{3} + 2 = 7$$
$$\frac{x}{3} + 2 - 2 = 7 - 2$$
$$\frac{x}{3} = 5$$
$$3 \times \frac{x}{3} = 5 \times 3$$
$$x = 15$$

c
$$\frac{x+3}{2} = 5$$
$$2 \times \frac{x+3}{2} = 5 \times 2$$
$$x + 3 = 10$$
$$x = 10 - 3$$
$$x = 7$$

d
$$\frac{5-2x}{3} = 7$$
$$3 \times \frac{5-2x}{3} = 7 \times 3$$
$$5 - 2x = 21$$
$$5 - 2x - 5 = 21 - 5$$
$$-2x = 16$$
$$\frac{-2x}{-2} = \frac{16}{-2}$$
$$x = -8$$

Exercise A7.2 Grade C

1 Solve these equations.

a $\frac{x}{3} = 3$ **b** $\frac{m}{4} = -2$ **c** $\frac{-n}{3} = 6$ **d** $\frac{m}{5} = 4$

2 Find the value of the unknown in each of these equations.

a $\frac{s}{3} + 5 = 8$ **b** $4 - \frac{t}{2} = 1$ **c** $\frac{u}{5} + 7 = 5$ **d** $16 = \frac{v}{4} + 13$

3 Solve these equations.

a $\frac{2x}{3} + 5 = 9$ **b** $\frac{3y}{2} - 5 = 4$ **c** $3 - \frac{2z}{5} = -3$ **d** $\frac{3q}{2} + 5 = -7$

4 Solve these equations.

a $\frac{x + 5}{3} = 2$ **b** $\frac{x - 3}{4} = 2$ **c** $\frac{x + 9}{2} = -4$ **d** $\frac{10 - x}{4} = 1$

5 Solve these equations.

a $\frac{2x + 1}{5} = 5$ **b** $\frac{3x - 2}{4} = 4$ **c** $\frac{11 - 2x}{3} = -1$ **d** $\frac{31 - 3x}{4} = 4$

Problems

A03

6 I think of a number.
I divide my number by 4 and add 6.

a Write an expression for 'I divide my number by 4 and add 6'.
Use n to represent the number.

$\frac{n}{\square} + \square$

b My answer is 10.
Using your expression from part **a**, write an equation to show this.

Expression **a** = 10

c Solve your equation to find the number, n.

7 Use the method in question **6** to write an equation and find the missing number in these problems.

a I think of a number.
I divide it by 3 and subtract 4.
The answer is 7.

b I think of a number.
I half it and add 8.
The answer is 3.

8 The perimeter of this equilateral triangle is $2x + 6$.

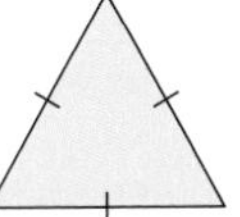

a Write an expression for the length of one side of the triangle.

Length of side = $\frac{\text{perimeter}}{3}$

b The length of one side of the triangle is 8cm.
Find the value of x.

9 The perimeter of this square is $4 + x$.
The length of one side is 10 cm.
Write an equation and solve it to find the value of x.

A7.3 Finding solutions from graphs

This spread will show you how to:

- Plot straight line graphs
- Use graphs to find solutions to equations

Keywords
Solution
Satisfy

- All the points on a graph line fit (or satisfy) the equation of the line.
  You could extend the graph an infinite distance.

You draw the graph line right to the edge of the grid, to show it continues.

- You can read x-and y-values from a graph.

Example

Here is the graph of $y = 3x - 2$.

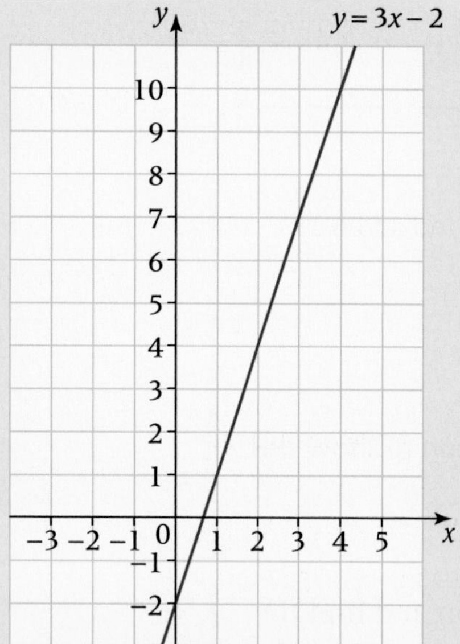

a Find the value of y when $x = \frac{1}{2}$.
b Find the value of x when $y = 7$.

a Draw a vertical line from $x = \frac{1}{2}$ to the graph.
Draw a horizontal line from the graph to the y-axis.
Read off the value of y.
When $x = \frac{1}{2}$, $y = -\frac{1}{2}$.

b Draw a horizontal line from $y = 7$ to the graph.
Draw a vertical line from the graph to the x-axis.
Read off the value of x.
When $y = 7$, $x = 3$.

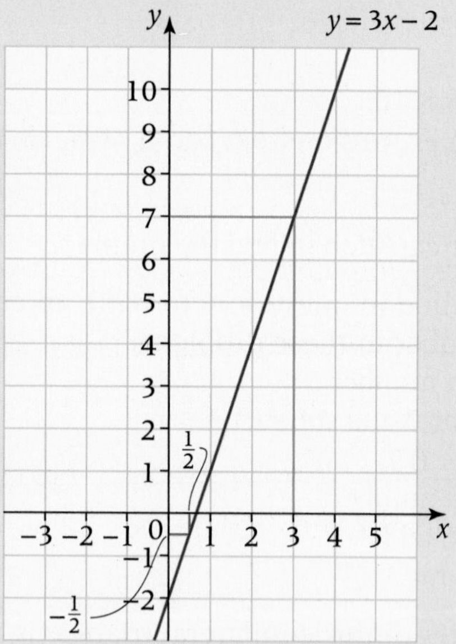

- You can use a graph to find **solutions** to equations.

Example

For each equation, **describe** how you could draw a graph to find the value of x.

a $2x + 6 = 10$.

b $-5x + 1 = 11$.

a Draw the graph of $y = 2x + 6$.
Read off the x-value when $y = 10$.

You do not need to draw the graph.

a Draw the graph of $y = -5x + 1$.
Read off the x-value when $y = 11$.

Exercise A7.3 Grade B/C

1 Here is the graph of $y = -2x + 3$.
Use the graph to find

a the value of y when $x = \frac{1}{2}$

b the value of y when $x = -2\frac{1}{2}$

c the value of x when $y = -1$

d the value of x when $y = 9$.

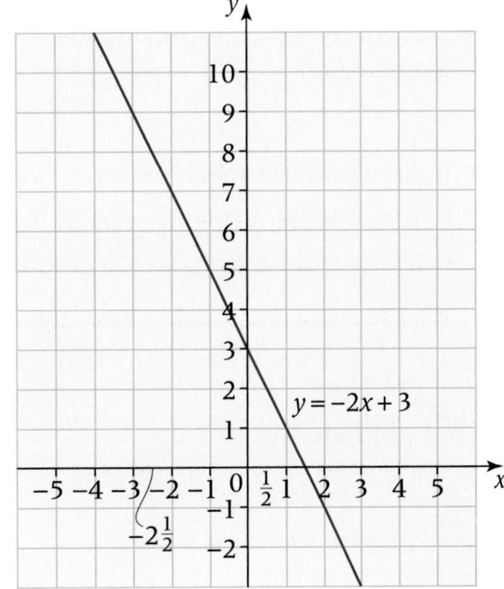

2 **a** Draw the graph of $y = \frac{1}{2}x + 3$.

b Point P on this line has y-coordinate 7.
Use your line to find the x-coordinate of point P.

c Which of these points lie on the line?

$(2, 4)$ $(3, 7)$ $(-3, 1\frac{1}{2})$ $(-4, 2)$

3 **a** What graph would you draw to find the solution to the equation $4x - 7 = -15$?

b Draw the graph and use it to find the value of x.

4 Write down three equations that you could solve using the graph in question **1**.
Use the graph to find a solution to each of your equations.

5 Draw the graph of $y = 3x + 2$.

a Use your graph to solve

i $3x + 2 = 6.5$ **ii** $3x + 2 = 17$ **iii** $3x + 2 = -7$.

b You can rewrite the equation

$$3x + 6 = 5$$

as

$$3x + 2 + 4 = 5$$

Subtract 4 from each side:

$$3x + 2 = 5 - 4 = 1$$

So $3x + 2 = 1$ is equivalent to $3x + 6 = 5$.
You can use your graph from part **a** to solve $3x + 2 = 1$.
Rewrite the equation $3x + 7 = 16$
as $3x + 2 = ?$
Find the value of x from your graph.

6 **a** Draw a graph to solve the equation $2x + 6 = 10$.
What is the value of x?

b Use your graph from **a** to solve

i $2x + 6 = 14$ **ii** $2x + 6 = -3$ **iii** $2x + 9 = 12$.

A7.4 Trial and improvement

This spread will show you how to:

- Use systematic trial and improvement to estimate the solutions of an equation

Keywords
Estimate
Improvement
Trial

- To solve equations with powers, you can use **trial** and **improvement**.
  - You **estimate** a solution and **try** it in the equation.
  - If your estimate doesn't fit, you **improve** it and try again.

Example

Use trial and improvement to find the value of x in this equation.

$x^2 = 87$

Give your answer to 1 dp.

p.232

$x^2 = 87$

An estimate for x is 9.2

Try 9.2 in the equation:	$9.2^2 = 84.64$	too small
Try 9.3 in the equation:	$9.3^2 = 86.49$	too small
Try 9.4 in the equation:	$9.4^2 = 88.36$	too big

So the solution is between 9.3 and 9.4.
Try the halfway value, 9.35: $9.35^2 = 87.42$ too big
So the solution is between 9.3 and 9.35.

too small ↓ 9.3 — 9.31 — 9.32 — 9.33 — 9.34 — 9.35 ↓ too big

The solution is 9.3 to 1 dp.

$9^2 = 81$, so estimate that x is a bit bigger than 9.

When the answer is too small, improve your estimate by choosing a slightly bigger value.

All these values between 9.3 and 9.35 round to 9.3

- When using trial and improvement you need to work systematically. You can show your trials in a table.

Example

The equation.

$x^3 + x = 33$

has a solution between 3 and 4.
Use trial and improvement to find the solution.
Give your answer correct to 1 decimal place.

p.234

x	x^3	$x^3 + x$	Too big or too small?
3.5	42.875	46.375	too big
3.2	32.768	35.968	too big
3.1	29.791	32.891	too small
3.15	31.225...	34.405...	too big

3.1 — 3.15 — 3.2

The solution is between 3.1 and 3.15.
The solution is 3.1 to 1 dp.

All the values between 3.1 and 3.15 round to 3.1.

Exercise A7.4

Grade D

1 Bina is using trial and improvement to find a solution to $x^2 = 29$.
She draws this table:

x	x^2	Too big or too small?
5.5	30.25	
5.4		

a Copy the table and fill in the rest of the rows for the values 5.5 and 5.4.

b What value could you try next?
Write this value in your table and complete the row.

c Improve your estimate and write the value in the table.
Complete the row for this estimate.

d Continue in this way until you have found a solution to 1 decimal place.

You may need to add extra rows to your table.

2 The equation $x^2 - x = 13$ has a solution between 4 and 5.
Copy and complete the table to find this solution to 1 decimal place.
Draw as many rows as you need.

x	x^2	$x^2 - x$	Too big or too small?
4.5			

3 The equation $x^3 + x = 146$ has a solution between 5 and 6.
Copy and complete the table to find this solution to 1 decimal place.
Draw as many rows as you need.

x	x^3	$x^3 + x$	Too big or too small?

4 **a** Substitute $x = 1$, $x = 2$ and $x = 3$ into the equation

$$x^3 - x = 9$$

b Use your answers from part **a** to help you estimate a solution to the equation $x^3 - x = 9$.

c Draw up a table for this equation.

d Use your answer from part **b** as your first estimate in your table.

e Find the solution to 1 decimal place.

Your table will be similar to the one in question **3**.

AO3 Problem

5 Use trial and improvement to find a solution to

$$x^3 + x = 73$$

Give your solution to 1 decimal place.

Summary

Check out

You should now be able to:

- Solve equations involving brackets, fractions and negative signs
- Use graphs to find solutions to equations
- Use systematic trial-and-improvement to find approximate solutions of equations.

Worked exam question

a Complete the table of values for $y = x^2 - 3x + 1$

x	−2	−1	0	1	2	3	4
y	11		1	−1			5

(2)

b On the grid, draw the graph of $y = x^2 - 3x + 1$ (2)

c Use your graph to estimate the values of x for which $y = 3$ (2)

(Edexcel Limited 2006)

a

$$
\begin{array}{llll}
 & y = x^2 & - 3x & + 1 \\
\text{When } x = 3 & y = 3^2 & - 3 \times 3 & + 1 = 1 \\
\text{When } x = 2 & y = 2^2 & - 3 \times 2 & + 1 = -1 \\
\text{When } x = -1 & y = (-1)^2 & - 3 \times -1 & + 1 = 5
\end{array}
$$

x	−2	−1	0	1	2	3	4
y	11	5	1	−1	−1	1	5

b

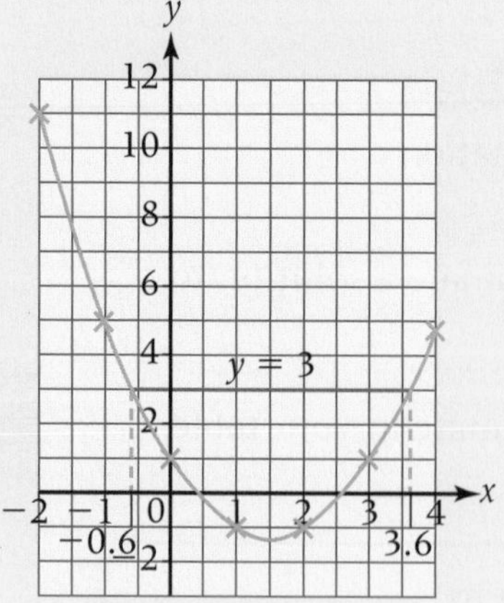

The y values will not be in a linear pattern because the graph is a quadratic curve.

Plot the points accurately.

The smooth curve must pass through all the points.

Draw the line $y = 3$ to show the method.

c When $y = 3$

$x = -0.6$ and $x = 3.6$

Exam questions

1 Solve the equations

a $4(x - 3) = 10$ (2)

b $\frac{x}{5} = -7$ (2)

2 By drawing a suitable graph, **estimate** the solution to the equation

$$2x - 3 = 1\tfrac{1}{2}$$ (3)

3 The equation

$$x^3 - x = 30$$

has a solution between 3 and 4.
Use a trial and improvement method to find this solution.
Give your answer correct to 1 decimal place.
You must show all your working. (2)

(Edexcel Limited 2007)

Functional Maths 8: Sport

Mathematics is used widely in sport, particularly when taking measurements and recording results.

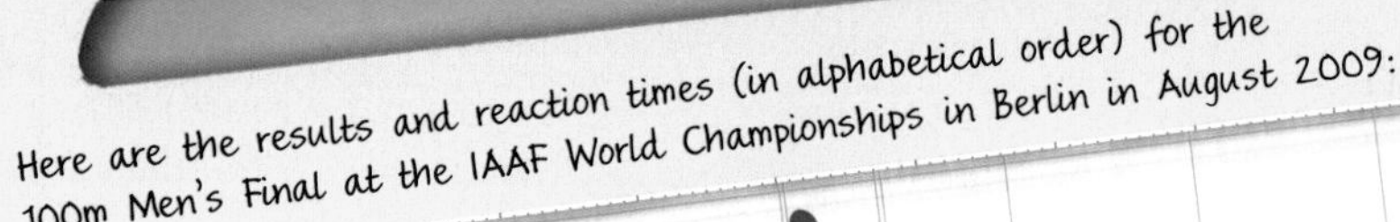

Here are the results and reaction times (in alphabetical order) for the 100m Men's Final at the IAAF World Championships in Berlin in August 2009:

Use the photo to order Bailey and Thompson as well as Burns and Chambers. What degree of accuracy is shown here?

Name	Nationality	Time (s)	Reaction (s)
Bailey	ANT	9.93	0.129
Bolt	JAM	9.58	0.146
Burns	TRI	10.00	0.165
Chambers	GBR	10.00	0.123
Gay	USA	9.71	0.144
Patton	USA	10.34	0.149
Powell	JAM	9.84	0.134
Thompson	TRI	9.93	0.119

What degree of accuracy is reported for
a) the result times
b) the reaction times?

Draw a stem-and-leaf diagram to show the result times of this race.

Calculate the
a) range b) median c) mean
of the reported results, giving your answers to an appropriate level of accuracy.

Which average do you think best represents these results? Explain your answer.

Here are the results and reaction times for the 100m Women's Final at the same World Championships:

Name	Nationality	Time (s)	Reaction (s)
Fraser	JAM	10.73	0.146
Stewart	JAM	10.75	0.170
Jeter	USA	10.90	0.160
Campbell-Brown	JAM	10.95	0.135
Williams	USA	11.01	0.158
Ferguson-McKenzie	BAH	11.05	0.130
Sturrup	BAH	11.05	0.137
Bailey	JAM	11.16	0.173

Use diagrams and statistics to compare the Men's and Women's reported results.

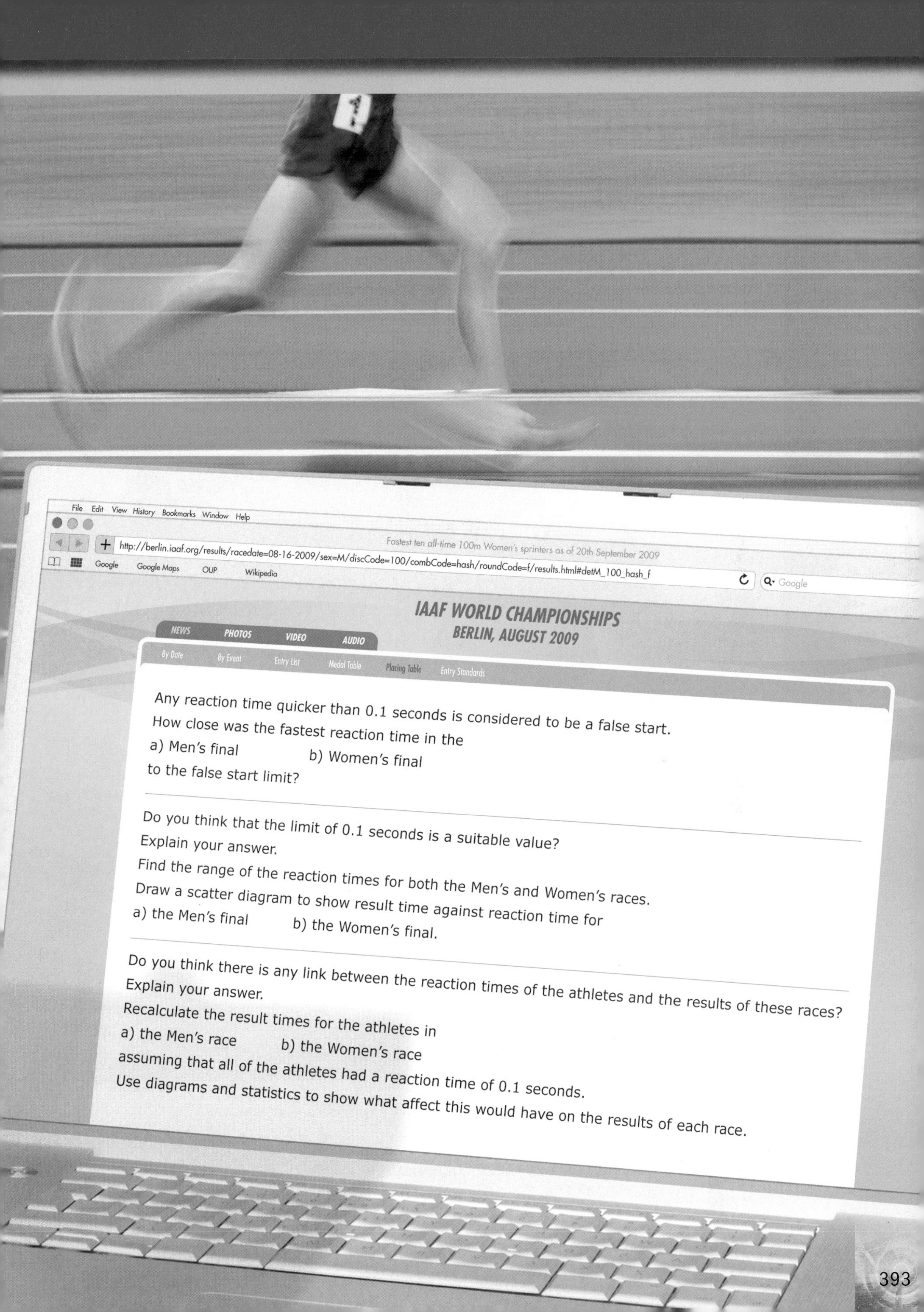

IAAF WORLD CHAMPIONSHIPS
BERLIN, AUGUST 2009

NEWS PHOTOS VIDEO AUDIO

By Date By Event Entry List Medal Table Placing Table Entry Standards

Any reaction time quicker than 0.1 seconds is considered to be a false start.
How close was the fastest reaction time in the
a) Men's final b) Women's final
to the false start limit?

Do you think that the limit of 0.1 seconds is a suitable value?
Explain your answer.
Find the range of the reaction times for both the Men's and Women's races.
Draw a scatter diagram to show result time against reaction time for
a) the Men's final b) the Women's final.

Do you think there is any link between the reaction times of the athletes and the results of these races?
Explain your answer.
Recalculate the result times for the athletes in
a) the Men's race b) the Women's race
assuming that all of the athletes had a reaction time of 0.1 seconds.
Use diagrams and statistics to show what affect this would have on the results of each race.

G7

Circles and Pythagoras

Introduction

Mountain rescue teams need to find the shortest distance to an accident in the mountains. They can calculate the distance on a map from their starting place to the accident using Pythagoras' Theorem.

What's the point?

Knowing the shortest distance between two locations enables you to get to your destination quicker – in some circumstances this can save lives.

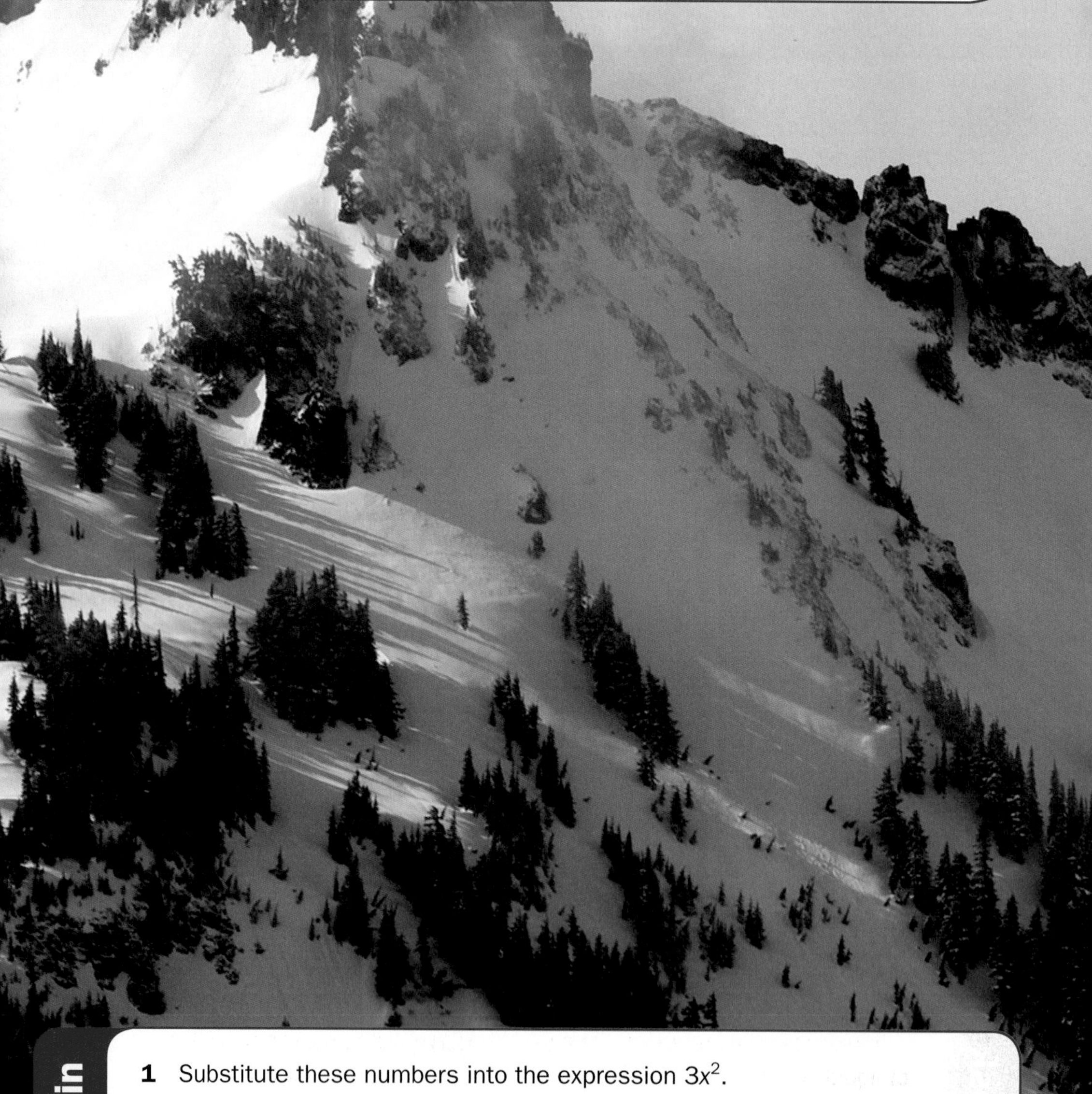

Check in

1 Substitute these numbers into the expression $3x^2$.

a 2 **b** 5 **c** 3.1 **d** -2

2 Calculate each of these quantities.

a $3^2 + 4^2$ **b** $7^2 - 5^2$ **c** $\sqrt{70}$ (to 1 d.p.)

Orientation

What I should know	What I will learn	What this leads to
G1 →	■ Calculate the circumference and area of a circle ■ Calculate the volume of right prisms ■ Understand, recall and use Pythagoras' theorem	→ Manufacturing and industrial design (eg packaging design); surveying

Rich task

A drinks company needs to design a container to hold exactly 360 ml of liquid. They are aware of environmental issues and want to minimise the surface area of the container.

a Design a container to hold exactly 360 ml which has the minimum surface area.

b Refine your design in light of any practical considerations.

G7.1 Circumference and area of a circle

This spread will show you how to:

- Calculate the circumference and area of a circle

Keywords
Centre
Circle
Circumference
Diameter
Pi (π)
Radius

In a **circle**:

- the **radius** is r
- the **diameter** is d
- the **circumference** is C.

C, d and r are all measures of length.

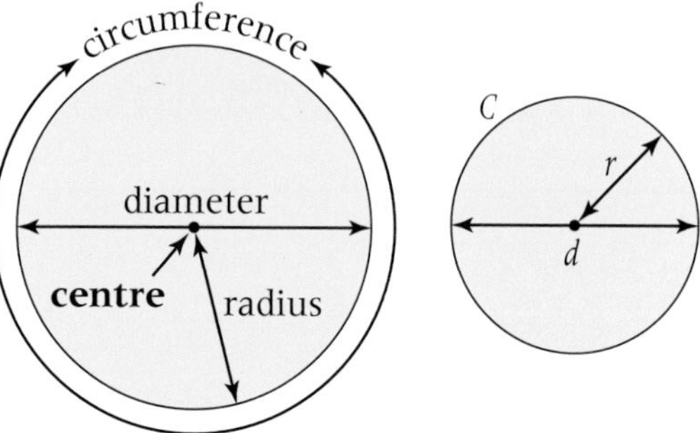

The perimeter of a circle is called the circumference.

- Diameter = 2 × radius

- $C = \pi \times \text{diameter} = \pi d = 2\pi r$

$d = 2 \times r$

$\pi = 3.14 \ldots$

Example

Calculate the circumference of this circle.

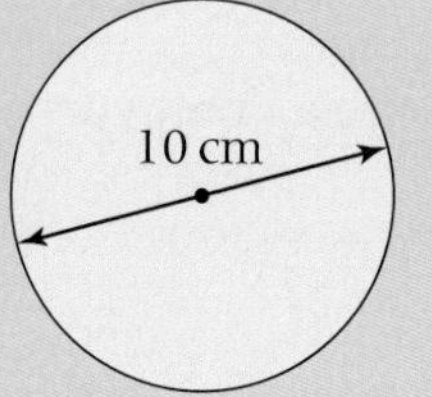

$C = \pi \times d$
$= 3.14 \times 10$
$= 31.4$ cm   Circumference is measured in units of length.

- Area of a circle = π × radius × radius
  $= \pi \times r \times r$ or πr^2

r^2 = means $r \times r$

Example

A circular lawn has radius 3 metres.

a Calculate the area of the lawn. State the units of your answer.

b Calculate the length of edging stones needed to fit all round the edge of the lawn.

Give your answer to a suitable degree of accuracy.

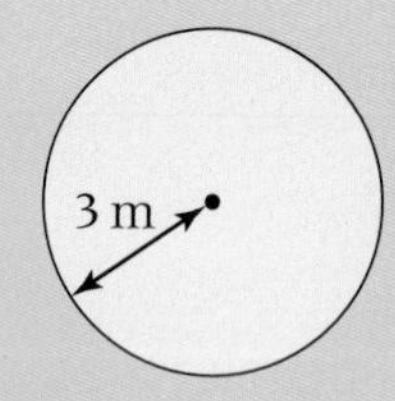

a Area $= \pi r^2$
$= 3.14 \times 3 \times 3$
$= 3.14 \times 9$
$= 28.26\,\text{m}^2$

b Circumference $= \pi d$
$= 3.14 \times 6$
$= 18.84$ m
So 19 m of edging stones are needed.

Area is measured in square units.

Exercise G7.1

Grade D

Take $\pi = 3.14$ for all questions on this page.

1 Calculate the circumferences of these circles. State the units of your answers.

a 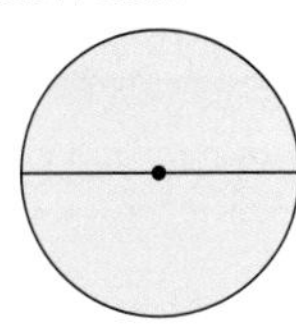
diameter = 10 cm

b 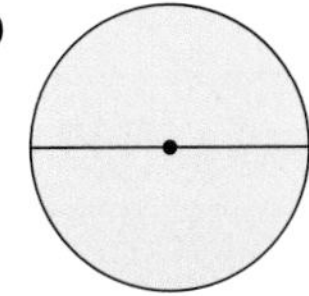
diameter = 8 m

c 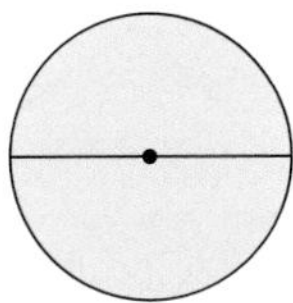
diameter = 12 cm

d 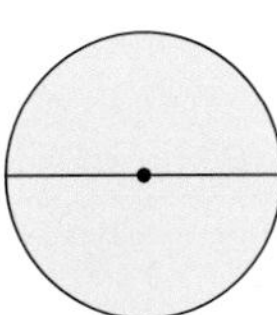
diameter = 20 m

e 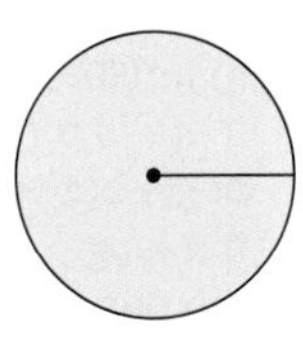
radius = 2 m

f 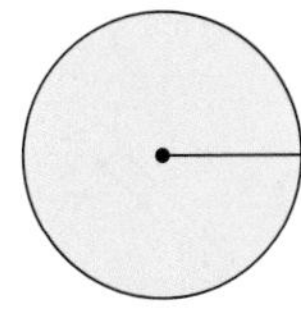
radius = 8 cm

g 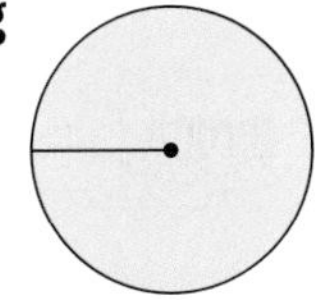
radius = 1.5 m

h 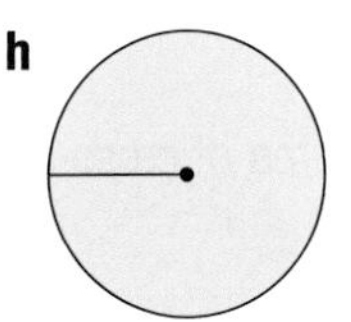
radius = 3.5 cm

2 Calculate the diameter of a circle, if its circumference is
a 18.84 cm **b** 15.7 m **c** 28.26 cm **d** 47.1 m **e** 314 cm

3 Calculate the perimeters and areas of these shapes. State the units of your answers.

a 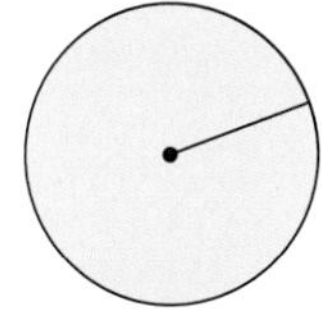
radius = 7 cm

b 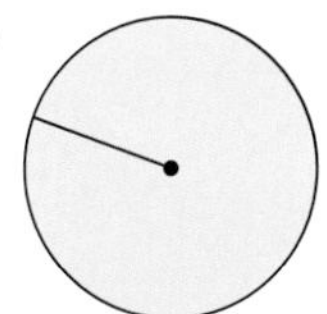
radius = 5 m

c
radius = 4 cm

d 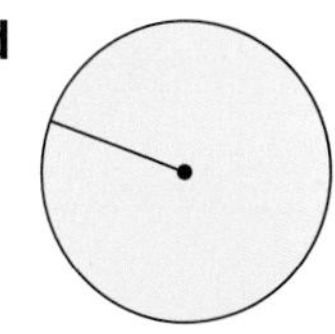
radius = 3 m

e 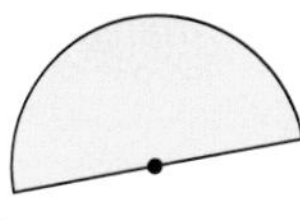
diameter = 20 m

f 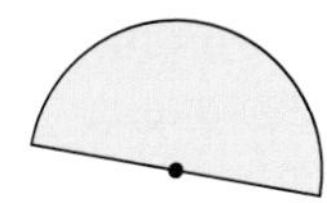
diameter = 16 cm

g 
diameter = 12 mm

h 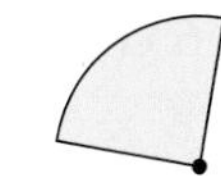
diameter = 18 cm

Functional Maths **AO2**

4 A garden pond is circular.
The radius of the pond is 1.5 m.
a Calculate the diameter of the pond.
b Calculate the circumference of the pond.
c Calculate the area of the pond.

Give your answers to a suitable degree of accuracy.

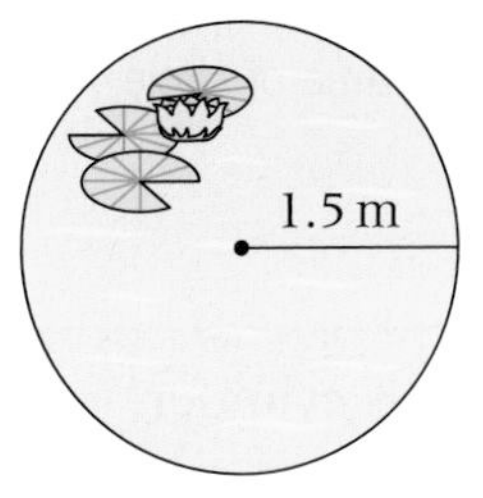

Challenge

5 A standard running track is 400 m in length.
Design a running track which includes
a two straight sections of 100 m each
b two semi-circular sections at opposite ends.
Give your answer as a scale drawing, with dimensions clearly marked.

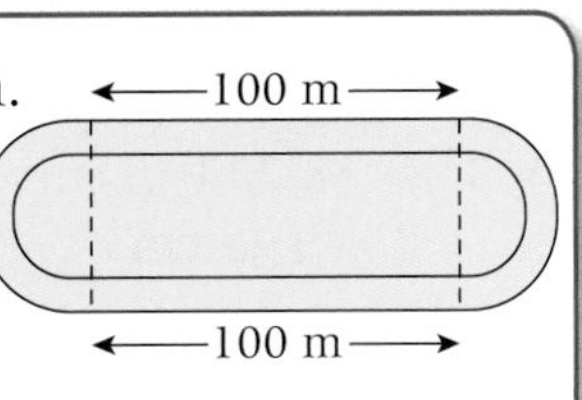

G7.2 Volume of a prism 2

This spread will show you how to:

- Calculate volumes of right prisms

Keywords
Cross-section
Cylinder
Prism
Volume

- A **prism** is an object with constant **cross-section**.

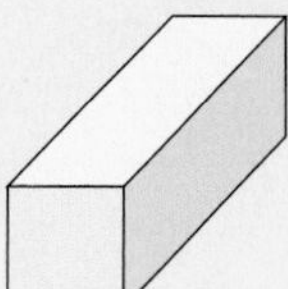

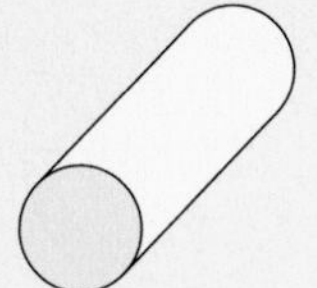

p.158

- **Volume** of a prism = area of cross-section × length.
  $= A \times l$

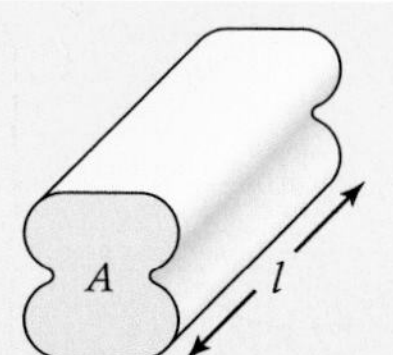

In a right prism there is a right angle between the length and the base.

Example

a Work out the volume of this cuboid.

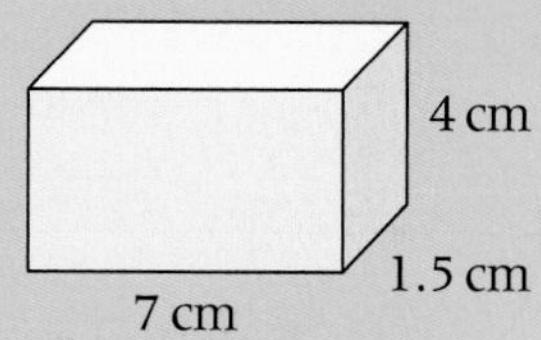

b Work out the volume of this prism.

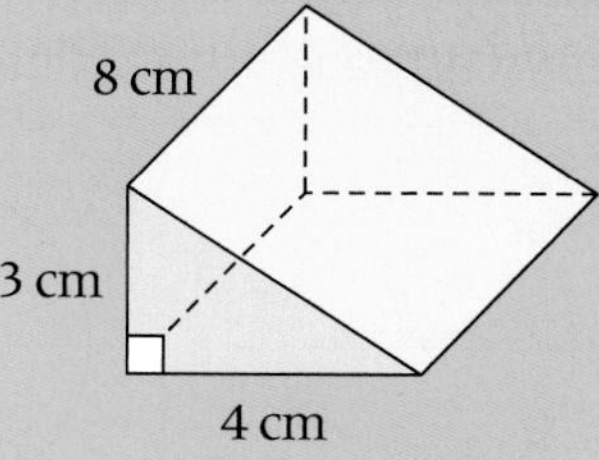

a Area of cross-section =
$4 \times 1.5 = 6\text{ cm}^2$
Volume $= 6 \times 7 = 42\text{ cm}^3$

b Area of cross-section =
$\frac{1}{2} \times 4 \times 3 = 6\text{ cm}^2$
Volume $= 6 \times 8 = 48\text{ cm}^3$

Area of triangle $= \frac{1}{2}bh$

- A cylinder is a prism with circular cross-section.
- Volume of a **cylinder** = area of circle × height

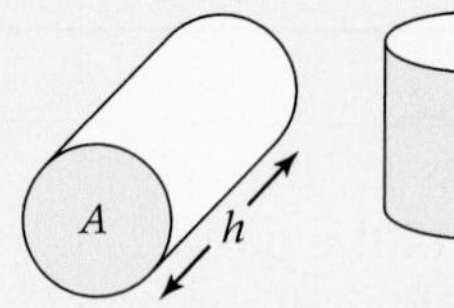

Example

Find the volume of this cylinder.

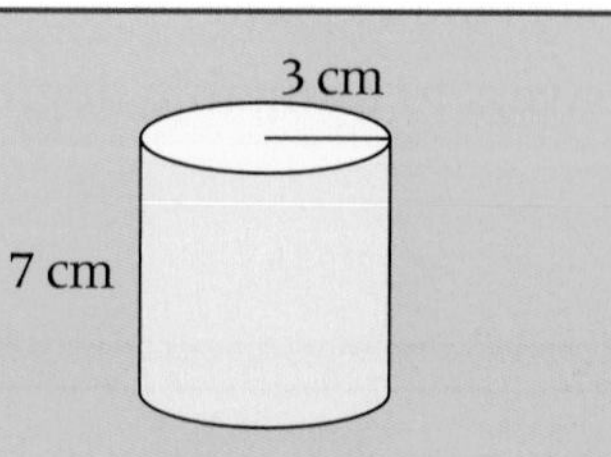

Area of circle $= \pi \times 3^2 = 28.274\ldots\text{ cm}^2$
Volume $= 28.274\ldots \times 7 = 198\text{ cm}^3$

Do not round intermediate steps of the calculation.

Give answers to a sensible degree of accuracy.

Exercise G7.2 Grade C

1 Find the volume of each cuboid.

a

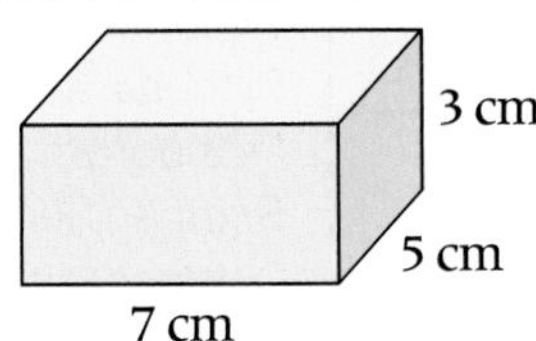

b

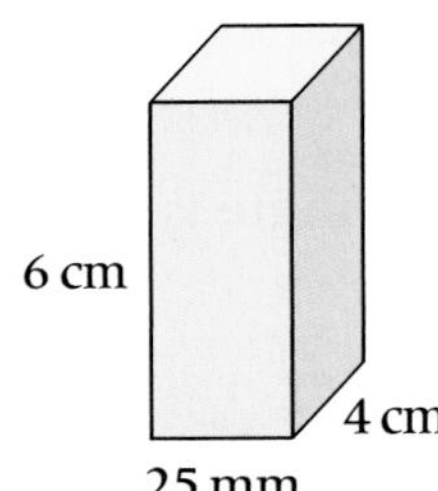

c

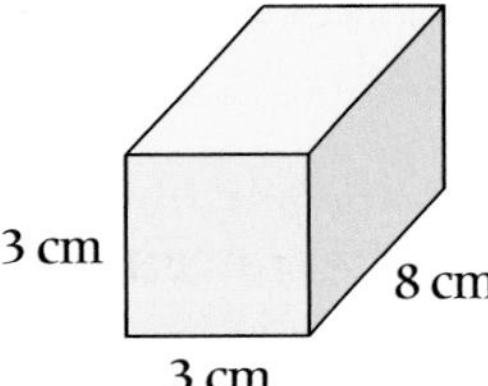

d

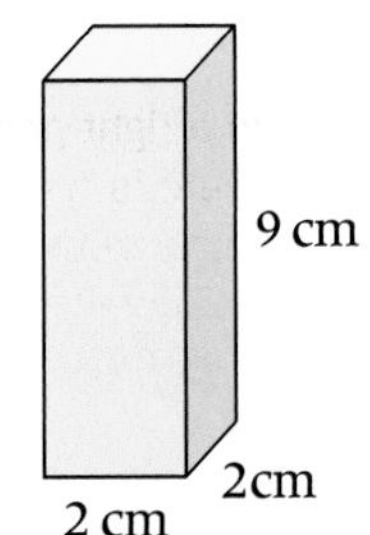

e

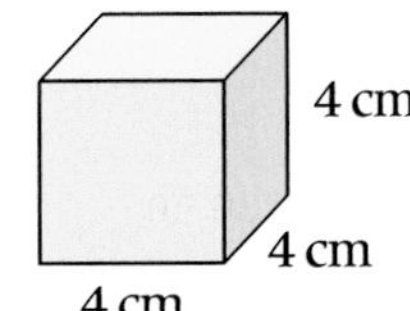

f

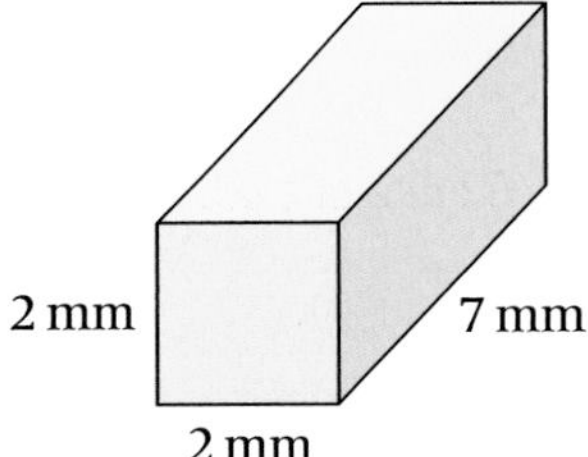

2 Find the volume of each cylinder.

a

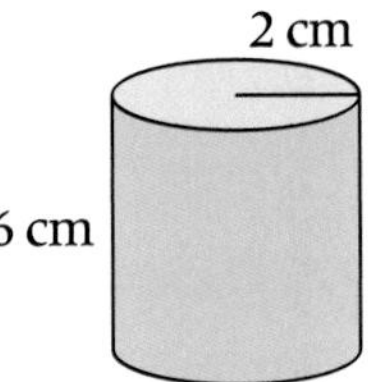

b

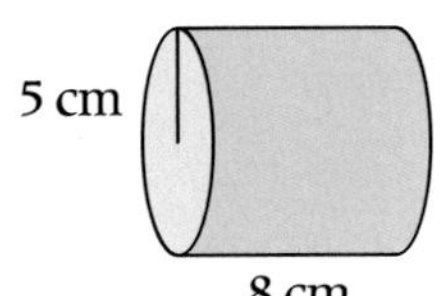

c

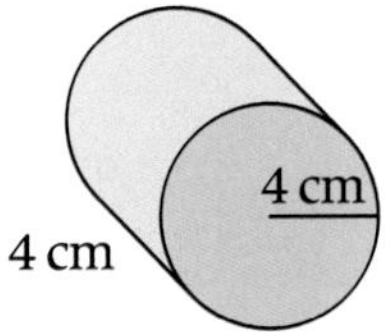

d

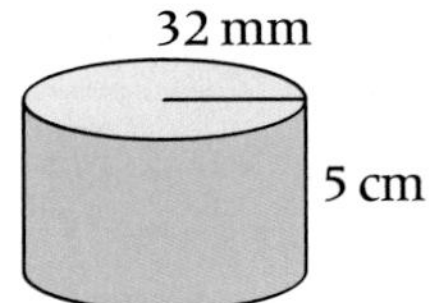

Be careful with units in part **d**.

3 Find the volume of each prism.

a

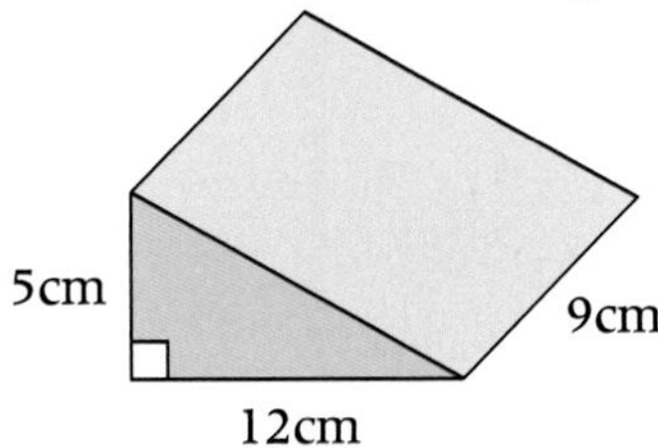

b

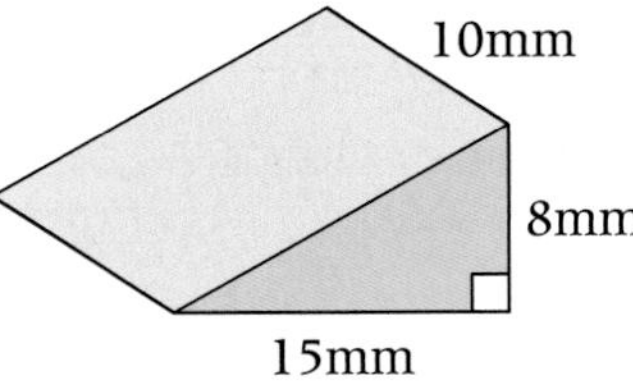

c

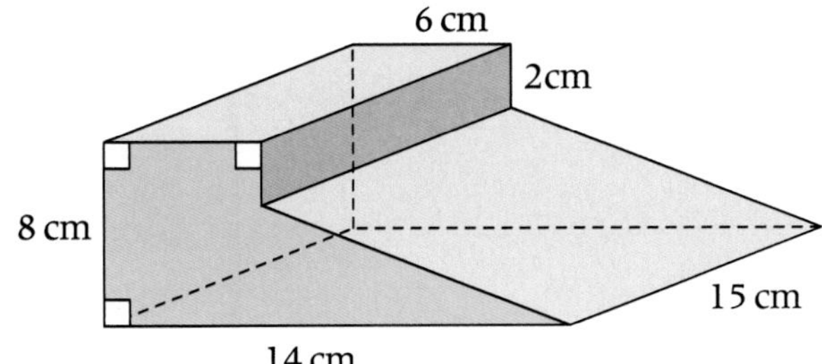

G7.3 Pythagoras' theorem

This spread will show you how to:

- Understand, recall and use Pythagoras' theorem

Keywords
Hypotenuse
Pythagoras' theorem
Right-angled triangle
Square
Square root

The longest side of a **right-angled triangle** is called the **hypotenuse**.

The hypotenuse is always opposite the right angle.

hypotenuse

This is a right-angled triangle.

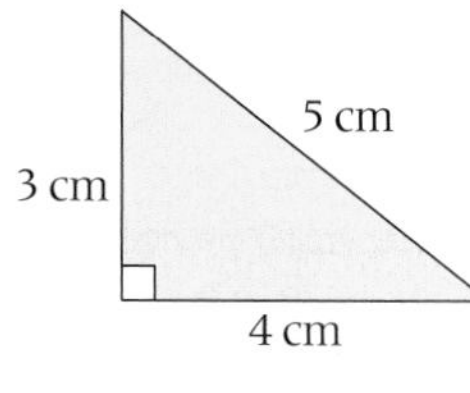

Draw the **squares** on each side.

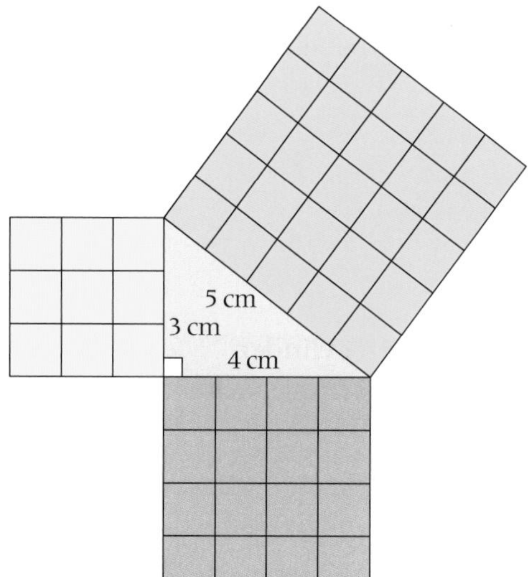

Calculate the areas of the squares.

Area of yellow square $= 3 \times 3 = 9\,\text{cm}^2$
Area of red square $= 4 \times 4 = 16\,\text{cm}^2$
Area of orange square $= 5 \times 5 = 25\,\text{cm}^2$

Area of orange square = area of yellow square + area of red square.

This is **Pythagoras' theorem**.

- In a right-angled triangle, $c^2 = a^2 + b^2$ where c is the hypotenuse.

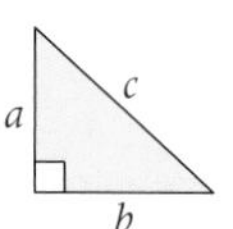

Example

Calculate the unknown lengths in these triangles.

a

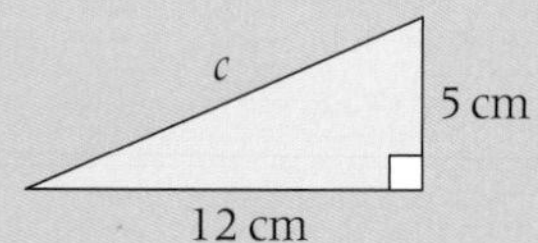

b

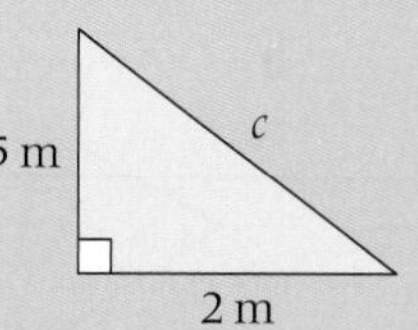

a Label the sides.

b Label the sides.

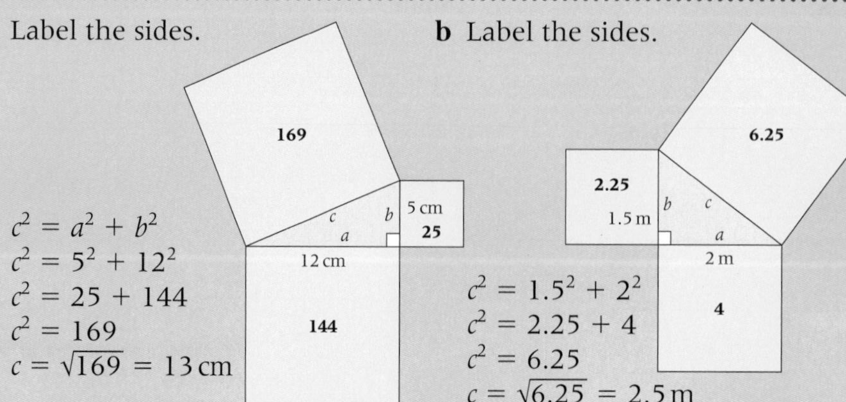

$c^2 = a^2 + b^2$
$c^2 = 5^2 + 12^2$
$c^2 = 25 + 144$
$c^2 = 169$
$c = \sqrt{169} = 13\,\text{cm}$

$c^2 = 1.5^2 + 2^2$
$c^2 = 2.25 + 4$
$c^2 = 6.25$
$c = \sqrt{6.25} = 2.5\,\text{m}$

$\sqrt{}$ means **square root.**

$\sqrt{169} = 13$ because $13 \times 13 = 169$.

Exercise G7.3 — Grade C

1 Calculate the area of these squares. State the units of your answers.

a 

8 cm

b 

10 m

c 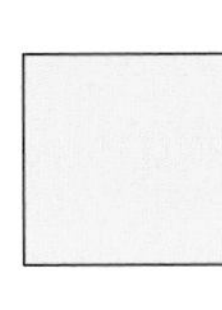

1.8 m

d 

36 mm

e 

4.5 m

2 Calculate the length of a side of these squares.
State the units of your answers.

a 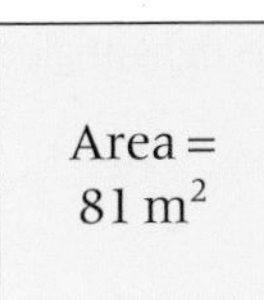

b 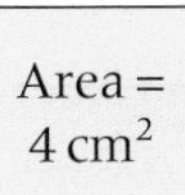

c 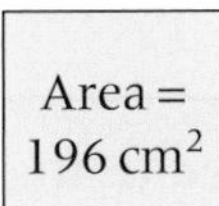

d 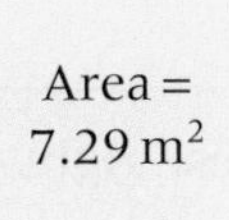

e 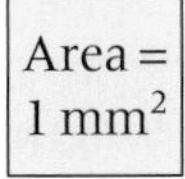

Did you know?

Pythagoras was a Greek mathematician most famous for his theorem, who taught his students that 'all things are numbers'.

3 Calculate the unknown area for these right-angled triangles.

a, **b** 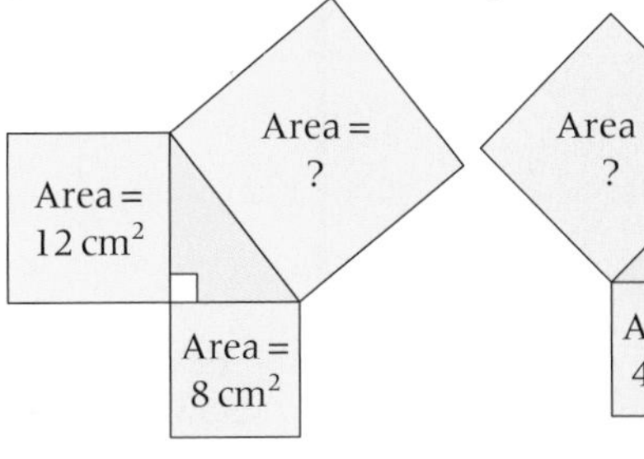

c 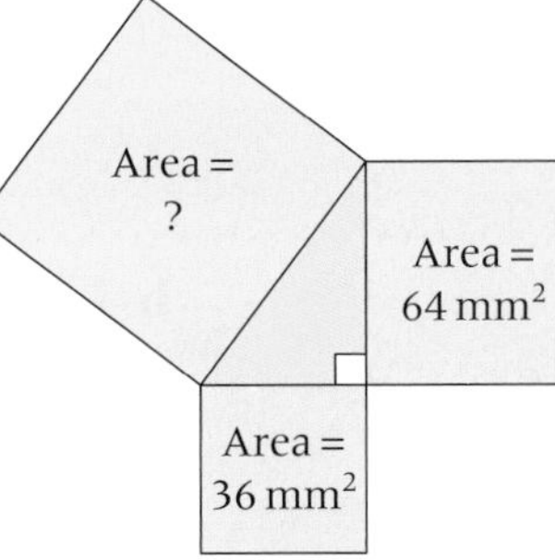

4 Calculate the length of the hypotenuse in these right-angled triangles. State the units of your answers.

a 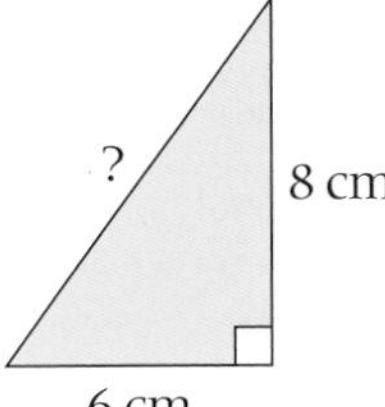

b 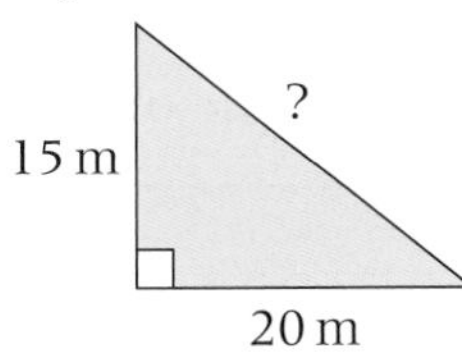

c 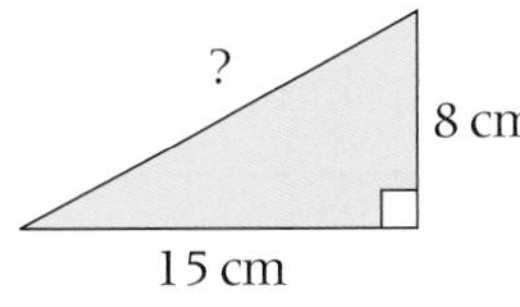

d 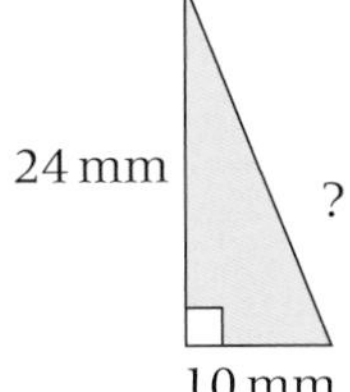

e 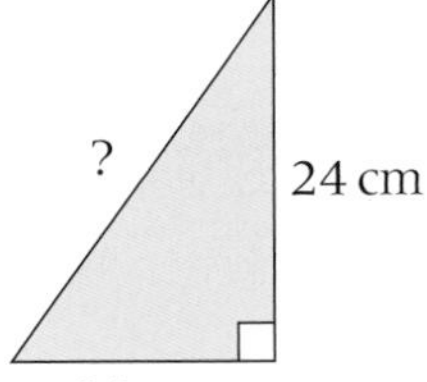

f 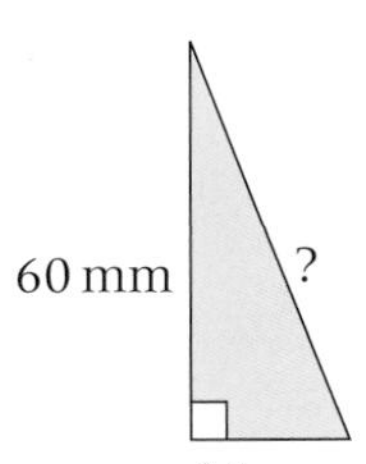

G7.4 More Pythagoras' theorem

This spread will show you how to:

- Understand, recall and use Pythagoras' theorem

Keywords
Hypotenuse
Pythagoras' theorem
Right-angled triangle
Square
Square root

- **Pythagoras' theorem** states

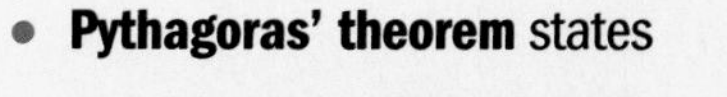

For any right-angled triangle, $c^2 = a^2 + b^2$ where c is the hypotenuse.

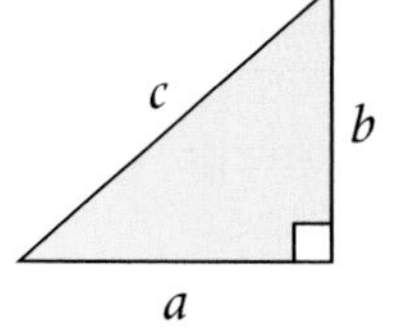

You can use Pythagoras' theorem to find a side given two other sides.

- You add to find the **hypotenuse**.
- You subtract to find the other sides.

The triangle must be right-angled.

Example

Calculate the unknown length in these right-angled triangles.

a

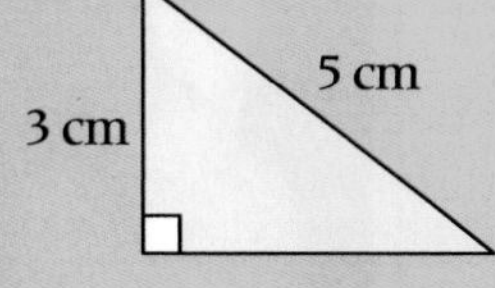

b

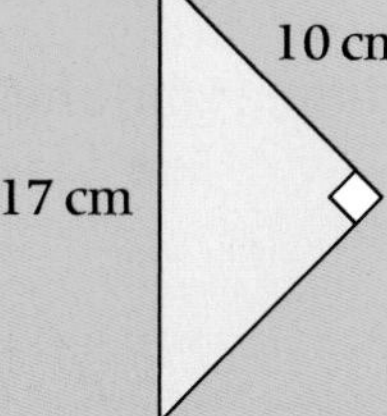

a Label the sides.

$a = ?, b = 3, c = 5$
$a^2 = c^2 - b^2$
$a^2 = 5^2 - 3^2$
$= 25 - 9$
$a^2 = 16$
$a = \sqrt{16} = 4\text{ cm}$

b Label the sides.

$a = 10, b = ?, c = 17$
$b^2 = c^2 - a^2$
$b^2 = 17^2 - 10^2$
$= 189$
$b = \sqrt{189}$
$= 13.7\text{ cm (to 1 dp)}$

You don't need to draw the squares on the sides.

You use Pythagoras' theorem to find the length of a line on a grid.

Example

Calculate the length of the **line segment** from (2, 4) to (5, 2).

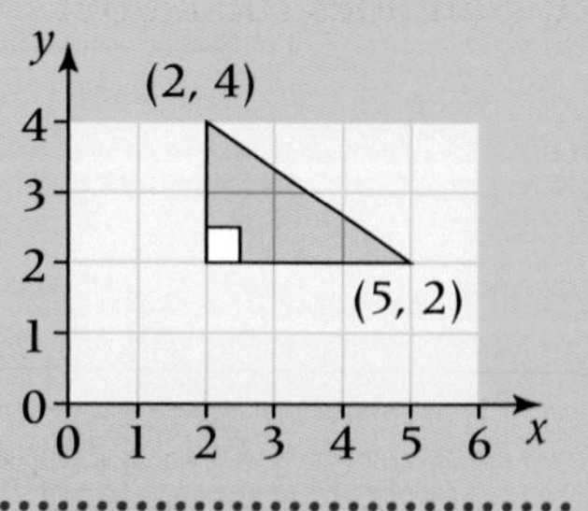

$c^2 = 2^2 + 3^2$
$c^2 = 4 + 9$
$c^2 = 13$
$c = \sqrt{13} = 3.60555 = 3.6\text{ units (to 1 dp)}$

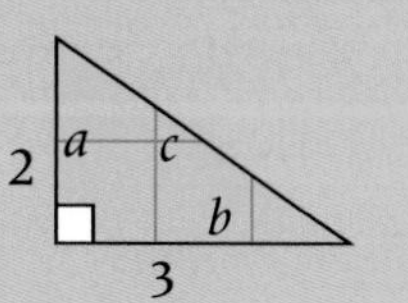

Label the sides.

Exercise G7.4 — Grade C

1 Calculate the area of the unknown square for these right-angled triangles.

a

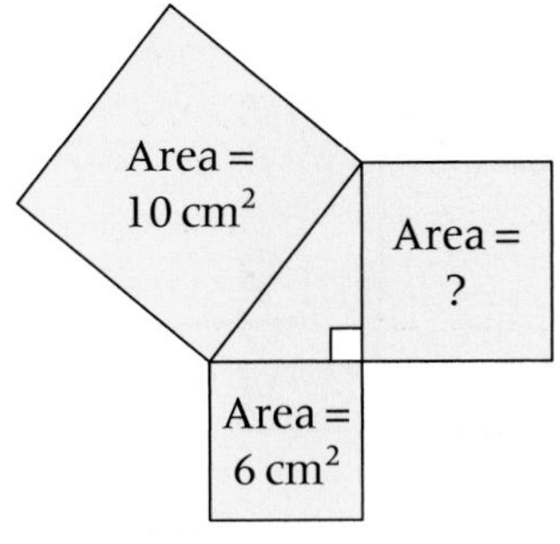

b

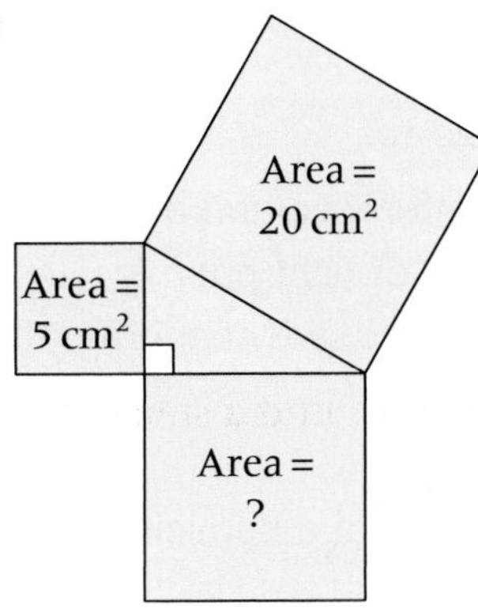

2 Calculate the unknown length in these right-angled triangles.
Give the units of your answers.

a **b**

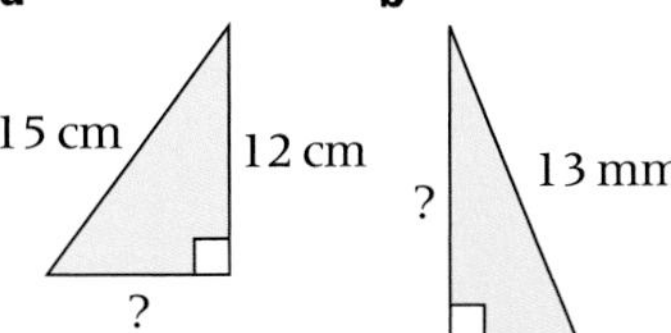

c

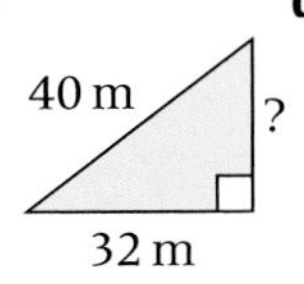

d **e**

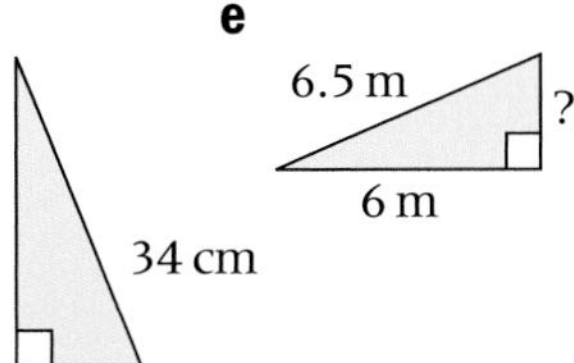

3 Calculate the distance between these points.
Give your answers to a suitable degree of accuracy.

a (1, 2) and (4, 6)
b (2, 2) and (6, 5)
c (1, 2) and (2, 5)
d (0, 5) and (4, 1)
e (3, 6) and (6, 0)

Functional Maths **A02**

4 A 4 metre ladder leans against a wall with its base 1.5 metres from the wall. How far up the wall does the ladder reach?

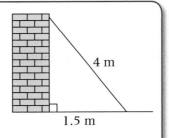

4 m
1.5 m

Summary

Check out

You should now be able to:

- Calculate the circumference and area of circles
- Calculate the volume of right prisms
- Understand, recall and use Pythagoras' theorem

Worked exam question

Here is a tile in the shape of a semicircle.

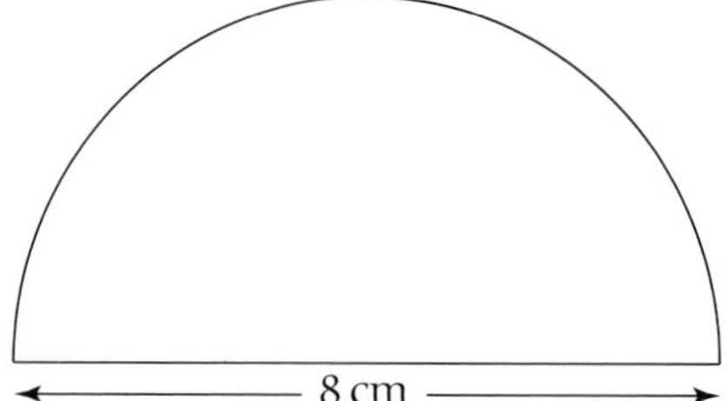

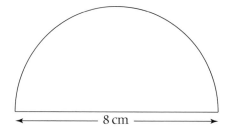

Diagram NOT accurately drawn

The diameter of the semicircle is 8 cm.

Work out the perimeter of the tile.
Give your answer correct to 2 decimal places. (3)

(Edexcel Limited 2009)

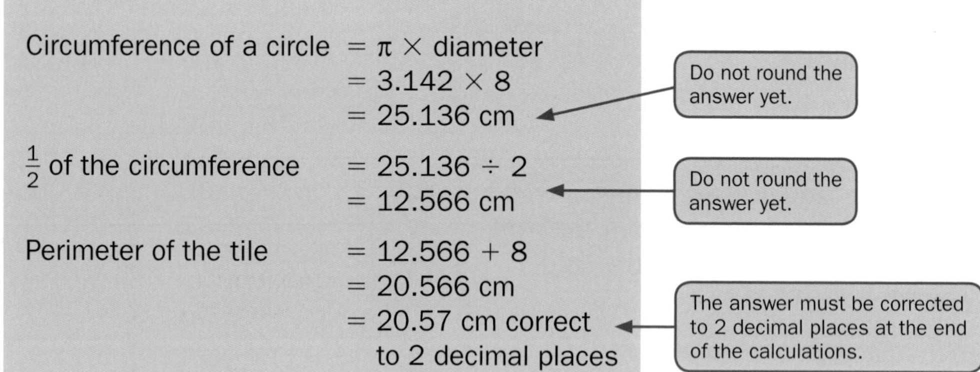

Circumference of a circle $= \pi \times \text{diameter}$
$= 3.142 \times 8$
$= 25.136$ cm

Do not round the answer yet.

$\frac{1}{2}$ of the circumference $= 25.136 \div 2$
$= 12.566$ cm

Do not round the answer yet.

Perimeter of the tile $= 12.566 + 8$
$= 20.566$ cm
$= 20.57$ cm correct to 2 decimal places

The answer must be corrected to 2 decimal places at the end of the calculations.

Exam questions

1 Here is a cuboid.

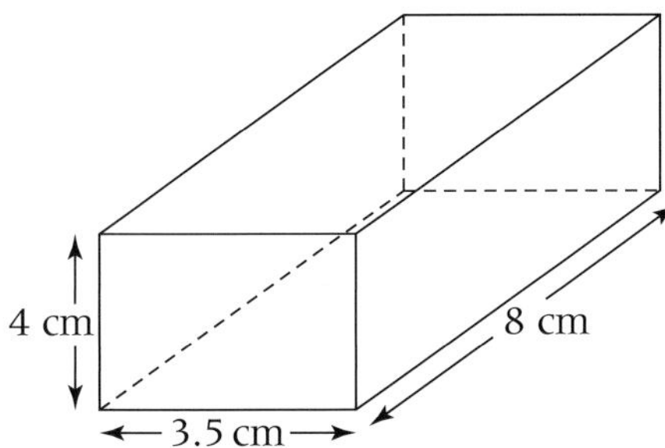

Diagram NOT accurately drawn

Calculate the volume of the cuboid. (2)

A03

2

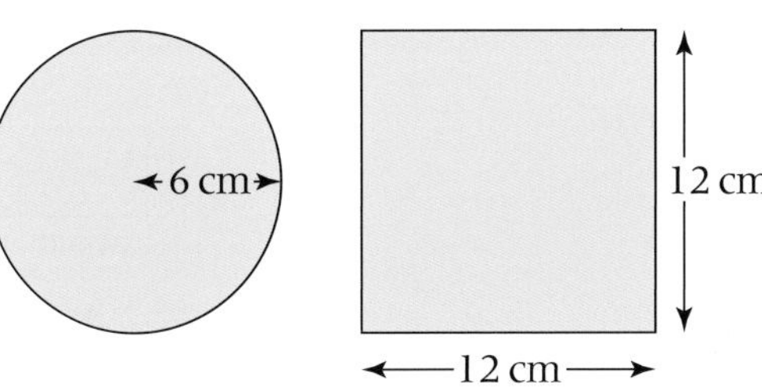

Diagram NOT accurately drawn

A circle has a radius of 6 cm.

A square has a side of length 12 cm.

Work out the difference between the area of the circle and the area of the square.

Give your answer correct to one decimal place. (4)

(Edexcel Limited 2008)

3

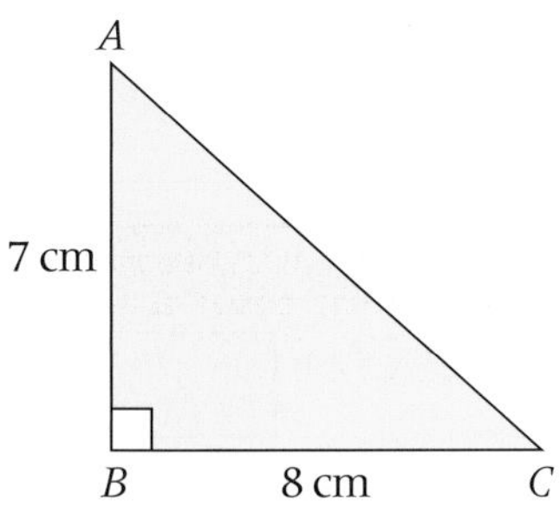

Diagram NOT accurately drawn

ABC is a right-angled triangle.
$AB = 7$ cm
$BC = 8$ cm

Work out the length of AC.
Give your answer correct to 2 decimal places. (3)

(Edexcel Limited 2008)

GCSE formulae

In your Edexcel GCSE examinations you will be given a formula sheet. Here are the formulae that you are given in your exams.

Area of a trapezium $= \frac{1}{2}(a + b)h$

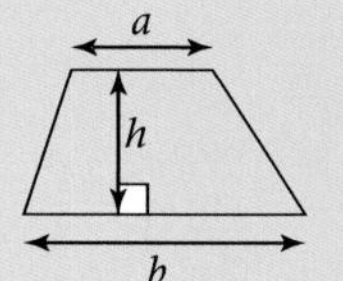

Volume of prism = area of cross section × length

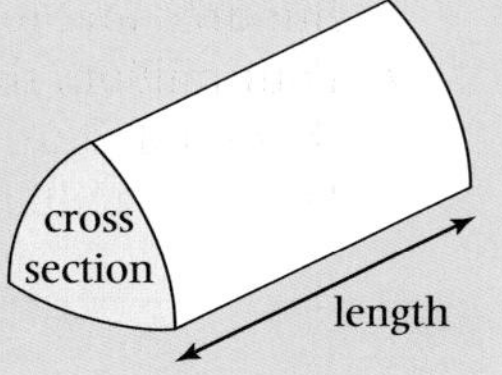

Here are some other formulae that you should learn.

Area of a rectangle = length × width

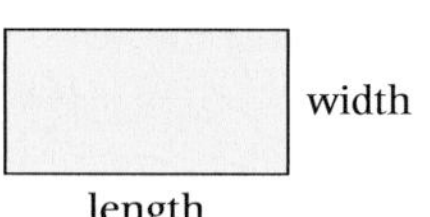

Area of a triangle $= \frac{1}{2} \times$ base × height

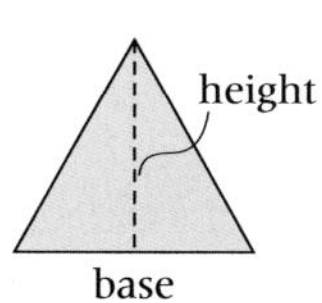

Area of a parallelogram = base × perpendicular height

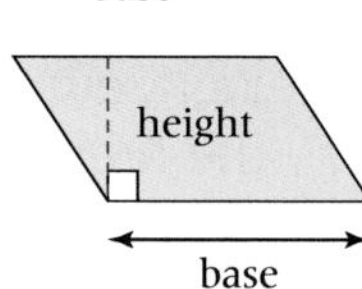

Area of a circle $= \pi r^2$

Circumference of a circle $= \pi d = 2\pi r$

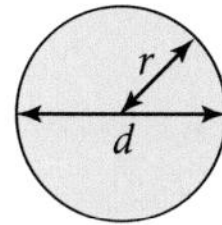

Volume of a cuboid = length × width × height

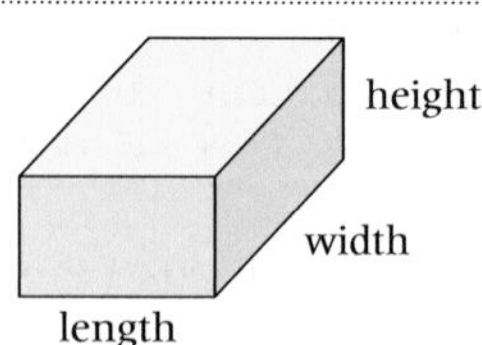

Volume of a cylinder = area of circle × length

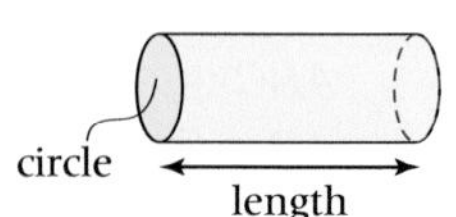

Pythagoras' theorem states,

For any right-angled triangle, $c^2 = a^2 + b^2$
where c is the hypotenuse.

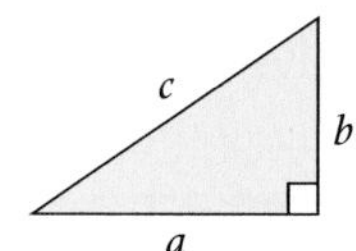

N1 Check in

1 −8, −5, −3, −1, 2, 4
2 a 7 b −10 c −12 d −3
3 1, 2, 3, 4, 6, 8, 12, 16, 24, 48

N1.1

1 a Four hundred and fifty-six
b Thirteen thousand, two hundred
c One hundred and fifteen thousand and twenty
d Four hundred and sixty thousand, three hundred and forty
e Four million, three hundred and twenty-five thousand, four hundred
f Fifty-five million, six hundred and seventy thousand, three hundred and forty-five
g Forty-five point eight
h Three hundred and sixty-seven point zero three
i Four thousand, five hundred and three point three four
j Two thousand seven hundred point zero two
2 a 538 b 2031 c 15 603 d 280 453
e 417.3 f 1 717 338 g 537.403
h 3.03
3 a 25.5 b 1.85 c 50 d 4.95
e 1.375 f 0.705
4 a 5.007, 5.099, 5.103, 5.12, 5.2
b 0.5, 0.509, 0.525, 0.545, 0.55
c 7.058, 7.302, 7.35, 7.387, 7.403
d 0.4, 0.42, 2.4, 4.2, 42
e 26.9, 26.97, 27.06, 27.1, 27.6
f 13.19, 13.3, 13.43, 14.03, 14.15
5 a 320 b 4 c 1.52 d 0.146
e 23.7 f 2430 g 0.0123 h 4.59
i 3400 j 135.6 k 0.0236 l 17.45
m 0.392 n 0.728 o 0.0124 p 8.14
6 a 96.6 b 937.3 c 22.23 d 24 140

N1.2

1 a 3.8 b 4.25 c 540 d 4.8
2 a 6.5 cm b 4.75 kg
c 1154 °C d 3.24 tonnes
3 a About 7.3 cm b About 68.3 ml
c About 46.7 mph d About 8.37 °C
e About 54 g f About 3.3 cm
g About 3.73 ml h About 2800 °C
4 a 13 : 59 b 15 : 21
c 2 h 7 min d 1 h 20 min

N1.3

1 a −13, −12, −6, 0, 15, 17
b −8, −7, −6, −5, −3, 0
c −5, −2, 1, 2, 3, 4
d −8, −3, −1.5, 2, 3, 9
e −5, −4.5, −3, −2, 2, 3
f −9, −1, 2, 3, 6, 8
g −4.5, −3, −2.5, −1, 0, 5.5
h −6, −5.8, −5.7, −5.4, −5.1, −5
2 a 16 b −7 c 4 d 37
e 17 f −7 g 9 h −11
i −8 j 21 k −8 l −2
m −18 n 4 o −5 p 2
q −20 r 10 s −8 t −28
3 a 31 b −11 c 4 d −7
e 5.5 f 2.5 g 7.5 h −0.5
4 a 6, 5, 4, 3
b 8, 9, 10, 11
c 13, 12, 11, 10, 9, 8
d 11, 12, 13, 14, 15, 16

Adding −1 is the same as subtracting 1, and subtracting −1 is the same as adding 1, etc.

5 a 8 b −2 c 9 d 0
e −13 f −14 g −14 h 20
i 12 j 3 k −5 l −6
m 4 n −25 o −1 p 1
q −9 r −23 s −9 t −23

N1.4

1 a −8, −12, −16 b −7, 0, 7, 14, 21, 28
2 a −2 b 2 c −3 d 3
e −4 f 4
3 a 6 b 30 c −21 d 8
e −20 f 24 g −24 h 42
i 16 j 50 k 5 l −8
m 5 n 5 o −9 p −63
q −49 r 72 s −9 t −6
u −4 v −10 w 9 x −56
y −13
4 a + × − = −, −20 c − × − = +, 30
d − × − = +, 28 f + × + = +, 40
g + × − = −, −35 h − ÷ − = +, 8
j − × − = +, 70
5 a −120 b 132 c −225 d −147
e −117 f −133 g −414 h −40
i −13 j −67.2

N1.5

1 ai 3490 aii 3500 aiii 3000
bi 3390 bii 3400 biii 3000
ci 14 850 m cii 14 900 m ciii 15 000 m
di £57 790 dii £57 800 diii £58 000
ei 92 640 kg eii 92 600 kg eiii 93 000 kg
fi £86 190 fii £86 200 fiii £86 000
gi 3440 gii 3400 giii 3000
hi 74 900 hii 74 900 hiii 75 000
2 a 4 b 29 c 469 d 369
e 20 f 27 g 101 h 0

3 ai 3.447 aii 3.45 aiii 3.4
bi 8.948 bii 8.95 biii 8.9
ci 0.128 cii 0.13 ciii 0.1
di 28.387 dii 28.39 diii 28.4
ei 17.999 eii 18.00 eiii 18.0
fi 10.000 fii 10.00 fiii 10.0
gi 0.004 gii 0.00 giii 0.0
hi 2785.556 hii 2785.56 hiii 2785.6

4 ai 8.37 aii 8.4 aiii 8
bi 18.8 bii 19 biii 20
ci 35.8 cii 36 ciii 40
di 279 dii 280 diii 300
ei 1.39 eii 1.4 eiii 1
fi 3890 fii 3900 fiii 4000
gi 0.008 37 gii 0.0084 giii 0.008
hi 2400 hii 2400 hiii 2000
ii 8.99 iii 9.0 iiii 9
ji 14.0 jii 14 jiii 10
ki 1400 kii 1400 kiii 1000
li 140 000 lii 140 000 liii 100 000

5 a $5 \times 6 = 30$ b $18 + 22 = 40$ c $\frac{6 \times 3}{9} = 2$
d $35 - 10 = 25$ e $\frac{33 \times 5}{3} = 55$
f $(10^2 + 9)^2 \approx 100^2 = 10\,000$

6 a £60 b 20p

N1 Summary

1 a −4°C b 7°C c 2°C

2 a 33 b 180 c and d correctly located

3 £36

G1 Check in

1 a 600 b 71 000 c 48 d 2630
e 4500 f 6 g 75 h 6.5
i 3.2

2 a 7.8 b 15.5 c 9

G1.1

1 a cm or m b ml or cl c kg d cm
e kg f km g ml or cl h litre
i tonne j g

2 a 2 cm b 4 m c 4.5 m d 4 km
e 5 mm f 4500 g g 6 kg h 6.5 kg
i 2.5 t j 3000 ml

3 a 10 miles b 25 miles c 55 miles
d 52.5 miles

4 a 2.5 cm b 12.5 cm c 15 cm
d 30 cm e 90 cm

5 a 4.4 lb b 88 lb c 110 lb
d 1.1 lb e 5.5 lb

6 a 180 g butter, 360 g caster sugar
b 240 g rice, 120 g raisins, 90 g sugar, 120 g currants
c 180 g self-raising flour, 60 g corn flour, 60 g cornflakes, 30 g drinking chocolate, 180 g margarine, 90 g sugar

7 112 km/h

G1.2

1 a 12 m, 8 m² b 19 cm, 12 cm²
c 39 mm, 81 mm² d 26.8 cm, 43.2 cm²
e 30.4 m, 38.4 m²

2 a 12 cm² b 30 m² c 14 cm²
d 72 mm² e 13.5 cm²

3 a 5 cm b 9 cm c 12 m

4 a 32 cm, 44 cm² b 42 cm, 74 cm²
c 56 cm, 188 cm²

G1.3

1 a 6 b 12 c 3 d 9

2 a 6 b 6 c 8 d 6

3 a 80 cm² b 800 m² c 120 mm² d 384 cm²

4 a 50 cm² b 375 mm² c 28 m² d 160 cm²

5 a 6 m b 14 cm c 8 mm d 8 cm

6 a $\frac{1}{2} \times 10 \times (10 + 20) = 150$ cm²
b $25 + 100 + 25 = 150$ cm²

G1.4

1 a 48 cm² b 32 cm² c 24 cm² d 208 cm²

2 a 136 cm² b 38 m² c 160 cm² d 118 cm²
e 188 cm²

3 a 24 cm² b 40 cm² c 32 cm² d 6 cm²
e 108 cm²

4 a 528 cm² b 189 cm²

G1 Summary

1 a 4.6 kg bi 2.2 lbs ii 11 lbs

2 169 cm²

3 Yes

A1 Check in

1 a 9 b −2 c 12 d 2

2

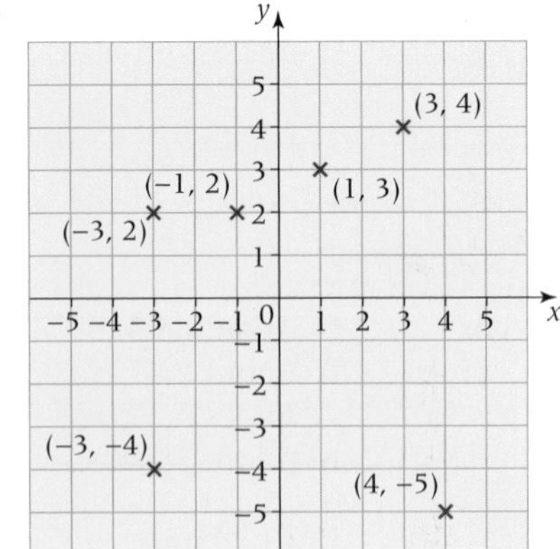

A1.1

1 a 0, 5, 10, 15 b 0.5, 1, 1.5, 2, 2.5
c −1, 1, 3, 5, 7 d −9, −5, −1, 3, 7
e −41, −36, −31, −26, −21 f −8, −2, 4, 10, 16

2 aii −4, −1, 2, 5, 8 bii −8, −3, 2, 7, 12
cii −7, −5, −3, −1, 1 dii −1, 3, 7, 11, 15

eii 2, 2.5, 3, 3.5, 4 **fii** −17, −14, −11, −8, −5
gii −3, −2.5, −2, −1.5, −1

3 b $y = 2x + 6$ **c** 0, 2, 4, 6, 8, 10, 12
d (−3, 0) (−2, 2) (−1, 4) (0, 6) (1, 8) (2, 10) (3, 12)

4 b $y = \frac{1}{2}x - 1$ **c** −2.5, −2, −1.5, −1, −0.5, 0, 0.5
d (−3, −2.5) (−2, −2) (−1, −1.5) (0, −1) (1, −0.5) (2, 0) (3, 0.5)

5 a (ii) (3) **b** (i) (5)
c (v) (1) **d** (iii) (4)
e (iv) (2)

A1.2

1 a $y = -3, 0, 3, 6, 9$
b (−2, −3), (−1, 0), (0, 3), (1, 6), (2, 9)
c–f

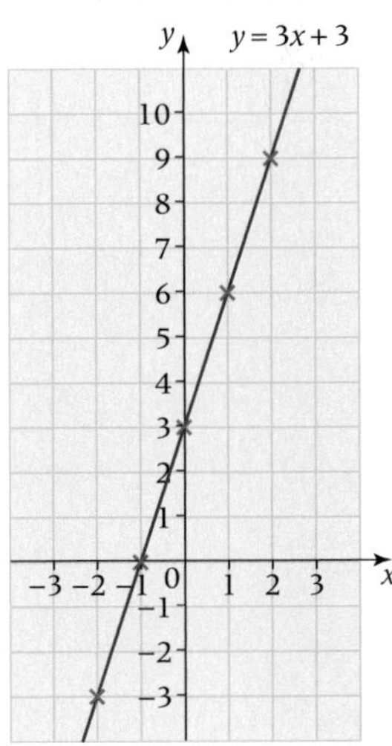

2 a $y = 5, 4, 3, 2, 1$
b (−2, 5), (−1, 4), (0, 3), (1, 2), (2, 1)
c–f

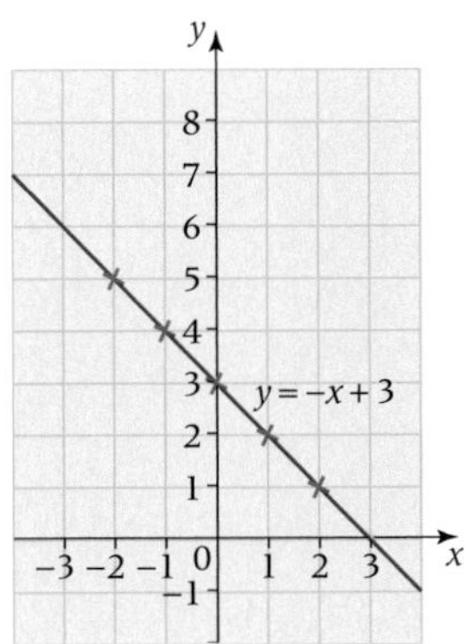

3 a $y = 8, 7, 6, 5, 4$
b (−2, 8), (−1, 7), (0, 6), (1, 5), (2, 4)
c–f

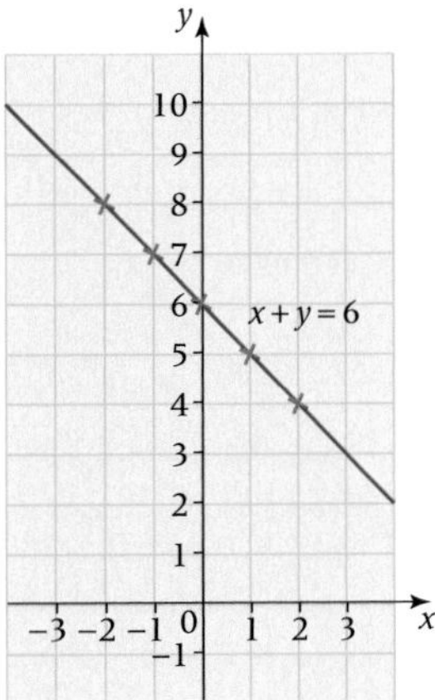

4 a $y = -9, -7, -5, -3, -1$
b (−2, −9), (−1, −7), (0, −5), (1, −3), (2, −1)
c–f

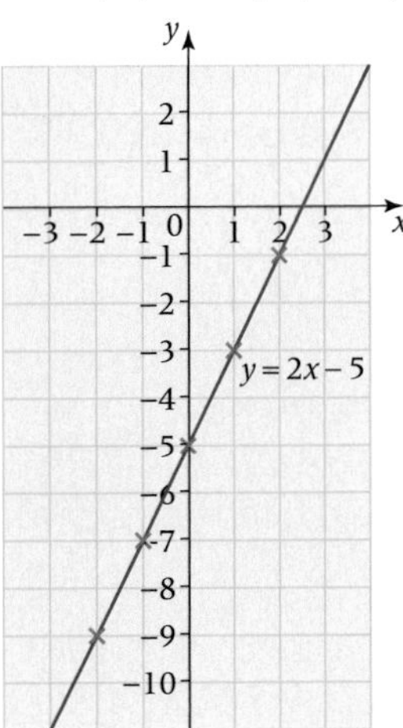

A1.3

1 a–d

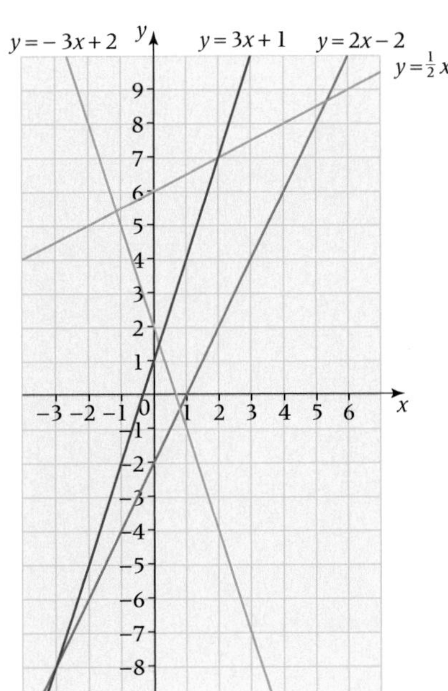

2 a–d

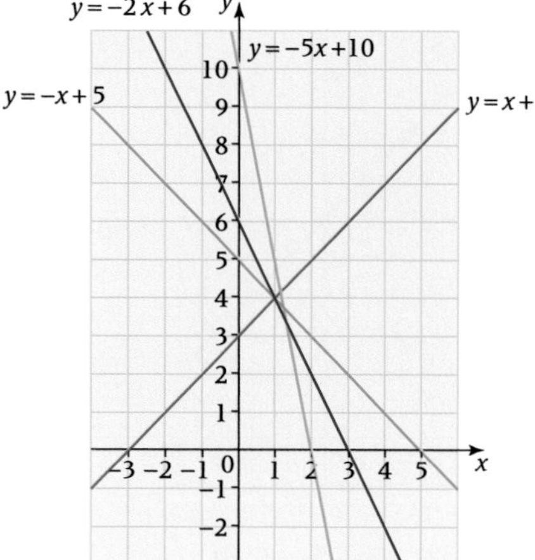

3 When $x = 0.5$, $y = 2$; when $y = 0$, $x = 1.5$

4 When $x = -0.5$, $y = -1$; when $y = 7$, $x = 1.5$

5 When $x = \frac{1}{2}$, $y = 2\frac{3}{4}$; when $y = 3\frac{1}{4}$, $x = -\frac{1}{2}$

6 When $x = -2$, $y = 0$; when $y = -5$, $x = 3$.

7 a–c

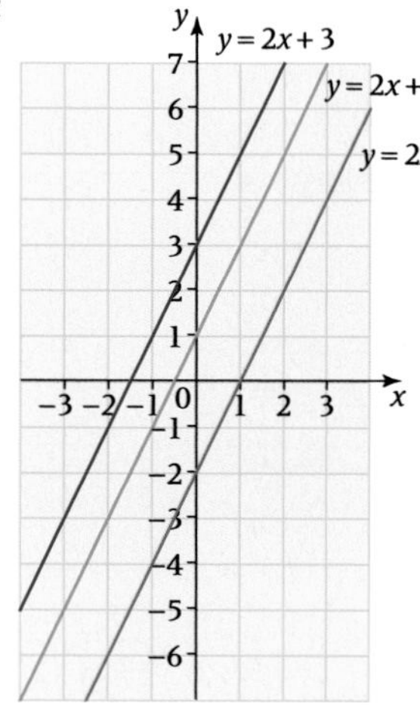

The lines are parallel.

8 a–c

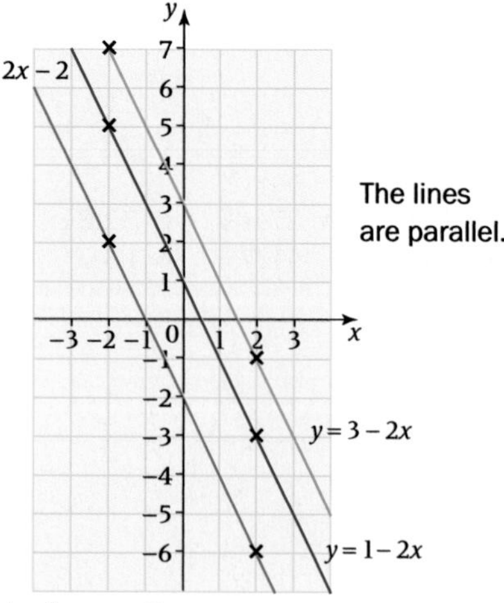

The lines are parallel.

9 a $y = 14$ **b** $x = -3$

A1.4

1 a $x = 4$ **b** $x = -2$ **c** $x = 1$ **d** $y = 5$
e $y = 3$ **f** $y = -1$ **g** $y = -3$ **h** $y = -5$

2 a–e

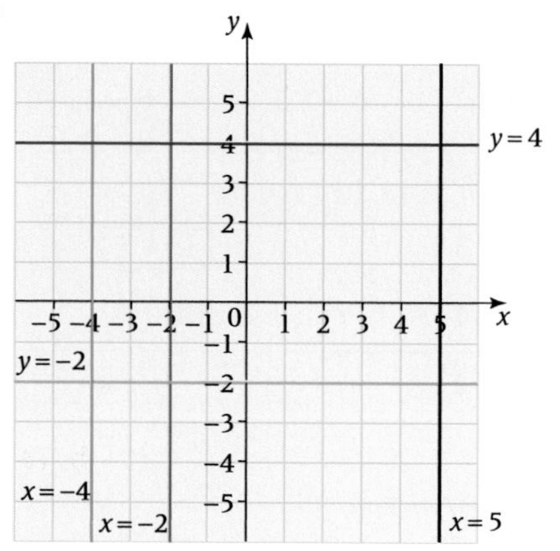

3

Horizontal lines	Vertical lines
$y = 4$	$x = 5$
$y = -10$	$x = 15$
$y = -2$	$x = -3$
$y = -6$	$x = 4$

4 a $(-2, 4)$ **b** $(5, -2)$ **c** $(-4, 4)$

5 a $(2, -3)$ **b** $(1, 6)$ **c** $(3, -1)$

6 For example, the lines $x = 2$, $x = -2$, $y = 2$ and $y = -2$ make a square.

7 b x-axis **c** y-axis

8 a–c

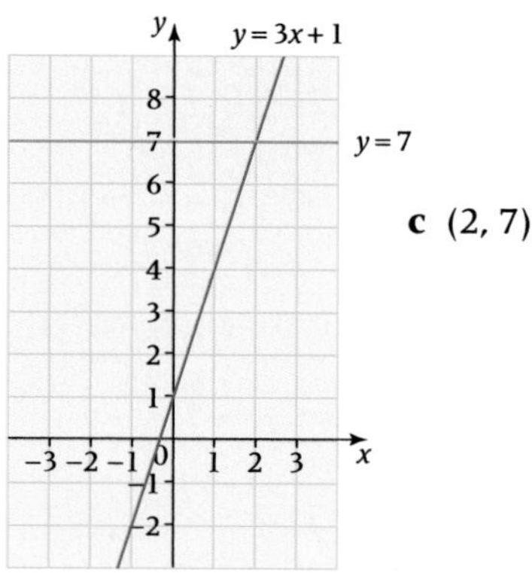

c $(2, 7)$

A1.5

1 a $m = 3$, $c = -1$ **b** $m = 2$, $c = 5$
c $m = 4$, $c = -3$ **d** $\frac{1}{2}$, $c = 2$
e $m = 5$, $c = 1$ **f** $m = -3$, $c = 7$

2 a ii **b** iii **c** i **d** iv **e** v

3 a $y = -x + 5$ **b** $y = x + 3$
c $y = -x - 2$ **d** $y = x - 3$
e $y = -2x + 6$ **f** $y = -5x + 9$
g $y = -3x - 2$ **h** $y = 2x + 5$
i $y = -\frac{1}{2}x + 2$ **j** $y = \frac{1}{2}x + 4$
k $y = -\frac{1}{2}x + 4$ **l** $y = -3x + 4$

4 a $y = x + 3$ and $y = x - 3$ (**b** and **d**)
b $y = -x + 5$ and $y = -x - 2$ (**a** and **c**)

c $y = -3x - 2$ and $y = -3x + 4$ (**g** and **l**)
d $y = -\frac{1}{2}x + 2$ and $y = -\frac{1}{2}x + 4$ (**i** and **k**)

5 **a** and **b**

6 $y = \frac{1}{2}x - 9$, $y = x + 11$, $y = 2x - 2$, $y = 3x + 1$, $y = 4x + 3$

7 $y = 3x + c$ for any c

8 $y = -4x + c$ for any c

9 $y = \frac{1}{2}x + 4$

10 Straight line through (−2, 2) and (2, −2); slopes down from left to right, as do all graphs with negative gradient

A1.6

1 **a**

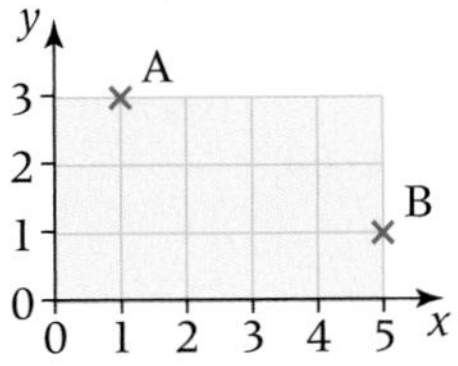

b (3, 2)

2 **a** (3, 3) **b** (2, 4) **c** (2, 1)
d (5, 4) **e** (2, 3)

3 $x = 5$, $y = 2$

4 **a** (1, −4) **b** (2, −4)

5 **a** (1, 4) **b** (2, 4)

A1 Summary

1 **a** −3, 3, 5, 7
b graph passing through (−1, −1) and (2, 5) – straight line
ci $y = -2$ **ii** $x = 2.5$

2 $y = 3x - 2$

N2 Check in

1 **a** 435 **b** 186

2 **a** 72 **b** 42 **c** 12 **d** $4\frac{23}{30}$
e 1392 **f** 17

N2.1

1 **a** 270 **b** 80 **c** 330 **d** 40
e 3800 **f** 70 **g** 210 **h** 390

2 **a** 63 **b** 0.6 **c** 0.69 **d** 2.7

3 **a** 355 **b** 560 **c** 950 **d** 808
e 567 **f** 889 **g** 14.3 **h** 20.7

4

+	2.9	4.8	3.9	2.5	5.9	5.7
3.1	6	7.9	7	5.6	9	8.8
6.5	9.4	11.3	10.4	9	12.4	12.2
8.2	11.1	13	12.1	10.7	14.1	13.9
4.9	7.8	9.7	8.8	7.4	10.8	10.6
7.1	10	11.9	11	9.6	13	12.8
9.6	12.5	14.4	13.5	12.1	15.5	15.3

5 **a** 248 km **b** 263 words
c 265 marks **d** 169 minutes

6 **a** 18.7; 8.7, 10; 5.2, 3.5, 6.5; 4.6, 0.6, 2.9, 3.6
b 25; 12.7, 12.3; 5.8, 6.9, 5.4; 3.7, 2.1, 4.8, 0.6

N2.2

1 **a** 36.8 **b** 78.3 **c** 27.1 **d** 42.1

2 **a** 6.2 **b** 7.1 **c** 8.5 **d** 27.9

3 **a** 10.72 **b** 19.72 **c** 18.11 **d** 141.99

4 **a** 8.05 **b** 4.73 **c** 38.74 **d** 18.68

5 **a** 34.06 **b** 44.71 **c** 3.51 **d** 24.59
e 17.98 **f** 28.89

6 **a** 22.08 **b** 47.34 **c** 83.17

7 **a** 61.98 kg **b** £221.80 **c** 5.87 m
d 30.73 kg **e** 3.525 kg

N2.3

1 **a** 56 **b** 7.2 **c** 9.4 **d** 240
e 72 **f** 0.675 **g** 465 **h** 63

2 **a** 460 **b** 1.7 **c** 127 **d** 0.0082

3 **a** 84 **b** 126 **c** 21 **d** 26
e 187 **f** 279 **g** 32 **h** 174
i 182 **j** 609 **k** 899 **l** 1485

4 **a** 17.6 **b** 168 **c** 79.2 **d** 86.8
e 126 **f** 76.8 **g** 206 **h** 79

5 **a** 153 **b** 207 **c** 25.3 **d** 97.9
e 46.2 **f** 111.3 **g** 114.3 **h** 716.1

6 **a** 86 **b** 22 **c** 568 **d** 216
e 32 **f** 948 **g** 96 **h** 28

7 **a** 244 **b** 36 **c** 128 **d** 24
e 14 **f** 15.3 **g** 10.5 **h** 12.2

8 **a** 46.2 **b** 46 **c** 18.2 **d** 60
e 6 **f** 2175 **g** 3 **h** 30

9 **a** 90 kg **b** £31

N2.4

1 **a** 216 **b** 588 **c** 2943 **d** 364
e 728 **f** 875 **g** 1610 **h** 3888
i 10 336 **j** 4642 **k** 5320 **l** 9222

2 **a** 26 **b** 23 **c** 33 **d** 38
e 37 **f** 68 **g** 15 r 5 **h** 46 r 3

3 **a** 38.4 **b** 108.1 **c** 147.2 **d** 120.9
e 153.6 **f** 649.7

4 **a** 20.02 **b** 27.68 **c** 32.81 **d** 34.5
e 141.81 **f** 61.56 **g** 83.3 **h** 511.92

5 **a** 319.7 **b** 688.5 **c** 1205.4 **d** 805.8
e 3365.3 **f** 1664.1

6 **a** £21.06 **b** £36.86 **c** £202.23
d 39 min 2.4 sec **e** £80.16

7 **a** 12 **b** 18 **c** 19 **d** 23
e 29 **f** 21

8 **a** 3.8 **b** 5.9 **c** 8.4 **d** 12.4
e 13.2 **f** 15.4 **g** 13.7 **h** 27.6

N2.5

1 **a** 26 **b** 37 **c** 52 **d** 10
e 33 **f** 5 **g** 180 **h** 9

2 **a** 28 **b** 72 **c** 5 **d** 16
e 2 **f** 75

3 a $5 \times (2 + 1) = 15$ b $5 \times (3 - 1) \times 4 = 40$
c $20 + 8 \div 2 - 7 = 17$ d $2 + 3^2 \times (4 + 3) = 65$
e $2 \times (6^2 \div 3) + 9 = 33$ f $(4 \times 5 + 5) \times 6 = 150$

4 a Pete, because the contents of the brackets are $2 \times 9 - 4 = 18 - 4 = 14$.
b No; $(5 \times 4)^2 = 20^2 = 400$, whereas $5 \times 4^2 = 5 \times 16 = 80$.
ci 55.7685 cii 55.8

5 a 1 b 2 c 2 d 14 e 40
f 7

6 a 14 b 10 c 2 d 12 e 91
f 112 g 70 h 37 i 11 j 3

7 a 170 b 0.58 c 1.78

N2.6

1 ai 2000 aii 1500 aiii 1550
bi 6000 bii 5800 biii 5790
ci 18 000 cii 17 800 ciii 17 790
di 35 000 dii 35 100 diii 35 130
ei 237 000 eii 236 900 eiii 236 870

2 ai 4.356 aii 4.36 aiii 4.4 aiv 4
bi 9.857 bii 9.86 biii 9.9 biv 10
ci 0.937 cii 0.94 ciii 0.9 civ 1
di 19.496 dii 19.50 diii 19.5 div 19
ei 26.808 eii 26.81 eiii 26.8 eiv 27
fi 20.000 fii 20.00 fiii 20.0 fiv 20
gi 0.005 gii 0.00 giii 0.0 giv 0
hi 3896.657 hii 3896.66
hiii 3896.6 hiv 3897

3 a 0.3 b 150 c 0.08 d 280
e 38 f 0.04 g 92.3 h 4460

4 a 10^2 b 0.01 c 0.01 d 1000
e 0.1 f 0.01

5 ai 9.48 aii 9.5 aiii 9
bi 27.7 bii 28 biii 30
ci 46.7 cii 47 ciii 50
di 388 dii 390 diii 400
ei 2.41 eii 2.4 eiii 2
fi 4910 fii 4900 fiii 5000
gi 0.009 48 gii 0.0095 giii 0.009
hi 3490 hii 3500 hiii 3000
ii 9.88 iii 9.9 iiii 10
ji 25.1 jii 25 jiii 30
ki 2310 hii 2300 hiii 2000
li 237 000 lii 240 000 liii 200 000

6 a 2.4 b 0.56 c 50 d 20
e 0.48 f 400

7 a $4 \times 4 = 16$ b $20 \times 20 = 400$
c $\frac{5 \times 8}{20} = 2$ d $54 \div 9 = 6$

8 a $\frac{30 \times 40}{3 \times 4} = 100$ b $\frac{16 \times 0.5}{0.2 \times 32} = 1.25$
c $(25 + 4)^2 \approx 30^2 = 900$ d $\frac{64 \times 4}{4} = 64$
e $\sqrt{2 \div 0.04} = \sqrt{50} \approx 7$ f $\sqrt{30 \div 0.6} = \sqrt{50} \approx 7$

N2 Summary

1 £19.50
2 £11.36, £22.99, £18, £91.82
3 a Pat b 7
4 a £90 b £6.75
5 2000 (or close)

G2 Check in

1 a 40° b 120°

G2.1

1 a 80° b 60° c 70° d 155°
e 27° f 120°

2 a 54° b 60° c 118°
d $d = 28°$, $e = 104°$ e $f = 37°$, $g = 71°$

3 a 23°, isosceles b 60°, equilateral
c 90°, right-angled

4 a 71° b 66° c 60°

G2.2

1 a 60°, equilateral b 90°, right-angled
c 33°, isosceles d 79°, scalene
e 45°, right-angled isosceles

2 a e.g. (1, 1) b e.g. (3, 0) c e.g. (3, 2)
d e.g. (−2, 0) e (1, 1.5) f e.g. (3, 0)

3 a 60°, 60°, 60° b 30°, 30°, 120°

4 a 5 b 5 c 5
d 5 e 5 f 5

5 a 6 cm² b 6 cm² c 6 cm²
d 6 cm² e 6 cm²

6 No, the angles sum to 180°, so none of the angles can be greater than 180°.

G2.3

1 a 50° b 50° c $c = 70°$, $d = 110°$
d 144° e 128°

2 a 90°, rectangle b 115°, kite
c 106°, parallelogram d 108°, rhombus
e 67°, isosceles trapezium

3 a 70° b 50° c 100°

G2.4

1 a 90° b $b = 100°$, $c = 80°$
c 10° d $d = 125°$, $e = 55°$
e 105° f $f = 110°$, $g = 70°$, $h = 110°$

2

Shape	Equal in length	Bisect each other	Perpendicular
Rectangle	✓	✓	✗
Kite	✗	✗	✓
Isosceles trapezium	✓	✗	✗
Square	✓	✓	✓
Parallelogram	✗	✓	✗
Rhombus	✗	✓	✓
Ordinary trapezium	✗	✗	✗

3 **a** $(-1, 2)$ **c** 6 square units

G2.5

1 **a** 47° (vertically opposite angles)
b 117° (vertically opposite angles)
c $c = 35°$ (vertically opposite angles), $d = 145°$ (angles on a straight line add to 180°)
d $d = 103°$ (vertically opposite angles), $e = 77°$, (angles on a straight line add to 180°), $f = 77°$ (vertically opposite angles)
e 60° (angles at a point add to 360°)

2 **a** 110° (corresponding angles)
b 47° (alternate angles)
c 115° (alternate angles)
d 63° (corresponding angles)
e 130° (corresponding angles)
f $f = 68°$ (corresponding angles), $g = 112°$ (angles on a straight line add to 180°)
g $h = 50°$ (angles on a straight line add to 180°), $i = 50°$ (corresponding angles)
h $j = 63°$ (alternate angles), $k = 63°$ (vertically opposite angles)
i $l = 118°$ (alternate angles), $m = 118°$ (vertically opposite angles)

3 **a** $a = 36°$ (alternate angles), $b = 63°$ (alternate angles), $c = 81°$ (angles on a straight line/in a triangle add to 180°)
b $a = 61°$ (corresponding angles), $b = 49°$ (corresponding angles), $c = 70°$ (angles in a triangle add to 180°)
c $a = 113°$ (alternate angles), $b = 67°$ (angles on a straight line add to 180°), $c = 113°$ (corresponding angles), $d = 67°$ (angles on a straight line add to 180°), $e = 113°$ (corresponding/alternate angles)

G2.6

1 **a** 47° (alternate angles)
b 63° (corresponding angles)
c $c = 56°$ (alternate angles), $d = 43°$ (corresponding angles)
d $e = 52°$ (alternate angles), $f = 48°$ (corresponding angles), $g = 80°$ (angles in a triangle/on a straight line add to 180°)
e 125°

2 **a** 45° **b** 54° **c** 40°
d $d = 75°$, $e = 105°$ **e** 70°

3 **a** $a = b = c = 61°$
b $d = e = f = 70°$, $g = 40°$
c $h = 36°$, $i = j = 108°$, $k = 36°$
d $l = m = n = o = p = 60°$
e $q = r = s = t = 25°$

4 **a** 75° **b** 82° **c** 34°

G2.7

1 Depends on handwriting, for example:

A B C D E F G H I
J K L M N O P Q R
S T U V W X Y Z

2 **a** 3 **b** 2 **c** 2 **d** 3
e 2 **f** 3 **g** 2 **h** 2
i 2 **j** 2

3 **a** 3 lines, 4 lines, 5 lines, 6 lines, 8 lines
b 3, 4, 5, 6, 8

4 **a**

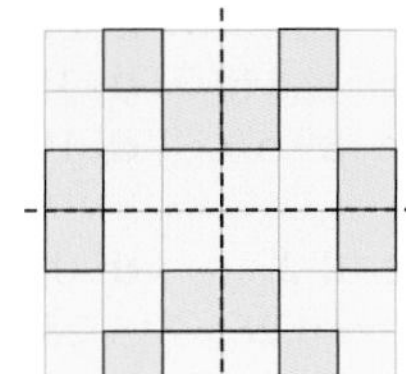

b

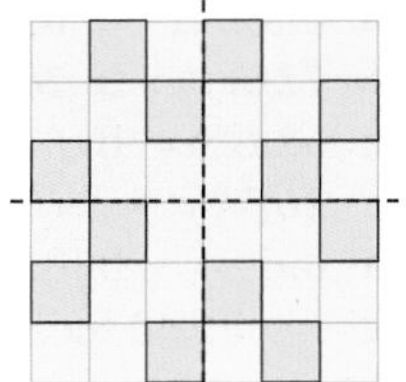

5 **a** $x = 3$ **b** $y = -1$

G2 Summary

1 122°

2 **ai** $x = 63°$
ii Corresponding or alternate angles

3 Last column on the right: 2nd and 3rd squares up

N3 Check in

1 0.1, $\frac{1}{4}$, $\frac{1}{2} = 0.5$, $23\% = \frac{23}{100}$

2 **a** 0.375 **b** $\frac{5}{6}$ or 0.83

N3.1

1 **ai** $\frac{8}{12}$ **aii** $\frac{2}{3}$
bi $\frac{14}{16}$ **bii** $\frac{7}{8}$
ci $\frac{12}{20}$ **cii** $\frac{3}{5}$
di $\frac{10}{15}$ **dii** $\frac{2}{3}$

2 **a** $\frac{1}{3}$ **b** $\frac{3}{4}$ **c** $\frac{3}{5}$ **d** $\frac{4}{9}$
e $\frac{5}{8}$ **f** $\frac{1}{3}$ **g** $\frac{4}{9}$ **h** $\frac{23}{93}$

3 **a** $\frac{3}{2}$ **b** $\frac{11}{3}$ **c** $\frac{35}{8}$ **d** $\frac{20}{9}$
e $\frac{41}{7}$ **f** $\frac{39}{5}$ **g** $\frac{96}{11}$ **h** $\frac{88}{7}$

4 **a** $1\frac{1}{4}$ **b** $1\frac{3}{5}$ **c** $1\frac{4}{7}$ **d** $2\frac{1}{4}$
e $2\frac{1}{5}$ **f** $2\frac{6}{7}$ **g** $4\frac{3}{5}$ **h** $3\frac{1}{9}$

5 **a** 8 **b** 27 **c** 56 **d** 56
e 2 **f** 90 **g** 85 **h** 7

6 **a** $\frac{2}{5} > \frac{1}{3}$ **b** $\frac{1}{3}$, $\frac{7}{18}$, $\frac{4}{9}$

7 **a** $\frac{2}{5}$ **b** $\frac{2}{3}$ **c** $\frac{4}{7}$ **d** $\frac{5}{6}$
e $\frac{4}{7}$ **f** $\frac{10}{7}$

8 a $\frac{3}{15}, \frac{1}{3}, \frac{2}{5}$ b $\frac{1}{2}, \frac{15}{28}, \frac{4}{7}$ c $\frac{7}{4}, \frac{5}{8}, \frac{9}{14}$

N3.2

1 a $\frac{3}{10}$ b $\frac{3}{5}$ c $\frac{16}{25}$ d $\frac{9}{20}$
e $\frac{3}{8}$ f $1\frac{2}{25}$ g $3\frac{19}{80}$ h $3\frac{1}{16}$

2 a 0.3 b 0.44 c 1.04 d 0.62
e 0.45 f 0.52 g 0.28 h 3.35

3 a 0.44 b 0.67 c 1.35 d 0.73
e 1.14 f 1.4 g 2.17 h 0.85

4 a $\frac{2}{5}$ b $\frac{9}{10}$ c $\frac{7}{20}$ d $\frac{13}{20}$
e $\frac{1}{100}$ f $3\frac{31}{50}$ g $\frac{61}{400}$ h $\frac{17}{800}$

5 a 54% b 40% c 85% d 52%
e 66.7% f 24% g 120% h 44%

6 a 0.37 b 0.07 c 1.89 d 0.45

7 a 72% b 20% c 125% d 3%

8 a 68.6% b 64% c 89.5% d 191.7%
e 26.3%

9 a $0.\dot{6}$ b $0.\dot{2}\dot{7}$ c $0.\dot{2}$ d $0.\dot{4}2857\dot{1}$

10 a $\frac{1}{7} = 0.142\ 857\ 142$ $\frac{2}{7} = 0.285\ 714\ 285$
$\frac{3}{7} = 0.428\ 571\ 428$ $\frac{4}{7} = 0.571\ 428\ 571$
$\frac{5}{7} = 0.714\ 285\ 714$ $\frac{6}{7} = 0.857\ 142\ 857$
b The first six decimal places recur.
c Again, the first six decimal places recur.

N3.3

1

Fraction	Decimal	Percentage
$\frac{3}{8}$	0.375	37.5%
$\frac{7}{25}$	0.28	28%
$\frac{3}{20}$	0.15	15%
$\frac{3}{8}$	0.375	37.5%
$\frac{4}{5}$	0.8	80%
$\frac{7}{40}$	0.175	17.5%

2 a $\frac{5}{8}$ b $\frac{4}{5}$ c $\frac{5}{7}$ d $\frac{3}{8}$
e $\frac{16}{11}$ f $\frac{14}{9}$ g $1\frac{7}{23}$ h $2\frac{8}{11}$

3 a $<$ b $>$ c $>$ d $>$

4 a 47%, $\frac{12}{25}$, 0.49 b 78%, $\frac{4}{5}$, 0.81
c $\frac{7}{12}, \frac{4}{5}$, 66% d 29%, 0.3, $\frac{5}{16}, \frac{7}{22}$

5 a $\frac{19}{28} = 67.9\%$ b $\frac{11}{16} = 68.8\%$
c $\frac{19}{28} = 79.2\%$ d $\frac{1}{3} = 33.3\%$

6 a German, as $\frac{37}{54} = 68.5\%$
b $\frac{7}{31} = 23\%$, so Sarah's class is in accord with the rest of the school.

N3.4

1 a $2\frac{1}{2}$ b 2 c $2\frac{2}{3}$ d $1\frac{6}{7}$ e 2 f $1\frac{1}{3}$

2 a 4 b $3\frac{3}{4}$ c 4 d $4\frac{2}{3}$ e $2\frac{1}{4}$
f $22\frac{2}{5}$ g $13\frac{1}{3}$ h $8\frac{5}{9}$

3 a $\frac{5}{4}$ kg b $3\frac{1}{2}$ kg c $7\frac{1}{5}$ litres d $14\frac{2}{5}$ kg

4 a €12 b £28 c $37\frac{1}{2}$ m d $36\frac{4}{7}$ km
e £375 f $58\frac{1}{3}$ mm g 1375 m h $18\frac{6}{13}$ g

5 a 264 kg b $4500 c 4.44 kg d 952 cups
e 21.67 tonnes f 96° g 139.35°
h 0.87 hours or 52 minutes i £260.67

6 a $\frac{2}{3}$ b $\frac{3}{5}$ c $\frac{1}{5}$ d $\frac{11}{60}$

7 a £24 b £7.50 c 73 days

8 a $\frac{1}{10}$ b $\frac{1}{8}$ c 3 d $\frac{4}{3}$
e $\frac{5}{4}$

N3.5

1 a £150 b 2 kg c £40
d 18.5 kg e £0.30 or 30p f 34.28 m

2 a £9 b 82 kg c $5
d £0.75 or 75p e £31.50 f 0.19 m

3 a £51 b 72 Mb c £45
d £40 e 136.5 m f £22
g 1099 mm h 6.3 kg i 31.5 mm

4 a Find 10% by dividing by 10; find 5% by halving 10%; add the two answers together.
b Find 10% and then halve it.
c Find 10% and times by 3; find 5% by halving 10%; add the two answers together.
d Find 10%; halve 10% to find 5%; halve 5% to find 2.5%; add the three answers together.
e Find 10% and halve it to find 5%; subtract 5% from 100% (the original amount).

5 a 11.2 Mb b 13.2 tonnes c 90.85 km
d £98.28

6 a £2.04 b 13.92 km c £3.04
d €108.80 e 11.05 m f 33.58 cm
g 125.8 m h £1.53 i £21.25

N3.6

1 a 4.5 kg b 10.2 m c 54°
d 0.74 cm e 331.5 ml f 63°
g 18.2 kg h 85.87 kg i 5.544 kg
j 3.96 m^2

2 a £385 b 70.3 kg c £550.20
d 491.4 km e 1128 kg

3 a £397.80 b 524.9 kg c £1758.96
d 599.56 km e $3423.55

4 New wage: £364, £296.92, £428.74, £217.64, £206.59

5 a 492.8 ml b £166.50 c £250 185
d 1081 students

N3 Summary

1 22

2 a £3.20 b 75% c £17

3 a £268.65 b $\frac{1}{30}$

D1 Check in

1 **a** $\frac{2}{3}$ **b** $\frac{1}{2}$ **c** $\frac{3}{4}$ **d** $\frac{1}{4}$ **e** 1
2 **a** 1 **b** 1 **c** $\frac{3}{10}$ **d** $\frac{2}{5}$
3 **a** 0.9 **b** 0.4 **c** 0.85
4 **a** 0.01 **b** 0.25 **c** 0.35 **d** 0.05 **e** 0.36

D1.1

1 Impossible: **b**, **c**, **e**; Certain: **a**, **d**
2 **a** head, tail **b** 1, 2, 3, 4
c c, h, a, n, g, e **d** yellow, green, blue
e Mon, Tue, Wed, Thu, Fri, Sat, Sun
3 **Aa** blue, blue, blue, blue
Ab 1
Ac 0
Ad blue
Ae red
Ba blue, blue, blue, red
Bb $\frac{3}{4}$
Bc $\frac{1}{4}$
Bd blue
Be red
Ca blue, blue, red, red
Cb $\frac{1}{2}$
Cc $\frac{1}{2}$
Cd–e equal chance of each colour
Da blue, red, red, red
Db $\frac{1}{4}$
Dc $\frac{3}{4}$
Dd red
De blue
Ea red, red, red, red
Eb 0
Ec 1
Ed red
Ee blue
4 **a** $\frac{1}{250} = 0.004$ **b** $\frac{10}{250} = \frac{1}{25} = 0.04$
5 **a** $\frac{48}{120} = \frac{2}{5}$ **b** $= \frac{3}{5}$

D1.2

1 **a** 0.0 **b** 0.5 **c** 1.0
2 **ai** $\frac{1}{10}$ **aii** $\frac{3}{10}$ **aiii** $\frac{6}{10} = \frac{3}{5}$
b Yellow 0.1, Green 0.3, Red 0.6
c Yellow **d** Red **e** 1
3 **ai** $\frac{6}{4} = \frac{3}{4}$ **aii** $\frac{2}{8} = \frac{1}{4}$
b Green 0.25, Pink 0.75
c Green **d** Pink **e** 1
4 0.99
5 0.6

D1.3

1 **a** Yes **b** Yes **c** No **d** Yes
e No **f** Yes **g** No **h** Yes
2 **a** $\frac{1}{4}$ **b** $\frac{1}{4}$ **c** $\frac{1}{2}$
3 **a** $\frac{2}{5}$ **b** $\frac{1}{2}$ **c** $\frac{1}{10}$ **d** $\frac{1}{2}$ **e** $\frac{3}{5}$
f 1
4 **a** $\frac{1}{5}$ **b** $\frac{1}{5}$ **c** $\frac{2}{5}$ **d** $\frac{2}{5}$ **e** $\frac{4}{5}$
5 **a** 30, 5, 5, 10
bi $\frac{3}{5}$ **bii** $\frac{1}{10}$ **biii** $\frac{3}{10}$

D1.4

1 **a** $\frac{20}{50} = \frac{2}{5}$ **b** $\frac{15}{50} = \frac{3}{10}$ **c** $\frac{10}{50} = \frac{1}{5}$ **d** $\frac{5}{50} = \frac{1}{10}$
2 **ai** 24 **aii** 8 **aiii** 16
aiv 6 **av** 18
bi $\frac{2}{24} = \frac{1}{12}$ **bii** $\frac{12}{24} = \frac{1}{2}$ **biii** $\frac{8}{24} = \frac{1}{3}$
biv $\frac{16}{24} = \frac{2}{3}$ **bv** $\frac{6}{24} = \frac{1}{4}$ **bvi** $\frac{18}{24} = \frac{3}{4}$
3 **a** $\frac{1}{10}$ **b** $\frac{5}{10} = \frac{1}{2}$ **c** 0 **d** $\frac{2}{10} = \frac{1}{5}$ **e** $\frac{8}{10} = \frac{4}{5}$

D1.5

1 75
2 80
3 9
4 **a** 15 **b** 20 **c** 25
5 **a** 0.15
bi 10, 15, 30, 20, 10, 15
bii 50, 75, 150, 100, 50, 75
biii 100, 150, 300, 200, 100, 150
6 £1

D1.6

1 **a** 11, 16, 14, 9 **b** Red
ci $\frac{11}{50} = 0.22$ **cii** $\frac{16}{50} = 0.32$ **ciii** $\frac{40}{50} = 0.28$
2 **a** 9, 10, 6, 9, 6 **b** 2 **c** 40
di $\frac{9}{40} = 0.225$ **dii** $\frac{10}{40} = \frac{1}{4} = 0.225$
diii $\frac{6}{40} = \frac{3}{20} = 0.15$ **div** $\frac{9}{40} = 0.225$
dv $\frac{6}{40} = \frac{3}{20} = 0.15$
e 15
3 **a** 50
bi $\frac{9}{50} = 0.18$ **bii** $\frac{14}{50} = \frac{7}{25} = 0.28$
biii $\frac{27}{50} = 0.54$
c 2 red, 3 green, 5 blue
d By increasing the number of times a ball is taken out.

D1.7

1 AB, AC, BC, BA, CA, CB
2 **a** AD, AE, AF, BD, BE, BF, CD, CE, CF

b $\frac{1}{9}$ **c** $\frac{4}{9}$

3 a HH, HT, TH, TT

b 1st spin 2nd spin

H ($\frac{1}{2}$) → H ($\frac{1}{2}$), T ($\frac{1}{2}$)

T ($\frac{1}{2}$) → H ($\frac{1}{2}$), T ($\frac{1}{2}$)

c $\frac{1}{4}$ **d** $\frac{3}{4}$ **e** 25

4 a Red Red, Red Black, Black Red, Black Black

b First selection Second selection

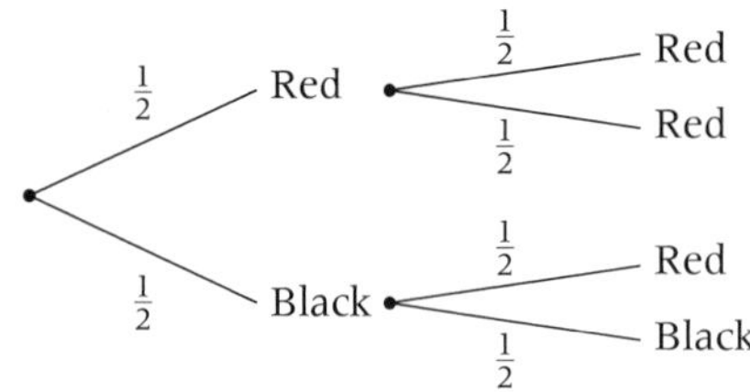

c $\frac{1}{2}$

D1.8

1 a RA, RB, RC, RD, RE, YA, YB, YC, YD, YE, GA, GB, GC, GD, GE, PA, PB, PC, PD, PE

b

	R	Y	G	P
A	(R, A)	(Y, A)	(G, A)	(P, A)
B	(R, B)	(Y, B)	(G, B)	(P, B)
C	(R, C)	(Y, C)	(G, C)	(P, C)
D	(R, D)	(Y, D)	(G, D)	(P, D)
E	(R, E)	(Y, E)	(G, E)	(P, E)

c $\frac{1}{20}$

2 a

	1	2	3	4
Heads	(1, H)	(2, H)	(3, H)	(4, H)
Tails	(1, T)	(2, T)	(3, T)	(4, T)

bi $\frac{1}{8}$ **bii** $\frac{1}{4}$

3 a

	Club (C)	Diamond (D)	Spade (S)	Heart (H)
Club (C)	(C, C)	(D, C)	(S, C)	(H, C)
Diamond (D)	(C, D)	(D, D)	(S, D)	(H, D)
Spade (S)	(C, S)	(D, S)	(S, S)	(H, S)
Heart (H)	(C, H)	(D, H)	(S, H)	(H, H)

b $\frac{1}{4}$

4 a

	1	2	3	4	5	6
1	(1, 1)	(2, 1)	(3, 1)	(4, 1)	(5, 1)	(6, 1)
2	(1, 2)	(2, 2)	(3, 2)	(4, 2)	(5, 2)	(6, 2)
3	(1, 3)	(2, 3)	(3, 3)	(4, 3)	(5, 3)	(6, 3)
4	(1, 4)	(2, 4)	(3, 4)	(4, 4)	(5, 4)	(6, 4)
5	(1, 5)	(2, 5)	(3, 5)	(4, 5)	(5, 5)	(6, 5)
6	(1, 6)	(2, 6)	(3, 6)	(4, 6)	(5, 6)	(6, 6)

P(Double six) = $\frac{1}{36}$

b 7 has the most outcomes

D1.9

1 a Any impossible event

b Any event that will definitely happen

2 a $\frac{2}{5}$ or 0.4 **b** $\frac{3}{5}$ or 0.6

3 a $\frac{3}{10}$, 0.35, $\frac{3}{8}$, $\frac{2}{5}$, 45%

b

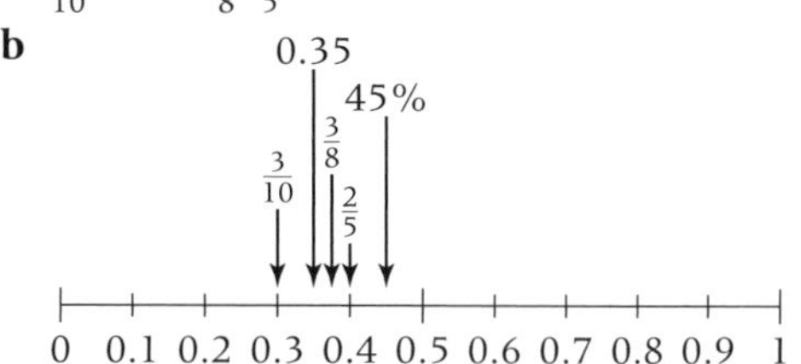

4 a $\frac{3}{8}$ **b** Red **c** Blue

d 8 red, 2 blue, 6 green

5 a Green 0.2, Red 0.27, Blue 0.25, Yellow 0.28

b 25

D1 Summary

1 a 25, 22, 46, 33 **b** $\frac{37}{100}$ or 0.37

c $\frac{24}{46}$ or $\frac{12}{23}$

2 40

3 (B,G), (B,Y), (G,B), (G,Y), (Y,B), (Y,G)

A2 Check in

1 a 5 **b** 9 **c** 4 **d** 10

2 ai 1, 2, 3, 6, 9, 18 **aii** 1, 2, 3, 4, 6, 12

aiii 1, 2, 3, 4, 6, 8, 12, 24

b 1, 2, 3, 6

A2.1

1 a $4b$ **b** $2y$ **c** $3a$

d $9p$ **e** $3x$ **f** $6z$

2 a $5p + 6q$ **b** $9x + 7y$ **c** $2m + 8n$

d $x + 5y$ **e** $8r - 6s$ **f** $2g - 4f$

g $2a + 6b + 5c$ **h** $5u - 2v + 3w$ **i** $3x - 4y + 5z$

j $6r + 5s + 2t$

3 a $6t$ **b** $3n$ **c** $4x$

4 a $4x$ **b** $4x + 8$

5 a $2m$ **b** $3m$ **c** $12m$

6 a $6c$ **b** $10d$ **c** $6c + 10d$

7 a $50f + 30g$ b $80j + 40k$
c $50x + 60y + 30z$
d $60p + 80q + 40r$

A2.2

1 a y^4 b m^6 c x^3 d p^2
2 a $3t^2$ b $4pq^2$ c $6v^2w^3$ d $2r^4s$
3 a $6m^2n$ b $8y^3z^2$ c $12gh^3$ d $10xy^4$
4 a $6m^2$ b $12p^3$ c $6xy^2$ d $10r^2s^2$
5 a n^5 b s^7 c p^4 d t^4
6 a x^7 b x^8 c x^9 d x^7
7 a r^2 b r c r^5 d r^3
8 a m^4 b x c t^2 d y^3
9 a x b m^2 c s^3 d v^3
e q^3 f t^4 g p h y^2
10 $2n^3 = 2 \times n^3$, $2 \times n \times n = 2n^2$, $n^2 = \frac{n^4}{n^2}$, $5 \times n = 5n$

A2.3

1 a $3m + 6$ b $4p + 24$ c $2x + 8$ d $5q + 5$
e $12 + 2n$ f $6 + 3t$ g $12 + 4s$ h $8 + 2v$
2 a $6q + 3$ b $8m + 4$ c $12x + 9$ d $6k + 2$
e $10 + 10n$ f $12 + 6p$ g $4 + 12y$ h $10 + 8z$
3 a $5p + 9$ b $7m + 8$ c $2x + 4$ d $10 + 5k$
e $9t + 10$ f $4r + 7$
4 a $5n + 12$ b $6p + 10$ c $10x + 10$ d $18n + 7$
5 a $n + 5$ b $3(n + 5)$
6 a $s + 6$ b $2(s + 6)$ c $2s + 19$
7 a $12y$ b $y + 2$ c $20(y + 2)$ d $32y + 40$
8 a $4x^2 + x$ b $m^3 + 2m$ c $2t^3 + 8t$ d $3p^3 + 3p$
9 a $4m^2 - 12m$ b $2p^2 - 12p$
c $-3x - 6$ d $-10m + 20$

A2.4

1 a $9r$ b $4m^2$ c $4x$ d $8tv$
e $10mn$ f $6xy^2$ g $2x^2 + x$ h $9w - 8$
i $z^3 + 3z + 1$
2 a $8y + 12$ b $6x - 4$ c $6k - 6$ d $4 - 4n$
3 a $k^2 + k$ b $m^2 + 7m$ c $10t + 5$
4 a $2m^2 - 6m$ b $8p^2 - 4p$ c $r^3 + 3r$ d $2s^3 - 8s$
5 a $5r + 4$ b $2s$ c $4j + 5$ d $15t - 9$
6 a $12m^2 - 9m - 3$ b $6p^2 - 14p + 4$
c $-10q^2 + 15q + 45$ d $8v^2 - 20v + 12$
7 a $n + 4$, $3(n + 4)$, $4n$, $4n - 2$, $2(4n - 2)$
b $5n - 16$

A2.5

1 a 1, 2 b 1, 2, 4 c 1, 2, 5, 10
d 1, 2, 3, 6 e 1, 3 f 1, 2
g 1, 2 h 1, 2, 4, 8
2 a 3 b 2 c 2 d 4
3 a y b s c m d $2y$
4 a $2(x + 5)$ b $3(y + 5)$ c $4(2p - 1)$
d $3(2 + m)$ e $5(n + 1)$ f $6(2 - t)$
g $2(7 + 2k)$ h $3(3z - 1)$
5 a $w(w + 1)$ b $z(1 - z)$ c $y(4 + y)$
d $m(2m - 3)$ e $p(4p + 5)$ f $k(7 - 2k)$
g $n(3n^2 - 2)$ h $r(5 + 3r)$
6 $4(x + 3) = 4x + 12$, $4x^2 - 3x = x(4x - 3)$,
$3(x - 4) = 3x - 12$, $4x + 3x^2 = x(4 + 3x)$
7 a $4(y - 3)$ b $x(2x + 3)$ c $y(3y - 1)$
d $5(3 + t^2)$ e $3m(1 + 3m)$ f $2r(r - 1)$
g $v(4v^2 + 1)$ h $3w(w + 1)$
8 a Kate
b Debbie should have an 8 in front of the x^2-term inside the bracket. If she had included this, she would have been able to take out more factors. Bryn should have $8x$ rather than $8x^2$ as the first term in the bracket. He can take out a further factor of 2.

A2 Summary

1 a $2p + 4q$ b $2y^2$ c $3c + 4d$ d $8pq$
2 a $4a$ b $6b - 3$ c c^3 d d^2
3 a 1 b −5
4 a $x(x - 5)$ b $(15x - 6)$
5 a $80x$ b $95y$ c $80x + 95y$
6 Possibilities include: $x + 3$, $x + 3$; $2x$, 6

D2 Check in

1 a 44, 47, 48, 55, 56, 59, 61, 65
b 0.5, 0.8, 1.5, 1.7, 2.1, 2.5
c 13.1, 13.2, 21.3, 23.1, 31.2, 32.1
2 a 81 b 179 c 105 d 205 e 441
f 74 g 135 h 177 i 219 j 41

D2.1

1 a 6, 7, 8, 5, 4 b i c u d 30
2 a 5, 4, 7, 4, 2, 2, 1, 2, 3 b 5 c 92 mm
3 a 9, 17, 11, 3 b 808
4 a 28 b 67

D2.2

1 a Controlled experiment b Observation
c Controlled experiment d Data logging
e Controlled experiment f Observation
g Observation h Data logging
i Observation j Data logging
2 a Observation b 1, 21; 2, 11; 3, 3; 4, 4; 5, 1
c 40 d 73
3 a Controlled experiment
b–c 1, 13; 2, 14; 3, 4; 4, 4; 5, 5; 6, 5
d 2 e 45
f Yes, the dice seems to be biased in favour of 1 and 2.
g By increasing the number of rolls.

D2.3

1 a Choices should be given.
b 'Recently' is too vague.
2 a Which is your favourite fruit? b 100

3 **a** 30 is in two options and over 40s are missing.
b The options are too vague.
c Using more than one shop would improve the reliability of the data.
d Examples:
How old are you?
Under 20 20–29 30–39 40 or over
How often do you go shopping?
At most once a month 3 times a month
At least once a week

4 **a** Which channel do you watch the most?
b 30
c There are far too many 'Other' possibilities.

5 **a** 'Regularly' is too vague.
b How many times a week do you buy a newspaper?
0 1 2 3 4 5 6 7
c There is no option for less than 1 year. If someone last bought a book a number of years ago, they are unlikely to remember how many years exactly. Better options are:
Less than a week ago 1–4 weeks ago
1–6 months ago More than 6 months ago

D2.4

1 **a** discrete **b** discrete **c** continuous
d discrete **e** continuous **f** discrete
g continuous **h** continuous **i** discrete
j discrete

2 **a** 4, 9, 16, 11, 10 **b** 50
3 **a** 8, 6, 7, 10, 3, 6 **b** 40
4 **a** 0, 4, 7, 6, 8 **b** 25
5 **a** 8, 13, 10, 9 **b** $1.0 < m \leqslant 2.0$ **c** 40

D2.5

1 **ai** 15 **aii** 12
bi 39 **bii** 22
c 58

2 Boys: 12, 5; Girls: 7, 8

3 **a–b** Example:

	Contract	Pay as you go
Black	25	30
Silver	30	15

4

	Sugar	No sugar
Tea		
Coffee		

5

	Part-exchange	Cash
Saloons		
Hatchbacks		

D2.6

1 **a** £220, £275, £310, £345, £350, £402, £437, £500, £549, £600
b All answers in GHz: 1.6, 1.8, 1.8, 2.0, 2.0, 2.0, 2.0, 2.16, 2.16, 2.53
c 3 **d** 10
ei 1, 4, 6–10 **ii** 2, 6, 8, 9, 10 **iii** 5–8
f 6

2 **a** Biased, as each name is not equally likely to be chosen.
b Biased, as each name is not equally likely to be chosen.
c Random, as each card is equally likely to be picked.
d Biased, as each height is not equally likely to be chosen.
e Biased, as each person is not equally likely to find the star.
f Biased, as only students 1 to 6 will have an equal chance of being selected.
g Biased, as student 30 has no chance of being picked.

D2 Summary

1 **a** £540 **b** £270 **c** Single
2 13, 19, 14, 38, 18, 27
3 any suitable data collection sheet

G3 Check in

1 **a** 40 cm² **b** 30 cm²
2 **a** 250 **b** 6300 **c** 41 **d** 250 **e** 3500
f 4 **g** 5.6 **h** 40 **i** 4.1 **j** 5.2

G3.1

1 **a** Triangular prism **b** Square-based pyramid
c Sphere **d** Cuboid
e Pentagon-based pyramid
f Cone **g** Cylinder
h Cube **i** Tetrahedron
j Pentagonal prism

2 **a** **b** **c**

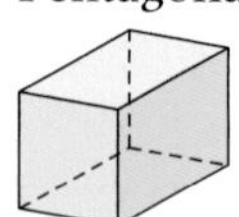
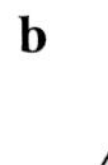
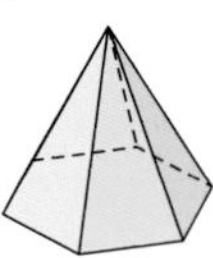
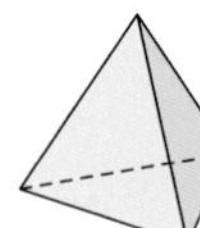

3 **a** 8 **b** 12 **c** 6

4 a

Name of solid	No. of faces (f)	No. of edges (e)	No. of vertices (v)
Triangular prism	5	9	6
Square-based pyramid	5	8	5
Tetrahedron	4	6	4
Pentagonal prism	7	15	10
Square-based prism	6	12	8
Cube	6	12	8
Hexagonal pyramid	7	12	7
Octagonal prism	10	24	16
Pentagonal pyramid	6	10	6

b $e + 2 = f + v$

5 For example,

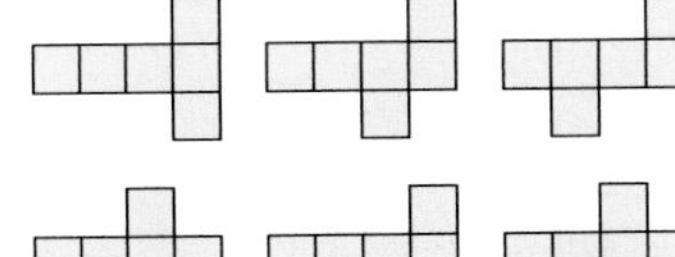

G3.2

1 **a** 36 cm³ **b** 250 m³ **c** 240 cm³
2 100
3 **a** 288 m³ **b** 76.9 cm³ **c** 55.3 cm³
4 6 cm
5 **a** 3 cm **b** 5.7 cm **c** 8.7 m
6 **a** 1500 cm³ **b** 440 cm³ **c** 324 cm³

G3.3

1 **a** 160 cm³ **b** 108 m³ **c** 134.4 m³
2 **a** 203.125 m³ **b** 9.3 cm³ **c** 3.125 m³
3 **a** 24 cm², 120 cm³ **b** 3 m², 30 m³
c 4 m², 20 m³ **d** 32 cm², 256 cm³
4 Yes

G3 Summary

1 **a** 8 **b** C
2 **a** various possibilities eg x = 150 cm, y = 170 cm, z = 200 cm
b various answers eg with the above, 5.1 m³

A3 Check in

1

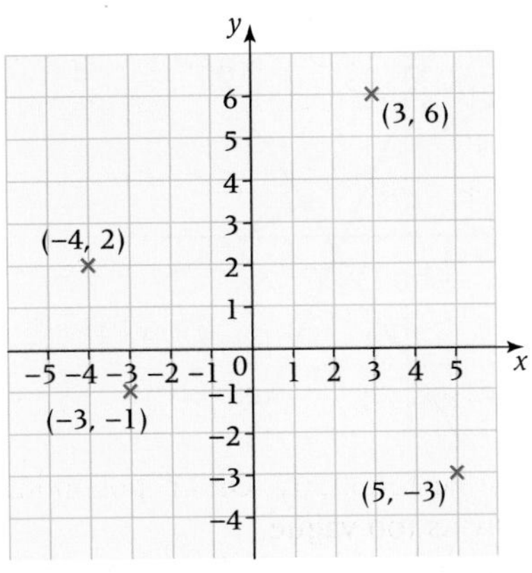

2 $y = 1, 3, 5, 7, 9$

A3.1

1 **a** $y = -1, 3, 5, 7, 11$
b

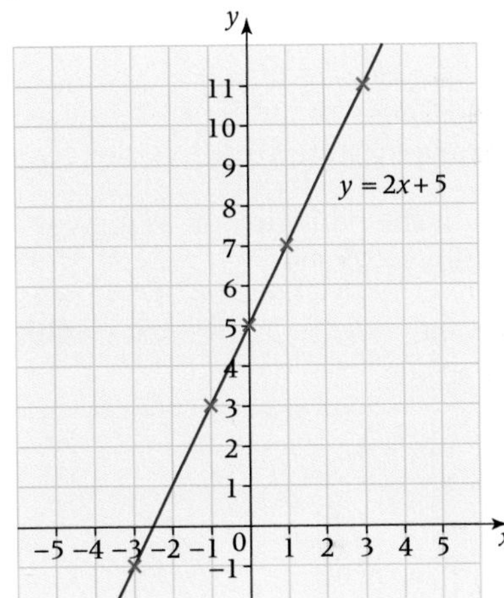

2 **a–d**

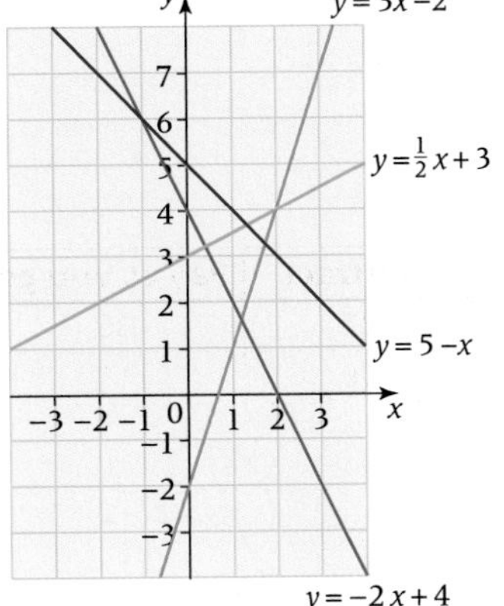

3 a–d

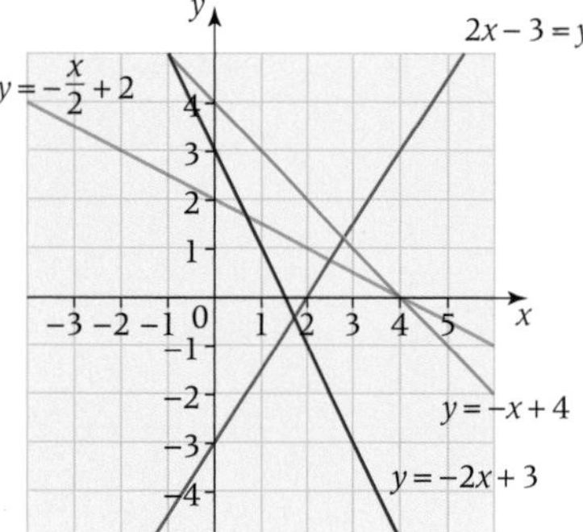

4 a–d

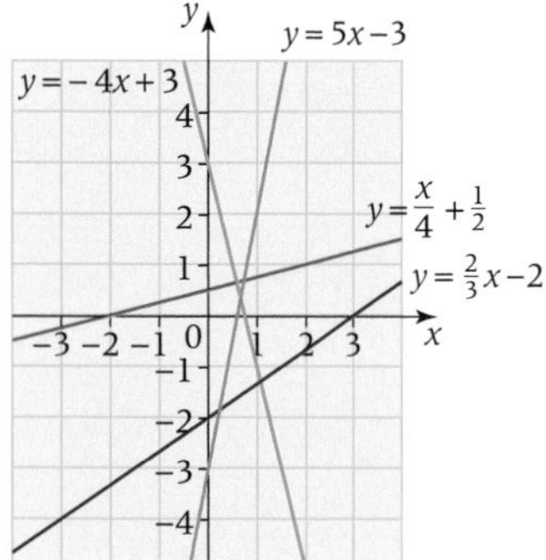

5 $4x+2y=1$ is the odd one out, as it gives $y=\frac{1}{2}-2x$ not $y=2x+\frac{1}{2}$

6 a

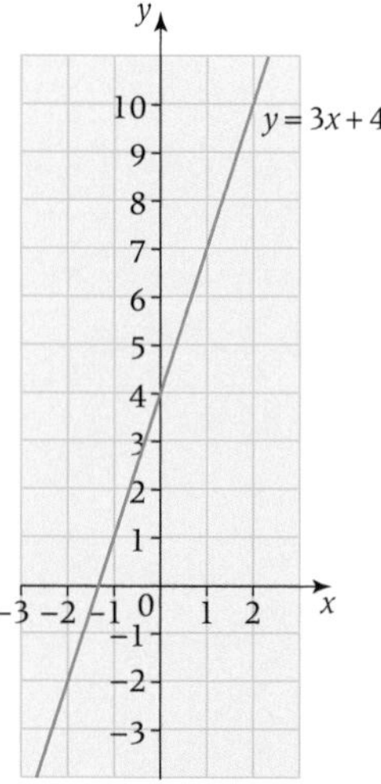

bi 5.5 **bii** −1.5

7 a–d

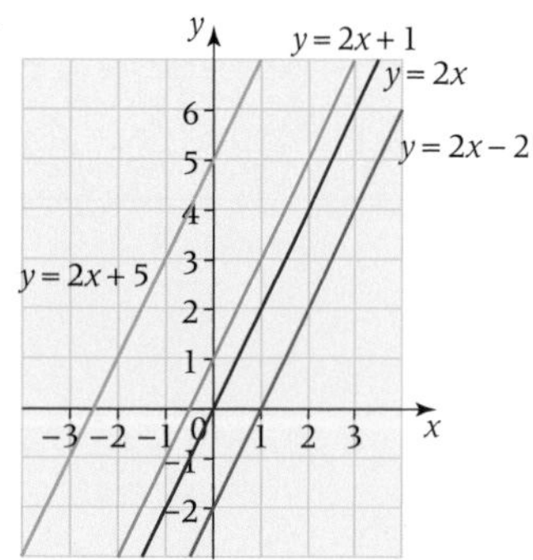

The lines are all parallel.

8 a–c

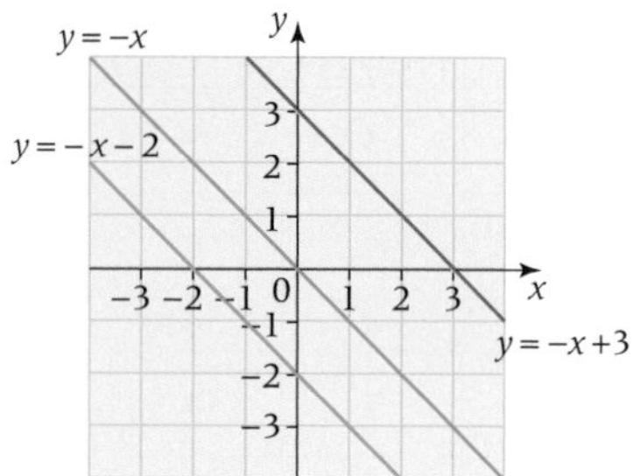

The lines are all parallel.
$y=-x+1$ would lie between $y=-x$ and $y=-x+3$, with the same slope and passing through (0, 1).

A3.2

1 A3, B1, C4, D2

2 Growth spurt at around 5, steadies down until next growth spurt at about 13–17 years (puberty) then steadies down again.

3

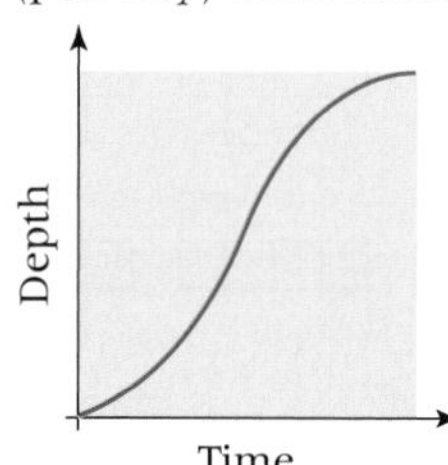

4 a

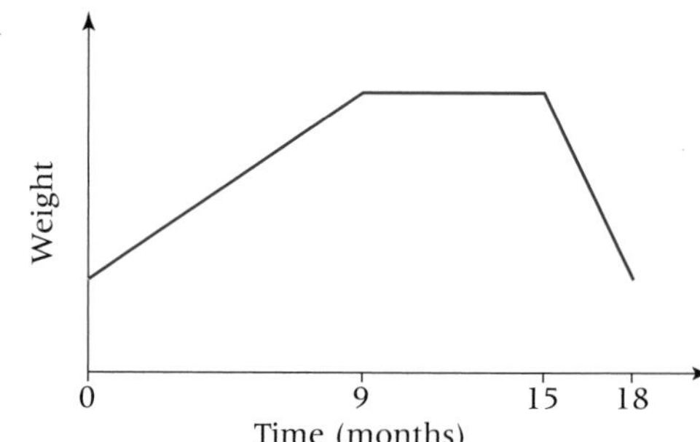

b

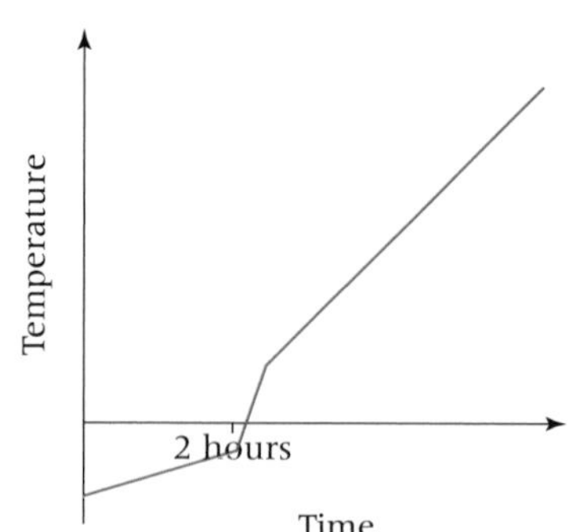

5 a

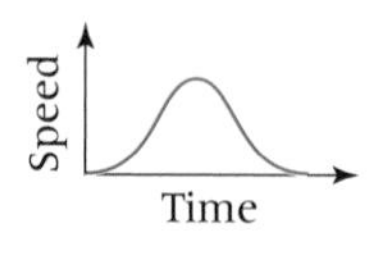

b

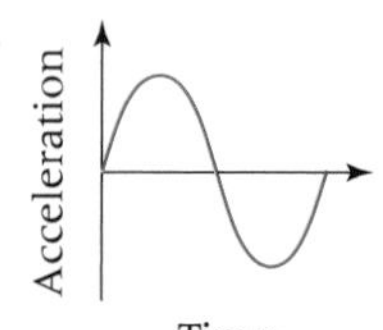

A3.3

1 **a** 4.8 km **b** 6.25 miles
c 7.2 km **d** 1.25 miles
1 mile is longer than 1 km.

2 **a** 2.7 kg **b** 4.5 kg **c** 8.8 lbs
d 4 lbs **e** 3.2 kg **f** 1 lb
g 5.5 kg **h** 11 lb
1 kg is heavier than 1 lb, as 1 kg ≈ 2.2 lb

3 **ai** 68 °F **aii** 14 °C **aiii** 86 °F **aiv** −7 °C
b 32 °F
c 28 °F, 36 °F, 43 °F, 54 °F, 75 °F

A3.4

1 **a** e.g. 0 cm = 0 mm, 10 cm = 100 mm
b 100 mm

2 **a** 0 lbs, 22 lb, 11 lb
ei 4.5 kg **eii** 2.3 kg
eiii 6.6 lb **eiv** 5.5 lb

3 **a** e.g. £0 = $0, £10 = $17, £20 = $34
b $51
di $8.50 **dii** £17.60

4 **b** The NZ cap is cheapest.

A3.5

1 2.5 mph

2 **a** 8 **b** 15 **c** 150 **d** 40 **e** 2.5

3 37.5 miles

4 **a** 320 **b** 175 **c** 270 **d** 50 **e** 125

5 2.5 hours

6 **a** 2 **b** 2.5 **c** 3.5 **d** 4.5 **e** 3.33

7 **a** 70 km/h **b** 14 km/litre

8 **a** 333.3 m/min **b** 5.6 m/s

A3.6

1 **a** 1 pm **b** 60 miles
c $1\frac{1}{2}$ hours **d** 25 miles
e

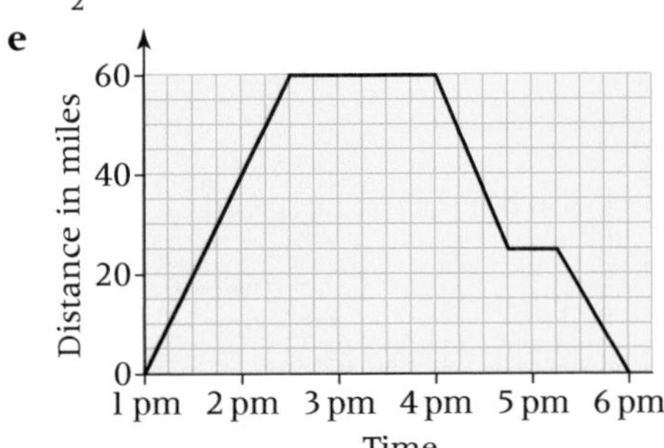

2 **a** F **b** C **c** D **d** A
e G **f** B **g** E

3 **a** 8 hours **b** 260 miles **c** 2 hours
d $\frac{1}{2}$ hour **e** 2 hours

A3.7

1 **a** 80 km **b** 5 hours **c** 16 km/h
d $\frac{50}{2}$ = 25 km per hour
e 15 km/h **f** first **g** faster

2 **a** 5 miles **b** $\frac{1}{2}$ hour
c 2:30 pm to 3 pm, as the graph is steeper here.
d 5 mph **e** 10 miles
f $\frac{1}{2}$ hour **g** 20 mph
h 15 miles
i

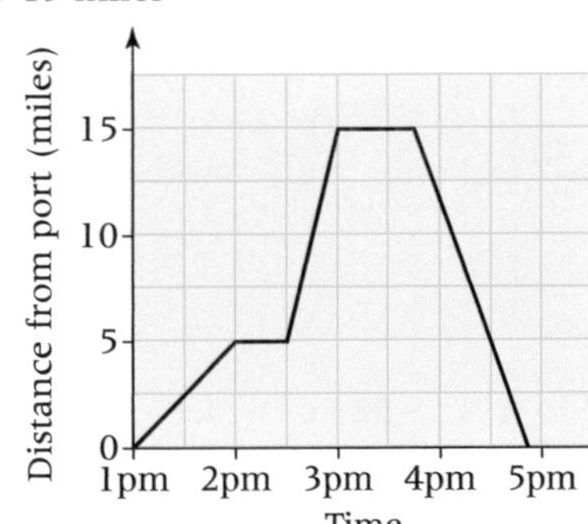

j 4:45 pm

3 **a** 2 km **b** 4 km/h
c

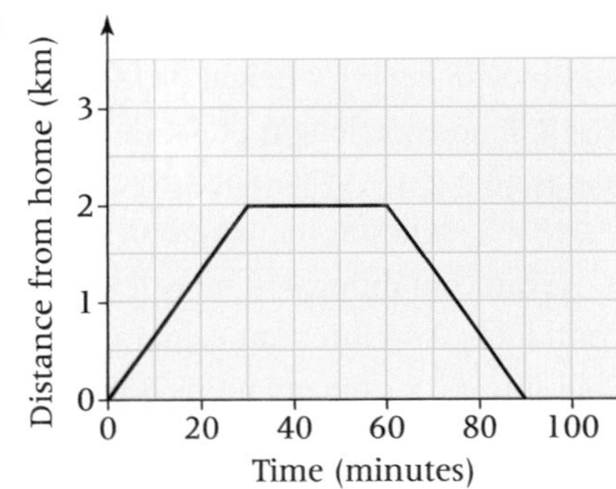

A3.8

1 **a** 200 **b** 225 **c** 25
d

e Sales rose sharply – due to Christmas season.
f Increase in sales

2 **a** 0.7 m **b** 0.5 m **c** 1.9 m **d** 0.1 m
e No, as growth has slowed down.
3 **a** iii **b** ii **c** i

A3 Summary

B, D, C, A, F, E

N4 Check in

1 240 miles
2 15 miles
3 **a** 0.23 m **b** 240 000 cm

N4.1

1 **a** 1 : 2 **b** 8 : 5 **c** 8 : 5 **d** 3 : 2
e 19 : 9 **f** 1 : 6 **g** 2 : 4 : 3 **h** 4 : 5 : 8
2 **a** 2 : 5 **b** 11 : 16 **c** 5 : 2 **d** 5 : 3
e 5 : 3 **f** 8 : 5
3 **a** 1 : 3 **b** 7 : 3 **c** 15 : 2 **d** 9 : 100
4 **a** 1 : 3 **b** 3 : 2 **c** 2 : 1 **d** 3 : 4
5 **a** 1 : 2.5 **b** 1 : 3.85 **c** 1 : 4.17 **d** 1 : 41.67
e 1 : 23.68 **f** 1 : 150 **g** 1 : 12.5
6 **a** 1 : 50 **b** 1 : 20 000 **c** 1 : 36
7 **a** 35 kg **b** 28 kg

N4.2

1 **b** 3 : 1; height of 144 cm = 3 × width of 48 cm; width of 48 cm = $\frac{1}{3}$ × height of 144 cm
c 16 : 7; limousine length of 6.4 m = $\frac{16}{7}$ × car length of 2.8 m; car length of 2.8 m = $\frac{7}{16}$ × limousine length of 6.4 m
d 3 : 4; can containing 330 ml = $\frac{3}{4}$ × can containing 0.44 litre; can containing 0.44 litre = $\frac{4}{3}$ × can containing 330 ml
2 **a** 15 girls **b** 88 kg
c 60 purple flowers **d** 504 students
3 **a** 1.2 cm **b** 44 teachers **c** 39 cm
4 **a** 325 m **b** 0.6 cm
5 **a** £27 : £63 **b** 287 kg : 82 kg
c 64.5 tonnes : 38.7 tonnes
d 19.5 litres : 15.6 litres
e £6 : £12 : £18

N4.3

1 **a** £40 : £35 **b** £350 : £650
c 260 days : 104 days **d** 142.86 g : 357.14 g
e 214.29 m : 385.71 m
2 **a** 42 women **b** 240 g
c 63 feet **d** 430 pages
3 **ai** 66.66% **aii** 360 cm
bi 120% **bii** 102 kg
4 **ai** 72 g **aii** 115 g Copper, 69 g Aluminium
b $\frac{11}{50}$
5 **a** 2.65 m **b** 2.55 m

N4.4

1 **a** 2.4 × (4.3 + 3.7) = 19.2
b 6.8 × (3.75 − 2.64) = 7.548
c (3.7 + 2.9) ÷ 1.2 = 5.5
d $(2.3 + 3.4^2) \times 2.7 = 37.422$
e 5.3 + 3.9 × (3.2 + 1.6) = 24.02
f 3.2 + 6.4 × (4.3 + 2.5) = 46.72
2 **a** 178.412 383 5 **b** 0.196 708 95
c 3.210 178 253 **d** 3.350 190 476
e 1.157 007 415 **f** 0.135 604 5
3 **ai** 15.3 m² **aii** £103.40 **b** £66.67
4 **a** £21.13 **b** £16.37
c Yes, the new bill is cheaper than the old bill.
5 **a** 30 h 21 m **b** 1821 m

N4 Summary

1 62.5 cm
2 1.4715...
3 Rob

G4 Check in

1 **a** (1, 3) **b** (1, −2) **c** (−3, −2) **d** (−1, 3)
2 **a** $x = 2$ **b** $y = 2$ **c** $y = -x$ **d** $y = x$

G4.1

1 **a**

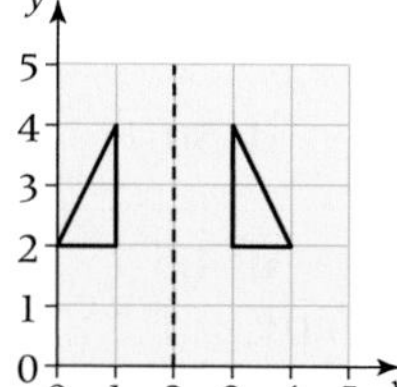

b

c

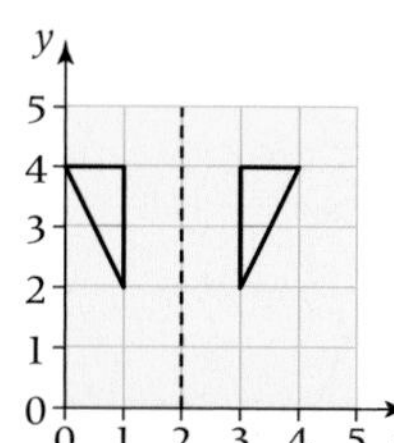

2 **a** $x = 3$ **b** $y = 1$ **c** $x = -1$
3 **a–b**

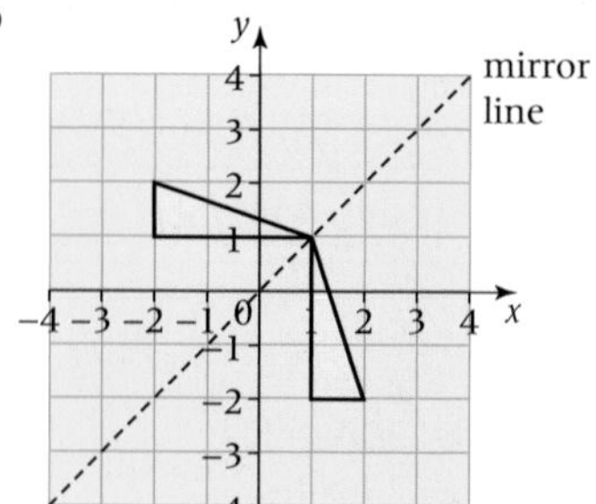

3 **c** $y = x$

4 a–c

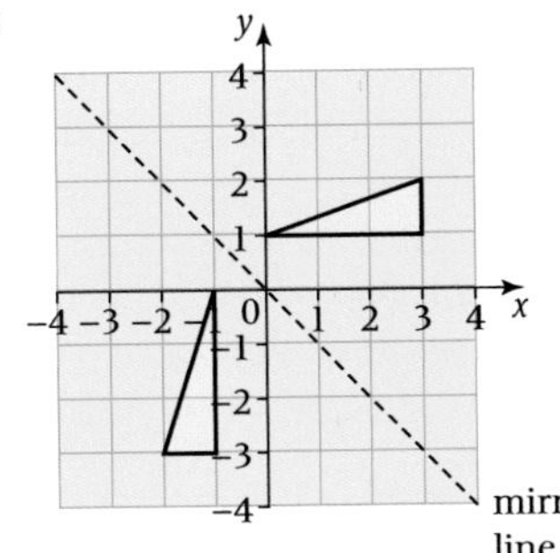

d (−1, 0), (−1, −3), (−2, −3) **e** $y = -x$

G4.2

1 a 90° anticlockwise **b** 90° clockwise
c 180° clockwise **d** 90° anticlockwise
e 90° clockwise **f** 90° clockwise
g 90° anticlockwise **h** 90° anticlockwise
i 180° clockwise **j** 90° clockwise
k 90° clockwise **l** 180° anticlockwise
m 90° clockwise **n** 180° clockwise
o 90° anticlockwise

2

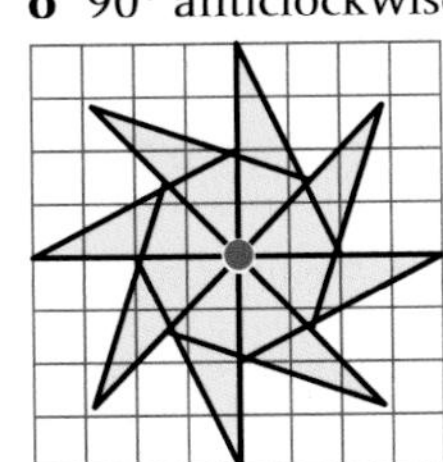

3 b Kite
c Image vertices: (0, 0), (−1, 2), (0, 3), (1, 2)
d (−1, 2) **e** Yes

4 c (−1, −1), (2, −1), (2, −3)

G4.3

1 D, F, H, J

2 A Translation $\begin{pmatrix}4\\3\end{pmatrix}$ **B** Translation $\begin{pmatrix}4\\3\end{pmatrix}$
C Translation $\begin{pmatrix}0\\3\end{pmatrix}$ **D** Translation $\begin{pmatrix}0\\-3\end{pmatrix}$
E Translation $\begin{pmatrix}4\\-3\end{pmatrix}$ **F** Translation $\begin{pmatrix}0\\-4\end{pmatrix}$
G Translation $\begin{pmatrix}-4\\3\end{pmatrix}$ **H** Translation $\begin{pmatrix}-4\\-3\end{pmatrix}$

3 a Translation $\begin{pmatrix}5\\0\end{pmatrix}$ **b** Translation $\begin{pmatrix}0\\4\end{pmatrix}$
c Translation $\begin{pmatrix}0\\-4\end{pmatrix}$ **d** Translation $\begin{pmatrix}2\\-6\end{pmatrix}$
e Translation $\begin{pmatrix}3\\2\end{pmatrix}$ **f** Translation $\begin{pmatrix}-5\\4\end{pmatrix}$
g Translation $\begin{pmatrix}-2\\6\end{pmatrix}$ **h** Translation $\begin{pmatrix}-5\\0\end{pmatrix}$
i Translation $\begin{pmatrix}-3\\-6\end{pmatrix}$ **j** Translation $\begin{pmatrix}5\\-4\end{pmatrix}$

4 a (−4, 2) **b** Isosceles trapezium
c Image vertices: (1, 0), (4, 0), (2, 2), (3, 2)
d Congruent **e** (1, 0)

G4.4

1 3

2 B

3 a–b

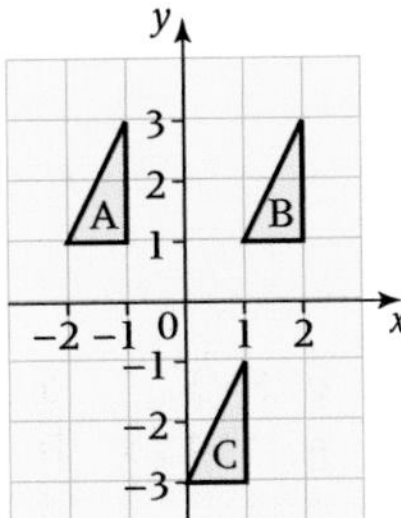

c Translation $\begin{pmatrix}1\\4\end{pmatrix}$

4 a–b

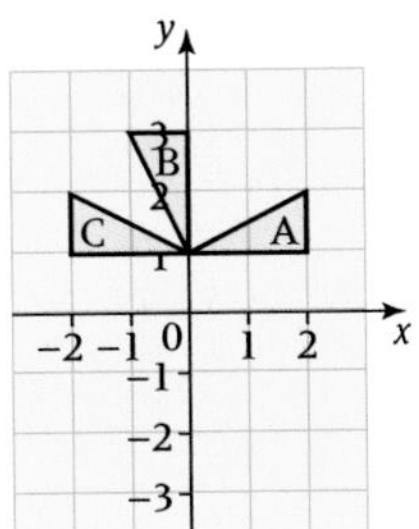

c Rotation through 90° clockwise

5 a–b

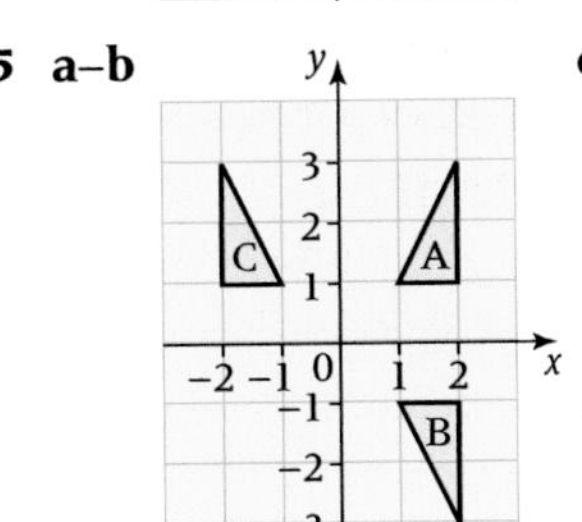

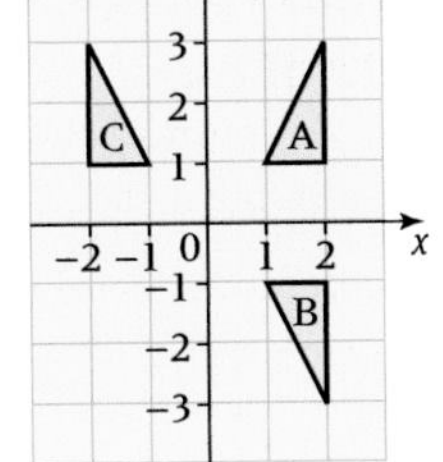

c Rotation through 180°

G4.5

1 a 2 **b** 3 **c** 2 **d** 2
e 2 **f** 3 **g** 5 **h** 2

2 a A: Yes, 2; D: Yes, 3; B, C, E: No **b** A, D

3 a A: Yes, 2; C: Yes, 3; B, D, E: No **b** A, C

G4.6

1 a 2 **b** 2 **c** 3 **d** 2

2 a

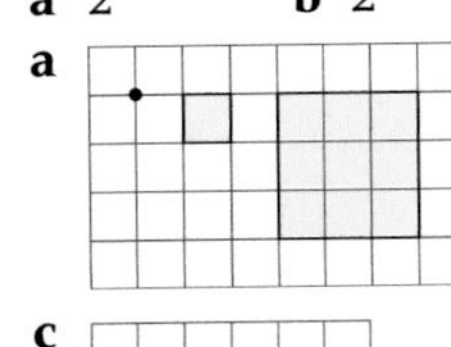

b

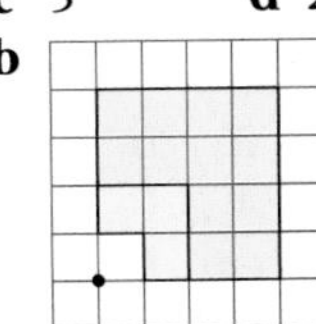

c

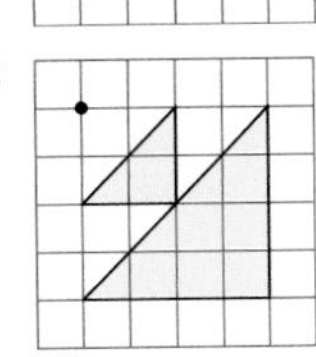

d

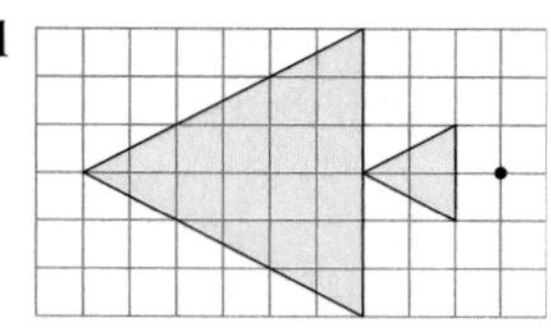

e

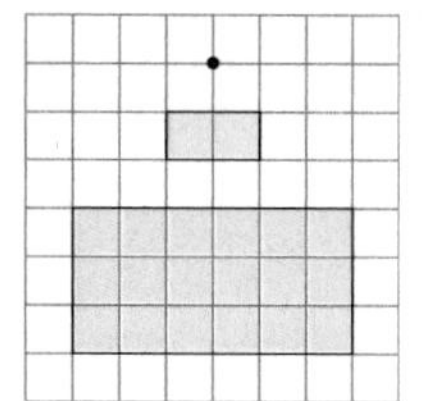

f

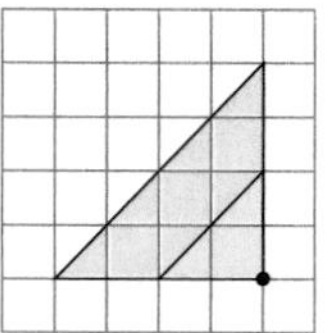

g

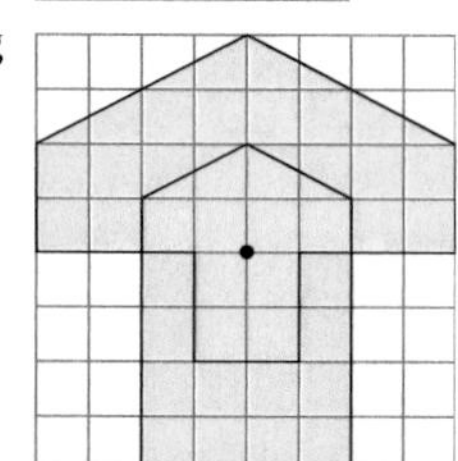

h

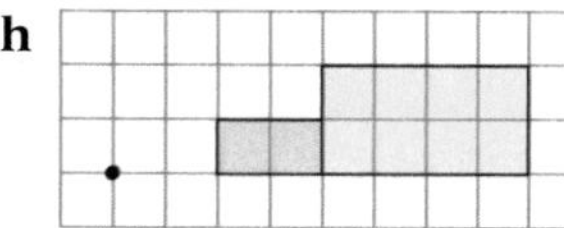

i

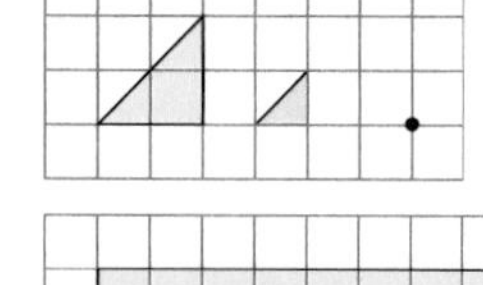

j

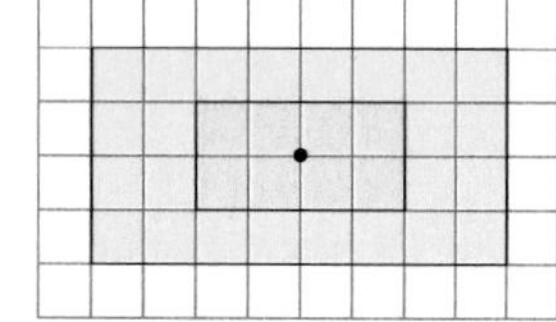

G4.7

1 a $a = 40°$, $b = 50°$
  b $c = 20°$, $d = 40°$
  c $h = 75°$, $i = 75°$, $j = 30°$, $k = 75°$, $l = 75°$
  d All 60°
2 a Yes, 2 **b** Yes, 5 **c** No **d** No
  e Yes, 4 **f** No
3 a 2, 8 cm **b** 3, 12 cm
4 circles, regular hexagons, squares, equilateral triangles

G4 Summary

1 a vertices of A are (−1, 5), (−1, 3) and (3, 3).
  b vertices of B are (1, −2), (5, −2) and (5, −4).
  c vertices of C are $(1, 1\frac{1}{2})$, (1, 4) and (2, 4).

A4 Check in

1 a 3 **b** 6 **c** 5 **d** 6
2 a 3 **b** 4 **c** 5 **d** 4
3 a 4, 8, 12, 16, 20, 24
  b 3, 6, 9, 12, 15, 18
  c 5, 10, 15, 20, 25, 30
  d 6, 12, 18, 24, 30, 36

A4.1

1 6, 10, 14, 18, 22; 26, 21, 16, 11, 6; 10, 7, 4, 1, −2; −6, −4, −2, 0, 2; −23, −16, −9, −2, 5
2 a 2, 4, 6, 8, 10 **b** 17, 19, 21, 23, 25
  c 4, 8, 12, 16, 20 **d** 24, 30, 36, 42, 48
  e 7, 12, 17, 22, 27 **f** 1, 4, 9, 16, 25
  g 2, 5, 10, 17, 26 **h** 2, 4, 8, 16, 32
3 a 4, 7, 10, 13, 16 **b** 25, 19, 13, 7, 1
  c 4, 8, 12, 16, 20 **d** 30, 22, 14, 6, −2
  e −16, −10, −4, 2, 8
4 ai 31, 38
  aii First term 3, increases by 7 each time
  bi 25, 33
  bii First term −7, increase by 8 each time
  ci −7, −4
  cii First term −19, increase by 3 each time
  di 11, 27
  dii First term 7, increase by 4 each time
  ei 11, 19
  eii First term 3, increase by 8 each time
  fi 1, −4
  fii First term 16, decrease by 5 each time
  gi −11, 1
  gii First term −11, increase by 3 each time
  hi 13, −1
  hii First term 13, decrease by 7 each time
5 ai 2, 3, 5, 8, 12
  aii First term 2, increase by 1, 2, 3, 4
  bi 18, 22, 25, 27, 28
  bii First term 18, increase by 4, 3, 2, 1
  ci −6, −5, −3, 0, 4
  cii First term −6, increase by 1, 2, 3, 4
  di 6, 8, 11, 15, 20
  dii First term 6, increase by 2, 3, 4, 5
  ei −24, −23, −21, −17, −9
  eii First term −24, increase by 1, 2, 4, 8 (powers of 2)
  fi −15, −7, −1, 3, 5
  fii First term −15, increase by 8, 6, 4, 2
6 a 1, 3, 5, 7, 9, 11, 13 and 4, 7, 10 (13 could go in the second sequence instead)
  b 2, 4, 8, 16, 32 and 7, 11, 15, 19, 23

A4.2

1 a 6, 11, 16; 51 **b** 11, 14, 17; 38
  c 4, 12, 20; 76 **d** −2, 4, 10; 52
  e 22, 20, 18; 4 **f** 10, 5, 0; −35
  g −13, −6, 1; 50 **h** −2, 2, 6; 34

2 a 14, 17, 23, 38 **b** −3, 3, 15, 45
3 a 5, 8, 13, 20, 29 **b** −1, 2, 7, 14, 23
c 2, 8, 18, 32, 50 **d** 11, 8, 3, −4, −13
4 a 12, 33, 108 **b** −2, 19, 94
c 15, 57, 207
5 a 5, 9, 13
b Each term is one more than a multiple of 4.
c No, 222 is not one more than a multiple of 4.
6 a 3, 9, 19 **b** $2 \times 5^2 + 1 = 51$ not 101
7 a 1, 4, 9, 16, 25 **b** +3, +5, +7, +9
c

4th square number	16	1 + 3 + 5 + 7
5th square number	25	1 + 3 + 5 + 7 + 9
6th square number	36	1 + 3 + 5 + 7 + 9 + 11

d 10th square number = 100

A4.3

1 a 8, 6, 4, 2, 0 **b** 1, 0, −1, −2, −3
c 14, 10, 6, 2, −2 **d** 13, 6, −1, −8, −15
e 13, 10, 7, 4, 1 **f** 1, −4, −9, −14, −19
g −7, −9, −11, −13, −15
h 25, 20, 15, 10, 5 **i** 5, 2, −1, −4, −7
j 4, −6, −16, −26, −36 **k** 5, 2, −3, −10, −19
l −8, −2, 8, 22, 40
2 a +4
b The *n*th term contains the term 4*n*.
c

Sequence	5	9	13	17	21
4*n*	4	8	12	16	20

d $4n + 1$
3 a $6n + 5$ **b** $9n - 8$ **c** $7n + 8$ **d** $4n - 14$
e $23 - 3n$ **f** $19 - 4n$ **g** $24 - 8n$ **h** $39 - 8n$
4 a $4n + 3$ **b** $4n - 10$ **c** $41 - 9n$ **d** $21 - 6n$
5 a Term 3 = 13, Term $n = 3n + 4$
b Term 4 = 14, Term 10 = 50, Term $n = 6n - 10$

A4.4

1 a **b** 8, 11, 14, 17, 20 **c** 35
2 a
× × × × × × × × × ×
× ×
× ×
× × × × × × × × × ×
b 10, 14, 18, 22, 26
c Four crosses are added each time – two to the top and two to the bottom
d +4 **e** $4n + 6$
3 a 13, 17 (add 4) **b** $4n - 3$ **c** 197
4 a 18, 22 (add 4); $4n + 2$; 202
b 9, 11 (add 2); $2n + 1$; 101
c 13, 16 (add 3); $3n + 1$; 151

A4.5

1 a 4, 7, 10, 13, 16
b $3n + 1$
c The *n*th pattern has three branches of *n* dots and one extra dot in the centre.
2 a 6, 11, 16, 21, 26 **b** $5n + 1$
c The *n*th pattern has five branches of *n* beads and one extra bead in the centre.
3 a 3 **b** 5, 8, 11, 14, 17 **c** $3n + 2$
d Start with two cards leaning against each other, then add three more cards each time (another pair of leaning cards and one bridging card).
e No, 52 is not two more than a multiple of 3.
4 a Add one vertical and two horizontal posts each time.
b 16
c $3n + 1$
d Start with one vertical post then add three posts each time.
e 79
5 a

Type of car	**Number of days**						
	1	**2**	**3**	**4**	**5**	**6**	**7**
Small	70	90	110	130	150	170	190
Medium	85	110	135	160	185	210	235
Large	100	130	160	190	220	250	280

bi $10 \times 30 + 70 = £370$
bii $14 \times 25 + 60 = £410$
biii $20n + 50$

A4 Summary

1 ai 5 **ii** 23 **b** $2 \times 100 - 1$
c pattern with 14 dots **d** 14, 17
2 $5n + 1$
3 eg 8,16; 7,11

N5 Check in

1 1, 2, 3, 4, 6, 8, 12, 24
2 2, 3, 5, 7, 11, 13
3 a 45 **b** 100

N5.1

1 a 2, 4, 5, 10, 20 **b** 2, 3, 4, 6, 8, 12, 16
c 5, 10, 15, 20 **d** 2, 3, 5, 17, 19
2 a 1 × 24, 2 × 12, 3 × 8, 4 × 6
b 1 × 45, 3 × 15, 5 × 9
c 1 × 66, 2 × 33, 3 × 22, 6 × 11
d 1 × 100, 2 × 50, 4 × 25, 5 × 20, 10 × 10
e 1 × 120, 2 × 60, 3 × 40, 4 × 30, 5 × 24, 6 × 20, 8 × 15, 10 × 12
f 1 × 132, 2 × 66, 3 × 44, 4 × 33, 6 × 22, 11 × 12
g 1 × 160, 2 × 80, 4 × 40, 5 × 32, 8 × 20, 10 × 16
h 1 × 180, 2 × 90, 3 × 60, 4 × 45, 5 × 36, 6 × 30, 9 × 20, 10 × 18, 12 × 15
i 1 × 360, 2 × 180, 3 × 120, 4 × 90, 5 × 72, 6 × 60, 8 × 45, 9 × 40, 10 × 36, 12 × 30, 15 × 24, 18 × 20

j $1 \times 324, 2 \times 162, 3 \times 108, 4 \times 81, 6 \times 54, 9 \times 36, 12 \times 27, 18 \times 18$
k $1 \times 224, 2 \times 112, 4 \times 56, 7 \times 32, 8 \times 28, 14 \times 16$
l $1 \times 264, 2 \times 132, 3 \times 88, 4 \times 66, 6 \times 44, 8 \times 33, 11 \times 24, 12 \times 22$
m $1 \times 312, 2 \times 156, 3 \times 104, 4 \times 78, 6 \times 52, 8 \times 39, 12 \times 26, 13 \times 24$
n $1 \times 325, 5 \times 65, 13 \times 25$
o $1 \times 432, 2 \times 216, 3 \times 144, 4 \times 108, 6 \times 72, 8 \times 54, 9 \times 48, 12 \times 36, 16 \times 27, 18 \times 24$

3 **a** 17, 34, 51 **b** 29, 58, 87
c 42, 84, 126 **d** 25, 50, 75
e 47, 94, 141 **f** 35, 70, 105
g 90, 180, 270 **h** 120, 240, 360
i 95, 190, 285 **j** 208, 416, 624

4 324

5 **a** 2 **b** 5 **c** 6 **d** 8
e 15 **f** 18 **g** 25 **h** 12
i 15

6 **a** 12 **b** 40 **c** 36 **d** 75
e 42 **f** 150

7 **a** 120 seconds **b** 18 cm × 18 cm

N5.2

1 **a** 25 **b** 121 **c** 225 **d** 289

2 **a** 16, 36 **b** 49 **c** 121, 144 **d** 225

3 **a** 256 **b** 13.69 **c** 2500 **d** 44.89
e 316.84 **f** 17.64 **g** 3.61 **h** 0.01
i 15.21 **j** 4.41 **k** 0.49 **l** 175.56

4 **a** ±23 **b** ±12.53 **c** ±6.40 **d** ±0.4
e ±2.6 **f** ±28.28 **g** ±36.67 **h** ±6.21
i ±84.22 **j** ±15.32

5 **a** 7 **b** 9 **c** 5 **d** 6
e 11 **f** 12 **g** 3 **h** 2

6 **a** $(2.645\,751)^2 = 6.999\,998$; 2.645 751 is only accurate to 6 d.p. so its square is not exactly 7.
b 56 and 57

7 **a** 4.5
bi 6.3 **bii** 7.7 **biii** 9.7

N5.3

1 **a** 343 **b** 1000 **c** 2197 **d** 6859

2 **a** Square: 4, 16; Cube: 27
b Square: 64, 144; Cube: 64
c Square: 196, 256; Cube: 216
d Square: 900; Cube: 1000

3 **a** 512 **b** 13.82 **c** 8000 **d** 59.32
e 1601.61 **f** −21.95 **g** 704.97 **h** 0.125
i −157.46 **j** 970.30 **k** −0.001 **l** 4784.09

4 **a** 9 **b** 4.64 **c** 4 **d** 4.41
e 1.97 **f** 1.39 **g** 1.1 **h** 3.83
i 23 **j** −6 **k** −4.12 **l** 0.25

5 **ai** 2.7 **aii** 3.7 **aiii** 4.3
aiv 5.3 **av** 6.7 **avi** 7.9
avii 9.7 **aviii** 11.4

N5.4

1 **a** 16 **b** 32 **c** 125 **d** 2401 **e** 729

2 **a** 3375 **b** 729 **c** 1024 **d** 217 678.23
e 2197

3 **a** 25 **b** 40 **c** 259 947
d 8000 **e** $\frac{2}{256}$ or 0.01953

4 **a** 3 **b** 4 **c** 4 **d** 7
e 23

5 **a** 340 **b** 76 600 **c** 0.085 **d** 23 000
e 312 000 **f** 56 200 **g** 2.96

6 **a** 3^4 **b** 7^5 **c** 2^{12} **d** 10^3
e 3^4 **f** 4^7 **g** 10^{10} **h** 7^6
i 2^6 **j** 10^5 **k** 4^0

7 **a** 5.4 **b** 3 **c** 10^4
d 1 730 000

8 **a** y^5 **b** 4^{10} **c** w^5 **d** 4^{y-2}
e g^4 **f** 576

N5.5

1 **a** 75 **b** 40 **c** 63 **d** 180 **e** 441

2 **a** 2×3^2 **b** $2^3 \times 3$ **c** $2^3 \times 5$
d 3×13 **e** $2^4 \times 3$ **f** 2×41
g $2^2 \times 5^2$ **h** $2^4 \times 3^2$ **i** $2^2 \times 3^2 \times 5$
j $3^2 \times 5 \times 7$ **k** $2^2 \times 3 \times 37$ **l** $2 \times 3^3 \times 5^2$

3 **a** 7 missing in the answer; $126 = 2 \times 3^2 \times 7$
b Divided 105 by 5 but recorded it as 3; $210 = 2 \times 3 \times 5 \times 7$
c 221 is not prime, so he should not have stopped; $221 = 13 \times 17$

4 **a** e.g. 8, 12, 20 **b** e.g. 16, 24, 54, 90
c e.g. 112, 120, 176, 200 **d** e.g. 64

5 **a** 3 **b** 5 **c** 6 **d** 48
e 3 **f** 17

6 **a** 72 **b** 120 **c** 72 **d** 60
e 180 **f** 432

7 **a** $\frac{3}{4}$ **b** $\frac{2}{3}$ **c** $\frac{5}{8}$ **d** $\frac{2}{3}$
e $\frac{9}{13}$ **f** $\frac{2}{5}$

N5 Summary

1 **ai** 25 **ii** 28 **iii** 5 and 20 **iv** 26 and 33
b $2^3 = 8$

2 **a** 64 **b** 9 **c** 200

3 **a** 7.2225 **b** 7

4 180

5 **a** $2 \times 2 \times 2 \times 7$ **b** 14

6 $2 \times 2 \times 2 \times 3 \times 11$

7 42

D3 Check in

1 **a** 90° **b** 130°

2 **a** 120 **b** 45 **c** 60 **d** 72
e 6 **f** 20 **g** 30 **h** 18
i 10

D3.1

1 **a** 1550
b 3 guitars, 2.5 guitars, 1.5 guitars

2 **a** 13 **b** 10°
c Win = 150°, Draw = 80°, Lose = 130°
d Pie chart with angles given in part **c**

3 **a** 6°
b Sunny = 90°, Cloudy = 108°, Rainy = 84°, Snowy = 18°, Windy = 60°
c Pie chart with angles given in part **b**

4 **a** 0.75°
b Pie chart with: Cod 90°, Plaice 75°, Haddock 72°, Sardines 87°, Mackerel 36°

D3.2

1 **a** 8, 8, 13, 6, 5
b–c

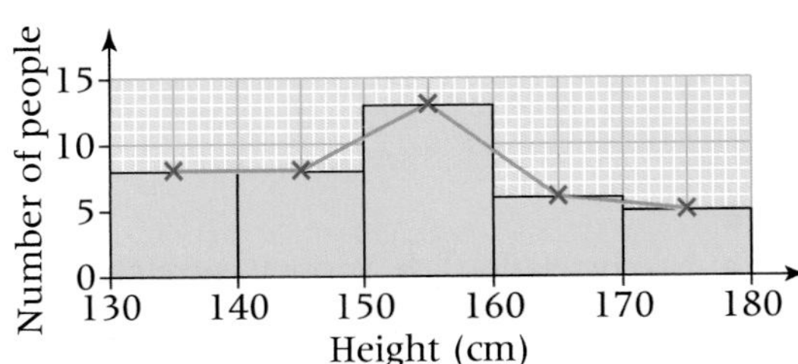

2

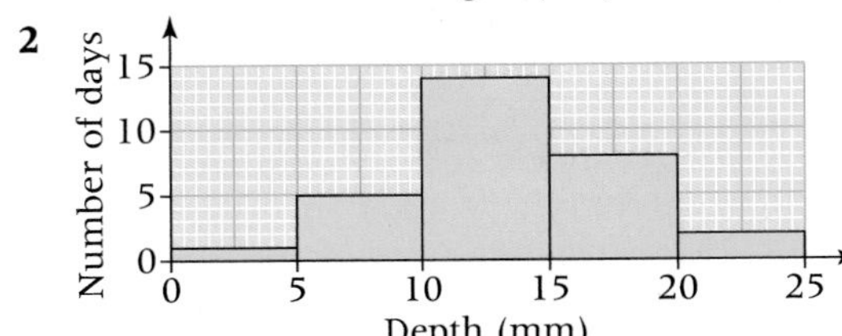

3

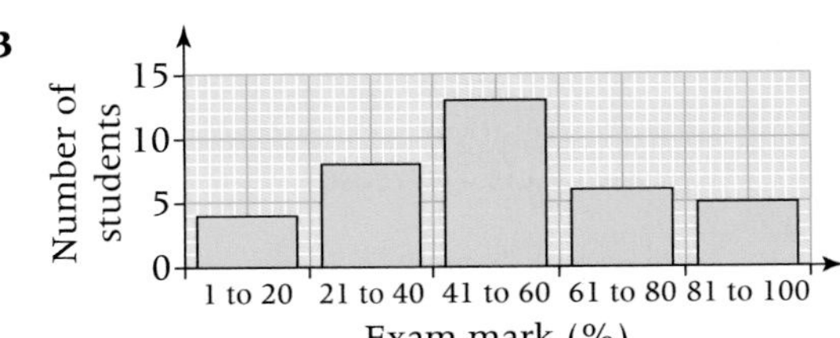

4 **b–c**

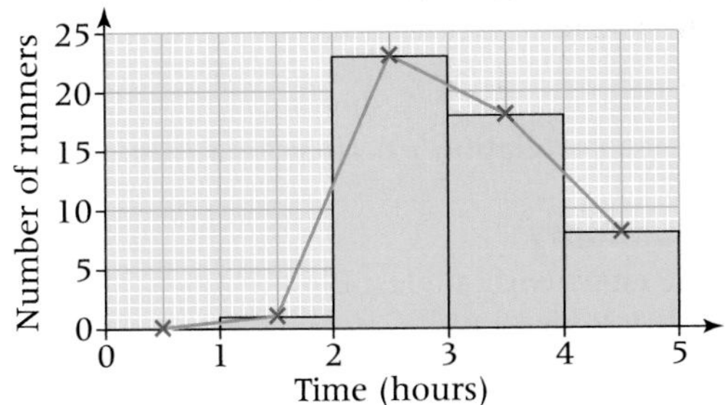

D3.3

1

100	8 8 8
110	0 0 1 2 6 7 7 9 9
120	0 0 1 1 5 5 6 6
130	0 1 4 5 6 7 8
140	0 2 4

Key: 120 | 5 means 125 seconds

2

43.0	0 2 3 8 8 9
44.0	0 1 3 4 5 7
45.0	0 0 1 2 6 9
46.0	0 1 3 5 5 9 9

Key: 44.0 | 7 means 44.7 seconds

3 **a**

10	0 4 4 4 7 9 9 9
20	0 0 0 1 2 2 3 3 3 4 5 6 6 6 6 7 8 9 9
30	1 2 4

Key: 10 | 7 means 17°C

b

50	0 7 7 7
60	3 6 6 6 8 8 8
70	0 2 2 3 3 3 5 7 9 9 9 9
80	1 2 4 4 8
90	0 3

Key: 50 | 7 means 57°F

D3.4

1

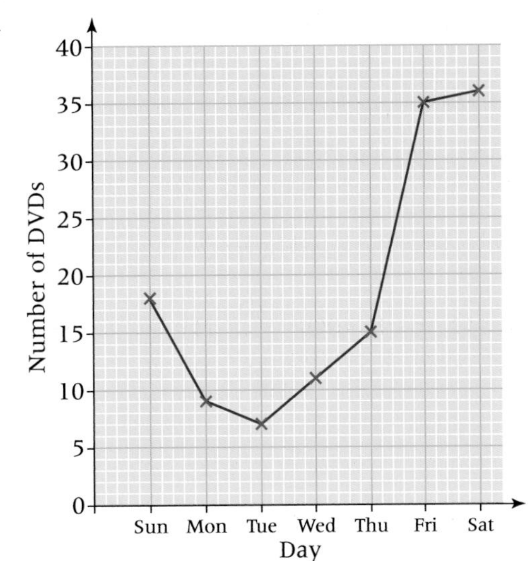

2

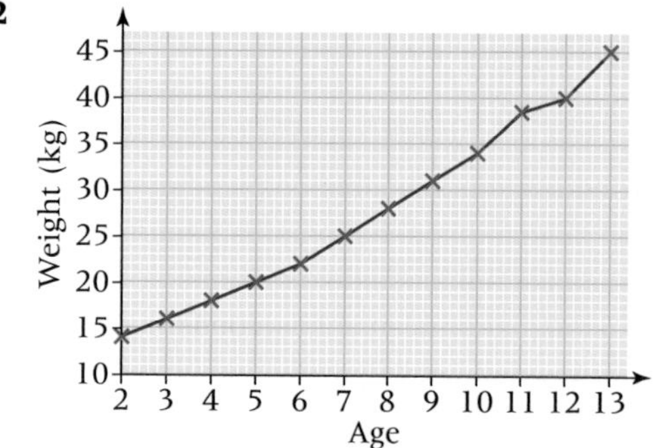

3

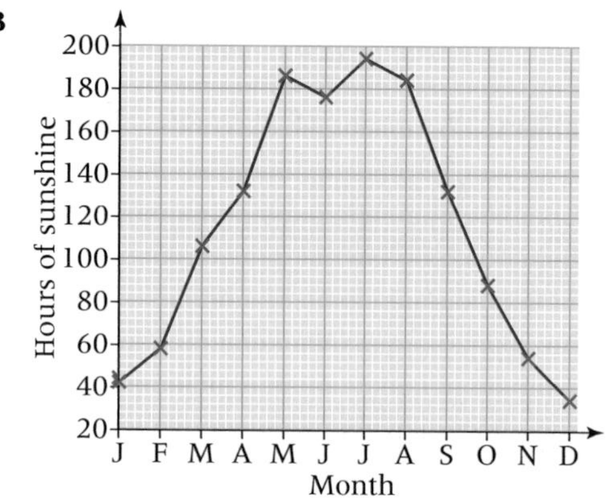

4

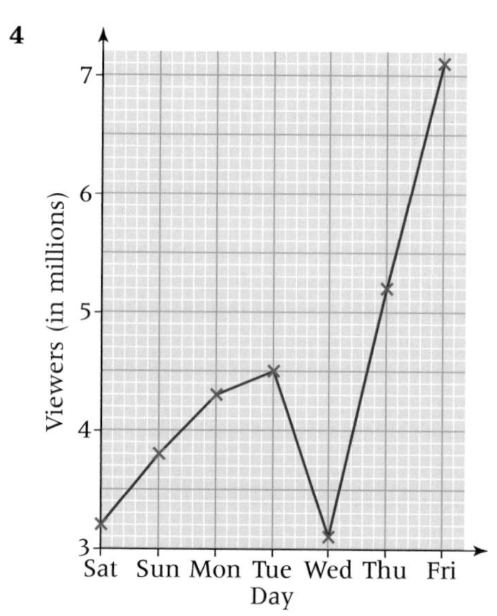

5

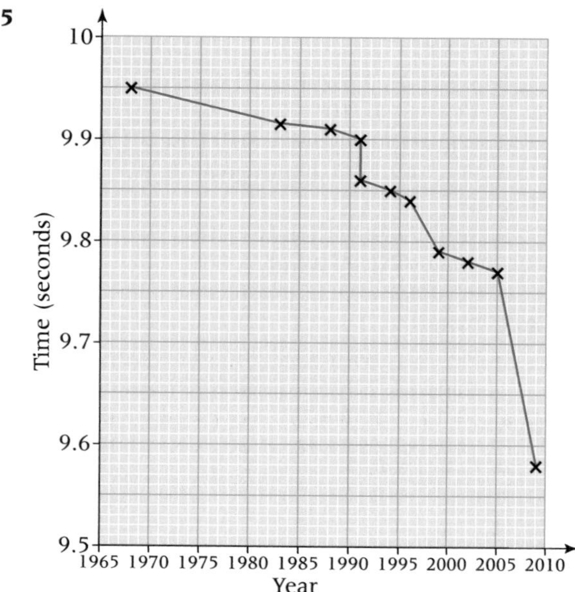

D3.5

1 **a** No correlation **b** Positive correlation
c Negative correlation

2 **a**

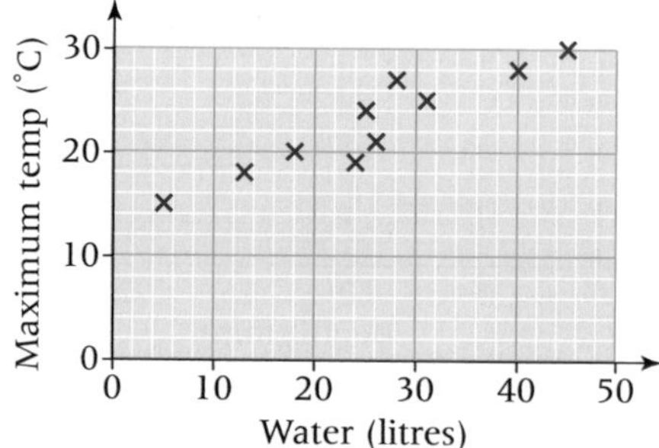

b Positive correlation
ci Increases **cii** Decreases

3 **a**

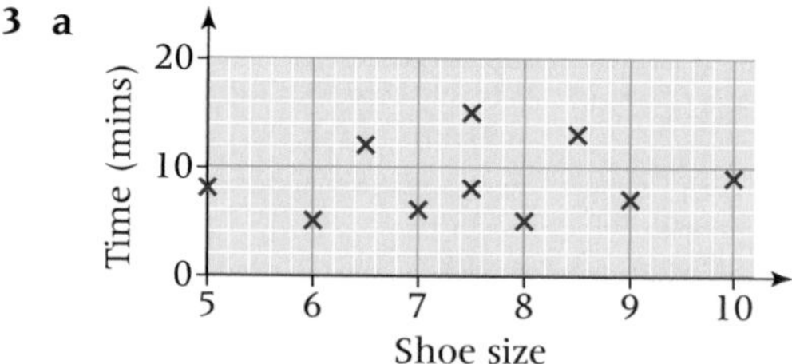

b No correlation **c** No relationship

D3 Summary

1 Pie chart with angles: Blue tit 144°, Chaffinch 128°, Redpoll 88°
2 Frequency polygon including points (5, 4), (15, 13), (25, 17), (35, 19) and (45, 7).
3 The pattern of crosses should run diagonally downwards left to right.

A5 Check in

1 16 cm
2 **a** x **b** m **c** $3n$ **d** $2p$

A5.1

1 **ai** 14 **aii** $28 \div 2 = 14$
bi 26 **bii** $33 - 7 = 26$
ci 21 **cii** $9 + 12 = 21$
di 42 **dii** $7 \times 6 = 42$

2 **a** $7 \rightarrow \times 3 \rightarrow 21$ **b** $35 \rightarrow \div 5 \rightarrow 7$
c $27 \rightarrow -8 \rightarrow 19$ **d** $6 \rightarrow \times 6 \rightarrow 36$
e $28 \rightarrow +12 \rightarrow 40$ **f** $7 \rightarrow \times 4 \rightarrow 28$
g $43 \rightarrow -7 \rightarrow 36$ **h** $52 \rightarrow \div 4 \rightarrow 13$

3 **a** $7 \leftarrow \div 3 \leftarrow 21$ **b** $35 \leftarrow \times 5 \leftarrow 7$
c $27 \leftarrow +8 \leftarrow 19$ **d** $6 \leftarrow \div 6 \leftarrow 36$
e $28 \leftarrow -12 \leftarrow 40$ **f** $7 \leftarrow \div 4 \leftarrow 28$
g $43 \leftarrow +7 \leftarrow 36$ **h** $52 \leftarrow \times 4 \leftarrow 13$

4 **a** $a = 14$ **b** $b = 25$ **c** $c = 16$ **d** $d = 56$
e $x = 8$ **f** $f = 40$ **g** $g = 8$ **h** $h = 196$
i $i = 31$ **j** $j = 25$ **k** $k = 19$ **l** $m = 56$

5 **a** $c = 8$ **b** $d = 41$ **c** $f = 9$ **d** $g = 24$
e $h = 20$ **f** $i = 42$ **g** $j = 9$ **h** $k = 22$
i $l = 15$ **j** $m = 6$ **k** $n = 48$ **l** $q = 7$
m $r = 32$ **n** $u = 72$

6 **a** $x - 12 = 11, x = 23$ **b** $\frac{x}{5} = 8, x = 40$

A5.2

1 **a** 5 **b** 32 **c** 10 **d** 1
e +5 **f** ×5

2 **a** $a = 6$ **b** $b = 9$ **c** $e = 28$ **d** $f = 18$
e $g = 30$ **f** $h = 16$

3 **a**

	×4	+3
1	4	7
2	8	11
x	$4x$	$4x + 3$
10	40	43

b

	÷3	−1
12	4	3
9	3	2
x	$\frac{x}{3}$	$\frac{x}{3} - 1$
24	8	7

c

	×5	−3
1	5	2
2	10	7
x	$5x$	$5x - 3$
11	55	52

4 **a** $a = 10$ **b** $b = 9$ **c** $e = 2$ **d** $f = 15$
e $g = 70$ **f** $i = 30$ **g** $j = 60$ **h** $k = 5$
i $m = 1.5$ **j** $p = -2$

5 **a** $3x - 1 = 11$ **b** $4n + 7 = 27$
c $5q + 3 = 33$ **d** $\frac{r}{3} + 15 = 22$

6 **ai** $2x + 7 = 15$ **aii** $x = 4$
bi $4x - 5 = 13$ **bii** $x = 4.5$
ci $\frac{x}{5} + 3 = 11$ **cii** $x = 40$

A5.3

1 **a** $x = 5$ **b** $x = 5$ **c** $x = 8$ **d** $x = 6$
e $x = 5.5$ **f** $x = 50$ **g** $y = 18$ **h** $z = 40$
i $y = 3$ **j** $p = 2$

2 **a** $m = 7$ **b** $p = -7$ **c** $n = 2$ **d** $q = 5$
e $r = -11$ **f** $k = 6$ **g** $m = 5$ **h** $a = 8$

3 $16p - 15 = 33$ ($p = 3$, $m = n = 8$)

4 **a** $6n + 6 = 36, n = 5$
b $5m - 6 = 54, m = 12$

5 **a** $2y + 16 = 36$ **b** $y = 10$

6 **a** 5 cm **b** 6 cm **c** 8 cm
In **c** all sides are equal.

A5.4

1 **a** $4x + 12$ **b** $2y - 8$ **c** $15 - 5a$ **d** $6 - 3b$

2 **a** $x = 4$ **b** $s = 6$ **c** $t = 3$ **d** $v = 3$

3 **a** $-2c - 8$ **b** $-3d + 9$ **c** $8m - 2$ **d** $12 - 8n$

4 **a** $a = -6$ **b** $b = -1$ **c** $c = 2$ **d** $d = -2$

5 **a** $e = 1.5$ **b** $f = \frac{2}{3}$ **c** $g = 0.75$ **d** $h = -0.5$

6 **a** $x = -8.5$ **b** $y = 2.5$ **c** $z = 2.5$
x is the odd one out.

7 **a** $3(x - 2)$ **b** $x = 6$

8 **a** $4(2y + 5)$ **b** $y = 1$

9 $4(z - 6), z = 8$

A5.5

1 **a** $m = 5$ **b** $p = 3$ **c** $t = 3$ **d** $n = 7$
e $q = 8$ **f** $s = 8$

2 **a** $s = -3$ **b** $t = -4$ **c** $u = -2$ **d** $v = -1$

3 **a** $a = 5$ **b** $b = -4$ **c** $c = 2.5$ **d** $d = -3$

4 **a** $x = 7.5$ **b** $x = -3$ **c** $x = 0.25$ **d** $x = -1.5$

5 **a** $21 = 2n + 5$ **b** $4n - 11 = 21$
c $2n + 5 = 4n - 11$ **d** $n = 8$

6 **a** $n = 10$ **b** $5n - 8 = 2n + 10, n = 6$
c $3n + 4 = 5n + 12, n = -4$

A5 Summary

1 **a** $x = 4$ **b** $y = 15$ **c** $z = 7$

2 26 cm

3 25°

G5 Check in

1 and **2** accurate drawings

G5.1

1 **a** 60° **b** 60°, 120°, 60°, 120° **c** 360°

2 **a**

Number of sides	Number of triangles	Sum of the interior angles
4	2	360°
5	3	540°
6	4	720°
7	5	900°
8	6	1080°
9	7	1260°
10	8	1440°

b $(n-2) \times 180$ c 2340

3 a 1080° b 135°

c

Number of sides	Name	Number of triangles	Sum of the interior angles	One interior angle
3	Equilateral triangle	1	180°	60°
4	Square	2	360°	90°
5	Regular pentagon	3	540°	108°
6	Regular hexagon	4	720°	120°
7	Regular heptagon	5	900°	128.6°
8	Regular octagon	6	1080°	135°
9	Regular nonagon	7	1260°	140°
10	Regular decagon	8	1440°	144°

G5.2

1 a 360 b 45°

c

Number of sides	Name	Sum of exterior angles	One exterior angle
3	Equilateral triangle	360°	120°
4	Square	360°	90°
5	Regular pentagon	360°	72°
6	Regular hexagon	360°	60°
7	Regular heptagon	360°	51.4°
8	Regular octagon	360°	45°
9	Regular nonagon	360°	40°
10	Regular decagon	360°	36°

2 a 18° b 360° c 20 d 20 sides

3 a 24° b 156°

4 a 146° b 115°

5 a 45° b 135° c Octagon

G5.3

1 a 120°

b 3 × 120° = 360°, so three hexagons fit together at a point.

2 $x = 135°$

3 $a = 60°$, $b = 120°$

4 $a = 30°$, $b = 60°$

5 a 120°

b The hexagon has equal angles, so it is regular.

6 No; the interior angle is 108°, which is not a factor of 360°.

G5.4

1 a

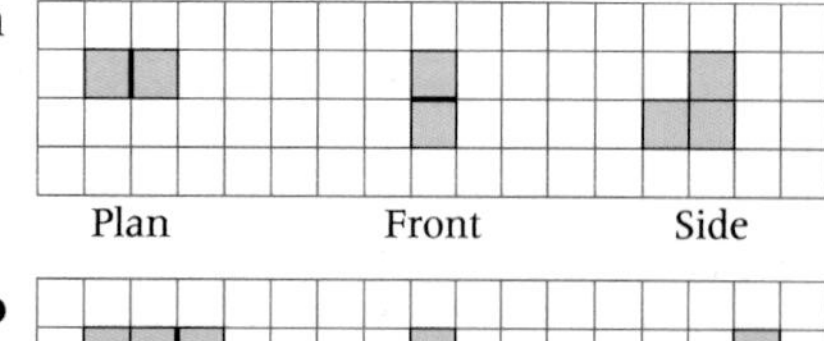

b

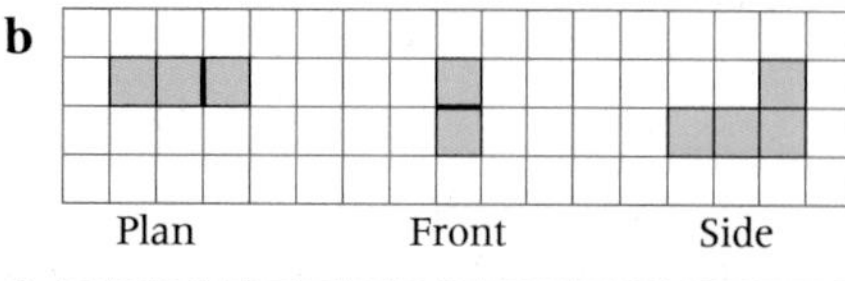

c

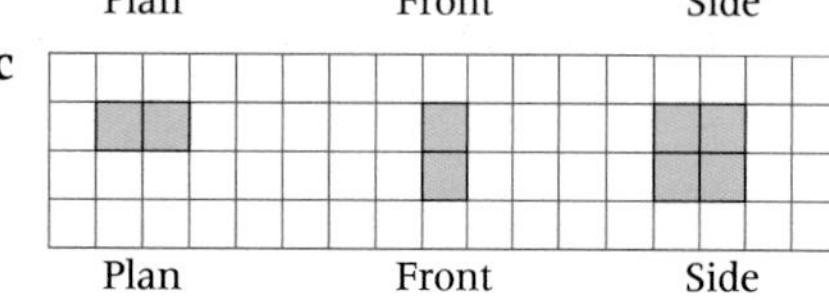

d

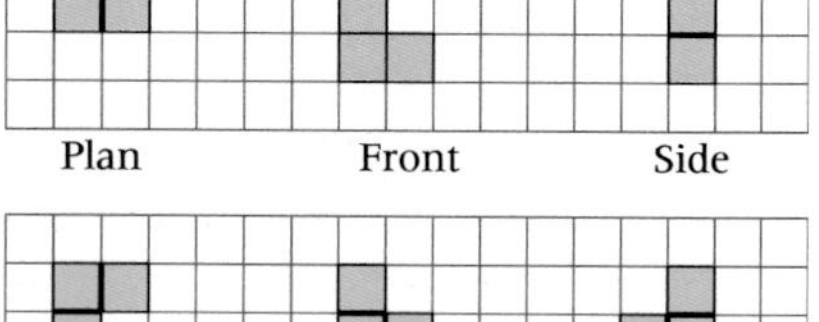

e

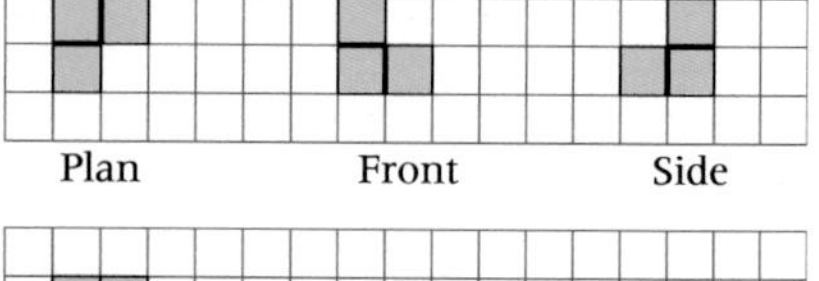

f

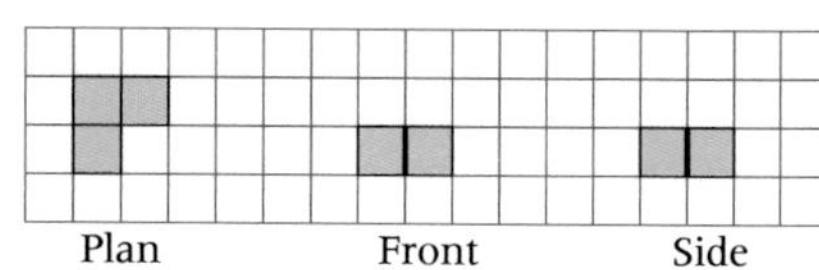

2 a

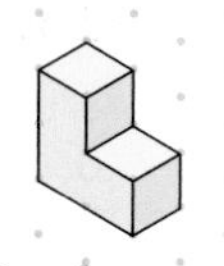

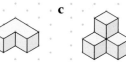

3 cubes

b

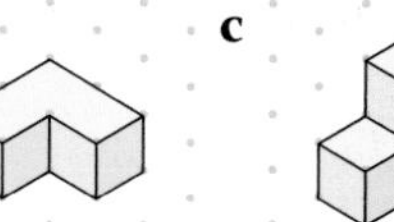

3 cubes

c

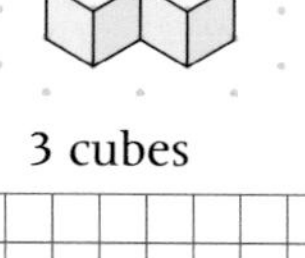

4 cubes

3 a

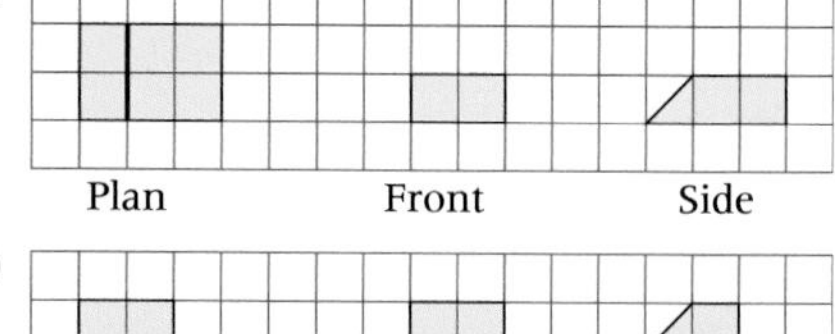

b

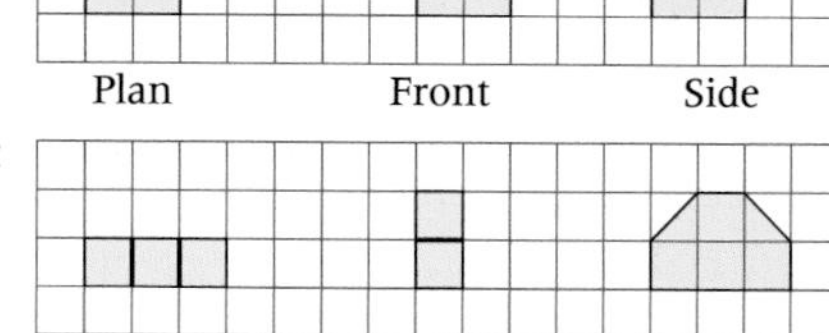

c

Plan Front Side

G5.5

1 a 1800 mm b 4.5 cm c 3.5 m
d 2 km e 3.5 km f 4.5 m
g 0.85 m h 250 cm i 2.5 m
j 0.8 km

2 a 8 m^2 b 80 000 cm^2

3 a 24 m^2 b 240 000 cm^2

4 a 400 mm^2 b 730 mm^2 c 1090 mm^2
d 250 mm^2 e 40 000 mm^2

5 a 6 cm^2 b 12 cm^2 c 8.5 cm^2
d 65 cm^2 e 100 cm^2

6 a 4 m^2 b 8.5 m^2 c 100 m^2
d 12.5 m^2 e 0.5 m^2

7 a 50 000 cm^2 b 100 000 cm^2 c 65 000 cm^2
d 77 500 cm^2 e 6000 cm^2

8 a 4 km^2 b 18 km^2 c 0.5 km^2
d 1.5 km^2

9 a 1000 litres b 6000 litres c 7500 litres

G5.6

1 a 16 cm b 12 cm^2
c Length = 30 cm, width = 10 cm
d 80 cm e 300 cm^2 f 5, 25

2 **a** 32 cm^3 **b** 6 cm, 12 cm, 12 cm
c 864 cm^3 **d** 27
3 **a** 30 cm^2 **b** 120 cm^2
4 **a** 250 cm^3 **b** 2000 cm^3
5

Scale factor	Multiplier for length	Multiplier for area	Multiplier for volume
4	4	16	64
5	5	25	125
6	6	36	216
7	7	49	343

6 56 cm, 160 cm^2

G5 Summary

1 sketch of a cube with a square-based pyramid on top
2 70 000 cm^2
3 No – there will be 90° gaps

N6 Check in

1 **a** 10 **b** 4
2 3
3 0.7, 0.75, 0.8, 0.875

N6.1

1 **a** $\frac{2}{3}$ **b** $\frac{5}{8}$ **c** $\frac{5}{11}$ **d** $\frac{13}{17}$
e $\frac{3}{23}$ **f** $\frac{13}{27}$
2 **a** 1 **b** $\frac{2}{3}$ **c** $1\frac{2}{11}$ **d** $\frac{7}{13}$
e $1\frac{2}{3}$ **f** $\frac{2}{3}$ **g** $2\frac{1}{3}$ **h** $3\frac{4}{7}$
3 **a** $\frac{5}{6}$ **b** $\frac{17}{20}$ **c** $\frac{4}{15}$ **d** $\frac{18}{35}$
e $\frac{23}{24}$ **f** $\frac{38}{45}$ **g** $\frac{59}{99}$ **h** $\frac{94}{105}$
4 **a** $\frac{1}{3}$ **b** $\frac{1}{6}$ **c** $\frac{3}{4}$ **d** $\frac{1}{3}$
5 **a** $1\frac{7}{15}$ **b** $2\frac{1}{10}$ **c** $2\frac{7}{12}$ **d** $1\frac{31}{35}$
e $2\frac{1}{15}$ **f** $1\frac{7}{8}$ **g** $1\frac{7}{12}$ **h** $\frac{43}{63}$
6 **a** $5\frac{11}{12}$ miles **b** $1\frac{13}{16}$ lb **c** $1\frac{79}{80}$ kg **d** $\frac{2}{15}$
ei $29\frac{9}{28}$ feet **eii** $62\frac{4}{45}$ feet **eiii** $16\frac{1}{9}$ m

N6.2

1 **a** $1\frac{1}{2}$ **b** 2 **c** $3\frac{1}{3}$ **d** $2\frac{1}{7}$
e $2\frac{1}{2}$ **f** $4\frac{1}{3}$
2 **a** 2 **b** 4 **c** $3\frac{1}{3}$ **d** $\frac{7}{12}$
e $\frac{3}{5}$ **f** 16 **g** 6 **h** $23\frac{3}{8}$
3 **a** 8 **b** 10 **c** 14 **d** 20
e 48 **f** 220
4 **a** $2\frac{4}{5}$ kg **b** $2\frac{1}{7}$ m
5 **a** 6 **b** $17\frac{1}{2}$ **c** $2\frac{2}{5}$ **d** 14
e 48 **f** $6\frac{3}{7}$ **g** 2 **h** $2\frac{1}{7}$
6 **a** $\frac{3}{10}$ **b** $\frac{9}{20}$ **c** $\frac{15}{28}$ **d** $\frac{12}{35}$
e $\frac{2}{3}$ **f** $\frac{7}{24}$ **g** $\frac{2}{3}$ **h** $2\frac{1}{4}$
i $\frac{9}{49}$ **j** $\frac{1}{2}$ **k** $2\frac{1}{3}$ **l** $1\frac{37}{40}$
7 **a** 10 **b** $\frac{5}{6}$ **c** $1\frac{1}{15}$ **d** $\frac{6}{7}$
e $\frac{27}{28}$ **f** $1\frac{1}{5}$ **g** $\frac{1}{4}$ **h** $\frac{4}{35}$
i $\frac{4}{55}$ **j** $2\frac{5}{8}$ **k** $1\frac{1}{6}$ **l** $1\frac{2}{25}$
m 2 **n** $3\frac{3}{8}$ **o** $1\frac{13}{15}$
8 **a** 3 **b** 4

N6.3

1 **a** 63 **b** 12.1 **c** 5.4 **d** 24.2
e 360 **f** 4.3 **g** 236 **h** 0.0078
2 **a** 15.4 **b** 189 **c** 58.3 **d** 114.8
e 133 **f** 63.6 **g** 49 **h** 69
i 35.2 **j** 173.6 **k** 134.1 **l** 784.3
m 112 **n** 34 **o** 18 **p** 19.8
3 **a** 11.9 **b** 65.1 **c** 111.2 **d** 93.6
e 100.8 **f** 211.2 **g** 43 **h** 73
4 **a** 11.6 **b** 35.6 **c** 148.6 **d** 153.9
e 140.4 **f** 100.3
5 **a** 49.3 **b** 726 **c** 67.2 **d** 66.7
e 26.6 **f** 67.5 **g** 12 **h** 40
6 **a** £116.91 **b** 30.38 m^2 **c** £35.76
ai 101 430 **aii** 1 014 300 **aiii** 1014.3
aiv 10.143 **av** 1.0143 **avi** 1014.3
avii 1.0143 **aviii** 0.10143
bi 65.49 **bii** 654.9 **biii** 3.7 **biv** 17.7
7 **ai** 9331 **aii** 0.9331 **aiii** 217 **aiv** 430
bi 78.72 **bii** 7872 **biii** 0.48 **biv** 16.4

N6.4

1 **a** 26.08 **b** 32.71 **c** 2.81 **d** 31.99
e 26.47 **f** 13.49 **g** 9.17 **h** 67.54
2 **a** 51 **b** 100.8 **c** 109.2 **d** 174.8
e 117.6 **f** 475.3
3 **a** 3.9 **b** 6.1 **c** 8.8 **d** 12.3
e 13.3 **f** 14.9
4 **a** 161.98 kg **b** 19.22 g **c** 1.102 kg
5 **a** 4.002 **b** 4.4 **c** 75.31 **d** 14.7
e 41.673 **f** 181.64 **g** 15.13 **h** 4.4712
i 3.5991
6 **a** £3.33 **b** £11.31 **c** 75 trees **d** £79.25

N6.5

1 **a** 0.166667 **b** 0.4 **c** 0.3
d 1.33333 **e** 0.833333
2 **a** 841 **b** 0.16 **c** 0.36 **d** 2.24 **e** 0.866
3 **a** $6\frac{28}{45}$ **b** $2\frac{15}{28}$ **c** $4\frac{21}{25}$
4 **a** 2401 **b** 1 000 000 **c** 3 **d** 2

5 a eg $0.5^2 = 0.25$, $1^2 = 1$

b eg $\sqrt{0.5} = 0.707$, $\sqrt{1} = 1$

6 digits left to right: 1, 3, 2

N6 Summary

1 a £458.40 b £14.50
2 a $\frac{1}{3}$ b $\frac{1}{8}$
3 33p
4 15
5 a 1566 b 156.6 c 15.66

A6 Check in

1 a 6 b 11 c 9 d 6
2 a $3x+3$ b $2x-2$ c $8x+12$ d $12x-6$
3 a $x=4$ b $y=6$
4 a $4(x+2)$ b $2(3x+1)$ c $3(y-3)$

A6.1

1 a 24 b 6 c 18 d 8
e 27 f 5 g −2 h 16
2 a −12 b 15 c 14 d 9
3 ai 19 aii −5 bi 2 bii −10
ci 12 cii 9 di 23 dii −13
ei 16 eii 4 fi 36 fii 12
4 a $x=6$ b $y=11$ c $x=-2$
d $y=1$ e $b=3$ f $c=-4$
g $f=2$ h $g=-4$
5 b $3x-6$ c $6+2x$ d $10-5x$
6 a $4(2m+1)$ b $3(4n-3)$ c $5(3p+11)$
d $q(q+2)$ e $4(4r-7)$ f $2q(2p-5)$
7 a Identity b Function c Formula
d Equation e Expression f Formula
g Formula h Function

A6.2

1 a 60 cm² b 100 cm² c 5 m² d 11.5 m²
2 ai £4 aii £7.25 aiii £3.10 b 10p
3 a £115 b £290
4 a 13 b 48
5 144
6 a 47.5 b 84
7 a 2 b 2
8 4
9 a 3 b 2
10 a 2 b 2
11 Paul; when $x=6$, $2x^2 = 2 \times 36 = 72$

A6.3

1 a $C = 35 + 20h$ b £95
2 a $C = 2 + 0.6m$ bi £5 bii £11
3 a $C = 75 + 35d$ b €320 c 12 days
4 a $P = 2b + 2$ b 12 pencils
c 18 pencils d 23
5 14 children
6 5 days
7 a $C = 3n + 1.5m$ b $m = 4 \times n$
c $C = 9n$ d 6 adults

A6.4

1 a 8 b −2
2 a 4 b 14
3 a 11 b 6.5
4 a 60 b 144
5 a $\frac{1}{2}$ b 4
6 a $x = \frac{y-c}{m}$ b $t = \frac{v-u}{a}$ c $x = 2(y-d)$
d $x = \frac{y-c}{m}$
7 a $t = \frac{s+6}{3}$ b $t = \frac{2x-9}{5}$ c $t = \frac{3x-12}{2}$
8 a $y = \frac{2-4x}{3}$ b $y = \frac{2x+6}{3}$ c $y = \frac{3x-z}{5}$
9 a $n = \frac{P-1}{4}$
bi 9 bii 13 biii 57
10 a 200 b 150 c 570

A6.5

1
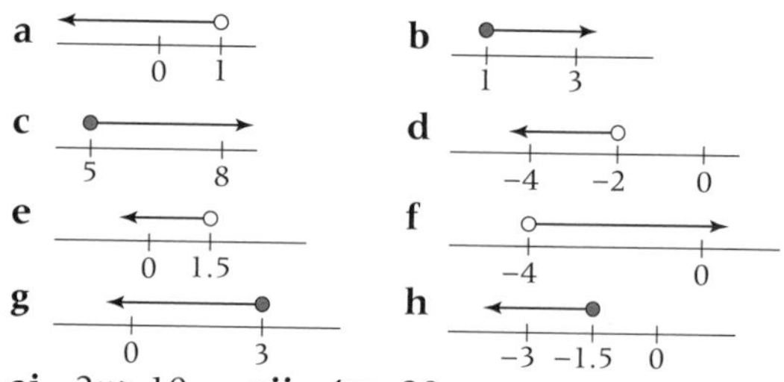

2 ai $2x > 10$ aii $4x > 20$
bi $3y < 18$ bii $5y \leqslant 30$
c $5x \geqslant -20$ d $6m < -18$
3 a $x \leqslant 2$ b $x < 5$ c $x > -2$ d $x \geqslant -4$
4 a $3x > 9, x > 3$ b $7x > 35, x > 5$
c $2x \leqslant 2, x \leqslant 1$ d $5x \geqslant 15, x \geqslant 3$
5 a $x \leqslant 5$ b $x \geqslant 6$ c $x \geqslant 2$ d $x < 4$
e $x \geqslant -1$ f $x \leqslant 3$ g $x > 3$ h $x \leqslant 2$
6 a $x \geqslant 3$ b $x > 2$ c $x \geqslant 0$ d $x > -1$
e $x \geqslant -2$ f $x \leqslant 4$ g $x \geqslant -2.5$ h $x < -7.5$
7 a ii b v c vi d i
e iv f iii

A6.6

1 a $x < 5$ b $y \geqslant 6$ c $y \leqslant 4$ d $r > 9$
e $w \leqslant 15$ f $s > 2$ g $u < -12$ h $v \geqslant -4$
2 a $x > 1, x < 5$ b $x > -5, x < -1$
c $x > -2, x < 4$ d $x \geqslant -6, x \leqslant -1$
e $x > 2, x < 7$ f $x \geqslant -1, x \leqslant 2$
3 a $-10 \leqslant x < 5$ b $5 < y < 12$
c $-2 < z \leqslant 6$ d $-4 \leqslant t \leqslant 2$
4
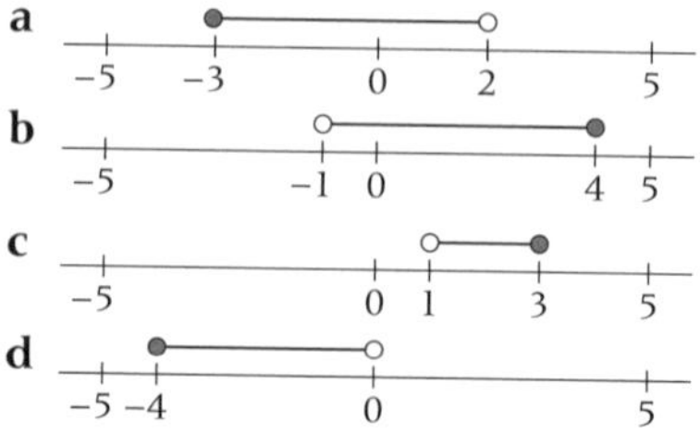

5 **a** −3, −2, −1, 0, 1 **b** 0, 1, 2, 3, 4
c 2, 3 **d** −4, −3, −2, −1

6 **a**, **b**, **c** and **e**

7 **a**

−5 −4 0 5

b −4, −3, −2, −1, 0, 1, 2, 3, 4

8 1, 2, 3, 4

9 **a** −2, −1, 0, 1, 2 **b** −1, 0, 1, 2, 3, 4
c 2, 3, 4, 5

A6.7

1 **a** $y = 9, 1, 0, 1, 9$

b–d

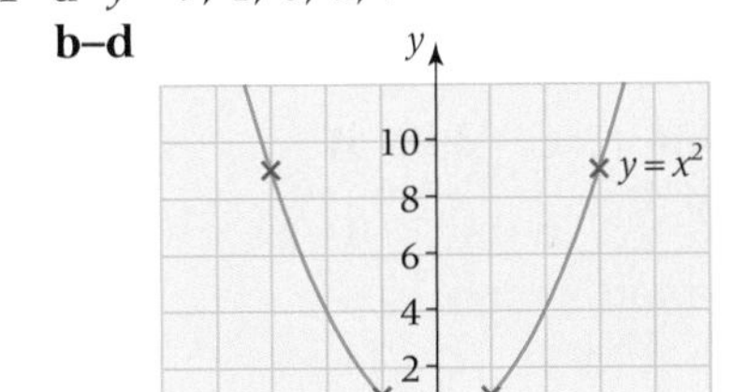

2

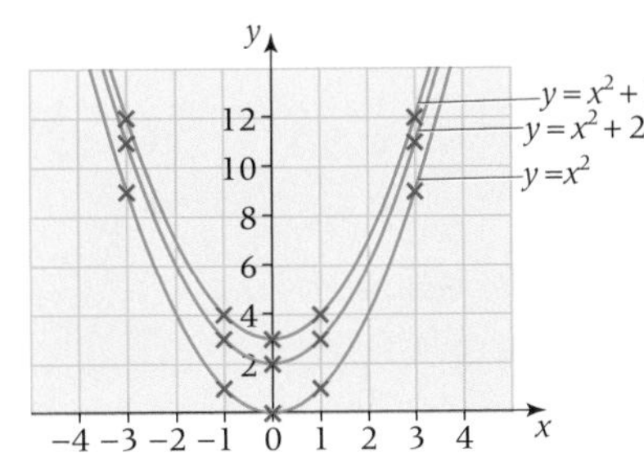

$y = x^2 + 2$ is the same shape as $y = x^2$ but shifted up 2; $y = x^2 + 3$ is the same shape as $y = x^2$ but shifted up 3.

3

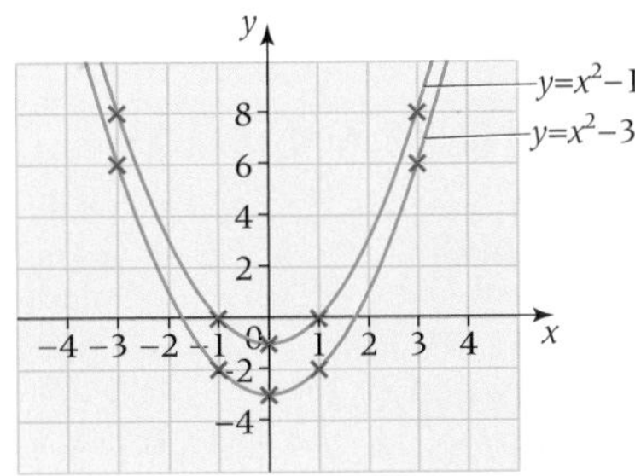

$y = x^2 - 1$ is the same shape as $y = x^2$ but shifted down 1; $y = x^2 - 3$ is the same shape as $y = x^2$ but shifted down 3.

4 **a** iv **b** i **c** ii **d** iii

5 **a**

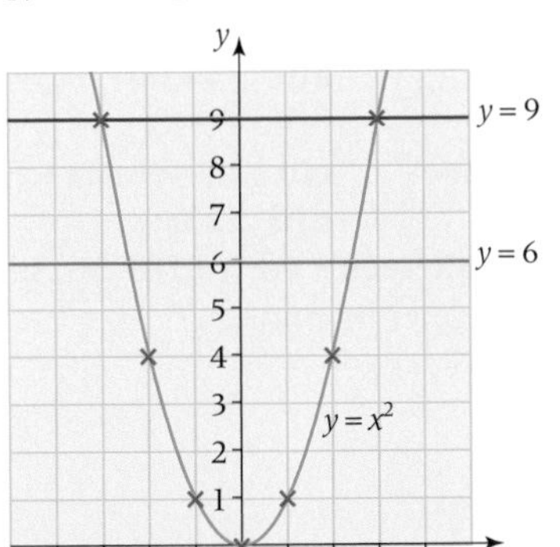

b (3, 9) and (−3, 9) **c** $x = -3, 3$
e $x = -2.4, 2.4$ **f** $y = 3$
g No, because the curve $y = x^2$ does not cross the line $y = -9$.

A6 Summary

1 **a** £155 **b** 6 **c** $p = 35h + 50$

2 **a** 80 **b** 29.5

3 **a** $x = -1\frac{1}{2}$ **b** $t = \frac{v-u}{5}$

4 **a** −3, −2, −1, 0, 1 **b** $x < -2$

G6 Check in

1 **a** 42° **b** 123° **c** 230°

2 Circle with 4.6 cm diameter

3 **a** 67 mm **b** 6.7 cm

G6.1

1 **a** Rectangle, 27.3 cm **b** Rhombus, 22.4 cm
c Rectangle, 27.9 cm

2 **a** 057° **b** 168° **c** 237° **d** 276° **e** 348°

3 **a**

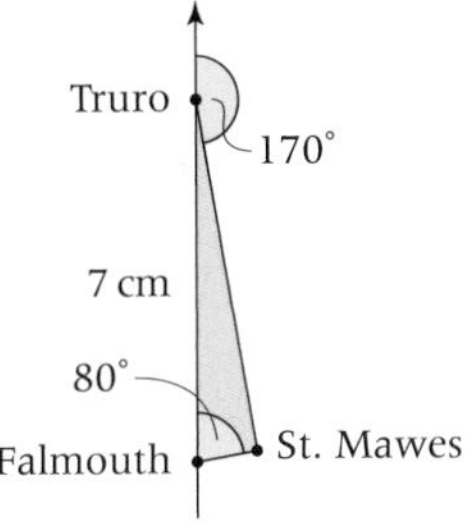

Scale: 1cm represents 2 km

b 2.4 km **c** 13.8 km

G6.2

1 **a** 8.2 cm **b** 5.3 cm **c** 11.6 cm

2 **a** 5.7 cm, 5.7 cm **b** 7.6 cm, 5.0 cm
c 5.8 cm, 3.4 cm

3 **a** 60° **b** 76° **c** 90°

4 **a** 5.7 cm, 55° **b** 6.0 cm, 45° **c** 6 cm, 67°

G6.3

For examples of constructing perpendicular bisectors, see page 246.

1 **d** 4 cm

4 **c** 90°

5 The diagonals are perpendicular bisectors of each other if each line is divided into two equal parts and they meet at right angles. Use your ruler, compasses and protractor to check.

G6.4

For examples of constructing angle bisectors, see page 248.

6 **c**

N
NW NE
W E
SW SE
S

7 **d** perpendicular
e The obtuse angles are equal (vertically opposite angles) and the acute angles are equal (vertically opposite angles). One acute angle and one obtuse angle sum to 180° (angles on a straight line). The angle between the bisectors is half an acute angle and half an obtuse angle, so it is half 180°, which is 90°.
8 **e** 2.2 cm

G6.5

See page 246, for examples of constructing perpendicular bisectors.
See page 248, for examples of constructing angle bisectors.
See page 250, for examples of loci and using loci in problem solving.

1 **b** Angle bisector
2 **b** Angle bisector
3 **b** Perpendicular bisector
4 Circle of radius 3 cm
5 A parallel line centred between the existing parallel lines
6 A semicircle of radius 2 m
7 **b** Perpendicular bisector
c The region to the left of the perpendicular bisector

G6.6

1 **a** 40 cm **b** 100 cm **c** 5 cm
d 65 cm **e** 125 cm
2 **a** 110 cm **b** 80 cm
3 75 cm by 200 cm
4 **a** 6 m, 9 m, 18 m **b** 162 m^2
5 **a** 1000 m **b** 4000 m **c** 5000 m
d 250 m **e** 7250 m

G6 Summary

1 **a** 130° **b** 185 km
c C should be 7 cm from B, on a bearing of 060° from B.
2 check angles are 60°.
3 perpendicular bisector of *PQ*

N7 Check in

1 £28.00
2 1.5
3 £68

N7.1

1 **ai** $\frac{3}{10}$ **aii** 30% **bi** $\frac{5}{8}$ **bii** 62.5%
ci $\frac{4}{9}$ **cii** 44.4% **di** $\frac{5}{12}$ **dii** 41.7%
ei $\frac{7}{25}$ **eii** 28%
2 **a** $\frac{3}{5}$, 61%, 0.63 **b** $\frac{17}{25}$, 69%, $\frac{7}{10}$, 0.71
c 34%, $\frac{7}{20}$, 0.36, $\frac{3}{8}$, $\frac{2}{5}$ **d** $\frac{2}{5}$, 42%, $\frac{3}{7}$
e 0.14, 15%, $\frac{3}{19}$, $\frac{1}{5}$ **f** 81%, $\frac{8}{9}$, 0.9, 0.93, $\frac{19}{20}$
3 **ai** $\frac{3}{5}$ **aii** 60% **bi** $\frac{13}{25}$ **bii** 52%
ci $\frac{3}{20}$ **cii** 15% **di** $\frac{7}{10}$ **dii** 70%
ei $\frac{4}{5}$ **eii** 80%

N7.2

1 **a** 5 **b** 8 **c** 7 **d** 4.5
e 1.5 **f** 3.3 **g** 3.1 **h** 7.2
i 6.7 **j** 8.6 **k** 1.8 **l** 1.4
2 **a** $\frac{1}{3}$ **b** $\frac{1}{2}$ **c** $\frac{3}{10}$ **d** $\frac{1}{4}$ **e** $\frac{3}{8}$
f $\frac{2}{5}$ **g** $\frac{1}{6}$ **h** $1\frac{1}{2}$ **i** 2
3 £50, £150, £1500, £1900, £2400
4 **a** £18.75 **b** £5.95 **c** £11.13
d £6.24 **e** £9.48 **f** 720 Mb
g £1.87 **h** 12 litres **i** £55.65

N7.3

1 **a** 2 **b** 3.5 **c** 3.5 **d** 3.33
2 **a** $\frac{1}{2}$ **b** $\frac{2}{7}$ **c** $\frac{2}{7}$ **d** $\frac{3}{10}$
3 **a** 2 **b** $\frac{1}{2}$
4 **a** 1.25 **b** $\frac{4}{5}$
5 **a** 1.6 **b** $\frac{5}{8}$
6 **a** £5.60 **b** $\times\frac{7}{5}$, £2.66
c $\times\frac{20}{9}$, £169.00 **d** 6300 g or 6.3 kg

N7.4

1 Leonard £7, Pavel £6.75, Andy £11.55
2 **a** £7.42 per hour
b 170 bricks per hour
c 55 km/h
3 £1 = 5 litas, £1 = 11.55 dollars, £1 = 6.3 riyals
4 €345.60, €1036.80, €9072
5 £250, £533.33, £1700

N7.5

1 Selling price: £10.20, £25.96, £7.96, £28.12, £176.49
2 **a** £116.33 **b** £2.10 **c** £36.74 **d** £21.89
3 **aii** 742.4 ml **aiii** 740 ml
bii 4.914 m **biii** 4.9 m
cii 2.7356 tonnes **ciii** 2.7 tonnes
dii 519.6 g **diii** 520 g
4 Payment by instalments costs £189.36, so cash payment is cheaper by 36p.

N7.6

1 a £612.50 b £2335.80 c £26 684.80
2 a £1358.20 b £8828.30 c £4658.63
d £2634.91
3 a £790 b £1109.25 c £54.60
d £132.43
4 a £477.30 b £14 105 c £149 582

N7.7

1 a £7.15 b £124.19 c £10.62 d £33.60
2 a Pie chart angles: Maximo Park 120°, Red Hot Chili Peppers 45°; Kaiser Chiefs 195°
b Pie chart angles: Walk 216°, Bus 60°, Cycle 24°, Taxi/minibus 48°, Car 12°
3 a 3.6 m b 12.5 miles c 13.9 m/s
d 18 mph e 0.014 m^2
4 9.6 cm, 7.2 cm
5 a £7 b £350

N7 Summary

1 £12.60
2 a 10 b £94
3 a 1530 b £94.12

D4 Check in

1 a 4, 5.5, 6.5, 7, 8
b 2.3, 2.4, 3.2, 3.4, 4.2, 4.3
c 7.5, 7.9, 8.3, 8.6, 9.1
2 a 6, 6, 7, 8, 8, 9, 9, 9, 9, 9
b 100, 100, 101, 102, 102, 104, 104, 104, 104, 104
3 a 110° b 35°

D4.1

1 a Discrete b Discrete c Continuous
d Continuous e Continuous f Discrete
g Continuous h Continuous i Discrete
j Continuous k Discrete l Discrete
2 a 5 b 4 c 9 d 1 e 7
f 5 g 17 h 7 i 2 j £3.85
3 a 2 b 3 c 30
4 41 kg
5 a 31 °F b 34 °F
c Athens hotter but Madrid more variable
6 23 or 42

D4.2

1 a 4
b–d

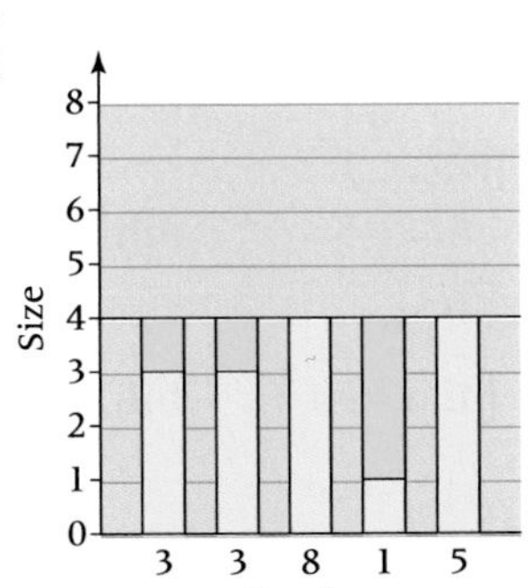

2 a 11, 4, 25 b Car
3 a 38p, 85p, £1.12, £2.15, £2.47 b £1.12
4 a 80.4 °F b 80 °F c 80 °F
5 a 5.0 b 5.8

D4.3

1 a 3, 3, 3, 3, 4, 4, 5, 5
b Range = 2, Mode = 3, Median = 3.5, Mean = 3.75
2 a 1, 1, 1, 1, 2, 2, 2, 2, 2, 2, 3, 3, 4, 4, 4, 4, 4, 5, 5, 5, 5, 5, 5, 5, 5
b 8
c Range = 4, Mode = 5, Median = 4, Mean = 3.28
3 a 2.4 b 1 c 2 d 3
4 a 2.7 b 4 c 3 d 3
5 a 3, 4, 0, 3, 3, 3, 3, 0
b Mean = 5.85, Mode = 4, Median = 6, Range = 7

D4.4

1 a 2, 4
b Number 47's data is more spread out than Number 45's.
2 a 1, 3, 4, 1, 1 b 1.8, 2, 2
c On average, houses in Ullswater Drive have more cars than those in Ambleside Close.
3 a Ireland: 22, 23, 24, 24, 24, 25, 26, 26, 26, 27, 27, 28
Spain: 2, 5, 6, 7, 10, 10, 10, 11, 11, 11, 11, 12
b Ireland 25.5, Spain 10
c On average, Ireland has more days of rain than Spain.
d Ireland 6, Spain 10
e There is a bigger spread or larger variation in the number of rainy days in Spain.

D4.5

1 a 1, 6, 8, 3, 3, 3 b 70 to 74 c 70 to 74
2 a 3 b 23, 28, 33, 38
c 23, 168, 66, 38; Mean speed = 29.5 mph
3 a 30 students b $160 < h \leqslant 170$
c $170 < h \leqslant 180$ d 163.3 cm

D4.6

1 ai 24 aii 12 aiii 36 aiv 4 av 76
b Cotton
2 ai £20 aii £10 b Children
c 4 × World Single Trip = £20, which is cheaper than World Annual insurance.
3 ai 1 person aii 3 people
b 28 tickets
4 a 120° b 3° ci 30 cii 50 ciii 40

D4.7

1 ai Cooking and washing up
aii Washing and ironing
bi Cooking and washing up bii DIY

2 **ai** 100 million **aii** 1000 million
b India **c** UK

3 **ai** 2 **aii** 1
b 85–90 m **c** 70–75 m **d** 10 athletes

4 The women jumped further, on average. The men had a greater spread of long jumps than the women.

D4.8

1 **a** 10, 16, 22, 22, 24, 26, 28, 29, 30
bi 23 **bii** 22 **biii** 24 **biv** 20

2 **a**

0	7 9
10	7 9 2 1 5 8 7
20	5 5 1 5 3
30	1 2 7
40	3 0 1

b

0	7 9
10	1 2 5 7 7 8 9
20	1 3 5 5 5
30	1 2 7
40	0 1 3

ci 23.4 **cii** 25 **ciii** 22 **civ** 36

3 **a** 128 sec **b** 120 sec **c** 126 sec **d** 31 sec

4 **a** 49 **b** 16 **c** $\frac{1}{4}$

5 **a** Long jump
b High jump 26 cm, long jump 15 cm; there is a greater spread of distances for the high jump than there is for the long jump.

D4.9

1 **a** Negative correlation **b** No correlation
c Positive correlation

2 **a** A: Poor exam mark, lots of revision; B: Very good exam mark, lots of revision; C: Very good exam mark, little revision; D: Poor exam mark, little revision; E: Average exam mark, average amount of revision
b A: Not much pocket money, equal eldest; B: Lots of pocket money, equal eldest; C: Lots of pocket money, equal youngest; D: Not much pocket money, equal youngest; E: Average pocket money, middle age
c A: Low fitness level, lots of hours in gym, B: Good fitness level, lots of hours in gym, C: Good fitness level, few hours in gym, D: Low fitness level, few hours in gym, E: Medium fitness level, medium hours in gym

3 **a** 16 **b** 24

4 **a, c**

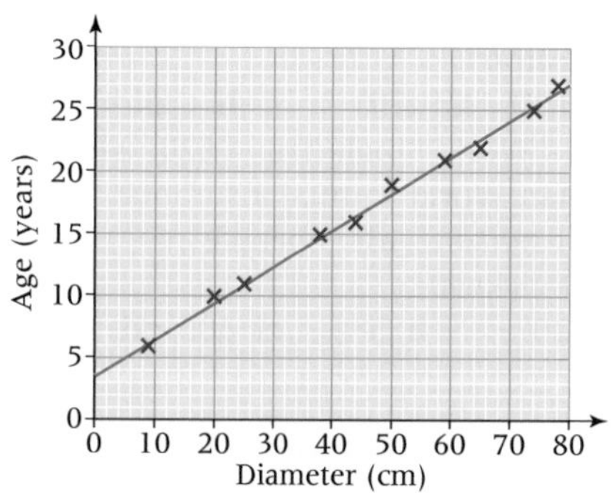

b Positive correlation **d** 20 years

D4 Summary

1 **a** 1 **b** 3 **c** 2.1

2 around 47 (draw a line of best fit)

A7 Check in

1 straight line graph passing through (0, −3) and (4, 1)

2 **a** 4 **b** 5.061 **c** −26.368

3 **a** $x = 7$ **b** $x = 10$

A7.1

1 **a** $r = 4$ **b** $s = -3$ **c** $t = 2$ **d** $v = -5$

2 **a** $a = 3$ **b** $b = -2$ **c** $c = 5$ **d** $d = -4$

3 **a** $x = 6$ **b** $y = -6$ **c** $z = 5.5$ **d** $m = 2$

4 **a** $e = 3.5$ **b** $f = 0.5$ **c** $g = -1.5$ **d** $h = -1$

5 **a–d**

	$3x-2$	$4x+1$	$8x-3$
$2(x+3)$	$x=8$	$x=2.5$	$x=1.5$
$4(2x-1)$	$x=0.4$	$x=1.25$	No solution
$3(4x+1)$	$x=-\frac{5}{9}$	$x=-0.25$	$x=-1.5$

6 **a** $3x + 9$ **b** $4x + 4$
c $4x + 4 = 3x + 9$ **d** $x = 5$

7 **a** $4(x + 2)$ **b** $8x = 4(x + 2)$ **c** $x = 2$

8 **a** $4m$ **b** $3(m + 2)$
c $4m = 3(m + 2)$, $m = 6$ **d** 8

A7.2

1 **a** $x = 15$ **b** $m = -8$ **c** $n = -18$ **d** $m = 20$

2 **a** $s = 9$ **b** $t = 6$ **c** $u = -10$ **d** $v = 12$

3 **a** $x = 6$ **b** $y = 6$ **c** $z = 15$ **d** $q = -8$

4 **a** $x = 1$ **b** $x = 11$ **c** $x = -17$ **d** $x = 6$

5 **a** $x = 12$ **b** $x = 6$ **c** $x = 7$ **d** $x = 5$

6 **a** $\frac{n}{4} + 6$ **b** $\frac{n}{4} + 6$ **c** $n = 16$

7 **a** $\frac{n}{3} - 4 = 7$, $n = 33$ **b** $\frac{n}{2} + 8 = 3$, $n = -10$

8 **a** $\frac{2x+6}{3} = 10$ **b** $x = 9$

9 $\frac{2+x}{4} = 10$, $x = 36$

A7.3

1 **a** $y = 2$ **b** $y = 8$ **c** $x = 2$ **d** $x = -3$

2 **a**

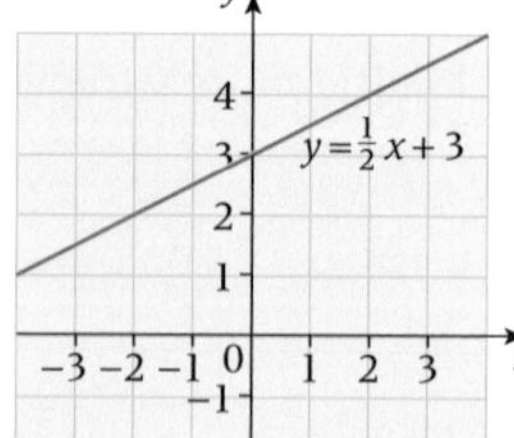

b $x = 8$
c (2, 4) and (−3, 1.5)

3 **a** $y = 4x - 7$ **b** $x = -2$

5 **ai** $x = 1.5$ **aii** $x = 5$ **aiii** $x = -3$
b $3x + 2 = 11$, $x = 3$

6 **a** $x = 2$
bi $x = 4$ **bii** $x = -4.5$ **biii** $x = 1.5$

A7.4

1 a

x	x^2	Too big or too small
5.5	30.25	Too big
5.4	29.16	Too big

d $x = 5.4$

2 $x = 4.1$

3 $x = 5.2$

4 a 0, 6, 24 b x is between 2 and 3.
e $x = 2.2$

5 $x = 4.1$

A7 Summary

1 a $x = 5\frac{1}{2}$ b $x = -35$

2 $x = 2\frac{1}{4}$

3 $x = 3.2$

G7 Check in

1 a 12 b 75 c 28.83 d 12

2 a 25 b 24 c 8.4

G7.1

1 a 31.4 cm b 25.12 m c 37.68 cm
d 62.8 m e 12.56 m f 50.24 cm
g 9.42 m h 21.98 cm

2 a 6 cm b 5 m c 9 cm
d 15 m e 100 cm

3 a 44.0 cm, 153.86 cm^2 b 31.4 m, 78.5 m^2
c 25.1 cm, 50.24 cm^2 d 18.8 m, 28.26 m^2
e 51.4 m, 314 m^2 f 41.1 cm, 200.96 cm^2
g 21.4 mm, 113.04 mm^2
h 32.1 cm, 254.34 cm^2

4 a 3 m b 9.4 m c 7.1 m^2

5 accurate scale drawing

G7.2

1 a 105 cm^3 b 60 cm^3 c 72 cm^3
d 36 cm^3 e 64 cm^3 f 28 mm^3

2 a 75.4 cm^3 b 628.3 cm^3 c 201.1 cm^3
d 160.8 cm^3

3 a 270 cm^3 b 600 mm^3 c 1080 cm^3

G7.3

1 a 64 cm^2 b 100 m^2 c 3.24 m^2
d 1296 mm^2 e 20.25 m^2

2 a 9 m b 2 cm c 14 cm
d 2.7 m e 1 mm

3 a 20 cm^2 b 8 cm^2 c 100 mm^2

4 a 10 cm b 25 m c 17 cm
d 26 mm e 30 cm f 65 mm

G7.4

1 a 4 cm^2 b 15 cm^2

2 a 9 cm b 12 mm c 24 m
d 16 cm e 2.5 m

3 a 5 units b 5 units c 3.2 units
d 5.7 units e 6.7 units

4 3.7 m

G7 Summary

1 112 cm^3

2 30.9 cm^2

3 10.63 cm

Index

A
accuracy, appropriate degrees of, 190
addition
  fractions, 292–3
  mental, 48–9
  negative numbers, 8–9
  order of operations, 56
  written, 50–1
algebra, brackets in, 126–7
algebraic expressions, 122–3
  simplifying, 122
alternate angles, 72, 74
angle bisectors, 330–1
angles
  alternate, 72, 74
  corresponding, 72, 74
  in parallel lines, 72–3
  properties, 64–5
  in quadrilaterals, 68–9
  vertically opposite, 64, 72
  see also exterior angles; interior angles
anticlockwise, 200
appreciation, 352
approximations, 58
arcs, 328, 330
area, 16–27, 284, 406
  circles, 396–7, 406
  parallelograms, 22–3, 406
  rectangles, 20–1, 406
  surface, 24–5
  trapeziums, 22–3, 406
  triangles, 20–1, 406
arithmetic sequences, 220
arrowheads
  angles, 68
  properties, 70
art, 338
average speed, 176–7
averages
  and charts, 358–79
  see also means
axes, horizontal, 252

B
balance method, 384
  equation solving, 264–5
bar charts, 96, 246, 370
  comparative, 372
bar-line charts, 246, 370
bases, 20, 22
bearings, 324–5
  three-figure, 324
Beaufort Scale, 45
best fit, lines of, 254, 376
bias, 110, 146
BIDMAS, 56, 128
bisectors
  angle, 330–1
  perpendicular, 328, 332
brackets, 128
  in algebra, 126–7
  expanding, 126, 266, 382
  order of operations, 56, 190
  solving equations with, 266–7, 382–3
Brahmagupta (598–668), 55
businesses, 242–3

C
calculator methods, 88, 90, 300–1
  RAN key, 146
  and ratios, 182–93
capacity, 18
categories, 246
centres, 396
  of enlargement, 208
  of rotation, 200
chances, 102
charts, 246–7, 364–5, 370–3
  and averages, 358–79
  bar-line, 246, 370
  pie, 246, 370
  tally, 136
  see also bar charts; diagrams; graphs
chunking method, 54
circles, 406
  area, 396–7, 406
circumference, 396–7, 406
class intervals, 142, 368
  midpoints, 248
clockwise, 200
coefficients, 220
columns, 144
common denominator, 292
common difference, 216, 220, 222
common factors, 130, 231
common multiples, 231
compasses, 330
compensation, 48, 296
compound measures, 172–3
congruence, 204–5
congruent shapes, 200, 202, 278
constructions, 322–37
  triangles, 326–7
continuous data, 142, 248, 360, 368
  grouped, 248, 372
controlled experiments, 138–9
conversion graphs, 168–9
  drawing, 170–1
conversions, 170
  units, 168
coordinate pairs, 30
coordinates, 40
correlations, 254, 376
  negative, 254, 376
  positive, 254, 376
corresponding angles, 72, 74
crop circles, 339
cross-sections, 158, 398
cube numbers, 234
cube roots, 234–5
cubes, 234–5
  properties, 154
cubic centimetres, 156, 282
cubic metres, 156, 282
cuboids
  properties, 154
  volume, 156–7, 398, 406
cylinders, 398
  volume, 406

D
data
  comparing, 366–7
  discrete, 142, 248, 360
  displaying, 244–57
  grouped, 142–3, 248, 368–9
  interpretation, 244–57
  ordered, 250, 374
  primary, 136
  secondary, 136
  types of, 360–1
  see also continuous data
data collection, 134–49
data logging, 138
data-collection sheets, 136, 138, 140
databases, and random sampling, 146–7
decimal places, 12
decimals, 2–15
  calculations, 46–61
  and fractions, 80–95, 290–303
  mental methods, 296–7
  ordering, 86–7
  and percentages, 80–95
  and proportion, 342
  recurring, 84
  terminating, 84
  written methods, 298–9
decomposition, prime factors, 238–9
decreasing sequences, 216
degrees, angles, 64
denominators, 82
  common, 292
  lowest common, 292
depreciation, 352
Descartes, René (1596–1650), 33
diagonals, 38, 274
diagrams, 246–7, 370–3
  grouped frequency, 248–9
  sample space, 114
  stem-and-leaf, 250–1, 374–5
  tree, 112
  see also charts; graphs
diameters, 396
digits, 4
  non-zero, 12
direct proportion, 344, 346
direction, 324
discrete data, 142, 248, 360
distance, 172, 174
distance–time graphs, 174–5
  speed from, 172
dividends, 54
division
  fractions, 294–5
  mental, 52–3
  negative numbers, 10–11
  order of operations, 56
  prime numbers, 238
  written, 54–5
divisors, 54
drawings, scale, 334–5

E
edges, 154
elevations, 280–1
  front, 280
  side, 280
enlargements, 206–9, 210, 284, 334
  centres of, 208
equally likely events, 114
equally likely outcomes, 100, 110, 112, 114, 116, 146
equations, 30, 258–71, 306–7, 314, 380–91
  and brackets, 382–3
  with brackets, solving, 266–7
  and fractions, 384–5
  satisfying, 386
  solving
    using balance method, 264–5
    using function machines, 260–1
  of straight lines, 38–9
  subjects of, 34
  two-step, 262–3
  with unknown on both sides, 268–9
equidistance, 198, 332
equilateral triangles
  angles, 64
  properties, 66
equivalent fractions, 82–3, 292
equivalents, 18
estimated means, 368
estimation, 6, 12, 58–9, 110, 388
events, 100, 116
  equally likely, 114
  successive, 112
  two, 112–15
exchange rates, 170, 348–9
expected frequencies, 108–9, 116
experiments, 110
  controlled, 138–9
explicit form, 34
explicit functions, 164
expressions, 120–33, 306
  simplifying, 128–9
  see also algebraic expressions
exterior angles, 74
  polygons, 276–7

F
faces, 24, 154
factor trees, 238
factorising, 130–1
factors, 52, 230–1
  common, 130, 231
  prime, 238–9
  scale, 206, 208, 210, 284–5, 334
fairness, 110
formulae, 306–7
  changing subjects of, 312–13

and inequalities, 304–21
substitution, 308–9
writing, 310–11
fraction key, 300
fractions
addition, 292–3
and decimals, 80–95, 290–303
division, 294–5
and equations, 384–5
equivalent, 82–3, 292
improper, 82
multiplication, 294–5
ordering, 86–7
and percentages, 80–95
and proportion, 342
of quantities, 88–9
subtraction, 292–3
unit, 294
frequencies
expected, 108–9, 116
relative, 110–11
frequency diagrams, grouped, 248–9
frequency polygons, 248, 372
frequency tables, 136–7, 144, 364
grouped, 142
front elevations, 280
function machines, equation solving, 260–1
functions, 30–1, 306
explicit, 164
and graphs, 34
implicit, 164
quadratic, 318–19

G
general terms, 218–19
gradients, 38
graffiti, 338
graphs
finding solutions from, 386–7
and functions, 34
horizontal, 36–7
line, 252
quadratic functions, 318–19
scatter, 254–5, 376–7
time series, 252–3
vertical, 36–7
see also charts; conversion graphs; diagrams; distance–time graphs; linear graphs; real-life graphs
greater than, 314
grid method, 54
grouped continuous data, 248, 372
grouped data, 142–3, 248
grouped frequency diagrams, 248–9
grouped frequency tables, 142

H
HCF (highest common factor), 230, 238
height, 156
perpendicular, 20, 22
highest common factor (HCF), 230, 238
histograms, 372
holidays, 194–5
horizontal axes, 252
horizontal graphs, 36–7
hypotenuse, 326, 400, 402
hypotheses, 140

I
identities, 306–7
imperial measures, 18–19
imperial units, 18
implicit form, 34
implicit functions, 164
improper fractions, 82
increasing sequences, 216
index laws, 124
index notation, 124
indices, 124–5
order of operations, 56
see also powers
inequalities, 314–15
and formulae, 304–21
two-sided, 316–17
integers, 2–15, 228–41, 294, 298, 316
intercepts, 38
interest, 352–3
simple, 352
interior angles, 74
polygons, 274–5, 276
inverse operations, 260, 262, 264
isosceles trapeziums
angles, 68
properties, 70
isosceles triangles
angles, 64
properties, 66

J
justification, 224

K
kites
angles, 68
properties, 70

L
LCM (least common multiple), 230, 238
least common multiple (LCM), 230, 238
length, 16–27
less than, 314
like terms, 122
line graphs, 252
line segments, 402
midpoints, 40–1
linear graphs, 28–43
drawing, 32–3, 164–5
linear relationships, 254, 376
linear sequences, 216
lines
of best fit, 254, 376
mirror, 198
number, 6
perpendicular, 328–9
of symmetry, 76
see also parallel lines; straight lines
litres, 282
loci, 322–37
lowest common denominator, 292

M
maps, 30, 334–5
mass, 18
means, 362, 364
estimated, 368
measures, 394–405
compound, 172–3
imperial, 18–19
metric, 18–19
three-dimensional, 282–3
two-dimensional, 282–3
median, 362, 364
memory keys, 300
mental addition, 48–9
mental division, 52–3
mental methods, 48, 88
decimals, 296–7
mental multiplication, 52–3
mental subtraction, 48–9
metric measures, 18–19
metric units, 18, 282
mid-values, 368
midpoints, 328
of class intervals, 248
of line segments, 40–1
mirror lines, 198
mixed numbers, 82
modal class, 368
modal values, 362
mode, 362, 364
models, 166
multiples, 52, 230–1
common, 231
multiplication
fractions, 294–5
mental, 52–3
negative numbers, 10–11
order of operations, 56
written, 54–5
multiplicative inverse, 294
multipliers, 206
mutually exclusive outcomes, 102, 104–5, 116

N
negative correlations, 254, 376
negative numbers
addition, 8–9
division, 10–11
multiplication, 10–11
subtraction, 8–9
nets, 24, 154
Nightingale, Florence (1820–1910), 247
non-zero digits, 12
***n*th term,** 218, 220
finding, 220–1
number lines, 6
numbers
cube, 234
mixed, 82
ordering, 8
square, 232
see also negative numbers; prime numbers
numerators, 82

O
observations, 138–9
Ohm's law, 313
operations
inverse, 260, 262, 264
order of, 56–7, 190
ordered data, 250, 374
ordering, fractions, decimals and percentages, 86–7
outcomes, 100, 112, 116
equally likely, 100, 110, 112, 114, 116, 146
mutually exclusive, 102, 104–5, 116

P
parallel lines, 38
angles in, 72–3
using, 74–5
parallelograms
angles, 68, 74
area, 22–3, 406
properties, 70
partitioning, 48, 52, 296
pattern sequences, 222–5
percentages
and decimals, 80–95
decrease, 92–3
and fractions, 80–95
increase, 92–3
ordering, 86–7
problems, 350–1
and proportion, 342
of quantities, 90–1
perimeters, 284
rectangles, 20–1
triangles, 20–1
perpendicular bisectors, 328, 332
perpendicular height, 20, 22
perpendicular lines, 328–9
pi (π), 396
pictograms, 246, 370
pie charts, 246, 370
place value, 4–5, 296
plans, 280–1
polygons
exterior angles, 276–7
frequency, 248, 372
interior angles, 274–5
position-to-term rules, 218
positive correlations, 254, 376
power key, 300
powers, 124, 228–41
order of operations, 56
of ten, 236
see also indices
primary data, 136
prime factors, decomposition, 238–9
prime numbers, 231
division, 238
prisms
properties, 154
volume, 158–9, 398–9, 406
probability, 98–119
theoretical, 110

probability scales, 102–3
problems, two-step, 262
products, 230
profit, 350
proofs, 74
proportion, 342–3
direct, 344, 346
problems, 354–5
and ratios, 346–7, 354
proportionality, 340–57
protractors, 326
pyramids, properties, 154
Pythagoras (c.580–500 BC), 401
Pythagoras' theorem, 400–3, 406

Q
quadratic functions, graphs, 318–19
quadrilaterals
angles, 68–9
properties, 70–1
see also rectangles
quantities
fractions of, 88–9
percentages of, 90–1
questionnaires, 140–1

R
radii, 396
radio maths, 288–9
RAN key, 146
random sampling, 138
and databases, 146–7
range, 360–1, 364
ratios, 344
calculations, 184–5
and calculator methods, 182–93
problem solving, 188–9
and proportion, 346–7, 354
simplest form, 184
unitary form, 184
reading scales, 6–7
real-life graphs, 162–81
interpretation, 178–9
reciprocal key, 300
reciprocals, 88
rectangles
angles, 68
area, 20–1, 406
perimeters, 20–1
properties, 70
recurring decimals, 84
recycling, 150–1
reductions, 334
reflection symmetry, 76
reflections, 198–9, 204
regular shapes, 66, 274, 278
relationships, 376
linear, 254, 376
see also correlations
relative frequencies, 110–11
representative values, 362
rhombuses
angles, 68
properties, 70
right-angled triangles, 326, 400
angles, 64
properties, 66
roots, 228–41
cube, 234–5
order of operations, 56
square, 232–3, 400
rotational symmetry, 76
order of, 76
rotations, 200–1, 204
centres of, 200
rounding, 12–13
rows, 144
rules
position-to-term, 218
term-to-term, 216–17

S
sample space diagrams, 114
sampling, 138–9
see also random sampling
sandwich shops, 96–7
scale drawings, 334–5
scale factors, 206, 208, 210, 284–5, 334
scalene triangles
angles, 64
properties, 66
scales, 168, 184, 186, 188
probability, 102–3
reading, 6–7
scatter graphs, 254–5, 376–7
secondary data, 136
sectors, 246, 370
sequences, 214–27
arithmetic, 220
decreasing, 216
increasing, 216
linear, 216
pattern, 222–5
shapes
congruent, 200, 202, 278
regular, 66, 274, 278
similar, 206, 210–11
three-dimensional, 152–61, 272–87
see also two-dimensional shapes
side elevations, 280
significant figures, 12
similar shapes, 206, 210–11
simple interest, 352
simplest form, ratios, 184
sliding, 202
solids, 154
solution sets, 314
speed, 172
average, 176–7
sport, 392–3
spread, 360, 366
square centimetres, 282
square key, 300
square metres, 282
square numbers, 232
square root key, 300
square roots, 232–3, 400
square units, 20
squares, 232–3, 400
angles, 68
properties, 70
standard method, 54
statistical keys, 300
stem-and-leaf diagrams, 250–1, 374–5
straight lines, 64
equations of, 38–9
subjects
of equations, 34
of formulae, 312–13
substitution, 30, 300
formulae, 308–9
subtraction
fractions, 292–3
mental, 48–9
negative numbers, 8–9
order of operations, 56
written, 50–1
successive events, 112
surface area, 24–5
surveys, 140–1
symmetry, 76–7
lines of, 76
reflection, 76
see also rotational symmetry
systematic approaches, 112

T
tables, 364–5
two-way, 106–7, 144–5
see also frequency tables
tally charts, 136
temperature, 44
ten, powers of, 236
term-to-term rules, 216–17
terminating decimals, 84
terms, 122
general, 218–19
like, 122
see also *n*th term
tessellations, 278–9
theoretical probability, 110
thousandths, 12
three-dimensional measures, 282–3
three-dimensional shapes, 152–61, 272–87
three-figure bearings, 324
time, 172, 174
time series graphs, 252–3
timetables, 6
transformations, 196–213
translations, 202–3, 204, 278
trapeziums
angles, 68
area, 22–3, 406
properties, 70
see also isosceles trapeziums
tree diagrams, 112
trends, 252
decreasing, 178
increasing, 178
trial-and-improvement method, 388–9
trials, 100, 108, 110, 116
triangles
angles in, 64, 66
area, 20–1, 406
construction, 326–7
perimeters, 20–1
properties, 66–7
see also equilateral triangles; isosceles triangles; right-angled triangles; scalene triangles
two events, 112–15
two-dimensional measures, 282–3
two-dimensional shapes, 62–79, 272–87
symmetry, 76
two-sided inequalities, 316–17
two-step equations, solving, 262–3
two-step problems, 262
two-way tables, 106–7, 144–5

U
unit fractions, 294
unitary form, ratios, 184
unitary method, 344–5
units
conversions, 168
imperial, 18
metric, 18, 282
square, 20

V
values
modal, 362
representative, 362
variables, 254, 376
vectors, 202
vertical graphs, 36–7
vertically opposite angles, 64, 72
vertices, 154, 208
volume, 282, 284, 406
cuboids, 156–7, 406
cylinders, 406
prisms, 158–9, 398–9, 406

W
weather, 44–5
whole numbers *see* integers
width, 156
wind, 45
written addition, 50–1
written division, 54–5
written methods, 50, 88, 90
decimals, 298–9
written multiplication, 54–5
written subtraction, 50–1

Y
y-intercept, 36, 38